VARIETIES OF PRACTICAL REASONI

VARIETIES OF PRACTICAL REASONING

edited by Elijah Millgram

A Bradford Book
The MIT Press
Cambridge, Massachusetts
London, England

This book was set in Times New Roman on '3B2' by Asco Typesetters, Hong Kong, and was printed and bound in the United States of America.

First printing, 2001

Library of Congress Cataloging-in-Publication Data

Varieties of practical reasoning / edited by Elijah Millgram.
      p.   cm.
"A Bradford book."
Includes bibliographical references and index.
ISBN 0-262-13388-1 (hc. : alk. paper) — ISBN 0-262-63220-9 (pbk. : alk. paper)
1. Reasoning. I. Millgram, Elijah.
BC177.V37 2001
160—dc21   00-054899

Contents

Sources and Acknowledgments

"Practical Reasoning: The Current State of Play" draws on material from "Practical Reasoning," in C. Eliasmith, ed., *Dictionary of Philosophy of Mind*, an online resource hosted by Washington University in St. Louis.

"Humean Doubts about Categorical Imperatives" is adapted from James Dreier, "Humean Doubts about the Practical Justification of Morality," in Garrett Cullity and Berys Gaut, eds., *Ethics and Practical Reason* (Oxford: Clarendon Press, 1997). Reprinted with the permission of Oxford University Press and James Dreier.

"Internal and External Reasons" was first published in Ross Harrison, ed., *Rational Action*. Copyright 1979 by Cambridge University Press. Reprinted with the permission of Cambridge University Press.

"Williams' Argument against External Reasons" was first published in *Analysis* 47, no. 1 (1987): 42–44. Reprinted with the permission of Brad Hooker.

"Skepticism about Practical Reason" was first published in *The Journal of Philosophy* 83, no. 1 (1986): 5–25. Reprinted with the permission of *The Journal of Philosophy* and Christine M. Korsgaard.

"The *Protagoras*: A Science of Practical Reasoning" was first published in Martha Nussbaum, *The Fragility of Goodness*. Copyright 1986 by Cambridge University Press. Reprinted with the permission of Cambridge University Press.

"Taking Plans Seriously" was first published in *Social Theory and Practice* 9, nos. 2–3 (1983): 271–287. Copyright 1983 by *Social Theory and Practice*. Reprinted by permission.

"Moderation and Satisficing" is excerpted from Sterling McMurrin, ed., *The Tanner Lectures on Human Values VII*, 1986, pp. 55–71. The text here was revised for Michael Slote, *Beyond Optimizing* (Cambridge: Harvard University Press, 1989). Reprinted by permission of the University of Utah Press and Harvard University Press.

"Choosing Ends" was first published in *Ethics* 104 (1994): 226–251, and was reprinted in David Schmidtz, *Rational Choice and Moral Agency* (Princeton: Princeton University Press, 1995). The text here was revised for the latter. Copyright 1994 by the University of Chicago. All rights reserved. Reprinted with the permission of the University of Chicago, Princeton University Press, and David Schmidtz.

"Deliberation Is of Ends" was first published in *Proceedings of the Aristotelian Society*, suppl. vol. 36 (1962). Copyright 1962 by the Aristotelian Society. Reprinted by courtesy of the editor of the Aristotelian Society and with the permission of David Wiggins.

"Deliberation and Practical Reason" was first published in *Proceedings of the Aristotelian Society* 76 (1975–1976): 29–51. The text here was revised for David Wiggins, *Needs, Values, Truth*, 3rd edition (Oxford: Clarendon Press, 1998). Copyright 1975 by the Aristotelian Society. Reprinted by courtesy of the editor of the Aristotelian Society and with the permission of David Wiggins.

"Consistency in Action" was first published in N. Potter and M. Timmons, eds., *Universality and Morality: Essays on Ethical Universality* (Dordrecht: Reidel, 1985), pp. 159–186. Copyright 1985 by D. Reidel Publishing Company. Republished with kind permission from Kluwer Academic Publishers. The text here was revised for Onora O'Neill, *Constructions of Reason* (Cambridge: Cambridge University Press, 1989). Used with the permission of Cambridge University Press.

"Pleasure in Practical Reasoning" was originally published in *The Monist* 76, no. 2 (1993): 394–415. Reprinted with the permission of *The Monist*.

"How to Make Decisions: Coherence, Emotion, and Practical Inference" includes material excerpted from Paul Thagard, *Coherence in Thought and Action*. Reprinted with permission from the MIT Press.

"The Idea of Perfection" was originally published in the *Yale Review* 53, no. 3 (1964): 342–380. Reprinted with the permission of Blackwell Publishers.

"Action, Norms, and Practical Reasoning" was originally published in *Philosophical Perspectives* 12 (1998): 127–139. Reprinted with the permission of Blackwell Publishers.

Preparation of this volume was supported by a fellowship from the Center for Advanced Study in the Behavioral Sciences. I am grateful for financial support provided through the Center by the Andrew W. Mellon Foundation.

VARIETIES OF PRACTICAL REASONING

Chapter 1

Practical Reasoning: The Current State of Play

Elijah Millgram

Practical reasoning is reasoning directed towards action: figuring out what to do, as contrasted with figuring out how the facts stand. The study of practical reasoning has been a rapidly changing area, in which the fortification and defense of a very small number of entrenched positions inherited from the great dead philosophers has given way to a healthy profusion of competing and largely new views, and in which important ideas and arguments turn up annually or semiannually—a rate that remakes a philosophical subspecialty over the course of a decade or so. The aim of this anthology is to provide an overview of the state of the field as it has shaped up over the 1980s and 1990s,[1] and the aim of this essay is to serve both as a guide to the articles in this volume and as a map of the area. The essay is also meant to provide very selective suggestions for further reading, and the notes will point you to the one or two items on a particular issue or topic that you might want to look at next.

Progress on practical reasoning is of great importance to ethics, and until not long ago, most work on practical reasoning took place inside one or another ethical system. The result has been to tie substantive moral theories in the great ethical traditions very tightly to different theories of practical reasoning. This suggests determining which tradition (if any) has gotten it right about the central moral questions (e.g., how one should treat one's fellow human beings) by figuring out which has the right account of practical reasoning. More generally, since a moral theory is (very roughly) a theory about what one should do, and a theory of practical reasoning is a theory of how to figure out what to do, the two kinds of theories are related as a theory of product to a theory of process. Not only should selecting the right process give you a way of choosing among the available products, but new, freestanding theories of practical reasoning can be expected to generate new moral and ethical theories. So advances in practical reasoning promise to break—or anyway, shake up —the long-lasting stalemate between the handful of very familiar moral and ethical positions.

We will see below how the theory of practical reasoning has consequences for philosophy of mind, for value theory, and for the social sciences. It is also connected to the old problem of freedom of the will. The connection is obvious enough in one direction: if one's will is not free, then the question of how to figure out what to do loses its urgency. But it has been argued that the connection runs in the other direction as well: that, surprisingly, not all theories of practical reasoning permit genuinely intentional action, and so, freedom of the will.[2]

The current debate in practical reasoning focuses on the question of what inference patterns are legitimate methods of arriving at decisions or intentions to act, or other characteristically practical predecessors of actions such as evaluations, plans, policies, and judgments about what one ought to do. (There are dissenting voices: Candace Vogler's essay reconstructs G. E. M. Anscombe's argument that this way of thinking about practical reasoning is wrong from the ground up.) The spectrum of competing theories ranges from the very minimal, allowing only one form of practical inference (or even none), to maximally permissive views that "let a thousand flowers bloom," and the remainder of this article surveys the most prominent positions on this spectrum.

Let me just mention a number of issues that this way of organizing the material leaves to one side. First, there is a family of traditionally very important questions about practical irrationality, those having to do not with what it takes to get the right conclusion but rather with what goes wrong when one has the right conclusion but still does the wrong thing.[3] Second, there are approaches that distinguish practical rationality from practical reasoning, and try to explain the former without first working up a substantive account of the latter: in this class are informed-desire theories (which hold, roughly, that a desire is rational if it is one you would have if you knew or thought more about it),[4] as is Elizabeth Anderson's expressivist account (on which actions make sense—are rational—when they express evaluations that would be reflectively endorsed from a suitable common point of view).[5] Third, I am not discussing earlier work on prudential (i.e., future-regarding) reasons; these were at the time regarded as a possible model for a treatment of altruistic reasons, and while interest in this (to my mind, still unexhausted) approach seems to have abated, it has a contemporary successor in attempts to look for reasons for action in one's self-conception or practical identity.[6]

While these problems will be getting less attention here than they are used to, one very much underdiscussed issue will get slightly more. I will wrap up by visiting a question to be repeatedly touched upon in reviewing the various theories of practical inference: how should one go about determining what the legitimate forms of practical reasoning are, in the first place?

NIHILISM

Nihilism about practical reasoning is the view that there are no legitimate forms of practical inference, and that consequently there is no such thing as practical reasoning: appearances notwithstanding, there is no mental activity that counts as figuring out what to do. Everyone acknowledges that there are considerations that are presented as reasons for action but that, on second glance, aren't really reasons after all (celebrity product endorsements, for example); the nihilist is someone who thinks that *all* would-be reasons for action are like those. The Practical Tortoise of James Dreier's chapter is a nihilist, and nihilism is canvassed as a possible form of irrationality in section 3 of Christine M. Korsgaard's essay.

The nihilist position is the most minimal on the spectrum of views about practical reasoning, and it suffers from a shortage of contemporary defenders. This is perhaps not surprising: suppose that the question of what the legitimate forms of practical reasoning are is itself a practical question (the question of *how* to think rationally); then if nihilism were true, there would be no good arguments for it. Likewise, it might seem hard to imagine how an argument against nihilism could fail to beg the question, and this may explain why there are so few attempts to refute it.[7] However, arguments for nihilism (treated as a view about the facts, rather than about what to do) can be found in Hume,[8] and the position was probably entailed by emotivism, the logical positivists' favored metaethics. If you think that what look like practical judgments are *merely* the expressions of emotions, understood as 'raw feels', then, as was pointed out at the time, it is hard to see how they could contradict each other; it is just as hard to see how they could entail one another.[9]

Nihilism should be regarded as the null hypothesis against which other accounts of practical reasoning must be defended. That may prove in the end to be an overly ambitious demand; as with other forms of radical skepticism, convincing refutations of nihilism may after a while start to look like an unattainable ideal. But, as with other forms of skepticism, we can expect the attempts at refutation to teach us a good deal about that whose existence we are trying to demonstrate.

INSTRUMENTALISM

Instrumentalism holds that all practical reasoning is means-end reasoning, that is, that figuring out what to do is entirely a matter of determining how to achieve one's goals or satisfy one's desires. Because infinite regresses are generally not thought possible in instrumental justification (finite creatures have only finitely many suitably distinct desires), and because circularity in instrumental justification is thought to be unreasonable, the instrumentalist position usually has it that practical justification bottoms out in desires one just has: you can reason about how to get what you want, but not about what to want in the first place. Instrumentalism is the default view in the field, and probably among philosophers in general;[10] it is represented in this volume by Christoph Fehige's essay.

An argument for a theory of practical reasoning explicitly or implicitly takes a stand on the question of how such arguments should work, and Fehige's chapter represents one widely held view on the question. Think of how field linguists construct a grammar for a language: quizzing native speakers about what particular utterances are grammatical (that is, collecting their linguistic intuitions) and formulating rules to cover most of the judgments about particular cases. Armed with the rules, they are then in a position to classify some utterances as ungrammatical (even if those utterances still sound fine to the native speakers). Nelson Goodman labeled the outcome of this process "reflective equilibrium" and used it as a model for reasoning about the rules of rational inference: "a rule is amended if it yields an inference we are unwilling to accept; an inference is rejected if it violates a rule we are unwilling to amend."[11] In the case at hand, if most of the practical inferences we regard as legitimate fall under the heading of means-end inference, a handful of exceptions can be ruled out as irrational on the basis of the account. We will see a further instance of this form of argument below.

There are other ways into instrumentalism as well. One of these, internalism, has taken on a life of its own, and I will discuss it shortly under its own heading. Perhaps the next most discussed is to see instrumentalism as tied to belief-desire psychology. The idea here is that we can establish what the mental states that make up practical reasoning must be, and doing so will restrict the forms of possible practical reasoning to one. While Fehige's version of instrumentalism makes how desires *feel* centrally important, this is a very unusual position in the contemporary debate (though it does try to capture what it is that the man in the street finds so gripping about his wants). The more common view is that desires need have no phenomenology at all. Beliefs and desires are distinguished from each other in terms of *direction of fit*: beliefs are supposed to fit the world and are changed when they don't; desires are what the world is supposed to fit, and the world gets changed when it doesn't match the desires. If it can be shown that a mental state that figures in practical reasoning must have one or the other of these directions of fit, but not both, then practical reasoning will have to proceed from desires, evidently by way of beliefs about how to satisfy them.[12]

This kind of argument for instrumentalism might seem unpromising, for a reason made vivid by an example of John Searle's: most shoes have one direction of fit (the shoe is supposed to fit the foot), but Cinderella's shoe had the other direction of fit (the Prince required the foot to fit the shoe).[13] That is, ordinary objects don't have intrinsic directions of fit; what the direction of fit is depends on the use to which the object is put. There's no reason to think that mental representations differ from ordinary objects in this regard, and so the question of what directions of fit they have is the question of how they are deployed—or, more carefully worded, since much of how we think is up to us, how they are *to be* deployed. But that question is just, What are the correct forms of reasoning, practical and otherwise? This means that we should not expect to be able to establish what the available mental states are without bringing to bear a theory of practical reasoning, which means, in turn, that the kind of argument we are considering will usually beg the question.[14]

Whether or not belief-desire psychology can be made to serve as a premise in an argument for instrumentalism, theories of practical reasoning and mental ontologies are very tightly linked. If, as I have been suggesting, the direction of explanation is from the former to the latter, the theory of practical reasoning is important not just for ethics but for philosophy of mind as well; arriving at a view as to how practical reasoning is to be done will tell you what kinds of items the mind contains.

Before we move on to the debate over internalism, note that there are a number of much more straightforward things to be said for the

instrumentalist position. Means-end reasoning is perhaps the least controversial form that practical reasoning has been alleged to take: we all know
what it is like to try to figure out how to achieve a goal, and we know
how to determine whether instrumental reasoning has been successful or
not. Dreier's essay argues that if nihilism is false—that is, if there are any
legitimate forms of practical reasoning—then means-end reasoning must
be one of them; Vogler argues elsewhere that means-end rationality is not
optional, because it is built into the structure of actions; and Korsgaard
argues that instrumental rationality is part and parcel of being an agent
at all.[15] Since instrumental reasoning proceeds from desires you have,
your stake in the results of such reasoning seems very clear—the actions
it tells you to take promise to get you things you already want. When
people do seem to act for reasons, it is generally possible to ascribe
to them an appropriate desire. And noninstrumental practical reasoning
would evidently allow one's ultimate desires to be corrected by others,
but as Bernard Williams reminds us in chapter 4, we are familiar with
such attempts at correction, and as a rule they are heavy-handed, dogmatic, and unconvincing. Accordingly, instrumentalists insist that the
burden of proof lies with their opponents.

INTERNALISM

A further way of getting instrumentalism off the ground is what nowadays often gets called *internalism*: to a first approximation, the idea that
reasons for action must invoke desires. After all, only desires, broadly
construed, can explain actions, and reasons for action must be able, in
suitable circumstances, to explain actions. The question of how reasons
for action are connected to motivations was the subject of an older debate
in the ethics literature about whether such reasons were "internal"; John
Robertson's essay in this volume lays out the main lines of that debate
(and sorts out the confusingly many different ways the labels "internalist"
and "externalist" have been used).

    The view that reasons for action bottom out in motivations was taken
up and developed by Bernard Williams in his influential essay "Internal
and External Reasons." (This reprinting is supplemented by further notes
that summarize the situation as he now sees it.) Much of the subsequent
controversy has had to do with how internalism is related to instrumentalism; Brad Hooker's brief reply (chapter 5), which usefully outlines the
argument in that essay, claims that the reasons Williams gives for inter-

nalism presuppose instrumentalism. Alternatively, internalism could be thought of as a more sophisticated successor to instrumentalism: one way of distinguishing the views arises from the thought, at work in "Internal and External Reasons," that there is more to desire-oriented practical reasoning than finding a *means* (where this is understood as a cause of the object of one's desire); a better view will be more generous about how practical reasons can be extracted from desires.[16]

The requirement that practical inference be driven by the agent's motivations was expected to discriminate against inference rules that purport to tell you what to do, *whatever* your motivations. But Korsgaard's essay, responding to Williams, argues that the internalist connection between motivation and reasons for action cannot be used to discriminate between one form of practical inference and another. If the internalist argument works against more-than-instrumental views (such as the Kantian practical reasoning she favors), then, she points out, it will also work against instrumental reasoning and leave you with nihilism. Conversely, if the internalist argument does not work against instrumental reasons, it will not work against (e.g.) Kantian reasons either.[17]

INCOMMENSURABILITY OF ENDS

Instrumental reasoning is *defeasible*, that is, an apparently satisfactory instrumental inference can be defeated by adding further premises. For instance, if my end is to have an espresso, a suitable means might be going to a particular café, but I might quite properly retract my decision when I learn that its management donates a percentage of the café's profits to a terrorist group. There are obviously indefinitely many defeating conditions of this kind, and if we want to understand how means-end reasoning works, we should be able to say under what circumstances a means-end inference ought (and ought not) to go through. (The issue is relevant to the correctness of instrumentalism; if it takes noninstrumental practical reasoning to settle which of various competing considerations is to take priority, then instrumentalism will have turned out to be mistaken.)

If the ends are commensurable—that is, intuitively, if their values are all measurable on a single scale—then one can choose the most important end (or rather, the collection of jointly satisfiable ends that is most important). In the instrumentalist picture, the relative importance of an end is a matter of how strongly it is desired. Full-fledged commensurability of ends is thus a matter of desires having something like numerically representable strengths. Whether ends or desires (and, for that matter, values) really *are* commensurable is controversial.[18] Martha Nussbaum's essay uses a reading of Plato's *Protagoras* to develop the idea that commensurability should be thought of not as a characteristic of our desires and the objects of our evaluative attitudes as they now stand but as a proposal for radical reform. If our desires and evaluations were made suitably homogenous by being redirected to a single commensurating end, then instrumental reasoning would work across the board. (On her reading, Socrates tries pleasure out for this role, but in principle, other ends with the right structure would do just as well.)

Nussbaum lays out both the benefits one might expect this kind of reform to deliver—first and foremost, that practical reasoning would become a far more systematized technique, one that delivered answers to hard questions about what to do routinely rather than exceptionally—and the price that we would have to pay for it. If, as I earlier suggested, the question of how to reason practically is itself a practical question, one would expect instrumentalists to demand cost-benefit analyses of the effects of reasoning instrumentally.[19] Nussbaum's argument responds to this demand, but if commensurability of ends really is a condition for instrumentalism's being workable, it amounts to an argument against instrumentalism.

Her discussion also highlights an important methodological issue: Is the question about what forms practical reasoning legitimately takes one of discovery or of invention? That is, are we looking for the immutable forms of practical logic that are, as it were, there already? Or are we trying to come up with a technique for figuring out what to do that works well for us, whether one of the several we have on hand or one of the indefinitely many we might make up?

SATISFICING

In 1976 Jimmy Carter ran for President on the slogan: "Why not the best?" One answer, given some time back by Herbert Simon, is that finding the best choice can be in various ways too expensive.[20] Another is that choice sets may fail to contain maximal elements; when there is no best choice, choosing the best is not an option.[21] One alternative to maximizing is satisficing, that is, choosing an option that is, while perhaps not the best, good enough. Satisficing is naturally thought of as instrumentalist in spirit, and is defended as a kind of second-level maximizing: the best first-level strategy, once typical information and computational costs are taken into account, may be satisficing rather than maximizing.[22] In chapter 10, Michael Slote defends satisficing as being in line with our intuitions about the rationality of particular choices; that is, like Fehige, he gives what looks like a reflective-equilibrium argument for his theory of practical reasoning. Perhaps the most important task facing satisficing accounts of practical rationality is coming up with a principled, usable method of determining what counts as good *enough*.

REASONING WITH MAIEUTIC ENDS

A standard objection to instrumentalism is that it makes ultimate ends come out arbitrary: your ultimate ends are the things you just happen to want; they are beyond the reach of deliberation and rational control. But we know from experience that this is not what our lives are like. A response to the objection can stay within the spirit of instrumentalism by appealing to maieutic ends. A second-order end (also called a second-order desire) is an end whose content consists of having other ends or desires. Maieutic ends are a kind of second-order end for, roughly, filling up affective space with ends. For example, you might want to have a career in medicine, for entirely financial reasons; in order to have the career, you have to care about the right things, e.g., healing the sick; so you come to want to have the end of healing the sick. As the example suggests, it is possible to reason about the desirability of wanting something, without expanding the repertoire of inference patterns beyond the instrumental. One can (it is held) adopt desires that are ultimate in the sense that their objects are not wanted as means to further ends; but one can also adopt these desires for instrumental reasons, because although the objects of the desires are not wanted as means to further ends, the desires themselves are so wanted. In chapter 11 David Schmidtz develops and defends this approach.

PLANS

On the planning view of rational deliberation advanced by Michael Bratman, practical reasoning consists largely in the adoption, filling in, and reconsideration of plans. In Bratman's usage, plans have two important characteristics that distinguish them from desires. First, they are typically *incomplete*: your plan for flying to Spain may include the intention of getting to the airport, but until the day arrives, it may well not include a subplan for getting to the airport, e.g., calling a taxi, waiting for it, getting in, and taking it there. Second, plans are supposed to be *stable*: normally, one reasons about how to execute and fill in one's plan, but not, unless special circumstances arise, about whether to reject the plan in favor of some other.

Practical reasoning that avails itself of plans has advantages over reasoning that uses only beliefs and desires. Because plans are stable, plans make the practical reasoning one has to do manageable by framing one's deliberations, and so restricting the number of options that need to be considered. Also because plans are stable, they can faciliate interpersonal and intrapersonal coordination.[23] Because plans are usually filled in as needed, they can efficiently take account of information that becomes available later rather than earlier.

Suppose that if you must reconsider every time a new bit of information turns up, your decision making task will swamp your cognitive resources, and that this makes rational a policy that triggers reconsideration of one's plans only on special occasions. Suppose that you adopt a plan because you believe, rationally, that it will best satisfy your desires. And suppose circumstances change so that it no longer does, but your rationally held policy for reconsidering plans does not take the change in circumstances to warrant reconsideration. Then the instrumentalist theory may hold that it is irrational for you to perform the actions dictated by the plan, because executing the plan will not best satisfy your current desires, whereas the planning theory will hold that it is rational, because you are rationally refusing to reconsider a rationally adopted plan. This means that the planning theory of practical rationality can deliver prescriptions for action that differ from those of the traditional instrumentalist theory.

SPECIFICATIONISM

Many of our ends—runs one objection to instrumentalism—are simply too vague or indefinite to serve as starting points for means-end reasoning, so practical reasoning must consist partly in further specifying the overly indefinite ends. For instance, I want to improve my looks, but before actually making purchases at the makeup counter, I need to figure out just what improvement in my looks would *be*. The early pivotal papers by Aurel Kolnai and David Wiggins appear in this volume. Kolnai, who thinks that Aristotle was an instrumentalist, develops specificationism as an alternative to Aristotle's view, while Wiggins attributes the specificationist view to Aristotle.

In contrast to the three immediately preceding positions, which remain instrumentalist in spirit, specificationism (like the further positions we will survey) is a full-fledged alternative to the view that all practical reasoning is means-end reasoning: only when supplemented with the rational specification of ends is instrumental reasoning viable at all. That said, the full-fledgedness needs to be qualified: some specification of ends (or rules, or whatever) can, of course, be merely instrumental. When my goal is to write a very good paper, much of the further specification that is necessary before I can actually start to write is noninstrumental (I still need a much more definite conception of what it is I want to write).[24] When my goal is to write my way through the paper I have thoroughly outlined, the point of the further specification—of the way I frame the sentences—is to serve the already fully specified goal. The reader is warned that this distinction is almost never made explicit in the literature, and that it is very easy to lose track of it.

The most important item on the specificationist agenda is to make out what distinguishes correct or rational specifications from incorrect or irrational specifications of an insufficiently definite goal. Sarah Broadie has pressed this point, agreeing that Aristotle holds that we move from less to more definite specifications of our ends, but denying that this could be *reasoning*: since the conclusions of such trains of thought have more content than their starting points, the starting points do not constrain the conclusions, and we have no way to distinguish correct specifications from incorrect specifications.[25]

Henry Richardson has taken up the challenge of showing where the added value comes from.[26] There is an additional, so-far-unmentioned reason for the specification of ends. Many of our ends conflict, but often those conflicts (whether between one's own ends or the ends of different people) can be removed by further specification of the ends in question. Since the point of cospecification is to remove conflicts between ends, specifications should be chosen that make the ends cohere with one another (and with other background elements of one's evaluative system). What this position comes to will depend on just what coherence is taken to be; evidently, this way of developing the specificationist view requires, first of all, the further specification of coherence.

Three remarks about the current state of specificationist theory. First, while Richardson's way of further specifying the specificationist view is, right now, the most developed, it may prove to be just one among several options. Perhaps the point is not always to *resolve* conflict; one might, for instance, sharpen up vague ends or rules in order to introduce conflict between them—say, in the name of brand differentiation or as a negotiating tactic or as a way of escalating hostilities.[27] Second, the specificationist view, which in its earliest formulations was too vague actually to be applied, has evolved by itself undergoing further specification—as one would expect if settling on the right way to do practical reasoning were itself an exercise in practical reasoning. But if that is what is going on, it is an especially delicate exercise. Until the view has been specified enough to be applied to this very problem, how can one tell whether one candidate specification or another is the right way to proceed? Third, the cases that have anchored and driven development of the approach have almost all been drawn from the domain of moral theory. This is surprising, since one would think that there are well-documented cases in other areas— for instance, the design of novel products and technologies—that would allow one to investigate specificationist reasoning without requiring one to cope with difficult moral questions at the same time.[28]

COHERENCE-DRIVEN REASONING

Practical reasoning is sometimes thought to be a matter of adjusting one's practical take on things in the direction of greater coherence. Just what this suggestion amounts to will depend both on what the elements of one's practical take on things are thought to be and on what the coherence of such elements with one another is supposed to consist in. For instance, if preferences are the relevant items, coherence might be understood to consist in the agent's preferences satisfying the conditions for his having a well-defined utility function. I'll return shortly to the expected-utility model; for the moment, the following problem will motivate looking at other ways of filling out the idea of coherence. No sense has been given to the notion of a set of preferences being *more* or *less* coherent; your preferences are either coherent (if they induce, that is, can be represented by, a utility function), or they are not. Thus the expected-utility approach to coherence specifies an ideal that is unattainable for human beings, without saying what it would be to move closer to it or farther away.

The elements of one's practical take on things might alternatively be thought to consist of goals, subgoals, and actions; emotions and values are two others that could be included in the mix. In this case, coherence-driven practical deliberation would amount to choosing the subset of the goals and actions under consideration that best cohere with one another (and with one's emotions or values, if those are part of the coherence problem). Practical reasoning of this kind can be described as *inference to the most coherent plan*. (In the event that finding the most coherent plan is impractical, the recommendation is to find as coherent a plan as one can.) The proposal is worth investigating for a number of reasons. It is likely to be more realistic in the demands it makes on an agent than other approaches; for instance, you do not need to know exactly how strong your desires are, or exactly what the utilities of the various outcomes are, or precisely what the relevant conditional probabilities are, in order to be in a position to make a pretty coherent choice. (This suggests that coherentist choice can sometimes bypass the incommensurabilities that, we saw, were a problem for instrumentalists.) Goals that hang together are likely to be more efficient in their use of resources, and coherent plans of action are more likely to work, than decisions to embark on nonoverlapping and competing courses of action. Plans of action are in some way or other constitutive of persons and of lives; a certain degree of coherence is necessary both to being a (unified) agent and to having a (single) life. So if being a person with a life is desirable, then so are coherent plans (though perhaps we do not always want maximally coherent lives; a life in which everything is too tightly locked into place is likely to be brittle). Coherence-driven accounts are another alternative to the instrumentalist paradigm; for example, goals can be adopted on the ground that they cohere with other goals that one already has, even if achieving them would not be a means to any end that one already has.

The most urgent issue in this area is the development of comparative notions of coherence that are precise enough to give clear answers to questions of the form "Of these competing plans, which is the most coherent?" Without notions of coherence that are usable in this way, appeals to coherence are empty, and the merits of coherence-driven accounts of practical reasoning cannot be assessed. Paul Thagard's essay describes one way of modeling deliberative coherence computationally, and the computational model gives us a precise rendering of (one version of) coherence.

UTILITY MAXIMIZATION

The common idea that expected-utility theory is a satisfactory rendition of practical reasoning is hard to place on the spectrum of views we are considering, because it is given two very different readings: on one, it is a kind of instrumentalism (where the agent's goal is to maximize his expected utility),[29] and on the second, it provides a formal notion of coherence (see above). Michael Mandler's essay explains the expected-utility formalism and the different interpretations it has been given, and he argues that the justifications for the different requirements on patterns of preferences presuppose differing interpretations of preference. (While chapter 17 is somewhat technical, it presupposes only high school algebra.)

As a matter of fact, the formalism may well be compatible with other positions on the spectrum as well. It is certainly compatible with nihilism, and the wide availability of personal computers has made this easy to see: to the computer-literate, the expected-utility formalism looks like a data compression technique, or perhaps an encryption device, rather than a representation of reasoning, or even of rationality in one's preferences. The formalism gives a way of *representing* one's preferences—provided that they satisfy a handful of actually quite demanding conditions—by assigning real numbers ("utilities") to outcomes, in such a way that selecting the action with the highest expected utility will be the choice conforming to one's preferences. That is, the formalism performs a function analogous to those of the popular ZIP and Compress programs: just as these programs store your information in a file formatted to take up less space on your hard disk than an uncompressed file, so the expected utility formalism allows you to encode unmanageably many preferences as much more manageable real numbers. Of course, there may be as many numbers as there were preferences in the first place, and if one is unlucky, these numbers may not be much more manageable than the preferences had been (in which case, one can think of the encoding as encryption rather than compression). Thought of in either of these two ways, however, retrieving your original preferences via an expected-utility calculation is no more practical reasoning than retrieving your original file by decompressing a "zipped" file (or by decrypting an encrypted file) is theoretical reasoning. And the formalism could be used to encode suitably structured preferences even if there were nothing that counted as practical reasoning at all, that is, even if nihilism were correct.

RESOLUTION OF PRACTICAL CONTRADICTIONS

One important aspect of theoretical reasoning (that is, reasoning directed toward belief) is resolving contradictions in one's system of beliefs, and freedom from contradiction is an important contributor to theoretical coherence.[30] How we revise our beliefs in the face of contradiction is not well understood, but we can expect that practical rationality will also require freedom from practical contradiction, that freedom from practical contradiction will be an important contributor to practical coherence,[31] and that practical reasoning will be directed at, among other things, resolving practical contradictions. The prior question here is, What is to be understood by *practical contradiction*?

One answer, canvassed by Onora O'Neill's essay, is that one can have incoherent intentions, as when one adopts an end but refuses to pursue the means to it. (A variation on the idea that intentions can be incoherent invokes universalizability, which I will discuss shortly.[32]) And a second answer suggests that practical contradictions can be generated in desires, on the model of so-called "Evening Star, Morning Star" cases.[33] Just as discovering that the Evening Star is also the Morning Star can introduce an explicit contradiction into one's system of beliefs (as, e.g., when one had believed that the Evening Star was habitable, but that the Morning Star was not), so discovering that the objects of a desire and of an aversion are identical can similarly bring one up short. A gentleman of two centuries ago, realizing suddenly that defending his honor would, in the circumstances in which he found himself, simply be murder, might give up either his practical commitment to his honor or his commitment to not committing murder, or he might adjust his understanding of those commitments in hard-to-anticipate ways.

UNIVERSALIZABILITY

Kantian theories of practical reasoning typically require that reasons be universalizable: roughly, that it be possible for everyone in like circumstances to act likewise on the basis of similar reasons. Universalizability is usually motivated by one or another understanding of the Principle of Sufficient Reason: that if satisfying a given description is a good enough reason for an action in one case, it must be a good enough reason in another case, and that one's practical reasons can be recast in the form of descriptions (rather than, say, proper names). O'Neill argues that the requirement imposes substantial constraints on what actions are permissible, and she explains how the requirement can be proceduralized. Universalizability acts as a filter through which proposed actions and the reasons for them are passed, but it can also be used to generate reasons on its own when not acting on a proposed reason would fail the universalizability test. Contemporary interest in universalizability is closely tied to the role it plays in Kantian moral theory, which today is one of the most prominent positions in ethics.[34]

PRACTICAL EMPIRICISM

On the views we have seen so far, the source of an agent's reasons for action lies *within*: in the agent's goals or ends or desires (instrumentalism, satisficing, maieutic ends), in the agent's intentions (the planning view, Kantian universalizability), or in how all these factors cohere with one another. On the instrumentalist view, for instance, experience can supply the facts needed to determine how to attain one's ends, but the ends themselves are set from inside, by one's desires. Against this, practical empiricism has it that it is both possible and necessary to learn what matters or what is important from experience, and that there is no reason to think that goals, priorities, evaluations and other like pieces of an agent's cognitive equipment will be useful guides to action if the world is not allowed to have its say in what they look like. The desires and intentions with which one comes to a situation may be simply irrelevant (likely when the circumstances are novel), or their objects may prove disappointing when obtained; successful agency requires an ability to correct one's assessments and agenda on the fly.

For instance, thirst is an apparently unproblematic desire, and it turns out to be hardwired in. In the environments in which people evolved, this was a sensible design move: a liquid you could drink was bound to be water; a person who is sufficiently dehydrated will die; so having dehydration trigger an overriding desire to drink seems like the right thing. Today, however, this design feature looks like a case of premature optimization. People are stranded in the Sahara on a fairly regular basis, and they end up drinking the motor fluids in their vehicle: the radiator fluid, the oil, the gasoline, and so on.[35] Here is a circumstance in which the overridingly strong desire to drink liquids is inappropriate, given that the point of being equipped with that desire is to maintain the organism's hydration levels. And this is something the victims can understand;

drinking motor oil is only going to make things worse. But since jeeps were not around when evolution "designed" human beings, and since evolution did not design human beings in the Sahara, it was not a circumstance that evolution was in a position to anticipate.

There are a number of outstanding issues for the practical empiricist, and I will highlight just three of them. First, the claim that one learns what matters from experience leaves open the question of what the inference patterns through which such learning takes place are. They must be inductive, in a very minimal sense, since the agent is generalizing from a past he has seen to a future he has not. But induction need not be—and probably should not be—induction by enumeration. Second, the practical empiricist needs to identify the indices used in learning what is important; my essay suggests that pleasure functions in human beings as an indicator of desirability, and Jennifer Hawkins has argued that desires are observations of, roughly, value. Finally, the practical empiricist owes an argument that learning what matters from experience is in fact practically rational.[36]

REDESCRIPTION AS PRACTICAL REASONING

To draw the right conclusion about what to do, you normally have to have an adequate description of your situation. Arriving at such a description is usually regarded as theoretical rather than practical reasoning; you are reasoning about the facts, rather than about the values. Iris Murdoch differs on this point: arriving at the description that is ultimately the basis for action is the important and hard part of practical reasoning (in part because facts cannot be distinguished from values—or, more interestingly, because the attempt to do so is itself the expression of a particular set of values).[37] Murdoch's views are the origin of contemporary particularism, an approach to moral philosophy that can claim figures such as John McDowell and Jonathan Dancy.[38]

Murdoch's discussion focuses almost entirely on one aspect of the process of redescription, that of overcoming the temptation to see situations in emotionally convenient ways. In her most famous example, a mother conquers her jealousy and learns to see her daughter-in-law as refreshing, simple, spontaneous, and delightfully youthful, rather than as vulgar, rude, undignified, and tiresomely juvenile. Murdoch's insight is important but incomplete: even if one agrees that redescribing one's situation is practical reasoning, it will be hard to accept that such redescription is all there really is to figuring out what to do; and it will be as hard to agree that all there really is to successful redescription is getting past the emotionally induced distortions.

Practical reasoning is reasoning directed towards action, and so there is a tendency in the literature to think that instances of practical reasoning must terminate in an action or in a decision to act. This cannot be right: just as one could engage in inconclusive theoretical reasoning (where one realizes that one does not have enough evidence to arrive at a conclusion), so one could engage in inconclusive practical reasoning (where one thinks things over but, quite correctly, fails to come to a decision). Murdoch provides a further corrective to this too-simple model. If you leave your deliberating until it is time to act, you will be insufficiently prepared and will end up making a leap in the dark. Acquiring the right descriptions—the right way of *seeing* matters—must be done ahead of time, probably long before you can anticipate the choices and decisions in which you will need to deploy those descriptions. Part of practical reasoning is building up a conceptual toolkit, or a kind of practical or moral expertise. A stretch of practical reasoning may end in adding a concept to your repertoire, and that concept may, for all you know, never actually be used to determine an action. If your practical reasoning is done ahead of time and stored up for when you need it, such reasoning, even if it is done properly, may never eventuate in a decision or an action.

INFERENTIAL EXPRESSIVISM

Robert Brandom holds that desire ascriptions merely express commitments to the "material" (i.e., substantive) correctness of practical inferences, inferences that do not themselves involve desires. For instance, to say that someone desires not to get wet is to make explicit his commitment to inferring "I will take my umbrella" from "It is going to rain." The desire, Brandom insists, is not a suppressed premise of the inference. This is tantamount to an argument against instrumentalism, to the effect that the instrumentalist position radically misconceives the point of ascribing desires to agents. The omnipresence of desires served by one's actions is not, as it has been taken to be, evidence for instrumentalism.[39] Rather, that one's practical inferences can generally be recast in a form that invokes desires is entirely *neutral* with respect to the question of what patterns of practical inference are legitimate. Brandom's view is the maximally permissive position on our spectrum: for all we know, there could be indefinitely many quite different kinds of legitimate practical inference.

THE QUESTION OF METHOD

In the course of reviewing the most important positions on the spectrum of substantive views about practical reasoning, we have also seen a number of different ways of arguing for views of this kind: reflective-equilibrium approaches, which appeal to intuitions about rationality; attempts to tie patterns of inference to structures of action or agency, or to views in the philosophy of mind; reflexive arguments (where the pattern of inference being argued for is used in that very argument); and so on. Evidently, entering into the debate about the right way to reason practically means entering into another, second-order debate as well, a debate regarding the right ways to *argue* about practical reasoning.

Although I have been surveying the field rather than conducting an argument, I nonetheless want to draw a couple of conclusions from what we have seen. The first and most obvious is that there are by now too many competing theories of practical reasoning out there for unreflectively adopting one to remain a respectable option—especially if, as I have suggested, important consequences, within philosophy and without, will follow from one's answer. The second and perhaps less obvious conclusion is that unreflectively adopting a mode of arguing about practical reasoning is no longer respectable either. My quick list of the competing modes of argument shows that although the second-order question has received surprisingly little attention, it can no longer be postponed.

Acknowledgments

This essay draws on material that previously appeared in my 1998. For comments on earlier drafts, I'm grateful to Jon Bendor, Jim Fearon, Christoph Fehige, Ariela Lazar, Jitka Maleckova, Tamar Schapiro, and David Schmidtz.

Notes

1. For an overview of earlier work, see Raz 1978 and Wallace 1990.

2. Buss 1999.

3. For a recent treatment that emphasizes these questions, see Searle forthcoming. Akrasia, or weakness of will, does come in for discussion in Nussbaum's chapter; perhaps the most influential article on this topic in the past thirty years or so is Davidson 1980. For a review of attempts to deny the possibility of akrasia, see Walker 1989. An extensive discussion of the problem of akrasia may be found in Mele 1987.

4. Christoph Fehige invokes a related device in his chapter. See Gibbard 1990, 18–22, for a brief critical overview of this approach.

5. Anderson 1993.

6. Nagel 1970, Parfit 1986, Korsgaard 1996b.

7. Railton (1997) tries out various answers one could give to someone toying with nihilism.

8. Hume 1739/1978, 413–418, 456–470. See Darwall 1983, 53, for this kind of take on Hume's position. For reconstructions of Hume's arguments, see Hampton 1995 and Millgram 1995.

9. For a *locus classicus* of emotivism, see Stevenson 1959. There's a delicate point here, which is that a dismissive view of the emotions is needed for the conclusion to stick. On a cognitively rich understanding of the emotions, emotivism need not entail nihilism.

10. Hume 1777/1975, 293, gives an early expression of the view. The position is often called Humeanism, and Hume's statement "Reason is, and ought only to be the slave of the passions" (1739/1978, 415) is (controversially) read as an instrumentalist slogan. However, we have already noted that Hume also provides arguments for nihilism, and still other views on practical reasoning have been discerned in Hume's writings as well. To prevent confusion, I'll just avoid using the locution "Humean."

11. Goodman 1979, 64; see also pp. 62–65.

12. For an argument along these lines, see Smith 1987; the argument is recapitulated in Smith 1994, chap. 4. In her essay in this volume, Vogler discusses the original purposes of Anscombe's distinction between the different directions of fit. Velleman (2000) points out that many kinds of mental attitude are about the way the world is (not just believing but, e.g., assuming), and many are about how the world is to be (not just desiring, but, e.g., fantasizing). It follows that there must be more to these mental states than a representation of a state of affairs plus the contrast between being about how the world is and being about how the world should be.

13. Searle 1983, 8, n.

14. For a related objection, see van Roojen 1995, esp. pp. 48–53. While arguments for instrumentalism from belief-desire psychology will work only if reasons for accepting the psychology can be found that are independent of one's theory of practical reasoning, one might still want to look further for reasons of this kind. David Lewis has appealed to the way in which the formalism of decision theory splits up practical considerations into probabilities and utilities; as an unusually articulate advocate of this not unusual line of defence, he is worth quoting: "Decision Theory is an intuitively convincing and well-worked-out formal theory of belief, desire, and what it means to serve our desires according to our beliefs. . . . Surely it is fundamentally right. If an anti-Humean Desire-as-Belief Thesis collides with Decision Theory, it is the Desire-as-Belief Thesis that must go" (2000, 45). Now when one puts forth such a consideration, it's very important to be clear

about what its force is. Is it an appeal to the elegance of a mathematical representation (which, after all, is what expressions like "intuitively convincing" often mean in contexts like this)? It then amounts to an argument only if one takes the elegance of a way of putting a claim to be an argument for its truth. Is it an appeal to a substantive view about practical reasoning? In that case, it is question-begging if the ultimate use of the point is to settle what the correct substantive view about practical reasoning is. One hopes that it is not simply an appeal to *prestige*. Another variation on the move is to argue, as does Gauthier, that "the maximizing conception of rationality is almost universally accepted and employed in the social sciences"; that conception, which invokes agents' preferences, "treats practical reason as strictly instrumental" (Gauthier 1986, 8, 25). Whether this consideration counts as a weighty reason for accepting instrumentalism depends on how happy one is with the current state of the social sciences. Gauthier is right to identify what is there called "Rational Choice Theory" as one of the dominant paradigms in the social sciences; this means that to reject instrumentalism as a theory of practical reasoning is to call for a change of method in the social sciences. We have here another way in which work on practical reasoning can have important and far-reaching consequences.

15. Vogler, forthcoming, Korsgaard 1997.

16. Three remarks. First, not everyone will agree that this is the right gloss on 'means'—rather than, say, a consideration whose point is given by the satisfaction of a desire. Second, the notion of internalism has also recently taken on a sense in which it insists only that something 'inside' an agent's psychology account for his actions, whether or not that something is particularly desire-like. On such a view, practical reasons that bottom out in a 'practical identity' (e.g., one's understanding of oneself as a philosophy professor, a Canadian, a "made man", and so on) would count as internal. (For practical identities as a source of reasons, see Korsgaard 1996b, p. 101 and *passim*.) Third, and perhaps surprisingly, whether or not it is possible to be an internalist without being an instrumentalist, it is possible to be an instrumentalist without being an internalist: Fehige's version of instrumentalism is an example of such a view.

17. Hampton (1998) has likewise argued that instrumental and other patterns of practical inference are equally metaphysically "queer," and that we cannot use the idea that desires and preferences are naturalistically respectable to decide between competing theories of practical rationality.

18. For a recent overview of the debate, see Chang 1997.

19. Stich (1990, esp. pp. 129–142, 145–149) argues that all cognitive techniques should be assessed in this way, though he does not seem to have practical reasoning specifically in mind.

20. Simon 1957, chaps. 14 and 15. For a more recent piece that places satisficing in the context of work on bounded rationality, see Simon 1990.

21. Fehige 1994; for applications of the point, see Landesman 1995; Schlesinger 1964; Nozick 1989, 225 f.

22. In fact, this approach is hard to spell out satisfactorily, because the second-order optimization problem is likely to be as hard or harder than the problem with which one started: finding the optimal strategy turns out to involve an infinite regress. See Conlisk 1996. Conlisk also provides a very useful survey of the literature and overview of the field.

23. Bratman's views have been elaborated over the past two decades, and in particular, his account of when it is rational to reconsider one's plans has undergone considerable flux. See Bratman 1987, 1999. Bratman's views were influenced by Gilbert Harman's earlier work on intentions (1976).

There is interesting related work focusing on intentions that is hard to place along the spectrum of positions we are surveying. Velleman (1989) has argued that intentions are self-fulfilling predictions (and so, practical reasoning is in fact a variety of theoretical reasoning). The predictions are self-fulfilling because agents desire to understand what they are doing, and acting on the basis of such a self-fulfilling prediction produces the requisite kind of self-understanding. Kavka (1983) considers limits on intending at will.

24. The example is due to Allen Coates.

25. Broadie 1987. It's curious that the criterion she invokes—that if a train of thought is to be reasoning, there can be nothing in the conclusion that was not already in the premises—seems obvious to contemporary authors, and that the very opposite seemed just as obvious not so long ago. John Stuart Mill, not atypically of his time and in line with much tradition, took it for granted that a train of thought could not count as reasoning unless there was *more* to the conclusion than to the premises (1973, 158–162).

26. Richardson 1994. Richardson 1990 focuses on the specification of rules.

27. I owe this suggestion to Curtis Bridgeman.

28. See, for instance, Abbate 1999 for a successful and very-well-known specification, or Latour 1996 for a failed (and so less-well-known) case.

29. For the instrumentalist interpretation, see, e.g., Gauthier 1986, 25. Against the claim that the interpretation is required, see Darwall 1983, 62–67.

30. It's usually taken for granted that freedom from contradiction is not just important but indispensible (e.g., Kornblith 1989, 210). However, freedom from contradiction may be too expensive, computationally and otherwise, to be insisted on. Thagard's accounts of coherence allow constraints generated by contradictory factors to be occasionally violated when doing so would satisfy other sufficiently weighty constraints.

31. For example, expected-utility theory, which can be interpreted as providing a coherence concept, standardly imposes the requirement that if x is preferred to y, then y is not (strictly) preferred to x.

32. O'Neill takes up this idea as well. For another treatment in very much the same spirit, see Korsgaard 1996a, 93–101. For an earlier but much less terse discussion, see Nell 1975. Kantians by and large address "contradictions in the will" and universalizability together, but the two are distinguishable, and so are presented separately here.

33. The suggestion is due to Candace Vogler, but to the best of my knowledge it has not found its way into print.

34. Korsgaard (1990) reconstructs Kant's reasons for insisting on the universalizability requirement. For work on spelling out universalizability conditions formally, see Rabinowicz 1979.

35. See Langewiesche 1996, 53, 149–152, 188.

36. Millgram (1997) develops an argument to the effect that induction in the practical domain is indeed reasoning. See also Hawkins 2000, esp. pp. 50 ff. For a predecessor of the view, see Stampe 1987, esp. pp. 358–381.

37. On this last point, see Diamond 1996.

38. See Dancy 1985, McDowell 1998, Dancy 1993. Murdoch's shorter philosophical work is collected in Murdoch 1999.

39. More carefully, on Brandom's view, desires are not quite omnipresent: some practical-inferential commitments are to be articulated using not desires but, e.g., "ought" statements. See also Brandom 1994, 243–253. His point is a relative of an older objection to the apparent omnipresence of desires due to Thomas Nagel (1970, 27–32).

References

Abbate, J. 1999. *Inventing the Internet.* Cambridge: MIT Press.

Anderson, E. 1993. *Value in Ethics and Economics.* Cambridge: Harvard University Press.

Bok, H. 1998. *Freedom and Responsibility.* Princeton: Princeton University Press.

Brandom, R. 1994. *Making It Explicit.* Cambridge: Harvard University Press.

Bratman, M. 1987. *Intention, Plans, and Practical Reasoning.* Cambridge: Harvard University Press.

Bratman, M. 1999. *Faces of Intention.* Cambridge: Cambridge University Press.

Broadie, S. W. 1987. "The Problem of Practical Intellect in Aristotle's Ethics." In J. Cleary, ed., *Proceedings of the Boston Area Colloquium in Ancient Philosophy*, vol. 3, pp. 229–252. Lanham: University Press of America.

Buss, S. 1999. "What Practical Reasoning Must Be If We Act for Our Own Reasons." *Australasian Journal of Philosophy* 77: 399–421.

Chang, R. 1997. *Incommensurability, Incomparability, and Practical Reason.* Cambridge: Harvard University Press.

Conlisk, J. 1996. "Why Bounded Rationality?" *Journal of Economic Literature* 34: 669–700.

Cullity, G., and B. Gaut 1997. *Ethics and Practical Reason.* Oxford: Clarendon Press.

Dancy, J. 1985. "The Role of Imaginary Cases in Ethics." *Pacific Philosophical Quarterly* 66: 141–153.

Dancy, J. 1993. *Moral Reasons.* Oxford: Blackwell.

Darwall, S. 1983. *Impartial Reason.* Ithaca: Cornell University Press.

Davidson, D. 1980. "How Is Weakness of the Will Possible?" In his *Essays on Actions and Events*, pp. 21–42. Oxford: Oxford University Press.

Diamond, C. 1996. "'We Are Perpetually Moralists': Iris Murdoch, Fact, and Value." In M. Antonaccio and W. Schweiker, eds., *Iris Murdoch and the Search for Human Goodness.* Chicago: University of Chicago Press.

Fehige, C. 1994. "The Limit Assumption in Deontic (and Prohairetic) Logic." In G. Meggle and U. Wessels, eds., *Analyomen 1.* Berlin: de Gruyter.

Gauthier, D. 1986. *Morals by Agreement.* Oxford: Clarendon Press.

Gibbard, A. 1990. *Wise Choices, Apt Feelings.* Cambridge: Harvard University Press.

Goodman, N. 1979. *Fact, Fiction, and Forecast*, 3rd ed. Indianapolis: Hackett.

Hampton, J. 1995. "Does Hume Have an Instrumental Conception of Practical Reason?" *Hume Studies* 21: 57–74.

Hampton, J. 1998. *The Authority of Reason.* Cambridge: Cambridge University Press.

Harman, G. 1976. "Practical Reasoning." *Review of Metaphysics* 29: 431–463.

Hawkins, J. 2000. *The Metaphysics of Value and the Normative Aspect of Experience.* Ph.D. thesis, Princeton University.

Hume, D. 1739/1978. *A Treatise of Human Nature.* Edited by L. A. Selby-Bigge and P. H. Nidditch. Oxford: Clarendon Press.

Hume, D. 1777/1975. *Enquiry Concerning the Principles of Morals.* Edited by L. A. Selby-Bigge and P. H. Nidditch. Oxford: Oxford University Press.

Kavka, G. 1983. "The Toxin Puzzle." *Analysis* 43: 33–36.

Kornblith, H. 1989. "The Unattainability of Coherence." In John Bender, ed., *The Current State of the Coherence Theory*, pp. 207–214. Dordrecht: Kluwer.

Korsgaard, C. 1990. *The Standpoint of Practical Reason.* New York: Garland.

Korsgaard, C. 1996a. *Creating the Kingdom of Ends.* Cambridge: Cambridge University Press.

Korsgaard, C. 1996b. *The Sources of Normativity.* Cambridge: Cambridge University Press.

Korsgaard, C. 1997. "The Normativity of Instrumental Reason." In Cullity and Gaut 1997, 215–254.

Landesman, C. 1995. "When to Terminate a Charitable Trust?" *Analysis* 55: 12–13.

Langewiesche, W. 1996. *Sahara Unveiled.* New York: Pantheon.

Latour, B. 1996. *Aramis, or the Love of Technology.* Translated by Catherine Porter. Cambridge: Harvard University Press.

Lewis, D. 2000. "Desire as Belief." In his *Papers in Ethics and Social Philosophy*, pp. 42–54. Cambridge: Cambridge University Press.

McDowell, J. 1998. "Virtue and Reason." In his *Mind, Value, and Reality,* pp. 50–73. Cambridge: Harvard University Press.

Mele, A. 1987. *Irrationality: An Essay on Akrasia, Self-Deception, and Self-Control.* Oxford: Oxford University Press.

Mill, J. S. 1973. *A System of Logic.* In his *Collected Works,* vol 7. London and Toronto: Routledge Kegan Paul and University of Toronto Press.

Millgram, E. 1995. "Was Hume a Humean?" *Hume Studies* 21: 75–93.

Millgram, E. 1997. *Practical Induction.* Cambridge: Harvard University Press.

Millgram, E. 1998. "Practical Reasoning." In C. Eliasmith, *Dictionary of Philosophy of Mind.* On-line resource maintained by Washington University in St. Louis. http://www.artsci.wustl.edu/~philos/MindDict/practicalreasoning.html.

Murdoch, I. 1999. *Existentialists and Mystics.* Edited by P. Conradi. New York: Allen Lane/Penguin.

Nagel, T. 1970. *The Possibility of Altruism.* Princeton: Princeton University Press.

Nozick, R. 1989. *The Examined Life.* New York: Simon and Schuster.

Nell (O'Neill), O. 1975. *Acting on Principle.* New York: Columbia University Press.

Parfit, D. 1986. *Reasons and Persons.* Oxford: Oxford University Press.

Rabinowicz, W. 1979. *Universalizability.* Dordrecht: Reidel.

Railton, P. 1997. "On the Hypothetical and Non-Hypothetical in Reasoning about Belief and Action." In Cullity and Gaut 1997, 53–79.

Raz, J. 1978. *Practical Reasoning.* Oxford: Oxford University Press.

Richardson, H. 1990. "Specifying Norms as a Way to Resolve Concrete Ethical Problems." *Philosophy and Public Affairs* 19: 279–310.

Richardson, H. 1994. *Practical Reasoning about Final Ends.* Cambridge: Cambridge University Press.

Schlesinger, G. 1964. "The Problem of Evil and the Problem of Suffering." *American Philosophical Quarterly* 1: 244–247.

Searle, J. 1983. *Intentionality.* Cambridge: Cambridge University Press.

Searle, J. Forthcoming. *Reason in Action.* Cambridge: MIT Press.

Simon, H. 1957. *Models of Man.* New York: John Wiley and Sons.

Simon, H. 1990. "Invariants of Human Behavior." In *Annual Review of Psychology* 41: 1–19.

Smith, M. 1987. "The Humean Theory of Motivation." *Mind* 96: 36–61.

Smith, M. 1994. *The Moral Problem.* Oxford: Blackwell.

Stampe, D. 1987. "The Authority of Desire." *Philosophical Review* 96: 335–381.

Stevenson, C. L. 1959. "The Emotive Meaning of Ethical Terms." In A. J. Ayer, ed., *Logical Positivism*, pp. 264–281. Glencoe: Free Press.

Stich, S. 1990. *The Fragmentation of Reason.* Cambridge: MIT Press.

Van Roojen, M. 1995. "Humean Motivation and Humean Rationality." *Philosophical Studies* 79: 37–57.

Velleman, J. D. 1989. *Practical Reflection.* Princeton: Princeton University Press.

Velleman, J. D. 2000. "The Guise of the Good." In *The Possibility of Practical Reason.* Oxford: Oxford University Press.

Vogler, C. Forthcoming. *Reason in Action.* Cambridge: Harvard University Press.

Walker, A. 1989. "The Problem of Weakness of Will." *Noûs* 23: 653–676.

Wallace, R. J. 1990. "How to Argue about Practical Reason." *Mind* 99: 355–385.

Chapter 2

Humean Doubts about Categorical Imperatives

James Dreier

Humeans are skeptical about the existence of categorical imperatives.[1] This skepticism emerges in their skepticism about morality, but it is not rooted in moral skepticism at all. Conversely, Humean skepticism about morality and its justification is rooted in a more general skepticism about the existence of categorical imperatives.

1 REASONS

Before I explain exactly what I mean by a categorical imperative, let me start with some more intuitive points. When someone offers me a reason to do something, the reason generally has a ground somewhere in some system of rules.[2] We may speak colloquially of various kinds of reasons. There are reasons of prudence, and these come from a system of rules that together form the rules of prudence. Saying that someone is acting imprudently is saying that he is flouting these rules. Telling someone that she has a reason of prudence to put away some money for a rainy day is approximately telling her that the rules of prudence demand that she put away some money for a rainy day. There are very many other sorts of rules, and with them come other sorts of reasons. For example, there are rules of baseball, and these generate reasons of baseball. We have a good reason not to send Smoltz to the mound, namely, that another player pinch-hit for him last inning. The rules of baseball forbid sending a player to the mound to pitch when he has already been yanked for a pinch hitter in the same game. There is nothing particularly mysterious about there being such a reason.

Similarly, I think, we might say that you have a reason to send a check for membership fees to the American Philosophical Association, even though they have lost their records and don't know whether you have already paid your dues. The reason is a reason of fairness. It would be unfair of you not to pay your dues, relying on the dues of others to provide the money for the APA to perform the services that you take advantage of every year. This reason is a reason of morality, and it comes from rules of morality. So far, there is nothing more mysterious about moral reasons than there is about reasons of baseball.

Still, it appears to make sense to ask whether this or that set of rules really does provide me with any reason. For example, the rules of good musicianship require (let's suppose) that I practice my scales daily. I might admit as much but still wonder whether I really do have any reason to practice my scales today. I might put it this way: do the rules of good musicianship really apply to me at all? Or this way: do I have any reason to follow those rules? Similarly for baseball reasons. Why on earth should I care about what the rules of baseball say? The request for a further justification certainly does make sense here, and often we think we can provide one. When the manager asks whether he has any reason to follow his baseball reasons, we can point out that he will not get very far in his career by flouting them, or that he's not going to get away with trying to bring Smoltz back into the game now, so there's no point in trying, or various other reasons that might be offered.

Sometimes it seems to be an open question, and an interesting and important one, whether we have any reason to follow a certain set of rules or, as we might put it, any reason to act on our reasons of such-and-such a kind. For example, it is an interesting question whether we have any reason to follow the laws of our own state. There is no mystery about what it means to tell me that I have a legal reason to pay my taxes. It means that legal rules (that is, laws) require me to pay my taxes. But I can wonder whether these rules have any justification, whether I have any reason to follow them.

When I try to answer this question, I look to other reasons, reasons external to the law itself. These other reasons have to tell me to follow laws, and they themselves have to be reasons that I really do have; otherwise the attempt to find reasons fails. The reasons I consider might be prudential, or they might be moral; either sort of reasons can be good candidates for explaining why I have reason to follow the laws of my state. Then the question can arise again, whether I have any reason to follow *these* reasons. If I don't follow the laws, then I am a criminal, but I can doubt whether this provides *me* with any reason to follow them. If legal obligations can be shown to be moral obligations, then if I don't follow laws I am immoral, but I can doubt whether these moral obligations provide me with any reason to follow the laws. If they are grounded in prudential reasons, then if I don't follow the laws I am imprudent, but I can doubt whether the rules of prudence really do provide me with reasons to follow the laws, whether I have any reason to avoid imprudence. Where might this regress of reasons end?

There is a fundamental sense, I think, of having a reason, and it is in this sense that we can wonder whether we have any reason to follow legal, moral, or prudential rules. But even in this more fundamental respect, there is no sense at all to be made of the question of whether we have any reason to follow the rules of rationality. Maybe rationality is itself nothing more than a system of rules, just as prudence and law and morality are. Even so, I will argue that rationality, and reasons of rationality, are unlike these other systems of rules and the reasons they generate. It always makes sense to think that there might be (or fail to be) reasons to follow moral, legal, or prudential rules. To think that there are or could be reasons to follow the rules of rationality is, I would say, to misunderstand what reasons are. Reasons are *in terms of* the rules of rationality. There is a reason to do something just in case it is rational to do it. That is why, in some contexts, there can be a need to justify morality or law or even prudence, but no similar need for a justification of rationality. The contrast here seems to me to be important. This paper argues that there really is such a contrast, and it tries to explain why.

2   CATEGORICAL IMPERATIVES

Humeans doubt that morality could be a set of categorical imperatives, and this doubt might even be thought of as their hallmark. Let me clarify what I mean by a categorical imperative. Following Foot (1972), I distinguish a couple of senses in which imperatives might be categorical. First, we might say that an imperative is categorical when our application of it to the behavior (or deliberations) of someone does not depend on any aim, on any desire, of that person. In this sense, the rule 'Practice your scales daily' is not categorical, since we should withdraw it upon learning that the addressee had no interest in learning to play the piano. There is little question that there are categorical imperatives in this sense: moral imperatives are a perfectly good example. Informing your critic that you aren't interested in according respect to other persons isn't going to make him withdraw the imperative to keep your promises. But this sense of 'categorical' is not the one that Humeans have their doubts about. We are interested rather in a second sense of 'categorical'. A rough try at expressing this sense is to say that a categorical imperative is one that each person has reason to follow, no matter what her desires. This is only a *rough* try because whether it succeeds in explaining the sense of 'categorical' in which Humeans deny that morality could be categorical depends on how we fill in an explanation of what it is to have a reason. But it will do for a start.

Humeans sometimes say that *no* imperatives are categorical. I think they are mistaken to say so, for reasons that will emerge. But let's focus first on the special case of moral imperatives. Why couldn't they be categorical, according to the Humean view?

Suppose that we want to explain why someone acted as he did. Suppose that he walked to the corner shortly before noon, and we want to explain why. Since he does it intentionally, we typically cite some mental states of the agent that rationalize the action. We could cite mental states of his that merely cause the behavior, but that is a different kind of explanation.[3] The classic form of explanation is the citing of a belief-desire pair. He walked to the corner shortly before noon because he wanted to eat a sandwich at noon and believed that by walking to the corner shortly before noon he could bring this state of affairs about. In this explanation we cite the agent's reason. His reason is a belief-desire pair. For short, we might say that his reason was that he wanted a sandwich, or that he thought that walking to the corner was the only way he could get a sandwich. Which is the sensible thing to say depends on context, of course. But it doesn't follow that what his reason really was depends on context. Moreover, I am denying that it depends on context. There are only pragmatic grounds, not deep ones, for describing the person's reason one way rather than another.

As I just admitted, in ordinary talk we can give reason-for-action explanations that do not make explicit reference to any desire. Maybe he walked to the corner shortly before noon because he believed that this was the only way to save his life. We would not ordinarily add, 'and he wanted to save his life'. But this is a shallow feature of ordinary talk. It is unusual but conceivable *not* to desire to save one's own life, and if indeed our agent does not, then citing his belief that walking to the corner shortly before noon was the only way to save his life provides no explanation of his walking, and so doesn't count as a reason in the explanatory sense of 'reason'. But it's also true that we sometimes seem to cite reasons for action without citing desires, when we aren't just failing to mention a desire that we assume must be present. Maybe the agent walked to the corner shortly before noon because he remembered his promise to meet his sister on the corner at noon. Do we need to add, 'and he wanted to keep his promise'? We might. But we might instead say, 'he believed that he had an obligation to keep the promise'. Then must we add, 'and he wanted to discharge his obligation'?

I think we *do* need to add *something*. For after all, some people recognize their obligations and do not act on them. What we need to add is something to the effect that this is a sort of person whom the thought of an obligation normally moves to action. The question I want to examine now is how this sort of thing, this sort of fact about a person, can sensibly and illuminatingly be described. Once that is done, we'll be in position to understand why Humeans think that moral imperatives couldn't be categorical.

3   MOTIVATING REASONS

A motivating reason is a reason that someone has to do something, where his doing it (if he does it) is explained by his having that reason. Following Michael Smith, among others, we can contrast this sort of reason with a normative reason. A normative reason is, to put it somewhat loosely, a reason that a person *ought* to do something. If she then does it, this is explained not by the fact that she had the reason but by the fact that she recognized this reason and was motivated by it. For example, I had a normative reason to wear a suit to my brother's wedding. And I did wear one. That I did is explained not by the fact that I had this reason but by the fact that I "accepted" it, we might say, that I cared about that sort of reason and recognized that I had it.

Suppose that a person has a belief and performs some action, he ϕs. What must the belief be, and what do we need to add to the belief in order to explain the action by citing the agent's reason for performing it? The simplest Humean view would be that the belief must have a content of the form 'By ϕ-ing, I will ψ', and we must add that the agent has a desire to ψ. This is Michael Smith's account in *The Moral Problem*. It requires a much longer defense than I can give here. But the main idea can be given fairly easily. The primary access that we have to the whole idea of a desire is that it is a state of mind characterized by its output in behavior. Let's allow ourselves a little weaseling: a desire to ϕ is a mental state that *normally* motivates its bearer to ϕ. 'Normally' statements are very suspicious, but for now at least we'll take it in a loose and intuitive way; we aren't offering an analysis or placing any great weight on the claim.

Putting the weasel aside, then, we have very good grounds to say that a person has a motivating reason to ϕ only when she has a desire to ψ and a belief that by ϕ-ing she will ψ. For suppose that she believed that by ϕ-ing she would ψ, and that this explains why she ϕs—that's what's necessary for her to have a motivating reason to ϕ. What do we have to add? We have to add that she had some motivation to do what she believed she would do by ϕ-ing. What state is that? A motivation to do what she believes she will do by ϕ-ing is a motivation to ψ (since that's what she believes she'll do by ϕ-ing). The state that explains this motivation is one which normally produces the motivation as its output. So it is a desire to ψ.

One might question whether this account of the desire to ψ is a correct analysis. I think this issue is probably a red herring. 'Desire' here is really a term of art. It covers what is covered in ordinary language by the notions of desire proper, wanting, valuing, having a goal, preferring, and probably many other things. What they have in common is precisely what the (weasely) analysis says.

So much for the Humean view of motivating reasons. I intend it to convince only temporarily. With it in place, we return to the question of why Humeans say that moral imperatives cannot be categorical.

A categorical imperative, I said, is one that each person has reason to follow, no matter what her desires. What kind of reason do we mean? Not a merely normative reason. Each person does have a normative reason to refrain from harming others, irrespective of what she wants. This is one sense of 'categorical', but not the one we want here. It seems that we want the sense of 'categorical' that results from plugging *motivating* reasons into the 'reason' slot of the formula. We can see now why anyone who accepts the Humean account of motivating reasons should think that what (motivating) reasons a person has depends entirely on what desires she has. For a person's having a motivating reason just is a matter of her having a belief and a desire. The reason that she has is a reason that she wouldn't have were she to lack the desire. This chunk of theory completes the simple Humean story. Let's recap.

Humeans doubt that morality could consist of categorical imperatives, because (i) a categorical imperative is one that you have reason to follow irrespective of your desires, and (ii) what you have motivating reason to do depends on your desires. If morality cannot consist of categorical imperatives, then a person can be given reasons to follow moral rules only if she has certain relevant desires. In particular, she must desire to follow moral rules, or desire what the moral rules tell her to pursue, or the like. What desires we have is a contingent fact about us. So whether a person has any reason at all to follow moral rules is a contingent matter. This is disappointing and falls short of the kind of justification we sometimes hope for. David Copp (1991) puts it this way: a justification for following moral rules that appeals to contingencies of the agent addressed is not a justification of morality per se but only a justification of morality for someone. Humeans think that this is a disappointment we will have to learn to live with.

There is a flaw in the reasoning of the last paragraph above. The conclusion, that the justification of morality is contingent, follows from the premise (let's call it a 'lemma', since it was independently established), that morality does not consist of categorical imperatives, only if the kind of reason that fills out the content of the conclusion is the same as the kind of reason that gives content to the lemma. Are the kinds of reason the same? In the lemma we are plugging motivating reasons into the 'reason' slot:

Lemma   Morality does not consist of categorical imperatives (imperatives that each person has reason to follow, no matter what her desires).

Conclusion   The justification of morality is contingent.

Is that the sort of reason we mean when we think about the justification of morality? This is still unsettled. We are thinking of reasons of rationality, which I argued are ultimate reasons in some sense. Motivating reasons are also ultimate, in a way. But it is not obvious that reasons of rationality and motivating reasons are the same thing. If they aren't, then it might be that morality can be justified to anyone, independent of her desires, because everyone has the reason of rationality to follow moral rules, even though whether a person has a motivating reason to follow moral rules is contingent.

Nearly all of the remainder of this paper is devoted to understanding the relation between motivating reasons and reasons of rationality. The next section is about motivating reasons. The section after that tries to explain the relation between accepting rules and desiring things. I will argue that generally speaking, rules give us reasons only when we "accept" them, and that *nearly* always, accepting a rule is a matter of desiring something or other. Only *'nearly'*, because there is a very important exception to this generalization. There is (at least) one rule whose acceptance cannot be a matter of desiring anything at all.

4   THE INTERPRETATION OF MOTIVATING REASONS

Are motivating reasons just the same as reasons of rationality? On the face of it, no. They do not seem to be the same *kind* of thing. Motivating reasons are psychologically real, since they are explanatory by nature. A motivating reason that you have is an empirical property that you bear, or how could it explain anything that you do? But a reason of rationality is something normative. For you to have a reason of rationality is for it to be the case that you *ought* to act in a certain way. As I said, citing a normative reason can be a kind of explanation, but it is only an explanation on the (tacit) assumption that the agent does, or at least is disposed to do, what she ought to do. As I have put it, citing a normative reason is explanatory only on the assumption that the agent *accepts* the norms in question. Here 'accepts' is really a term of art; there is a sense of 'accepting a reason', no doubt, according to which one may accept a reason and have not even the slightest tendency to act on it. But I am using 'accepts' for whatever it takes to be actually motivated by the kind of reason in question.

Since reasons of rationality are, after all, normative, they are not the same kind of thing as motivating reasons, so the Humean argument does not go through as sketched. I think this is an important fact, so let me support my claim. Someone might think that reasons of rationality are not really normative at all. Maybe standards of rationality are something like canons of interpretation, so that acting rationally is just a matter of being interpretable. In that case, to say that someone has a reason of rationality to ϕ might just be to say that in case she does ϕ, her ϕ-ing is interpretable as intentional action. While I think there must be something to this idea, it can't be correct as stated. For there is such a thing as irrational action. There is such a thing as fallacious reasoning. People do reason incorrectly, not merely from false premises, and when they do, they are reasoning precisely as they *ought not* to reason. They have good reasons not to draw the conclusions they draw. What sorts of reasons could these be? Reasons of rationality. I will give examples below, but it seems to me that the point is clear enough in the abstract. Reasons of rationality are normative.

Here is a suggestion for why motivating reasons and normative reasons of rationality might be conflated. We are calling 'motivating reasons to ϕ' those belief-desire pairs of the following form: the desire to ψ and the belief that by ϕ-ing, I will ψ. So we have this claim:

(MR) A has a motivating reason to ϕ iff there is some ψ such that A desires to ψ and A believes that by ϕ-ing, she will ψ.

Now in fact I think this claim can be understood in two different ways. According to one reading, it is really a normative claim. It says, in effect, that you ought to perform the necessary and sufficient means to your desired ends. You might not do this. You might, at least on occasion, find yourself lacking the motivation to perform the necessary and sufficient means to some end you desire. This would be a fault of yours, a failure of rationality. Glossing over some distinctions, we might say that your failure would be a failure of instrumental reason. So this reading of (MR) takes it to be a statement of the norm of instrumental reason.

Second, the claim could be understood in a different way. It might be a partial analysis of desire and belief; it might be a purported analytic truth. A motivating reason, according to this reading, would be something that actually does motivate you. The claim would be that unless you are in fact motivated to ϕ, there is no ψ such that you desire to ψ and you believe that by ϕ-ing, you will ψ. According to the analysis, a crude functionalist analysis, it is of the very essence of the desire to ψ that, when combined with the belief that by ϕ-ing you will ψ, it produces a desire in you to ϕ; and it is of the very essence of the belief that by ϕ-ing you will ψ that, when combined with the desire to ψ, it produces in you the desire to ϕ. Let's call this the 'constitutive' reading. According to it, belief and desire are partly constituted by their stated roles in the production of motivation.

I object to the second reading, for reasons I have just given. It implies that it is impossible to desire to ψ, believe that by ϕ-ing you will ψ, and yet fail to desire to ϕ. But this does not seem to be impossible; it seems to be irrational. When I say how it seems, I am admittedly reporting my intuitions, and the very existence of seriously held philosophical views to the contrary of mine demonstrates that these intuitions aren't universally shared. My intuitions are hardly unique, though. Kant says,

Who wills the end, wills (so far as reason has decisive influence on his actions) also the means which are indispensibly necessary and in his power. So far as willing is concerned, this proposition is analytic. (Ak 417)

It could alike be said 'Who wills the end, wills also (necessarily, if he accords with reason) the sole means which are in his power.' (Ak 417–8)

The parenthetic condition, in each case, is crucial. The crude functionalist reading of (MR) would in effect leave out that condition and say that willing the end *is* willing the means.[4]

Not to leave the point resting on my intuitions and the authority of Kant, let me give some theoretic backing to my objection. The desire to ψ and belief that by ϕ-ing I will ψ do, I admit, have conceptual connections to the desire to ϕ. Can we imagine someone who under no circumstances would come to have the latter desire on the basis of the former desire plus the belief? Perhaps not. Maybe this would be a case of someone so wildly irrational that we could not think of her as an agent at all. But it is a long jump to conclude that there is a universal necessary connection between beliefs and desires of the sort postulated by the second reading of (MR). For desire has other conceptual facets. For instance, in us sophisticated linguistic creatures, beliefs and desires are normally available to introspection. So I ought to know whether I desire a french fry and whether I believe that the one and only way to get one is by ordering some. So my sincere report that I so believe and so desire might be enough to ground the attribution to me, even if I don't order some french fries (or even want to order any). Good functionalist analyses ought to respect the plurality of links that mental states have to other states, to actions and linguistic behavior, to perceptual inputs, and the like. That is why I called the second reading of (MR) "crude."

But finally, even if my objection is not convincing, I want to insist on a weaker claim. We cannot have both readings of (MR) at once. They are exclusive. If, as I deny, (MR) can be read as a kind of functionalist analysis of belief and desire, then it cannot also be normative, it cannot be an expression of an instrumentalist conception of rationality. For norms are things that it is possible to violate. The idea of a norm that it is logically impossible to violate makes no sense. So reasons of rationality, which are normative, cannot be the same sorts of things as motivating reasons, which are explanatory of action. Hence (MR) defines motivating reasons only on the second, functionalist reading, and it defines a normative means/ends principle only on the first reading.

To conclude this section, let's recall why this distinction between motivating reasons and normative reasons of rationality is important.

(1) An imperative is categorical if and only if a person has reason to follow it that is independent of what she desires.

(2) A person's having reason to ϕ depends on there being some ψ such that she desires to ψ and believes that by ϕ-ing, she will ψ.

(3) So any reason a person might have depends on a desire of hers.

(4) So there are no categorical imperatives.

This argument goes through just in case 'reason' can be understood univocally in the premises (1) and (2). Premise (2) was offered and defended as a conception of motivating, explanatory reasons (though I cast some doubt on it even when construed that way). But premise (1) cannot be understood to be about motivating reasons, because if it were, then it would be perfectly obvious and trivial that there are no categorical imperatives, including moral imperatives, since it is perfectly obvious that what *motivating* reasons you have depends on your desires. We don't deny that people sometimes behave immorally. If an imperative could be categorical only if each and every person could, in fact, be motivated to follow it by arguments alone, then there would be no question of even moral imperatives being categorical.

The ground for skepticism about categorical imperatives, then, is very shaky. At least as I have presented it so far, skepticism relies on a dubious conflation of two kinds of reasons. We may doubt that there are any motivating reasons to follow moral rules that each person has necessarily and independently of what she happens to desire, but that in itself doesn't provide any ground for doubting that moral rules are categorical, since categorical imperatives are justified by *normative* reasons.

I think that skepticism is called for nonetheless. I will argue that there is something special about exactly the kind of norms of rationality that Humeans accept.[5] This special status confers a kind of necessity on the Humean norms that we may properly doubt can accrue to other sorts of norms. The request for justification, I will argue, is intelligible as a demand for reasons bearing just that kind of necessity. And we may properly doubt that the demand for moral justification can be satisfied. So we may properly doubt that moral imperatives are categorical, but we must allow that some imperatives are categorical.

5   RULES AND DESIRES

Suppose that we tell Ann that she ought to ϕ. She asks why. We cite some rules R that tell her to ϕ. She shrugs. These rules have no grip on her. She can see that the rules do tell her to ϕ, but she doesn't accept the rules, they don't motivate her. We might think, she is missing something. What is she missing? What must be true of her, that isn't, for her to be motivated by our explanation? Insofar as we think there is something wrong with Ann for failing to be motivated by the belief that she is required by R to ϕ, we will think that her missing this something is exactly what's wrong with her.

Schematic as this story is, there is an almost entirely general answer that we can give. Ann is missing a desire. How can we know this? How do we know that what she's missing isn't a capacity of some other sort, or a belief? Couldn't what's wrong with Ann be that she believes something false or that she fails to believe some truth? We know that what's missing is a desire, because we have enough characterization of the missing state to see that it is a desire with a certain specifiable content. Since she believes that were she to ϕ, she would comply with R and we want a state that gets her from that belief to the motivation to ϕ, we know that the state is the desire to comply with R. That's what the desire to comply with R *is*.

We have to be a bit careful here. We have already rejected the simple functionalist definition of desire, so we can't say that S is a desire to ψ iff S is a state producing a desire to ϕ upon input of a belief that by ϕ-ing, one will ψ. The means-end rule, (M/E), is a normative principle of rationality:

(M/E) If you desire to ψ and believe that by ϕ-ing, you will ψ, then you have a reason to ϕ.

Given that Ann is means/ends rational, all we need to give her in order to get her to ϕ is the desire to comply with R.

I said that the missing-desire answer is *almost* an entirely general answer to the question raised in the schematic story. Why only almost? We're taking it as a kind of methodological axiom that whatever is missing when someone has a belief and lacks a certain motivation is a desire of some sort or other. There doesn't seem to be any room for exceptions.

Suppose that Ann's case is like this. We tell her that she ought to take a prep course for the LSATs. She asks why. We point out that she wants to raise her chances of getting into a competitive law school, and she can raise her chances by taking the prep course. She admits as much, but she still isn't motivated to take the prep course. So we cite a rule, (M/E). Now suppose that Ann agrees that this rule does indeed instruct her to take the prep course (or at least it tells her that she has some reason to take it), given what she believes and desires, but she shrugs and doesn't accept the rule.

We must now conclude that there is something wrong with Ann. She *ought* to take (or at least to have some motivation to take) the prep course, given what she believes and wants, but she doesn't take (and doesn't even have motivation to take) the course.[6] The story is an instance of the schematic story. We can ask ourselves what exactly Ann is missing. What state does she lack whose absence explains what's wrong with her? Isn't it a desire of some sort? For we thought that any state that bridges the gap between a belief and a motivation must be a desire. But not this one. What Ann is missing can't be any desire.

The desire that is supposed to bridge the gap between believing that a rule requires her to ϕ and being motivated to ϕ is the desire to comply with the rule. But suppose that Ann's mental inventory were supplemented with a desire to comply with the rule, in this case to comply with (M/E). Could this complete the picture? Were she to desire to comply with (M/E), would she then be motivated to take the LSAT prep course? By hypothesis, Ann suffers from this failure of practical reason: she fails to be motivated by the acknowledged means to her desired ends. So adding a desire (complying with (M/E)) does not in her bring about the motivation to perform an acknowledged means to her end of doing well in the LSAT. We cannot bring about in Ann the motivation to perform an action acknowledged by her to be a means to a certain end, by getting her to desire that end. This is a good way to motivate normal, rational agents, but in Ann's case it is futile. But this futile attempt is exactly what we would be engaged in if we were to try to bring Ann to desire to take the LSAT prep course by giving her a desire (complying with (M/E)) that would motivate her to take the prep course. So what Ann is missing cannot be a desire. Call this the Tortoise argument (for a reason I will explain shortly).

Maybe this argument looks too quick. We do agree that what's wrong with Ann is that she is missing some sort of state. And that state takes the input of belief (that taking the prep course is a necessary means to improving her chances of getting into a competitive law school) and desire (to get into a competitive law school) to the output of motivation or action. And such states just *are* desires, one might say. After all, we are being broad in our classification of desires. What prevents us from counting this state, whatever its ordinary description, as a desire?[7] What prevents us is that desires are typed by their content. When asked which desire Ann needs, we have to be able to say something like "The desire that p" or "The desire to ϕ." We can't just cite inputs and outputs. No doubt what Ann is missing is very much like a desire in certain respects, but if it isn't a desire to ____ or a desire that ____ or even a desire for ____, then it is no desire at all. But as soon as some content is given to this purported missing desire, then the Tortoise argument shows that it could not be what Ann is missing.

I call this the Tortoise argument by analogy to Lewis Carroll's story of Achilles and the Tortoise (Carroll 1895). I'll use a minor variant of the story to explain. The Tortoise considers an argument of this form:

(a) If these two sides are equal to the same, then they are equal to each other.

(b) These two sides are equal to the same.

(z) They are equal to each other.

He claims to believe the two premises, (a) and (b), but to be unsure about the conclusion, (z). Achilles assures him that (z) really does follow from the premises. The Tortoise asks him to add a statement of this entailment explicitly to the premises, so Achilles writes,

(a) If these two sides are equal to the same, then they are equal to each other.

(b) These two sides are equal to the same.

(c) If (a) and (b) are both true, then (z) must also be true.

(z) They are equal to each other.

The Tortoise claims again to accept all of the premises but still to be unsure of whether to believe the conclusion. He asks Achilles to add another premise:

(d) If (a) and (b) and (c) are all true, then (z) must also be true.

But adding this premise, and an indefinitely long list of further premises that the reader may supply, will not help the Tortoise reach the desired conclusion. His problem is not a lack of premises; clearly (a) and (b) are perfectly sufficient premises for the conclusion to be reached! The Tortoise's problem, his irrationality, was that he did not draw the logical conclusion of an argument whose premises he accepted and whose reasoning was valid and simple. What state was he missing? He did not accept the inference rule, modus ponens. There is no temptation here to suppose that what the Tortoise was missing was a desire of any sort,[8] but there might be *some* temptation to think that his failure to accept the rule was a matter of his lacking a certain belief. At least, Achilles was so tempted. Achilles tried to get the Tortoise to believe that (an instance of) modus ponens is valid (that's what (c) says, after all: it says that the modus ponens inference from (a) and (b) to (z) is valid). And he succeeded! But futilely. For from this additional, otiose premise, the Tortoise was still unable (or unwilling?) to draw the logically implied conclusion. I find this parallel striking.

Now we've singled out the (M/E) rule as special. Once you accept the (M/E) rule, what you need to get you to accept other rules is one or another desire. But no desire will get you to accept the (M/E) rule itself. (Compare modus ponens. Once you have modus ponens, what you need to get you to accept other rules is a belief in some conditional. But a belief in a conditional won't get you modus ponens itself.) So means-ends rationality has a special status. But is this special status relevant to the question at hand?

When someone asks for a justification of practical rules, for example, morality, she is asking to be given a reason to follow them. Telling someone why he should do something is giving him reasons, normative, practical reasons. Since they are normative reasons, they are grounded in some set of rules, some norms. When we give a justification, we are either explicitly citing or adverting to some norms. But we can't just cite any old bunch of norms. Which norms count toward justification? The problem is that if we simply cite a bunch of rules, the agent may well ask, what are those rules to me? She may ask for a reason to follow them. And we can't just shrug this off. Suppose that someone cited the laws of India in support of moral principles. We ourselves recognize that this sort of justification is useless. We have to say why the rules we cite are better.

If we cite the laws of India and our subject asks what reason she has to follow them, we understand what she's asking. She's again asking for reasons. She doesn't see any force in the rules we've cited. She's missing whatever it takes to be motivated by the belief we've instilled, namely, that the laws of India require her to abide by moral norms. That state is a desire. We can understand how someone might lack that desire. Asking for a reason in this context makes perfectly good sense.

If our subject were asking for some reason to follow (M/E), the matter would be different. Suppose that she isn't motivated to ϕ when she believes that by ϕ-ing she will ψ and she desires to ψ. So she asks what reason she has, and when we cite the (M/E) principle, she asks what reason she has to follow that. But now, I think, we are at a loss. Not merely at a loss to provide a compelling answer, but at a loss to know what to think of such a person. What would *count* as a reason, by her lights? As long as she accepts (M/E), we know what would count as a reason: the fact that by following the rule to be justified, she would achieve some end she desires.

Compare Carroll's theoretic case. Suppose that someone asks for a theoretic justification of some proposition q. We could try to get her to believe that p, and that if p then q. We know what's required; it's a matter of getting her to believe the right things, the propositions from which she can infer that q. But what about the Tortoise? We can't give him a justification to believe the conclusion, not one that he can see to be a justification. We can't give him a reason that he will see as a reason. That's because there doesn't seem to be anything that counts as a reason for the Tortoise. Those conditionals we count on to give reasons have no effect on the Tortoise.

We give you reasons to believe something by finding things you believe and getting you to draw inferences. If you can't draw those inferences, then nothing counts as a reason for you. And similarly for practical reasons. We can give you practical reasons by finding things you want and some things you believe and getting you to draw practical inferences. If you can't draw the practical inferences, not even the fundamental (M/E) kind, then nothing counts as a reason for you. This is why (M/E) has a kind of ground-level normative status. I think it also counts as a categorical imperative. Of course, the particular reasons that (M/E) generates are all hypothetical reasons. But (M/E) itself is not hypothetical. Its demands must be met by you, insofar as you are rational, no matter what desires you happen to have. That is why I said earlier that I think Humeans are mistaken to say that there are no categorical imperatives at all.

The main context in which we might hope that there are categorical imperatives is the context of giving moral reasons. We would like to be able to give a justification for morality, in the sense of being able to give someone reasons for abiding by moral rules. Some people already want to abide by moral rules. Those people already have reasons. But their reasons seem to depend on their contingent wants. A satisfying justification of morality would give reasons that are independent of contingent wants. Humeans doubt that there is any such justification, because they doubt that there are any such reasons. For suppose that someone cited a reason for complying with moral rules. Citing a reason is referring or adverting to some norm. If the reason cited is grounded in an arbitrary norm, say in the laws of India, then it can't count as a justification, precisely because we may perfectly sensibly ask what reason there is to comply with *that* norm. Nor is this a facile tactic of demanding that reasons be given ad infinitum. The laws of India clearly do not count as a reason to comply with moral rules, even if they entail that we ought to comply with moral rules. Admittedly, reasons must end somewhere. But they may not end just anywhere. Humeans may plausibly claim that instrumental reasons are ground-level reasons. But instrumental reasons are never independent of our contingent desires. This is the ground for Humean skepticism about the categorical imperatives in the context of morality.

In closing, some prospects for combating the skepticism. I have claimed a kind of sine qua non status for (M/E). Giving a means-end reason counts as giving a reason if anything does; if it doesn't count, then the request for reasons is empty. But no principle other than (M/E) has this status. So the only ultimate sort of reasons are instrumental reasons. And this means that (M/E) is categorical in one sense, namely, that its force must be felt by anyone who is capable of acting for reasons at all. No particular means-end reasons are categorical, though. Any particular means-end reason counts as a reason for someone only if the end it cites is an end that person happens to have. And moral rules are not categorical; they depend for their compelling force on contingent desires. So I claimed. I can see two ways that an anti-Humean could resist.

First, she might claim that there are other sorts of practical principles with the same status as (M/E). Maybe these other principles could yield enough content, independent of contingent aims, to provide justification for moral rules. I think this is one way of seeing "transcendental" Kantian arguments. One might think that something of this sort happens in the case of theoretic reason when we wonder about the justification of induction. On the one hand, the demand that we provide a reason to believe, for example, that the future will resemble the past does get some grip, since the skeptic is willing to count *deductive* reasons as reasons and points out that all the deductive grounds for induction are question-begging. Inductive principles of reasoning are independent of deductive ones. On the other hand, arguably, the willingness to infer future predications from past ones is as much embedded in the functional character of belief as modus ponens is embedded in the functional character of a conditional belief (by which I mean only a belief whose content is a conditional). Are there practical principles apart from (M/E) that have a similar status?

Second, and to my mind more plausibly, she might claim that there are *alternatives* to (M/E). Let me explain. The first line of resistance insists that (M/E) is only one of a set of principles, all of which must be accepted if the idea of a reason is to make sense at all. But instead it might be that (M/E) is only one of a set of principles, *one* of which must be accepted if the idea of a reason is to make sense at all. To illustrate, think again of Carroll's theoretic analog. A person (or Tortoise) who doesn't accept modus ponens can't be brought to accept it by supplying him with some conditional premises. But modus ponens is not unique in this respect. Our subject might accept disjunctive syllogism, for example. Then we could get him to believe that q, when he believes already that p and that if p then q, by adding the premise $\neg(p \rightarrow q) \vee (\neg p \vee q)$, which is, after all, a tautology. He could then reach $(\neg p \vee q)$ from $(p \rightarrow q)$, which he believes, plus the second premise; and q from p, which he believes, plus the intermediary conclusion. The point is that you need some inference rule or other, in addition to your beliefs, to draw inferences, but there isn't any particular inference rule you need. It is not obvious what practical rules one might use as a general alternative to (M/E).[9] This strategy *might* yield a principle, one having a status at least equal to (M/E), which itself has substantial moral content.

It might, but I doubt it. When we first looked at (M/E), we noted that it can be thought of in two ways. According to the constitutive reading, (M/E) says that someone who desires an end and believes that some action is a necessary means to that end cannot fail to desire the means. It would count decisively against attributing to someone the instrument-belief and the end-desire that she did not desire the means. I argued that the constitutive reading is false—as stated, it is too strong a condition. I also said, though, that something like the constitutive reading seems right, something suitably weakened. The output of the means-desire is *partly* constitutive of the combined functions of the end-desire and the instrument-belief. Bringing about the means-desire in someone when she has the end-desire is a part of the concept of an instrument-belief, but the connection may fail and the state still be attributable, as long as there are some other conceptual connections in place, and as long as there is some story surrounding the failure that makes it understandable.

We might say that failure of means-end rationality cannot be "global," that an agent cannot be generally and always means-end irrational, or we could not see him as having those beliefs and those desires. Failure of means-end rationality can be local, so long as the surrounding story gives us enough material to attribute the instrument-belief and the end-desire.

Other inferential principles do not seem to have this feature. If they don't, it's hard to see how an alternative to (M/E) could be established.

Let me forestall a possible misunderstanding of my argument. It is *not* that you had better use (M/E) or you will be unintelligible as having reasons. This, I think, is a dubious argument. It suggests that everyone after all will want to be intelligible as having reasons, whatever else she wants.[10] Rather, my argument is that a request for reasons makes sense only if there is something that could count as a reason. Of course, in one sense the project of justifying morality straightforwardly fails if nothing counts as a reason at all. But the reason that Humeans doubt that there are categorical imperatives is that there are (possible?) beings who can recognize reasons, who act on reasons, who are moved by reasons, but who are not moved by the imperatives in question. A justification would show them what reason they have. So long as a person is means-end rational, there are reasons she can act on, reasons that can motivate her, reasons that she accepts as reasons. If we cannot provide her with a reason to abide by moral rules, then we cannot justify morality. The problem of justifying morality stands in stark contrast to the problem of justifying the (M/E) principle itself. Someone who doesn't accept the (M/E) principle cannot be given reasons of any sort. That we cannot justify our principle to such a person is no more troubling than our inability to justify principles of deduction.

This argument has a transcendental feel about it quite alien to Humeanism. As a Humean myself, I think we should be up front about this. The special status of instrumental reason is due to its being the sine qua non of having reasons at all. We shouldn't be embarassed to take the insights of Kantian philosophizing to heart. Certain aspects of the Humean position deserve to be abandoned. We should abandon a hard-line metaphysical position according to which the very idea of practical reason is mysterious. Our skepticism should consist in doubts that the content of practical reason is anything like the content of morality, doubts, indeed, that its content outruns the bare (M/E) principle.[11] We should be contesting the normative ground, not contesting its very existence.

Notes

1. 'Humean', as I use it, is the name of a kind of philosophical theory of practical reason. I do not address the historical question of whether Hume had a theory of this kind. Nor will I give any explicit definition of the kind.

2. In saying that reasons are always grounded in *rules*, I might be begging an important question against other conceptions. For example, a virtue ethicist might say that our ethical reasons are grounded in facts about the characters of virtuous agents, and that such character is not reducible to following a set of general rules. But for my purposes, the generality of the rules is not important. Even if there is a different particular rule for each situation in which we find ourselves, that will be fine for my purposes.

3. This is not to say that rationalizing explanations aren't also causal. I don't see how they could fail to be causal. I don't think this point matters to the main argument in the text.

4. Quite possibly, the distinction between desiring and willing is important here.

5. See Millgram 1995 on whether Hume is a Humean in this sense.

6. This point is made in Hampton 1992.

7. Simon Blackburn put this objection to me.

8. But see Railton 1992. Railton's (1997) use of the Tortoise is for a different, though related, end. See also Dreier 1994 for the relevance of the Tortoise to the views presented by Railton.

9. But see Thagard and Millgram 1996.

10. See Railton 1997; also relevant is Blackburn 1995.

11. This kind of skepticism is mentioned and distinguished, but *not* discussed, in Korsgaard 1986 (this volume, chap. 6).

References

Blackburn, S. 1995. "Practical Tortoise Raising." *Mind* 104: 695–711.

Carroll, L. 1895. "What the Tortoise Said to Achilles." *Mind* 4: 278–280.

Copp, D. 1991. "Moral Skepticism." *Philosophical Studies* 62: 203–233.

Dreier, J. 1994. "Perspectives on the Normativity of Ethics." *Noûs* 28: 514–525.

Foot, P. 1972. "Morality as a System of Hypothetical Imperatives." *Philosophical Review* 81: 305–316.

Hampton, J. 1992. "Hobbes and Ethical Naturalism." In J. Tomberlin, ed., *Ethics*, Philosophical Perspectives, no. 6, pp. 333–353. Atascadero, Calif.: Ridgeview Publishing Co.

Kant, I. 1964. *Groundwork of the Metaphysics of Morals*. Translated by H. J. Paton. New York: Harper and Row. Originally published as *The Moral Law* (London: Hutchinson and Co.). Page references are given using the standard pagination of the Academy edition of Kant's works.

Korsgaard, C. 1986. "Skepticism about Practical Reason." *Journal of Philosophy* 83: 5–25. Reprinted in this volume, chap. 6.

Millgram, E. 1995. "Was Hume a Humean?" *Hume Studies* 21: 75–93.

Railton, P. 1992. "Some Questions About the Justification of Morality." In J. Tomberlin, ed., *Ethics*, Philosophical Perspectives, no. 6, pp. 27–53. Atascadero, Calif.: Ridgeview Publishing Co.

Railton, P. 1997. "On the Hypothetical and Non-hypothetical in Reasoning about Belief and Action." In B. Gaut and G. Cullity, eds., *Ethics and Practical Reason*, pp. 53–79. New York: Oxford University Press.

Smith, M. A. 1994. *The Moral Problem*. Oxford: Blackwell.

Thagard, P., and E. Millgram. 1996. "Inference to the Best Plan: A Coherence Theory of Decision." In D. Leake and A. Ram, eds., *Goal-Driven Learning*, pp. 439–454. Cambridge: MIT Press.

Chapter 3

Instrumentalism

Christoph Fehige

Instrumentalism is the doctrine that the choice of means to our ends can be more or less rational, but our ends themselves can't.[1] Except where the extent to which we attain our ends is at stake, reason will not require us to harbor or pursue one end rather than another. *De finibus non est disputandum.*

The meaning and the merit of this claim will depend on what we have in mind when speaking of a person's ends. In particular, whether we buy the instrumentalist refusal to pick out "rational" ends from among them will depend on how rich our notion of an end is all by itself. The bulk of this paper will sketch one view of endhood and a view of practical rationality based on it. If these views are plausible, we will find out how instrumentalist we should be by finding out how instrumentalist they are.

1 MATTERS OF THE HEART

1.1 Basics

Some things are dear to our hearts. To act rationally, I submit, means in essence: to look after these things, as best we can. I call this view, or rather the version of it that I will begin to spell out and inspect for evidence of instrumentalism, the Hearty View.

By saying that things are close to our hearts, I mean, roughly, that they affect us in a certain way. Somewhat less roughly, to think of them is pleasant, to think of their opposite unpleasant. The person to whom it is important that her children will be happy is the person who is delighted with the thought that they will be, and sad at the thought that they won't. These affects, the pleasures or pains of thinking that this and that is the case or is not the case, are the stuff of the heart. Less poetically speaking, if processed properly, they constitute the fact that a person cares about certain things, that she values them, that they matter to her.

These pronouncements need elaborating. To begin with, if matters of the heart are to be the contents of pleasant thoughts, then the contents must indeed play their part in this business. In particular, nothing follows from the fact that the *words* "My children will be happy" flash through my mind and make me happy. Maybe the words make no sense to me at all, or no sense that at that moment I realize. We have to make sure that I get the semantics right, too, that I know what I'm talking about or thinking about. I must grasp, correctly represent to myself, the fact at issue. My being pleased will count as being pleased *at* a certain prospect, rather than pleased undirectionally or at another prospect, only if the prospect is there—only if it is before my mind's eye, only if I'm fully and vividly aware of it.[2] It should be thoughts in this sense whose pleasantness counts.

A second point might appear opposed to the first. Something can be close to a person's heart even when the person has different things on her mind altogether. Suppose that I'm a loving father and a plumber, and that right now I'm concentrating on repairing a dripping tap and hence not thinking of my children. Our theory should not force us to conclude that my children are, at this moment, not dear to me. My children may well be dear to me all the time—I just cannot think of them all the time. Not, for instance, while repairing a dripping tap in order to be able to afford their college fees. Thus, instead of asking *whether* a person is thinking of p, we should ask what would be happening *if* she were.[3]

Combining this point with the previous one, about pleasant thoughts, we can venture a slogan. A state of affairs p is dear to a person if and only if the following holds true of her: if she fully represented p to herself, she'd be pleased.

1.2 Complications

Complications abound. Cases come to mind that threaten our slogan as follows. They seem to invite the description that a person fully represents to herself that p and is pleased while or because of doing so, but they leave us hesitant or unwilling to say that p is dear to her heart. What, for instance, if Mary is thrilled to hear that p just because she knows that p will serve as a means to things dear to her heart? What if she has been given a drug that makes her enthusiastic about p, or a drug that makes her enthusiastic no matter whether she thinks of p or non-p? What if she

is half asleep and is having pleasant dreams, daydreams, fantasies about
p? And what if she's enthusiastic about p, but unenthusiastic about being
enthusiastic about p?

We can also think of scenarios that work the other way round. In these
cases, it appears that a person fully represents to herself that p and fails
to be pleased, but we may still want to say that p is dear to her heart. For
instance, what if Mary is in such a lousy mood to begin with that her full
representation of p, while making her noticeably less unhappy, fails to go
all the way and make her happy? What if her belief that p is out of reach
dampens her enthusiasm and turns the thought of p itself, a p that "deep
in her heart" she is still enthusiastic about, into a sad one? And what do
we make of force of habit? What if the thought of living in a nice cozy
flat doesn't currently make Mary enthusiastic for the sole reason that,
having lived in such a flat for years, she has got used both to the fact and
the prospect of doing so?

All these issues call for legislation.[4] Many of them will go away if
we ask whether, *in a cool hour, when she's sober, awake, undisturbed by
other thoughts*, Mary would be happy fully representing to herself that p.
Others will go away if we switch to the comparative question: would she
be happier fully representing to herself that p than she would be fully
representing to herself that non-p? These are just examples of refinements
we may want to introduce.

They *can* be introduced, which is the main thing. If we can come up
with a problematic scenario, we can ipso facto exclude it from the concept we're explicating. Moreover, once we know that we want some such
concept of being dear to someone's heart to loom large in our notion of
rationality, there is nothing to stop us from fine-tuning the former with
a view to the latter. The details can be rigged so that they enable the
concept to play the role.

1.3 Desire

Hearts or not, we may as well employ the standard term from debates on
rationality. We can address the notion that is beginning to emerge as a
notion of desire. Desires are, very roughly speaking and in the sense
explained, pleasant thoughts. They are affects.

This view of desire has a pedigree that I cannot fully unfold here. We
find it more or less clearly articulated in Aristotle, Augustine, Descartes,
Spinoza, and Kant.[5] The Brits tend to concur. Hobbes, for one, says that
"all ... desire ... is accompanied with some delight"; James Mill, that

desires are "ideas ... which it is agreeable to have"; his son, that "to desire anything, except in proportion as the idea of it is pleasant, is a physical and metaphysical impossibility."[6] Later, the view acquires a large following among such German-speaking thinkers as Wundt, Schneider, von Giżycki, Sigwart, Ziehen, von Ehrenfels, Pfänder, and Meinong;[7] most notably, Moritz Schlick develops it at some length in chapter 2 of his *Fragen der Ethik*.

Modern proponents of the affective theory also include: Karl Duncker, who says that, as presented in anticipation, a situation that is desired "becomes aglow with an empathetical feeling tone of pleasantness"; J. C. B. Gosling, who develops a notion of wanting as "viewing with pleasure, or being pleased at the thought of"; Richard Brandt and Jaeg-won Kim, who treat it as essential for the meaning of "wanting that p" that the agent would feel joy if she received the unexpected news that p, and disappointment if she received the unexpected news that non-p. More recently, Galen Strawson has developed the thought that "the link to the notion of affect dispositions is internal to and fundamentally con-stitutive of the notion of desire in a way that the link to the notion of be-havioral dispositions is not."[8]

Brandt's and Kim's reference to disappointment reminds us to count in the tradition of Plato, John Locke, Schopenhauer, and others who see desiring as essentially connected with uneasiness and pain.[9] In as far as such explications refer to a negative feeling caused by the thought that a certain object is absent, they converge with the proposal at hand—see the remarks about matters of the heart from sec. 1.1 and about comparativity in sec. 1.2. It would thus be more accurate, albeit more cumbersome and potentially misleading, to say, not that desires are pleasant thoughts, but that desires are pleasant or unpleasant thoughts.

It has also been observed more than once that this conception treats us to a notion of strength. If joy turns a thought into a desire, a strong joy will turn a thought into a strong desire.[10] The "strong joy", we should add, is joy that would be strong under the proper circumstances; all the provisos from sections 1.1 and 1.2 carry over. So does the remark that, if somebody experiences the opposite of joy at the thought of the opposite of p, this, too, will have a say.

Like most products of philosophical concept-mongering, our concept of desire does not fully coincide with one particular previous usage. We have seen, however, that the affective view is not, as some people might want to put it, "revisionist". Let's be clear about who is: those authors who saw off the phenomenal part of desire. They leave us with a torso of the concept, with a behavioral persiflage of desire. Their desire is desire as instantiated in robots, or in thermostats.

1.4 Desire and Pleasure

Two more words on the relation of desire to pleasure. On the one hand, our view runs no risk of collapsing into hedonism. The desideratum itself can be entirely nonhedonic and nonexperiential, and this can be known to the desirer. For instance, the thought that flowers will grow on my grave can please me, and will then count as a desire to have flowers growing on my grave. Furthermore, and as is illustrated by the same example, the joy we are talking about when we call desires joyful representations is not necessarily anticipated joy. To desire that *p*, I need not believe that *p* either entails or would cause pleasure for me or anybody else. Hedonism fails to ensue because there is no reason to think that if desires are pleasant thoughts they can only be thoughts *of* pleasure, in which case only pleasure could be desired. Saying that pleasure is the mode is not saying that pleasure is the content.[11]

On the other hand, although our explication does not entail that pleasure alone is desired, it does entail that pleasure is desired—a claim that, over the centuries, has often been made, less often denied, and still less often argued for.[12] Here is one argument. According to the Hearty explication of desire, I desire the things that it would be pleasant for me to imagine. Now, my imagining that I am in a certain pleasant state of consciousness must involve an imagining of that state, and, as with all states of consciousness, nothing that doesn't involve that state itself *counts* as an imagining of it. (Anything that involved only different states would at best count as an imagining of those states or as a misimagining of the one at issue.) But if my imagining to be in a certain pleasant state of consciousness involves that very state and is therefore pleasant itself, then it constitutes a desire to be in that state. In other words, for every pleasant state of consciousness, it holds true on conceptual grounds, given the concept of desire that has been outlined here, that I desire, pro tanto, to be in that state.

1.5 Jargon

As to terminology: the things close to our hearts are our projects, ends, goals, or purposes, the contents of our pro-attitudes and inclinations; they matter to us; we care about them, we appreciate, cherish, desire, prefer, value, want, and wish them. At times, there may be good reasons to distinguish between some of these expressions; for present purposes, however, we can treat them as by and large synonymous. The relation we're talking about, no matter by which name, is the relation that bottoms out in affects—along the lines proposed.

Moreover, the relation is, as has been briefly indicated in sec. 1.2, a desiring of the intrinsic kind, where states of affairs are desired for their own sake and not just as a means to other ends. Finally, when we say that a preference or desire is fulfilled or satisfied or frustrated, we do not in general imply that the preferrer's consciousness is affected thereby; but only, that what the preferrer has wished for is, or is not, the case. In this by now well-established terminology, "fulfillment" etc. do not serve as psychological notions.

1.6   The Picture Thus Far

In moving on from our concept of desire as a real or hypothetical affect, we are leaving behind unfinished business. The substance is there, but some details are missing. I pointed out in sec. 1.2 that various borderline cases remain to be settled. I have paid little tribute to the importantly different *ways* in which thoughts can be pleasant or unpleasant—witness anger, fear, hope, love, remorse, sympathy, and the like. I haven't stopped to criticize the wide-spread view that the "if" clause of a dispositional analysis should equip the agent not just with a full *representation* of the proposition at issue, but also with far-reaching *information* about the world.[13] I haven't discussed the objections against employing certain kinds of hypothetical constructs to characterize what the agent "really" wants,[14] let alone the more general philosophical issues of emotions and pleasure, of counterfactual conditionals, consciousness, and mental representation.

Still, some simple truths point our way. The person who would feel indifferent to the news that he will have to die tomorrow doesn't *care* to live. His *feeling* indifferent *is* his indifference, his not caring, his not desiring. Similarly, the child who pictures herself on a new bicycle, and revels in the prospect, desires to have the bicycle. Her reveling is not a symptom or concomitant. It *is* the desire. If we take away the reveling, both the real and the counterfactual, we take away the desire. In that case, the child might still exhibit bicycle-acquiring behavior. But if so, she is, as far as that desire is concerned, a zombie.

Desire, value, and the like are anchored in sentience. Launder the affects and modify the *experimentum crucis* as much as you like—at the end of the day we should ask, in one form or the other, how the subject would feel about *p*. When we ask this question, we're not using a metaphor.

2   COMPETING NOTIONS OF DESIRE

It was worth dwelling on our notion of a desire. For one thing, we will be talking about desires a great deal, with our whole conception of rationality pivoting on them. Besides, other notions of desire tend to give desire-based normative rationality, and the readings of instrumentalism associated with them, a bad name.

Suppose, for instance, that, whenever a person puts some thought into the question of what to do, we call the upshot of her deliberation, at least if she acts accordingly, a desire. Thus, if she comes to a conclusion like "I'd better ϕ (should ϕ, have more reason to ϕ than not to, herewith decide to ϕ)" and then ϕs, she has ipso facto desired to ϕ. Suppose also that we plug this notion of desire into a desire-based conception of rationality.

The result would be unsatisfactory.[15] The category of the rational would simply duplicate the category of the intentional or the deliberate. But clearly some intentional actions, some actions that arise from some thinking, are irrational. Thinking as such doesn't render an action rational; at best, correct thinking does. We must specify *what* the agent should have taken into account, and *how*, before we can call her action rational.

Next, suppose that by a desire we mean a disposition to act and that we make desires in this sense the foundations of normative rationality. This, too, would be peculiar. I might have who knows what tendencies. How could my mere tendency to ϕ constitute a normative reason to ϕ?[16]

More or less the same question arises if we use the term "desire" for *causes* of our actions. Imagine that scientists find out that the quivering of my pineal gland causes me to ϕ. Why should we say that the gland's quivering provides me with a normative reason to ϕ? And if in the realm of causes we switch from glands to thoughts, things look no better. For imagine that the thought, or the physical substrate of the thought, that a certain action would maximize the number of garden chairs in the world causes me to perform that action. Again, why should that make it *reasonable* for me to perform it?

Finally, suppose that, following the crowd, we say that a desire is an attitude characterized by its "direction of fit". What makes an attitude a desire is that, if somebody has the attitude towards a proposition p, then the world should be, or should be made by that person, a p-world.[17] To use the canonical comparison, desire resembles a shopping list: the question of what goes into your shopping basket should be governed by the list. Belief, on the other hand, resembles the list drawn up by a detective watching you shop: her list should be governed by what goes into your basket. That's the difference. Desire is what the world should track (it has the world-to-mind direction of fit), whereas belief is what should track the world (it has the mind-to-world direction of fit). And suppose this time that we base rationality on desire thus defined.

What, however, are we going to make of the word "should" in these characterizations? One option would be to give it something like a statistical reading. What makes an attitude a desire for p, we would then be saying, is that people who have the attitude tend to try to make the world a p-world. That way, the direction-of-fit approach will collapse into the disposition-to-act approach, which we have already rejected. Alternatively, we could give the "should" a normative reading. What makes an attitude a desire, we would then be saying, is that for people who have the attitude it is *rational* to make the world a p-world. Putting desires-in-this-sense to the service of rationality, we will get a notion of rationality based on desire based on rationality. We will have gone full circle: it is rational to do what it is rational to do. "Direction of fit" doesn't help.

All these unhappy episodes can be merged into one. Upon your return from the weekend shopping I notice that you bought, say, an early Rembrandt. "Was it wise of you to buy that painting?", I might well ask. As we have seen, some theories of practical reason—some theories based on certain conceptions of desires—would commit you to answers like these:

- Yes, for I did it intentionally.
- Yes, for I had a tendency to.
- Yes, for my pineal gland caused me to.
- Yes, for I'm sure what caused me to was a thought.
- Yes, for I did.
- Yes, for it was wise to.

The answers are bizarre. This one is not: "Yes, for I had set my heart on it."

3   EFFICACY

3.1   What Reasons Cause

We have severed, or rather denied, various conceptual links between reasons and causes—between normative reasons on the one hand and what are sometimes called motivating, explanatory reasons on the other. It is one thing to ask what it would be wise for you to do; several others, what you have a tendency to do and what causes this tendency, let alone what you end up doing and what causes you to.

This notoriously invites all sorts of questions. What about acting *for* a reason? Shouldn't we be able to say of an agent that she did it *because* it was the rational thing to do?[18] Don't we see ourselves as creatures often influenced by reasons? And if our reasons have no causal power, why make so much fuss about them? Why deliberate?

These worries concern the efficacy of practical reason. There are two ways we might try to lay them to rest. If we accept the requirement that practical reason must in some sense or other be efficacious, we should now stop to investigate how the Hearty View fares with respect to that challenge. Not badly, we would probably find out, at least as far as the challenge concerns human beings on planet Earth. Surely, myriads of people do myriads of things that they believe will best fulfill their desires—desires in the Hearty sense. And frequency is a clue to causality.

However, I plead for a more radical response. We should not accept requirements of efficacy, not, at any rate, as constraints on a theory of normative reason. In saying this, I'm not denying that it would be a good thing if we acted for reasons; in several respects, it would. Nor am I denying that we act for reasons; as indicated in the previous paragraph, I suspect that we frequently do. I'm only denying that the extent to which we do should have a say in what *counts* as a reason. Rationality is an ideal. As with every ideal, the causal world can trample on it, but not refute it. If we don't live up to the ideal, that is too bad. But too bad for us, not for the ideal.

3.2   What Beliefs about Reasons Cause

Do things look any different if we turn our attention from reasons to beliefs about reasons? If I *believe* that I have, all things told, a reason to ϕ, I will tend to ϕ—doesn't this conditional qualify as a conceptual truth?

I don't see why. Who says that I *necessarily* am a creature driven, at least ceteris paribus, by its own beliefs about its reasons for action? The possibility that I'm not should hardly be ruled out on the grounds that I shudder to think of it.

To be sure, if my behavior is immune to the results of my deliberation, there is no point in deliberating, and I may just as well—provided that at least this belief of mine translates into action—stop it. But this, too, neither is nor justifies a change of my beliefs about the underlying ideal. If the behavior is irrational, it is irrational, and that's that. We shouldn't knight knaves just because they prevail. Thus, while it might be true that, if beliefs about reasons were causal flops, we would have no reason to reason, neither would we have a reason to change our conception of a reason.

Efficacy, I suggest, must remain contingent. We may get good news or bad news about it, but no conceptual guarantees. There is really not much merit in the idea of putting practical reason in the driver's seat by withholding the title of reason from anything that doesn't happen to be in the driver's seat.

4   GOOD FOR US

We have begun to explicate desires as affects (sec. 1), and we have begun to see that this notion of desire matches normative reasons far better than its competitors do (sec. 2), worries about the efficacy of the resulting reasons notwithstanding (sec. 3). We now turn to another route that leads to desire-based rationality.

4.1   The Welfare Argument

The argument takes a bit of a run-up. It starts with the question what it is for a person's life to go well. What do we mean by a person's "good" or "welfare"?[19] Clearly, something that is moored to her mind in one way or another. For consider a run-of-the-mill fact from the world out there, say that the sun is shining. This state of affairs may in various ways affect a person's welfare, but will not by itself constitute it. We can imagine a person who has no interest in this fact, a person who, even if the matter is brought to her attention, is indifferent to it (ex ante, ex post, and in flagrante) and to everything that comes with it. Sunshine is of no use to such a person. It would not make her better off. Our notion of welfare must include a subjective element; it must include "getting something out of it".

This requirement, the interest requirement, leaves us with two candidates. One is pleasure or, more precisely and in well-known words, "pleasure and the absence of pain". The candidate succeeds. No doubt everybody is ceteris paribus better off feeling good than feeling bad; no doubt everybody is ceteris paribus worse off with a toothache than without. Pleasure is a component of welfare.

But is it the only one? Suppose it were. Then we would be doing people a favor if, one night while they're asleep, we connected them to a pleasure machine for the rest of their lives.[20] We'd have to say that this would do them good—good all things told—even if, consulted beforehand about this option, they had vehemently declined it. This sounds implausible.

Or imagine a writer (if it helps, a philosopher) who desires her last book to be read even after her death, at least for a while. This is what she lives for, so that even in the final months of agony she battles to finish the work. And the minute she has breathed her last, you dump the typescript in the rubbish bin. Have you harmed her? I think you have. You have frustrated a desire she had. Her desire was for her book to be read—not for herself to believe it would be read, and not for herself to feel as good as she would if she believed it would be read. She desired a fact, not, at any rate not just, the pleasure that the fact or the belief in the fact would cause her. Thwarting her wish, I suggest, would make her worse off even without affecting her pleasure.[21] Thus, in addition to pleasure, we have to count in the second candidate that meets the interest requirement: people's getting what they want. Desire fulfillment, too, is a component of welfare.

Pleasure *and* desire fulfillment have a say, then, in what constitutes one's welfare. But, as we recall from sec. 1.4, it follows from general considerations about desiring that a person's pleasure ranks among the things she desires. Hence, every instance of pleasure, even if the subject hasn't so much as thought of it, is an instance of desire fulfillment. To say that pleasure *and* desire fulfillment count is, then, not wrong but wordy—like saying that Safeway sells apples *and* fruit. From the true claim that welfare is a matter of pleasure and desire fulfillment, we may proceed to a claim that is just as true but shorter: welfare is desire fulfillment.

At this point, an argument for desire-based rationality drops into our laps. Rationality has to do with the good life. Most of us would agree that the person who believes an action to be best for him, but doesn't perform it, is irrational—stupid, as laymen tend to put it. In other words, it is rational for him to do what he believes is best for him. As we have just argued, "best for him" means "best fulfills his desires". Thus, it is rational for him to do what he believes would best fulfill his desires. Ditto for each of us.

4.2   The Welfare Argument Annotated

These ruminations will profit from a handful of postscripts. First of all, note how welfare and rationality dovetail. They deal in the same currency: desire fulfillment. What fulfills our desires is good for us to get, what we believe fulfills our desires is rational for us to do. Rationality is prudence. It is the intelligent pursuit, within the limits of the available information and resources, of our goals and projects, and thus of our own good.

Second, since our explication of desire from section 1 captures what it is for something to matter to somebody, it also applies to the case of *welfare* as desire fulfillment. So the argument from section 4.1, the welfare argument, leads us not just to desire-based rationality, but all the way to desire-in-the-Hearty-sense-based rationality. It is an argument for the Hearty View.

Third, if desire is defined in terms of full representation, and desire fulfillment is both rational for you to seek and good for you to get, it doesn't follow that full representation itself is rational or good. Full representation can be a nuisance and should be avoided much of the time. It can spoil our fun or peace of mind, and it can distract us from effecting the means to our ends. Still, we had better engage in it every now and then to make sure we're still on target. While we don't want to spend our days being charmed by our ends, neither do we want to wake up to the fact that we've been working for ends that ceased to charm us ten years ago.

Fourth, pleasure once again. Our plea for seeing welfare as desire fulfillment appealed to the desires for pleasure, whose conceptually guaranteed existence had been explained earlier. These desires, while not tailor-made for the occasion, come in handy. For often real or alleged divergences between *pleasure* and desire fulfillment get quoted as divergences between *welfare* and desire fulfillment. Pleasure is at issue when some instances of desire fulfillment are claimed to be no good for us (say that the fulfillment of a desire disappoints) and when, vice versa, some things that are good for us are claimed not to fulfill a desire (say that we experience a pleasure that we hadn't known or thought of before).[22] To such claims, the standing desires for one's own pleasure provide the right answers.

Last, in having rationality linked to considerations about the agent's welfare, we're not embracing the doctrine of rational egoism, at least not in any sense that would make it objectionable. Egoists are not defined as people who follow their hearts, but as people whose hearts are cold. They are not defined as people who go by their desires, but as people who fail to have or go by desires of a certain type—by desires, of at least a certain strength, that others fare well. Imagine, for instance, a rational philanthropist who ardently and intrinsically desires to help others and acts accordingly. We would hardly call this person an egoist. And if by some terminological caprice we did, then egoism thus defined, with Mother Teresa among its representatives, would cease to be a spectre.

5   THE DYNAMICS OF DESIRE

Desires are the alpha and omega, but desires can change. This raises two questions: what to make of changes, and what changes to make.

5.1   When Desires Change

The first of these questions, how to *respond* to changes of desire, translates into three subquestions. Assuming that I have the relevant knowledge, should I take into account now desires that I had in the past, but have no longer?[23] What about desires that I will have in the future, but do not have now?[24] And what about my "asynchronic desires"—desires that are not around, either not yet or no longer, when their contents come true?[25]

On the one hand, different trios of answers to these questions define significantly different versions of our central claim that desires rule the roost. On the other hand, the questions do not challenge that claim. So we may keep things simple here. Let us pretend that we answer all three questions in the affirmative. Let us pretend that, if my desires have a say in my rational decisions, then so do my past, future, and asynchronic desires. The truth, I repeat, may be different and less homogeneous.[26] We simplify in order to concentrate on the big picture.

5.2   When Desires Should Be Changed

This takes us from changes of preference that befall us to those we can bring about—clearly an issue of immense import for the debate about instrumentalism. The disciple of a desire-based view, it is sometimes held, tends to overlook this issue. By having everything hinge on desires, he forgets that we can revise them. He forgets that we can, and quite frequently should, develop, drop, modify, or reverse a desire.

This reproach, however, lacks all foundation. As David Hume and many others have pointed out, devotion to desire fulfillment does not entail indifference between one pattern of desires and another.[27] Quite the contrary. Since some patterns would be more conducive to desire fulfillment than others, the seeker of desire fulfillment has a serious stake in the existence of the right patterns. He will try to overcome his preference for cigarettes, for Beatrices who don't respond to his advances, and so forth. His self-improvement manuals will include Ovid's *Remedia amoris*, Seneca's *De vita beata*, and Albert Ellis's *Practice of Rational-Emotive Therapy*. Without forgetting that *some* frustration paves the way to satisfaction, he will cultivate preferences that are satisfiable—jointly satisfiable, to be precise. Desire fulfillment is not a conservative or passive ideal that leaves us stuck with our orectic lot; it is the rational guide for the revision of desires.

I say "the" rational guide, because I know of no others. Where *is* the case in which a change of desire fails to promise more desire fulfillment, yet is recommended by reason?

Could it be a case where lack of imagination, or of this or that concept, prevents the desire from existing? Where the subject hasn't looked at a possible state of affairs, or hasn't looked carefully enough?[28] It can't, since (remember sec. 1.1) desires are already defined in terms of what would be the case if all the imagining and representing took place. Could it be a case where desires have been manipulated or distorted? It can't, since (remember sec. 1.2) desires are already defined in terms of what would go on in the agent's mind if no undue interference, by herself or others, by moods or drugs or whatnot, occurred. Could it be a case where the false belief that p is impossible stifles the desire? Or where an extrinsic desire is erected on a false belief? These can't be the problems either, since (remember secs. 1.2 and 1.5) our view makes desires immune, in more than one respect, to the beliefs the desirer happens to have.

Could it be a case where my desires have been formed by dreary circumstances? I doubt it. To be sure, preference formation can go badly wrong for me. But when this has happened, it seems that my only reason for a change would be that I'd be better off with the new set of desires. And since (remember sec. 4) "better off" is a matter of desire fulfillment, so is that reason. Could it be a case, then, where not to acquire the desire, or not to dispose of it, harms me in any way? Same answer as before: since harm is a dent in my welfare, and welfare is desire fulfillment, this would be an argument from desire fulfillment.

Could it be a case of "genuine novelty"? This is Elijah Millgram's concern. Unlike your typical philosopher, Millgram believes that "our world is full of new and surprising things". Quite often, he argues, these things render "the desires, aims, and interests we already have ... suddenly obsolete". Therefore, "we must be able to learn new interests from experience".[29]

But why can't the novelties be handled by an appeal to how we would have felt if we had vividly imagined them, however difficult the imagining might be? And surely, even if they can't, the preference changes Millgram would recommend will be changes that, given the new circumstances, would be good for us. In which case, as has been pointed out above, the preference party fully agrees that we should try to bring them into effect.

5.3   Too Much of a Good Thing?

Oddly enough, friends of desire-based rationality get to hear the opposite reproach as well. The charge now is not that they change their desires too rarely, but that they might end up changing them all the time. Suppose that frequently, whatever project you have at that time, you find out that you could reap more desire fulfillment if you gave up that project and adopted a new one. Would reason require you to change your projects like socks?[30]

As with socks, you shouldn't overdo it, and nobody is asking you to. Given how the mind and the world work, continuous desire hopping, if psychologically feasible at all, would not pay (not in terms of desire fulfillment, that is), and will thus not be recommended by a desire-based theory. The reasons why it wouldn't pay are manifold. Different desires require different resources, including different dwellings, friends, jobs, skills, tools; so you'd have to continuously chase after these things as well. Besides, changing the desires will tend to hurt, one way or the other. And after the umpteenth change, you won't be able to muster up much enthusiasm for project umpteen plus one—not, at any rate, without playing certain tricks upon yourself that may well harm you elsewhere. True, significant drawbacks like these needn't always exist, and this leaves us with conceivable and real cases in which the seeker of desire fulfillment would change his desires if he could. But with the significant drawbacks out of the way, isn't that exactly the right thing for him to do? Why *not* change one's desires if it helps? You should "want the events to happen as they do happen," Epictetus recommends, "and your life will go well".[31] Surely he has a point. The goal is harmony between the will and the world. Making a habit of attuning them *both* qualifies as wisdom.

There is one limit. You could change your desires so radically that the person with the new desires would no longer be you. That, of course, is a limit the theory observes. For if the person with the new desires wouldn't be you, then the new desires wouldn't be yours, and neither would their fulfillment. In saying that your rational actions serve *your* welfare, desire-based rationality will hardly advise you to adopt desires whose adoption would blot you out.[32]

5.4   The Hearty View

Thus ends the sketch of one view of practical rationality. A sketch indeed, since much remains to be filled in. I have not yet linked these thoughts to the technicalities of rational decision theory,[33] and I haven't discussed the paradoxes of rational decision making.[34] I haven't asked whether the beliefs that render an action rational (say the belief that, if I press the yellow button, the machine will start) must be rational in their own right: sound, say, and warranted by the available evidence.[35] Some thorny issues concerning rationality and time haven't received their due, and neither has the place of *moral* reasons in this picture.

But we have made headway. While parts of the sketch fitted desire-based views in general, the mainstay of the Hearty View was one particular explication of desire. To desire something is to be touched by it. Or rather, to be disposed to be touched by the thought of it. Or rather, to be disposed to be delighted at the prospect of its being the case. More delighted, at any rate, than by the opposite prospect. In approximately this sense of "desire", the rational thing to do is the thing you believe would best fulfill your desires.

The Hearty View pinpoints what matters and puts it center stage. It goes by what the agent cares about. It explains why pleasure is a final end, and why it is not the only one. It observes the distinctions between justification and explanation, advice and prediction, "should" and "is", norms and facts. It dovetails with our considered judgements on welfare, and honors the appropriate links between what is rational for us to do and what is good for us. It is not egoistic. Finally, it tells us how to adjust not merely our actions to our desires, but also our desires themselves.

6   THE VERDICT

We now have at our disposal the outline of a theory of ends, namely of desires, and their role in practical rationality. As befitted the occasion, we paid particular attention to the strong requirements that govern the very notion of an end as well as to the malleability of ends. Most of the evidence being in, we can try our hands at a verdict. Drawing both on general reflections and on the particulars of the view that has emerged, we return to the big question: Should we be instrumentalists? Should we claim, and if so, in what sense, that we can reason about the best means to our ends, but not about the ends themselves?

6.1   The Pull

The most uncontroversial part of the answer says that we sometimes sit down with a pretty clearly defined goal in mind and ask ourselves how to get there. This is not exactly a rare occurrence. There can be little doubt, and there is little doubt in the literature, that the session such a question calls for merits the name of practical reasoning. The choice of what one takes to be the most efficient means to one's ends constitutes one large chunk of practical rationality.

Moreover, consider what would happen if somebody told us: that he wants to get rid of a toothache; that he could take aspirin; that this, but nothing else, would help; that taking it wouldn't conflict with any other project of his—and that he does *not* find it advisable to take it. We would suspect that the toothache is the least of his problems. Consider also the mirror image of that person: the man who is right in believing that no past, present, or future desire of his would be fulfilled by his taking an aspirin. Shouldn't we agree that he has no reason to take the tablet? If he asked us, "Why should I take it?", we would be hard pressed for an answer.

So there's a strong pull from desires to reasons, and a strong pull from the absence of desires to the absence of reasons. Far be it from us to jump to conclusions. As with UFOs, open-mindedness is the name of the game. Every alleged sighting of a case that does not conform to the basic pattern deserves our attention. Such cases would include desires one shouldn't act on or one should get rid of; desires one should have; and things one should do though one does not desire either them or their expected consequences. We ought to check every such report, dismiss or accept it, and maybe modify our Humean leanings in order to accommodate it. If we proceed like this, the present paper has suggested and partly shown, a desire-based view will indeed prevail. The view can indeed be classified, this I hope to point out in a moment, as at least mildly instrumentalist.

6.2   Neutrality

With our emphasis on means-ends rationality, we follow in the footsteps of the Enlightenment. When one woman's meat is another woman's poison, this should hardly entail that one of these women is irrational. It would be presumptuous for a conception of rationality to give its blessing, other things being equal, to a desire to collect stamps, but not to a desire to collect coins.

This tolerance extends to all cases of that *form*. In particular, it also extends to the more eccentric predilections from the philosophical folklore. Well-known examples include the intrinsic desires to count blades of grass, to have a saucer of mud, or to drink paint.[36] To be sure, here our advice that the agent decide with a view to *all* her desires acquires a certain urgency. She may well have strong desires to survive, or not to be stared at. Still, if the fulfillment of no other desires were at stake, and if the agent had really set her heart, full representation and all, on one of these puzzling activities, then it would be only fitting for her to go ahead. It is just as rational for some people to act on desires that amaze me as it is for me to act on desires that no doubt amaze them. It takes many desires to make a world. Reason, like the state, should be neither dictatorial nor discriminatory. Both of them should say: *chacun à sa façon*.

6.3   Moderate Instrumentalism

The view of practical rationality sketched earlier in this paper has similar implications. To determine how instrumentalist this view is, I propose to collect, but not to reargue, the relevant points from the sections that lie behind us.

Most notably, desires—in the sense explained, in which "desire" captures what it is for something to matter to somebody—have the last word. Every such desire, and nothing but such a desire, counts. These desires are "given", not just in the sense that their existence or non-existence need not always be in our power, but also in the sense that, if such a desire is really there, no rational critique can set its normative force to zero. Once their strength has been taken into account, all these desires are equal. There will be no reason to acquire, to keep, to act upon, or to act as if one had, a desire of one content rather than another —unless it is a reason that itself has to do with the number and strength of fulfilled desires. Furthermore, desires, and thus reasons, can vary; for a large class of propositions p, it is quite possible that one rational person desires p while another does not.

This list should suffice to warrant the use of the term "instrumentalism". It should be a cautious use, though, since some other features of rationality as it has been pictured here may sound inviting to the noninstrumentalist. For instance, finding out what our ends are, in the rationally relevant sense of "end", can be hard work, and some ways of going about it are more reasonable than others. (Concentrating, and then calling up and rotating a candidate for endhood before our mind's eye will often be more promising than consulting a psychic or the Bible.) In this sense, the sense of detecting rather than generating or eliminating, we reason about final ends, and face a genuine danger of getting the answer wrong. To some extent even in the other senses. We can have reasons to adopt, or to make ourselves adopt, new desires and to dispose of existing ones. These reasons, however, will themselves be accountable to nothing but the quantity of desire fulfillment. They will bottom out, say, in our desire to have, or not to have, certain desires, or in the fact that certain desires cannot, or cannot jointly, be satisfied.

On balance, features traditionally conceived of as instrumentalist dominate this view. If somebody disagreed and decided to say that the points from the previous paragraph amount to a denial of instrumentalism, he would have a hard time naming a single instrumentalist, dead or alive —a prospect that should raise further doubts as to the point of cutting up the field his way. Should we still hesitate to adopt the label "instrumentalism", then perhaps "moderate instrumentalism" is the solution.

6.4 Pseudoinstrumentalism?

We get an appropriate coda to all this by looking at one possible objection. "With your full-representation requirement", a critic might say pointing back to secs. 1.1 and 1.2, "you have simply strengthened the notion of an end. Ends can't be irrational on your account for the sole reason that you have hidden the rationality in the notion of an end itself. So you did come round to noninstrumentalism in substance and are only keeping up a façade of instrumentalism."

The underlying question here is how to interpret the force of full representation. When you fully represent things to yourself, what can this effect? Some, whom we can call the *revisionists*, have it that full representation or some such process can change your desires, and, let us assume, rationally so. For example, you have a desire, fully represent, and end up with another desire, acquired and required by reason. If we accepted this answer, which we shouldn't, then the criterion of rationality endorsed by the Hearty View, as well as the criteria endorsed by various other views that appeal to full representation, would look anti-instrumentalist. Rationality or full representation would require preference changes all over the place.

Nonrevisionists, on the other hand, grosso modo exclude this. They say that only what would survive or emerge from full representation *is* a desire.[37] In that case, things will look different. The expression "rational desire" has become more or less pleonastic. Since, so to speak (and only so to speak), nothing but a "rational desire" counts as a desire to begin with, rationality will never change desires—except, of course, to secure larger *amounts* of fulfillment.

Let me illustrate the dissent with two examples. John McDowell considers cases of the following type. I have what seems like a desire to ϕ (say to tell the truth), discover that, in the situation at hand, ϕ-ing would amount to an act of category ψ (say betraying a friend's secret), and this discovery has the effect that I no longer have what seems like a desire to ϕ. What has been going on? McDowell answers with the revisionists. My discovery, or what for present purposes we can as well call my full representation, has "silenced" my desire to ϕ.[38] The Hearty View denies this. Full representation has helped me find out that I *have* no desire to ϕ, but at best a desire to ϕ in a way that does not amount to ψ-ing. Notice that when we come to criteria of rational action, the upshot is the same either way. Notice also that, as McDowell is right to emphasize, the case at hand should not be confused with a different type, in which a desire exists and survives, but is outweighed by another one.

Some writings of what has been dubbed the "specificationist" school lend themselves to a similar analysis. Take Henry Richardson's tale of a politician's catharsis—written, I believe, before the author moved to Washington, D.C. The plot goes as follows. A politician plans to impress his electorate by showing off how he helps the homeless. But chewing the prospect over, he comes to perceive their condition as truly appalling. The whole idea of using the homeless merely as a means in his campaign becomes disgusting to him. At the end of this "mental 'experiment'", as Richardson calls it, the politician wants to help street people, no matter whether he gets elected. Richardson says, with the revisionists, that deliberation has made the politician adopt a new final end.[39] The Hearty View says, against the revisionists, that the politician has discovered what his ends are. They both want to say that the rational thing for this politician to do is to go and help the homeless.

Both parties should agree in at least one more respect: the "subjectivity" or "objectivity" of practical reasons. A revisionist should not be misled by her claim that certain changes of preference are required or effected by reason. This claim might make it sound (to resort to our brief discussion of McDowell for this purpose) as if *everybody* who fully represented to himself the issue of ϕ-ing-and-thereby-ψ-ing had, on pain of irrationality, to lose interest in ϕ-ing. This is not so. Some might rationally lose interest, and some might rationally not.[40] How a subject feels about ϕ-ing, and before, during, or after undergoing a full representation of ϕ-ing-and-thereby-ψ-ing, is, just as the words suggest, a subjective matter if ever there was one.

Where does this leave us? The objection we've been considering said that our instrumentalism is pseudo. We have identified the underlying dissent about the role of full representation: the revisionist says that it shapes desires; the nonrevisionist, that it detects them. It should be clear by now that, *if* revisionism is wrong, the objection backfires. For if revisionism is wrong, then what is pseudo is an *anti*-instrumentalism based on it. Such an anti-instrumentalism will only bid us to revise or ignore our pseudo-ends, not our ends.

As far as I can tell, the "if" clause is indeed true and revisionism wrong. We will see this if we return to the beginning of this paper. Desires, we said there and it is hardly controversial to say, have a content. Now, if we permitted ourselves to say that simply *grasping* the content could change a desire, then in what sense can it ever have been a desire *with that content*? In what sense does somebody desire p (p, and not nothing or something else) who, if only he looked at p a little harder, would desire it "no longer"? What on earth did his desiring of *it* ever consist in? Here revisionists have a lot of explaining to do. While waiting for them to do the explaining, we had better remain nonrevisionists. And moderate instrumentalists.

Acknowledgments

The thoughts in this paper have profited from the comments of countless friends and colleagues over the years. I'm grateful to every one of them and will express this more fully when I express the thoughts themselves more fully. Thanks are also due to the Deutsche Forschungsgemeinschaft and the Alexander von Humboldt Stiftung for research grants, and to Stanford University for its hospitality.

Notes

1. Examples of by and large instrumentalist creeds include: Allais 1953, sec. 47; Anscombe 1957, secs. 34 and 38; Aristotle, *Nicomachean Ethics*, 1112b; Audi 1989, chap. 4; Gauthier 1975, end of sec. 1, 1986, pp. 25 f.; Hempel 1961–1962, esp. sec. 2.3; Hubin 1991 and 1999; Hume 1739–1740, secs. 2.3.3 and 3.1.1; Hutcheson 1734–1737, vol. 1, p. 38; Luce and Raiffa 1957, p. 21; James Mill 1829, vol. 2, p. 262 (this covers father and son—more on their instrumentalism in Millgram 2000, p. 289); von Mises 1949, sec. 1.4; Rawls 1971, sec. 64; Resnik 1987, p. 5; Russell 1954, p. 8; Schmidtz 2000; Stampe 1987; Weber 1922, chaps. 2.1, 10, and pp. 597–613. Some of these are paradigm cases, some borderline cases, of instrumentalism.

2. Similarly, Brandt 1979, beginning of chap. 6, as well as sec. 3.4; von Ehrenfels 1897, secs. 20 f.; Lewis 1989, p. 121; Sidgwick 1874, p. 112.

3. Appeals to counterfactual conditionals in this and related contexts are standard; some classical sources are given in the previous note, more in Fehige 2000, sec. 1.2.

4. And many of them have received it, one way or the other—see, for instance, Brandt 1979, sec. 3.4, and 1998.

5. Aristotle, *De anima*, 2.2 f. and 3.7–3.13; Augustine, *De civitate dei*, sec. 14.7; Descartes 1649, secs. 87 and 91 f.; Spinoza 1677, part 3, esp. theorem 36 and definition 32; Kant 1797, beginning of the introduction. A handful of the sources I mention in this and the next section can be found, along with brilliant discussion, in Katz 1986.

6. Hobbes 1651, sec. 1.6.11; James Mill 1829, vol. 2, pp. 190 f.; John Stuart Mill 1861, towards the end of chap. 4.

7. Wundt 1874, secs. 17.1.a, 17.4.b, 17.4.c; Schneider 1880, pp. 75–77; von Giżycki 1883, sec. 1.8; Sigwart 1886, sec. 1.3; Ziehen 1891, chap. 16; von Ehrenfels 1897, esp. secs. 20 f. and 79; Pfänder 1900, sec. 1.4; Meinong 1902, secs. 53–56, esp. p. 321, 1921, p. 667.

8. Duncker 1941, p. 416; Gosling 1969, p. 97 and passim, esp. chaps. 6 f.; Brandt and Kim 1963, p. 427; Strawson 1994, sec. 9.8.

9. Plato, *Gorgias*, 496d, *Symposium* 34c–36b; Spinoza, *loc. cit.*; Locke 1689, secs. 2.20.6 and 2.21.31 f.; Condillac 1754, sec. 1.3; Schopenhauer 1844, sec. 57 of book 3; Duncker 1941, sec. 14; for a discussion, see Sidgwick 1874, pp. 46 f. as well as secs. 1.4.4 (endnote) and 4.1.2 (first footnote). Descartes states the symmetry, concerning desire, of joy about *p* and sorrow at non-*p* particularly clearly (loc. cit.), and so do Gosling 1969, pp. 97 and 121, as well as, loc. cit., von Ehrenfels, von Giżycki, Pfänder, Schlick, Sigwart, and Ziehen.

10. See the various quantitative phrases in Locke 1689, secs. 2.20.6 and 2.21.31; similarly, Green 1883, sec. 105; Sidgwick 1874, last sentence of p. 47, as well as, loc. cit., von Giżycki, Schlick, Schneider, and Ziehen.

11. In Carolyn Morillo's words, pleasure is the anchor, not necessarily the focus, of desire (1995, passim). The two claims have been run together by many authors, including the Mills: 1829, vol. 2, pp. 192 f., 327, 361, and 1861, end of chap. 4. Early clarifications include: von Ehrenfels 1897, sec. 9; MacKenzie 1892, sec. 1.2.5 (and note to sec. 1.1.3); Rashdall 1907, vol. 1, sec. 1.2 (esp. pp. 17, 28–32); Schlick 1930, sec. 2.8; Sidgwick 1874, last sentence of p. 47, and, loc. cit., Sigwart, von Giżycki, and Pfänder.

12. MacIntyre 1965 discusses the issue and the literature.

13. As Richard Brandt's theory does; on the difference, see Lewis 1989, p. 124, and Murphy 1999.

14. See, e.g., Gibbard 1990, pp. 18–22; Johnston 1989; Rosati 1995; Velleman 1988; some of these authors list further critics.

15. I am paraphrasing very loosely Thomas Nagel's much-quoted protest from 1970, sec. 5.2. For works on the concept of desire, see the bibliography in Fehige and Wessels 1998.

16. A question asked forcefully in Quinn 1993, sec. 2.

17. The idea, as well as the shopping basket we are about to encounter, go back to Anscombe 1957, sec. 32; for a discussion of much of the literature, see Humberstone 1992.

18. See, for instance, Davidson 1963; Smith 1994, sec. 5.2; Williams 1980, pp. 78, 82 f., and 1989, pp. 38 f. Emphatically affirmative answers to this question have given birth and publicity to a form of instrumentalism that concentrates on "desires" conceived of as causes of actions—see the previous section. I'm not the only skeptic about these answers. Korsgaard 1986 contains similar misgivings in a different terminology, and Schueler 1995, chap. 2, a plea to keep explanatory and justificatory reasons strictly apart.

19. The thoughts in this section ride roughshod over various complications discussed in Parfit 1984, part 2, but could be brought in line with that discussion; see below, sec. 5.1. Some of the moves that follow—especially the rejection of "objective list" accounts as well as of hedonistic accounts of welfare—are standard; see, e.g., Parfit 1984, appendix I. For other works on the relation of welfare to desire fulfillment, see the bibliography of Fehige and Wessels 1998.

20. Nozick 1974, pp. 43–45.

21. The view is developed more fully in Feinberg 1977; Goldstick 1988; Lockwood 1979; and Solomon 1976.

22. For such objections, see, e.g., Grice 1967, sects 1.2 and 1.4, and Katz 1986, sec. 2.2. See also the discussions above, sec. 1.4, and below, sec. 5.1.

23. See Bricker 1980, esp. pp. 389 f., and Parfit 1984, chap. 8.

24. See the works mentioned in the following note as well as Bricker 1980; Broome 1994; Nagel 1970, part 2; Parfit 1984, part 2 and appendix F; Sidgwick 1874, pp. 124 and 381; Weirich 1981. Some of these works deal with the discounting of *other* people's future welfare, but the problems are related.

25. See Arneson 1990, pp. 164–167; Brandt 1982, sec. 8; Bykvist 1998, chap. 4; Hare 1981, sec. 5.6; and Maslen 2000.

26. In particular, Parfit's present-aim theory (1984, part 2) is a strong candidate. The theory would complicate the discussions in secs. 1.4, 4, and 5.2 f. of this paper. For a simplification similar to the one I'm opting for, see Hare 1981, p. 105.

27. Hume 1741, p. 5 and essay 18. Long before, the Buddha and the Stoics said the same. Later statements include Bricker 1980, secs. 4 f.; Bykvist 1998, chap. 5; the editors' introduction to *possible* preferences in Fehige and Wessels 1998; Mill 1838, p. 98; Schelling 1978; Schmidtz 1994.

28. This and some of the following points are discussed more fully, with references, in Fehige 2000, sec. 6.

29. This is the topic of Millgram 1997, esp. chap. 5; quotations from pp. 89, 103, and 6.

30. See the numerous references in Wessels 1998, note 57.

31. Epictetus, *Encheiridion*, sec. 8.

32. Bricker 1980, p. 400.

33. Luce and Raiffa 1957 and Resnik 1987 are two of many introductions.

34. See, e.g., Blackburn 1998, chap. 6; Bratman 1999; Parfit 1984, parts 1 f.; Sidgwick 1874, sec. 2.3.

35. See Hempel 1961–1962, sec. 2.2; Weber 1922, pp. 432–438.

36. Rawls 1971, pp. 432 f.; Anscombe 1957, sec. 37; Davidson 1963, p. 4.

37. For a complication I will have to ignore here, see Lewis 1989, p. 117.

38. McDowell 1978, pp. 90 f., 1979, p. 56. Like the Hearty View, Hubin 1999, pp. 35 f., favors the opposite answer.

39. Richardson 1994, sec. 13, anticipating much of what happens with the hero of John Grisham's *Street Lawyer* (1998). More on specificationism in the introduction to this volume.

40. For most *representata*, at any rate. The remarks on pleasure in sec. 1.4 suggest an exception.

References

Allais, M. 1953. "Fondements d'une théorie positive des choix comportant un risque et critique des postulats et axiomes de l'école américaine". *Econométrie* 40.

Anscombe, G. E. M. 1957. *Intention*. Second ed.: Oxford, 1963.

Aristotle. *De anima*. In vol. 1 of *Aristotelis opera*. Vol. 1: Berlin, 1831.

Aristotle. *Ethica nicomachea*. In vol. 2 of *Aritstotelis opera*. Vol. 2: Berlin, 1831.

Arneson, Richard J. 1990. "Liberalism, Distributive Subjectivism, and Equal Opportunity for Welfare". *Philosophy and Public Affairs* 19.

Audi, Robert. 1989. *Practical Reasoning*. London.

Augustine. *De civitate dei*. Turnhout, 1955.

Blackburn, Simon. 1998. *Ruling Passions*. Oxford.

Brandt, Richard B. 1979. *A Theory of the Good and the Right*. Oxford.

Brandt, Richard B. 1982. "Two Concepts of Utility". In his *Morality, Utilitarianism, and Rights*. Cambridge, 1992.

Brandt, Richard B. 1998. "The Rational Criticism of Preferences". In Christoph Fehige and Ulla Wessels, eds., *Preferences*. Berlin.

Brandt, Richard B., and Jaegwon Kim. 1963. "Wants as Explanations of Actions". *Journal of Philosophy* 60.

Bratman, Michael E. 1999. *Faces of Intention*. Cambridge.

Bricker, Phillip. 1980. "Prudence". *Journal of Philosophy* 77.

Broome, John. 1994. "Discounting the Future". *Philosophy and Public Affairs* 23.

Bykvist, Krister. 1998. *Changing Preferences*. Ph.D. dissertation, Uppsala University.

Condillac, Étienne Bonnot de. 1754. *Traité des sensations*. In vol. 1 of his *Œuvres philosophiques*. Vol. 1: Paris, 1947.

Davidson, Donald. 1963. "Actions, Reasons, and Causes". In his *Essays on Actions and Events*. Oxford, 1980.

Descartes, René. 1649. *Les passions de l'âme*. In vol. 11 of his *Œuvres*. Vol. 11: Paris, 1909.

Duncker, Karl. 1941. "On Pleasure, Emotion, and Striving". *Philosophy and Phenomenological Research 1*.

Ehrenfels, Christian von. 1897. *System der Werttheorie*. Vol. 1. In vol. 1 of his *Philosophische Schriften*. Vol. 1 of the *Schriften*: München, 1982.

Epictetus. *Encheiridion*. In his *Discourses, Books III–IV; Fragments; Encheiridion*. Cambridge, Mass., 1928. The English wording I use is inspired by Nicholas White's translation. Indianapolis, 1983.

Fehige, Christoph. 2000. "Justice beyond Desires?" In Victoria Davion and Clark Wolf, eds., *The Idea of a Political Liberalism*. Totowa, N.J.

Fehige, Christoph, and Ulla Wessels, eds. 1998. *Preferences*. Berlin.

Feinberg, Joel. 1977. "Harm and Self-Interest". In P. M. S. Hacker and J. Raz, eds., *Law, Morality, and Society*. Oxford.

Gauthier, David. 1975. "Reason and Maximization". In his *Moral Dealing*. Ithaca, N.Y., 1990.

Gauthier, David. 1986. *Morals by Agreement*. Oxford.

Gibbard, Allan. 1990. *Wise Choices, Apt Feelings*. Oxford.

Giżycki, Georg von. 1883. *Grundzüge der Moral*. Leipzig.

Goldstick, D. 1988. "The Welfare of the Dead". *Philosophy* 63.

Gosling, J. C. B. 1969. *Pleasure and Desire*. Oxford.

Green, Thomas Hill. 1883. *Prolegomena to Ethics*. Third ed.: Oxford, 1890.

Grice, Geoffrey Russell. 1967. *The Grounds of Moral Judgement*. Cambridge.

Hare, R. M. 1981. *Moral Thinking*. Oxford.

Hempel, Carl G. 1961–1962. "Rational Action". *Proceedings and Addresses of the American Philosophical Association* 35.

Hobbes, Thomas. 1651. *Leviathan*. Indianapolis, 1994.

Hubin, Donald C. 1991. "Irrational Desire". *Philosophical Studies* 62.

Hubin, Donald C. 1999. "What's Special about Humeanism?" *Noûs* 33.

Humberstone, I. L. 1992. "Direction of Fit". *Mind* 101.

Hume, David. 1739–1740. *A Treatise of Human Nature*. Oxford, 1978.

Hume, David. 1741. *Essays: Moral, Political, and Literary*. Indianapolis, 1985.

Hutcheson, Francis. 1734–1737. *A System of Moral Philosophy*. London, 1755. Written by Hutcheson between 1734 and 1737 for his lectures in Glasgow and published posthumously.

Johnston, Mark. 1989. "Dispositional Theories of Value". *Proceedings of the Aristotelian Society*, suppl. vol. 63.

Kant, Immanuel. 1797. *Metaphysische Anfangsgründe der Rechtslehre*. Part 1 of *Die Metaphysik der Sitten*. In vol. 6 of *Kant's gesammelte Schriften*. Vol. 6: Berlin, 1907.

Katz, Leonard David. 1986. *Hedonism as Metaphysics of Mind and Value*. Ph.D. dissertation, Princeton University.

Korsgaard, Christine. 1986. "Skepticism about Practical Reasoning". In this volume.

Lewis, David. 1989. "Dispositional Theories of Value". *Proceedings of the Aristotelian Society*, suppl. vol. 63.

Locke, John. 1689. *An Essay concerning Human Understanding*. Oxford, 1975.

Lockwood, Michael. 1979. "Singer on Killing and the Preference for Life". *Inquiry* 22.

Luce, R. Duncan, and Howard Raiffa. 1957. *Games and Decisions*. New York.

MacIntyre, Alisdair. 1965. "Pleasure as a Reason for Action". *Monist* 49.

MacKenzie, John S. 1892. *A Manual of Ethics*. Sixth ed.: London, 1929.

Maslen, Cei. 2000. "Humeanism and Nagel's Persimmon". Unpublished typescript.

McDowell, John. 1978. "Are Moral Requirements Hypothetical Imperatives?" In his *Mind, Value, and Reality*. Cambridge, Mass., 1998.

McDowell, John. 1979. "Virtue and Reason". In his *Mind, Value, and Reality*. Cambridge, Mass., 1998.

Meinong, Alexius. 1902. *Über Annahmen*. Second ed.: 1910. Vol. 4 of the *Gesamtausgabe*. Vol. 4: Graz, 1977.

Meinong, Alexius. 1921. *Ethische Bausteine*. Fragment published posthumously in vol. 3 of the *Gesamtausgabe*. Vol. 3: Graz, 1968.

Mill, James. 1829. *Analysis of the Phenomena of the Human Mind*. Second ed.: London, 1878.

Mill, John Stuart. 1838. "Bentham". In vol. 10 of his *Collected Works*. Vol. 10: Toronto, 1969.

Mill, John Stuart. 1861. *Utilitarianism*. In vol. 10 of his *Collected Works*. Vol. 10: Toronto, 1969.

Millgram, Elijah. 1997. *Practical Induction*. Cambridge, Mass.

Millgram, Elijah. 2000. "Mill's Proof of the Principle of Utility". *Ethics* 110.

Mises, Ludwig von. 1949. *Human Action*. New Haven.

Morillo, Carolyn R. 1995. *Contingent Creatures*. Lanham, Md.

Murphy, Mark C. 1999. "The Simple Desire-Fulfilment Theory". *Noûs* 33.

Nagel, Thomas. 1970. *The Possibility of Altruism*. Oxford.

Nozick, Robert. 1974. *Anarchy, State, and Utopia*. New York.

Parfit, Derek. 1984. *Reasons and Persons*. Rev. edition. Oxford, 1989.

Pfänder, Alexander. 1900. *Phänomenologie des Wollens*. Leipzig.

Plato. *Gorgias*. In his *Lysis; Symposium; Gorgias*. Cambridge, Mass., 1925.

Plato. *Symposium*. In his *Lysis; Symposium; Gorgias*. Cambridge, Mass., 1925.

Quinn, Warren. 1993. "Putting Rationality in Its Place". In his *Morality and Action*. Cambridge.

Rashdall, Hastings. 1907. *The Theory of Good and Evil*. Oxford.

Rawls, John. 1971. *A Theory of Justice*. Cambridge, Mass.

Resnik, Michael D. 1987. *Choices*. Minneapolis.

Richardson, Henry S. 1994. *Practical Reasoning about Final Ends*. Cambridge.

Rosati, Connie S. 1995. "Persons, Perspectives, and Full Information Accounts of the Good". *Ethics* 105.

Russell, Bertrand. 1954. *Human Society in Ethics and Politics*. London.

Schelling, T. C. 1978. "Egonomics, or the Art of Self-Management". *American Economic Review* 68.

Schlick, Moritz. 1930. *Fragen der Ethik*. Frankfurt am Main, 1984.

Schmidtz, David. 1994. "Choosing Ends". In this volume.

Schmidtz, David. 2000. "Reasons for Reasons". Unpublished typescript.

Schneider, Georg Heinrich. 1880. *Der thierische Wille*. Leipzig.

Schopenhauer, Arthur. 1844. *Die Welt als Wille und Vorstellung*. Vol. 2. Vol. 2 of his *Werke*, third ed. Vol. 2 of the *Werke*: Zurich 1994.

Schueler, G. F. 1995. *Desire*. Cambridge, Mass.

Sidgwick, Henry. 1874. *The Methods of Ethics*. Seventh ed.: London, 1907.

Sigwart, Christoph. 1886. *Vorfragen der Ethik*. Freiburg im Breisgau.

Smith, Michael. 1994. *The Moral Problem*. Oxford.

Solomon, Robert C. 1976. "Is There Happiness after Death?" *Philosophy* 51.

Spinoza, Benedictus de. 1677. *Ethica*. In vol. 2 of his *Opera*. Vol. 2: Heidelberg, 1925.

Stampe, Dennis W. 1987. "The Authority of Desire". *Philosophical Review* 96.

Strawson, Galen. 1994. *Mental Reality*. Cambridge, Mass.

Velleman, J. David. 1988. "Brandt's Definition of 'Good'". *Philosophical Review* 97.

Weber, Max. 1922. *Gesammelte Aufsätze zur Wissenschaftslehre*. Sixth ed.: Tübingen, 1985. Papers published between 1903 and 1922.

Weirich, Paul. 1981. "A Bias of Rationality". *Australasian Journal of Philosophy* 59.

Wessels, Ulla. 1998. "Procreation". In Christoph Fehige and Ulla Wessels, eds., *Preferences*. Berlin.

Williams, Bernard. 1980. "Internal and External Reasons". In this volume.

Williams, Bernard. 1989. "Internal Reasons and the Obscurity of Blame". In his *Making Sense of Humanity*. Cambridge, 1995.

Wundt, Wilhelm. 1874. *Grundzüge der physiologischen Psychologie*. Sixth, rev. ed., vol. 3: Leipzig, 1911.

Ziehen, Th. 1891. *Leitfaden der physiologischen Psychologie*. Tenth ed.: Jena, 1914.

Chapter 4

Internal and External Reasons

Bernard Williams

Sentences of the forms '*A* has a reason to ϕ' or 'There is a reason for *A* to ϕ' (where 'ϕ' stands in for some verb of action) seem on the face of it to have two different sorts of interpretation. On the first, the truth of the sentence implies, very roughly, that *A* has some motive which will be served or furthered by his ϕ-ing, and if this turns out not to be so the sentence is false: there is a condition relating to the agent's aims, and if this is not satisfied it is not true to say, on this interpretation, that he has a reason to ϕ. On the second interpretation, there is no such condition, and the reason-sentence will not be falsified by the absence of an appropriate motive. I shall call the first the 'internal', the second the 'external', interpretation. (Given two such interpretations, and the two forms of sentence quoted, it is reasonable to suppose that the first sentence more naturally collects the internal interpretation, and the second the external, but it would be wrong to suggest that either form of words admits only one of the interpretations.)

I shall also for convenience refer sometimes to 'internal reasons' and 'external reasons', as I do in the title, but this is to be taken only as a convenience. It is a matter for investigation whether there are two sorts of reasons for action, as opposed to two sorts of statements about people's reasons for action. Indeed, as we shall eventually see, even the interpretation in one of the cases is problematical.

I shall consider first the internal interpretation, and how far it can be taken. I shall then consider, more sceptically, what might be involved in an external interpretation. I shall end with some very brief remarks connecting all this with the issue of public goods and free-riders.

The simplest model for the internal interpretation would be this: *A* has a reason to ϕ iff *A* has some desire the satisfaction of which will be served by his ϕ-ing. Alternatively, we might say ... some desire, the satisfaction of which *A* believes will be served by his *φ*-ing; this difference will concern us later. Such a model is sometimes ascribed to Hume, but since in fact Hume's own views are more complex than this, we might call it *the sub-Humean model*. The sub-Humean model is certainly too simple. My aim will be, by addition and revision, to work it up into something more adequate. In the course of trying to do this, I shall assemble four propositions which seem to me to be true of internal reason statements.

Basically, and by definition, any model for the internal interpretation must display a relativity of the reason statement to the agent's *subjective motivational set*, which I shall call the agent's *S*. The contents of *S* we shall come to, but we can say:

(i) An internal reason statement is falsified by the absence of some appropriate element from *S*.

The simplest sub-Humean model claims that any element in *S* gives rise to an internal reason. But there are grounds for denying this, not because of regrettable, imprudent, or deviant elements in *S*—they raise different sorts of issues—but because of elements in *S* based on false belief.

The agent believes that this stuff is gin, when it is in fact petrol. He wants a gin and tonic. Has he reason, or a reason, to mix this stuff with tonic and drink it? There are two ways here (as suggested already by the two alternatives for formulating the sub-Humean model). On the one hand, it is just very odd to say that he has a reason to drink this stuff, and natural to say that he has no reason to drink it, although he thinks that he has. On the other hand, if he does drink it, we not only have an explanation of his doing so (a reason why he did it), but we have such an explanation which is of the reason-for-action form. This explanatory dimension is very important, and we shall come back to it more than once. If there are reasons for action, it must be that people sometimes act for those reasons, and if they do, their reasons must figure in some correct explanation of their action (it does not follow that they must figure in all correct explanations of their action). The difference between false and true beliefs on the agent's part cannot alter the *form* of the explanation which will be appropriate to his action. This consideration might move us to ignore the intuition which we noticed before, and lead us just to legislate that in the case of the agent who wants gin, he has a reason to drink this stuff which is petrol.

I do not think, however, that we should do this. It looks in the wrong direction, by implying in effect that the internal reason conception is only concerned with explanation, and not at all with the agent's rationality, and this may help to motivate a search for other sorts of reason which are connected with his rationality. But the internal reasons conception is concerned with the agent's rationality. What we can correctly ascribe to him in a third-personal internal reason statement is also what he can ascribe to himself as a result of deliberation, as we shall see. So I think that we should rather say:

(ii) A member of S, D, will not give A a reason for ϕ-ing if either the existence of D is dependent on false belief, or A's belief in the relevance of ϕ-ing to the satisfaction of D is false.

(This double formulation can be illustrated from the gin/petrol case: D can be taken in the first way as the desire to drink what is in this bottle, and in the second way as the desire to drink gin.) It will, all the same, be true that if he does ϕ in these circumstances, there was not only a reason why he ϕ-ed, but also that that displays him as, relative to his false belief, acting rationally.

We can note the epistemic consequence:

(iii) a. A may falsely believe an internal reason statement about himself, and (we can add)

    b. A may not know some true internal reason statement about himself.

(b) comes from two different sources. One is that A may be ignorant of some fact such that if he did know it he would, in virtue of some element in S, be disposed to ϕ: we can say that he has a reason to ϕ, though he does not know it. For it to be the case that he actually has such a reason, however, it seems that the relevance of the unknown fact to his actions has to be fairly close and immediate; otherwise one merely says that A would have a reason to ϕ if he knew the fact. I shall not pursue the question of the conditions for saying the one thing or the other, but it must be closely connected with the question of when the ignorance forms part of the explanation of what A actually does.

The second source of (iii) is that A may be ignorant of some element in S. But we should notice that an unknown element in S, D, will provide a reason for A to ϕ only if ϕ-ing is rationally related to D; that is to say, roughly, a project to ϕ could be the answer to a deliberative question formed in part by D. If D is unknown to A because it is in the unconscious, it may well not satisfy this condition, although of course it may provide the reason why he ϕ's, that is, may explain or help to explain his ϕ-ing. In such cases, the ϕ-ing may be related to D only symbolically.

I have already said that

(iv) internal reason statements can be discovered in deliberative reasoning.

It is worth remarking the point, already implicit, that an internal reason statement does not apply only to that action which is the uniquely preferred result of the deliberation. 'A has reason to ϕ' does not mean 'the action which A has overall, all-in, reason to do is ϕ-ing'. He can have reason to do a lot of things which he has other and stronger reasons not to do.

The sub-Humean model supposes that ϕ-ing has to be related to some element in S as causal means to end (unless, perhaps, it is straightforwardly the carrying out of a desire which is itself that element in S). But this is only one case: indeed, the mere discovery that some course of action is the causal means to an end is not in itself a piece of practical reasoning.[1] A clear example of practical reasoning is that leading to the conclusion that one has reason to ϕ because ϕ-ing would be the most convenient, economical, pleasant etc. way of satisfying some element in S, and this of course is controlled by other elements in S, if not necessarily in a very clear or determinate way. But there are much wider possibilities for deliberation, such as: thinking how the satisfaction of elements in S can be combined, e.g. by time-ordering; where there is some irresoluble conflict among the elements of S, considering which one attaches most weight to (which, importantly, does not imply that there is some one commodity of which they provide varying amounts); or, again, finding constitutive solutions, such as deciding what would make for an entertaining evening, granted that one wants entertainment.

As a result of such processes an agent can come to see that he has reason to do something which he did not see he had reason to do at all. In this way, the deliberative process can add new actions for which there are internal reasons, just as it can also add new internal reasons for given actions. The deliberative process can also subtract elements from S. Reflection may lead the agent to see that some belief is false, and hence to realise that he has in fact no reason to do something he thought he had reason to do. More subtly, he may think he has reason to promote some development because he has not exercised his imagination enough about what it would be like if it came about. In his unaided deliberative reason, or encouraged by the persuasions of others, he may come to have some more concrete sense of what would be involved, and lose his desire for it, just as, positively, the imagination can create new possibilities and new desires. (These are important possibilities for politics as well as for individual action.)

We should not, then, think of S as statically given. The processes of deliberation can have all sorts of effect on S, and this is a fact which a theory of internal reasons should be very happy to accommodate. So also it should be more liberal than some theorists have been about the possible elements in S. I have discussed S primarily in terms of desires, and this term can be used, formally, for all elements in S. But this terminology may make one forget that S can contain such things as dispositions of evaluation, patterns of emotional reaction, personal loyalties, and various projects, as they may be abstractly called, embodying commitments of the agent. Above all, there is of course no supposition that the desires or projects of an agent have to be egoistic; he will, one hopes, have non-egoistic projects of various kinds, and these equally can provide internal reasons for action.

There is a further question, however, about the contents of S: whether it should be taken, consistently with the general idea of internal reasons, as containing *needs*. It is certainly quite natural to say that A has a reason to pursue X, just on the ground that he needs X, but will this naturally follow in a theory of internal reasons? There is a special problem about this only if it is possible for the agent to be unmotivated to pursue what he needs. I shall not try to discuss here the nature of needs, but I take it that insofar as there are determinately recognisable needs, there can be an agent who lacks any interest in getting what he indeed needs. I take it, further, that that lack of interest can remain after deliberation, and, also that it would be wrong to say that such a lack of interest must always rest on false belief. (Insofar as it does rest on false belief, then we can accommodate it under (ii), in the way already discussed.)

If an agent really is uninterested in pursuing what he needs; and this is not the product of false belief; and he could not reach any such motive from motives he has by the kind of deliberative processes we have discussed; then I think we do have to say that in the internal sense he indeed has no reason to pursue these things. In saying this, however, we have to bear in mind how strong these assumptions are, and how seldom we are likely to think that we know them to be true. When we say that a person has reason to take medicine which he needs, although he consistently and persuasively denies any interest in preserving his health, we may well still be speaking in the internal sense, with the thought that really at some level he *must* want to be well.

However, if we become clear that we have no such thought, and persist in saying that the person has this reason, then we must be speaking in another sense, and this is the external sense. People do say things that ask to be taken in the external interpretation. In James' story of Owen Wingrave, from which Britten made an opera, Owen's father urges on him the necessity and importance of his joining the army, since all his male ancestors were soldiers, and family pride requires him to do the same. Owen Wingrave has no motivation to join the army at all, and all his desires lead in another direction: he hates everything about military life and what it means. His father might have expressed himself by saying that *there was a reason for Owen to join the army.* Knowing that there was nothing in Owen's S which would lead, through deliberative reasoning, to his doing this would not make him withdraw the claim or admit that he made it under a misapprehension. He means it in an external sense. What is that sense?

A preliminary point is that this is not the same question as that of the status of a supposed categorical imperative, in the Kantian sense of an 'ought' which applies to an agent independently of what the agent happens to want: or rather, it is not undoubtedly the same question. First, a categorical imperative has often been taken, as by Kant, to be necessarily an imperative of morality, but external reason statements do not necessarily relate to morality. Second, it remains an obscure issue what the relation is between 'there is a reason for A to ...' and 'A ought to ...'. Some philosophers take them to be equivalent, and under that view the question of external reasons of course comes much closer to the question of a categorical imperative. However, I shall not make any assumption about such an equivalence, and shall not further discuss 'ought'.[2]

In considering what an external reason statement might mean, we have to remember again the dimension of possible explanation, a consideration which applies to any reason for action. If something can be a reason for action, then it could be someone's reason for acting on a particular occasion, and it would then figure in an explanation of that action. Now no external reason statement could *by itself* offer an explanation of anyone's action. Even if it were true (whatever that might turn out to mean) that there was a reason for Owen to join the army, that fact by itself would never explain anything that Owen did, not even his joining the army. For if it was true at all, it was true when Owen was not motivated to join the army. The whole point of external reason statements is that they can be true independently of the agent's motivations. But nothing can explain an agent's (intentional) actions except something that motivates him so to act. So something else is needed besides the truth of the external reason statement to explain action, some psychological link; and that psychological link would seem to be belief. A's believing an external reason statement about himself may help to explain his action.

External reason statements have been introduced merely in the general form 'there is a reason for A to ...', but we now need to go beyond that form, to specific statements of reasons. No doubt there are some cases of an agent's ϕ-ing because he believes that there is a reason for him to ϕ, while he does not have any belief about what that reason is. They would be cases of his relying on some authority whom he trusts, or, again, of his recalling that he did know of some reason for his ϕ-ing, but his not being able to remember what it was. In these respects, reasons for action are like reasons for belief. But, as with reasons for belief, they are evidently secondary cases. The basic case must be that in which A ϕ's, not because he believes only that there is some reason or other for him to ϕ, but because he believes of some determinate consideration that it constitutes a reason for him to ϕ. Thus Owen Wingrave might come to join the army because (now) he believes that it is a reason for him to do so that his family has a tradition of military honour.

Does believing that a particular consideration is a reason to act in a particular way provide, or indeed constitute, a motivation to act? If it does not, then we are no further on. Let us grant that it does—this claim indeed seems plausible, so long at least as the connexion between such beliefs and the disposition to act is not tightened to that unnecessary degree which excludes *akrasia*. The claim is in fact *so* plausible, that this agent, with this belief, appears to be one about whom, now, an *internal* reason statement could truly be made: he is one with an appropriate motivation in his S. A man who does believe that considerations of family honour constitute reasons for action is a man with a certain disposition to action, and also dispositions of approval, sentiment, emotional reaction, and so forth.

Now it does not follow from this that there is nothing in external reason statements. What does follow is that their content is not going to be revealed by considering merely the state of one who believes such a statement, nor how that state explains action, for that state is merely the state with regard to which an internal reason statement could truly be made. Rather, the content of the external type of statement will have to be revealed by considering what it is to *come to believe* such a statement—it is there, if at all, that their peculiarity will have to emerge.

We will take the case (we have implicitly been doing so already) in which an external reason statement is made about someone who, like Owen Wingrave, is not already motivated in the required way, and so is someone about whom an internal statement could not also be truly made. (Since the difference between external and internal statements turns on the implications accepted by the speaker, external statements can of course be made about agents who are already motivated; but that is not the interesting case.) The agent does not presently believe the external statement. If he comes to believe it, he will be motivated to act; so coming to believe it must, essentially, involve acquiring a new motivation. How can that be?

This is closely related to an old question, of how 'reason can give rise to a motivation', a question which has famously received from Hume a negative answer. But in that form, the question is itself unclear, and is unclearly related to the argument—for of course reason, that is to say, rational processes, can give rise to new motivations, as we have seen in the account of deliberation. Moreover, the traditional way of putting the issue also (I shall suggest) picks up an onus of proof about what is to count as a 'purely rational process' which not only should it not pick up, but which properly belongs with the critic who wants to oppose Hume's general conclusion and to make a lot out of external reason statements—someone I shall call 'the external reasons theorist'.

The basic point lies in recognising that the external reasons theorist must conceive *in a special way* the connexion between acquiring a motivation and coming to believe the reason statement. For of course there are various means by which the agent could come to have the motivation and also to believe the reason statement, but which are the wrong kind of means to interest the external reasons theorist. Owen might be so persuaded by his father's moving rhetoric that he acquired both the motivation and the belief. But this excludes an element which the external reasons theorist essentially wants, that the agent should acquire the motivation *because* he comes to believe the reason statement, and that he should do the latter, moreover, because, in some way, he is considering the matter aright. If the theorist is to hold on to these conditions, he will, I think, have to make the condition under which the agent appropriately comes to have the motivation something like this, that he should deliberate correctly; and the external reasons statement itself will have to be taken as roughly equivalent to, or at least as entailing, the claim that if the agent rationally deliberated, then, whatever motivations he originally had, he would come to be motivated to ϕ.

But if this is correct, there does indeed seem great force in Hume's basic point, and it is very plausible to suppose that all external reason statements are false. For, *ex hypothesi*, there is no motivation for the agent to deliberate *from*, to reach this new motivation. Given the agent's earlier existing motivations, and this new motivation, what has to hold for external reason statements to be true, on this line of interpretation, is that the new motivation could be in some way rationally arrived at, granted the earlier motivations. Yet at the same time it must not bear to the earlier motivations the kind of rational relation which we considered in the earlier discussion of deliberation—for in that case an internal reason statement would have been true in the first place. I see no reason to suppose that these conditions could possibly be met.

It might be said that the force of an external reason statement can be explained in the following way. Such a statement implies that a rational agent would be motivated to act appropriately, and it can carry this implication, because a rational agent is precisely one who has a general disposition in his S to do what (he believes) there is reason for him to do. So when he comes to believe that there is reason for him to ϕ, he is motivated to ϕ, even though, before, he neither had a motive to ϕ, nor any motive related to ϕ-ing in one of the ways considered in the account of deliberation.

But this reply merely puts off the problem. It reapplies the desire and belief model (roughly speaking) of explanation to the actions in question, but using a desire and a belief the content of which are in question. *What* is it that one comes to believe when he comes to believe that there is reason for him to ϕ, if it is not the proposition, or something that entails the proposition, that if he deliberated rationally, he would be motivated to act appropriately? We were asking how any true proposition could have that content; it cannot help, in answering that, to appeal to a supposed desire which is activated by a belief which has that very content.

These arguments about what it is to accept an external reason statement involve some idea of what is possible under the account of deliberation already given, and what is excluded by that account. But here it may be objected that the account of deliberation is very vague, and has for instance allowed the use of the imagination to extend or restrict the contents of the agent's S. But if that is so, then it is unclear what the limits are to what an agent might arrive at by rational deliberation from his existing S.

It *is* unclear, and I regard it as a basically desirable feature of a theory of practical reasoning that it should preserve and account for that unclarity. There is an essential indeterminacy in what can be counted a rational deliberative process. Practical reasoning is a heuristic process, and an imaginative one, and there are no fixed boundaries on the continuum from rational thought to inspiration and conversion. To someone who thinks that reasons for action are basically to be understood in terms of the internal reasons model, this is not a difficulty. There is indeed a vagueness about 'A has reason to ϕ', in the internal sense, insofar as the deliberative processes which could lead from A's present S to his being motivated to ϕ may be more or less ambitiously conceived. But this is no embarrassment to those who take as basic the internal conception of reasons for action. It merely shows that there is a wider range of states, and a less determinate one, than one might have supposed, which can be counted as A's having a reason to ϕ.

It is the external reasons theorist who faces a problem at this point. There are of course many things that a speaker may say to one who is not disposed to ϕ when the speaker thinks that he should be, as that he is inconsiderate, or cruel, or selfish, or imprudent; or that things, and he, would be a lot nicer if he were so motivated. Any of these can be sensible things to say. But one who makes a great deal out of putting the criticism in the form of an external reason statement seems concerned to say that what is particularly wrong with the agent is that he is *irrational*. It is this theorist who particularly needs to make this charge precise: in particular, because he wants any rational agent, as such, to acknowledge the requirement to do the thing in question.

Owen Wingrave's father indeed expressed himself in terms other than 'a reason', but, as we imagined, he could have used the external reasons formulation. This fact itself provides some difficulty for the external reasons theorist. This theorist, who sees the truth of an external reason statement as potentially grounding a charge of irrationality against the agent who ignores it, might well want to say that if Wingrave *père* put his complaints against Owen in this form, he would very probably be claiming something which, in this particular case, was false. What the theorist would have a harder time showing would be that the words *meant* something different as used by Wingrave from what they mean when they are, as he supposes, truly uttered. But what they mean when uttered by Wingrave is almost certainly *not* that rational deliberation would get Owen to be motivated to join the army—which is (very roughly) the meaning or implication we have found for them, if they are to bear the kind of weight such theorists wish to give them.

The sort of considerations offered here strongly suggest to me that external reason statements, when definitely isolated as such, are false, or incoherent, or really something else misleadingly expressed. It is in fact harder to isolate them in people's speech than the introduction of them at the beginning of this chapter suggested. Those who use these words often seem, rather, to be entertaining an optimistic internal reason claim, but sometimes the statement is indeed offered as standing definitely outside the agent's *S* and what he might derive from it in rational deliberation, and then there is, I suggest, a great unclarity about what is meant. Sometimes it is little more than that things would be better if the agent so acted. But the formulation in terms of reasons does have an effect, particularly in its suggestion that the agent is being irrational, and this suggestion, once the basis of an internal reason claim has been clearly laid aside, is bluff. If this is so, the only real claims about reasons for action will be internal claims.

A problem which has been thought to lie very close to the present subject is that of public goods and free riders, which concerns the situation (very roughly) in which each person has egoistic reason to want a certain good provided, but at the same time each has egoistic reason not to take part in providing it. I shall not attempt any discussion of this problem, but it may be helpful, simply in order to make clear my own view of reasons for action and to bring out contrasts with some other views, if I end by setting out a list of questions which bear on the problem, together with the answers that would be given to them by one who thinks (to put it cursorily) that the only rationality of action is the rationality of internal reasons.

1. Can we define notions of rationality which are not purely egoistic?
Yes.
2. Can we define notions of rationality which are not purely means-end?
Yes.

3. Can we define a notion of rationality where the action rational for *A* is in no way relative to *A*'s existing motivations?

No.

4. Can we show that a person who only has egoistic motivations is irrational in not pursuing non-egoistic ends?

Not necessarily, though we may be able to in special cases. (The trouble with the egoistic person is not characteristically irrationality.)

Let there be some good, *G*, and a set of persons, *P*, such that each member of *P* has egoistic reason to want *G* provided, but delivering *G* requires action *C*, which involves costs, by each of some proper sub-set of *P*; and let *A* be a member of *P*: then

5. Has *A* egoistic reason to do *C* if he is reasonably sure either that too few members of *P* will do *C* for *G* to be provided, or that enough other members of *P* will do *C*, so that *G* will be provided?

No.

6. Are there any circumstances of this kind in which *A* can have egoistic reason to do *C*?

Yes, in those cases in which reaching the critical number of those doing *C* is sensitive to his doing *C*, or he has reason to think this.

7. Are there any motivations which would make it rational for *A* to do *C*, even though not in the situation just referred to?

Yes, if he is not purely egoistic: many. For instance, there are expressive motivations—appropriate e.g. in the celebrated voting case.[3] There are also motivations which derive from the sense of fairness. This can precisely transcend the dilemma of 'either useless or unnecessary', by the form of argument 'somebody, but no reason to omit any particular body, so everybody'.

8. Is it irrational for an agent to have such motivations?

In any sense in which the question is intelligible, no.

9. Is it rational for society to bring people up with these sorts of motivations?

Insofar as the question is intelligible, yes. And certainly we have reason to encourage people to have these dispositions—e.g. in virtue of possessing them ourselves.

I confess that I cannot see any other major questions which, at this level of generality, bear on these issues. All these questions have clear answers which are entirely compatible with a conception of practical rationality in terms of internal reasons for action, and are also, it seems to me, entirely reasonable answers.

Notes

1. A point made by Aurel Kolnai: see his 'Deliberation Is of Ends' (this volume, chap. 12). See also David Wiggins, 'Deliberation and Practical Reason' (this volume, chap. 13).

2. It is discussed in 'Ought and Moral Obligation', in Bernard Williams, *Moral Luck* (Cambridge: Cambridge University Press, 1981), pp. 114–123.

3. A well-known treatment is by M. Olson Jr. *The Logic of Collective Action* (Cambridge, Mass., 1965). On expressive motivations in this connexion, see S. I. Benn, 'Rationality and Political Behaviour', in S. I. Benn and G. W. Mortimore, eds., *Rationality and the Social Sciences* (London, 1976). On the point about fairness, which follows in the text, there is of course a very great deal more to be said: for instance, about how members of a group can, compatibly with fairness, converge on strategies more efficient than everyone's doing *C* (such as people taking turns).

Postscript

Some Further Notes on Internal and External Reasons

Bernard Williams

A good deal has been written about this question since this article appeared in 1980, and I have added two pieces myself.[1] The editor of the present collection has given me the opportunity of adding some remarks about the present state of the issue, as I see it; I shall do so in the form of some brief notes on what I take to be the central issues, rather than by attempting anything like a review of the literature.

1

The formulation of the internalist position which I now prefer[2] is: A has a reason to ϕ only if there is *a sound deliberative route* from A's subjective motivational set (which I label "S," as in the original article) to A's ϕ-ing. Whether this is also a sufficient condition of A's having a reason to ϕ is a question which I have left aside; the essence of the internalist position is that it is a necessary condition. It is natural to take the condition as implying not just that A has a reason to ϕ, but that he or she has more reason to do that than to do anything else. This is the case I shall take as central.

2

There is no attempt to give an account of what counts as "a sound deliberative route" except to the extent that this is required by the demands of internalism. I have assumed that if an agent's conclusion in favour of a certain action is essentially based on a false belief (as in the gin and petrol example) the agent has no reason to do that action, though he thinks that he has. The basis for "correcting" his deliberation in the direction of the truth is that he indeed wants to take the correct means to his ends—this is indeed part of his *S*. In general, the aim of getting things right in such ways is part of any agent's interest as a rational deliberator, and the aim can be assumed to figure in any rational agent's *S* (though there can be exceptional cases in which an agent has a reason to sustain a false belief). However, we cannot simply assume that moral considerations, for instance, or long-term prudential concerns must figure in every agent's *S*. For many agents, as we well know, they indeed do so, if not altogether securely; but a philosophical claim that they are necessarily part of rational agency needs argument.

There is, then, no attempt to exclude altruistic or other ethical considerations from the rational agent's *S*. For most agents, those patterns of motivation appear there together with many others—desires, projects, sympathies and so on. Nor does the account constrain the relation between the action and the agent's *S* to some narrow instrumental connection; actions can express and flow from various elements in the agent's *S* without being means to some separate end. Equally, the account is not committed to the formulations of classical rational decision theory, to the effect that all the input to a decision can be made explicit and is subjected to an algorithmic process. There is room for the imagination in deciding what to do, and correspondingly in saying what someone else has reason to do. Indeed, the stance towards the agent that is implied by the internalist account can be usefully compared to that of an imaginative and informed advisor, who takes seriously the formula "If I were you . . . ."

3

It is a consequence of the account that the question whether a given person has a reason to act in a certain way may have no entirely determinate answer. This consequence is entirely welcome: there are indeed many and unclear stages on the path between cases in which it is manifestly and overwhelmingly clear that an agent has reason to do a certain thing, and cases in which my telling him what he has reason to do constitutes influencing him or getting him to see things in a new light. A realistic account should accept that there is an essential indeterminacy in this area.

It follows from the account that in more than one way, an agent may be mistaken about what he has reason to do (one example we have already noticed is that of false belief). This is essential to preserving the point that statements of what people have reason to do have normative force; no account that excludes this can be adequate. Some writers make a distinction between "normative" and "explanatory" reasons, but this does not seem to me to be helpful, because normative and explanatory considerations are closely involved with one another. On the one hand, if it is said, in the normative mode, that A has a reason to ϕ, the speaker must envisage the possibility of A's ϕ-ing for that reason, in which case the reason will figure in the explanation of what A does. (I appeal to this connection in the argument against external reasons.) On the other hand, if we explain what A does in terms of his reason for doing that thing, which is one type of giving a reason why he did it, we rationalize his conduct (in the phrase familiar from Davidson's work): that is to say, we cite a consideration which was effective in his coming to act because it made normative sense to him. Its making normative sense to him implies that it made normative sense in terms of his S. This does not mean that when an agent has a thought of the form "that is a reason for me to ϕ," he really has, or should really have, the thought "that is a reason for me to ϕ *in virtue of my S.*" The disposition that forms part of his S just is the disposition to have thoughts of the form "that is a reason for me to ϕ," and to act on them.

4

I do not deny, and it would be absurd to deny, that sentences of the form "*A* has a reason to ..." (or "There is a reason for you to ..." and so on) are used in ways that do not satisfy the internalist condition. My claim is, first, that when they are so used and are not merely mistaken, the speaker intends some roughly specifiable other thing which does not mean the same in general as "*A* has a reason to ...," such as "We have a reason to want *A* to ..."; and, second, that there is no principled and convincing way of distinguishing the basic sense of "*A* has a reason to ..." from these other things other than an internalist interpretation.

This raises the question of what an externalist account of such sentences and their truth conditions will be. I say in the article reprinted here that the externalist wants, specifically, to be able to say that someone who resists a correct externalist claim is *irrational*. I accept that this is too strong.[3] But the question remains, of what it is that those who believe in true externalist claims about people's reasons take those claims to say. There seem to be three principal approaches to this question. One is broadly Kantian, to the effect that the structure and not simply the content of practical reason can ground reasons. This is the type of idea which, as I said in discussing the "correction for error" in section 2 above, needs to be made good independently. Moreover, if it could be made good (which I doubt) I think that what it would yield would be a limiting version of internalism. If it were true that the structure of practical reason yielded reasons of a certain kind as binding on every rational agent, then it would be true of every rational agent that there was a sound deliberative route from his or her S to actions required by such reasons.[4]

The second approach is very broadly speaking Aristotelian, and constructs a truth condition for externalist claims in terms of the reasons that would be recognized by an ideal, "well brought up," or at least improved, agent—an agent, that is to say, for whom these would indeed be internal reasons. I have argued that this approach gives the wrong answer.[5] Just because I am, and can know myself to be, an imperfect agent, it may be that I have reason not to try things which a better agent would indeed have reason to do; and problems of this type can always in principle arise, until the distance between the actual and the imaginary improved agent has been reduced to zero, and we are back with internalism.

A third line of argument, which has been advanced in various different forms, is roughly to the effect that what counts as a reason for certain actions is an institutional or social question, and not an individual or psychological question as internalism seems to suggest. This line seems to me to take up something true, but not to deliver it at the right place. What can rationalize or render intelligible various kinds of action is certainly a social, and in some part an institutional, matter. It can be a question of historical, anthropological, and philosophical interpretation, how far these various practices are, also, variable and local. But whether they are local or more widely spread, it will equally be true that they need a basis in individual psychologies. There can be an institution of promising, for example, only because enough people enough of the time have (internal) reason to do something because they have acted in a way that counts as promising to do that thing.[6] There is thus no problem in understanding the exchange of reason claims between people who have internalized the practice. But we are still owed an account of what is being said when the reason claims are directed to people who are known not to have internalized the practice, or to be insufficiently responsive to it—that is to say, in cases where an externalist interpretation is definitively required. It is much too late in the day, historically and politically, to suppose that a socially sanctioned reason gets a hold on a given agent simply because he finds himself within the boundaries of a society in which that reason is widely recognized.

We need a realistic account, social and psychological, of what is going on when seemingly externalist claims, referring to a social or institutional reason, are directed at recalcitrant or unconvinced agents. In the present paper I suggest, vaguely, that those who make claims about people's reasons in such circumstances are often "entertaining an optimistic internal reasons claim." In a later paper[7] I suggested a more detailed account by which seemingly externalist reason claims (I was particularly concerned with blame) work "proleptically": the claim that A has a reason to ϕ is not strictly true, by internalist standards, at the moment that it is made, but the very fact that it is made can help to elicit a more general motivation from the agent's S, such as the desire to have the respect of people like the speaker, and this motivation together with the recognition of those people's desire or demand that he should ϕ can indeed bring it about that he (now) has a reason to ϕ. This is the merest sketch, but it is only by invoking some such mechanisms that we can bridge the gap between genuinely internalist reason claims, and externalist claims which, unless they can get some help in social and psychological terms, there may be no reason to see as more than bluff and brow-beating.

5

I have made the point that there are many things that critics of an agent may say other than that he has reason to behave differently—for instance, that he is inconsiderate, or cruel, or selfish, or imprudent. In the course of a notably constructive contribution to the discussion,[8] T. M. Scanlon has said:

These criticisms ... involve accusing [the agent] of a kind of deficiency, namely a failure to be moved by certain considerations that we regard as reasons. (What else is it to be inconsiderate, cruel, insensitive and so on?) If it is a deficiency for the man to fail to see these considerations as reasons, it would seem that they must be reasons for him. (If they are not, how can it be a deficiency for him to fail to recognize them?)

This is not, and it is not intended to be, a knock-down argument against the internalist position. I agree that the agent's faults can be understood in terms of a failure to see certain considerations as reasons, just as the opposed virtues can be understood as dispositions to see those considerations as reasons. I also agree that if we think of this as a deficiency or fault of this man, then we must think that in some sense these reasons *apply* to him; certainly he cannot head off the criticism by saying that the reasons do not apply to him because he does not have that kind of S, as someone else might appropriately say that the fact that a brilliant new opera is being staged in New York is not a reason for him to go there, because a taste for opera is no part of his S. This is a point about the (special kind of) universality of (this kind of) reasons.

But none of this implies that these considerations are already the defective agent's reasons; indeed, the problem is precisely that they are not. Let ⌐N⌐ stand in for some normative term: if the critic expresses himself by saying "There is a reason for this man to behave differently to these people," then what he says is of the form "There are considerations about these people's welfare, interests, and so on such that it is ⌐N⌐ that this man should treat those considerations as reasons." What can we take ⌐N⌐ to be? It does not seem to me that there is anything in this way of putting the situation which takes us beyond understanding ⌐N⌐ as, very roughly speaking, "better." We can make this significantly more determinate by explaining that the improvement would lie in the agent's coming to count as reasons considerations which we, other citizens, humane people in general, count as reasons, but while this may help to explain why we, as critics, express ourselves by saying "There is a reason for A to behave differently," it does not make that statement, or the ⌐N⌐ that it implicitly contains, any more a matter of A's reasons.

If we take ⌐N⌐ itself to introduce the notion of a reason, so that we are saying that the agent has a reason to come to treat these considerations as reasons, then we are back with the familiar question of how the project of coming to do that is related to his existing S. Scanlon himself has some interesting remarks about the "reflective modification" of one's S, which may be controlled by certain dispositions in one's existing S without being a deliberative satisfaction of one's S. This will be another example of the psychological material that can help, as I put it in the last section, to bridge the gap between internalist claims, and externalist claims which come to no more than bluff and brow-beating. As I believe Scanlon would agree, exploring this territory is an important contribution to breaking down the age-old sharp distinctions between reason on the one hand and force, coercion and mere persuasion on the other—distinctions which in their more extreme forms have been not just philosophically confusing but ethically and politically disastrous.

Notes

1. "Internal Reasons and the Obscurity of Blame," first published 1989 and reprinted in Williams 1995 and in a section of my "Replies" in Altham and Harrison 1995, pp. 186–194.

2. As in Williams 1995.

3. Altham and Harrison 1995, p. 192.

4. This was why I said in Williams 1995, at note 3 to p. 37, that in this respect I had "no basic disagreement with Christine Korsgaard's excellent paper 'Skepticism about Practical Reason'." Her paper appears as chapter 6 in the present volume.

5. In Altham and Harrison 1995, against a suggestion of John McDowell's, which I took—perhaps a little simplistically—to be to this effect.

6. I discuss some questions about the individual psychological base of institutional and other socially described actions in "Formal and Substantial Individualism," reprinted in Williams 1995.

7. Williams 1995, esp. pp. 41 ff.

8. Scanlon 1998, pp. 363–373; the cited passage is at p. 367. Scanlon makes several other valuable points, which I shall not try to take up here.

Bibliography

Altham, J. E. J., and Ross Harrison, eds. 1995. *World, Mind, and Ethics: Essays on the Ethical Philosophy of Bernard Williams.* Cambridge: Cambridge University Press.

Scanlon, T. M. 1998. *What We Owe to Each Other.* Cambridge: Harvard University Press.

Williams, Bernard. 1995. *Making Sense of Humanity.* Cambridge: Cambridge University Press.

Chapter 5

Williams' Argument against External Reasons

Brad Hooker

Bernard Williams, in his article 'Internal and External Reasons' (reprinted in this volume, chap. 4), attacks the view that there can be external reasons for action—that is, reasons that are not relative to the agent's 'subjective motivational set' (p. 78). Williams wants to be fairly permissive about what goes into this subjective motivational set: he mentions not only desires but also 'dispositions of evaluation, patterns of emotional reaction, personal loyalties, and various projects, as they may be abstractly called, embodying commitments of the agent' (p. 81). Williams' argument against the possibility of external reasons might now be reconstructed roughly as follows.

1. Given that one had made oneself aware of the relevant empirical facts, including (perhaps through imagination) facts about what some alternative outcome would be like, one would be engaging in rational practical deliberation if one were (a) ascertaining what way of satisfying some element in one's subjective motivational set would be best in the light of the other elements in the set, (b) deciding which among conflicting elements in one's subjective motivational set one attaches most weight to, or (c) 'finding constitutive solutions, such as deciding what would make for an entertaining evening, granted that one wants entertainment'. (This account of rational practical deliberation can be distilled from pp. 78–81.) Thus rational practical deliberation in each of its forms has as its starting point the subjective motivational set had by the agent prior to this deliberation.
2. A reason is *internal* just if it can be reached by rational practical deliberation which starts from the agent's antecedent subjective motivational set.
3. From (1) and (2) it follows that any reasons the agent arrives at *by rational practical deliberation* will be internal reasons. (That is, if I could,

by means of deliberating in any of the ways mentioned in (1), arrive at a new belief about what there is reason for me to do, then there was an internal reason for me to do the act in question to begin with [p. 85].)

4. What there is reason for me to do is determined by what I would, if I deliberated rationally (and knew all relevant empirical facts), find there is reason for me to do.

5. From (3) and (4) it follows that there are no such things as external reasons.

Not surprisingly, Williams anticipates the reply his opponent (whom he calls 'the external reasons theorist') is most likely to try:

> It might be said that the force of an external reason statement can be explained in the following way. Such a statement implies that a rational agent would be motivated to act appropriately, and it can carry this implication, because a rational agent is precisely one who has a general disposition in his S [subjective motivational set] to do what (he believes) there is reason for him to do. So when he comes to believe that there is reason for him to ϕ, he is motivated to ϕ, even though, before, he neither had a motive to ϕ, nor any motive related to ϕ-ing in one of the ways considered in the account of deliberation (p. 85).

But Williams complains that this explanation employs a belief the content of which is in question. He then asks, rhetorically,

> *What* is it that one comes to believe when he comes to believe that there is a reason for him to ϕ, if it is not the proposition, or something that entails the proposition, that if he deliberated rationally, he would be motivated to act appropriately? (p. 85)

Though at first this rhetorical question seems to be a witty refutation of the external reasons theory, on further reflection it seems to be either question-begging or impotent. Which fault it has depends on how 'deliberated rationally' is meant. It is question-begging if Williams means by 'rational deliberation' his own conception of rational deliberation, outlined in (1) above. The external reasons theorist will not only reject Williams' claim that external reasons are impossible but also be dissatisfied with Williams' conception of rational practical deliberation—in contrast to Williams, the external theorist is likely to think that (at least some) rational deliberation about reasons for action starts not from the agent's own subjective present motivations, but from some objective ('external') values or requirements, fixed independently of the agent's present motivations. So, the external reasons theorist will deny that the content of the proposition that there is a reason for one to ϕ is to be captured by the proposition that, if one deliberated rationally according Williams' conception of rational deliberation, one would be motivated to ϕ.

But now suppose Williams doesn't want to beg any questions by his reference to rational practical deliberation. Suppose, that is, that he wants the reference to be taken in a neutral way which does not rule out the external reasons theorist's own conception of rational practical deliberation. In this case, the external reasons theorist will be able to accept that the proposition that one has a reason to ϕ entails the proposition that, if one were rational and deliberated rationally, one would be motivated to ϕ. But now Williams' rhetorical question is impotent. For accepting this entailment does not undermine the possibility of external reasons.

Williams is aware of the point that his argument against the possibility of external reasons turns on his account of practical deliberation (pp. 85 f.). But what we need is an answer to the question this point raises: what is wrong with those views which hold that (at least some) rational practical deliberation starts from something external to the agent's present subjective motivational set?

The dispute between Williams and the external reasons theorist is ultimately over the starting points of practical deliberation. Obviously I have not tried to show that the external reasons theorist is, as against Williams, right about this. What I have argued is that Williams does not show, at least in the article in question, that there cannot be external reasons.

Acknowledgments

The central idea in this article is due to Robert Gay, to whom I am naturally very grateful. No doubt if he had written up his idea into an article, the result would have been much superior to mine. I also want to thank Madison Powers and Roger Crisp for helpful comments on an earlier draft.

Chapter 6

Skepticism about Practical Reason

Christine M. Korsgaard

The Kantian approach to moral philosophy is to try to show that ethics is based on practical reason: that is, that our ethical judgments can be explained in terms of rational standards that apply directly to conduct or to deliberation. Part of the appeal of this approach lies in the way that it avoids certain sources of skepticism that some other approaches meet with inevitably. If ethically good action is simply rational action, we do not need to postulate special ethical properties in the world or faculties in the mind, in order to provide ethics with a foundation. But the Kantian approach gives rise to its own specific form of skepticism, skepticism about practical reason.

By *skepticism about practical reason,* I mean doubts about the extent to which human action is or could possibly be directed by reason. One form that such skepticism takes is doubt about the bearing of rational considerations on the activities of deliberation and choice; doubts, that is to say, about whether "formal" principles have any content and can give substantive guidance to choice and action. An example of this would be the common doubt about whether the contradiction tests associated with the first formulation of the categorical imperative succeed in ruling out anything. I will refer to this as *content skepticism.* A second form taken by skepticism about practical reason is doubt about the scope of reason as a motive. I will call this *motivational skepticism.* In this paper my main concern is with motivational skepticism and with the question whether it is justified. Some people think that motivational considerations alone provide grounds for skepticism about the project of founding ethics on practical reason. I will argue, against this view, that motivational skepticism must always be based on content skepticism. I will not address the question of whether or not content skepticism is justified. I want only to establish the fact that motivational skepticism has no independent force.

I

Skepticism about practical reason gets its classical formulation in the well-known passages in the *Treatise of Human Nature* that lead Hume to the conclusion that

Reason is, and ought only to be the slave of the passions, and can never pretend to any other office than to serve and obey them.[1]

According to these passages, as they are usually understood, the role of reason in action is limited to the discernment of the means to our ends. Reason can teach us how to satisfy our desires or passions, but it cannot tell us whether those desires or passions are themselves "rational"; that is, there is no sense in which desires or passions are rational or irrational. Our ends are picked out, so to speak, by our desires, and these ultimately determine what we do. Normative standards applying to conduct may come from other sources (such as a moral sense), but the only standard that comes from reason is that of effectiveness in the choice of means.

The limitation of practical reason to an instrumental role does not only prevent reason from determining ends; it even prevents reason from ranking them, except with respect to their conduciveness to some other end. Even the view that those choices and actions which are conducive to our overall self-interest are rationally to be preferred to self-destructive ones is undermined by the instrumental limitation. Self-interest itself has no rational *authority* over even the most whimsical desires. As Hume says:

'Tis not contrary to reason to prefer the destruction of the whole world to the scratching of my finger. 'Tis not contrary to reason for me to chuse my total ruin, to prevent the least uneasiness of an *Indian* or person wholly unknown to me. 'Tis as little contrary to reason to prefer even my own acknowledg'd lesser good to my greater, and have a more ardent affection for the former than the latter. (*T* 416)

Under the influence of self-interest [or of "a general appetite to good, and aversion to evil, consider'd merely as such" (*T* 417)] we may rank our ends, according to the amount of good that each represents for us, and determine which are, as Hume puts it, our "greatest and most valuable enjoyments" (*T* 416). But the self-interest that would make us favor the greater good need not itself be a stronger desire, or a stronger reason, than the desire for the lesser good, or than any of our more particular desires. Reason by itself neither selects nor ranks our ends.

Hume poses his argument as an argument against "the greatest part of moral philosophy, ancient and modern" (*T* 413). Moral philosophers, Hume says, have claimed that we ought to regulate our conduct by reason, and either suppress our passions or bring them into conformity with it; but he is going to show the fallacy of all this by showing, first, that reason alone can never provide a motive to any action, and, second, that reason can never oppose passion in the direction of the will. His argument for the first point goes this way: all reasoning is concerned either with abstract relations of ideas or with relations of objects, especially causal relations, which we learn about from experience. Abstract relations of ideas are the subject of logic and mathematics, and no one supposes that those by themselves give rise to any motives. They yield no conclusions about action. We are sometimes moved by the perception of causal relations, but only when there is a pre-existing motive in the case. As Hume puts it, if there is "the prospect of pleasure or pain from some object," we are concerned with its causes and effects. The argument that reason cannot oppose a passion in the direction of the will depends on, and in fact springs directly from, the argument that reason by itself cannot give rise to a motive. It is simply that reason *could* oppose a passion only if it could give rise to an *opposing motive*.

What is important to notice in this discussion is the relation between Hume's views about the possible content of principles of reason bearing on action and the scope of its motivational efficacy. The answer to the question what sorts of operation, procedure, or judgment of reason exist is presupposed in these passages. In the first part of the argument Hume goes through what by this point in the *Treatise* is a *settled* list of the types of rational judgment. The argument is a sort of process of elimination: there are rational judgments concerning logical and mathematical relations; there are empirical connections such as cause and effect: Hume looks at each of these in turn in order to see under what circumstances it might be thought to have a bearing on decision and action. In other words, Hume's arguments against a more extensive practical employment of reason depend upon Hume's own views about what reason is—that is, about what sorts of operation and judgment are "rational." His motivational skepticism (skepticism about the scope of reason as a motive) is entirely dependent upon his content skepticism (skepticism about what reason has to *say* about choice and action).

Yet Hume's arguments may give the impression of doing something much stronger: of placing independent constraints, based solely on motivational considerations, on what might count as a principle of practical reason. Hume seems to say simply that all reasoning that has a motivational influence must start from a passion, that being the only possible source of motivation, and must proceed to the means to satisfy that passion, that being the only operation of reason that transmits motivational force. Yet these are separate points: they can be doubted, and challenged, separately. One could disagree with Hume about his list of the types of rational judgment, operation, or possible deliberation, and yet still agree with the basic point about the source of motivation: that all rational motivation must ultimately spring from some nonrational source, such as passion. At least one contemporary philosopher, Bernard Williams, has taken something like Hume's argument to have this kind of independent force, and has so argued in his essay "Internal and External Reasons,"[2] which I will take up later in this paper.

The Kantian must go further, and disagree with Hume on both counts, since the Kantian supposes that there are operations of practical reason which yield conclusions about actions and which do not involve discerning relations between passions (or any pre-existing sources of motivation) and those actions. What gives rise to the difficulty about this further possibility is the question of how such operations could yield conclusions that can motivate us.

II

The problem can best be stated in some terms provided by certain recent discussions in moral philosophy. W. D. Falk, William Frankena, and Thomas Nagel, among others, have distinguished between two kinds of moral theories, which are called "internalist" and "externalist."[3] An *internalist* theory is a theory according to which the knowledge (or the truth or the acceptance) of a moral judgment implies the existence of a motive (not necessarily overriding) for acting on that judgment. If I judge that some action is right, it is implied that I have, and acknowledge, some motive or reason for performing that action. It is part of the sense of the judgment that a motive is present: if someone agrees that an action is right, but cannot see any motive or reason for doing it, we must suppose, according to these views, that she does not quite know what she means when she agrees that the action is right. On an *externalist* theory, by contrast, such a conjunction of moral comprehension and total unmotivatedness is perfectly possible: knowledge is one thing and motivation another.

Examples of unquestionably external theories are not easy to find. As Falk points out (125–26), the simplest example would be a view according to which the motives for moral action come from something wholly separate from a grasp of the correctness of the judgments—say, an interest in obeying divine commands. In philosophical ethics the best example is John Stuart Mill (see Nagel 8–9), who firmly separates the question of the proof of the principle of utility from the question of its "sanctions." The reason why the principle of utility is true and the motive we might have for acting on it are not the same: the theoretical proof of its truth is contained in chapter IV of *Utilitarianism*, but the motives must be acquired in a utilitarian upbringing. It is Mill's view that *any* moral principle would have to be motivated by education and training and that "there is hardly anything so absurd or so mischievous" that it cannot be so motivated.[4] The "ultimate sanction" of the principle of utility is *not* that it can be proved, but that it is in accordance with our natural social feelings. Even to some who, like Mill himself, realize that the motives are acquired, "it does not present itself ... as a superstition of education, or a law despotically imposed by the power of society, but as an attribute which it would not be well for them to be without."[5] The modern intuitionists, such as W. D. Ross and H. A. Prichard, seem also to have been externalists, but of a rather minimal kind. They believed that there was a distinctively moral motive, a sense of right or desire to do one's duty. This motive is triggered by the news that something is your duty, and only by that news, but it is still separate from the rational intuition that constitutes the understanding of your duty. It would be possible to have that intuition and not be motivated by it.[6] The reason why the act is right and the motive you have for doing it are separate items, although it is nevertheless the case that the motive for doing it is "because it is right." This falls just short of the internalist position, which is that the reason why the act is right is the reason, and the motive, for doing it: it is a practical reason. Intuitionism is a form of rationalist ethics, but intuitionists do not believe in practical reason, properly speaking. They believe there is a branch of theoretical reason that is specifically concerned with morals, by which human beings can be motivated because of a special psychological mechanism: a desire to do one's duty. One can see the oddity of this if one considers what the analogue would be in the case of theoretical reasoning. It is as if human beings could not be convinced by arguments acknowledged to be sound without the intervention of a special psychological mechanism: a belief that the conclusions of sound arguments are true.

By contrast, an internalist believes that the reasons why an action is right and the reasons why you do it are the same. The reason that the action is right is both the reason and the motive for doing it. Nagel gives as one example of this the theory of Hobbes: the reason for the action's rightness and your motive for doing it are both that it is in your interest. The literature on this subject splits, however, on the question of whether the Kantian position is internalist or not. Falk, for instance, characterizes the difference between internalism and externalism as one of whether the moral command arises from a source outside the agent (like God or society) or from within. If the difference is described this way, Kant's attempt to derive morality from autonomy makes him a paradigmatic internalist (see Falk 125, 129). On the other hand, some have believed that Kant's view that the moral command is indifferent to our desires, needs, and interests—that it is categorical—makes him a paradigmatic externalist.[7] Since Kant himself took the categorical character of the imperative and autonomy of the moral motive to be necessarily connected, this is a surprising difference of opinion. I will come back to Kant in section VII.

This kind of reflection about the motivational force of ethical judgments has been brought to bear by Bernard Williams on the motivational force of reason claims generally. In "Internal and External Reasons" Williams argues that there are two kinds of reason claims, or two ways of making reason claims. Suppose I say that some person P has a reason to do action A. If I intend this to imply that the person P has a motive to do action A, the claim is of an internal reason; if not, the claim is of an external reason. Williams is concerned to argue that only internal reasons really exist. He points out (82–83) that, since an external-reason claim does not imply the existence of a motive, it cannot be used to explain anyone's action: that is, we cannot say that the person P did the action A because of reason R; for R does not provide P with a motive for doing A, and *that* is what we need to explain P's doing A: a motive. Nagel points out that if acknowledgment of a reason claim did not include acknowledgment of a motive, someone presented with a reason for action could ask: Why do what I have a reason to do? (9; see also Falk 121–22). Nagel's argument makes from the agent's perspective the same point that Williams makes from the explainer's perspective, namely, that unless reasons are motives, they cannot prompt or explain actions. And, unless reasons are motives, we cannot be said to be practically rational.

Thus, it seems to be a requirement on practical reasons, that they be capable of motivating us. This is where the difficulty arises about reasons that do not, like means/end reasons, draw on an obvious motivational source. So long as there is doubt about whether a given consideration is able to motivate a rational person, there is doubt about whether that consideration has the force of a practical *reason*. The consideration that such and such action is a means to getting what you want has a clear motivational source; so no one doubts that this is a reason. Practical-reason claims, if they are really to present us with reasons for action, must be capable of motivating rational persons. I will call this the *internalism requirement*.

III

In this section I want to talk about how the internalism requirement functions—or, more precisely, malfunctions—in skeptical arguments. Hume winds up his argument by putting the whole thing in a quite general form. Reason is the faculty that judges of truth and falsehood, and it can judge our ideas to be true or false because they represent other things. But a passion is an original existence or modification of existence, not a copy of anything: it cannot be true or false, and therefore it cannot in itself be reasonable or unreasonable. Passions can be unreasonable, then, only if they are accompanied by judgments, and there are two cases of this kind. One is when the passion is founded on the supposition of the existence of objects that do not exist. You are outraged at the mocking things you heard me say about you, but I was talking about somebody else. You are terrified by the burglars you hear whispering in the living room, but in fact you left the radio on. It is of course only in an extended sense that Hume can think of these as cases where a passion is irrational. Judgments of irrationality, whether of belief or action, are, strictly speaking, relative to the subject's beliefs. Conclusions drawn from mistaken premises are not *irrational*.[8] The case of passions based on false beliefs seems to be of this sort.

The second kind of case in which Hume says that the passion might be called unreasonable is

when, in exerting any passion in action, we chuse means insufficient for the design'd end, and deceive ourselves in our judgment of causes and effects. (*T* 416)

This is in itself an ambiguous remark. Hume might, and in fact does, mean simply that we base our action on a false belief about causal relations. So this is no more genuinely a case of irrationality than the other. Relative to the (false) causal belief, the action is not irrational. But it is important that there is something else one might mean in this case, which is that, knowing the truth about the relevant causal relations in the case, we might nevertheless choose means insufficient to our end or fail to choose obviously sufficient and readily available means to the end. This would be what I will call *true irrationality*, by which I mean a failure to respond appropriately to an available reason.

If the only possibility Hume means to be putting forward here is the possibility of action based on false belief about causes and effects, we get a curious result. Neither of the cases that Hume considers is a case of true irrationality: relative to their beliefs, people *never* act irrationally. Hume indeed says this:

... the moment we perceive the falsehood of any supposition, or the insufficiency of any means, our passions yield to our reason without any opposition. (*T* 416)

But it looks as if a theory of means/end rationality ought to allow for at least one form of true irrationality, namely, failure to be motivated by the consideration that the action is the means to your end. Even the skeptic about practical reason admits that human beings can be motivated by the consideration that a given action is a means to a desired end. But it is not enough, to explain this fact, that human beings can engage in causal reasoning. It is perfectly possible to imagine a sort of being who could engage in causal reasoning and who could, therefore, engage in reasoning that would point out the means to her ends, but who was not motivated by it.

Kant, in a passage early in the *Groundwork*, imagines a human being in just such a condition of being able to reason, so to speak, theoretically but not practically. He is talking about what the world would have been like if nature had had our happiness as her end. Our actions would have been controlled entirely by instincts designed to secure our happiness, and

if, over and above this, reason should have been granted to the favored creature, it would have served only to let it contemplate the happy constitution of its nature. (G 395)

The favored creature is portrayed as able to see that his actions are rational in the sense that they promote the means to his end (happiness);

but he is not motivated by their reasonableness; he acts from instinct. Reason allows him to admire the rational appropriateness of what he does, but this is not what gets him to do it—he has the sort of attitude toward all his behavior that we in fact might have toward the involuntary well-functioning of our bodies.

Being motivated by the consideration that an action is a means to a desirable end is something beyond merely reflecting on that fact. The motive force attached to the end must be transmitted to the means in order for this to be a consideration that sets the human body in motion—and only if this is a consideration that sets the human body in motion can we say that reason has an influence on action. A practically rational person is not merely capable of performing certain rational mental operations, but capable also of transmitting motive force, so to speak, along the paths laid out by those operations. Otherwise even means/end reasoning will not meet the internalism requirement.

But the internalism requirement does not imply that nothing can interfere with this motivational transmission. And generally, this is something there seems to be no reason to believe: there seem to be plenty of things that could interfere with the motivational influence of a given rational consideration. Rage, passion, depression, distraction, grief, physical or mental illness: all these things could cause us to act irrationally, that is, to fail to be motivationally responsive to the rational considerations available to us.[9] The necessity, or the compellingness, of rational considerations lies in those considerations themselves, not in us: that is, we will not necessarily be motivated by them. Or rather, to put the point more properly and not to foreclose any metaphysical possibilities, their necessity may lie in the fact that, when they do move us—either in the realm of conviction or in that of motivation—they move us with the force of necessity. But it will still not be the case that they necessarily move us. So a person may be irrational, not merely by failing to observe rational connections—say, failing to see that the sufficient means are at hand—but also by being "willfully" blind to them, or even by being indifferent to them when they are pointed out.[10]

In this respect practical reason is no different from theoretical reason. Many things might cause me to fail to be convinced by a good argument. For me to be a theoretically rational person is not merely for me to be capable of performing logical and inductive operations, but for me to be appropriately *convinced* by them: my conviction in the premises must carry through, so to speak, to a conviction in the conclusion. Thus, the internalism requirement for theoretical reasons is that they be capable of convincing us—insofar as we are rational. It is quite possible for me to be able to perform these operations without generating any conviction, as a sort of game, say, and then I would not be a rational person.

Aristotle describes the novice in scientific studies as being able to repeat the argument, but without the sort of conviction that it will have for him later, when he fully understands it. In order for a theoretical argument or a practical deliberation to have the status of reason, it must of course be capable of motivating or convincing a rational person, but it does not follow that it must at all times be capable of motivating or convincing any given individual. It may follow from the supposition that we are rational persons and the supposition that a given argument or deliberation is rational that, if we are not convinced or motivated, there must be some explanation of that failure. But there is no reason at all to believe that such an explanation will always show that we had mistaken reasons, which, if true, would have been good reasons. Many things can interfere with the functioning of the rational operations in a human body. Thus there is no reason to deny that human beings might be practically irrational in the sense that Hume considers impossible: that, even with the truth at our disposal, we might from one cause or another fail to be interested in the means to our ends.

IV

My speculation is that skepticism about practical reason is sometimes based on a false impression of what the internalism requirement requires. It does not require that rational considerations always succeed in motivating us. All it requires is that rational considerations succeed in motivating us insofar as we are rational. One can admit the possibility of true irrationality and yet still believe that all practical reasoning is instrumental. But once this kind of irrationality is allowed in the means/end case, some of the grounds for skepticism about more ambitious forms of practical reasoning will seem less compelling. The case of prudence or self-interest will show what I have in mind. I have already mentioned Hume's account of this matter: he thinks that there is "a general appetite to good, and aversion to evil" and that a person will act prudently insofar as this calm and general passion remains dominant over particular passions. It is under the influence of this end that we weigh one possible satisfaction against another, trying to determine which conduces to our greater good. But if this general desire for the good does not remain predominant, not only the motive, but the reason, for doing what will conduce to one's greater good, disappears. For Hume says it is not contrary to reason to prefer an acknowledged lesser good to a greater.

Suppose, then, that you are confronted with a choice and, though informed that one option will lead to your greater good, you take the other. If true irrationality is excluded, and you fail to take the means to some end, this is evidence either that you don't really have this end or that it is not the most important thing to you. Thus, in this imagined case, where you do not choose your greater good, this is evidence either that you do not care about your greater good or that you do not care about it as much as you do about this particular lesser good. On the other hand, if you do respond to the news that one option leads to your greater good, then we have evidence that you do care about your greater good. This makes it seem as if your greater good is an end you might care about or not, and rationality is relative to what you care about. But, once we admit that one might from some other cause fail to be responsive to a rational consideration, there is no special reason to accept this analysis of the case. I do not mean that there is a reason to reject it, either, of course; my point is that whether you accept it depends on whether you *already* accept the limitation to means/end rationality. If you do, you will say that the case where the lesser good was chosen was a case where there was a stronger desire for it, and so a stronger reason; if you do not, and you think it *is* reasonable to choose the greater good (because prudence has rational authority), you will say that this is a case of true irrationality. The point is that the motivational analysis of the case *depends* upon your views of the content of rational principles of action, not the reverse. The fact that one might or might not be motivated to choose a certain course of action by the consideration that it leads to the greater good does not by itself show that the greater good is just one end among others, without special rational authority, something that some people care about and some people do not. Take the parallel case. The fact that one might or might not be motivated to choose a certain course of action by the consideration that it is the best available means to one's end does not show that taking the means to one's ends is just one end among others, an end some people care about and some people do not. In both cases, what we have is the fact that people are sometimes motivated by considerations of this sort, and that we all think in the latter case and some think in the former case that it is rational to be so motivated.

The argument about whether prudence or the greater good has any special rational authority—about whether it is a rational consideration—will have to be carried out on another plane: it will have to be made in terms of a more metaphysical argument about just what reason does, what its scope is, and what sorts of operation, procedure, and judgment are rational. This argument will usually consist in an attempt to arrive at a general notion of reason by discovering features or characteristics that theoretical and practical reason share; such characteristic features as universality, sufficiency, timelessness, impersonality, or authority will be appealed to.[11] What the argument in favor of prudence would be will vary from theory to theory; here, the point is this: the fact that someone might fail to be motivated by the consideration that something will serve her greater good cannot by itself throw any doubt on the argument, whatever it is, that preferring the greater good is rational. If someone were not convinced by the logical operation of conjunction, and so could not reason with conviction from "A" and from "B" to "A and B", we would not be eager to conclude that conjunction was just a theory that some people believe and some people do not. Conjunction is not a theory to believe or disbelieve, but a principle of reasoning. Not everything that drives us to conclusions is a theory. Not everything that drives us to action need be a desired end (see Nagel 20–22).

V

An interesting result of admitting the possibility of true irrationality is that it follows that it will not always be possible to argue someone into rational behavior. If people are acting irrationally only because they do not know about the relevant means/end connection, they may respond properly to argument: point the connection out to them, and their behavior will be modified accordingly. In such a person the motivational path, so to speak, from end to means is open. A person in whom this path is, from some cause, blocked or nonfunctioning may not respond to argument, even if this person understands the argument in a theoretical way. Aristotle thinks of the incontinent person as being in a condition of this sort: this happens to people in fits of passion or rage, and the condition is actually physiological.[12] Now this is important; for it is sometimes thought, on the basis of the internalism requirement, that if there is a reason to do something it must be possible to argue someone into doing it: anyone who understands the argument will straightaway act. (The conclusion of a practical syllogism is an action.) Frankena, for example, argues against an internalist construal of the moral "ought" on the grounds that even after full reflection we do not always do what is right (71). But if there is a gap between understanding a reason and being motivated by it, then internalism does not imply that people can always be argued into reasonable conduct. The reason motivates someone who is capable of being motivated by the perception of a rational connection. Rationality is a condition that human beings are capable of, but it is not a condition that we are always in.

It is for this reason that some ethical theories centered on the idea of practical reason are best thought of as establishing ideals of character. A person with a good character will be, on such a view, one who responds to the available reasons in an appropriate way, one whose motivational structure is organized for rational receptivity, so that reasons motivate in accord with their proper force and necessity. It is not an accident that the two major philosophers in our tradition who thought of ethics in terms of practical reason—Aristotle and Kant—were also the two most concerned with the methods of moral education. Human beings must be taught, or habituated, to listen to reason: we are, as Kant says, imperfectly rational.

In fact, the argument of the last section can be recast in terms of virtues. Suppose that it *is* irrational not to prefer the greater good: this need have nothing at all to do with having the greater good *among* your desired ends. It is of course true that some people are more steadily motivated by considerations of what conduces to their greater good than others: call such a person *the prudent person*. The fact that the prudent person is more strongly motivated by reasons of greater good need not be taken to show that he has stronger reasons for attending to his greater good. (People have varying theoretical virtues too.[13]) We may indeed say that the prudent person "cares more" about his greater good, but that is just another way of saying that he responds more strongly to these kinds of consideration, that he has the virtue of prudence. It need not be taken to imply that his greater good is a more heavily weighted end with him and that, therefore, it really does matter more to him that he achieve his greater good than it does to another person, an imprudent person, that he achieve his. It makes more sense to say that this other person ignores reasons that he has. Again, take the parallel: some people respond much more readily and definitely to the consideration that something is an effective means to their end. We might call such a person a *determined* or *resolute* person. Presumably no one feels like saying that the determined or resolute person has a stronger reason for taking the means to her ends than anyone else does. We all have just the same reason for taking the means to our ends. The fact that people are motivated differently by the reasons they have does not show that they have different reasons. It may show that some have virtues that others lack. On a practical-reason theory, the possibility of rationality sets a standard for character; but that standard will not always be met. But this is not by itself a reason for skepticism about the scope of the deliberative guidance that reason *can* provide. This is a reason for skepticism only about the extent to which that guidance will ever be taken advantage of.

VI

Nevertheless, the fact that a practical reason must be capable of motivating us might still seem to put a limitation on the scope of practical reason: it might be thought that it is a subjective matter which considerations can motivate a given individual and that, therefore, all judgments of practical reason must be conditional in form. In Hume's argument, this kind of limitation is captured in the claim that motivation must originate in a passion. In the means/end case, we are able to be motivated by the consideration that action *A* will promote purpose *P* because, and only if, we have a pre-existing motivational impulse (a passion) attached to purpose *P*. As Hume says, a relation between two things will not have any motivational impact on us unless one of the two things has such impact. This does not limit practical reason to the means/end variety, but it might seem to impose a limitation of this sort: practical-reason claims must be reached by something that is recognizably a rational deliberative process from interests and motives one already has. This position is advocated by Bernard Williams in "Internal and External Reasons." Williams, as I have mentioned, argues that only internal reasons exist; but he takes this to have a strong Humean implication. Williams takes it that internal reasons are by definition relative to something that he calls the agent's "subjective motivational set": this follows from the fact that they can motivate. The contents of this set are left open, but one kind of thing it will obviously contain is the agent's desires and passions. Internal reasons are reasons reached by deliberation from the subjective motivational set: they can motivate us because of their connection to that set. Means/end deliberation, where the end is in the set and the means are what we arrive at by the motivating deliberation, is the most characteristic, but not the only, source of reasons for action. Williams calls the means/end view the "sub-Humean model," and he says this:

The sub-Humean model supposes that ϕ-ing [where ϕ-ing is some action we have a reason for doing] has to be related to some element in [the subjective motivational set] as causal means to end (unless, perhaps, it is straightforwardly the carrying out of a desire which is itself that element in [the subjective motivational set].) But this is only one case.... there are much wider possibilities for deliberation, such as: thinking how the satisfaction of elements in [the subjective motivational set] can be combined, e.g. by time ordering; where there is some irresoluble conflict among the elements of [the subjective motivational set], considering which one attaches most weight to ... or, again, finding constitutive solutions, such as deciding what would make for an entertaining evening, granted that one wants entertainment. (80–81)[14]

Anything reached by a process of deliberation from the subjective motivational set may be something for which there is an internal reason, one that can motivate. External reasons, by contrast, exist regardless of what is in one's subjective motivational set. In this case, Williams points out, there must be some rational process, not springing from the subjective motivational set and therefore not relative to it, which could bring you to acknowledge something to be a reason and at the same time to be motivated by it. Reason must be able to produce an entirely new motive, the thing that Hume said could not be done.

Thus, Williams takes up one part of the skeptic's argument: that a piece of practical reasoning must start from something that is capable of motivating you; and drops the other, that the only kind of reasoning is means/end. One might suppose that this limits the operations of judgments of practical reason to those functions which are natural extensions or expansions of the means/end variety, and the things Williams mentions in this passage, such as making a plan to satisfy the various elements in the set, or constitutive reasoning, are generally thought to be of that sort. But in fact this is not Williams' view, nor is it necessitated by his argument, as he points out.

The processes of deliberation can have all sorts of effect on [the subjective motivational set], and this is a fact which a theory of internal reasons should be very happy to accommodate. So also it should be more liberal than some theorists have been about the possible elements in [the subjective motivational set]. I have discussed [the subjective motivational set] primarily in terms of desires, and this term can be used, formally, for all elements in [the subjective motivational set]. But this terminology may make one forget that [the subjective motivational set] can contain such things as dispositions of evaluation, patterns of emotional reaction, personal loyalties, and various projects, as they may abstractly be called, embodying commitments of the agent. (81)

Williams can accommodate the case of someone's acting for reasons of principle, and in this case the form the deliberation will take is that of applying the principle or of seeing that the principle applies to the case at hand. The advocate of the view that all deliberation is strictly of the means/end variety may claim to assimilate this case by the formal device of saying that the agent must have a desire to act on this principle, but this will not change the important fact, which is that the reasoning in this case will involve the application of the principle, which is not the same as means/end reasoning.[15]

In this kind of case, Williams' point will be that in order for the principle to provide reasons for a given agent, acceptance of the principle must constitute part of the agent's subjective motivational set. If the principle is not accepted by the agent, its dictates are not reasons for her. Reasons are relativized to the set. If this is true, it looks at first as if all practical reasons will be relative to the individual, because they are conditioned by what is in the subjective motivational set. Reasons that apply to you regardless of what is in your subjective motivational set will not exist.

This argument, however, having been cut loose from Hume's very definite ideas about what sort of rational operations and processes exist, has a very unclear bearing on claims about pure practical reason. If one accepts the internalism requirement, it follows that pure practical reason will exist if and only if we are capable of being motivated by the conclusions of the operations of pure practical reason as such. Something in us must make us capable of being motivated by them, and this something will be part of the subjective motivational set. Williams seems to think that this is a reason for doubting that pure practical reasons exist, whereas what seems to follow from the internalism requirement is this: if we can be motivated by considerations stemming from pure practical reason, then that capacity belongs to the subjective motivational set of every rational being. One cannot argue that the subjective motivational set contains only ends or desires; for that would be true only if all reasoning were of the means/end variety or its natural extensions. What sorts of items can be found in the set does not limit, but rather depends on, what kinds of reasoning are possible. Nor can one assume that the subjective motivational set consists only of individual or idiosyncratic elements; for that is to close off without argument the possibility that reason could yield conclusions that every rational being must acknowledge and be capable of being motivated by. As long as it is left open what kinds of rational operations yield conclusions about what to do and what to pursue, it must be left open whether we are capable of being motivated by them.

Consider the question of how an agent comes to accept a principle: to have it in her subjective motivational set. If we say that the agent comes to accept the principle through reasoning—through having been convinced that the principle admits of some ultimate justification—then there are grounds for saying that this principle is in the subjective motivational set of every rational person: for all rational persons could be brought to see that they have reason to act in the way required by the principle, and this is all that the internalism requirement requires. Now this is of course not Williams' view: he believes that the principles are acquired by education, training, and so forth, and that they do not admit of any ultimate justification.[16] There are two important points to make about this.

First, consider the case of the reflective agent who, after being raised to live by a certain principle, comes to question it. Some doubt, temptation, or argument has made her consider eliminating the principle from her subjective motivational set. Now what will she think? The principle does not, we are supposing, admit of an ultimate justification, so she will not find that. But this does not necessarily mean that she will reject the principle. She may, on reflection, find that she thinks it better (where this will be relative to what other things are in her motivational set) that people should have and act on such a principle, that it is in some rough way a good idea—perhaps not the only but an excellent basis for community living, etc.—and so she may retain it and even proceed to educate those under her influence to adopt it. The odd thing to notice is that this is almost exactly the sort of description Mill gives of the reflective utilitarian who, on realizing that his capacity to be motivated by the principle of utility is an acquirement of education, is not sorry. But Mill's position, as I mentioned earlier, is often taken to be the best example of an *externalist* ethical position.

More immediately to the point, what this kind of case shows is that for Williams, as for Hume, the motivational skepticism depends on what I have called the "content skepticism." Williams' argument does not show that if there were unconditional principles of reason applying to action we could not be motivated by them. He only thinks that there are none. But Williams' argument, like Hume's, gives the appearance of going the other way around: it looks as if the motivational point—the internalism requirement—is supposed to have some force in limiting what might count as a principle of practical reason. Whereas in fact, the real source of the skepticism is a doubt about the existence of principles of action whose content shows them to be ultimately justified.

VII

The internalism requirement is correct, but there is probably no moral theory that it excludes. I do not think that it even excludes utilitarianism or intuitionism, although it calls for a reformulation of the associated views about the influence of ethical reasoning on motivation. The force of the internalism requirement is psychological: what it does is not to refute ethical theories, but to make a psychological demand on them.

This is in fact how philosophers advocating a connection between morality and practical reason have thought of the matter. From considerations concerning the necessity that reasons be internal and capable of motivating us which are almost identical to Williams', Nagel, in the opening sections of *The Possibility of Altruism*, argues that investigations into practical reason will yield discoveries about our motivational capacities. Granting that reasons must be capable of motivating us, he thinks that if we then are able to show the existence of reasons, we will have shown something capable of motivating us. In Nagel's eyes, the internalism requirement leads not to a limitation on practical reason, but to a rather surprising increase in the power of moral philosophy: it can teach us about human motivational capacities; it can teach us psychology.[17]

As Nagel points out, this approach also characterizes the moral philosophy of Kant. By the end of the Second Section of the *Groundwork*, there is in *one* sense no doubt that Kant has done what he set out to do: he has shown us what sort of demand pure reason would make on action. Working from the ideas that reasons in general (either theoretical or practical) must be universal, that reason seeks the unconditioned, and that its binding force must derive from autonomy, he has shown us what a law of pure reason applying to action would look like. But until it has been shown that we can be motivated to act according to the categorical imperative, it has not been completely shown that the categorical imperative really exists—that there really is a law of pure practical reason. And this is because of the internalism requirement. The question how the imperative is possible is equated to that of "how the constraint of the will, which the imperative expresses in the problem, can be conceived"

(*G* 417). Thus, what remains for proof by a "deduction" is that we are capable of being motivated by this law of reason: that we have an autonomous will. In the *Groundwork III*, Kant does try to argue that we can be motivated by the categorical imperative, appealing to the pure spontaneity of reason as evidence for our intelligible nature and so for an autonomous will (*G* 452). In the *Critique of Practical Reason*,[18] however, Kant turns his strategy around. He argues that we know that we are capable of being motivated by the categorical imperative and therefore that we know (in a practical sense) that we have an autonomous will. Again, explorations into practical reason reveal our nature. It is important, however, that although in the *Critique of Practical Reason* Kant does not try to argue *that* pure reason can be a motive, he has detailed things to say about *how* it can be a motive—about how it functions as an incentive in combatting other incentives.[19] Something is still owed to the internalism requirement: namely, to show what psychological conclusions the moral theory implies.

It may be that we are immune to motivation by pure practical reason. But, for that matter, it may be that we are immune to motivation by means/ends connections. Perhaps our awareness of these in cases where we seem to act on them is epiphenomenal. In fact we are quite sure that we are not immune to the reasons springing from means/ends connections; and Kant maintained that, if we thought about it, we would see that we are not immune to the laws of pure practical reason: that we know we can do what we ought. But there is no guarantee of this; for our knowledge of our motives is limited. The conclusion is that, if we are rational, we will act as the categorical imperative directs. But we are not necessarily rational.

VIII

I have not attempted to show in this paper that there is such a thing as pure practical reason, or that reason has in any way a more extensive bearing on conduct than empiricism has standardly credited it with. What I have attempted to show is that this question is open in a particular way: that motivational considerations do not provide any reason, in advance of specific proposals, for skepticism about practical reason. If a philosopher can show us that something that is recognizably a law of reason has bearing on conduct, there is no special reason to doubt that human beings might be motivated by that consideration. The fact that the law might not govern conduct, even when someone understood it, is no reason for skepticism: the necessity is in the law, and not in us.

To the extent that skepticism about pure practical reason is based on the strange idea that an acknowledged reason can never fail to motivate, there is no reason to accept it. It is based on some sort of a misunderstanding, and I have suggested a misunderstanding of the internalism requirement as a possible account. To the extent that skepticism about pure practical reason is based on the idea that no process or operation of reason yielding unconditional conclusions about action can be found, it depends on—and is not a reason for believing—the thesis that no process or operation of reason yielding unconditional conclusions about action can be found. To the extent that skepticism about pure practical reason is based on the requirement that reasons be capable of motivating us, the correct response is that if someone discovers what are recognizably reasons bearing on conduct and those reasons fail to motivate us, that only shows the limits of our rationality. Motivational skepticism about practical reason depends on, and cannot be the basis for, skepticism about the possible content of rational requirements. The extent to which people are actually moved by rational considerations, either in their conduct or in their credence, is beyond the purview of philosophy. Philosophy can at most tell us what it would be like to be rational.

Acknowledgments

I would like to thank Timothy Gould, Charlotte Brown, and audiences of an earlier version of this paper at Columbia and the University of Chicago, for comments on and discussions of the issues of this paper, from which I have learned a great deal.

Abbreviations

C2 Immanuel Kant, *Critique of Practical Reason* (1788), trans. Lewis White Beck. The Library of Liberal Arts, 1956. Formerly published in Indianapolis by Bobbs-Merrill, now published in New York by Macmillan.

G Immanuel Kant, *Groundwork of the Metaphysics of Morals* (1785), trans. Lewis White Beck as *Foundations of the Metaphysics of Morals*. Library of Liberal Arts, 1959.

T David Hume, *A Treatise of Human Nature* (1739), 2nd edition, edited by L. A. Selby-Bigge and P. H. Nidditch. Clarendon Press, 1978.

Notes

1. David Hume, *Treatise of Human Nature* p. 415. Hereinafter cited as "*T*" followed by page reference.

2. This paper was originally published in Ross Harrison, ed., *Rational Action* (New York: Cambridge, 1980), and is reprinted here as chapter 4. Page references are to this volume.

3. Actually, Falk and Frankena speak of internalist and externalist senses of 'ought'. See Falk, "'Ought' and Motivation," in his *Ought, Reasons and Morality: The Collected Papers of W. D. Falk*, chapter 1 and Frankena's discussion, "Obligation and Motivation in Recent Moral Philosophy," *Perspectives on Morality: Essays of William K. Frankena*, chapter 6. Nagel's discussion is in *The Possibility of Altruism*, part I.

4. *Utilitarianism*, p. 30.

5. Mill, *Utilitarianism*, p. 33.

6. See Prichard, "Duty and Interest," in his *Moral Obligation and Duty and Interest*. Falk's original use of the distinction between internal and external senses of 'ought' in "'Ought' and Motivation" is in an argument responding to Prichard's paper.

7. See Frankena, "Obligation and Motivation," p. 63, for a discussion of this surprising view.

8. I am ignoring here the more complicated case in which the passion in question is parent to the false beliefs. In my examples, for instance, there might be cases such as these: irritation at me predisposes you to think my insults are aimed at you; terror of being alone in the house makes you more likely to mistake the radio for a burglar. Hume does discuss this phenomenon (*T* 120). Here, we might say that the judgment is irrational, not merely false, and that its irrationality infects the passions and actions based on the judgment. If Hume's theory allows him to say that the judgment is irrational, he will be able to say that some passions and actions are truly irrational, and not merely mistaken, although he does not do this.

9. "Available to us" is vague, for there is a range of cases in which one might be uncertain whether or not to say that a reason was available to us. For instance there are (1) cases in which we don't know about the reason, (2) cases in which we couldn't possibly know about the reason, (3) cases in which we deceive ourselves about the reason, (4) cases in which some physical or psychological condition makes us unable to see the reason, and (5) cases in which some physical or psychological condition makes us fail to respond to the reason, even though in some sense we look it right in the eye. Now no one will want to say that reason claims involving reasons people do not know about are therefore external, but as we move down the list there will be a progressive uneasiness about whether the claim is becoming external. For toward the end of the list we will come to claim that someone is psychologically incapable of responding to the reason, and yet that it is internal: capable of motivating a rational person. I do not think there is a problem about any of these cases; for all that is necessary for the reason claim to be internal is that we can say that, if a person did know and *if nothing were interfering with her rationality*, she would respond accordingly. This does not trivialize the limitation to internal reasons as long as the notion of a psychological condition that interferes with rationality is not trivially defined.

10. I have in mind such phenomena as self-deception, rationalization, and the various forms of weakness of will. Some of these apply to theoretical as well as practical reason, and for the former we can add the various forms of intellectual resistance or ideology (though "willful" is not a good way to characterize these). For some reason, people find the second thing that I mention—being indifferent to a reason that is pointed out to you—harder to imagine in a theoretical than in a practical case. To simply shrug in the face of the acknowledged reason seems to some to be possible in practice in a way that it is not in theory. I think part of the problem is that we can push what the practically paralyzed person accepts over into the realm of theory: he *believes* "that he ought to do such-and-such," although he is not moved to; whereas there seems to be nowhere further back (except maybe to a suspense of judgment) to push what the theoretically paralyzed person accepts. It may also be that the problem arises because we do not give enough weight to the difference between being convinced by an argument and being left without anything to say by it, or it may be just that what paralysis *is* is less visible in the case of belief than in the case of action.

11. Universality and sufficiency are appealed to by Kant; timelessness and impersonality by Nagel, and authority by Joseph Butler.

12. *Nicomachean Ethics*, VII.3, 1147b 5–10.

13. The comparisons I have been drawing between theoretical and practical reason now suggest that there should also be something like an ideal of good theoretical character: a receptivity to theoretical reasons. The vision of someone free of all ideology and intellectual resistance might be such an ideal.

14. Williams uses the designation '*S*' for 'subjective motivational set', but I have put back the original phrase wherever it occurs; hence the brackets.

15. It is true that the application of a principle may be so simple or immediate that it will be a matter of judgment or perception rather than deliberation. In such a case there will be some who want to deny that practical reason has been used. On the other hand, the reasoning involved in applying a principle may be quite complicated (as in the case of the contradiction tests under the categorical imperative), and so be such that anyone should be willing to call it reasoning. If the fact that you hold the principle gives motivational force to either the insight or the deliberative argument to the effect that this case falls under the principle, then the result is a practical reason.

16. Williams himself remarks that the "onus of proof about what is to count as a 'purely rational process' . . . properly belongs with the critic who wants to oppose Hume's general conclusion and to make a lot out of external reason statements" (84). Although I think he is quite right in saying that the burden of proof about what is to count as a purely rational process—about *content*—belongs to Hume's opponents, I am arguing that there is no reason to suppose that if this burden is successfully picked up the reasons will be external.

17. *The Possibility of Altruism*, p. 13. Nagel calls this a "rebellion against the priority of psychology" (11) and accordingly distinguishes two kinds of internalism: one that takes the psychological facts as given and supposes that we must

somehow derive ethics from them in order to achieve an internalist theory, and one that supposes that metaphysical investigations—investigations into what it is to be a rational person—will have psychological conclusions. Hobbes would be an example of the first kind and Kant of the second.

18. See especially *C2* 30, 41–50.

19. In Chapter III of the Analytic of the *Critique of Practical Reason*, where Kant's project is "not ... to show a priori why the moral law supplies an incentive but rather what it effects (or better, must effect) in the mind, in so far as it is an incentive" (*C2* 72).

Bibliography

Aristotle. *The Nicomachean Ethics.* Translated by David Ross and revised by J. L. Ackrill and J. O. Urmson. Oxford: Oxford University Press, 1980.

Falk, W. D. *Ought, Reasons, and Morality: The Collected Papers of W. D. Falk.* Ithaca: Cornell University Press, 1986.

Frankena, William K. *Perspectives on Morality: Essays of William K. Frankena.* Edited Kenneth E. Goodpaster. Notre Dame: University of Notre Dame Press, 1976.

Hume, David. *A Treatise of Human Nature.* 2nd edition. Edited by L. A. Selby-Bigge and P. H. Nidditch. Oxford: Clarendon Press, 1978.

Mill, John Stuart. *Utilitarianism.* Edited by George Sher. Indianapolis: Hackett, 1979.

Nagel, Thomas. *The Possibility of Altruism.* Oxford: Clarendon Press, 1970. Reprinted in Princeton: Princeton University Press, 1978.

Prichard, H. A. *Moral Obligation and Duty and Interest: Essays and Lectures by H. A. Prichard.* Edited by W. D. Ross and J. O. Urmson. Oxford: Oxford University Press, 1968.

Chapter 7

Internalism, Practical Reason, and Motivation

John Robertson

INTRODUCTION

The terms 'internalism' and 'externalism' have come in to use to mark off positions at the intersection of three areas of interest in philosophy. One area is the issue of the possibility of practical reason. We apply norms freely in speaking of what people ought to want, to hope for, and to believe, but the familiar epithets of rational appraisal—'true', 'well-supported', 'mistaken', and the like—apply most perspicuously to belief, and through it to belief-involving states. It is irrational to fear mice to the extent of wanting above all else to live in a mouse-free environment, because it is foolish to believe mice pose much of a threat. Here fear and desire inherit their irrationality from the irrationality of the belief on which they are based. If reason is practical, actions and action-involving states like intentions and desires are subject to norms of rationality that are *not* in this way derivative from the norms of rational belief.

A second area is the theory of motivation, that is, of the kinds of items that must be referred to in the explanation of intentional action. The third is the question of whether morality is autonomous: whether, and in what sense, moral considerations derive their force, either as motivating or as rational, from something outside morality, as opposed to possessing this force intrinsically. Though the first two issues are logically independent of the third, it is only recently that they have begun to receive much attention on their own.

The topic offers the prospect of laying out the three issues in a perspicuous way, one that reveals their interrelations and takes us some distance toward settling them. But conflicting accounts of what internalism is and which historical figures are internalists can lead anyone to wonder if this hope is misplaced. Thus authors as various as Hobbes, Hume, and Kant have been termed 'internalist' by some authors, 'externalist' by others; and these conflicting classifications do not seem to reflect differences in interpretations of the figures in question. Sometimes, as the following quotations show, one person's internalism seems to be as near as makes no difference another's externalism:

Internalism is the view that an agent who judges something good should feel a pull towards promoting it, whether or not she does in fact.[1]

Externalists ... hold that the truth of a normative claim does not depend on its being the case that the person to whom the claim applies would be motivated under any conditions other, of course, than those in which she is moved as she ought to be.[2]

At least for the case of a true judgement of the form 'I ought to ϕ', these characterizations appear to coincide.

I think that clarity can be achieved by considering this cluster of issues together, though to evaluate the case for this, some preliminary philosophical and terminological clarification will be required. The first part of this essay is devoted to this exegetical chore. In the second, I consider four lines of argument concerning the positions identified in the first part that have appeared frequently in the literature.

FALK'S TWO SENSES OF 'EXTERNAL'

The terms 'internal' and 'external' were introduced into contemporary discussions two generations ago by W. D. Falk in his criticisms of Prichard's "Duty and Interest."[3] Prichard opens that essay with the question of why philosophers—he takes as examples Plato and Butler—find it necessary to argue that right action will be for our own good. These efforts, he feels "are out of place, so that the real question is not so much whether they are successful, but whether they ought ever to have been made" (1968, 204). Prichard traces their attention to this question to their assumptions that "to stimulate a man into doing some action, it is not merely insufficient but even useless to convince him that he is morally bound to do it, and that, instead, we have to appeal to his desire to be better off" (1968, 222). But, he argues, the assumption is unwarranted and the arguments unnecessary if there is a desire to do what is right because it is right. Such a desire, if strong enough, will lead one to act on what one knows to be right without involving a desire to be better off.

Falk's objection to Prichard, though obscure in some details, is clear in its general features. There seems to Falk to be a mismatch between the question Prichard poses and his answer to it. On the one hand, the question 'Why ought I to do my duty when I have no wish to?' uses 'ought', Falk thinks, to express a demand of practical reason, or perhaps practical necessity. Such a "motivational" sense of 'ought' expresses "an impulse ... which a person would have if he both acquainted himself with the facts ... and tested his reactions to them, *and* which he would have necessarily, i.e. unalterably by any repetition of these mental operations" (1986, 38). But Prichard's answer appeals only to an "external" 'ought', a demand that Falk at first characterizes as issuing "from outside the agent" (1986, 32) but later as "a requirement from outside, or an inner compulsion of a special quality" (1986, 40). Prichard's answer does not address the question he set himself.

Now there is much to question in these criticisms. What matters for our immediate purpose is that Falk characterizes the external 'ought' in two different ways: first as a demand issuing from outside the agent, then as a requirement from outside *or* an inner compulsion of a special quality. We have in these two characterizations of 'external' the source of two of the interpretations of what internalism comes to in the contemporary literature. On the first ("outside the agent"), Hume is an internalist: the calm passions that constitute moral bedrock on his theory are psychological facts; for similar reasons Kant will be an internalist. Prichard, who holds that moral obligations consist of nonpsychological facts, will be an externalist. The second characterization, which adds "an inner compulsion of a special quality" as a source of *external* 'oughts' changes things entirely. The point now seems to be to contrast 'oughts' that are the rationally binding products of practical reason with the sentimentalists' moral passions and Prichard's desire to do what is right. This moves Hume to the externalist camp, for Hume's 'ought', while internal to the psyche of the agent, is not produced by practical reason. By this standard, Kant remains an internalist.

To this we can add a third interpretation, deriving from Frankena, who takes the externalist to hold that obligation "represents a fact or requirement which is external to the agent in the sense of being independent of his desires and needs."[4] This has the effect of moving Kant, who contrasts the requirements of practical reason with such desires and needs, into the *externalist* camp, while leaving Hume with the internalists.

SOME POSSIBLE POSITIONS

These terminological inconsistencies make it difficult to see what is at issue. Let us stipulate the following generic formulation of internalism, intended to capture the idea that motivation and justification are conceptually connected, so that reasons must motivate a rational agent. It is a conceptual truth that

(RMR) A consideration C is a reason for an agent to ϕ if and only if the agent would be motivated to ϕ if she were rational and aware of C.

In what follows I will refer to this biconditional as (RMR) ("Reasons must Motivate Rational persons").

There are two quite different sorts of theorists who will accept (RMR) with respect to moral considerations. What we will call a "robust" internalist will accept it because she holds that moral considerations are intrinsically motivating, guaranteed by their content to affect the motivation of anyone who is rational and aware of them. But (RMR) will also be accepted by what I will call an "attenuated" internalist about moral considerations. An attenuated internalist denies that moral considerations have such intrinsic motivating power. They motivate a rational agent only given contingent facts about that agent's desires.[5] Such a theorist will still accept (RMR), since she denies that C is a reason for an agent unless the agent happens to be motivated by C upon due consideration.

The difference corresponds to the two ways in which one might interpret (RMR). Robust internalists construe the left-hand as bearing the explanatory weight: reflection on what one has reason to do is independent of, and gives direction and content to, one's motivations if one is rational. (Hereafter I refer to this as the "left-weighted" reading.) Attenuated internalists give interpretative priority to the right-hand side: facts about someone's motivation, just by themselves, determine and limit the claims about what there is a reason for him to do. (Hereafter this will be the "right-weighted" reading.) On the attenuated version a reason claim can be *defeated* just because it fails to motivate someone, however good its credentials otherwise, but on the robust version this will show only that the person is irrational.

Some of the terminological confusion in discussions of internalism in moral philosophy comes from the tendency of each of these parties to characterize the other as externalists. On the robust internalist view of things, the attenuated internalist takes motivation to consist in facts about an agent's psychological makeup *external to* considerations that are reasons. The attenuated internalist takes the status of being a reason to be something *conferred on* a consideration by the motivation of the agent, rather than intrinsic to the consideration itself.[6] From the attenuated internalist's point of view, however, the robust internalist is one who holds that the status of a consideration as a reason is *external to* the motivation of the person to whom the reason claim is addressed.[7] And on the attenuated internalist's view, the presence in every rational agent of a tendency to be motivated by some consideration would mean that everyone had an internal reason to be motivated by it. On the robust internalist's view, this could be a mere psychological fact, since it leaves unaddressed the further question of whether the motivation is rational. The latter question can be settled only by an examination of the motivating consideration itself.[8]

Undoubtedly, anyone who believes in practical reason at all will be at least tempted to be a robust internalist about some concerns but not others. It seems plausible to suppose that one's health, for example, gives one reasons, whatever one's actual motivation—this corresponds to the left-weighted reading of (RMR). But only the fact that one happens to care about pursuits like chess or bee keeping can, it seems, make facts relevant to success at these activities reasons to do anything—this corresponds to the right-weighted reading. Some of the interesting alternatives, with respect to those who accept (RMR), seem to be these:

· Accepting only the right-weighted reading—understanding that any consideration, including health and morality, counts as a reason only for those who happen to care about them, because they care about them.
· Accepting the left-weighted reading for morality and the right-weighted reading for everything else.
· Accepting the left-weighted reading for important self-interested concerns and the right-weighted reading for morality and other concerns that matter to us, if they do, because we care about them.

Those who give (RMR) the right-weighted reading with respect to moral reasons are likely to understand the requirement of rationality on the right-hand side quite differently from those who interpret it left-to-right. On the right-weighted reading, rationality is interpreted procedurally.[9] Rational evaluation does not extend to an agent's basic motivations, but applies just to how derivative motivations arise from them as the result, for example, of instrumental reasoning. On the left-weighted reading, rationality is a substantive matter, extending to an agent's basic motivations. This shows that rationality is a contested concept, not that the agreement on (RMR) is specious.

I shall understand moral externalism to be the position that holds moral reasons are not subject to (RMR). Such a theorist holds, as Prichard did, that moral considerations give normative or justifying reasons, but that this has no conceptual tie to rational motivation. An externalist agrees with the attenuated internalist that it is a contingent matter whether a rational person is motivated by a moral consideration C, but he agrees with the robust internalist that this does not undermine C's standing as a reason for A to act. He may say, for example, that C is a reason for anyone to act because acting on it would be approved by someone judging from the moral point of view, but claim it is rational, though immoral, to refuse to judge things from that point of view.[10]

According to externalists questions of moral justification and questions of motivation are distinct in at least the following ways. What makes it *true* that someone morally ought to do a particular act is not some fact about the motivation of that person. What *justifies* a moral claim need not motivate a rational person to whom that claim applies. Whether a consideration is a *reason* for someone to do something is a distinct question from whether that consideration *moves* him upon due consideration. An externalist may claim that even an ideally rational and fully informed agent might not be motivated by a moral claim or its justification. An ideally rational agent necessarily *believes* a justified moral claim, but whether he is motivated by it is a question of what he happens to want. Falk's assumption that the truth of a moral claim, or the adequacy of its justification, could be tested by its power to motivate anyone who grasped it, is a mistake on this view, and the notion that morality is a requirement of practical rationality is a myth.

The relations between these positions can be represented schematically as in table 1. Let us consider what each position has to say about moral reasons as they apply to an agent who suffers a permanent loss of moral motivation, and about his rationality. The externalist's and attenuated internalist's agreement on (3) means both accept that this need not indicate any irrationality. Because they disagree at (1), however, they disagree on (2), about whether such a loss of motivation means there is a change in the agent's reasons for acting morally. The externalist and the robust internalist agree that such a change does not change an agent's reasons for acting morally—hence their 'No' at (2). Their answers to (3) diverge,

Table 1
Three positions on the relation between moral reasons and motivation

	Robust internalism	Attenuated internalism	Externalism
1. Conceptual tie between moral reasons and motivation?	Yes	Yes	No
2. Moral reasons depend upon contingent facts about motivation?	No	Yes	No
3. Moral motivation rationally optional?	No	Yes	Yes

reflecting their disagreement about the conclusions one can draw about an agent's rationality from such a lapse in moral motivation. The robust internalist and the attenuated internalist agree that one cannot separate questions about the moral reasons that apply to someone and his motivation in the way the externalist has at (1), but they disagree about what a lapse in moral motivation means with respect to the moral reasons that apply to an agent—this is their disagreement at (2)—and they disagree as well about what it means for the rationality of the agent, i.e., about (3).

Of recent writers, Korsgaard (1986) and Nagel (1970) are robust internalists; Williams (1981) and Foot[11] attenuated internalists; Railton (1992, 1993), Copp (1995a), and Parfit (1997) are externalists.

Some writers lump those who answer 'Yes' to question (3) under the 'externalist' label.[12] This masks their deep disagreement at (1) and (2), for theorists may agree "that . . . it is a contingent and rationally optional matter whether an agent who believes that it is right to act in a certain way is motivated to act accordingly"[13] and yet disagree on the bearing this has on the reasons an agent has to act. Others lump those who answer 'Yes' at (1) together as internalists, but ignore the difference between those who give (RMR) a left-weighted reading and those who interpret it right-to-left. Frankena collapses into the externalist camp all those who say 'No' at (2) on the grounds that they refuse to let moral reasons be held hostage to the vagaries of individuals' desires. This has the odd result that Kant and Mill, or Korsgaard and Parfit, who take opposed positions on (1) and (3), are classed together. The moral is that agreement on just one of the above questions does not identify an interesting position, though the agreements and differences are genuine.

FOUR ISSUES

I turn now to four issues that continue to play a role in contemporary discussions. The aim in the first three sections is to disentangle unrelated questions and dispose of question-begging or otherwise misguided objections. In the fourth I identify what seems to separate the best version of attenuated internalism from robust internalism and try to indicate what might settle the very large issue between them. I conclude with some observations on the historical roots of the contemporary dispute that will, I hope, help put them in a new light.

1 Judgement Internalism

The two internalisms identified above differ over how a moral consideration achieves the status of a reason and over the relations between a consideration with that status and motivation. The robust internalist takes the status to be intrinsic to moral considerations, and the motivation that derives from an awareness of them to be rationally required rather than a contingent psychological fact. The attenuated internalist demurs on both counts. These are differences concerning how the content of moral considerations figure as reasons and the role of those contents in motivation. Both internalisms need to be sharply distinguished from a position, termed 'judgement internalism' by Darwall and 'appraiser internalism' by Brink, that holds that for someone to *make* a sincere moral judgement, or to be in a state that could be expressed by such a judgement, she must be motivated to some extent to act on it.[14]

Judgement internalism seems to be supported by certain parallels one might expect between normative and nonnormative assertions.[15] For nonnormative claims, assertion involves a commitment to the truth of the content asserted. This commitment exactly matches the content of the state of mind expressed by the assertion—a belief that the content is *true*. And it is natural to conclude that assertion here involves a commitment to the truth of what is asserted *because* that commitment is involved in the state of mind that is expressed in assertion. It is because to believe is to believe true, on the one hand, and assertion expresses belief, on the other, that nonnormative assertion involves a commitment to truth.

In the case of normative assertions, one might expect the state of mind expressed must match the commitments of the assertions as well. Normative, and in particular moral, assertions appear to involve commitments to motivation and feelings of approval and disapproval: someone whose apparently sincere normative utterances never, or rarely, matched his dispositions to behavior and his tendencies to approve and disapprove would somehow, one might think, have failed to understand what he was saying. The tempting conclusion is that the state of mind expressed by normative assertions involves, as a conceptual matter, motivation and tendencies to approval and disapproval. This conclusion, however, is inconsistent with the existence of states, like depression and acedia, that leave the agent's capacity to sincerely assert normative claims intact while eliminating her capacity to be motivated in accordance with them. Recent formulations of judgement internalism have accordingly modified the original idea: it is a conceptual truth, the suggestion is, that a *practically rational* person is motivated by the normative judgements she accepts.[16]

Though perhaps there is no outright inconsistency between judgement internalism and either of our internalisms, it seems more natural for those who hold either of the latter to reject it. Both our internalisms need to allow for someone who sincerely but *mistakenly* judges that some consideration gives him reason to act. An attenuated internalist, for example, will take such a case to be one in which the agent is mistaken about his motivation or (more likely) mistaken about the bearing that facts about his motivation have on the reasons there are for him to act. It seems possible, for example, for Owen Wingrave, in Williams's example, to accept his father's judgement that there is a reason for him to join the army, while still having no motivation to do so.[17] If our attenuated internalist is also a judgement internalist, he must take Owen's failure to be motivated as evidence of further irrationality on his part, beyond whatever irrationality is involved in mistakenly believing his father's judgement to be a reason. This seems odd, since on his account the father's judgement does not give Owen a reason to do anything in the first place. One would think that failure to be motivated by something that isn't a reason could never count against one's *practical* rationality; if anything, one would expect it to count *for* it.[18]

The awkwardness of combining the positions emerges if we consider an Owen who is both credulous and unduly conscientious. Because he is credulous, he accepts his father's false claim that there is a reason to join the army, and because he is conscientious, he comes to be motivated by this belief. The judgement internalist must count this an *improvement* in Owen's practical rationality: now he is "rational by his own lights," motivated to do what he believes he has reason to do.[19] The attenuated internalist should, I think, regard this as a *deterioration* in his practical rationality: Owen now not only believes his father's false reason claim, but is also motivated by it.

The problem of combining either of our internalisms with judgement internalism is not surprising. Even so "subjectivist" a theory of reasons as attenuated internalism is a normative and *substantive* theory, in the sense that whether a consideration really is a reason is a separate matter from whether someone takes it to be one. Judgement internalism has historically been offered as an alternative to substantive accounts, one according to which reasons are simply considerations toward which one takes a certain sort of attitude. The posited attitude can be assessed in many ways, and from many points of view, but it is not true or false. The problem of sincerely but mistakenly taking something to be a reason cannot arise, and consequently, the related notions of correcting or improving a reason judgement have presented a challenge to these views. On substantive accounts, it can arise, and there seems little incentive for attenuated internalists to allow failing to be motivated by mistaken reason judgements to weigh against someone's practical rationality.

2   The Alleged Incompleteness of Externalist Justifications

A line of criticism of externalism originated by Falk aims to show externalist moral justifications must be incomplete. Prichard claimed that the person persuaded he had a duty would, if he thought about it, find that he had some desire to do it. Falk objected, "It seems paradoxical that moral conduct should require more than one kind of justification: that having first convinced someone that regardless of cost to himself he was morally bound to do some act we should then be called upon to convince him as well that he had some and some sufficiently strong reason for doing this same act."[20] This is repeated by Nagel, who puts it as follows: "[Given externalism, the motivation for acting morally] is not supplied by ethical principles and judgements themselves, and ... an additional psychological sanction is required to motivate our compliance.... Such views are, it seems to me, unacceptable on their surface, for they permit someone who has acknowledged that he should do something and has seen *why* it is the case that he should do it to ask whether he has any reason for doing it."[21]

The objection involves a confusion to which Falk is prone: that of taking the desires Prichard and other externalists introduce to explain what moves us to act as further justifying factors.[22] On the externalist view, someone persuaded that something is a duty may be rational and yet not *act* if he lacks the desire to do his duty. Only on *internalist* assumptions—specifically, (RMR) above—will this support the additional claim that he has not been given a reason to do it. Indeed, it may seem an objection to the externalist view that, if it is right, someone *cannot* cite his lack of motivation as a reason against doing what he should do. On that view, facts about motivation aren't *relevant* to what there is a moral reason to do. (I take up the implications of the fact that people sometimes seem to think of their lack of motivation as relevant in the following section.)

The externalist position amounts, it is sometimes claimed, to moral skepticism.[23] I doubt this line of argument can be made out without assuming (RMR), and thus begging the question. Still, it points to something interesting. Its force is not quite grasped, I think, even by Frankena. In the concluding pages of his paper he supposes an externalist may agree that "There is in fact a psychological gap between obligation and motivation," but "all that follows is that, if externalism is true, human beings may sometimes lack all motivation to do what they apprehend is right."[24] But this concession implies that when someone *is* motivated to do what she apprehends is right, the motivation derives not from the apprehension, but from a desire of the sort Falk disparages as an "inner compulsion." This would not be troubling if the idea of rationally required motivation were a myth. If we suppose that it is not a myth, that an agent is rationally required to be motivated by considerations of self-interest but *not* by morality, for example, then externalism about moral reasons implies something quite troubling: that moral motivation is rationally optional in a way that motivation by some other concerns is not.[25]

Externalism about moral reasons fits comfortably with (though it does not require) a moral-realist metaphysics and a commonsense (and Humean) view of motivation. It deserves to be the default position, absent a showing that some stronger notion of practical moral reason makes sense. But it is also the natural concomitant of an account of morality that explains its requirements in terms of institutional and social needs, and that explains our responses to those requirements in terms of socialization.[26] Such an account is deflationary: it has been the aspiration of much moral theory since Socrates to use the standards of practical rationality to explain and justify the hold moral requirements seem to have. It is their readiness to abandon this project that underlies the suspicion that externalist moral theorists deserve to be classified as moral skeptics.

3   The Humean Theory of Motivation: Rationally Optional Desires and Whims

What we might term the "core" of Hume's theory of motivation is often thought to favor either attenuated internalism or externalism over robust internalism. On Hume's theory, any intentional action is to be explained by appeal to two quite distinct kinds of states of the agent: a belief and a desire. The most persuasive argument for the core theory is by example: A given belief will set you in motion at one time, not at another. What makes this difference in particular cases? Why does the belief that there is no beer in the refrigerator send you to the store at one point but have no effect at another? Surely, the difference is that you *desire* beer at that time. Why does the desire for beer at one time send you to the refrigerator, at another time to the store? Surely, the difference is that in the first case you *believe* there is beer in the refrigerator, in the second that there is not. If desire is held constant, differences in actions are explained by differences in beliefs, and if beliefs are held constant, differences in actions are explained by differences in desires. I have given examples in which the beliefs are about instrumental means to a goal, but that is accidental: the same belief/desire pattern is required where the agent believes that the action is an instance of a kind of act he wants to do, or a constituent of an instance of a kind he wants.

On this theory, desire is a generic notion covering any mental state with "world to mind direction of fit."[27] It is a theoretical state, in the sense that it is attributed to subjects on the basis of inferences from observed behavior, including verbal behavior, and such attributions go hand in hand with attributions of other theoretical states, in particular, beliefs. It is central to this sense that desire is related to belief and action such that if A ϕs and A believes that by ϕing A will π, and A would not have ϕed without that belief, then A desires to π. This conception of desire leaves open whether a desire is introspectively available to an agent motivated by it, what its causal origins are, what its standing with relation to practical reason is, and indeed, whether it is a propositional attitude at all.

Hume's core theory does not rule out robust internalism. This much of Hume's theory is an account of what figures in the explanation of action, of the "hardware" of motivation.[28] Robust internalism, by contrast, is an account of the nature and role of reasons as they figure in deliberation, as normative considerations favoring and disfavoring a course of action. The distinctive claims of robust internalism are, first, that moral considerations do not owe their status as reasons to contingent psychological facts about an agent, and second, that there is an element of *rational* necessity in their motivational power. Though attenuated internalism and externalism are inconsistent with these claims, Hume's core theory is not. So though verbs of desiring and wanting may be indispensable in stating our aims and the reasons for them, this fact does not support attenuated internalism. At most it testifies to the truth of the core Humean theory: that if deliberation is to *produce* an action, it must produce a desire. Attenutated internalism is the view that the states that control this deliberation—the most fundamental practical states at least so far as morality goes—are rationally optional desires. Robust internalism is inconsistent with this; it is not inconsistent with the core Humean theory.[29]

The widespread assumption that the Humean core by itself favors attenuated internalism may derive from a mistaken interpretation of the fact that it requires a desire as an element in any complete explanation of an action. If an agent's deliberations are to explain his actions, it may seem, his desires must figure as distinct elements in his deliberations, thus counting on their own as considerations favoring or disfavoring an action.[30] But the central cases in which our desires *do* appear naturally in our deliberations are paradigms of the rationally optional: 'I just wanted to' figures most naturally as a reason for wearing one dress rather than another, or ordering the fish rather than the pasta. This may have created the impression that the Humean core by itself involves a commitment to the view that reasons depend on rationally optional desires. Worse, it may seem that if attenuated internalism is true, even our deepest commitments should *seem* to us to be nothing more than relatively powerful and stable whims.

Appeals to a desire or a lack of desire as a constituent of a reason are frequently inapt. This fact helps explain what is so chilling in an example from Williams (though, as we shall see, nothing much can be concluded from it). Williams asks us to suppose that a husband were to respond, when told there are reasons for him to treat his wife decently, with the words 'I don't care. Don't you understand? I really do not care.'[31] That he does not care tells us that he *will* not treat his wife decently. In putting this forward where we expect a *reason*, he represents her happiness as having no greater claim on his deliberations than any whim of others that he happens not to share.[32] The example belies Williams's characterization of it: he remarks, "There is *nothing* in [the husband's] motivational set that gives him a reason to be nicer to his wife as things are." One naturally wants to ask why we should look *there* for reasons, and the example can seem in this way to support externalism or robust internalism.

What the example shows, however, is that anyone who accepts the Humean core, and the attenuated internalist in particular, must treat the role of desires in deliberation with some delicacy. They must put some distance between the idea that desires always play a role in deliberation, to which they are committed, and the idea that desires are always represented as deliberative steps, to which they are not. This does not seem hard to do: the uncaring husband shows himself as such not by reasoning from his indifference as a premise but by assigning considerations other than his wife's happiness greater importance. He may additionally be disposed to display his contempt by using such words as Williams imagines, but that is neither here nor there. In the typical case, desires manifest themselves in practical deliberation in the considerations the agent takes to be reasons and the weight he assigns them. Their content is completely expressed in those considerations. Adding explicit reference to desire in an account of the content of an agent's deliberative reasons would at best be redundant and at worst suggest that the reasons are no more than whims.[33] But it is compatible with all this that any particular desire is rationally optional.

Whims are paradigm cases in which someone's desires figure explicitly in his deliberative reasons. They are paradigms because the consideration that moves someone who acts on a whim will not by itself give him a reason, or a good reason. In contexts of explanation of action, reference to desire sometimes carries the suggestion of inadequate rational support as well. In general, just insofar as one aims to explain someone's action, the merit of his reasons is simply not relevant. Good or bad, they are the reasons that explain his action. Where explanation is the only point, it is natural to cite his desire. But sometimes both explanation and evaluation are pertinent. In such cases if we wish to endorse the reason, it is more natural, because it informs our audience of our endorsement, to cite the reason alone.[34] This too can create the impression, in those contexts where the merit of reasons is in question, that one cites a desire as a reason only when one thinks the consideration on which an agent acts is in some way unable to fully rationalize the agent's action. Why, after all, use a form of words that does not carry endorsement if you think the reasons sufficient? Why say the weaker thing when you can say the stronger?

The phenomenon is quite general. I may explain your believing *q* for the reason *p* either by referring to your *believing p* or simply by *citing p*. The latter commits me to *p* (and to *p*'s being a reason to believe *q*), and the former does not. It would clearly be a mistake to infer that someone's believing p, as opposed to p itself, is a reason for his believing q when p is a somewhat weak reason, and that when someone's reasons for believing q are very good, it is the reasons, not his believing them, that explain his believing q.[35] Philosophers have, however, drawn such conclusions when desires are referred to in explanations of action. In both cases this is to mistake points that have to do with the pragmatics of explanation, in particular the devices for marking a speaker's commitments in giving an explanation, with points about explanatory factors.

4 Robust Internalism and the Rational Stability of Reasons

Williams has considerably sharpened the issue between attenuated internalism and its rivals by asking what the sense could be of a claim that someone has a reason to ϕ in the absence of a "sound deliberative route" that would lead her to be motivated to ϕ. On even the most generous view of the resources available to the deliberating agent, some putative reasons must, one would suppose, leave some agents cold. The robust internalist in particular must explain what it means to insist that nevertheless there is a reason for such an agent to ϕ, that is, what it would be for her to come to acquire this motivation rationally. In particular, the explanation must give some content to the idea that the agent is missing a *reason*. It is not enough just to identify a defect of character that accounts for her indifference: such defects of character, on the attenuated internalist view, will serve only to modify the reason claims that can be made about her.

John McDowell, among others, has recently called in question the emphasis in this debate on the acquisition of motivation through deliberation.[36] The attention it has received from both sides is really quite odd. Our confidence in the rationality of our motivational states often has nothing to do with how they came about. We do not deliberate our way into enjoying twelve-tone music or raw oysters, much less moral virtue, and our confidence often, and rightly, persists even in the face of knowledge that the states arose as the result of bad reasoning. We can test the rationality of our motivation directly, it seems, and if so, we can bypass worries about whether sound deliberation led to it.[37] We can thus give sense to the idea of an external reason, one that motivates us because we are—in Williams's phrase—"considering matters aright", though we could not have reached that motive by deliberating from motivation we already had.[38] At or close to the "heart of the matter," McDowell claims, is this: "We do not conceive our values as owing their authenticity, and their relevance to what we do, to our motivational makeup or to anything in the psychological genesis of our coming to have them; and that, together with our managing to sustain confidence in them through reflection, is all that it takes for us to suppose they yield reasons."[39]

I doubt that this is the heart of the matter. First, as we have seen, it is our whims and the like that we conceive of as owing their authenticity to our makeup, and Williams need not assimilate our reasons to these. More important, attenuated internalism should take our most fundamental practical states each to involve at once desires, patterns of evaluation, and emotional responses, no one of which is, as an expression of that state, primary. One's sexual orientation is an uncontroversial example of this. Moral motivation seems part of such a state, a state that itself arises from something like Aristotelian habituation. The robust internalist's "recognition that a consideration is a reason" does not seem to describe any step in such habituation. If it fits anything, it seems to fit the upshot, the virtuous state of character, and it fits this as an expression of that state, rather than as an achievement of practical reason that leads to it. Similarly, finding someone attractive expresses a state that includes, but doesn't lead to, sexual desire. And in both cases it is natural to use the language of reasons causally and normatively to explain desire: if I can't see what you see in her, there are things you can say that may help, and if I can't see why you oppose right-to-work laws, there are things you can point to that may bring me round.[40]

Now, few think that the process of maturation that produces a sexual orientation leads to the grasp of a reason that does not owe its authenticity to our motivational makeup, presumably because the phenomenon is biologically based. But something needs to be said to explain why biological maturation and Aristotelian habituation are relevantly different, and Williams, in demanding a sound deliberative route, seems to be looking in the right place. The problem confronting McDowell's position arises, I suspect, for any theory of practical rationality that conceives of practical reasons substantively rather than procedurally, as justified by their content rather than by the deliberative route to them. One might suppose that a moderately high level of physical fitness is a requirement of substantive practical rationality, and one might try to defend this claim by pointing to the range of activities that only the physically fit can undertake and enjoy. But undertaking these activities with enjoyment is a characteristic expression of physical fitness, and insufficiently independent of the state itself to recommend it to the unfit. Aristotle recognized a gap of this sort between the satisfactions typical of the virtuous person and what can serve to recommend a virtuous state of character, and he sought to fill it with the argument that virtue is the function of man. Without something to play this role, McDowell's points seem inconclusive. Reasons that are external in McDowell's sense remain rationally optional, however compelling they are to those motivated by them, and whether or not it would be better if more of us were responsive to them.

What may speak in favor of a motivation's being rationally required is, I think, that the motivation is rationally stable. That is, if only conditions that uncontroversially undermine rationality can undermine a motivational state, that state is rationally required.[41] One might, without irrationality, simply lose one's taste for Prokofiev—his irony comes to strike one as shallow and superficial, perhaps—and discover a preference for Schubert. One might, perhaps, lose one's interest in large questions of social justice and, no longer caring about them, no longer have any reason to care. If robust internalism is right about any moral reasons, it must be true that at least some moral motivation is not like this.[42] Though one can always cease to be responsive to moral considerations, the case for the view that some responsiveness is rationally required cannot be made out without a showing that some such changes must involve a departure from rationality.[43]

Though there isn't space to explore this line of thought here, it may be that the motivation involved in the attitude of resentment satisfies these requirements.[44] On the one hand, it is a fundamental practical state, one that someone could not reach simply by deliberation. Whole cultures have come into existence in which only an elite, if anyone, exhibits the attitude at all. It seems then to require socialization into a favorable and quite distinctive social structure. On the other hand, it involves, in contrast to dislike or displeasure, the thought that one has been treated as one ought not to have been, and so a commitment to general, though not necessarily universal, standards of treatment that are typical of morality.

It is important to resist the temptation to a moralizing interpretation of these facts. The capacity to respond to some mistreatment with resentment has for most of our history been tied to status, and the thought that simply being a person is a status sufficient to ground duties is a comparatively recent arrival. In its commonest forms, historically and I suspect today, the general standards of appropriate treatment and concern have been restricted by race, gender, or tribe. Someone impressed by the slow and unsteady pace of the elimination of such restrictions, and the role in this of (often painful) social experience, is unlikely to find it plausible that anything deserving the name 'practical reason' could be at work.[45] Someone convinced of the existence of practical reason can be tempted to underestimate the role of contingency in this process. But there need be no conflict here. It may be that sheer historical accident frequently plays a decisive role in removing irrelevant restrictions, on the one hand, and practical rationality accounts for the stability of such achievements, on the other.

To return to the individual case, it seems probable that one who has developed the capacity for resentment could not simply lose it without being subjected to the sorts of trauma one associates with Stockholm syndrome or similar forms of abuse. The case for robust internalism is incomplete without evidence that this stability is not, like the taste for alcohol or refined sugar, just a species-wide psychological quirk, but is somehow rooted in the content of the attitude itself. Furthermore, the case needs evidence that insusceptibility to the attitude is rationally unstable, and tends to appear only in conditions that promote practical irrationality generally. These are optimistic liberal speculations, of course, and empirical speculations at that. But with these issues, it has never been a question of banishing the empirical altogether, but only a question of finding the right entry point for it. And the optimism, restricted as it is to the special case of motivation that is rationally stable, doesn't seem in danger of getting out of hand.

In conclusion, or perhaps in lieu of a conclusion, I venture an observation on the general point at issue, as Falk saw it, between these internalisms and externalism. The fundamental question at issue is whether standards of practical rationality are social or individual. We are the heirs of three traditions. The externalist tradition—starting (probably) with the conservative sophist Protagoras[46] and Aristotle, and continuing through Burke's "Reflections on the Revolution in France,"[47] Mill, and Bradley's "My Station and Its Duties"[48]—insists on the priority of social standards of practical reason as the measure of the individual's aims and interests.[49] The standards are external in a straightforward sense: they are the laws, customs, interests, and ideals of a society, sometimes expressed formally in its institutions, but sometimes only informally in traditions, including dissenting traditions.

Contemporary internalisms seem to have two quite distinct sources. Robust internalism arises with Socrates and the radical sophists, reappears with the major figures of the romantic movement, in particular Kant and Rousseau, and continues as a strain in the various subjectivisms of the twentieth century. Common to all these is the thought that animates robust internalism, that the ultimate arbiter of what a person has reason to do is some standard he finds he must rationally accept. The source of attenuated internalism is the sentimentalist school of thought, whose major figure is Hume, a tradition with an empiricist and naturalist bent and little interest in testing the rationality of society's demands. The skepticism about reason that pervades the sentimentalist tradition survives in attenuated internalism, making it quite an odd bedfellow for the robust version. It is, in fact, a conservative position, far closer to externalism in its general import, if only because the actual motivations from which it constructs reasons will match, for most people most of the time, the requirements of any viable society. If this is so in fact, what we go on to say about the few sensible knaves who fall through the cracks really doesn't matter terribly much. On either view, their existence can't threaten our claims to be justified in rejecting their outlooks. The challenge they present is to be met not with arguments but with such devices as better bicycle locks and a more powerful Securities and Exchange Commission.

Many moral philosophers regard the sensible knaves not as mere nuisances but as presenting a challenge to the good person's claim to be living a good life. It was Falk's point that if either externalism or attenuated internalism gives the right account of reasons, the idea of such a challenge doesn't make much sense.[50] Nothing in either view supports the idea that a good person's reasons can be tested by the power of those reasons to motivate those who appear indifferent to them. If there really is a challenge, some version of robust internalism must be the right account of at least some reasons, and the question whether it is the right account of some moral reasons remains.

Acknowledgments

I wish to thank the editor, Emily Robertson, and Seth Shabo for discussion and comments on earlier drafts.

Notes

1. Smith 1995, 280.

2. Darwall 1995, 12.

3. "'Ought' and Motivation" is in Falk 1986, 21–41. "Duty and Interest" is in Prichard 1968. (References in the text are to these volumes.)

4. "Obligation and Motivation in Recent Moral Philosophy," in Frankena 1976, 51.

5. Parfit's characterization of internalism thus fits only my attenuated internalism: "Internalists derive conclusions about reasons from psychological claims about the motivation that, under certain conditions, we would in fact have" (Parfit 1997, 102). It seems to me a weakness of Parfit's treatment of this question that he nowhere separates robust and attenuated internalism. It is symptomatic of this that his schema (1997, 103) distinguishes only an externalist position, according to which we always have reason to do our duty (whatever our motivation), and an internalist position, which "*restricts* morality to those who have moral motivation" (1997, 104; emphasis added). The robust internalist who thinks motivation is produced by grasping the content of moral considerations will not regard this as a restriction.

6. Thus David Brink: "Externalism claims that the motivational force and rationality of moral considerations depend on factors external to the considerations themselves" (1989, 42). Note that Brink's use of this terminology seems to be inconsistent (see Goldsworthy 1992, esp. 47–49). The same characterization of externalism figures in Korsgaard's exposition of Ross's views in Korsgaard 1989, esp. 54.

7. Here is Bernard Williams's sense of an external interpretation of a reason claim: "The external reasons statement ... will have to be taken as roughly equivalent to, or at least entailing, the claim that if the agent rationally deliberated, then, whatever motivations he originally had, he would come to be motivated to ϕ" (Williams 1981; this volume, 85). This position is usually characterized as a species of internalism (see Wallace 1990, 376, n. 48). Parfit (1997, 100) takes it to be definitive of externalism that for some reasons it *denies* the entailment Williams mentions.

8. This is not a condition Christine Korsgaard places on what she terms the "internalism requirement" in Korsgaard 1986 (this volume, 109). Her statement of the requirement, like (RMR), is intended to fit both robust and attenuated forms of internalism.

9. Parfit draws this contrast (1997, 101) but (mistakenly, I think) associates substantive rationality just with externalism.

10. See Railton 1992 and 1993.

11. See Foot 1972. She has recently changed her position, however (see Foot 1995).

12. For example, Smith 1994, 71. Smith's "strong" externalist affirms (3) and denies the further claim that one who judges an act right is motivated to do it or is irrational. I turn to the latter claim in the next section.

13. Smith 1994, 71.

14. Darwall 1983, 54; Brink 1989, 40. Judgement internalism is most recently defended in Gibbard 1990 and Dreier 1990. The quotes from Smith and Darwall (above, p. 128) that initially seem so close differ here. Smith is defending judge-

ment internalism, and Darwall is characterizing externalism. On the former, one ought to be motivated by whatever one takes to be a reason. On the latter, one ought to be motivated by what actually is a reason.

15. The parallels are suggested in Hare 1952, 19–20, and Davidson 1980, 86.

16. Smith 1994, 62. Alternatively, one may follow Dreier, who restricts the conceptual claim to normal contexts (see Dreier 1990).

17. Williams 1981; this volume, 82. The objection that Owen can't *really* accept his father's judgement unless he is motivated is commonly made at this point. If successful, this objection will keep judgement internalism and attenuated internalism consistent. I think the objection conflates the conversational implication of *saying* one ought to do something with *accepting* the judgement that one ought to do it, but my present point is just that the alliance is somewhat strained.

18. Copp 1995b.

19. Smith 1994, 62. Owen, in my example, is motivated by what Smith terms a *de dicto* desire; that is, the quantifier binding 'what there is reason to do' in 'Owen desires to do what there is reason to do' has narrow scope (1994, 71–76). Smith characterizes such motivation as fetishistic, but that doesn't affect the present point: judgement internalism will have to count some cases of fetishistic motivation as improvements in practical rationality.

20. Falk 1986, 29.

21. Nagel 1970, 9. Korsgaard cites this with approval (this volume, 108). See also Goldsworthy 1992, 43, on the "logical gap" between natural facts and decisions. The argument is well criticized by Frankena (see 1976, 71–72).

22. Falk's intuition that "the connection between duty and motivation is too close to be merely contingent" (1986, 29) is a particularly clear case of this: it is obviously true if "motivation" means "justification" and controversial if it means "desire."

23. Goldsworthy 1992, 56.

24. Frankena 1976, 72.

25. This seems to be the conclusion Falk is himself inclined to draw; it is strongly suggested by Foot (1972).

26. The point is made in Falk 1986, 32.

27. Smith 1987.

28. An assumption common to those who reject the core Humean theory on behalf of robust internalism is one we find in Falk's criticism of Prichard: that if desire is a causal condition for action distinct from belief, it must also be a distinct reason. That is, if the thought that you need help won't move me unless I have the corresponding desire, the thought itself can't be the whole reason for helping you when I do. Sometimes the assumption is rather that the thought can't be a *practical* reason if it relies on desire for motivational efficacy (Korsgaard 1989, 54). In either case, the theorists are led to construe belief as sufficient at least sometimes for motivation, which is certainly contrary to the Humean core.

The resulting position has odd results in the philosophy of mind: either those who are unmoved by the thought someone needs help turn out not to have that thought (McDowell 1979, 16); or they do have it, and the thought by itself is *sufficient* to explain their actions when it moves them, *though it may sometimes fail to do so* (Dancy 1993; Nagel 1970, 67, especially n. 1). The former response is ad hoc, and the latter attributes to moral belief the quaint causal features of an Aristotelian *dunamis* or "power."

29. See Wallace 1990, 370, on the "desire out–desire in" principle.

30. Stephen Darwall argues that desires do not figure in reasons in this way (see 1983, 2–4). Simon Blackburn has long insisted on the point (see Blackburn 1998, 254, on "the leading characteristic mistake of a whole generation of theorists wanting to go beyond Hume"). (See also Pettit and Smith 1990, 565–592.) Williams often expresses himself in ways that suggest he thinks that internal-reason statements involve deliberation from one's desires (e.g., Williams 1981, this volume, 85; and the example cited in the next paragraph). This is not essential to anything he says but has misled some (e.g., Schueler 1995, 72–73).

31. Williams 1995, 39.

32. Compare Melville's tale "Bartleby," which exploits the eeriness of the 'I don't care to' response to great effect.

33. Hence the thought that someone who does his duty both because it is his duty and because he wants to is not taking duty seriously enough. Both the redundancy and "mere whim" complaints are made by T. M. Scanlon (1998, chap. 1).

34. Compare "To protect the Albanians NATO bombed Belgrade" and "NATO bombed Belgrade because it wanted to protect the Albanians."

35. Edgley 1965, especially 180–183. I owe many of the points in the last two paragraphs to Edgley.

36. McDowell 1995.

37. Falk's "motivational" sense of 'ought' cited above, p. 129, is an example.

38. Williams 1981; this volume, 84 f.

39. McDowell 1995, 81; see also Scanlon 1998, 367.

40. These similarities suggest that Nagel's oft-invoked distinction between "motivated" and "unmotivated" desires involves a serious oversimplification (see Nagel 1970, chap. 5).

41. It is important that the characterization of irrationality involved be uncontroversial. The attenuated internalist has no problem accommodating specialized uses of 'irrational' of the sort a fan of twelve-tone music might use against the man who has never gotten past Schubert. Here I disagree with McDowell, who disparages "the craving for a kind of rationality independently demonstrable as such" (1979, 346), in terms of which the virtuous person's view can be shown to be rational. Without such a neutral notion of rationality I can see nothing that will distinguish McDowell's view from a nuanced version of attenuated internalism such as that espoused by Simon Blackburn.

42. It seems quite likely that some important forms of moral motivation will be like this. The attenuated internalist is surely right that some moral considerations, including some that are important to society, are reasons for us only because we happen to care about them.

43. Though the question of the deterioration of virtuous character exercised Aristotle and has received much attention since the appearance of Michael Stocker's classic essay (1979), the emphasis seems to me to have been misplaced. The disturbing question raised by Stocker's examples is not whether the states of character he describes are possible but whether they are rational—whether the politician who has lost interest in the suffering of those other than his friends and family (1979, 741) has, because of this, lost any reason to be interested.

44. Nagel 1970, 83 ff.; Korsgaard 1996b, 142 ff.

45. Moore 1978 provides a valuable survey of historical cases worth mulling over in this connection.

46. As he is presented in Plato 1997, 320c–328c.

47. Burke 1975.

48. Bradley 1927, 160–213.

49. Thus Burke: "We are afraid to put men to live and trade each on his own private stock of reason; because we suspect that the stock in each man is small, and that the individuals would do better to avail themselves of the general bank and capital of nations and of ages" (1975, 354).

50. Falk 1986, 40–41. I am interpreting freely here, since I do not think it helpful to follow Falk in casting the question in terms of senses of 'ought'.

References

Blackburn, S. 1998. *Ruling Passions.* Oxford: Clarendon Press.

Bradley, F. 1927. *Ethical Studies.* Oxford: Oxford University Press.

Brink, D. 1989. *Moral Realism and the Foundations of Ethics.* Cambridge: Cambridge University Press.

Burke, E. 1975. "Reflections on the Revolution in France." In *Edmund Burke on Government, Politics, and Society*, edited by B. W. Hill. New York: International Publications Service.

Copp, D. 1995a. *Morality, Normativity, and Society.* New York: Oxford University Press.

Copp, D. 1995b. "Moral Obligation and Motivation." In Couture and Nielsen 1995, 187–219.

Couture, J., and Nielsen, K. 1995. *On the Relevance of Metaethics. Canadian Journal of Philosophy*, suppl. vol. 21. Calgary: University of Calgary Press.

Dancy, J. 1993. *Moral Reasons.* Oxford: Blackwell.

Darwall, S. 1983. *Impartial Reason.* Ithaca: Cornell University Press.

Darwall, S. 1995. *The British Moralists and the Internal 'Ought'*. New York: Cambridge University Press.

Davidson, D. 1980. *Essays on Actions and Events.* New York: Oxford University Press.

Dreier, J. 1990. "Internalism and Speaker Relativism." *Ethics* 101: 6–26.

Edgley, R. 1965. "Practical Reason." *Mind* 74: 174–191.

Falk, W. D. 1986. *Ought, Reasons, and Morality*. Ithaca: Cornell University Press.

Foot, P. 1972. "Morality as a System of Hypothetical Imperatives." *Philosophical Review* 81: 305–316.

Foot, P. 1995. "Does Moral Subjectivism Rest on a Mistake?" *Oxford Journal of Legal Studies* 15: 1–14.

Frankena, W. 1976. "Obligation and Motivation in Recent Moral Philosophy." In his *Perspectives on Morality*, edited by K. Goodpaster. Notre Dame: University of Notre Dame Press.

Gibbard, A. 1990. *Wise Choices, Apt Feelings.* Cambridge: Harvard University Press.

Goldsworthy, J. 1992. "Externalism, Internalism, and Moral Skepticism." *Australasian Journal of Philosophy* 70: 40–60.

Hare, R. M. 1952. *Language of Morals*. Oxford: Oxford University Press.

Korsgaard, C. 1986. "Skepticism about Practical Reason." *Journal of Philosophy* 83: 5–25. Reprinted in this volume, chapter 6. Page references in the notes are to this volume.

Korsgaard C. 1989. "Kant's Analysis of Obligation: The Argument of *Groundwork* I." *Monist* 72: 311–340. Reprinted in Korsgaard 1996a. Page references in the notes are to this edition.

Korsgaard, C. 1996a. *Creating the Kingdom of Ends*. Cambridge: Cambridge University Press.

Korsgaard, C. 1996b. *The Sources of Normativity.* Cambridge: Cambridge University Press.

McDowell, J. 1978. "Are Moral Requirements Hypothetical Imperatives?" *Proceedings of the Aristotelian Society*, suppl. vol. 52: 13–29.

McDowell, J. 1979. "Virtue and Reason." *Monist* 62: 331–350.

McDowell, J. 1995. "Might There Be External Reasons?" In J. E. J. Altham and Ross Harrison, eds., *World, Mind, and Ethics,* pp. 68–85. Cambridge: Cambridge University Press.

Moore, B. 1978. *Injustice: The Social Bases of Obedience and Revolt.* New York: Pantheon.

Nagel, T. 1970. *The Possibility of Altruism*. Princeton: Princeton University Press.

Parfit, D. 1997. "Reasons and Motivation." *Proceedings of the Aristotelian Society,* suppl. vol. 71: 99–130.

Pettit, P., and Smith, M. 1990. "Backgrounding Desire." *Philosophical Review* 99: 565–592.

Plato. 1997. *Protagoras.* Translated by Stanley Lombardo and Karen Bell. Indianapolis: Hackett.

Prichard, H. A. 1968. *Moral Obligation and Duty and Interest.* Oxford: Oxford University Press.

Railton, P. 1992. "Some Questions about the Justification of Morality." *Philosophical Perspectives* 6: 27–54.

Railton, P. 1993. "What the Non-cognitivist Helps Us to See the Naturalist Must Help Us to Explain." In Haldane and Wright, eds., *Reality, Representation, and Projection*, pp. 279–300. New York: Oxford.

Scanlon, T. 1998. *What We Owe Each Other.* Cambridge: Harvard University Press.

Schueler, G. 1995. *Desire.* Cambridge: MIT Press.

Smith, M. 1987. "The Humean Theory of Motivation." *Mind* 96: 36–61.

Smith, M. 1994. *The Moral Problem.* Oxford: Blackwell.

Smith, M. 1995. "Internalism's Wheel." *Ratio*, n.s. 8: 277–302.

Stocker, M. 1979. "Desiring the Bad." *Journal of Philosophy* 76: 738–753.

Wallace R. 1990. "How to Argue about Practical Reason." *Mind* 99: 355–385.

Williams, B. 1981. "Internal and External Reasons." In his *Moral Luck.* Cambridge: Cambridge University Press. Reprinted in this volume, chapter 4. Page references in the text are to this volume.

Williams, B. 1995. "Internal Reasons and the Obscurity of Blame." In his *Making Sense of Humanity and Other Philosophical Papers, 1982–1993*, pp. 35–45. Cambridge: Cambridge University Press.

Chapter 8

The *Protagoras*: A Science of Practical Reasoning

Martha Nussbaum

And look: I gave them numbering, chief of all the stratagems.

Prometheus, in Aeschylus [?], *Prometheus Bound*

Every circumstance by which the condition of an individual can be influenced, being remarked and inventoried, nothing ... [is] left to chance, caprice, or unguided discretion, everything being surveyed and set down in dimension, number, weight, and measure.

Jeremy Bentham, *Pauper Management Improved*

They did not want to look on the naked face of luck (*tuchē*), so they turned themselves over to science (*technē*). As a result, they are released from their dependence on luck; but not from their dependence on science.

Hippocratic treatise *On Science* (*Peri Technēs*), late fifth century B.C.

The *Antigone* spoke of a life lived 'on the razor's edge of luck'. It warned against overambitious attempts to eliminate luck from human life, displaying both their internal failures and their problematic relation to the richness of values recognized in ordinary belief. Its conclusion appeared conservative: human beings had better stay with 'established conventions' in spite of the risks these leave in place. Both Aeschylean and Sophoclean tragedy have, in this way, combined a keen sense of our exposure to fortune with an awareness that some genuine human value is inseparable from this condition. This recognition left, it seems, little room for decisive progress on our problems.

The late fifth century in Athens, the time of Plato's youth, was a time both of acute anxiety and of exuberant confidence in human power. If human life seemed more than ever exposed to *tuchē* in all its forms, Athenians were also more than ever gripped by the idea that progress might bring about the elimination of ungoverned contingency from social life. This hope found expression in an antithesis and a story: the contrast between *tuchē*, luck,[1] and *technē*, human art or science; and the accompanying frequently told story of human progress against contingency through the reception or discovery of the *technai*. Plato's *Protagoras*, set in that time, tells the story, criticizes a conservative Athenian interpretation of it, and proposes a philosophical addition: Socrates argues that really decisive progress in human social life will be made only when we have developed a new *technē*, one that assimilates practical deliberation to counting, weighing, and measuring.

Throughout the dialogues that we shall study here, Plato's elaboration of radical ethical proposals is motivated by an acute sense of the problems caused by ungoverned luck in human life. The need of human beings for philosophy is, for him, deeply connected with their exposure to luck; the elimination of this exposure is a primary task of the philosophical art as he conceives it. His conception of this art in the *Protagoras* differs in certain ways from the conception worked out in dialogues of his 'middle' period.[2] But his sense of the nature and urgency of the problems behind philosophy remains constant. So does the belief that these problems can only be solved by a new kind of expert: one whose knowledge will take practical deliberation beyond the confusion of ordinary practice, fulfilling an aspiration to scientific precision and control already contained within ordinary belief. That is why the *Protagoras*, which takes as its explicit subject the human hope for science and the relationship between science and ordinary belief, is a good place to begin our investigation of Plato's relationship to the problems of *tuchē*, as ordinary belief depicts them.

The dialogue stages a competition between two figures, each of whom claims to be the herald of a social or political *technē* that will add a new chapter to the story of human progress through the *technai*. We should, therefore, prepare ourselves to appreciate the force of their proposals by telling ourselves this story, as a reader of the dialogue would know it.[3]

Once, a long time ago, human beings wandered over the surface of the earth and had no way to make themselves safe. Everything that happened was a threat. Rain drenched their uncovered skin; snow stung; hail slashed. The sun's dry heat brought searing thirst and fever to their unprotected heads. Helpless, they huddled in sunless caves beneath the ground. No hunting or farming skills gave them a stable source of food; no tame animals plowed or carried. No weather-diviner's art prepared them for the next day. No medical science healed their vulnerable bodies.

Nor could they turn for help to their fellow human beings, undertaking cooperative projects, communicating in shared language. Speechlessness and wilderness kept them apart. Isolated, silent, naked, they could neither record the past nor plan for the future; they could not even comfort each other in their present misery. 'Like shapes in dreams, they mixed up everything at random as their lives went on.' But so shapeless, without stability or structure, it could hardly have felt like a life.

These proto-humans (for their existence is so far more bestial than human) would soon have died off, victims of starvation, overexposure, the attacks of stronger beasts. Then the kindness of Prometheus (god named for the foresight and planning that his gifts make possible) granted to these creatures, so exposed to *tuchē*, the gift of the *technai*. House-building, farming, yoking and taming, metal-working, shipbuilding, hunting; prophecy, dream-divination, weather-prediction, counting and calculating; articulate speech and writing; the practice of medicine; the art of building dwelling-places—with all these arts they preserved and improved their lives. Human existence became safer, more predictable; there was a measure of control over contingency.

But still, in these cities of human beings (for now we are entitled to call them that), *tuchē* was not defeated. Many of their most cherished pursuits (especially their social pursuits) were vulnerable to uncontrolled happenings. Nor was there any stable harmony among the diverse commitments and values that characterized an ordinary human life. Furthermore, humans regularly found themselves 'overcome', as if by an alien power, by the force of their own passions, which both distorted their view of the good and blocked its effective pursuit. In all these ways their experience threw them into confusion, so that in their actions and choices, both of great things and of small, they felt themselves to be in continual danger. Such a life did not seem worth living for an artful creature like the human being. They searched for another life-saving art.

It is a story of gradually increasing human control over contingency. Its general outlines are familiar to us from the *Antigone*. Socrates and Protagoras will compete to fill out its final chapter. The dialogue presents us with a view of the problems that such a science must solve and offers us two deeply divergent views of what it can and should be. Socrates' proposal, in which numbering and measuring are central, is motivated, I shall argue, by the inability of the Protagorean 'art' to solve pressing problems with which both thinkers are concerned. The dialogue as a whole is a complex reflection about the relationship of sciences to problems, *technē* to *tuchē*; about the way in which science both saves us and transforms us, helps us attain our ends and reshapes the ends themselves. We can begin, then, by seeing how its characters and dramatic setting bring into focus the problems that the new science is supposed to solve. Then (after making some observations about the background conception of *technē*) we shall approach the rival proposals.

I

Plato chooses to set this dialogue right on the 'razor's edge'. It is a time of pride and prosperity—about two years before the outbreak of the Peloponnesian War, three years before the great plague that devastated Athens, both physically and morally.[4] Diseases of the body, diseases of character, the disease of war—all, we know, will shortly strike, unforeseen, this intelligent city that prides itself so much on artfulness and foresight. Since the reader, by hindsight, is aware that a vulnerable moral consensus is soon to be unhinged by external pressures, by the pull of conflicting obligations, by the strength of the appetitive desires, since he knows that among this dialogue's characters some will soon be dead and others will soon be killing, he will feel impatience with the lack of foresight that says that things in Athens are all right as they are. He will look for signs of disease beneath the optimism; he will look for a pessimistic and radical doctor.

In this dialogue Socrates is young—thirty-six in 433, and relatively little-known. His defeat of Protagoras may be his first public 'success'. Plato's dramatic portrait shows that, in other ways as well, he is not the Socrates of the *Symposium* (dramatic date 416) or even of the *Republic* (422).[5] A friend stops him on the road and asks him where he is coming from. Without even waiting for an answer, the friend knows: 'It's obvious that it's from your hunt [the word is the word for giving chase with a pack of dogs] after the beauty of Alcibiades.' (How, we wonder, is it obvious? Because that's his constant preoccupation? Is he distracted from all other pursuits by this hunt, like the characters disdainfully described by Diotima in the *Symposium*?[6]) This friend—not much like later friends of Socrates, but accepted here as a friend nonetheless—now teases him, saying that the boy is past his prime: he's already growing a beard. 'What of it?' Socrates replies, entering into the spirit of erotic gossip. After all, Homer (whose authority he seems happy to cite) says that this is the most delicious age of all. The friend, who seems to be a regular recipient of

Socrates' erotic confidences, now presses him: how, then, is the seduction progressing? (For Socrates here is the needy searching *erastēs*, Alcibiades the beautiful *erōmenos*, though these roles were later to be reversed.) Socrates is optimistic: Alcibiades is both kind and helpful. We are struck by the degree of Socrates' erotic responsiveness to the particularity of a single bodily individual; such everyday eroticism will figure in his *Symposium* speech only as an unacceptable way of living that philosophy helps us to avoid. Socrates says there that he was *persuaded* by Diotima to undertake the ascent, which promised freedom from the slavish love of unpredictable individuals; he acknowledges that he was different before this persuasion. Here we catch a glimpse of that difference.

But in Socrates' next remarks, we also see evidence that the ascent is in progress. His desire for the (alleged) wisdom of Protagoras made him, he says, completely forgetful of Alcibiades, even in his physical presence. And he considers the beauty of wisdom to be 'more beautiful' than Alcibiades' personal charm. It is important that he is willing already to treat this personal beauty as comparable, apparently along a single quantitative scale, with the beauty of philosophy or understanding. This is a crucial feature both of the *Protagoras* science of measurement and of the *Symposium* ascent, and a salient element of continuity between them. Socrates' remarks are in part ironic, since the conversation with Protagoras has already taken place and he knows that he has nothing to learn from Protagoras. But we do not need to doubt the sincerity of his assertions about the beauty of wisdom and his commitment to its pursuit. Young Socrates, then, is and is not persuaded by Diotima; he goes in and out of focus. But his vestigial love for the individuality of pieces of the physical world seems to be yielding increasingly to the judgments that will ground the science.

Something similar happens in the (dramatically) nearly contemporary *Charmides*.[7] At one point Socrates, inflamed by passion at the sight of Charmides' naked body inside his loose cloak, loses all control over himself and his practical judgments, becoming like a lion in pursuit of a fawn (155D–E, cf. 154B). But both before and after this moment he is pressing the view that beauties of soul and body are similar and commensurable, and that the soul is of far greater importance. Such a view, as we shall see, is good medicine for such losses of control.

Having praised wisdom, the Socrates of the *Protagoras* now takes a seat formerly occupied by a slave-boy (even as his slavish passion for Alcibiades yields place to his love of philosophy) and narrates the rest of the story (310A). It is the story of a competition for a soul. Hippocrates, a well-born, naïve young man, came to Socrates' house before dawn, full of eagerness to go and enroll himself as a pupil of the visiting sophist Protagoras. He is, strikingly, a namesake of the great doctor, leading practitioner and theorist of the new medical science, whose works extol the progress made by this *technē*. The connection of names is prominently stressed by Socrates, who also draws an elaborate parallel between Hippocrates' science and the alleged science of the sophist (331B ff., 313C ff.). After some brief questioning, it emerges that Hippocrates views his relationship to Protagoras as analogous to that of patient to doctor. He and Socrates now agree that there is a therapy of the soul that is analogous to the doctor's therapy of the body: as one goes to a doctor to get physically healed, so the proper end of philosophy (sophistry) is the healing of the soul. Socrates warns Hippocrates of the need for circumspection before he turns over his soul to an alleged expert for cure. Since the treatment will change the soul for better or worse, it is important to ask questions about the doctor's knowledge and the healing it promises.

What diseases of the soul are recognized by these seekers after therapy? For if we can be clear about the dialogue's depiction of human problems we will be better able to assess the competing solutions. (To some extent we must use hindsight, looking in the opening sequence for examples of difficulties that are explicitly recognized later on.) We see here a high degree of confusion about values, about what ought to be pursued and what not. Socrates and his friend disagree about what beauty is and what beauties are important. Socrates himself is confused about his erotic and philosophical motivations. Hippocrates has rushed off in pursuit of wisdom, of which he knows nothing, just because it sounds attractive. He doesn't understand, either, why he did not come earlier to tell Socrates about this runaway slave (310E): he knows he was distracted by something else, but he doesn't seem at any point to have made a deliberate choice in accordance with any clear criterion. We recognize, then, a need later stressed by Socrates (356C–E): the need for an orderly procedure of choice that will save us from being buffeted by the 'appearances' of the moment. Ordinary deliberation looks confused, unsystematic, and consequently lacking in control over both present and future.

This general problem grows out of and is linked to several that are more specific. We notice here, in fact, versions of all three of our problems of *tuchē*. First, we notice the vulnerability of these people to luck through their attachment to vulnerable objects and activities. The love affair with Alcibiades may go well or badly; this is not in Socrates' control. Insofar as he attaches importance to a pursuit and an object that are not in his grasp or even readily manipulable, he puts his own life at the mercy of luck. He does not know or control his future. (He cannot be, as he later is (361D), the new Prometheus.)

We see, too, that the values pursued by these people are plural. They see no clear way of rendering them commensurable or of avoiding serious conflicts among them. The hunt after Alcibiades pulls against the pursuit of philosophical discourse; a competing claim makes Hippocrates lose sight of the problem of the runaway slave. No common coin of value gives them a purchase on these conflicts, making them less stark.

We see, finally, the power of passion and need to derail practical planning. Socrates' pursuit of Alcibiades has often eclipsed all his other pursuits; the friend is more interested in love affairs than in anything else; the erotic and disorderly personality of Alcibiades dominates the scene. Hippocrates is 'overcome' and distracted from his plans by bodily need too: not, in his case, by *erōs*, but by the need for sleep (310C8–D2). Erotic need and the need for sleep are two features of ordinary human life conspicuously absent from the 'cured' Socrates of the *Symposium*.

Those are the diseases. The correct *technē* of practical choice would seem to be the one that could cure them.

II

Protagoras and Socrates agree that we need a *technē* governing practical choice.[8] They differ, at first, concerning the nature of the science required. The argument ends with agreement of all present that only a practical *technē* of the type favored by Socrates can 'save the lives' of human beings. Before we can assess their proposals we must understand what they are proposals about. What is the common notion of which the two are producing rival specifications? To ask this requires a historical digression, but one necessary for the adequate pursuit of our main line of argument.

The word *technē* is translated in several ways: 'craft', 'art', and 'science' are the most frequent. Examples of recognized *technai* include items that we would call by each of these three names. There are house-building, shoemaking, and weaving; horsemanship, flute-playing, dancing, acting, and poetry-writing; medicine, mathematics, and meteorology. The Greek word is more inclusive than any one of these English terms. It is also very closely associated with the word '*epistēmē*', usually translated 'knowledge', 'understanding'; or 'science', 'body of knowledge' (depending on whether it is being used of the known or of the cognitive condition of the knower). In fact, to judge from my own work and in the consensus of philologists, there is, at least through Plato's time, no systematic or general distinction between *epistēmē* and *technē*.[9] Even in some of Aristotle's most important writings on this topic, the two terms are used interchangeably.[10] This situation obtains in the *Protagoras*.[11]

The best place to begin searching for the ordinary conception of *technē* is the *technē/tuchē* antithesis, which both displays, and, by its pervasiveness, shapes it. Traces of the antithesis are evident already in Homer; by the time of Thucydides and the Hippocratic writer, it is a commonplace. The contrast is between living at the mercy of *tuchē* and living a life made safer or more controlled by (some) *technē*. *Technē* is closely associated with practical judgment or wisdom (*sophia*, *gnōmē*), with forethought, planning, and prediction. To be at the mercy of *tuchē* where *technē* is available is to be witless (e.g. Democritus B197); indeed, Democritus goes so far as to say that the whole notion of *tuchē*'s power is just an excuse that people have invented to cover up for their own lack of practical resourcefulness (B119).

Technē, then, is a deliberate application of human intelligence to some part of the world, yielding some control over *tuchē*; it is concerned with the management of need and with prediction and control concerning future contingencies. The person who lives by *technē* does not come to each new experience without foresight or resource. He possesses some sort of systematic grasp, some way of ordering the subject matter, that will take him to the new situation well prepared, removed from blind dependence on what happens.

To go further in setting out criteria for *technē* in the fifth and early fourth centuries, we can turn above all to the earlier treatises of the Hippocratic corpus, especially the treatises *On Medicine in the Old Days* (*Peri Archaiēs Iētrikēs*, abbreviated *Vet. Med.*), and *On Science* (*Peri Technēs*, or *De Arte*)—both probably to be dated late in the fifth century. For here we find what we do not find in contemporary literary and philosophical texts, namely a systematic *argument* that some human enterprise, in this case medicine, really deserves the title of *technē*. Criteria that remain implicit elsewhere are here explicitly stated. A similar list of criteria emerges, much later, from Aristotle's reflection on *technē* (especially the medical *technē*) in *Metaphysics* I.I. I shall refer to this discussion as well, since, though considerably after the *Protagoras* in date, its aim is to articulate a shared ongoing conception, a task which Aristotle here performs with his usual sensitivity. His results agree remarkably well with the medical texts; they may display Aristotle's own medical background. We find, in these sources, four features of *technē* stressed above all: (1) universality; (2) teachability; (3) precision; (4) concern with explanation.

1. *Universality* 'A *technē*', writes Aristotle, 'comes into being when from many notions gained by experience a universal judgment about a group of similar things arises' (981a5–7). He contrasts a hypothesis about what helped this particular case of disease with a general theory about a group of cases judged relevantly similar. Only the latter can be *technē*; and in virtue of this universality it can deliver true predictions concerning future cases. The fifth-century evidence stresses this same feature. The *Epidemics*, among the earliest Hippocratic texts, was exciting precisely because it gathered the experience of many similar cases into a general unitary theory of the disease that could provide physicians with an antecedent grasp of the prognosis for a new case. The authors of *On Science* and *On Medicine in the Old Days* answer charges that patients are healed by luck, not *technē*, by pointing to the reliable and general connection between a certain sort of treatment and a certain result: their procedures, they say, are not a series of *ad hoc* maneuvers, but 'A principle and a charted course' (*Vet. Med.* 1.2; *De Arte* 4). Xenophon, similarly, praises the ability of a person of *technē* to make a systematic unity of disparate elements.[12]

2. *Teachability* The universality of *technē* yields the possibility of teaching (Ar. *Metaph.* 981b7–8). Unordered experience can only be *had*, as chance brings it about; but *technē* can be communicated in advance of the experience, since it has grouped many experiences together and produced an account. The Hippocratic doctors make a similar point. The reason that some doctors are good and others are bad is that some have studied something that the others have not (*Vet. Med.* 1); the doctor must say this in order to support the claim of medicine to be a *technē*.

3. *Precision Technē* brings precision (*akribeia*) where before there was fuzziness and vagueness. The notion of *akribeia* is extremely important in fifth-century debates over *technē*. Originally connected, apparently, with true, precise construction of some manufactured object, *akribeia* comes to be associated, in medical debates, both with lawlike regularity or invariance and with fidelity to data: medicine is precise, *akribēs*, to the extent that its rules hold true, without exception, of all the cases, no matter how many and how varied they are. The acquisition of *akribeia* is frequently

linked with the notion of having a *measure* or a *standard*. The carpenter gets a precise fit by measuring correctly; measuring helps him to make his art more artful.[13] The doctor (on the defensive here, as we might expect) apologizes for the lack of *akribeia* in his art by pointing out that the measure to which he must, *faute de mieux*, refer is something far more elusive than number or weight—namely, the perceptions of each patient's body (*Vet. Med.* 9; cf. also the later *On Sterile Women*, which argues that treatment cannot be a matter of weighing). This means that the best he can hope for is to make only small mistakes.

4. *Concern with explanation* Finally, *technē* brings with it a concern for explaining: it asks and answers 'why' questions about its procedures (cf. *Vet. Med.* 20, Ar. *Metaph.* 981a28–30). A doctor who has learned the medical *technē* differs from his more *ad hoc* counterpart not just in his ability to predict what will happen if a certain treatment is applied, but also in his ability to explain precisely why and how the treatment works. The person of mere experience could tell you that on various occasions eating a lot of cheese gave the patient a stomach-ache. One stage further on, we find a doctor who says 'Cheese is a bad food, because it gives a stomach-ache to the person who eats a lot of it' (*Vet. Med.* 20). The author of *Vet. Med.*, and Aristotle, insist that this second person's knowledge would still fall short of *technē*: 'He must say what sort of pain it is and why it arises and what part of the human being is badly affected.' In numerous examples this medical author stresses that the doctor must be able to isolate the element *in* the food or the treatment that causes good or harm, and to explain how (through what sort of causal interaction with the body) the effect takes place. This ability, he points out, is closely linked to the goals of prediction and control: for without this information 'he will not be able to know what will result [sc. from a given treatment] or to use it correctly'.

These four features all bear upon the goal of mastering contingency; all are taken to be necessary features of *technē* on account of the relation in which they stand to this goal. Universality and explanation yield control over the future in virtue of their orderly grasp of the past; teaching enables past work to yield future progress; precision yields consistent accuracy, the minimization of failure. A person who says (as many did in the fifth century) that practical reasoning should become a *technē* is likely, then, to be demanding a systematization and unification of practice that will yield accounts and some sort of orderly grasp; he will want principles that can be taught and explanations of how desired results are produced. He will want to eliminate some of the chanciness from human social life.

One reason why it has been necessary to set this background out is that there has recently been an attempt to give the demand for a practical *techne* a much narrower interpretation. This issue must now be confronted, since it will decisively affect the interpretation of the *Protagoras*. In *Plato's Moral Theory*, Terence Irwin has claimed that '*techne*', like English 'craft', includes as a part of its meaning the notion of an external end or product, identifiable and specifiable independently of the craft and its activities.[14] What the craft does is to provide instrumental means to the realization of this independently specifiable end. Any claim that practical deliberation is, or can be, a *techne*—or any analogy between deliberation or virtue and any of the recognized *technai*, whether gymnastics, flute-playing, medicine, or shoemaking—is, on Irwin's reading, the specific, and dubious, claim that there is a human good that can be identified and desired independently of deliberation and the virtues; and that practical rationality is merely the finding of instrumental means to this external good.[15]

It is easy to see how crucial this issue is for a reader of the *Protagoras*. For both characters propose and wish to teach a practical *techne*; and Socrates' proposal, as we shall see, conforms to Irwin's constraints while Protagoras's does not. Irwin's picture implies, then, that Protagoras is not putting forward anything that has even a *prima facie* claim to be *techne*; he, and anyone who takes him seriously, will just be misunderstanding the meaning of the word. Besides the fact that we do not wish a serious interlocutor to be starting from a silly verbal mistake, it is also curious that none of the other highly intelligent characters, not even Prodicus, enamored of verbal fine points, charges him with this error. Nor, on Irwin's account, is the debate for the soul of Hippocrates a genuine debate: for assuming that what is wanted is a *techne* of practical reason, Socrates wins hands down. It will be as if Hippocrates came to an appliance store and, asking for the best vacuum cleaner, was offered, by two salesmen, a choice between a vacuum cleaner and an electric fan. It would be more philosophically interesting, and more worthy of Plato, if Socrates and Protagoras were putting up two serious rival candidates each of which might with some force be defended as a *techne*.

Now in fact the evidence about the ordinary conception of *techne* gives no support to Irwin's claim. No major scholar writing on the subject has even entertained such a theory; intellectual historians of the stature of

Dodds, Edelstein, and Guthrie concur in sketching a different story, the one I have attempted to flesh out above.[16] Nor is there a single prominent ancient author who speaks of 'techne' only in connection with craft production of a separately specifiable product. Even Xenophon, who so often shows sympathy with an instrumentalist view of deliberation, answers a question about the ends of the *techne* of household management by insisting that the activity of managing the house well is itself the end.[17] Aristotle makes a point of saying that there are *some* arts in which the work or *ergon* is a product external to the artist's activities— for example, housebuilding; and *others* in which the activities are themselves ends, for example mathematics, flute-playing, lyre-playing.[18] The Hellenistic divisions of the *technai* tell the same story.

If we now consider not statements about *techne* but examples of recognized *technai*, with ordinary beliefs about them, we find that several types are well represented. There are, first, the clearly productive *technai* such as shoemaking and housebuilding, where the product can indeed be specified (and desired) apart from any knowledge of the craftsman's activities. Even here, however, we note that what makes shoemaking *artful* and *good*, rather than merely adequate, may not be specifiable externally and in advance: for once the art exists, its own activities—fine stitching, elegant ornamentation—tend to become ends in themselves. The Greeks recognized this from the time of Homer. Achilles did not value his shield simply because it served well the requirements he could have set down antecedently. It is an example of high *techne* just because the craftsman has done so much more than Achilles' untutored imagination could have conceived or requested.

Next, there are arts like the medical art, where there is a vague end, health, that the layman can specify as desirable, and towards which, as a product, the practitioner's activity aims. But here one crucial part of the practitioner's work will be to get a more precise specification of the end itself. If he has no theory of what health is, it will be impossible for him to work out instrumental means to health. When a doctor prides himself on his *techne*, he includes his work on the end as well as his investigation of productive means.[19]

Finally, there are arts that seem to have purely internal ends: flute-playing, dancing, athletic achievement. Here there is no product at all: what is valued is the artful activity in itself. And yet, because of the disciplined, precise, and teachable character of these practices, they are unhesitatingly awarded the title of *techne*.[20] They are forms of order imposed upon the previously unordered and ungrasped continua of sound and motion.[21]

There are, then, several varieties of *techne*, with several structures. This digression, necessary to remove an obstacle to reading the *Protagoras* as a serious debate about the varieties of political *techne*, has also prepared us to understand the force of Protagoras's internal-end proposal. But now, surveying the full range of the fifth-century arts in the light of their underlying corporate aim, the elimination of *tuche*, we can make some observations that will prepare us, too, to understand why Socrates rejects it. Let us ask which arts are, so to speak, the most artful: which best deliver the goods of control, prediction, precise grasp. Now we discover that there may be desiderata towards this goal that are not present in all of the recognized arts. Here the force of Irwin's idea begins to become clear; it is not adequate as an account of the general conception of *techne*, but it singles out an important feature that helps certain arts to make striking advances in subduing *tuche*. For if there is something *external*, clear, and antecedently specifiable that counts as the end result of an art, its search for procedures can, it seems, be more definite and precise than in the arts where the end consists in acting in certain ways. A competition in shoemaking (abstracting from its aesthetic side) can be adjudicated with precision, because the externality of the end provides a clear measure of the activities' success. A competition in the art of flute-playing is much more elusive, since part of what is at stake is what we shall count as the end. We can easily feel in such cases more as if there is no decisive victory over *tuche*, no clear progress. Then again, *singleness* in an end appears more tractable than plurality; for if ends are plural we may need some further criterion or measure to adjudicate among them. Finally, an end which permits of *quantitative measure* seems to yield more precision than an end that cannot be so measured. (We shall return to this important idea later.)

If we put all this together, we can say that it is possible to have a *bona fide techne* that will be qualitative, plural in its ends, and in which the art activities themselves constitute the end; but such a *techne* seems unlikely to yield the precision and control that would be yielded by an art with a single, quantitatively measurable, external goal. Someone who was deeply gripped by problems of *tuche* would naturally prefer a *techne* of this kind, which would promise more decisive progress beyond unsystematized human judgments. Where and to what extent this sort of *techne* is possible and appropriate remains, however, a matter of dispute.[22]

Such, I shall now argue, is the shape of the debate in the *Protagoras*. Protagoras, conservative and humanistic, wants a *technē* that stays close to the ordinary practice of deliberation, systematizing it only a little. Socrates, more deeply gripped by the urgency of human practical problems, finds this insufficient. We must go further, be more thoroughly scientific, if we are to 'save our lives'—even if science makes those saved lives different.

III

Protagoras claims to teach a *technē* of practical reasoning. To display the nature of his art, he tells a story of human progress.[23] Its early sections show the power of *technai* to save the lives of living creatures generally; its last describes the progress made (and still being made) by human beings through an art of deliberation and the social excellences. We might at first think that only the last section gives us insight into the progress offered by the sophist himself. But his characterization of progress earlier in the speech reveals his conception of the relationship between arts and ends, life-saving and life-living. This is an important aspect of his teaching, which prepares us for the conservative nature of his social proposal and gives us some questions to ask, on his behalf, about Socrates' more radical strategy.

The story begins with the creation by the gods of mortal creatures, creatures vulnerable to contingency. Formed from a mixture of earth and fire, they live inside the earth until the appointed time for their emergence

Table 1

	Shoe making	Flute playing	Medicine	Land measuring	Protagorean deliberation	Socratic deliberation
End single	Yes	No	?	Yes	No	Yes
End external (specifiable apart from the art activities)	Yes	No	Partly (see above)	Yes	No	Yes
Measure quantitative	Partly	No	No	Yes	No	Yes

Note: This table is offered without further comment as an introduction to this and the next sections of this chapter.

into the light. At this point, Titans Prometheus and Epimetheus are charged with the task of distributing 'to each kind' powers or capabilities that will enable its members to survive and reproduce. Distinctions among the kinds appear, then, to pre-exist the distribution of arts and capabilities. The gods talk of kinds, even of allotting suitable powers to each kind; but the species, mere lumps of material stuff, are not yet in possession of any of the distinctive capabilities and ways of acting that currently constitute them as the species we know. To these characterless subjects the gods assign the powers that will enable the kind to survive, 'being careful by these devices that no species should be destroyed' (320E–321A). The strangeness of this story—a strangeness which, as we shall suggest below, seems to be intentional—forces closer inspection.

We are asked to imagine an uncharacterized object: a lump of earth and fire, named, let us say, 'horse'. This object now gets made into the speedy, hooved, oat-eating, high-spirited creature we know. We are, then, invited to believe that horses might have been otherwise, had the gods made different decisions. They might, for example, have been timid, seed-eating, nest-dwelling creatures capable of flying through the air. The same goes for the particular species member: the same Bucephalus we admire might have lived in a nest and eaten worms. We discover, as we are meant to, that this is incoherent. A creature that did not have the ability to run in a certain horsy way and to live a characteristic horsy life would not be a horse. If it had the 'arts'[24] of a bird, it would just be a bird. Nor would Bucephalus be one and the same creature if he were to undergo a change with respect to these central characteristics. There might be a Bucephalus in the trees; but it would only be homonymous, not identical, with the one on which Aristotle's pupil rode. When we pick Bucephalus out and trace him through space and time, we pick him out under a kind-concept, not as a bare lump; our practices implicitly rule out his having or coming to have the characteristic capabilities of birds. Central to our conception of his kind are the 'arts', abilities, and ways of life that ostensibly get distributed *to* species already constituted. Before the distribution there was just a lump; after that there is a horse and horsiness. We begin, then, to see, as we try to follow Protagoras' story straight, and fail, to what extent the 'arts', broadly construed as the creature's characteristic abilities and ways of functioning in the world, make living things the things they are.[25]

The incoherence and its moral might, of course, be inadvertent; but there are signs that Protagoras is well aware of the two different ways his account might be read and is deliberately provoking these reflections. For now we encounter this sentence: 'Epimetheus, not being altogether wise, didn't notice that he had used up all the capabilities on the non-rational creatures; so last of all he was left with the human kind (*to anthrōpōn genos*) quite unprovided for.' Here the oddness is blatant and sounds like a deliberate pointer. What can it mean, we wonder, to speak of using powers up on the *non-rational*, so that there is nothing left for *the human being*, when we know (and will be told again) that the human being (or whatever it currently is) is not yet a rational being? The distinction between the rational and the non-rational is presupposed in the very story of the gift of rationality. Protagoras lets us see that there is no coherent way of talking about the human being, and contrasting him with the rest of nature, without mentioning the distinctive capabilities and ways of acting that make him the creature he is. Rationality is not just an instrument given to a creature already constituted with a nature and natural ends; it is an essential element in this creature's nature, a central part of the answer to a 'What is it?' question about that creature; and it is constitutive of, not merely instrumental to, whatever ends that creature forms.

In each of these first two stages, then, 'arts' were given to creatures ostensibly to *save* those creatures' lives. What happened instead was that the art *created* a form of life, and creatures, that had not previously existed. We now must inquire about the status of the 'art' most central to this dialogue, the social or political art. Are the 'gifts of Zeus' a *technē* that merely serves previously existing human ends, or does Protagoras depict them as functions that go to make us what we are? To answer this we must, like Hippocrates, continue to listen to the story.

We now have beings that look something like human beings, living a life that looks something like a human life; they have houses, clothing, farming, religious ceremonies. They are still having trouble about survival. Apparently they do live in clusters—for they use speech, reproduce, and worship. Later references to the role of the 'expert' in these Promethean *technai* suggest even some elementary form of social organization, a simple, art-based division of labor. What they lack are laws, civic education, the institution of punishment. About their emotional and interpersonal lives we are told nothing, except that they wronged one another. We do not know what sorts of feelings and attachments, if any, bound them to one another. We may suppose, as does Hume in his parallel story, that the sexual tie gave rise to some attachments; perhaps also, again with Hume, that there were some ties of affection, even of acknowledged obligation, between parents and children.

We might now feel that we have a great deal, if not all, of our characteristic human nature and ends. At this point, there are two directions that our imaginary history of the arts might take. We might decide that what we have so far given these people is sufficient to make them human beings, their nature and ends human nature and ends. Then we would say that any further arts these creatures discover to help them in the war against contingency will be correctly understood as arts instrumental to a pre-set external end: the maintenance and protection of characteristically human life. The political art is a tool in the service of an end already constituted. Such is Hume's account of the origin and function of justice. Justice figures as an 'artificial virtue' in the service of ends separate from it; it is natural only insofar as it is a necessary means to natural human ends, and it is human nature to be resourceful in devising the necessary means to these.[26] This account tells us that we can coherently imagine a really *human* life in which human beings lack justice and political institutions. Such a life might be full of danger and difficulty, but it would still be recognizably ours. It would have all our natural ends in it. We would treat such people as members of our community; we would recognize in them the nature that we share. The human being is not by nature a political creature.[27]

Protagoras might, on the other hand, give an account of justice that would treat it as more like rationality than like shoemaking. He would then concede that there was a time when creatures bearing some resemblance to human beings lived without political institutions; he might even concede that these institutions arose at some point in history, in response to particular pressures. But he would insist that these institutions and these associated feelings have so shaped the lives of the creatures who have them that we cannot describe their *nature* without mentioning their membership in these institutions and their attachment to them. Nor can we enumerate the ultimate ends of this creature without mentioning his love of his city, his attachment to justice, his feelings of reverence for and obligation to other human beings. Our nature is a political nature.[28] Protagoras's account of justice is of this second kind. His genetic story, far from showing how easy it is to view the various *technai* as instrumental and so separable from human nature, actually shows how difficult it is to describe a recognizably human creature unless one endows him not only with rationality, but also with political aims and attachments.

A Humean view of the 'origin' of justice would characterize it as a means to human survival and flourishing, where these can be completely characterized without reference to the social. The gifts of Zeus are indeed introduced as means to the survival of mankind. Zeus is said to be moved by fear that 'our kind (*genos*) would be totally wiped out' (322C); this implies that a human kind pre-exists the gift of justice. But it is striking that as soon as Zeus's gifts are distributed, even the apparently pre-set end of human survival is no longer characterized in a way that separates survival from the city. Zeus's gifts are now called 'the principles of organization of cities, and the bonds of friendship' (322C); 'cities could not come into being' if they were distributed differently (322D); the law-breaker is a 'plague on the city' (322D5); if all do not share in the social excellences, 'there can be no city at all' (323A; cf. 324E1, 327A1, A4). What we thought was an external end begins to look internal, as though the arts of Zeus have transformed and now help to constitute this being's nature.

Again, a Humean teacher, if he were to give an honest account of his *ultimate purposes* in dealing with justice, must exclude from the description of the end all reference to social and political virtue, speaking only of whatever pleasure, success, wealth, and happiness are specifiable and desirable apart from the *polis*. But Protagoras's announced goal is, through his *technē*, to 'make human beings good citizens', teaching them good deliberation both about their household and about the affairs of the city. Although Hippocrates desires to become renowned, Protagoras promises him instead that he will be 'better' (*beltiōn*). He claims 'to excel all others in making people fine and good'—never (as was common at the time) to excel in helping people to realize ends that are separable from those of the community. He characterizes 'the excellence of a man' (*andros aretēn*) as a blend of justice, moderation, and piety—all civic excellences and gifts of Zeus.

The rest of his speech fills out this non-Humean picture of social virtue. Moral education is characterized as answering to a need that is part of our nature. Zeus gave us a natural tendency towards justice; but it must be developed by communal training.[29] 'All of human life stands in need of the proper rhythm (*euruthmias*) and harmonious adjustment' (326B5); the adjustment is not natural, but the need for it is. Thus the correction of children is compared to the straightening of wood that is gnarled and bent (325D); the implication is that moral training promotes healthy and natural growth, attacking problems which, left unattended, would blight the child's full natural development. Like Pindar's plant, the child needs external assistance to reach its natural ends. Moral training is the straightening of the tree, moral excellence its straightness—an excellence thoroughly intrinsic to our account of what it is to be a healthy, normal tree. (On a Humean view, the social excellences would be more like sun and rain: necessary but external, and replaceable by other means, should these be found.) Similarly, the punishment of the older offender is said to make him 'better' (*beltiōn*) and more healthy (contrast *aniaton*, 'incurable', 325A). This greater health consists in a reluctance, resulting from learning, to 'commit injustice again'. Social excellence is, then, to our psychological nature as health is to our bodily nature—an intrinsic (non-instrumental) good, which is deeply involved in all our other pursuits: 'what every person must have and with which he must do anything else he wants to learn or to do' (325A).[30] Protagoras's hypothetical citizens say of the person who does not share in them, not that he is stupid, not that he is a public menace, but that he is not one of them; he 'should not be among human beings at all'.[31]

Protagoras's question was, what *technē* do we have, or can we find, that has the power to make human beings good at deliberation and in control of their lives? In answer, he has told us a story about the fundamental role played by arts and capabilities in constituting the characteristic ways of life of living creatures. His story has shown us, in particular, that a capability for social excellence and for its proper development are a deep part of our human nature and way of life. But where, in all this, is the science? What expertise does Protagoras claim to teach? He recognizes that there is a *prima facie* problem about reconciling his insistence that all adults are teachers with his claim to be an expert. But he insists that there need be no contradiction, using, appropriately, an analogy to the learning of language (328A–B). Even if all adults are competent native speakers and teach the language to their children, there is still room for an expert who can take people 'a little further along the road'— presumably by making the speaker more explicitly and reflectively aware of the structures of his practice and the interconnections of its different elements. Even so, an expert ethical teacher can make the already well-trained young person more aware of the nature and interrelationships of his ethical commitments. It seems fair to view this very speech as a contribution to that sort of education. Protagoras's modest claim is not unlike the claim that Aristotle will make on his own behalf; and Aristotle too will insist that this sort of teaching can lead to the improvement of practice. But we must now ask: *how*? What progress could Protagoras's historical and descriptive teaching help us to make with the problems to which the dialogue has already directed our attention?

We can claim on behalf of this speech that it brings to the surface for reflection some important features of our practices of identifying individuals and kinds; in the process it offers us a deeper understanding of the place of the social and political in our own self-conception. It shows us explicitly the arts and orderly practices with which we already, in our cities, save our lives from the pain of conflict and the disorder of passional weakness. By raising current practice to a new level of self-awareness, by giving a general account of human nature and the place of the social excellences in it, Protagoras may fairly claim to be teaching a *technē*, an orderly understanding of a subject matter that displays connections, offers explanations, and has a certain degree of universality and communicability. And to some extent such a *technē*, or such an explicit and general formulation of the implicit *technē* of ordinary practice, can surely help us in the face of the practical dilemmas from which we turned to art.

A clearer articulation of our human self-conception gives us some standards for choice among competing and confusing value alternatives. Far from being relativistic or subjectivistic, this speech provides, in its general account of human nature and needs, some universally fixed points with reference to which we could assess competing social conceptions.[32] It shows us the relationship between a conception of the human being that many of Protagoras's hearers can be expected to share and certain concrete social practices that may be more subject to debate; *if* the listeners agree about the view of humanness, they may be led by his arguments to opt, for example, for one scheme of punishment rather than another. But if practical disagreements are as bitterly divisive as they in fact were in this period of crisis for Greece, they will be very likely to arise concerning the conception of humanness as well; progress is limited. When we turn to our specific problems of *tuchē*, we see its limits even more clearly.

(1) Protagoras allows us to continue to recognize and value vulnerable activities and objects: friends, families, the city itself. In fact, he insists strongly on the importance of these attachments. (And we shall see that his failure to render different attachments commensurable contributes in no small way to their ongoing vulnerability.) (2) Conflicts of values are made possible, in the first place, by the recognition of a plurality of distinct values. Protagoras's pupils will see more clearly how different major human ends support and in general complement one another. A Protagorean legislator can, further, minimize direct conflict between major components of the city's value system—for example, by structur-

ing civic and religious institutions in such a way as to prevent confrontation between the unwritten laws of family worship and the decrees of civil government. But because Protagoras denies the unity of the virtues, maintaining against Socrates that they are irreducibly heterogeneous in quality, he keeps alive the possibility of tragedy. (3) Finally, the speech recognizes the power of the passions as an ongoing danger for public morality. Here he speaks of the need for punishment; later he will hold that it is a shameful thing if passions can cause people who know the better to choose the worse action (352C–D).[33] The scheme of public and family education which he defends will go a long way towards training the passions and instilling virtuous dispositions; but it will not completely render them innocuous, nor does Protagoras think that it will.

We could say, then, that Protagoras's *technē* follows Tiresias's advice. It leaves our original problems more or less where it found them, making small advances in clarity and self-understanding, but remaining close to current beliefs and practices. He can claim to teach a *technē* that increases our control over *tuchē*; but the internality and plurality of its ends, and the absence of any quantitative measure, seem to leave his art lacking in precision and therefore in potential for decisive progress.

One reason for the conservatism is satisfaction. Protagoras has lived the prime of his life in the greatest age of Athenian political culture. He still seems to us to be a part of this glorious, relatively happy past; he stresses the fact that he is old enough to be the father of anyone else present. He is not gripped by the sense of urgency about moral problems that will soon characterize the writing of younger thinkers, for example Euripides, Thucydides, Aristophanes. The setting, with its allusions to the plague, its metaphors of disease, works to make this jolly conservatism seem anachronistic, inappropriate to the seriousness of impending contemporary problems. We hear it the way we might now hear a speech in praise of the Great Society made at the beginning of the Vietnam War— with our hindsight, and in the knowledge that failures of practical wisdom being made at that very time would erode the moral consensus the speaker was praising. We suspect that young Hippocrates, even without hindsight, will be less contented with things than his would-be mentor, inclined to look for stronger medicine. And if he is still content, the reader cannot be. It is no surprise that the dialogue compares Socrates' interview with these sophists to a living hero's visit to the shades of dead heroes in the underworld. It is a dead generation, lacking understanding of the moral crisis of its own time. Socrates compares himself to artful wily Odysseus,[34] deviser of life-saving stratagems; compared with him, his rivals are without resource.

Protagoras's story, however, suggests to us a more serious reason for his conservatism. He has shown us how thoroughly the identity and ways of life of a species are formed by the arts and abilities it possesses. In a time of deep need, feeling that our very survival is at stake, we may turn ourselves over to a new art. Sometimes this art will simply do what we ask of it, providing efficient instrumental means to the ends that we already have. Sometimes, however, as with the gifts of Zeus, the art will so deeply transform ways of life that we will feel that it has created a new type of creature. If, then, we contemplate curing our current ethical diseases by a new art, we must imagine, as well, and with the utmost care, the life that we will live with this new art and the aims and ends that go with it. For we may not want a radical solution, if its cost will be to be no longer human. This would hardly count as saving *our* lives.

IV

There is a *technē* that has made human beings capable of taking things quite different in kind and comparing them with respect to some property in which they are interested. It is a precise and orderly *technē*; it has given them the power to manipulate objects with far greater exactness than would have been available through the exercise of their unaided faculties. It is made by human beings; it appears to be a natural extension of ordinary activities, in the service of standing interests. It thus seems to involve no promise of making our human nature into something else. But it is capable, apparently, of endless progress and refinement. This art is the art or science of weighing, counting, and measuring.

Already in the *Euthyphro*, Socrates sees its attractions as a model for practical deliberation:

Socrates What sorts of disagreements, my good man, produce enmity and anger? Look at it this way. If you and I disagreed about which of two groups of items was more in number, would this disagreement make us enemies and cause us to be angry with one another? or wouldn't we count them up and quickly be released from our differences?

Euthyphro Of course.

Socrates And if we disagreed about the larger and smaller, wouldn't we turn to measurement and quickly stop our disagreement?

Euthyphro Right.

Socrates And by turning to weighing, I suppose, we would reach agreement about the heavier and the lighter?

Euthyphro How else?

Socrates But what is it that, if we should disagree about it and prove unable to turn to a criterion, would give rise to enmity and anger with one another? Perhaps you don't have the answer ready, but see if you don't agree that it is the just and unjust, the fine and shameful, the good and bad. Aren't these the things that, when we differ about them, and prove unable to turn to any sufficiently decisive criterion, lead to our becoming enemies to one another, whenever this happens—both you and I and all other human beings? (7B–D)

Evidently, then, a science of deliberative measurement would be an enormous advantage in human social life. And this is an idea for which the tradition of Greek reflection about *technē* and human understanding has by Plato's time prepared the way. The connection between numbering and knowing, the ability to count or measure and the ability to grasp, comprehend, or control, runs very deep in Greek thought about human cognition.[35] Already in Homer, the poet associates knowing with the ability to enumerate: the Muses give him their knowledge of the warring armies by imparting a catalogue of their numbers and divisions. To answer a 'how many?' question is to demonstrate a praiseworthy grasp of that to which one's attention is directed. We find in Homer contrasts between the *andrōn arithmos*, the denumerable company of heroes whose story can therefore be told, and the *dēmos apeirōn*, the mass of the undemarcated, whose lives will never be grasped and set down in a definite way.[36] The denumerable is the definite, the graspable, therefore also the potentially tellable, controllable; what cannot be numbered remains vague and unbounded, evading human grasp.

These connections are old and pervasive; they had more recently been given enormous impetus by the remarkable development in the *technai* of mathematics and astronomy, which became paradigms for science generally. The fifth-century *Prometheus Bound* calls numbering 'chief of all the stratagems', expressing a popular view that number is somehow a, or even the, chief element in *technē*, or the *technē par excellence*. Pythagorean epistemology of the fifth century (of which Plato is known to have been a serious student) explicitly argued that something was graspable only insofar as it was countable or numerically expressible. An examination of fifth- and early fourth-century uses of words associated with measure and quantitative commensurability shows that they come freighted with heavy cognitive and ethical associations: what is measurable or commensurable is graspable, knowable, in order, good; what is without measure is boundless, elusive, chaotic, threatening, bad.[37] The story that Hippasus of Metapontum was punished by the gods for revealing the secret of mathematical incommensurability gives evidence of the fear with which educated Greeks of this time regarded this apparent absence of definite *arithmos* at the heart of their clearest of sciences. (Our own mathematical terms 'rational' and 'irrational' are translations, and give further evidence of the way these things were seen.)

Given this situation, it is hardly surprising that someone who wanted to claim that he had developed a rational *technē* in some area would feel himself obliged to answer questions about number and measurability. Plato reflects this situation when he has Euthyphro, an interlocutor with no special interest in number, respond to Socrates' characterization of the arts as entirely obvious.[38] The author of *On Medicine in the Old Days* recognized, as we saw, that the absence of a quantitative measure in his art doomed it to deficient precision and therefore to error. He was still able to claim *technē* status for it. But some years later it will be forcefully argued that any *technē* at all, to be *technē*, must deal in numbering and measuring. The common concern of all *technē* and *epistēmē* whatever, insofar as it is *technē*, is 'to find out the one and the two and the three— I mean, to sum up, number and calculation. Or isn't it this way with these things, that every *technē* and *epistēmē* must of necessity participate in these?' The author is, of course, Plato; the text is the seventh book of the *Republic*.[39] It is absurd, Socrates there continues, for Aeschylus to represent Palamedes as claiming to have improved the art of generalship by the introduction of number; for surely if enumeration was not there, there could be no generalship at all. The *Epinomis* (977D ff.) develops a similar position with reference to the *technē–tuchē* antithesis: insofar as there is numbering and measuring in a practice, there is precise control; where numbering fails there is vagueness of grasp, therefore guesswork, therefore an element of *tuchē*.[40]

This Platonic argument is the natural development of a long tradition of reflection about the arts and human progress; it is adumbrated in Homer, developed in the *Prometheus Bound*; it haunts the Hippocratic writer. Plato's Pythagorean connections provide additional explanation for his endorsement of the position; or, better, his sense of the urgency of the problems of *tuchē* explains the attractiveness, for him, of Pythagorean arguments.

The idea that deliberation is, or could become, a kind of measuring is not itself alien to ordinary conceptions. It is as common for a Greek as for us to speak of weighing one course against another, measuring the possibilities. Even the Homeric gods, when they need to make a decision, put competing possibilities into the scales, judging by a single standard. Creon spoke of commensurability (387—cf. n. 44). Aristophanes ends the poetic contest in the *Frogs* with a travesty of this popular picture of deliberation. When he wants to decide which of two great tragic poets to prefer and restore to life, Dionysus's natural response is to put their verses (or rather the things mentioned in their verses) into the scale, weighing their enormously different themes and styles by a single measure. Aeschylus speaks of chariots, corpses, death; Euripides of light ships, speeches, persuasion. Aeschylus, therefore, weighs in as the victor. This is ridiculous. And yet it is a natural extension of a deeply held idea of rationality; the comic hero, surrogate of the ordinary man, goes for it. If deliberating is to become better, surer, more scientific, it is natural to suppose that change must proceed in this direction. (Aristophanes shows the danger of this picture, as well as its power.)

Such a science would offer several important advantages. First, things different in kind would become commensurable, as ungraspable qualitative differences are reduced to quantitative differences. The science presupposes agreement on the scale and units of measure; this achieved, many other things fall into place. Commensurability brings with it, as well, that singleness and externality in the end that promised to make procedures of choice clear and simple. For if we set ourselves to gauge, in each situation, the quantity of a single value and to maximize that, we eliminate uncertainty about what is to count as good activity. Choosing what to do becomes a straightforward matter of selecting the most efficient instrumental means to maximization, not the far messier matter of asking what actions are good for their own sake. And measurement, being precise, will also deliver a definite verdict about the instrumental alternatives, by a clear public procedure that anyone can use.

We readily grasp the relevance of measurement to the removal of serious value conflict. For instead of choosing, under circumstantial pressure, to neglect a different value with its own separate claims, one will merely be giving up a smaller amount of the same thing. This seems far less serious. And commensurability may be relevant to the elimination of our other problems as well. For if we really saw all ends as different quantities of one and the same thing, we would be likely to *feel* differently about them. This could modify our attachments to the vulnerable and our motivations for acts of passional disorder. This possibility we shall soon explore.

We can begin our examination of Socrates' project by looking at its conclusion, where he tells us what he claims to have shown:

Haven't we seen that the power of appearance leads us astray and throws us into confusion, so that in our actions and our choices between things both great and small we are constantly accepting and rejecting the same things, whereas the *technē* of measurement would have cancelled the effect of the appearance, and by revealing the truth would have caused the soul to live in peace and quiet abiding in the truth, thus saving our life? Faced with these considerations, would human beings agree that it is the *technē* of measurement that saves our lives, or some other *technē*?

Measurement, he agreed.[41] (356D–E)

Socrates claims to have enabled us to see our deep and pressing need for an ethical science of measurement. If we grasp the cost of lacking one and the great benefits of having it, we will, he thinks, agree that it is a matter of the first urgency to do what is needed to get one going. Protagoras, former defender of a plurality of values, proves the point by his agreement. Argument about whether, in fact, our values are commensurable on a single scale is, then, replaced by argument to the conclusion that they *must* be. Underlying the passage is the implicit agreement that what we cannot live with is being at the mercy of what happens, and that what we badly want is peace and quiet. If only measurement can take us from the one to the other, that is sufficient reason for us to 'turn ourselves over to' such a *technē*, whatever else it involves. Measurement is portrayed as the answer to a practical demand and the fulfillment of a pre-scientifically shared ideal of rationality.

Superficially, this agreement about the science follows an agreement that pleasure is the end. But the adoption of this single end is notoriously hasty and unargued. Only Socrates' final conclusion, I now want to claim, reveals the deep motivation behind this maneuver. The *Protagoras* has long been found anomalous among Plato's early and middle dialogues because of Socrates' apparent endorsement of the thesis that pleasure is the only intrinsic end or good.[42] Nowhere else does Socrates appear to be a single-end hedonist; and the nearly contemporary *Gorgias* is devoted, in part, to the refutation of a hedonist thesis. And yet none of the various attempts to explain the hedonism away has been successful. I want to suggest that both the adoption of the hedonistic premise (essential to Socrates' argument) and the vagueness surrounding this strategy can be best understood in the light of Socrates' goal of finding the right *sort* of practical *technē*, one that will do what the arts of Protagoras could not. We will be saved only by something that will assimilate deliberation to weighing and measuring; this, in turn, requires a unit of measure, some external end about which we can all agree, and which can render all alternatives commensurable. Pleasure enters the argument as an attractive candidate for this role: Socrates adopts it because of the science it promises, rather than for its own intrinsic plausibility.[43]

This begins to emerge clearly if we contrast the role of hedonism in this dialogue with the way it figures in later fourth-century thought. Eudoxus and Epicurus both argue for the intrinsic attractiveness of pleasure as the end or good, pointing to the natural pleasure-seeking behavior of animals and children. The *Protagoras* shows no trace of these concerns; nor, indeed, do any texts of the fifth and early fourth centuries. What we do find prominently expressed, as we have already seen in the *Antigone*, is the concern to find *a* standard or measure that will render values commensurable, therefore subject to precise scientific control. The need for measurement motivates the search for an acceptable measure.[44] What we need to get a science of measurement going is, then, an end that is single (differing only quantitatively): specifiable in advance of the *technē* (external); and present in everything valuable in such a way that it may plausibly be held to be the source of its value. Weight, as Aristophanes saw, has singleness, externality, and omnipresence; but it is short on intuitive appeal in the ethical sphere. Pleasure is a far more attractive placeholder. It is one of the few things we value that turns up in just about everything; it is also something to which we might think we could reduce every other value. For these reasons, it has traditionally remained the most popular candidate for the role of single measuring-stick of value, whenever someone has wanted badly enough to find one.

There are textual reasons to believe that pleasure, in the *Protagoras*, plays such a place-holding role. First, the subject of the entire dialogue, as introduced in the beginning of Protagoras's speech, is the *technē* of good deliberation. Our need for such a *technē*, and the various problems standing in the way of our success, have been brought forward before the introduction of hedonism and are its background. Second, the lengthy intervening discussions of the unity of the virtues reveal Socrates' strong interest in showing that there can be a single qualitatively homogeneous standard of choice. He correctly finds in the plurality and apparent incommensurability of the virtues a troublesome feature of Protagoras's so-called *technē*, one that impedes the solution to certain pressing problems. But only the introduction of the science of measurement, which requires and proceeds by way of the hedonistic assumption, shows us how we are to envisage the unity that will solve these problems. We can see, furthermore, that Socrates' introduction of the notion of scientific practical knowledge, and his denial both of conflict and of *akrasia*, in fact precede the introduction of hedonism: in commenting on Simonides' poem, which may well be a reflection on cases of what we have called tragic conflict (certainly it concerns a case where circumstances force a good person to do something shameful against his will), Socrates asserts that 'doing badly is nothing other than being deprived of knowledge (*epistēmē*)' (345B) and that 'all who do shameful and bad things do so involuntarily (*akontes*)' (345D–E). But his only argument to this conclusion turns out to require hedonism (or some other similar premise) for its success.

Finally, we can derive support from a fact that has troubled all commentators: the absence of any sustained exploration of the nature of pleasure and of its suitability as a standard of choice. Problems that trouble Plato not only in the late *Philebus*, but also in the *Gorgias*—the plurality of pleasures, the resistance of subjective feelings to precise measurement—do not even surface here. When Plato does turn to these difficult issues, he concludes that hedonism, as a theory of the good, is deeply defective. Many commentators have, therefore, tried to explain hedonism here as merely an *ad hominem* assumption for use against Protagoras, or as a belief of 'the many', not seriously endorsed by Socrates. But these suggestions are inadequate to explain its role in the argument. It is only with the aid of the hedonistic assumption that Socrates is able to reach conclusions that he clearly claims as his own.[45] It is difficult to see the thesis as *ad hominem*: Protagoras, a defender of the plurality of ends, proves initially quite resistant to Socrates' suggestion. As for the 'many', they and their view of *akrasia* are not introduced until long after the interlocutors agree about hedonism. Where hedonism *is* introduced, the ordinary view, which calls 'some pleasant things bad and some painful things good' is, in fact, *contrasted* with the view of Socrates: 'What I say is, insofar as things are pleasant, are they not to that extent good, leaving their other consequences out of account?' (351C).[46] The summary of the argument again asserts hedonism as Socrates' own view, connecting it with the life-saving project: 'Since we have seen that the preservation of our life depends on a correct choice of pleasure and pain, be it more or less, larger or smaller ...' (357A). None of the interlocutors ever doubts that this position is Socrates' own. As the dialogue draws to a close, he expresses in the strongest terms his identification with the figure of Prometheus, saying he takes thought for the entirety of his life in a Promethean fashion (361D). But only the science, based on pleasure, enabled him to do this correctly.[47]

We are, then, in the peculiar position of being unable to get rid of hedonism as a view of the character Socrates without distortion of the text, but unable, also, to see why such a controversial and apparently un-Platonic thesis should be allowed, undefended and even unexplored, to play such a crucial role in a major argument for important and well-known Platonic conclusions. A reading of the argument that takes Socrates' fundamental concern to be the establishment of a deliberative science of measure offers a solution. Knowing in a general way what sort of end we need to get the science going, Socrates, *pro tempore*, tries out pleasure. At the end of the dialogue he concedes that the content of this value has been left unspecified: 'Now *which technē*, and *what epistēmē*, we shall inquire later. But this suffices to show that it is *epistēmē*' (357B–C). If we find it odd that Socrates can feel so confident about the form of the science before establishing that there is a candidate for the end that is unitary and universal in the way required, we might begin to reflect that perhaps Socrates is less interested in our current intuitions about ends than he is in giving us a gift that will save our lives. Zeus did not require that justice be already a central human concern when he decided to make the attachment to justice a linch-pin of his saving *technē*.

It is worth pausing at this point to remark that the drive towards hedonism and utilitarianism in nineteenth-century moral philosophy had a very similar motivation. In both Bentham and Sidgwick,[48] we find that distaste for the plurality and incommensurability of common-sense values gives a powerful push towards the selection of an end that is, admittedly, not believed to be a supreme good in the intuitive deliverances of common sense. Bentham's arguments that only such a science of measure would eliminate contingency from social life show deep Platonic sympathies and are well worth study for any student of this dialogue and of Greek thought about ethical *technē*. Sidgwick's discussion of the reasons for moving beyond common sense to single-standard utilitarianism is of enormous interest to us as well, since it reveals so clearly that the central motivation towards hedonism is a need for commensurability in order to deal with messy deliberative problems. Happiness or pleasure, Sidgwick concedes, is not recognized by common sense to be the single end of choice.[49] But:

If, however, this view be rejected, it remains to consider whether we can frame any other coherent account of Ultimate Good. If we are not to systematize human activities by taking Universal Happiness as their common end, on what other principles are we to systematize them? It should be observed that these principles must not only enable us to compare among themselves the values of the different non-hedonistic ends which we have been considering, but must also provide a common standard for comparing these values with that of Happiness.[50]

It is, he continues, our 'practical need of determining whether we should pursue Truth rather than Beauty', this value rather than that, that leads us to hedonism, despite its problematic relation to common sense. If it be objected that it is inappropriate to depart to this extent from our intuitions, it can be replied that this is what happens whenever a science is born:

But it must be borne in mind that Utilitarianism is not concerned to prove the absolute coincidence in results of the Intuitional and Utilitarian methods. Indeed, if it could succeed in proving as much as this, its success would be almost fatal to its practical claims; as the adoption of the Utilitarian principle would then become a matter of complete indifference. Utilitarians are rather called upon to show a natural transition from the Morality of Common Sense to Utilitarianism, somewhat like the transition in special branches of practice from trained instinct and empirical rules to the technical method that embodies and applies the conclusions of science; so that Utilitarianism may be presented as the scientifically complete and systematically reflective form of that regulation of conduct, which through the whole course of human history has always tended substantially in the same direction.[51]

I want to claim that the *Protagoras* shows a similar motivation towards hedonism and a similar picture of the relation of science to ordinary beliefs. Ethical science is continuous with ordinary belief in that it fulfills an ideal of rationality embodied in ordinary belief: thus there is a 'natural transition' from ordinary belief to scientific practice. To make this transition, clearly, science's choice of an end must also have *some* continuity with ordinary beliefs about ends: this is why hedonism is plausible and Aristophanes absurd. But if it is to be worth something as science, and not 'a matter of complete indifference', it must go beyond the ordinary. To complain about this would be as retrograde as to complain that a

Hippocratic doctor does not administer the same old remedies your parents used to make.

We must now confront the argument in which Socrates purports to show us that the phenomenon commonly called *akrasia* does not, as described, occur: scientific knowledge of the overall good is sufficient for correct choice. Much has been written about this argument, whose structure now seems to be rather well understood.[52] It falls into three stages: first, a description of the problem; second, an argument that this problem does not really arise; third, an alternative diagnosis of practical error. The problem is a familiar one. *A* can do either *x* or *y*. *A* knows that *x* is better (overall), but chooses *y*, because he is overcome by pleasure. (The first statement of the problem adds, as alternatives, pain, love, and fear—but Socrates, quite reasonably in light of the hedonist agreement, speaks only of quantities of pleasure in what follows. This is important.) Knowledge, then, is 'dragged around like a slave'.

Protagoras and Socrates have explicitly agreed, from the outset, on two crucial premises:

(H) Pleasure is identical with the good.

(H₁) *A* believes pleasure to be identical with the good.

Now, in the crucial second phase of the argument, Socrates uses these premises, substituting 'good' for 'pleasant' to produce an absurdity in the description of what allegedly happens: *A* knows *x* is more good than *y*; *A* chooses *y*, because he is overcome by (desire for) the good in *y*. 'What ridiculous nonsense', Socrates now remarks, 'for a person to do the bad, knowing it is bad [i.e. inferior], and that he ought not to do it, because he was overcome by good.'

At first we do not see clearly what the absurdity is: for isn't this, in a way, just what happens? This other good over here exerts a special kind of pull that draws us to it so that we just neglect our commitment to the good that is better overall. But we get more information when Socrates himself explains the absurdity, showing us what he means by 'overcome'. Is the good in *y*, he asks, *a match for* the badness involved in missing out on *x*? No: for this would contradict the description of the case, according to which there is, and is known to be, *more* good in *x* than in *y*. But then if *y* really offers a smaller *amount* of good, an amount that is not *a match for* the good in *x*, then what *A* is doing is choosing a smaller package of pleasures and giving up a larger package. But how absurd that *A* should, with full knowledge, give up the larger package because he was overwhelmed by the smaller amount in the smaller package. It becomes like saying, '*A*, offered the choice between $50 and $200, chose the $50, even though he knew that $200 was more than $50, because he was overcome by the quantity of the $50.' And that does seem absurd. In short, notions of *amount* and of qualitative homogeneity seem to be doing some work here in producing the absurd result. We shall shortly see how central their place is.

How could such an absurd mistake occur? Socrates can explain it only as the result of a mistaken judgment about the size of the packages. Just as adverse physical conditions sometimes give rise to false beliefs about size, nearer items appearing taller or larger, so nearer pleasures, too, can strike us as bigger and more important just on account of their nearness. The nearness of the present pleasure produces a false belief about size that temporarily displaces the agent's background knowledge about the real sizes involved. It is clear that, with pleasure as with size, a science of measurement would suffice to put an end to our errors.

Our attention must now be drawn to Socrates' premises in the second, absurdity-producing part of the argument. For the explicit hedonistic assumptions are clearly not enough to get Socrates to his conclusion. He is making tacit use of at least two further assumptions:

(M) Whenever *A* chooses between *x* and *y*, he weighs and measures by a single quantitative standard of value.

(C) *A* chooses *x* rather than *y* if and only if he believes *x* to be more valuable than *y*.[53]

(M) gives us the use of a quantitative standard in each particular case. (H) gives us the singleness of the standard across all cases. (C) gives us the reliable connection between the beliefs that are the outcome of the weighing and the agent's actual choices. Together they yield the conclusion Socrates wants: if *A*'s choice is not the result of a correct weighing, and is not made under external duress (ruled out in the description of the case), then it must result from an incorrect weighing. For this is the only reason why someone who could have more would choose to have a smaller quantity of the same thing.

Each of these premises has a certain plausibility as an account of our deliberative procedures *some* of the time. Yet anyone who accepts the initial description of the case as the account of an actual human occurrence should take issue with them. For together they succeed in telling us that a problem by which we are intuitively gripped and troubled does not exist. *Akrasia* was supposed to be a case where ordinary deliberative rationality breaks down. What Socrates has done is not so much to prove that there can never be such breakdowns as to clarify the relationship between a certain picture of deliberative rationality and the *akrasia* problem. If we believe in a single end or good, varying only in quantity, and always deliberate by weighing or measuring (quantitatively), *and* always choose to act in accordance with our beliefs about the greater overall quantity of good, then *akrasia* will not happen. So, we are tempted to say: as long as rationality works it doesn't break down. We didn't need the genius of Socrates to tell us *that*.

At this point, many interpreters dismiss the entire argument. Seeing that the premises are not empirically acceptable as accounts of what we do in all cases (after all, their failure to hold was just what our ordinary belief in *akrasia* articulated), then, so these interpreters say, it looks as if Socrates had better do some more looking at the way people actually live and think. Socrates' conclusion, however, should make us suspect that something more is going on here. What he told us, and Protagoras agreed, is that only an ethical science of measurement will save our lives. If we accept his diagnosis of our problems and their urgency, and agree that we want to save our lives, it may occur to us that we are given, in Socrates' argument, an advertisement, as it were, for its premises. The argument does not rely on the common-sense intuitive acceptability of the premises. (Socrates stresses his disdain for the confused intuitions of the ordinary human being.) It shows us a connection between these premises and the disappearance of more than one problem. An agent who thinks the way these premises describe has no confusion about choice, no possibility of contingent conflict between incommensurables, *and*, it is claimed, no problem of *akrasia*. The whole thing, premises and all, appears to be the Socratic *technē* of practical reasoning, the life-saving art. The most astonishing claim implied by this argument is that the acceptance of the qualitative singleness and homogeneity of the values actually modifies the passions, removing the motivations we now have for certain sorts of irrational behavior. *Akrasia* becomes absurd—not a dangerous temptation, but something that would never happen. To see how this is supposed to be so, we need to return to Socrates' talk of packages and amounts and to enter more deeply into the life and the views of his hypothetical agent.

An ordinary case of *akrasia* looks like this. Phaedra knows that if she eats a bagel just before she goes running she will get a cramp and cut down the distance she can complete. She will be angry with herself later and she will find her health less good than it would have been had she run further and eaten less. She knows, then, let us say, that it is better all things considered not to eat the bagel now, but instead to go running directly. But she is very hungry, and the bagel looks so very appealing, sitting there hot and buttered on its plate. Its appeal to her is quite distinct and special; it does not look like a little bit of exercise or a small package of health. It looks exactly like a buttered bagel. And so (swayed by the desires it arouses) she eats it.

Contrast the following case. Phaedra's rational principle, for some reason, is to maximize her bagel-eating. Standing in the middle of the room, she sees on a table on one side a plate containing two fresh bagels, toasted and buttered. On the other side of the room, on a similar table, is a plate containing one toasted buttered bagel. The bagels are the same variety, equally fresh, equally hot, buttered in the same way. She can go for either one plate or the other, but (for some reason) not both. She knows that, given her rational principle, she ought to eat the two bagels. But, overcome by desire, she eats the one. Now this does seem highly peculiar, in a way that our first case did not. We must comprehend that there is *no* respect in which the single-bagel plate differs from the two-bagel plate, except in the number of bagels it contains. The bagels are in no way qualitatively different. Nor is the arrangement of bagels on plate or plate on table somehow more aesthetically appealing. The single-bagel plate is not even nearer, it is the same distance away. What could make Phaedra's choice anything but absurd, given that she really has the principle we say she has? I find myself imagining, as I try to understand her action, that there must after all be *some* distinguishing quality to that single bagel. It looked so cute, with its little burned spot on the crust. Or: it was from New York, and the other two were not. Or: she remembers eating bagels with her lover at *this* table, and not at that one. Or: she is a mathematician and she thinks that the single bagel in the middle of its plate exhibits a more pleasing geometrical arrangement. Or: it is so funny to see a bagel sitting on an elegant Lenox plate (the others being on a plain kitchen plate): it reminds her of the contradictions of existence. We could go on this way. But I mean to rule out every one of these sources of qualitative specialness in the description of the case. I insist on absolute qualitative homogeneity: the alternatives seem to her to differ in quantity only. And then, I believe, we do get the result Socrates wants. It is absurd.

It would never happen; the motivating desires would never arise; nobody who really saw the choice that way would choose that way.

What Socrates gets us to see, if we dig deep enough, is the connection between our *akrasia* problem and the way we ordinarily see things—the enabling role played by our belief in an incommensurable plurality of values in getting the problem going. *Akrasia* as we know and live it seems to depend upon the belief that goods are incommensurable and special: that this bagel, this person, this activity, though in some sense less good over all than its rival, has nonetheless a special *kind* of goodness that pulls us to it, a goodness that we could not get in just the same way by going in the other direction. It's one thing to be unfaithful through passionate desire for a lover whom one sees as a special and distinct individual. But suppose him to be a clone of your present lover, differing qualitatively in no feature (and let us suppose not even in history—as would be true of lovers in the ideal city), and the whole thing somehow loses its appeal.[54]

We might say, then, returning to the premises, that if we really have (H₁) and (M), (C) falls out as a natural consequence. (C) is not true as an empirical description of the workings of desire. It does, however, appear plausible as a description of the desires of agents who really believe to the bottom of their souls in the qualitative homogeneity of all of their alternatives. (For our case is, after all, only the shallowest beginning; what we ultimately must get ourselves to imagine is that Phaedra sees *every one* of her choices this way, *and* that in every choice it is one and the same measure of value that she recognizes. There is no heterogeneity at all, even across cases.) The recognition of heterogeneity, the dialogue tells us, is a necessary condition for the development of irrational motivations; in its absence, they will simply not develop; or, if once developed, will wither away.

In short, I claim that Socrates offers us, in the guise of empirical description, a radical proposal for the transformation of our lives. Like the other gifts mentioned by Protagoras, this science of measurement will enter into and reshape the nature and attachments of the being who receives it. It is now not surprising that he tells us little about the intuitive acceptability of his proposed end: for it may not be something that can be properly assessed from our ordinary viewpoint. From our ordinary viewpoint, things do look plural and incommensurable. But this viewpoint is sick. We want, and know we need, the viewpoint of science.

Now we understand, too, why love and fear drop out when the premises come in: because if we really accept these premises, love and fear, as we know them, do drop out. Here is another benefit of the science: it restructures our attachments so that they are far less fragile, even taken singly. Beautiful Alcibiades, irreplaceable, is a risky thing to love. But if one measure of (H) goes away to another lover, it is no difficult task to acquire another similar measure. Thoroughgoing commensurability yields a readily renewable supply of similar objects. The science that eliminated the possibility of contingent conflict and removed *akrasia* did so by eliminating, or denying, just that special separateness and qualitative uniqueness that is also a major source of each single attachment's exposure to fortune. Measurement is even more versatile than we thought.[55]

V

This dialogue is deeper than any work of utilitarian or hedonistic moral theory that proceeds as if it *were* straightforwardly describing ordinary beliefs and practices. Such works prove immediately vulnerable to the common-sense objection. Socrates (like Sidgwick) shows us what motivates a movement beyond the ordinary. The common-sense objection does not meet this argument, at least in the form in which I have stated it. How, then, can it be assessed?

Protagoras's myth suggested that a good way to understand the contribution of a new, allegedly life-saving art is to imagine the lives of the creatures to whom it was given, both before and after their receipt of the gift. This thought-experiment allows us to ask who these creatures were when they needed an art, and whether they were the same creatures after the art saved lives. This might help us to see whose lives, what sort of lives, the cure will save. Since Socrates here picks up the motif of life-saving, he invites us to imagine a Socratic conclusion to the Protagorean story, fleshing out the vague ending we sketched at the opening of this chapter. We shall now begin to answer that invitation: although an adequate response would be fuller and more storylike than this brief sketch.

Still human beings lived in confusion in their cities. In spite of the gifts of Zeus, they lacked precise control over their choices and actions. Whenever they disagreed about numbers, lengths, or weights, they could appeal to the arts of counting, measuring, or weighing to settle their disputes. But when they were confused about justice, nobility, or goodness, they had no art to arbitrate their quarrel. They became angry and violent; they insulted and wronged one another.

Even when they could agree, the primitive confusion of their value system often gave rise to serious conflicts: piety could seem to dictate one course of action, courage or love another. Then these unfortunate creatures were deeply torn; lamenting, they would cry out, saying things like, 'Which of these is without evils?' And, stricken by after-pain, things like, 'The laborious memory of pain drips, instead of sleep, before the heart.' They had no art that could cure this pain. Worse still, even when they did have settled beliefs about the right course of action, even when there was a single, unconflicted course of action available, they could still, in their disorderly and artless condition, be swayed by the lure of other nearer goods that were the objects of some passion. In their bewilderment they said that they must have been 'overcome' by pleasure, fear, or love. So, frightened and confused, torn by regret and perplexed by uncertainty, they wandered through their cities without understanding of their past actions, without the ability to guarantee their future. They even invented an art form which they called tragedy, in which they explored their pain. From these works one can quickly conclude that they found life not worth living in this state. 'Not to be born is the best of all'—this was the judgment of their most eminent poet and teacher, Sophocles, after surveying these difficulties.

Now Apollo, god of sunlight and rational order, god of numbering and of firm boundaries between one thing and another, the god revered by Pythagoras, looked down at their plight. He did not wish the entire race to perish. So he decided to give them an art that could save their lives. Through his resourceful messenger Socrates, he revealed to them his marvelous gift: the art or science of deliberative measurement, together with the single metric end or good, which is pleasure. With this art, they would be able, in any choice, to calculate precisely the amount of long-term pleasure to be realized by each alternative and so to weigh it against rival alternatives. The human partisans of this art could, then, set themselves, each one, to maximize the long-term pleasure enjoyed in the entire city.

With the gift of this saving art, a wonderful change came over the lives of these creatures, previously so helpless. Thanks to the art, what had seemed to be many and incommensurable values were now truly seen as one. The significance of this new orderliness for all their ways of life was immense. It was as if the clarity of Apollo's sunlight had dispelled all of their troubles. Even the face of the natural world looked different: more open, flatter, clearly demarcated, source of no threatening incommensurables. And the city took on, too, in this way, a new order and beauty. Before this, they had disagreed and quarreled; now they had only to work through the publicly established procedures of pleasure-computation to arrive at an answer in which all good citizens easily concurred. Every circumstance by which the condition of an individual can be influenced being remarked and inventoried, nothing was left to chance, caprice, or unguided discretion. Everything was surveyed and set down in dimension, number, weight, and measure. Before this, again, old-fashioned thinkers like Protagoras had taught that justice was an end in itself; even if it conflicted with another valued end there was no avoiding or denying its claims. Now these beings correctly saw that virtue is all one: justice, courage, and piety are all simply functions of pleasure, and the virtuous action in each case is the one that maximizes total pleasure. Children were raised with a correct, scientific teaching that developed their inner capability to see things in terms of a single measure; by punishing the recognition of incommensurables, civic teachers straightened the young tree towards adult rationality. These children came to see, as they grew, that the 'individuals' around them, parents and teachers, were, all alike, valuable sources and centers of pleasure, entirely comparable one with another.[56] They seemed not separate self-moving souls, but parts of a single system; not qualitatively special, but indistinguishable. Pleasures obtained from them and pleasures rendered to them are all still quantities of pleasure: this is, precisely, the value of persons, that they give so much pleasure to the city's total. If these citizens ever read those tragedies, artifacts of the earlier race, the ways of life depicted seemed strange to them. Here is a character, Haemon, inflamed with what he calls passionate love, killing himself because this one woman, Antigone, whom he loves, has died. This is incomprehensible. Why does he think that she is not precisely replaceable by any other object in the world? Why doesn't he understand that there are other exactly comparable and qualitatively indistinguishable sources of pleasure to whom he can, in return, give a comparable pleasure, thus augmenting the city's sum? In this play Creon is the only character in whom they can recognize themselves: for Creon says of this irrational young man's 'love': 'There are other furrows for his plow.'

And in the light of this change in beliefs and therefore passions, they obtained a further and greater benefit. The deep old-fashioned problem that used to be called *akrasia* is no longer a problem for these people, because in the absence of incommensurable values, and without recognition of the uniqueness of persons, the passions that most gave rise to *akrasia*—love, hatred, anger, fear—no longer have the same nature, or the same force. When everything is seen in terms of a single value, it is enormously easier to control one's desire for a smaller quantity of the same.

So, through science, these creatures have saved their pleasant existence. And if any citizen shows himself unable to perform acts of measurement, if he or she insists on inventing separate sources of value or unique objects of feeling, if he or she manifests desires other than the rational desire for the single good, he or she must be cast aside and put to death as a plague on the city. Each year in spring they celebrate a festival at the time of the old festival of Dionysus, where tragedies were presented. It is called the festival of Socrates. The works of art they present are the clear, reasonable prose dialogues that have taken the place of tragic theatre; they celebrate Socrates' courageous search for the life-saving art.

This dialogue, we see, shows more than a competition for a young soul. It shows us (ironically, since its protagonist wishes to bring about the death of tragedy) a tragedy of human practical reason. For it shows us an apparently insoluble tension between our intuitive attachment to a plurality of values and our ambition to be in control of our planning through a deliberative *technē*. The nature of its arguments is not straightforward. It does not simply try to convince us that such-and-such is the true or correct view of practical reason. It instead displays to us (to Hippocrates) the relationship between certain urgent needs and a certain sort of art or science, showing us at the same time the changes and (from a certain point of view) the losses that this art would entail. We thought that the science of measurement was a science that simply provided instrumental means to an external, agreed-on end. We have now come to see that a deep modification of ends is itself a part of the art—that Socrates' *technē*, like the arts of Zeus, creates new values and new dependencies. We supposed, naïvely, that we could go on recognizing our rich plurality of values and also have the precision and control offered by a quantitative social science. (Some utilitarian works are still naïve in this way, hardly ever asking what a person would be like who really saw the world that way, and more or less assuming that he or she would be just like us.) Plato tells us with his characteristic sternness that this does not look to be the case. Science does change the world. If part of our humanness is our susceptibility to certain sorts of pain, then the task of curing pain may involve putting an end to humanness.

In one way, the dialogue offers us (Hippocrates) a choice, sternly defining the alternatives, but leaving it to us to choose between them. At the end, we do not know whether Hippocrates will choose to make progress with Socrates or to muddle along with Protagoras—or whether he will reject the choice philosophically, by arguing that the alternatives are badly set up, or whether he will reject the choice unphilosophically, by going back to his accustomed thoughts and ways. The argument does not coerce him. It simply clarifies the nature of the situation. He sees more clearly the way the world links cure with disease, progress with cost.

But the argument also forces him to ask, who is he to choose? All the interlocutors agree, by the end, in rejecting Protagoras's 'The human being is the measure of all things', in favor of the Socratic 'All things are *epistēmē*' (361C). Protagoras, earlier, agreed to let the issue be judged by Socratic rationality (cf. 336A); and Socratic rationality insists that the intuitions of the ordinary person are unreliable. Socrates reminded us that in a competition between alternative ethical positions it is crucial to select an appropriate judge. If the judge is inferior to the contending philosophers, that is clearly no good; if he is an equal, why should the rivals take *his* word? So, clearly, it must be the person who is superior to both of them in knowledge or application. This means, for Hippocrates and for us, that ordinary intuitions and attachments cannot carry the day. We are asked by the dialogue to become suspicious of our own Protagorean evaluation and to look, in ourselves or in another, for a way of seeing, intellectually pure and precise. The dialogue allows us to respond with ordinary human judgment, and then reminds us that some types of judgment are higher than that. The troublesome questions raised by this Platonic move will not vanish from view.

Acknowledgments

I am indebted to the questions and criticism of several groups of students; I do not mean to slight others by singling out Robin Avery, John Carriero, Arnold Davidson, and Nancy Sherman. I am grateful, too, to Stanley Cavell, with whom I taught and often discussed this material. To Geoffrey Lloyd I am grateful not only for his comments, but also for allowing me, in the last stages of revision, to read and refer to his 'Measurement and mystification,' now published in *The Revolutions of Wisdom* (Berkeley: University of California Press, 1987), a fundamental study whose range and richness cannot be indicated in brief references.

Notes

1. On *tuchē*, see also Martha Nussbaum, *The Fragility of Goodness: Luck and Ethics in Greek Tragedy and Philosophy* (Cambridge: Cambridge University Press, 1976), chap. 1, p. 3. (This work is hereafter cited as Nussbaum, *Fragility*.) *Tuchē* does not imply randomness or absence of causal connections. Its basic meaning is 'what just happens'; it is the element of human existence that humans do not control.

For this reprinting, the scholarly apparatus has been much abridged. The reader will find extensive bibliographical resources and discussion of the relevant literature in the notes to the original publication.

2. For an account of the most important elements of continuity and discontinuity, see Nussbaum, *Fragility*, Interlude 2.

3. My version of the story is largely taken from Prometheus's speech in the *Prometheus Bound* (whose disputed authorship makes no difference to our reflections here). For other influential versions of the story, see Solon 13 (West), 43 ff.; Gorgias, *Apology of Palamedes*; and of course the chorus on the human being in the *Antigone*—cf. Nussbaum, *Fragility*, chap. 3. The *Prometheus Vinctus* story does not include mastery of internal passions.

4. On the problem of the dramatic date, see A. E. Taylor, *Plato* (London, 1926) 236, W. K. C. Guthrie, *A History of Greek Philosophy*, vol. IV, 214, C. C. W. Taylor, *Plato: Protagoras* (Oxford, 1976) 64, all of whom concur on a date of approximately 433. The reference at 327D to a play produced in 420 is an anachronism. As for the date of composition, this dialogue has sometimes been taken to be among the very earliest; but a majority of recent scholars have argued that it is a transitional work, later than the briefer aporetic dialogues and earlier than *Meno* and *Gorgias*.

5. It is worthy of note that the four dialogues considered in the section of *Fragility* from which this chapter is drawn form a chronological continuum in dramatic dates as well as in dates of composition. This does not hold true in general; but it may be significant that dialogues which I have singled out for their thematic continuity (all deal in some way with the relationship between philosophical expertise and our problems of *tuchē*, all are centrally concerned with 'madness' or control by the passions, all are concerned with the commensurability or harmony of different values) should also illustrate a dramatic development in the character of Socrates, in his relationship to these issues. The significance of the changing dramatic portrait is discussed in each of the four chapters of Nussbaum, *Fragility*, part II, most extensively in chaps. 6–7. We also notice that in three of the four dialogues Alcibiades plays a central role (for the relationship between Phaedrus and Alcibiades, cf. chap. 7, 212–13); in the *Republic*, the tyrannical soul plays a similar role.

6. On the metaphor of hunting as expression of a pervasive picture of practical intelligence setting itself against contingency, see M. Detienne and J.-P. Vernant, *Les Ruses de l'intelligence: la Mètis des grecs* (Paris, 1974); cf. *Fragility*, chap. 1, where I criticize their sharp opposition between the 'hunter' and the philosopher and examine some related aspects of Plato's imagery. In this dialogue the continuity between ordinary *erōs* and the philosophical ascent is forcefully stressed, as Socrates the hunter of Alcibiades becomes Socrates the wily new Odysseus, saving lives through the philosophical art. For a related discussion of hunting as an ethical image, see Nussbaum, "Consequences and Character in Sophocles' *Philoctetes*," *Philosophy and Literature* 1 (1976–1977): 25–53. On Socrates as *erastēs*, later *erōmenos*, see *Fragility*, chap. 6; on this erotic relationship in general, see Dover, *Greek Homosexuality* (Cambridge, 1978).

7. The *Charmides* is probably close in date of composition as well, coming late in the group of 'aporetic' early dialogues. For a fuller discussion of the history of the analogy between philosophy and medicine, see Nussbaum, *The Therapy of Desire: Theory and Practice in Hellenistic Ethics* (Princeton, 1994).

8. For Protagoras's claim, see 316D, and esp. 318E–319A.

9. See for example Isnardi Parente, *Technē* (Florence, 1966) 1; R. Schaerer, *Epistēmē et Technē* (Lausanne, 1930), *passim* (who notes, however, that *epistēmē* is used more often than *technē* to designate the cognitive condition of the agent). Dodds concludes that the concept of *technē*, in the late fifth century, is the concept of 'the systematic application of intelligence to any field of human activity' (11); cf. Guthrie, *History*, III, pt. I, 115, n. 3: 'It [sc. *technē*] includes every branch of human or divine skill, or applied intelligence, as opposed to the unaided work of nature.' These informal results are confirmed and supplemented by the rigorous and extensive linguistic analysis of the entire semantic field of the Greek verbs *epistasthai*, *gignōskein*, *eidenai*, and their related nouns *epistēmē*, *technē*, and *gnōsis* in J. Lyons, *Structural Semantics: an Analysis of Part of the Vocabulary of Plato* (Oxford, 1963). Lyons shows that *technē* and names of specific *technai* function semantically as the most common direct object of the verb *epistasthai*; he observes that '*epistēmē* and *technē* are very frequently, if not always, synonymous

in the contexts in which they occur in colligation with adjectives of class At', that is to say, with *-ikē* adjectives naming some art or science (187). He shows how productive this class is, how easily a Greek writer could thus give the name *technē* to any sort of organized know-how, anything which might be the object of *epistasthai*. His examples show the breadth and the heterogeneity of this class. He does observe that *epistēmē* is broader than *technē* in one way: it can sometimes be used interchangeably with *gnōsis*, where *technē* cannot. Lyons's argument concerning *gignōskein* and *gnōsis* is that they cover the area of personal acquaintance and familiarity, an area in which we do not find the verb *epistasthai*. So the point is that *technē* goes everywhere *epistasthai* does; it stops short of the area of personal familiarity, an area into which the noun *epistēmē* can enter. Although Lyons's analysis deals only with the Platonic corpus, it seems to me likely that his results in this respect would also describe the use of *technē* and *epistēmē* in the late fifth century and in other writers contemporary with Plato.

10. The passage of *Metaphysics* I with which we shall be concerned is a salient case of this. In one passage (*Ethica Nicomachea* 1140b2 ff.) Aristotle does explicitly distinguish *epistēmē* and *technē*, associating the latter entirely with productive art. (Cf. also 1112b7.) The same distinction is made in *Magna Moralia* 1197a33, which may not be genuine; this passage, however, says explicitly that in some of the arts that we shall see Plato calling *technai*, e.g., lyre-playing, the activity itself is the end. Aristotle's verbal distinctions are not dogmatically or even consistently maintained in this area: the distinction between *praxis* and *poiēsis* is one clear example of this. It is also not uncommon for him to use a word in both a wide and a narrow sense—both for the genus and for one of its sub-species: he does this explicitly with '*phronēsis*' and '*dikaiosunē*', implicitly, as I argue, with '*aisthēsis*' (cf. Nussbaum, *Aristotle's De Motu Animalium* [Princeton, 1978], Essay 5). It is clearly impossible to make the narrow *Ethica Nicomachea* sense of '*technē*' fit the rest of his usage, above all in *Metaphysics* I; the fact that this book is devoted to the views of predecessors helps to explain why his usage here remains close to the traditional usage.

11. Cf. esp. 356D ff., where there are repeated verbal shifts back and forth between the two, so that it is frequently difficult to tell to which noun the adjective '*metrētikē*' refers. In an earlier passage, Protagoras refers to his *technē* and to a *mathēma*, apparently interchangeably (316D, 318E, 319A).

12. Xenophon, *Memorabilia* III.10; for other examples, see Schaerer, *op. cit.*, D. Kurz, *Akribeia: das Ideal der Exaktheit bei den Griechen bis Aristoteles* (Göppingen, 1970). The *Gorgias* denies the title of *technē* to anything that cannot give a general *logos* of its procedures; its distinction between *empeiria* (experience, an empirical knack) and *technē* corresponds closely to the distinction of *Metaphysics* I. The question of how we make the transition from an accumulation of experience to a general account remained a central problem in Greek medical theory. Galen's *On Medical Experience* records a debate that uses a form of the Sorites paradox: if n medical observations are not sufficient for *technē*, surely $n + 1$ will not be sufficient; one observation is clearly not sufficient. From these premises we can show that no number, however large, will be sufficient, and so medicine, so

grounded, cannot be a *techne*. The empirical doctor replies in an interesting way: he points to the success of his practice and of his empirically based generalizations in curing disease. The point seems to be that if it works well against *tuche*, it is *techne* enough.

13. Cf. also Euripides, *Electra* 367 ff., where the absence of *akribeia* in human judgment is associated with the absence of a sure standard of judgment; and this, in turn, is traced to inner upheavals caused by elements of human nature.

14. Irwin (Oxford, 1977), *passim*, esp. III.9–11. Section III.9 contains a good discussion of some of the Platonic associations between craft and knowledge, and between both of these and the ability to give accounts. The crucial claim about *techne* is made on pp. 73–74: every person of *techne* 'produces a product which can be identified without reference to his particular movements'. Here Irwin must clearly be talking about the ordinary conception rather than about some divergent Socratic use, since he uses this account as a basis to interpret the force of analogies to the *technai* in the dialogues, even when Socrates is not using the word '*techne*'. His point is that any craft analogy will evoke in the mind of the reader a certain picture.

15. It is very important that Irwin be correct about what is implied by the word '*techne*' and by the presence of *techne* examples. His explicit evidence for an instrumental conception of excellence in the early dialogues is slight: one premise from an argument in the *Lysis*, a dialogue of a highly aporetic character: and then, as we shall see, the evidence of the latter half of the *Protagoras*—which, however, does not provide, by itself, any evidence for an instrumental reading of other early dialogues. Forceful objections to this reading have been brought forward by G. Vlastos, both in a review of Irwin in the *Times Literary Supplement* ('The virtuous and the happy', *TLS* 24 Feb. 1978, pp. 230–231) and in 'Happiness and virtue in Socrates' moral theory', *Proceedings of the Cambridge Philological Society* 210, NS 30 (1984) 181–213.

16. See E. R. Dodds, *The Ancient Concept of Progress and Other Essays on Greek Literature and Belief* (Oxford, 1971); L. Edelstein, *The Concept of Progress in Classical Antiquity* (Baltimore, 1967); and Guthrie, *History*.

17. Xenophon, *Oeconomicus* I; cf. Schaerer, *Episteme* on Xenophon's use of '*techne*' and '*episteme*'.

18. *Ethica Eudemia* 1219a12 ff., *Magna Moralia* 1211b28, 1197a9–11 (on which see above n. 10). For the Hellenistic view, see esp. Cicero, *de Finibus* III.24.

19. At *Ethica Eudemia* 1219a12 ff., Aristotle contrasts medical science with mathematical science: in the former there is an end, health, that is not identical to the activity of healing; in the latter the activity of *theoria* is an end in itself. But in *Metaphysics* VII.7 he clearly states that the activity of the doctor involves producing a further specification of the 'parts' or elements of the end itself.

20. Irwin is troubled by the prominence of these examples in Plato. He never disputes that they are, for Plato, central cases of *techne*. He produces an odd

solution: the flute-player 'still produces a product which can be identified without reference to his particular movements. When we can recognize a tuneful sound in music ... we can decide if certain movements are good flute-playing ...; a tuneful sound is not a good product *because* it is the result of good production, but the production is good because of the product' (73–74). This seems to be a desperate stratagem; even if this position has occasionally been defended in aesthetics, it seems plainly false. (Is Horowitz a great artist because he is efficient at fulfilling the instrumental conditions to the production of a 'tuneful sound' that we would desire and value as much if it were made by a machine? Could we adequately characterize the ends of piano-playing without mentioning hands, fingers, feet, imagination, and the piano?) Furthermore, such a position is completely unparalleled in this historical period: Aristotle regards it as entirely uncontroversial and self-evident that in the musical arts the performer's activities are ends in themselves. Irwin makes no attempt to argue that his conception is one that could have been held by a Greek thinker at this time; nor does he defend it as a plausible one for ours.

21. This element of music and other *technai* is explored in the *Philebus*.

22. C. C. W. Taylor, trans. and comm., *Plato: Protagoras* (Oxford, 1976), claims that an art that is *not* productive, i.e. one in which the ends of the art are up for debate within the art, cannot avoid collapsing into subjectivism (83). This surprising claim mars the general excellence of his discussion of Protagoras's speech. Though false, this sort of claim is illustrative of the sort of worry that motivates the push towards an external-end *technē*, in modern as well as in ancient moral philosophy.

23. Protagoras divides his speech into the 'story' (*muthos*) and the 'argument' or 'account' (*logos*); but it is by no means clear how he understands this division. The *logos* begins only at 324D—and yet the immediately preceding section (323A–324D) seems to belong, stylistically, with what follows rather than with the preceding story. G. B. Kerferd, 'Protagoras' Doctrine of Justice and Virtue in the *Protagoras* of Plato', *Journal of Hellenic Studies* 73 (1953): 42–45, concludes that 323A ff. is a summary of the *muthos*. We might also suspect that Protagoras does not have a firm or careful grasp of the categories of his own discourse.

It was at one time customary to read this speech as derived from the historical Protagoras's 'On the way things were in the beginning'. It is even printed in Diels–Kranz, though under the section 'Imitation'. I shall here treat the speech simply as the speech of a Platonic character; though we should not ignore the possibility that Plato is showing us how the issues of the dialogue grow out of the intellectual currents of his own day.

24. I use scare quotes because these powers are clearly not *technai* in the sense specified above; nor are they called this by Protagoras. They have in common with *technē* that they are resources with which a living creature is enabled to make its way in the world, defending itself against its dangers.

25. It is hardly necessary to mention that the 'What is it?' question is a, if not the, central question of the early tradition of Greek natural science. Asked about a

changing thing, this question is often phrased as a question about its *phusis*: what is the thing's essential nature, as this is revealed in its characteristic mode of life and growth? Cf. E. Benveniste, *Noms d'agent et noms d'action en indo-européen* (Paris, 1948) 78; D. Holwerda, *Commentatio de vocis quae est* φύσις *vi atque usu* (Groningen, 1955); F. Heinimann, *Nomos und Phusis* (Basel, 1945), esp. 89 ff.; C. Kahn, *Anaximander and the Origins of Greek Cosmology* (New York 1960) 200–203. Aristotle tells us that the 'What is it?' question (to which he himself gives an answer that stresses capabilities to function in certain characteristic ways) is *the* question that has been 'a perpetual subject of inquiry and perplexity' for his entire tradition (*Metaphysics* VII 1028b2 ff.). So it is not surprising—though it has rarely been noticed—that Protagoras should draw upon and illuminate this tradition of speculation. On the importance of kinds and kind-terms in answering the 'What is it?' question, see D. Wiggins, *Sameness and Substance* (Oxford, 1980), esp. chaps. 2 and 3—with reference to the Aristotelian view and its antecedents.

26. D. Hume, *A Treatise of Human Nature* (Oxford, 1978), Bk. III, Pt. II, Sections 1–2.

27. Furthermore, it seems to follow from the Humean account that we have reason to be just and law-abiding only when we are convinced that it is advantageous, in terms of other, more fundamental ends, to be so. Such an account seems unable to offer any reason why I should not act unjustly in my own interest in a particular case where (a) it is to my advantage to be unjust, (b) I am convinced that I will not be found out and punished, and (c) I believe with good reason that my unjust action will not undermine the generally useful practice of justice.

28. For Aristotle's criticism of such an account of human ends, see Nussbaum, *Fragility* chap. 12. A number of similarities between Protagoras and Aristotle emerge: the general anthropocentrism about ethics; the view that social excellence is a combination of shared natural sociability and social training; the view that *philia* is an important civic value, holding cities together; the view that all adults in a city are in some sense teachers of excellence, but that there is still room for a teacher to advance our reflective awareness of our practices; the view that what it is to be a certain sort of creature is to have certain functional capabilities. Some of these similarities have frequently been noticed: see, for example, Guthrie, *History* III, 67; D. Loenen, *Protagoras and the Greek Community* (Amsterdam, 1940) 103–26 with references.

29. This agrees with the view expressed by the historical Protagoras (Hermann Diels, *Die Fragmente der Vorsokratiker*, 6th ed., revised by Walther Kranz [Berlin, 1952], cited as DK; B3): 'Teaching needs nature and practice.'

30. These 'must's are said, it is true, partly with a view to the city's survival; but this is not enough to make the point a Humean one. Survival is not an external end in the Humean sense; even here, the *city* is the entity whose survival is desired.

31. In the same way, the traveler set down among apolitical savages is said by Protagoras to feel not *fear* (as he would among less restrained fellow humans),

but *loneliness* and *homesickness*, appropriate to one who does not see around him beings of his own kind. It is not altogether clear, in these two cases, whether the people described lack the (innate) *sense* of justice, or only its effective development. Even in the latter case they might be so hopelessly 'gnarled' and 'crooked' as to be unrecognizable.

32. The assimilation of this speech to relativism or subjectivism has come about in three ways: (1) by an unjustified assimilation of this dialogue to the 'Protagorean' doctrine of the *Theaetetus*; (2) by mistaking Protagoras's defense of law for a defense of each particular system of laws (whereas the speech plainly implies that a system of laws could be criticized for failure to perform the general function of law); (3) by the assumption (see n. 22 above) that any *technē* in which ultimate ends are up for debate must be hopelessly relativistic.

33. By this point Protagoras somewhat passively joins Socrates in attacking the 'many'; but his own earlier view of education gave a central place to correct shaping of the passions (356A–B), and his explanation of residual error, though sketchy, seems to invoke the incomplete training of these elements—since it is to these, more than to the intellect, that punishment as teaching is addressed.

34. Cf. 315B, where a Homeric quotation links Socrates to Odysseus, Hippias to the shade of Heracles; 315C, where Prodicus is, similarly, compared to Tantalus. The comparisons are unlikely to indicate particular similarities of character or achievement—for Prodicus is portrayed as a dignified and morally concerned person; the central point is that there is only one daring, resourceful, living man here, among the resourceless, artless dead.

35. On this see Nussbaum, 'Eleatic conventionalism and Philolaus on the conditions of thought', *Harvard Studies in Classical Philology* 83 (1979): 63–108, esp. 89–91, with references both textual and secondary. Valuable studies of early Greek thought about *arithmos* and its importance include O. Becker, *Zwei Untersuchungen zur antiken Logik, Klassisch-Philologische Studien* 17 (1957) 20 ff.; J. Stenzel, *Zahl und Gestalt* (Leipzig, 1933) 25 ff.; J. Annas, *Aristotle's Metaphysics M and N* (Oxford, 1976).

36. *Iliad* II.488, XXIV.776; for other texts, see Nussbaum, 'Eleatic conventionalism' 90–91.

37. See, for example, *ametrētos* at *Odyssey* XIX.512, XXIII.249, etc.; Euripides, *Electra* 236, 433; *ametria* and *ametros*, Democritus DK B70, C3; *summetron* as 'appropriate', 'suitable', Aeschylus, *Eumenides* 532, Isocrates 4.83, etc.; *summetria* as 'due proportion' at Democritus B191, cf. Pythag. DK D4, Crit. B6. In Plato these ethically charged uses are extremely common: cf. for example, *Gorgias* 525A, *Timaeus* 86C, 87D, *Republic* 486D, *Sophist* 228C, *Laws* 690E, 820C, 918B. On the *Philebus* see Nussbaum, *Fragility*, chap. 5. The central importance of '*metrios*' as an ethical term requires no exemplification.

38. The sentiment is close to one expressed in Gorgias's apology of Palamedes (30): 'Who was it who made human life resourceful from resourcelessness, and ordered from disorder ... discovering ..., and measures and weights, resourceful adjudications of our dealings ...?'

39. 522B ff.; the words '*technē*' and '*epistēmē*' are used without differentiation.

40. 987C ff. Even if this is not a genuine work of Plato (as I believe it is) it develops a recognizably Platonic position. Here again, the author switches back and forth between '*technē*' and '*epistēmē*' without distinction, so that it is not possible to tell to which noun the adjectives in *-ikē* refer. Cf. also *Laws* 819–20, where lack of knowledge of the commensurable and incommensurable is called 'a condition not human but more appropriate to certain swinish creatures', concerning which the Stranger declares himself 'ashamed not only on my own behalf but also on behalf of all Greeks' (819D). It should be observed, however, that the greatest problem, according to the Stranger, is that people believe things to be commensurable when really they are *not*. This, together with the fact that he acknowledges shame on his own behalf, may indicate a later criticism of the single science of measurement, in keeping with shifts in Plato's thought discussed in Nussbaum, *Fragility*, chap. 7. See Nussbaum, 'Plato on commensurability and desire', in *Love's Knowledge* (Oxford, 1990).

41. Below, this point is explicitly applied to the question of measuring by pleasure as the coin of ethical value.

42. The literature on this issue is large. Much of it deals with questions about the relationship between this dialogue and other early dialogues, and between both and the views of the historical Socrates. I shall not take up either of these large questions here; for the present I shall regard this dialogue as a self-contained work of Plato, continuous in its problems and concerns with other Platonic works.

43. Thus my position is similar to those of R. Crombie, *An Examination of Plato's Doctrines*, vols. 1–2 (London, 1962–1963), and R. Hackforth, 'Hedonism in Plato's *Protagoras*', *Classical Quarterly*, n.s. 22 (1982): 39–42, both of whom see Plato as 'trying out' hedonism out of certain background concerns with practical knowledge. Zeyl, 'Socrates and hedonism: *Protagoras* 351B–358D', *Phronesis* 25 (1980): 250–269, though he describes his position as 'anti-hedonist' and claims that the choice of pleasure as end is *ad hominem*, comes close to my position when he points out that to establish his conclusion Socrates needs not hedonism as such, but some premise that ensures singleness and commensurability (260).

44. Creon spoke of commensurability (387)—though without any precise quantitative account of the end in question: cf. Nussbaum, *Fragility*, chap. 3. Cf. also the *Philoctetes* of Sophocles, where the Chorus's anxious demand to be shown a practical *technē* leads them ultimately to sympathize with the consequentialist view of Odysseus, which judges actions right insofar as they contribute to a single final good (see *Fragility*, chap. 3, and Nussbaum, 'Consequences'). This is clearly, in the plays' terms, a modern progressive view, associated with Odyssean artfulness and resourcefulness. It challenges a traditional view which is similar to Protagoras's in its emphasis on action as a value in itself and on the importance of a plurality of intrinsic ends. The play testifies to the contemporary interest in a

revisionary ethical science; Neoptolemus's conservatism, like Protagoras's here, is attacked as retrograde.

45. Vlastos, *Plato's Protagoras* (Indianapolis, 1956) adds an important methodological point; it is uncharacteristic of Socrates to argue to an important conclusion of his own using a premise that he himself regards as unreliable (xl, n. 50).

46. This could also be translated 'what I mean'—though I find this translation less plausible, especially when the phrase is repeated at 351E1–2. So the 'I say' does not settle the issue on its own; but the *egō* of C4 is very emphatic, and seems to tell against an *ad hominem* reading.

47. Cf. also 360A. Zeyl, 'Socrates and hedonism', argues for his *ad hominem* reading by pointing out that it is possible to see Socrates as playing an *ad hominem* role straight through to the end. Since this involves ascribing to him non-sincere statements about several important matters, it appears to raise more interpretative problems than it solves (cf. above n. 45).

48. For Bentham's preoccupation with the elimination of contingency and connections between this and his obsessive concern with number and measure, see C. Bahmueller, *The National Charity Company* (California, 1981), which contains many fascinating citations from the unpublished MSS. For the epigraph to this chapter, see p. 83. For discussion of Sidgwick's views about the relationship between Utilitarian morality and common sense, see J. B. Schneewind, *Sidgwick and Victorian Morality* (Oxford, 1977).

49. *Methods of Ethics*, 7th ed. (London, 1907) 401. Cf. also the section 'Hedonism as a method of choice' in J. Rawls, *A Theory of Justice* (Cambridge, Mass., 1971) 554–560.

50. Sidgwick, *Methods* 406; cf. 478–479.

51. Sidgwick, *Methods* 425.

52. On the argument, see especially Irwin, *Plato's Moral Theory*, chap. 4, to whose account I am indebted; see also Zeyl, *op. cit.*, C. C. W. Taylor, *Plato: Protagoras*. A somewhat different account is in G. Santas, 'Plato's *Protagoras* and explanations of weakness', *Philosophical Review* 75 (1966): 3–33, reprinted in G. Vlastos, ed., *The Philosophy of Socrates* (Garden City, 1971).

53. Cf. 358D, where this principle is stated. My formulation here is indebted to Irwin, *Plato's Moral Theory*.

54. For further discussion of this issue, see Nussbaum, 'Plato on commensurability and desire'. A similar connection between incommensurability and weakness is developed in D. Wiggins, 'Weakness of will, commensurability and the objects of deliberation and desire', in *Proceedings of the Aristotelian Society* 79 (1978–1979) 251–277. I read this article in 1975 before starting work on this manuscript, and discovered its relationship to my point in 1982, while making this most recent revision. Thus my impression that I made an independent discovery of this point probably should be qualified.

55. For further discussion of these connections, see Nussbaum, *Fragility*, chaps. 5, 6, 11. (See also chap. 5, sec. V; chap. 6, pp. 181, 196–197.)

56. The children would learn these things most readily if, like children in the Ideal City, they were raised not by parents but by (interchangeable) public functionaries, and if, furthermore, they lived in a society that mandated full communism of property and did away with the exclusivity of sexual relations. Plato correctly sees that psychological changes this profound cannot be effected by lectures; they require a thorough restructuring of human experience. See Nussbaum, 'Plato on commensurability' for further discussion of these points. I ignore here the possibility raised there, that a thoroughgoing belief in commensurability would deprive people of the logical/metaphysical basis for individuating objects.

Chapter 9

Taking Plans Seriously

Michael Bratman

We are planning creatures. We frequently settle in advance on more or less complex plans concerning the future, and then these plans guide our later conduct. My plan for today includes beginning the day by preparing my lecture for my afternoon class, turning to some work on this paper, meeting Howard at the Faculty Club for lunch, giving my lecture, talking with John if he is in his office and, finally, picking up a manuscript at the computer center on the way home. As the day proceeds I execute my plan though, of course, I also must make further decisions (which route should I take to the computer center?) and could always reconsider my plan.

In this paper I try to sketch answers to two questions. First, what is involved in having such garden-variety plans? Second, what are the general outlines of a theory of practical rationality that takes such plans seriously?

1   PLANS: WHY WE BOTHER AND WHAT THEY ARE

I have spoken of my plan for the day. But this is ambiguous. On the one hand, I could mean an appropriate abstract structure—some sort of partial function from circumstances to actions, perhaps. On the other hand I could mean an appropriate state of mind, one naturally describable in terms of such structures. A more careful usage might reserve "plan" for the former and "having a plan" for the latter; but this is frequently stylistically awkward. In this paper I will use "plan" to mean "having a plan"—that is, a state of mind. Thus, plans are in the same category as though (for reasons that will emerge) different from desires and beliefs.

I want to know what is involved in having a plan of the garden-variety sort just described, and how such plans figure in a plausible conception of practical rationality. To do this I think we need to ask yet another question: Why, anyway, do we bother with such plans for the future?[1] Why don't we just cross our bridges when we come to them?

Part of the answer is that we thereby avoid the need for deliberation at the time of action. If I have settled on no relevant plan I will have to figure out what to do when I come to the bridge. But if I have settled on a plan to cross, and the situation at the bridge is at least roughly as I expected it to be, such deliberation will not be necessary. This can be quite useful in cases in which there will be limited opportunity for reflection when I get there.

But this is not the only or even the most important reason why we bother with such plans. We settle on such plans as a way of *coordinating* various activities. Plans facilitate coordination both of my own activities over time, and of my activities with yours. The ability to settle on such plans thereby enables us to achieve complex personal and social goals we would not otherwise be able to achieve.

For example, my plan for today enables me to coordinate various activities—including lecture-writing, paper-writing, and other errands—so as to achieve a complex mix of goals. And it is because both Howard and I are planning to meet each other for lunch that we are able to coordinate our otherwise disparate activities so as to achieve a common goal.

But how does this work? Just by *deciding* or *settling* at the beginning of the day on a plan for the rest of the day I do not ensure coordination. Such coordination requires, at the least, that there be some influence on my (and Howard's) later conduct. And my decision, at the beginning of the day, does not reach its ghostly hand over time to influence what I do later. Rather, it sets up a new state—a kind of decision "trace"—which somehow has the needed influence. This is the state of having a plan.[2] We make progress in understanding what it is to have a plan by reflecting on those features of this state which enable it to support such coordination.

Consider Howard and me. My plan to meet him at the Faculty Club is based on my expectation that he will be there, an expectation in turn based on my knowledge of his plan to be there. Howard's plan is in turn based on his expectation that I will be there, an expectation based on his knowledge of my plan. Now, how is it that my knowledge of Howard's plan to go to the Faculty Club at lunch time can support a reasonable expectation that he will?

A natural conjecture here is that this is in part because Howard's plan tends to motivate him to act as planned. It is a *pro-attitude* in at least the very general sense in which desires, inclinations, goals, and valuations are, and ordinary beliefs are not. Pro-attitudes in this very general sense play a motivational role: in concert with our beliefs they can move us to act. Thus, in knowing Howard's plan I know of a state that will tend to lead to his going to the Faculty Club at lunch time.

But this is not enough to support the kind of expectation that underlies such garden-variety cases of interpersonal coordination. Here we need to distinguish between two kinds of pro-attitudes. Suppose I desire a milkshake for lunch, recognize that the occasion is here, and am guilty of no irrationality. Still, I might not drink a milkshake; for my desire for a milkshake still needs to be weighed against conflicting desires—say, my desire to lose weight. Even though my desire for a milkshake *influences* what I do at lunch time, in the normal course of events I still might not drink one.

Let us say that my desire is merely a conduct-*influencing* pro-attitude. Now, the motivational role of *plans* seems different; plans seem not to be *merely* conduct-influencers. Suppose that this morning I settled on a plan that included my having a milkshake at lunch. Lunch-time arrives, my plan remains, and nothing unexpected happens. In such a case I do not need yet again to tote up the pros and cons concerning milkshake drinking. Rather, in the normal course of events I will simply proceed to execute this part of my plan and order a milkshake. My plan will not merely influence my conduct, it will *control* it: it is a conduct-*controlling* pro-attitude.

This difference in motivational roles helps explain how plans facilitate coordination. If I only knew that Howard had a conduct-influencing pro-attitude in favor of lunch at the Faculty Club I would have a much harder time determining whether I could reasonably expect him to be there. I would have to know much more about Howard's psychology: what his other goals and desires were, how they ranked in importance, how he tended to weigh up conflicting considerations, and so on. Interpersonal coordination would be rather difficult.

But in fact I know more than this, and this is why such coordination can work so smoothly. I know that in the normal course of events Howard's plan to lunch at the Faculty Club will *control* his conduct at lunch time, so long as he does not change his mind. If he continues to have this plan and recognizes the occasion he will at least try to go there, without having to weigh this plan against other desires, goals, and what-not. Howard has a conduct-controlling pro-attitude in favor of going to the Faculty Club, not merely a conduct-influencing one; and this helps support the expectations needed for coordination.

Plans are conduct-controlling pro-attitudes, and that is partly why they are able to play the role they do in interpersonal coordination. But this is still not the whole story. None of this would work if plans did not have a certain *stability*. I need to know that Howard's plan can be expected to stay around until lunch time. Of course, there is no reason to suppose that his plan is absolutely immune to change if something unexpected happens. But my reasonable expectation that he will be at the Faculty Club does not need such a supposition of rigidity. It just needs the sup-position (roughly) that the plan will be stable within most of the sorts of variations in Howard's beliefs, desires and circumstances that are realis-tically possible between now and lunch.

What is it for a plan to be stable, in the sense that is relevant here? First, in the normal course of events it will not vary in response to ordi-nary, nonrational bodily processes, unlike my desires to eat and drink. Second, and most important, having a plan will involve a strong dispo-sition *not to reconsider* it except in the face of a significant problem—as we might say, following John Dewey, except in the face of a "problematic situation." (Of course, Howard may fill in his plan, or make adjustments in its sub-plans, without reconsidering it.)

This associated disposition not to reconsider one's prior plan will play a significant role in later discussion, so let me say a bit more about it right away. Reconsidering a plan is something one *does*. It is not merely for the thought of acting differently to occur. Typically, to reconsider a plan is to reason with the aim of seeing whether some other plan would be better. In contrast, when I do *not* reconsider a plan of mine that is not normally an action of mine at all; normally it is just the absence of an action of reconsidering. Of course, there will be some cases in which I explicitly decide not to reconsider my plan, and intentionally refrain from reconsidering it. But normally not reconsidering does not involve intentionally refraining from reconsidering. Stability involves primarily a disposition not to reconsider, and only secondarily a disposition inten-tionally to refrain from reconsidering.

Plans, then, support interpersonal coordination, of the sort Howard and I are attempting, in part because they are relatively stable, conduct-controlling pro-attitudes. What about *intra*personal coordination? My plan for the day, I have said, facilitates the coordination of a complicated array of my activities over time. How?

In a way analogous to the interpersonal case. I begin the day by working on my lecture in part because of my expectation that I will get to work on this paper later in the day. Otherwise I would feel compelled to work on this paper right away, given the pressing deadline and my ability to give an acceptable lecture without any preparation. My plan grounds this expectation. It does this despite my known proclivity to get caught up in lecture preparations. It grounds this expectation in part because it is a conduct-controlling pro-attitude, and so normally need not be weighed against conflicting considerations when the time to turn to this paper arrives. (If it did need to be weighed in this way I might be considerably less confident that I *will* turn to this paper, knowing my tendency to be overly impressed with the importance of detailed lecture-preparations when I am in their midst.) It grounds this expectation also because it is a relatively stable state. I am disinclined to reconsider it in the light of minor variations in my situation—including variations in the degree to which I am attracted to working on the lecture.[3]

It is at least in part because plans are relatively stable, conduct-controlling pro-attitudes that they are so *useful* to us in facilitating both interpersonal and intrapersonal coordination. The ability to have such plans is, for us, a kind of "universal means," useful in our pursuit of a wide variety of different ends.

2   PLANS AND INTELLIGENT ACTIVITY

What would a theory of practical rationality look like if it took such plans, and their coordinating role, seriously? Part of the answer would consist of an account of constraints of consistency and coherence that are applicable to a person's plans both in isolation and together with his beliefs. Here I will draw on my earlier discussion of these matters.[4]

To serve their coordinating role well my plans will need, other things equal, to be both *consistent with each other* and *consistent with my beliefs*. It should be possible for my plans taken together to be successfully executed in a world in which my beliefs are true. Further, other things equal, my plans should also be *means-end coherent*. They should be filled in with appropriate sub-plans concerning how I am to do what I plan to do, sub-plans at least as extensive as I believe is now required to do what I plan. For example, at some point my plan may need to be filled in to include a sub-plan concerning my route home at the day's end.

The demand for means-end coherence is connected with the characteristic *incompleteness* of plans. Consider three ways in which the plans people like us normally have are *partial*. First, they do not specify what to do in *every* conceivable circumstance. My plan for the day does not tell me what to do in the event of an earthquake; though I might have another "stand by" plan for dealing with such an untoward eventuality. Second, plans will not normally specify what to do down to the most detailed, physical level. My plans will typically be at a level of abstraction appropriate to my habits and skills. I may need a detailed plan for shooting a jumpshot, a plan that specifies which foot to jump off from, when to break my wrist, and so on. In contrast, Dr. J's plan may be just to shoot a jump shot and then to steal the ball on the in-bounds play. Third, when initially formulated a plan may only provide a relatively general specification of some later conduct, a specification the agent knows will need to be filled in prior to the time of action. My initial plan may only tell me to stop at the computer center on the way home. But I know I will need later to settle on a specific route.

The demand for means-end coherence arises from this third way in which plans are partial. It is not a demand to complete my plans with respect to every conceivable circumstance or physical movement I might make. It is only a demand to fill in my plans with specifications of how I am to do what I am planning to do, specifications that are only as detailed as is, on my view, needed for me successfully to execute my plan. Nor is it a demand that these specifications be filled in all at once. They need only be provided at appropriate later stages in the on-going construction of my plan. I can leave until later the choice of a specific route home.

My view, then, is that there is a pragmatic rationale, rooted in the coordinating role of plans, for demands for consistency and means-end coherence on those plans. In being subject to these demands, plans differ from ordinary desires. I might desire to have a milkshake for lunch, and desire to run four miles after lunch (which is not to say that I desire to have a milkshake and to run) all the time knowing that if I do the former I will not be able to do the latter. Yet there need be no irrationality here. It is just a conflict of a sort that occurs countless times in the life of a reasonable person. If, however, my *plans* include both actions then I *am* guilty of a criticizable form of inconsistency. Again, simply desiring to stop at the computer center on the way home places me under no rational requirement to settle on some means to doing so, in the way in which planning to stop there would.

Let us turn now to action. How should we think of rationality in action if we are going to take plans seriously?

On one dominant tradition, inspired by Hume, rationality in action is a matter of fit between the action and the agent's desires and beliefs, values and expectations, utilities and probabilities, or some similar conative-cognitive pair. Strict Humeans confine themselves to the agent's desires and beliefs at the time of action. Others see as also relevant what desires and beliefs the agent will have, or would have under certain conditions (for example, certain kinds of reflection).

Such approaches involve a *two-parameter* conception of practical reason. But our discussion of plans should make us skeptical that such a two-parameter conception will provide a complete picture. After all, my *plans* seem somehow relevant to whether I am acting reasonably when I am executing them. Yet having a plan seems an importantly different sort of state than having a desire or a belief. Plans are conduct-*controlling* attitudes, not merely conduct-*influencing* ones, as are ordinary desires. Plans are subject to consistency and coherence constraints to which ordinary desires are not subject. And, as pro-attitudes, plans differ significantly from beliefs in their motivational role.[5]

The very idea that we have plans that are—and reasonably so—both *partial* and relatively *stable* will force us to complicate our account of rationality in action. You can see this in two ways. Consider, first, stability. To be stable is, in part, to resist reconsideration. So we will want to know when such resistance to reconsideration, and the conduct in which it issues, is reasonable. Now add partiality. A partial plan will need to be filled in later, prior to action. Given that the plan is relatively stable, the practical reasoning aimed at filling it in will take its main outlines for granted. This means that options will be seen as relevant only if they are compatible with those main outlines. We will want a theory of rationality in action somehow to illuminate the structure of such reasoning and the appropriate standards of reasonableness.

To make progress here let us reflect further on the role of deliberation and plans in intelligent activity. "Deliberation," Dewey teaches us, "has its beginnings in troubled activity."[6] The implicit contrast here is between smooth, on-going activity in which no further deliberation is called for, and cases in which deliberation is needed to "resolve entanglements in existing activity."[7] The phenomenon of plan-execution provides us with a special case of this general contrast.

On the one hand, there are cases in which the agent is engaged in an on-going activity involving the execution of a prior plan. He recognizes no problem for his plan; he runs into no "entanglements." He simply proceeds to execute it without further reconsideration of its merits. This is a case of *nondeliberative plan-execution*. On the other hand, there are cases in which the agent deliberatively weighs the pros and cons in favor of and against several conflicting options that present themselves for choice. He deliberates because he has run into some "entanglement" in executing some plan, or because he has been presented with a choice of a sort not anticipated in any such plan. This is a case of *deliberative decision*.

When we come to assess the agent's conduct in such cases we will need to ask slightly different questions. To keep track of these differences let us say that deliberative decisions are more or less *rational*, while in nondeliberatively executing a prior plan one is acting more or less *reasonably*. Thus, as I am using these terms, "rational" and "reasonable" are terms of assessment that apply to different objects: the former to deliberative decisions, the latter to cases of nondeliberative plan execution.[8]

Having said this, an important complexity should be noted immediately. Cases of "pure" deliberative decision or nondeliberative plan-execution are clearly atypical extremes. Most real cases of intelligent activity are a *hybrid*, involving elements of both.

This is because plans will typically have both a *hierarchical* and a *linear* structure. More general plans will embed more specific plans; as when my day's plan embeds a specific plan for getting to the computer center. And more extensive plans will organize various less extensive sub-plans either in sequence or meshed in some more or less complicated way. This is what my plan for the day does with my sub-plans concerning writing this paper and giving my lecture. Suppose, then, I am nondeliberatively executing a plan at a certain level of generality and extensiveness. I still might, at the same time, be deliberatively weighing the pros and cons concerning various ways of resolving a problem that has arisen at a more specific or more limited level. I might be faced with a problem with the writing of my lecture that requires some deliberative decision even while nondeliberatively executing my more general and more extensive plan for the day.

Indeed, it seems that most cases of deliberative decision are like this: they take place within the framework of the nondeliberative execution of a plan at a more general and/or more extensive level. This plan provides a background framework for the deliberative weighing of pros and cons. It does not merely influence one's decision between options, in the way that ordinary desires do. Rather, the background plan constrains what options are *relevant* options. Thus, I deliberate between different ways of presenting the Prisoner's Dilemma to my afternoon class; I do not consider putting down my lecture notes and going for a four-mile run. So long as I do not reconsider my more general plan I treat it as providing a fixed framework within which my more specific sub-plans are to be fit.

Of course, I *might* reconsider my more general plan for the day, and actually consider whether to run instead. Given a plan at any level of generality or extensiveness that one is nondeliberatively executing, it is always possible to reconsider and bring that plan into question. But we would cease to be planning creatures if we constantly reconsidered all our plans—if we always started from scratch. Typically we will be nondeliberatively executing some plans even while deliberating among various options, options duly constrained by the plans being executed.

This means that even cases of deliberative weighing will typically raise two sorts of questions: Was the agent's deliberative decision rational? And at the level at which the agent was nondeliberatively executing a plan, did his conduct satisfy plausible standards of reasonableness? A conception of rationality in action will need to address both such questions.

Within the Humean tradition cited above, it is common to see the rationality of a deliberative decision between several options presented for choice as a matter of the fit between those options and the agent's desires and beliefs. For example, it is common to suppose that a rational decision will favor that option with highest "expected utility." Now, I do not want to try to settle here on the merits of this conception. Rather, I want to point out than even if it were accepted as a conception of rational deliberative decision, we would still need a more elaborate framework for a full theory of rationality in action. This is because we would still be in need of an account of reasonable plan execution. I want now to try to sketch the outlines of such an account.

3 REASONABLE STABILITY

We have noted that for plans to play their characteristic role in coordination they need to have a certain stability. We need to say something more about what such stability involves and about when the stability of a plan is more or less reasonable.[9]

The stability of my plan for the day is largely a matter of my associated disposition not to reconsider it. This disposition may be rather minimal: I might be inclined to reconsider my plan given only a slight divergence between the way the world is when I come to act and the way I expected it to be when I first settled on my plan. Or the disposition might involve substantial rigidity, as when I would only reconsider it in the face of some extreme divergence from my expectations—an earthquake, for example.

A plan might be stable in some respects and not in others. Perhaps my discovery that there is a special lecture today at lunch time would not trigger reconsideration of my plan, whereas my discovery that this paper is due a month later than I had thought would. In contrast, things might be the other way round for you. My plan might be unstable in a respect in which yours is relatively stable, and vice versa.

The stability of my plan may be rooted in a further, "second-order" plan, but it need not. I may actually plan to reconsider my day's plan if I learn of a change in the deadline. But I need not have such a further plan in order to be *disposed* to reconsider in such circumstances.

The stability of a plan is generally a long-term feature of that plan: I do not constantly adjust the stability of my plans. To do that would undermine the point of having plans, for I would then be constantly reconsidering their merits. Further, I normally do not *decide* how stable my plan is to be. Generally, I do not, having settled on a plan, begin to reason yet again about how stable my plan should be (though in special cases I might). Rather, the stability of my plan is largely determined by general, underlying dispositions of mine.

The stability of my plans will generally not be an isolated feature of those plans, but will be linked with other features of my psychology. For example, if I am the sort of person who is constantly on the alert for dangers in my environment, my plans are likely to have a kind of instability they would not have if I were a person too engrossed in my projects to be very sensitive to such dangers.[10] I might be more likely than most to reconsider my planned route home upon hearing of a smog alert in the area. Frequently, the extent of stability of my plans will be connected with underlying tendencies to *take notice* of certain sorts of things and not others—to see certain features of my environment as *salient*. I may be more likely to take notice of certain kinds of hazards than you, and this fact may well be tied to a certain kind of instability that my plans have and yours do not.

In light of this discussion, what can we say about when a plan is *appropriately* stable? *not stable enough* in certain respects? *too stable* in other respects? Most generally, what can we say about when the stability of a plan is *reasonable*? Here I do not have as much an answer as the sketch of an answer—an answer that is broadly consequentialist in structure.

Return for a moment to rational deliberative decision. As noted, we might see this, in the Humean tradition, as a matter of fit with relevent desires and beliefs. Or, taking a somewhat different tack, we might see the rationality of such a decision as a matter of its expected impact on the agent's overall good. I will not try to resolve such differences here. What I do want to point out is that such conceptions share a certain structure. They assess the rationality of a deliberative decision by appeal to its expected impact on some central *goal*: desire-satisfaction, the agent's overall good, or perhaps something else.

Given such a goal, we may proceed in an analogous way in assessing plan stability. Suppose that I have a plan that is stable in certain ways. We can consider the general disposition to have one's plans of this sort be stable in such ways. We can then ask about the expected impact on the goal we have singled out, of my having this general disposition. The better this expected impact the more reasonable is the stability of my plan. The stability of my plan is reasonable *simpliciter* when this expected impact exceeds an appropriate threshold.

The expected impact of such a disposition towards stability will itself depend on a variety of factors. It will depend on what psychological traits are involved in such plan stability. It will depend on what sort of plan is in question: for example, how general the plan is. It will depend on general facts about my social and environmental circumstances. And, finally, it will depend on general facts about my particular psychology that may vary even while the disposition towards such stability remains fixed. For example, it will depend on the extent of my general abilities to reason carefully and quickly in the face of the unexpected.

Note that it is not only the impact on my *actions* that matters. This will, of course, be one of the main considerations relevant to our assessment of the stability of my plan. But there are other ways in which stability, and its associated psychological traits, can have a relevant impact. Suppose, for example, that the goal in terms of which we are assessing stability is the agent's long-term good. And suppose I have a high sensitivity to certain kinds of environmental hazards, a sensitivity associated with certain kinds of plan instability. Now, these kinds of instability may in fact conduce to certain kinds of useful preventive activity. But they may also conduce to a kind of apprehensive and fearful consciousness that will undermine my good. And that impact also is relevant to the assessment of such instabilities.

Another point to notice is that there will, in general, be a kind of social pressure towards increased stability. This is because the stability of my plans is one of the things that makes me a reliable partner in various schemes of interpersonal coordination—schemes that are to everyone's advantage.

So we have the following picture. A conception of rational deliberative decision can be expected to cite a central goal in terms of which such decisions are to be assessed. Given such a goal we may proceed to assess plan stability in a similarly consequentialist vein. This means that conceptions of rational deliberative decision can be *paired*, in a natural way, with conceptions of reasonable plan stability.

4   REASONABLE PLAN EXECUTION

With this treatment of reasonable stability in hand, let us return to our question of when an agent acts reasonably in nondeliberatively executing a prior plan. Recall that this phenomenon is not limited to cases in which there is no deliberation between alternative options. In many cases such deliberation will take place within the context of the nondeliberative execution of a more general plan. In such cases the options seen as relevant will be constrained by the more general plan. Once in the classroom, I might stop my lecture for a moment and try to figure out which of several ways of making a certain point will work best. But, unless I reconsider my more general plan, I will not stop to determine whether it would be better to stop the lecture in the middle and head over to the gym. What we want to know is when such nondeliberative execution of my more general plan, even when accompanied by deliberation at a less general level, is reasonable.

My strategy will be to construct an answer in terms of two ideas that have already received some discussion: reasonable plan stability and rational deliberative decision. I will assume we have some conception of when a deliberative decision, between several options presented for choice, is rational. This conception will be paired with a corresponding conception of reasonable plan stability. Given these two conceptions, what is it for my activity in nondeliberatively executing my plan to be reasonable?

My plans are constructed over time in different stages. We may suppose that at each stage in the construction of a plan I make a deliberative decision between different options, options themselves constrained by the structure of my plan as so far formed. Now let us consider a particular present plan of mine and suppose that the following conditions are satisfied. First, at each stage in the construction of my plan my deliberative decision, in favor of one element rather than others, was rational. Second, I have, until now, been successfully executing the earlier components of this plan. Third, my present plan, as so far formed, both satisfies our requirements of consistency and means-end coherence and is stable in various ways. Fourth, this stability is reasonable. Fifth, and finally, my present situation does not involve the sort of problem or "entanglement" that triggers reconsideration of my plan, given the ways in which it is stable. Given these conditions, I proceed nondeliberatively to execute part of my plan. What can we say about the reasonableness of my conduct in such a case?

It seems to me that, at least on one commonsense form of assessment, I am acting in a way that is not subject to a serious form of rational criticism: I am acting *reasonably* in so executing my plan. After all, I am engaged in the kind of plan-execution characteristic of the sort of planning creature I am—the sort of plan-execution the capacity for which we have seen to be so useful. And each element in my activity passes muster: my plan is the product of a sequence of rational deliberative decisions; it is now consistent, coherent and reasonably stable; and it is because of that stability that it is now being executed without further reconsideration.

I think, then, that we have here plausible sufficient conditions for reasonable, nondeliberative plan execution. A full account would provide plausible necessary conditions as well. But here I am content with a partial account that provides only sufficient conditions.

While only partial, this view of reasonable plan execution has several important consequences. First, my nondeliberative execution of my plan may be reasonable even though, as it happens, in this particular case it would have been better if I had reconsidered. (By "better" I mean better in terms of the expected impact on the goal by reference to which deliberative decisions are to be assessed—desire-satisfaction, perhaps.) This may be so even taking into account the inconvenience and other costs associated with reconsideration.

For example, suppose it is true that if upon hearing of the special lecture I had stopped and reconsidered my plan to meet Howard, then I would have seen that I could persuade Howard to meet me there. This option would have been slightly better, even taking into account the costs of reconsideration, than my proceeding nondeliberatively with my original plan. Nevertheless, my disposition not to reconsider my original plan in the face of this new information about the lecture might well be a kind of stability that is quite reasonable for me. After all, a general tendency to reconsider my plans in such cases, in which only marginal improvements are likely, will have obvious disadvantages. We are not very good at detecting slight differences in the pros and cons of various options, so reconsideration in such cases will many times just lead to inefficient delay. And the more inclined we are in favor of such reconsideration, the more difficult will be various forms of coordination. So it may well be that I act reasonably in proceeding nondeliberatively with my plan to meet Howard at the Faculty Club. If my plan had been considerably less stable I would have reconsidered; and on this particular occasion that would have been fortunate. But then my plan may well have been unreasonably unstable.

A second corollary is that two people, Smith and Jones, can be quite similar in their desires, beliefs and plans, and yet still differ in ways important to a theory of rational conduct. This is because their plans can still differ in stability, or be similar in stability but this stability be reasonable for one person but not for the other. Suppose, first, that Smith's plan is stable in ways in which Jones's is not. Given differences in their abilities, however, both plans are *reasonably* stable. (Perhaps Jones is just better at reasoning quickly in the face of the unexpected: he is a better improviser.) Jones might then reconsider his plan in a situation in which Smith would not. Jones might proceed rationally to diverge from his prior plan, while Smith would have proceeded to act reasonably in nondeliberatively executing that plan. So Smith and Jones would act differently and yet the former act reasonably and the latter rationally. Same beliefs, desires, and plans. Different actions. Yet both act in ways that are not criticizable by our theory.

Again, Smith's and Jones's plans may be quite similar in their stability yet, because of differences in their abilities, Smith's plan might be reasonably stable while Jones's is not. So, when they both proceed nondeliberatively to execute their plan it may be well that Smith acts reasonably while Jones does not. Same desires, beliefs, and plans. Same action. Yet one acts reasonably and the other does not.

The reasonableness of an agent's activity will depend, then, on his plans, the stability of these plans, and on the reasonableness of this stability. (Of course, it will depend on other things as well.) A theory of rationality in action that ignores this role of plans and their stability will be importantly incomplete.

5 INTENTIONS AND PLANS

I began this paper by asserting that we are planning creatures. I have been arguing that we need to take this fact seriously in our accounts of the motivation and assessment of intelligent activity. This argument applies both to commonsense and to scientific psychology. Both a plausible reconstruction of the former, and a reasonable candidate for the latter will, it seems to me, need to include something like plans among the states that play a motivational role.[11] (This is not, of course, to say that *all* intentional activity is motivated by prior plans.) Such plans are importantly different sorts of states than ordinary desires and beliefs. And facts about them and their stability will play a basic role in an acceptable theory of practical rationality.

I conclude with a brief remark about intention. Anscombe begins her justly famous monograph[12] by distinguishing between intending to do something and doing something intentionally. She then proceeds to treat the latter as basic for the theory of action, and leaves us without a clear treatment of the former. Many treatments of intention in the wake of Anscombe's monograph have more or less gone along with this theoretical decision and treated intentional action as the basic case for our understanding of intention.[13] Once we take plans seriously, however, a different strategy recommends itself. Rather than try to understand intending to act in terms of the purportedly more basic phenomenon of intentional action, we turn to the phenomenon of future-directed plans. We understand what it is to intend to do something in large part in terms of such plans; for future intentions are, at least typically, elements in such larger plans. This is to follow the strategy of *the methodological priority of future intentions and plans*. I conjecture that in this way we will gain a better understanding of the distinctive role intentions play in our lives.[14]

Acknowledgments

I want to thank Allan Gibbard for extremely helpful conversations on some of the topics of this paper, and for allowing me to see an as-yet unpublished paper of his on related issues. I also want to thank Patrick Suppes for providing detailed comments on an earlier draft that were immensely useful. I am also indebted to Robert Audi, Arnold Davidson, and Adrian Piper for many helpful comments. Initial work on this paper was supported by a summer research grant from the National Endowment for the Humanities.

Notes

1. I do not mean to be asking here about our specific reasons for settling on a prior plan in a particular case. My concern is, rather, with the general role such plans play in our lives.

2. Thus plans provide the connection between decision and future action decided upon, just as a "memory trace" may be thought to provide the connection between remembering and the past event remembered. Concerning the notion of a "memory trace," see C. B. Martin and M. Deutscher, "Remembering," *Philosophical Review* 75 (1966): 161–96.

3. Though plans normally support expectations of their successful execution as part of their contribution to coordination, there may still be cases in which I plan to A but do not believe I will. Though I will not pursue the point in this paper, I suspect that we have here a basis for a resolution of debates concerning the possibility of intending to A without believing I will. For conflicting views on this matter see Donald Davidson, "Intending," in *Essays on Actions and Events* (New York: Oxford University Press, 1980), pp. 83–102; and Paul Grice, "Intention and Uncertainty," *Proceedings of the British Academy* 57 (1971): 263–279.

4. In "Intention and Means-End Reasoning," *Philosophical Review* 90 (1981): 252–265 esp. pp. 259–260.

5. As indicated below, I see future intentions as, at least typically, elements in such plans. So what I am saying here amounts to a rejection of the sort of reductive approaches to intention offered by Audi, Beardsley, and Churchland. These philosophers try to analyze an intention to A as a complex of desires and beliefs. My remarks in this paragraph suggest some reasons for being wary of such attempts. But in the end I think the main argument for seeing plans—and so, intentions—as distinctive psychological phenomena lies in the theoretical usefulness of this approach. I take the present paper to be part of an argument for such utility. See Robert Audi, "Intending," *Journal of Philosophy* 70 (1973): 387–403; Monroe Beardsley, "Intending," in *Values and Morals: Essays in Honor of William Frankena, Charles Stevenson, and Richard Brandt*, ed. Alvin Goldman and Jaegwon Kim (Dordrecht, Holland: Reidel, 1978), pp. 163–184; and Paul Churchland, "The Logical Character of Action-Explanations," *Philosophical Review* 79 (1970): 214–236.

6. John Dewey, *Human Nature and Conduct* (New York: Random House, 1957), p. 187.

7. Dewey, p. 187.

8. I will be extending the scope of "reasonable" somewhat in the discussion to follow.

9. Here I am extending the scope of "reasonable" in the obvious way.

10. This example is derived from an example of Allan Gibbard's.

11. Atkinson and Birch seem inclined toward a similar conclusion in reflecting on the limitations of their theory when they write: "One reader of an early draft ... was concerned with how the *planning* and *scheduling* of activities, which distinguishes human from animal behavior, is to be taken into account. And so are we. At this writing, we consider planning a covert conceptual activity of considerable motivational significance, although we have not, as yet, encompassed the topic in any systematic way." *The Dynamics of Action* (New York: John Wiley and Sons, 1970), p. 95 n.

12. G. E. M. Anscombe, *Intention* (Ithaca: Cornell University Press, 1963).

13. This is even true of Davidson's work in the theory of action, even though he famously *dis*agrees with Anscombe on the issue of whether reasons are causes. See my essay "Davidson's Theory of Intention," reprinted in Michael Bratman, *Faces of Intention* (Cambridge: Cambridge University Press, 1999), pp. 209–224.

14. I expand on this point in "Two Faces of Intention," *Philosophical Review* 93 (1984): 375–405.

Chapter 10

Moderation and Satisficing

Michael Slote

It is widely assumed by philosophers (and of course others as well) that individualistic or extramoral practical rationality is subject to a condition of maximization: that the rational egoist, or the average non-egoist under conditions where the welfare of or commitments to others are not at issue, will seek to maximize her own good, or well-being. Utilitarians like Sidgwick and anti-utilitarians like Rawls both seem to assume that it is egoistically, individualistically, irrational not to maximize one's satisfactions and seek one's own greatest good.[1] More recently, however, some explicitly non-maximizing conceptions of personal well-being over time have been suggested by Amartya Sen and Charles Fried, who have, with differing degrees of vehemence, defended the notion that considerations of equality in the intertemporal distribution of goods in a single life have some independent weight in the reckoning of the goodness of lives.[2] The rational individual will wish to consider how much good for himself given courses of action will produce but also how evenly or equally the resultant good or satisfaction will be distributed across different times of his life, and he will allow for trade-offs between total amount of satisfaction and equality of distribution of satisfaction in deciding what courses of action to follow.

But even such non-maximizing conceptions of human good and the rational planning of lives never suggest that the egoistic individual, or the non-egoistic individual in situations where only his own well-being is at issue, should ever do anything but optimize; what gives way in such conceptions is the idea that the course of action yielding the most good or satisfaction is always best for a given individual, but the assumption that the rational individual does the best he can for himself remains unscathed. Fried and Sen in effect tell us that human well-being must be more complexly reckoned than simple (or non-gimmicky) maximizing accounts permit, but they do not propose that the rational egoistic individual, in sometimes seeking *less than the most* available good or satisfaction for herself, might also seek what is *less than best* for herself (both at an isolated given time or over a lifetime). However, I want to argue for just this sort of possibility. In doing so, I know that I shall be defending views which, in the light of unbroken philosophical tradition, will at least initially seem bizarre and implausible. But I think a variety of examples drawn from ordinary life help to underscore the coherence and intuitive force of the idea that we may rationally seek less than the best for ourselves and sometimes even reject what is better for ourselves for what is good enough. However, a number of conceptual and other objections naturally arise in connection with these theses and I hope that by providing answers to those specific objections I may persuade you that we are not going to fall into conceptual confusion or contradiction by rejecting or questioning the view that individualistic rationality requires us to maximize or, more broadly, to optimize with respect to our own good.

I

The idea that a rational individual might seek less than the best for himself was originally developed, I believe, in the literature of economics. The term "satisficing" was coined for the discussion of such behavior, and I shall make use of the term here. What the economists have done, however, is point to an aspect of human behavior (both individually and in groups) that philosophers have traditionally ignored, and I shall be discussing and articulating the idea of satisficing in an attempt to give an adequate philosophical account of this phenomenon. The emphasis will be on conceptual and moral-psychological issues, rather than on the sort of technical economic-theoretic development of the notion of satisficing that can be found in the literature of economics.

Consider an example borrowed from economics.[3] An individual planning to move to a new location and having to sell his house may seek, not to maximize his profit on the house, not to get the best price for it he is likely to receive within some appropriate time period, but simply to obtain what he takes to be a good or satisfactory price. What he deems satisfactory may depend, among other things, on what he paid for the house, what houses cost in the place where he is relocating, and on what houses like his normally sell at. But given some notion of what would be a good or satisfactory price to sell at, he may fix the price of his house at that point, rather than attempting, by setting it somewhat higher, to do better than that or do the best he can. His reason for not setting the price higher will not, in that case, be some sort of anxiety about not being able to sell the house at all or some feeling that trying to do better would likely not be worth the effort of figuring out how to get a better price. Nor is he so rich that any extra money he received for the house would be practically meaningless in terms of marginal utility. Rather, he is a "satisficer" content with good enough and does not seek to maximize (optimize) his expectations. His desires, his needs, are moderate, and perhaps knowing this about himself, he may not be particularly interested in doing better for himself than he is likely to do by selling at a merely satisfactory price. If someone pointed out that it would be better for him to get more money, he would reply, not by disagreeing, but by pointing out that for him at least a good enough price is good enough.

Such a person apparently fails to exemplify the maximizing and optimizing model of individual rationality traditionally advocated by philosophers. But I think he nonetheless represents a possible idea of individual rationality, and much of the literature of economics treats such examples, both as regards individuals and as regards economic units like the firm, as exemplifying a form of rational behavior. Though one might hold on to an optimizing or maximizing model of rationality and regard satisficing examples as indications of the enormous prevalence of irrational human behavior, economists have not done so and I think philosophers would have even less reason to do so. For there are many other cases where satisficing intuitively seems rational, or at least not irrational, and although some of these are purely hypothetical, hypothetical examples are the stock-in-trade of ethical and moral-psychological theory even when they are of little or no interest to economists.

Imagine that it is midafternoon; you had a good lunch, and you are not now hungry; neither, on the other hand, are you sated. You would enjoy a candy bar or Coca-Cola, if you had one, and there is in fact, right next to your desk, a refrigerator stocked with such snacks and provided gratis by the company for which you work. Realizing all this, do you, then, necessarily take and consume a snack? If you do not, is that necessarily because you are afraid to spoil your dinner, because you are on a diet, or because you are too busy? I think not. You may simply not feel the need for any such snack. You turn down a good thing, a sure enjoyment, because you are perfectly satisfied as you are. Most of us are often in situations of this sort, and many of us would often do the same thing. We are not boundless optimizers or maximizers, but are sometimes (more) modest in our desires and needs. But such modesty, such moderation, is arguably neither irrational nor unreasonable on our part.

Of course, moderation has been exalted as a prime virtue in many religious and philosophical traditions. But when, for example, the Epicureans emphasized the rationality of moderation in the pursuit of pleasure, they recommended modesty in one's desires only as a means to an overall more pleasurable, or less unpleasant, life, and in the example mentioned above, moderation is not functioning as a means to greater overall satisfaction or pleasures. One is not worried about ruining one's figure or spoiling one's dinner, and the moderation exemplified is thus quite different from the instrumental virtue recommended by the Epicureans. The sort of moderation I am talking about, then, is not for the sake of anything else.

But then isn't the moderate individual who is content with less a kind of ascetic? Not necessarily. An ascetic is someone who, within certain limits, *minimizes* his enjoyments or satisfactions; he deliberately leaves himself with less, unsatisfied. The moderate individual, on the other hand, is someone content with (what he considers) a reasonable amount of enjoyment; he wants to be satisfied and up to a certain point he wants more enjoyments rather than fewer, to be better off rather than worse off; but there is a point beyond which he has no desire, and even refuses, to go. There is a space between asceticism and the attempt to maximize pleasure or enjoyment—do the best one can for oneself—a space occupied by the habit of moderation. And because such moderation is not a form of asceticism, it is difficult to see why it must count as irrational from the standpoint of egoistic or extra-moral individual rationality.[4]

Now the kind of example just mentioned differs from the case of house selling in being independent of any monetary transaction. But the example differs importantly in another way from examples of satisficing mentioned in the literature of economics. Economists who have advocated the model of rational satisficing for individuals, firms, or state bodies have pointed out that—quite independently of the costs of gaining further information or effecting new policies—an entrepreneur or firm may simply seek a satisfactory return on investment, a satisfactory share of the market, a satisfactory level of sales, rather than attempt to maximize or optimize under any of these headings. But this idea of rational satisficing implies only that individuals or firms *do not always seek* to optimize or are *sat-*

isfied with attaining a certain "aspiration level" less than the best that might be envisaged. It does not imply that it could be rational actually to *reject* the better for the good enough in situations where both were available. In the example of house selling, the individual accepts less than he might well be able to get, but he doesn't accept a lower price when a higher bidder makes an equally firm offer. And writers on satisficing generally seem to hold that satisficing only makes sense as a habit of not seeking what is better or best, rather than as a habit of actually rejecting the better, when it is clearly available, for the good enough. Thus Herbert Simon develops the idea of aspiration level and of satisficing, but goes on to say that "when a firm has alternatives open to it that are at or above its aspiration level, it will choose the best of those known to be available."[5]

However, the example of the afternoon snack challenges the idea that the satisficing individual will never explicitly reject the better for the good enough. For the individual in question turns down an immediately available pleasure, something he knows he will enjoy. He isn't merely not trying for a maximum of enjoyments, but is explicitly rejecting such a maximum. (It may be easier to see the explicitness of the rejection if we change the example so that he is actually offered a snack by someone and replies: no thank you, I'm just fine as I am.) And I think that most of us would argue that there is nothing irrational here. Many of us, most of us, occasionally reject afternoon snacks, second cups of tea, and so on, not out of (unconscious) asceticism, but because (to some degree) we have a habit of moderation with regard to certain pleasures. The hypothetical example of the afternoon snack thus takes the idea of rational satisficing a step beyond where economists, to the best of my knowledge, have been willing to go.

At this point, however, it may be objected that the example may be one of rational behavior but is less than clear as an example of satisficing. The individual in question prefers not to have a certain enjoyment and certainly deliberately rejects the maximization of his enjoyments. But it is not clear that the moderate individual must think of himself as missing out on anything *good* when he forgoes the afternoon snack. For although he knows he would enjoy the snack, the very fact that he rejects such enjoyment might easily be taken as evidence that he doesn't in the circumstances regard such enjoyment as a good thing. In that case, he would be satisficing in terms of some quantitative notion of pleasure or enjoyment, but not with respect to some more refined or flexible notion of (his own) individual good, and the example would provide no counterexample to the idea that it is irrational to choose what is less good for oneself when something better is available.

But it would be a mistake to move too quickly in this direction. It is being granted—and how can it be denied?—that the person who turns down a snack would have enjoyed one. But doesn't that mean—in the circumstances as we have described them and barring irrelevant opportunity costs—that things would at least briefly have gone more enjoyably for him if he had taken a snack? If so, then in common-sense terms it seems undeniable that, in the short term, things would have gone at least slightly better for him if he had done so. (Or don't things go even slightly better with Coke?) However, even if the rejection of a snack does count as the rejection of a personal good—and of a personally better course of events—such facts may be obscured by the very smallness or triviality of the good in question. So it may be useful at this point to consider other examples, more purely hypothetical than the present one, where the good forgone through satisficing is larger and perhaps more obvious.

How do we react to fairy tales in which the hero or heroine, offered a single wish, asks for a pot of gold, for a million dollars, or, simply, for (enough money to enable) his family and himself to be comfortably well off for the rest of their lives? In each case the person asks for less than he might have asked for, but we are not typically struck by the thought that he was irrational to ask for less than he could have, and neither, in general, do the fairy tales themselves imply a criticism of this sort; so, given the tendency of such tales to be full of moralism about human folly, we have, I think, some evidence that such fairy-tale wishes need not be regarded as irrational. (In not regarding them as irrational, we need not be confusing what we know *about* fairy-tale wishes with what the individual *in* a given tale ought to know. In some fairy tales, people who ask for too much fail to get their wish or have it realized in an unacceptable way. But there is no reason to suppose that we consider the person who in a given fairy tale asks for enough to be comfortable not to be irrational, only because we mistakenly imagine him to have some evidence concerning the possible risks of asking for more than he does.)

Now the individual in the fairy tale who wishes for *less* than he could presumably exemplifies the sort of moderation discussed earlier. He may think that a pot of gold or enough money to live comfortably is all he needs to be satisfied, that anything more is of no particular importance to him. At the same time, however, he may realize (be willing to admit) that he could do better for himself by asking for more. He needn't imagine himself constitutionally incapable of benefiting from additional money or gold, for the idea that one will be happy, or satisfied, with a certain level of existence by no means precludes the thought (though it perhaps precludes *dwelling* on the thought) that one will not be as well off as one could be. It merely precludes the sense of wanting or needing more for oneself. Indeed the very fact that someone could actually explicitly wish (for enough money) to be comfortably well-off is itself sufficient evidence of what I am saying. Someone who makes such a wish clearly acknowledges the possibility of being better off and yet chooses—knowingly and in some sense deliberately—a lesser but personally satisfying degree of well-being. And it is precisely because the stakes are so large in such cases of wishing that they provide clearcut examples of presumably rational individual satisficing. But, again, the sort of satisficing involved is not (merely) the kind familiar in the economics literature where an individual seeks something other than optimum results, but a kind of satisficing that actually rejects the available better for the available good enough. Although the individual with the wish would be better off if he wished for more, he asks for less—we may suppose that if the wish grantor prods him by asking "are you sure you wouldn't like more (money or comfort or sheer felicity) than that?" he sticks with his original request. If we have any sympathy with the idea of moderation, of modesty, in one's desires, we shall have to grant that the satisficing individual who wishes for less is not irrational. Perhaps we ourselves would not be so easily satisfied in his circumstances, but that needn't make us think him irrational for being moderate in a way, or to a degree, that we are not.[6]

But at this point some doubt may remain about our description of the moderate individual's response to being granted a wish. It is not obvious that an individual who wishes for less than the most money (or comfort or well-being) he could ask for is satisficing in the strong sense defended earlier. He may make the seemingly modest wish he does because he is afraid of offending the wish grantor or in order to avoid being corrupted (or rendered blasé) by having too much wealth, and acting with such motives he will not exemplify the sort of satisficing moderation whose rationality I have tried to defend: he *will* be seeking what is best for himself under a refined conception of personal good that goes beyond mere wealth or material comfort.[7]

With this I can absolutely agree. An individual who asks for less than she could may indeed be motivated by factors of the above sort. My main point is, and has been, that there is no reason to insist or assume that such factors are always present when an individual asks for less than the most or best he can obtain. From the standpoint of the phenomenology of our own lives, it doesn't seem as if such factors are always present— we find it humanly understandable and not intuitively unreasonable that someone should lack an interest in the greatest heights of well-being or happiness and should actually reject the latter in favor of moderate or sufficient comfort or well-being. Why insist that some factors must always be present to turn putative cases of satisficing into cases, fundamentally, of optimization or maximization of the individual's (perceived) good?

The situation here resembles what is often said for and against psychological egoism. Many people—even philosophers—have argued as if it were practically a matter of definition that individuals seek their own greatest good, even when they appear to be sacrificing that good for the good of others. But nowadays philosophers at least seem to recognize that altruism and self-sacrifice cannot be ruled out a priori. Nonetheless, it in some sense remains empirically open that human altruism may turn out to be an illusion. It is conceivable, let us suppose, that a powerful enough psychological theory backing the universal selfishness of human behavior might eventually be adopted. But in the absence of such a theory, philosophers have been, I think, quite right to insist upon taking altruistic motivation seriously. Any moral psychology that wishes to remain true to our common or everyday understanding of things, to life as most of us seem to lead it, will assume that there is a phenomenon of altruistic motivation to explore and better understand, both conceptually and in its ethical ramifications.

Similar points can, I believe, be made about satisficing, or moderation in the sense delineated earlier. Some day economists and psychologists may show definitively that the best explanation of why humans act as they do requires us to assume that they are always maximizing or optimizing and thus that apparent examples of satisficing or moderation are illusory. But until and unless that happens, we should recognize—something philosophers have not previously noticed or admitted—that the common-sense understanding of our own lives leaves a definite recognizable place for occasional, perhaps even frequent, satisficing moderation. For in fact the phenomenon of moderation is not limited to fairy-tale examples, though I believe such examples allow one to see certain issues large enough and in sufficient isolation so as to make it easier to recognize moderation in the more muddied waters of everyday life. Even the example of the person selling a house need be altered only in minor ways in order to turn it from an example of not seeking the best for oneself into an example of actually rejecting the expectable better for the expectable good enough.

Imagine, for instance, that the person selling the house has a real-estate agent who has received a firm bid on the house that falls within the range the seller considers good enough. The agent tells the prospective buyer that it may take him three or four days to get in touch with the seller because he believes the latter is temporarily out of town; the buyer says he is in no hurry; in fact, the seller has not gone away and the agent conveys the bid to him on the same day it is made. The seller then tells the agent to let the prospective buyer know that his offer is acceptable, but the agent, who (we may assume) is not a satisficer, tells the seller that he really ought to wait a few days before accepting the offer that has been made. After all, he says, the offer is firm, and if you wait a few days before telling the prospective buyer that you agree to his terms, a better offer may come in.

Now in the circumstances as I have described them, the seller's likely benefit is greater if he waits—we are assuming that the seller is not rich, that the offer already made is firm, and that there is no reason to worry that the person who has made the offer may get cold feet (he doesn't expect his offer to be received for a couple of days). Yet the seller may tell the real-estate agent to convey his acceptance of the terms on offer without delay. Again, the reason may simply be that he considers the offer good enough and has no interest in seeing whether he can do better. His early agreement may not be due to undue anxiety about the firmness of the buyer's offer, or to a feeling that monetary transactions are unpleasant and to be got over as quickly as possible. He may simply be satisficing in the strong sense of the term. He may be moderate or modest in what he wants or feels he needs.

One cannot at this point reasonably reply that if the man doesn't want the (chance of) extra money for his house, then that cannot represent a good thing, a personal good that he gives up by immediately accepting the offer that has been made. An important distinction has to be made between what someone (most) wants and what advances his well-being (or represents a personal good for him). And, once again, a comparison with issues that arise in connection with altruism and moral behavior generally may help us to see the point. If altruism makes sense, then presumably so too does the notion of self-sacrifice. But the idea of deliberate self-sacrifice involves the assumption that what a person (most) wants need not be what advances his own personal well-being, what is (in one everyday sense) best for him. And this conceptual point carries over to discussions of moderation and satisficing. Just because the moderate individual asks for less money than he possibly could doesn't, for example, mean that additional wealth wouldn't be a good thing for him. The wishing and house-selling examples—as well as the earlier example of the rejected afternoon snack—indicate, instead, that an individual who does not want or care about a particular thing and who chooses not to have it, need not automatically regard that thing as not a personal good.[8] There is conceptual space for and human understandability in the idea of a personal good or element of one's own well-being that one simply doesn't care about or wish to have—and that one actually rejects—because one feels well enough off without it. It is a mere confusion, therefore, to say (as I have heard it said) that the person who turns down a certain good is nonetheless inevitably seeking her own good in some more refined sense, because she is maximizing the satisfaction of her weighted preferences on the whole, among which, after all, is presumably the preference not to have that unnecessary good (or the general preference not to have more than she needs). The same form of argument would be laughed out of court if applied in the area of morality and altruism: we all know by now that it would be absurd to argue that the individual who sacrifices his life for others must be seeking his own greatest good in doing so, because in doing so he is maximizing his weighted preferences, one very powerful one being the preference that he should die so others may live.[9] The only reason why a similar move is not instantly rejected in the area of individualistic rationality in connection with putative examples of moderation is that moderation as described earlier is a much neglected moral-psychological phenomenon. But once we get our sea legs on this topic, I think the sorts of objections to the phenomenon that naturally arise will be seen (at least in the cases mentioned above) to be as groundless as the sorts of objections to psychological altruism that abounded in earlier periods of philosophy but are now largely discredited.

On the other hand, once we become aware of the distinction between seeking our own greatest good and attempting to maximize the fulfillment of our self-regarding preferences, we may seek to understand individualistic rationality solely in the latter terms. We may claim, that is, that an individual is self-regardingly rational if and only if she maximizes the expectable satisfaction of her (firm, consistent, transitive) self-regarding desires/preferences. Such a view would indeed allow us to regard satisficing moderation, as described above, as rational, since the moderate individual may firmly and consistently prefer to forgo certain personal goods, certain heights of well-being or happiness. But this understanding of practically individualistic rational choice nonetheless clashes with some of our most deep-seated ideas and intuitions about rational choice, and in the end is no more adequate to common-sense views of rationality than optimizing/maximizing views that focus on personal good.

The preference-maximizing standard of rationality—once it is clearly detached from the idea of optimizing the agent's own good—allows one to treat the moderate individual as rational, but it also forces one to regard the thoroughgoing non-instrumental ascetic as completely rational. The preference-maximizing model has no way of ruling out the possibility of an individual with a fundamental consistent preference (within limits dictated by health) for the least comfort, the fewest enjoyments; and yet because our ordinary thinking tends to assume a connection between self-regarding rationality and the agent's good, we naturally regard the ascetic (but not the moderate individual) as perversely, irrationally, *thwarting* his own good. So any attempt to cast maximizing rationality loose from agential good and conceive it entirely in terms of the maximization of whatever preferences the agent (fundamentally, consistently, and so on) has will be unable to capture some of our deepest common-sense intuitions about self-regarding rationality.[10]

II

Of course, we have also seen that optimizing/maximizing views of rationality that focus on the agent's good have difficulty accounting for our intuitions about satisficing moderation. But despite those intuitions, the defender of optimization can nonetheless argue in various ways for the irrationality of rejecting the personally better for the personally good and sufficient, or good enough. For example, in response to my account of satisficing moderation, Philip Pettit has claimed that the person who rejects what is better for himself in favor of what he considers good enough may have a reason for choosing what he chooses—what he chooses is, after all, good enough—but has no reason to choose what he chooses in preference to what he rejects. There may be a reason to wish for or choose moderate wealth or well-being, but there is no reason for the moderate individual I have described to choose moderate wealth or well-being over great wealth or well-being, and for that reason, according to Pettit, his choice counts as irrational or unreasonable.[11]

This objection, however, is extremely problematic. It is not, to begin with, a general condition of rationality that in choosing between two options one has a reason to choose one of those options rather than the other—otherwise, we would sometimes really be in the position of Buridan's ass. When two equally (or incommensurably) good or self-beneficial options present themselves, it need not be irrational to choose one of them, even though one has no reason to prefer it to the other. (I have somewhere read that Arthur Balfour once spent twenty minutes trying to decide whether there was any reason for him to go up a stair-case to the left or one to the right in order to join a soirée to which he had been invited.) In the second place, reasons can be relative to an individual's concerns, her world view, or even her habits; and from the distinctive standpoint of the moderate individual, there may well be a reason to prefer moderate wealth (well-being) to great wealth (well-being). The fact that great wealth is much more than she needs (or cares about) can count, for such an individual, as a reason for rejecting great wealth and choosing moderate wealth, but of course such a reason will not motivate, or even occur to, someone who always seeks to optimize. The moderate individual will thus sometimes possess a statable reason for preferring what is less good for herself, but a reason precisely of a kind to lack appeal to the maximizing temperament.[12]

But this is not to claim that the moderate individual *always* chooses less than the best for himself. Other things being equal he will prefer what is better for himself to what is less good for himself; but from his particular standpoint, other things are not equal when what is less good for himself is good and sufficient for his purposes, and what is better for himself is much more than he needs or cares about. In such circumstances he can articulate a reason—a reason I think you and I can understand and empathize with—for choosing what is less good for himself. But faced, for example, with the choice between great wealth and dire poverty, he would have reason to choose the former (the moderate individual is not an ascetic) and indeed with respect to most choices between better and worse for himself he would (be able to) prefer the better-for-himself to the less-good-for-himself.

Moreover, although we have up till now been focusing on examples having to do with the appetites or material possessions, the idea of satisficing moderation has application to desires and projects that lie outside the pursuit of personal good or well-being narrowly conceived. Certain desires for achievement, such as the desire to solve a mathematical problem, may be neither morally motivated nor primarily focused on the good of the individual; but in some sense they are self-regarding (one doesn't simply desire that *someone* should solve the problem), and it is certainly possible to pursue such desires in a satisficing manner. One may have a personal ideal, such as the desire to be a really fine lawyer, without wishing to be better than other lawyers or the best lawyer possible or even the best lawyer it is possible for one to be. One's mother may have been an excellent lawyer, and one may simply want to emulate her. When asked "Don't you want to be the best lawyer you can possibly be?" one may reply "No, I just want to be a really fine lawyer, like my mother; I have no desire for anything beyond that," and this reply may express an inherently understandable compound of ambition and its limits, rather than a concern that too much devotion to the law might interfere with other, more important, life goals.

Notes

1. See Henry Sidgwick, *The Methods of Ethics* (London: Macmillan, 1907), 7th ed., pp. 119–122, 381–382, 497–509; and John Rawls, *A Theory of Justice* (Cambridge: Harvard University Press, 1971), pp. 23–27, 416–424.

2. See Amartya Sen's "Utilitarianism and Welfarism," *Journal of Philosophy* 76 (1979), 470–471; and Charles Fried's *An Anatomy of Values* (Cambridge: Harvard University Press, 1970), pp. 170–176.

3. For relevant discussions in the economics literature of satisficing, see, for instance, Herbert Simon, "A Behavioral Model of Rational Choice," *Quarterly Journal of Economics* 69 (1955): 99–118; Simon, "Theories of Decision Making in Economics and Behavioral Science," *American Economic Review* 49 (1959): 253–283; Simon, *Administrative Behavior* (New York: Macmillan, 1961), 2nd ed.; and R. Cyert and J. March, eds., *A Behavioral Theory of the Firm* (Englewood Cliffs: Prentice-Hall, 1963).

4. *Rational* satisficing seems to require not only a disinclination to optimize, but a reasonable sense of when one has enough. To be content with much less than one should be is (can be) one form of *bathos*. Moreover, as Peter Railton has pointed out, to have many strong desires and be willing to satisfice only at some high level of desire satisfaction is to fail to be moderate in one's desires. In speaking of satisficing moderation, I shall at least for the moment assume the absence of these complicating conditions.

5. Simon, "Theories of Decision Making," p. 264.

6. In fact, it is hard to see how any specific monetary wish can be optimizing if the individual is unsure about his own marginal utility curve for the use of money. And it may well be that we are *necessarily* satisficers in situations where we can wish for whatever we want, unless, perhaps, we are allowed to wish for our own greatest well-being in those very terms. If satisficing were irrational, would that mean that anything other than such an explicitly optimizing wish would be irrational? I discuss some of these issues in *Beyond Optimizing* (Cambridge: Harvard University Press, 1989), chapter 5.

It has been suggested that the intuitive force of the wish example may depend on the absence of a well-defined upper bound to what one may request. But even if there is no limit to how much money one may request and no such thing as one's greatest possible well-being, one cannot use those facts to explain why it seems to make sense for the person in the example to reject greater heights of well-being for a more moderate level of well-being.

7. Some of these points are made by Philip Pettit in reply to an earlier paper of mine. See his "Satisficing Consequentialism," *Proceedings of the Aristotelian Society*, suppl. 58 (1984): 175.

8. A quite similar point, that the virtuous individual who forgoes something that can only be obtained unjustly need not deny that he is forgoing a good thing, is made in my *Goods and Virtues* (Oxford: Oxford University Press, 1983), chap. 5. On the present view, a person may reasonably turn down the chance of getting more money (say, $90,000) for his house and simply accept what he takes to be a good price (say, $80,000). Does it follow (as Alan Donagan and Jonathan Glover have both suggested) that the moderate individual might (should) turn down a firm $90,000 when $80,000 is on offer? Certainly not. If $80,000 really is a good and sufficient price, then holding out for and striving after a higher amount may seem a form of "grubbing" with little to recommend it. But no such grubbing is involved when the higher price is firmly on offer, and in such a situation nothing need stand in the way of accepting the higher price. Note too that in the normal course of events it will never be clear that that one won't need the extra $10,000, so the case where both $80,000 and $90,000 are firmly on offer is also different from the fairy-tale example where one can wish for enough money to be moderately well off for the rest of one's life and where it is assumed that there will definitely be no need for any more than one is actually wishing for. Once again, there may be reason to take the firm $90,000, even if the moderate individual has no reason to ask for more than moderate wealth in an idealized fairy-tale situation.

9. Compare with Amartya Sen, "Rational Fools: A Critique of the Behavioral Foundations of Economic Theory," *Philosophy and Public Affairs* 6 (1977), *passim*.

10. In *Morals by Agreement* (Oxford: Oxford University Press, 1986), chap. 2, David Gauthier puts forward a pure preference-maximization view of rational choice. He argues for the subjectivity of values and on that basis denies that the content of preferences can be subjected to rational assessment. But he also recognizes that most people are not subjectivists about value and that they are inclined to criticize certain sorts of (consistent, firm, and so forth) preferences as irrational.

The view he is proposing is not supposed to be compatible with our ordinary thinking about individualistic rational choice.

11. See Pettit, "Satisficing Consequentialism," p. 172.

12. Similarly, non-egoistic reasons for helping others or doing the honorable thing will not appeal to the egoistic temperament, but this hardly shows that such reasons are illusory. See John McDowell, "The Role of *Eudaimonia* in Aristotle's Ethics," in A. Rorty, ed., *Essays on Aristotle's Ethics* (Berkeley: University of California Press, 1980), pp. 359–376.

Chapter 11

Choosing Ends

David Schmidtz

'Reason' has a perfectly clear and precise meaning. It signifies the choice of the right means to an end that you wish to achieve. It has nothing whatever to do with the choice of ends.

Bertrand Russell (1954, p. 8)

THREE KINDS OF ENDS

Rational choice, on a means-end conception, involves seeking effective means to one's ends. From this basic idea, the social sciences have developed an instrumental model of rationality. The instrumental model goes beyond a means-end conception by inferring from it not only that rational choice involves seeking effective means to one's ends but also that rational choice involves nothing beyond this. Ends must be taken as given, as outside the purview of rational choice. All chains of justification eventually come to an end in something unjustified.

Or so the story goes. This chapter, though, shows that it is possible to have a chain of means and ends whose final link is rationally justified. One might assume that justifying final ends requires a conception of justification foreign to rational choice theory. It does not. Admittedly, defenders and critics alike agree that "the theory of rational choice disclaims all concern with the ends of action."[1] But such quietism about ends is not necessary. A means-end conception of rationality can be consistent with our intuition that we can be rational in a more reflective sense, calling into question ends we happen to have and revising them when they seem unfit.

One could define ends as items we *ought* to pursue, but I define ends descriptively, as items we do pursue, which leaves open whether it is possible to have ends we not only pursue but which were rational to adopt as items to pursue. This chapter looks beyond a purely instrumental model to something more reflective, a model in which agents choose and criticize ends as well as means.

There is, of course, a problem. The instrumentalist model is standard equipment in the social sciences, in part because it is useful, but also in part because it is hard to imagine an alternative. Evaluating a proposed means to a given end seems straightforward. We simply ask whether it would serve the given end. But when we talk about being reflectively rational, we are talking about evaluating ends as such. Now, we evidently can and do judge some ends as not worth pursuing, but how?

My answer draws on distinctions between four kinds of ends, three of which are well-known among philosophers. Suppose I wake one morning wanting to go for a two-mile run.

1. Perhaps I have this goal as an end in itself; I want to run two miles just for the sake of being out there running. In this case, the goal of running two miles is a *final* end.
2. Or perhaps I want to run for the sake of some other goal. I run because I want to be healthy. In this case, running two miles is an *instrumental* end, instrumental to the further end of being healthy.
3. Or suppose I want to run two miles because I want some aerobic exercise. In this case, running two miles is not exactly a mere means to the further end of getting some exercise. Rather, running two miles constitutes getting some exercise. So, in this third case we can speak of going for a run as a *constitutive* end.[2]

A variety of subsidiary criteria often help us to assess the relative merits of alternative constitutive ends. For instance, if my further goal is to get some aerobic exercise, and it occurs to me that I could ride my stationary bicycle rather than run two miles, I could ask myself which is easier on my knees, which will use less time, whether the bicycle's noise will bother the neighbors at that hour, and so on. If subsidiary criteria do not tell the difference between alternative constitutive ends, then the best I can do is to pick a form of exercise and get on with it.

The three categories are not mutually exclusive. An end like running two miles could be both final and instrumental, pursued for its own sake as well as for the sake of further ends. Nevertheless, distinguishing among these three kinds of ends is useful. For one thing, the distinction makes it easy to see how we can rationally choose some of our ends. In particular, we can choose instrumental and constitutive ends as means to further ends, and so such ends can be rational in the sense that choosing to pursue them can serve further ends. By the same token, we criticize such choices by asking whether pursuing the chosen end really helps to secure the further end, or whether pursuing it truly constitutes pursuing the further end.

The final end that terminates a chain of justification, though, cannot be justified in the same way we justify the links leading to it. Final ends as such are neither constituents of nor instrumental to further ends. They are pursued for their own sake. Thus, the justification of final ends will be a different kind of story, a story that cannot be told within the confines of an instrumentalist model.

A FOURTH KIND OF END

Suppose that, for Kate, becoming a surgeon is an end. Perhaps it is an end because Kate thinks becoming a surgeon will be prestigious, in which case becoming a surgeon is an instrumental end. Kate becomes a surgeon in order to do something else, namely, to secure prestige. But maybe, for Kate, becoming a surgeon is an end in itself. How could a career in medicine come to be a final end?

Maybe it happened like this. When Kate was a teenager, she had no idea what she wanted to do with her life, but she knew she wanted to do something. She wanted goals to pursue. In particular, she wanted to settle on a career and thus on the goal or set of goals that a career represents. At some point, she concluded that going to medical school and becoming a surgeon would give her the career she wanted. So she went to school to pursue a career in medicine. She has various reasons to pursue this goal, of course, but she also pursues it as an end in itself, much as I might run just for the sake of being out running.

The interesting point is that Kate's story introduces a fourth kind of end, an end of acquiring settled ends, an end of choosing a career in particular. The goal of choosing a career is what I call a *maieutic* end—an end achieved through a process of coming to have other ends. People sometimes describe Socrates as having taught by the maieutic method (that is, the method of midwifery). The idea is that students already have great stores of knowledge in inchoate form, so the teacher's job is to help students give birth to this latent knowledge. I use the term 'maieutic' to suggest that we give birth to our final ends in the process of achieving maieutic ends.[3] In this case, Kate achieves a maieutic end by coming to have particular career goals. As we said, she settles on a career by deciding to pursue a career in medicine. Thus, just as final ends are the further ends for the sake of which we pursue instrumental and constitutive ends, maieutic ends are the further ends for the sake of which we choose final ends.

The immediate worry here is that there may appear to be an inconsistency in the way the terms are defined. I said we could choose a final end as a way of achieving a maieutic end. On the contrary, one might respond, if Kate chooses a career in medicine as a way of achieving a maieutic end, she must be pursuing that career not as a final end but rather as an instrumental end. This would be a natural response. It may even seem indisputable. However, it misses the distinction between *pursuing* a final end (which by definition we do for its own sake) and *choosing* a final end (which we might do for various reasons). By definition, final ends are pursued for their own sake, not for the sake of maieutic ends. Yet, even if Kate pursues an end purely for its own sake, it can still be true that there was, in Kate's past, a process by which she acquired that end. It can also be true that going through the process (of acquiring the new goal) served ends she had at the time. The supposition that the choice process is a means to an existing end leaves open whether the outcome of the process, the chosen end, will be pursued as a means to the same end. The new end may well be something Kate subsequently pursues for its own sake. The distinction between reasons for choosing and reasons for pursuing an end thus allows us to speak coherently of choosing a final end for the sake of further ends.

Against the distinction, one might object that when we choose an instrumental or a constitutive end, we necessarily pursue it for the same reason we originally chose it, namely, the further end to which we chose it as a means. Analogously, the objection continues, when we choose a final end we thereby take it to be good in itself. Consequently, our grounds for choosing X specifically as a final end must necessarily be the same as our grounds for pursuing X specifically as a final end—its being good in itself.[4]

This objection is more complicated than it looks. The alleged relation of identity between reasons for choosing and reasons for pursuing an end is by no means analytic. Even if it is true by definition that an instrumental end is both chosen and pursued as a means to a further end, it does not follow that the further end for which we chose it is identical to the further end for which we pursue it. It may be a safe assumption that they will be identical, but it is nevertheless an assumption, one that rests on further assumptions about human psychology. It is an empirical issue whether people tend to pursue ends for the same reasons they originally chose those ends as ends.

Similarly, even though it is true by definition that final ends are pursued for their own sake, it remains an open question whether further purposes were served by the process of coming to have final ends. For example, I may write in part because I love to write, but that supposition leaves open a possibility that other purposes were served by the process of becoming so devoted to writing. Developing that kind of devotion may have been what made it possible for me to get a job at a research-oriented university in the first place. I may even have been aware that good things happen to people who love to write when I began doing the things that led me to develop my taste for writing. My point here is that these are empirical matters. Some might insist that my reasons for choosing to pursue an end simply cannot—cannot possibly—differ from my subsequent reasons for pursuing that end. If that is true at all, though, it is a truth grounded in human psychology rather than in analysis of terms. Let us look more closely, then, at the psychological assumptions underlying this objection to the distinction between reasons for choosing and reasons for pursuing final ends.

My own understanding is that an act of adopting something as an end often changes our attitude toward it. If so, then it is a mistake to assume that our future grounds for pursuing X will be like our present grounds for adopting X as an end. My student may feel ambivalent about each of the subjects in which she might major, but if she anticipates coming to view the study of philosophy as good in itself, then her anticipation of this new attitude can be grounds for choosing to study philosophy in the first place. Similarly, part of the point of choosing a career is that we want—*and do not yet have*—the set of attitudes that goes with pursuing a particular career in a wholehearted way. We might have reasons to choose an end in part because of reasons we expect to develop for pursuing that end.

Observe, then, how the relation between maieutic and final ends differs from the relation between final and constitutive ends. The end of getting some aerobic exercise is schematic; we cannot do what it tells us to do until we choose a specific way of getting exercise, such as a two-mile jog.[5] Choosing specifics is a necessary preface to achieving the end. This is not how it works, though, when the further end is a maieutic end. Choosing specifics is not merely a preface to achieving a maieutic end. On the contrary, a maieutic end just is a goal of settling on a specific end. In settling on a specific goal and thereby meeting the maieutic end's demand, one is achieving the maieutic end, not merely choosing a specific way of pursuing it.

For example, my attempt to jog two miles constitutes my attempt to get some exercise, but Kate's attempt to become a surgeon does not constitute her attempt to choose a career goal. On the contrary, when Kate goes to medical school in an attempt to become a surgeon, she is not just attempting to choose a career goal. At that point, she has already chosen a career goal, namely, to be a surgeon. In the jogging case, I pursue goal A as a way of pursuing goal B. In the second case, Kate *chooses* goal A as a way of *achieving* goal B. Note that in the jogging case, A is the constitutive end, while in the other case, B is the maieutic end. Therefore, even if the relation between A and B were the same in both cases (which it is not), constitutive ends and maieutic ends would still be different, for the two kinds of ends are found at opposite ends of the relation.

We also can see how the relation between maieutic and final ends differs from the relation between final and instrumental ends. When one end is pursued purely for the sake of another end, then the rationale for its pursuit depends on its ongoing relation as a means to the further end. For example, if pursuing a career in medicine is merely a means of securing prestige, and Kate one day loses her desire for prestige, then she also loses her grounds for becoming a surgeon. The rationale for her career depends on the persistence of the further end of securing prestige. In the other scenario, though, the rationale for her career does not depend on the persistence of the teenage end of settling on a career. On the contrary, her evolving set of career goals *replaces* the teenage end with something quite different. As long as Kate is settled in her career as a surgeon, she has attained the goal (of settling on a career) that she had as a teenager, thus eliminating the earlier goal as an item to pursue. For Kate, the maieutic end of settling on a career reemerges (as an item to pursue) only if Kate at some point rejects her career as a surgeon and begins to long for something new.

Some readers might worry that a maieutic end is never really eliminated and that the new end it spawns is subsequently pursued, implicitly if not explicitly, as a means to the maieutic end. When Kate settles on a career, her subsequent pursuits might be motivated by the same concerns that drove her as a teenager to settle on a career. My response is that of course this will be true in some cases; some people, after settling on a career, subsequently pursue their careers as instrumental ends (instrumental to the further end of making money) or constitutive ends (constitutive of the further end of keeping busy). In other words, maieutic ends can give birth not only to final ends but to other kinds of ends as well.[6] But such cases are beside the point. If our task were to explain how instrumental or constitutive ends could be rationally chosen, then such cases would be relevant. Our actual objective, though, is to explain how final ends can be rationally chosen. Accordingly, we need to focus on cases in which the chosen ends are subsequently pursued as ends in themselves. We need to concentrate on the role maieutic ends play in giving birth to final ends, for it is in that role that maieutic ends are relevant to the puzzle of how final ends can be rationally chosen.

But, a critic might persist, how can we be sure that maieutic ends *ever* give birth to final ends? One could argue that, if the desire to have a career is what leads Kate to choose a career, then that same desire will be the further end for the sake of which she pursues her career. If she chooses a career as a mere means to the further end, then she will pursue the career for the same reason. In response, we need not deny that there can be a value that Kate attaches to having a career that persists through her choice and pursuit of a particular career. To say Kate eliminates "settling on a career" as an end (that is, as an item to pursue) is not to say she ceases to value having a career. We need to distinguish between something being valuable and something being an item to pursue. For example, my car is valuable to me. And if I leave it parked on a hill and the parking brake fails, then it also becomes an item to pursue. The car is valuable to me both before and after I secure it, but it ceases to be an item to pursue after I secure it. Similarly, if Kate already has a career, then having a career may be valuable to her, but it is not an item to pursue; it is an item she already has. In fact, it is not clear that having a career was ever an item to pursue. Before settling on a career, Kate pursued the goal of settling on a career. After settling on a career, Kate pursues her particular career, period; she does not pursue "having a career." And if her career is ever in jeopardy, then *securing* her career may well become an item to pursue. Of course, Kate continues to value having a career even as she pursues one, but this is no reason to doubt that she now has goals, acquired in the course of settling on her particular career, that she pursues for their own sake.

Maieutic ends are not the only kind of end that can be eliminated as an item to pursue, but their elimination has a unique upshot. In the means-end relation between instrumental and final ends, eliminating the further end renders the means pointless; it robs the means of normative significance. In contrast, in the means-end relation between final and maieutic ends, eliminating the further end is an essential part of the process by which final ends acquire their characteristic normative significance.

Maieutic ends are not merely a theoretical postulate. They are real. The drive to find a career or a spouse can be powerful, even painful, and such drives are drives to settle on a particular career or a particular person. Recall what it was like to choose a major subject in college or to choose a career. One way or another, we had to choose something, and, for some of us, not having done so yet was an occasion for considerable anxiety. Some of us had hardly any idea of what we really wanted, but it felt better to settle on some end or other than to let that part of our lives remain a vacuum. Of course, there were institutional and parental pressures as well, and some of us felt only those, but many of us also felt palpable pressure from within.

None of this denies that some people are simply gripped by particular final ends.[7] Perhaps such ends are not acquired by choice. If not, then questions about how they could be rationally chosen are moot. But that does not mean all questions are moot, for we can still ask whether further ends are served by the process of coming to have a final end. Whether ends are deliberately selected from a set of alternatives, my model has something to say. It addresses the question of whether an end's acquisition serves further ends.

That, then, is my theory about how an end, pursued as a genuinely final end, could nevertheless have been rationally chosen. There are ends —I call them maieutic ends—to which a final end could be chosen as a means. In passing, note that although the four kinds of ends are conceptually distinct, the four categories are not mutually exclusive. An end could be final, pursued for its own sake, and at the same time could be instrumental, pursued as a means to some further end. Later, I present three formal models of reflective rationality, the first of which models a maieutic end as a final end and the third of which models a maieutic end as an instrumental end. That an end falls into one category does not preclude it from falling into others.

In the next section, I explain how unchosen ends might serve as parts of a framework for judging a choice of ends. I then consider whether explaining the rational choice of one final end presupposes further and still unexplained final ends. Either way, we have seen how final ends could be rationally chosen, but are "loose ends" inevitable?

THE ROLE OF UNCHOSEN ENDS

Although some of our ends are chosen, some are not. For most of us, the goal of survival is a goal with which we simply find ourselves. Likewise, we want to be good at what we do, and this goal also seems to be unchosen, something we simply have. We want to be competent.[8] We do not need reasons to choose our unchosen ends, since we do not choose them. We simply have them. Even unchosen ends can be rejected, of course, but to rationally reject them, one needs a reason to reject them. Unchosen final ends, therefore, have a certain normative inertia, which means they can be part of a relatively stable frame of reference in terms of which we can evaluate ends we might acquire by choice. Not every pursuit, for instance, would be conducive to survival.

Harry Frankfurt goes a bit farther, holding that fixed ends are a *necessary* part of a normative frame of reference. The problem of choosing ends presupposes a frame of reference against which one assesses one's options, and not all of this framework can be an endogenous product of choice. As Frankfurt puts it, "It is only if his volitional nature is in certain respects already fixed that a person can effectively consider what his final ends should be—what is to be important to him, or what to care about. He will not be in a position to inquire into the question of how he should live unless it is already the case that there are some things about which he cares" (1992, p. 17). Frankfurt has a point. We need a fairly stable frame of reference to get started in assessing prospective ends.

At the same time, the stable foundation need not, as Frankfurt himself notes, "be fixed unalterably" (1992, p. 18). Although I accept Frankfurt's point, three related complications bear mentioning. First, the stable foundation need not be permanently fixed. Indeed, it might be something that has to be left behind. Childhood is the foundation for adulthood, but childhood is something we outgrow. Second, in the long run, the foundation might not be fixed independently of choice. Rather, some parts of the foundation (character traits, in particular) might arise and change through a process of habituation driven by ongoing patterns of choice. Third, even when an end is acquired by choice, the process of settling on that end may not be a simple act of will. On the contrary, often we settle on something as an end partly by habituating ourselves toward aiming at it. For instance, we want to have someone to love. This is a maieutic end that we achieve when we come to love particular people and when we accept spending time with them and making them happy as ends worth pursuing for their own sake. But coming to love and be devoted to a person is not a simple act of will but rather a matter of growing into a commitment, step by step.

So, some items come to be pursued as final ends through a process of habituation. Although Kate's character is stable with respect to particular decisions, it is also part of her that, over the long run, she shapes in incremental ways through her choices. If all goes well, she will grow into the career (and the husband) she chose, and the person she becomes will some day find that career (and that husband) intrinsically worthy of her ongoing commitment.

Of course, circumstances help determine whether a prospective end is appropriate. Indeed, circumstances determine whether a particular option even exists. A given activity counts as a prospective career, for example, only if there is a market for that kind of activity. (Does becoming a chess player count as settling on a career?) The nature of maieutic ends also depends on circumstances. For example, settling on a spouse can be a maieutic end only if a certain kind of social structure exists to render that end intelligible. To a large extent, culture dictates both the range of maieutic ends one could have and also the range of final ends whose choice would achieve a given maieutic end.

Another part of a framework for assessing prospective ends is supplied by an aspect of maieutic ends that we have yet to discuss. A maieutic end is an end of bringing ends into existence, of giving oneself ends to pursue. To have ends to pursue is to have something to live for. If we have a single overarching and maybe unchosen maieutic end, I would say it is the end of finding things to live for.[9] The various maieutic ends (settling on a major subject in college and then a career, defining ideals, choosing a spouse, finding ways of contributing to the community, and so on) are all species of a generic and overarching maieutic end of finding things to live for, ends to which one can devote oneself. In different words, the end of finding something to live for is the end of acquiring ends in general, the end of having one's life be spent on something rather than nothing.

That does not mean we are always looking for things to live for. Sometimes our existing corpus of ends gives us plenty to do, leaving us with neither the need nor the opportunity to look for more. Sometimes feeding ourselves (or our children) is a serious challenge; it keeps our hands so full that taking time to ask what we are living for is out of the question. To have no time for ends beyond bare survival is to have no need for ends beyond bare survival. But when day-to-day survival becomes too easy to keep us busy, that is when we need something else to aim at, lest we find ourselves with plenty of time to ponder the fact that there is nothing for the sake of which we are surviving.

In effect, insofar as bare survival originally presents itself as a final end, we need to convert it into something else, a form of survival that has instrumental value as well. When we do this, we change survival from something we happen to seek as a matter of descriptive biological fact into something with normative weight—a goal we have reason to seek. In this way, we redeem survival as a goal. But to do this, we need to settle on further ends to which survival can serve as means.[10] The next section incorporates these ideas into a model of reflective rationality.

A NEW MODEL

Means-end conceptions of rationality posit instrumental ends. Sophisticated versions also posit constitutive ends. A means-end conception also posits final ends, which rationally justify instrumental and constitutive ends. Instrumental or static rationality involves seeking effective means to given ends. The essence of reflective rationality is that, although it involves means-end reasoning, it goes beyond instrumental rationality because it does not take ends as given. Reflectively rational choosers realize that their preference functions change over time and that some changes will serve their current ends better than others. To be reflectively rational is to manage one's changing preference function, to do what one can to become the sort of person one wants to become. In figure 1, F, c, and i stand for final, constitutive, and instrumental ends. An arrow from c to F signifies that pursuing c is a means to F.

There will be as many chains of justification as there are final ends, and instrumental or constitutive ends pass as rational only if they are links within one or more chains, which is to say they serve as means to one or more final ends. The final ends that top the chains, though, are not justified, and final ends as such cannot be justified according to the instrumentalist conception of rational choice. (One might think of the latter as a Humean conception of reason.)

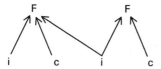

Figure 1
The means-end conception

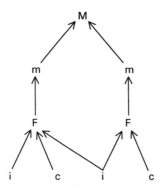

Figure 2
The reflective model, taking the overarching end as given

A model of reflective rationality adds the following elements to the means-end conception of rational choice. The point is to embellish the means-end conception rather than to supplant it, in the process showing how even final ends can be subject to rational choice. First, the model posits particular maieutic ends. Insofar as settling on final ends is our way of achieving maieutic ends, the choice is rational if it serves the purpose. Second, we pursue particular maieutic ends (like the end of choosing a career) as constitutive ends relative to the overarching maieutic end of finding something to live for. Getting a career is a way of getting something to live for (see figure 2). In figure 2, an arrow from i to F signifies that pursuing i is a means to F. An arrow from F to m signifies that choosing F is a means to a particular maieutic end m. An arrow from m to M signifies that pursuing m is a means to the overarching maieutic end M.

The model that emerges from this has several variations. We will look at three. In the first version, this is where we stop. We take the overarching maieutic end as a final end that is simply given. This first model

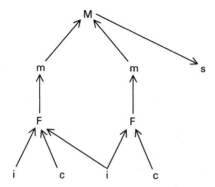

Figure 3
The reflective model, taking survival as given

is noteworthy in two ways. It explains how an end, pursued for its own sake, could nevertheless be rationally chosen. Second, the model identifies and characterizes further ends to which the choice of final ends could be a means. The model takes at least one final end as given, though, and so from a theoretical standpoint is not entirely satisfying. It goes beyond the instrumentalist model by showing how even final ends (most of them, at least) could be rationally chosen, but it shares with instrumentalist models the property of leaving us with loose ends—terminal ends not justified within the model.

Judging from the first model, then, it still seems reasonable to suppose that, as Bernard Williams writes, "There will have to be at least one reason for which no further reason is given and which holds itself up" (1985, p. 113).[11] The second model, however, goes further. Instead of taking the overarching maieutic end as given, we note that finding reasons to live improves our survival prospects. To whatever extent we care about survival, and to whatever extent finding things to live for strengthens our will to survive and thereby improves our survival prospects, we have a rationale for the overarching end. Finding things to live for is instrumental to the further end of survival. In the second model, we stop here. We take survival as a given final end (see figure 3). In figure 3, an arrow from M to s signifies that pursuing the overarching end M is a means to the end of survival.

Should we take the end of survival as given? Since we are given the end of survival as a matter of biological fact, why not? One problem is that we would still be left with a theoretical loose end, an end accounted for in descriptive biological terms but not in normative terms. There is also a practical reason why we cannot take survival as given. We cannot take it as given because, as a matter of fact, our commitment to the biologically given end of survival is not an all-or-nothing matter. Our commitment is a matter of degree, variable even within persons. The point is not that some people do not have the end of survival. (Even if some people lack the end of survival, this need not affect its normative force for the rest of us.) The more crucial fact is that, even for those of us who have the end of survival, the strength of our will to survive can change. Further, the strength of our will to survive is in part a consequence of our choices.

Accordingly, the third model goes one more step. Survival is a final end with which we begin as a matter of biological fact, but it will be subverted as an end if we cannot we find something that survival is *for*, that is, if we cannot find reasons to live. With some ends, of course, a threat of subversion would not matter. For example, if Ulysses expects the Sirens to subvert his desire for broccoli, he shrugs his shoulders and plans to eat something else. But in contrast, if Ulysses expects the Sirens to subvert his desire to survive, he binds himself to the mast. He wants to survive his encounter with the Sirens no matter how he will feel about survival when the time comes. Therefore, broccoli and survival are different. Unlike a desire for broccoli, the biologically given desire for survival happens to have a certain intransigence. It resists its own extinction. It drives us to find things to live for, as proof against its own subversion.

As we find things to live for, the goal of survival with which we begin as a biological instinct becomes something more than that. It becomes a means to final ends acquired in the process of achieving maieutic ends. And as those new goals insert themselves into our corpus of ends, the goal of bare survival evolves into something else. There comes a time when bare survival is no longer what we are after. By acquiring the final ends that make life instrumentally valuable, we convert bare survival from something we happen to pursue into something we have reason to pursue as part of an increasingly complex hierarchy of ends.[12]

This suggests a circular chain of reasoning (a nonvicious circle, since several and perhaps all of the links have empirical content). Constitutive and instrumental ends are justified as means to final ends. We pursue final ends for their own sake, and the *choice* of final ends is justified as a means of achieving particular maieutic ends. Particular maieutic ends are then justified as constitutive means to the overarching maieutic end of finding something to live for. Finding something to live for is instrumen-

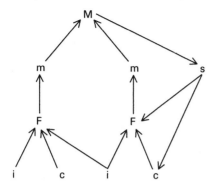

Figure 4
The reflective model, with no loose ends

tally justified to the extent that, given our psychology, achieving the overarching maieutic end (and thus producing reasons to live) helps us survive. And to close the circle, survival and the implied preservation of the ability to pursue goals has come to be instrumentally justified as a means to the pursuit of final ends (see figure 4).

In this model, survival is a means in the sense of being needed for the sake of other goals. To be an instrumental end, and thus an item to pursue, there must also be something one needs to do to secure it. As I use the terms, being an instrumental end entails being a means, but not vice versa. Survival is not unique in this respect. For example, suppose Tom needs a car in order to attend a concert. If Tom already has a car, though, then having a car is not an item to pursue and thus not an end and thus not an instrumental end, even though it is a means of attending the concert.

We might think there is an easier way to close the circle. That is, we could eliminate maieutic ends from the picture and suppose more simply that survival is justified as a means to our final ends while our final ends are justified by the fact that acquiring those ends gives us reason to live and thereby improves our survival prospects. But how could acquiring final ends improve our survival prospects? We can explain the point of acquiring final ends without reconstructing them as merely instrumental ends (which by hypothesis is not what they are) by saying that in acquiring final ends, we come to have reasons to live. And it is in virtue of giving us reasons to live that acquiring final ends improves our survival prospects. Therefore, the circle cannot close except by way of maieutic ends. Maieutic ends enter the picture even if the name I gave them does not.[13]

Does this mechanism drive the emergence of everyone's corpus of ends? It is hard to say. In any event, the models are not really meant to be descriptive in that sense. They are meant to show how someone, starting even from something as mundane as the survival instinct, could have reason to develop the complicated set of ends that beings like us actually have. The models are also meant to show how each element of an emerging corpus of ends can come to have its own normative force without any end's normative force begin simply taken as given. Survival enters the second model as a biological given, but the third model depicts a process by which this biological given eventually becomes something more than that. The third model thus exhibits a striking completeness, since within it there are no loose ends. The chain of justification has a beginning, but it need not come to an end. One might be tempted to ask for a justification of the chain as a whole, but to justify every link is to justify the whole chain. The chain metaphorically represents a series of choices wanting justification in rational choice terms, together with interrelationships that help them justify each other. When one forges the chain in such a way that no link is without justification (that is, no choice is without justification, including basic existentialist choices such as to seek survival or to cultivate ends beyond survival), then no issue of rational choice remains to be represented by the metaphorical chain as a whole.

Even as astute a critic of foundationalism as Bernard Williams joins foundationalists in embracing the least plausible implication of the foundationalist metaphor, namely, the idea that starting points are what subsequently erected edifices must rest upon.[14] We should not be fooled by the metaphor. We should realize that our starting points can be more like launching pads than like architectural foundations. A launching pad serves its purpose by being left behind. Even if we inevitably begin by taking some ends as given, it remains open whether a corpus of ends will always include ends taken as given.

Further, survival is not the only descriptively given end capable of launching the normative rocket. If the primeval desire for survival does not drive a person to develop a corpus of ends, something else might. A desire for happiness also can drive us to find things to live for, because we secure happiness by pursuing ends we care about for their own sake. (If we did not independently care about achieving those ends, then there would be nothing in the achievement to be happy about.) A primeval desire to avoid boredom might have similar consequences.[15] To launch the normative rocket, all we need is some sort of given desire that gives us reasons to find things to live for. I prefer to use survival as an example of such a primeval desire, partly because it is in fact biologically given, partly because it is relatively clear how bare survival could start out as a biologically given final end only to drive the process by which it evolves into a complicated instrumental end, thereby leaving us with no loose (that is, simply given) ends.

Perhaps it is somewhat curious that organisms would have a survival instinct in the first place. The reason why they have it, presumably, is this. Organisms having no instincts other than an instinct to replicate would not be good at replicating and thus would have declining representation in successive generations. The goal of replicating, the ultimate biological given, is better served in organisms who combine or replace that goal with other goals: to survive, to have sex, to eat, and so forth. Obviously, not every organism is guaranteed to have more offspring in virtue of having a complex corpus of ends, but whether the rule has exceptions is not the issue. The issue is whether the probability of replication goes up or down as a corpus of ends becomes complex.

Sociobiological speculation aside, it remains the case that, having posited an initial goal of bare survival, we can see why this goal would fall away as a driving force in just the way launching pads are supposed to fall away, to be replaced by a set of ends comprising a commitment to survive in a particular way, as a being with a particular hierarchy of ends. In circumstances like ours, to have the thinner goal is to have reason to try to replace it with its thicker analog. (The reason is that the end of bare survival is too thin to sustain itself as a corpus of ends. Unless survival acquires instrumental value, our commitment to it will decay.) It would have been simpler to posit a thicker goal (of surviving in a humanly dignified way, for example, or of having a life filled with happiness) as a biologically given final end, but that would have made the model at once much less interesting and much more controversial.

One might find it odd to model final ends as ends we acquire by conscious choice. Recall, then, that models of reflectively rational choice do not presume we acquire final ends only by conscious choice. We sometimes make choices unintentionally, habituating ourselves toward aiming at an end without realizing that we are doing so. Some of our ends seem simply to captivate us. Nor is anything necessarily wrong with acquiring ends unintentionally. When we find ourselves simply gripped by an end, we have no practical need to formulate a rationale for our ends. (There is a saying: "If it ain't broke, don't fix it.") Nevertheless, there might be a rationale for one's final ends whether one has reason to identify it. Final ends can give us something to live for whether we think of them as serving that purpose.

Thus, the three models have a normative force pertaining not only to ends one acquires by deliberate choice but also to ends by which one is simply gripped. They explain not just how we could come to have final ends but how we could come to have *rationally chosen* final ends, and such an explanation can have justificatory force even when it is not descriptively accurate.[16] For example, if Kate is simply gripped by the end of learning to play jazz guitar, then since she did not choose it at all, she cannot be said to have rationally chosen it either. Nevertheless, we can say her end is rational if the process of adopting it served an end she had at the time and, in particular, if adopting the end gave her something to live for. We can say this even when she neither chooses nor pursues the end with that further purpose in mind.

We have seen how final ends could be rationally chosen. In addition, the third model shows that it is not necessary for a chain of ends to terminate in an end that is simply given rather than rationally chosen. Note that these models rely only on the ordinary and well-understood means-end conception of rational choice. The choice of instrumental, constitutive, final, and maieutic ends are all explained as means to further ends. (By definition, the pursuit of final ends cannot be so explained, but even so, the choice of final ends can be.) This shows that the means-end conception of rational choice has the resources to go beyond the instrumentalist model. I do not assume that means-end reasoning is the only kind of rationality there is. Rather, the point of the exercise is to show how even this narrowest of conceptions of rational choice has the resources to explain the rational choice of ends, and further, to do so without leaving loose ends.

Aristotle (*Nicomachean Ethics*, 1112b11–12) said we deliberate not about ends but about ways and means.[17] But I believe we have maieutic ends. And if we deliberate about means to maieutic ends, then by that very fact we deliberate about ends. It is through means-end deliberation with respect to maieutic ends that final ends are brought within the purview of rational choice. To belabor the obvious, though, only choices can fall within the purview of rational choice. Therefore, the intent of this chapter's argument is to show how rationality is conferred on final ends as choices, not as ends per se. Even when there is nothing to say about the rationality of ends as ends, it remains possible to rationally choose final ends in the sense that choosing them can serve further ends.

Notes

1. David Gauthier (1986, p. 26). Michael Resnik puts it dramatically: "Individual decision theory recognizes no distinction—either moral or rational—between the goals of killing oneself, being a sadist, making a million dollars, or being a missionary" (1987, p. 5).

2. The distinction between instrumental and constitutive ends is formalized by J. L. Ackrill (1980, p. 19). I am also borrowing from a recent article by Scott MacDonald (1991).

3. I leave open whether, prior to our choosing them, we already have final ends in inchoate form. This sometimes does appear to be the case, though. There sometimes seems, for example, to be a grain of truth in describing a person as having been born for a particular pursuit.

4. I thank Scott MacDonald for suggesting this objection.

5. Constitutive ends can be either specific ways of pursuing a more formal further end (Putting on a suit can be constitutive of being well-dressed) or constituent parts of the further end (Putting on a tie can be a constituent of putting on a suit). See also Scott MacDonald's discussion of ends as specifications (1991, p. 59).

6. I thank Lainie Ross for helping me see this.

7. The issue came up in discussions with Ruth Marcus and Michael Della Rocca.

8. It is not a conceptual truth that human beings desire to be competent, but nor is that desire merely a local phenomenon. Probably, it is conspicuously present in all societies. Robert White (1971) says exploratory and playful behavior in children and even young animals serves to develop competence in dealing with the environment and that a sense of competence is a vital aspect of self-esteem. Sarah Broadie says the joy human beings take in doing things well "is so natural that people set up all sorts of trivial ends in order to have the satisfaction of achieving them correctly" (1991, p. 92).

9. I speak interchangeably of having, finding, getting, or coming to have something to live for.

10. It seems that some people would rather die than live without goals they consider worth living for. Suicide often might be understood not as a repudiation of the unchosen end of survival but rather as the ultimate confirmation of the intolerability of failing to achieve the maieutic end of finding something to live for.

11. Bernard Williams expresses skepticism about the "linear model" of reason-giving at issue in the cited passage, but his belief that it is impossible for rationales to go "all the way down" is unwavering.

12. For those with no desire to live in the first place, this argument does not get off the ground unless they have some other desire that can play a similar role in the model. But we are not concerned here with the likelihood that some people's ends cannot be rationally justified in this way. Perhaps some ends cannot be rationally justified at all. Be that as it may, the objective is to show how a final end could be rationally chosen. We do not need to argue that *all* ends are rationally chosen.

13. Another way of closing the circle invokes standard instrumental reasons for wanting some of our ends to be final ends. For example, we might be healthier if we eat broccoli as an end in itself—just for the taste—rather than for the sake of our health. (I thank Sara Worley for this point.) Merely acquiring the goal of eating broccoli does not by itself achieve the further end of being healthy, though. The further end persists as an item to pursue, which means the newly acquired end forms an intermediate link in an existing chain. In contrast, maieutic ends are achieved, not merely furthered, by the process of acquiring final ends. Having been achieved, maieutic ends drop away as items to pursue, breaking the circle and leaving the acquired end in the chain's terminal position, which explains how even the link that terminates a chain of ends could have been rationally chosen.

14. See Williams (1985, pp. 113–17).

15. I thank Harry Frankfurt for this suggestion. See also Frankfurt (1992, p. 12).

16. Alan Nelson (1986) discusses the relation between explanation and justification.

17. Aristotle believed that we deliberate about constitutive as well as instrumental means, and some commentators (for example, Terence Irwin in the notes to *Nicomachean Ethics*, 1985, p. 318) suggest that if we deliberate about a constitutive means to a final end, we thereby deliberate about the final end. On the contrary, we may deliberate about whether to run two miles without deliberating about whether to get some exercise. We may deliberate about whether to wear a maroon tie without deliberating about whether to wear a suit. And so on. We do not get to a perspective from which to assess final ends merely by deliberating about constitutive means.

References

Ackrill, J. L. 1980. "Aristotle on Eudaimonia." In *Essays on Aristotle's Ethics*, edited by Amélie O. Rorty. Berkeley: University of California Press.

Aristotle. 1985. *Nicomachean Ethics*. Translated by Terence Irwin. Indianapolis: Hackett. First published ca. 340 B.C.

Broadie, Sarah. 1991. *Ethics with Aristotle*. New York: Oxford University Press.

Frankfurt, Harry. 1992. "On the Usefulness of Final Ends." *Iyyun* 41: 3–19.

Gauthier, David. 1986. *Morals by Agreement*. Oxford: Oxford University Press.

MacDonald, Scott. 1991. "Ultimate Ends in Practical Reasoning: Aquinas's Aristotelian Psychology and Anscombe's Fallacy." *Philosophical Review* 100: 31–65.

Nelson, Alan. 1986. "Explanation and Justification in Political Philosophy." *Ethics* 97: 154–76.

Resnik, Michael. 1987. *Choices*. Minneapolis: University of Minnesota Press.

Russell, Bertrand. 1954. *Human Society in Ethics and Politics*. London: George Allen and Unwin.

White, Robert. 1971. "The Urge towards Competence." *American Journal of Occupational Therapy* 25: 271–74.

Williams, Bernard. 1985. *Ethics and the Limits of Philosophy*. Cambridge: Harvard University Press.

Chapter 12

Deliberation Is of Ends

Aurel Kolnai

1

To attack Aristotle's famous proposition '*Deliberation is of means*' may perhaps amount to flogging a dead horse, but the horse in question may after all not be quite dead and may deserve another course of flogging in order to be securely put out of harm's way or possibly to be proved immortal in some sense. Aristotle's argument for his thesis lies in the apparent constancy and indisputability of certain ends, the pursuit of which may give rise to deliberation: a deliberation by which the respective foregiven ends are not called in question. The relevant passage (*Ethica Nicomachea*, book III, 1112b) runs thus:

We deliberate not about Ends, but Means to Ends. No physician, e.g. deliberates whether he will cure, nor orator whether he will persuade, nor statesman whether he will produce a good constitution, nor in fact any man in any other function about his particular end; but having set before them a certain end they look how and through what means it may be accomplished.... And plainly not every search is deliberation, those in mathematics to wit, but every deliberation is a search.

It might well be asked whether 'to have set before them a certain end' did not already involve deliberation.

The three examples—the physician, the orator, the statesman—are all of a different logical status; the last obviously sounds least convincing, while the first is the most plausible (and has therefore most often been quoted). Whereas to cure and to persuade can at first sight easily be conceived of as pre-established ends requiring only the appropriate means to be attained, a 'good constitution' has no definite meaning by virtue of which to function as a logical premise; before the question of means can be gone into, it requires a definition or, rather, a determination of its content. Conservative liberals, radical democrats, communist totalitarians and fascist totalitarians might at the very best be said to pursue the self-same end of human happiness (or of the thriving of their respective countries) by different means, but they certainly do not aim at bringing about the selfsame 'good constitution' by different means: what they differ about is the *conception* of a 'good constitution'. Whoever denies that their *ends* are different and conflicting actually denies that there can be such a thing as different and conflicting ends. Apart from its being blatantly absurd, this is hardly Aristotle's own opinion: witness the *Politics* with its emphasis on class quarrels. As regards orators, we may certainly distinguish between the invariable formal 'end' of persuasion and the manifold and contingent 'means' preferred in different techniques of eloquence. But, as the 'ends' are necessarily controversial and persuading must be persuading of *something*, from which a rival orator is intent on *dissuading* the same hearers, it is here again less clear than in the physician's case that the deliberation preceding the performance seems to be underlain and governed by one strictly preconceived end. The doctor we *may* presume to be always out to cure his patient: is he, then, in doubt only as regards the means conducive to such a result, and does he deliberate, if at all, about means?

The answer, I submit, is No. So far as the physician confines himself to the determination of suitable curative means—often followed, in simple cases, by their application there and then—he does not deliberate but performs the theoretical activities of recalling to mind his relevant knowledge, looking up textbooks for more information, considering the peculiarities of the case in hand, weighing probabilities, comparing the average efficacy of various methods in similar cases and so forth. He does what a consulting physician, not responsible for any *decision*, might do just as well for him. The knowledge he brings to his practical task is ampler and more exact but not of a logically different nature than my wholly unpractical knowledge of the probability that, if streptomycin and some other recent therapies had been known in the middle of the last century or at least in the beginning of ours, Chopin or at least James Elroy Flecker would not have died so early of consumption. Aristotle says himself that enquiry or research is not deliberation; but he seems disposed to think that research about practically relevant matters is inseparable from deliberation, and in particular that because indeed practice necessarily bears upon 'singulars', all knowledge of and research about singulars must be intimately bound up with a practical intent and thus intertwined with deliberation. That is plainly not so, although it may be worth while to note that our thinking about such historical matters as vividly interest us will often entice us into bouts of 'quasi-' or 'phantasy' deliberation: Should I reject Parmenio's counsel of moderation if I were Alexander the Great? What should I have done in Sir Edward Grey's place in the fateful July days of 1914? However, physicians do have to deliberate a great deal, not because of the imperfection of their medical knowledge in general or owing to the incertitude of its application to the singular case, but because the *end* their decisions are ordained to, 'the cure of the patient', is not unequivocal except in a *prima facie* schematic sense, while in fact it is largely ambiguous, admitting of different interpretations, and requiring to be more closely determined according to the peculiar features of the situation in all but the simplest cases. Thus, the most effective cure here and now might appear harmful to the patient's health considered in a wider perspective, or possibly prejudicial from the point of view of public health; a radical operation or the use of some potent drug may imperiously commend itself yet at the same time entail grave risks; perhaps the doctor cannot fully devote his time and energies to the effective treatment of one case of middling gravity without unduly neglecting others, and many similar 'doctor's dilemmas'. In all of them, conflicting ends are involved (i.e. a choice between alternative goods is imposed); whether or not these ends can be regarded as 'means' to some higher ends and comparable with one another in terms of such an instrumentality, they cannot be construed as means to the one fixed and unproblematic end of 'curing the patient'. Their emergence bursts the bonds of that unique and isolated teleological constant, though of course the theme of curing the patient is in no wise invalidated thereby. Deliberation, then, arises not in virtue of the multiplicity of conceivable and available means but in virtue of the multiplicity of *other ends* as affected by the envisaged use of means in the service of *one given end*, and partly at least as implicit in the *conception* of that one end here and now endowed with a thematic primacy.

In the very passage quoted, Aristotle all but reveals this fairly simple truth, only to miss it owing to his utilitarian-rationalistic outlook. The paragraph is concluded by this sentence:

And if in the course of their search [*scil.* for appropriate means to an end] men come upon an impossibility, they give it up: if money, for instance, is necessary, but cannot be got; but if the thing appears possible then they attempt to do it.

No doubt, these clear-cut situations occur: 'the cure' for some dreadful (and some rather innocuous) diseases has not so far been found and thus the cases, to put it somewhat crudely, are 'given up', but if research should some day find the cure for one or the other of them it will be applied; I might fancy owning a well-staffed palatial house but as I literally couldn't get the money necessary to achieve this end, I utterly abstain from pursuing it. But this description is out of touch with the way things usually happen in life, and misses the real point. Money *is* in one sense a pure means, more so than Aristotle (unacquainted, I suppose, with our fiat money, lacking all intrinsic usefulness or beauty) could possibly have known; yet precisely for that reason, by virtue of its quite indeterminate and neutral convertibility, it actually stands for an indefinite manifoldness of *ends*. If I buy this dress, I cannot buy that encyclopaedia; if I make this trip to the South, I shall have to live on porridge and cigarettes alone for two months. I 'have got' the necessary money for any one or several of a hundred purchases I desire to make, but not for all of them or many of them. Economy does not mean not spending the money one hasn't got, it means not spending the money one has got—or spending it in awareness of having to face the consequences. It is a question, not of possessing or not possessing the means to an end, but of having to choose between goods, i.e. of renouncing the pursuit of one end for the sake of another.

2

It has been implicitly accorded above that the search for suitable means and the finding of such may sometimes quasi-automatically lead up to action, i.e. to the (attempted) realization of a preconceived end. Theoretical observation and calculation as such do not issue in action; hence, compared with these, the quest for means to a given end may look as if it amounted in itself to deliberation. Moreover, to contemplate almost any kind of means may involve a weighing of ends against ends (an analgesic tablet would relieve my neuralgic pain but might upset my stomach), so much so that any reference to possible means may give our practical thought a deliberative turn. Enquiry about facts or data and their numerical and causal connections is not deliberation, whether or no it happens to subserve directly or indirectly a practical object, and whether or no it is prompted or commandeered by a concrete end in view. Any purely theoretical piece of thinking may unexpectedly be turned to some practical use in a later situation, without retroactively changing its non-deliberative intrinsic nature; and the doing of a sum is no more an act of deliberation if it refers to bits of a debt I owe to somebody and intend to discharge forthwith than if it occurs just in the context of an algebraic problem.

That the technical preamble to action—the quest for means as such—is intrinsically different from deliberation is expressed in the fact that the former does not, whereas the latter does, constitute a field for the exercise of free-will. In finding out what I *can* do with a view to obtaining some effect, any intervention of my free choice cannot but falsify and invalidate the result of my quest: if I have to add, say, 33, 19 and 7, any sum other than 59 will represent an error, and it is pointless to say that I can reduce the total to 53 if I so will. I can, of course, *write* the false sum 53 underneath the column of addends if I so will. Supposing them to be items of a debt, I may do so with the object of cheating my creditor for example, having *deliberated* about whether I prefer saving 6 units of currency to keeping honest, and attach more weight to the chance of succeeding than to the risk of being caught in a disgraceful act; and having arrived at a morally objectionable and, very likely, a practically foolish decision. Whereas, then, the discovery or invention of means and the ascertaining of their foreseeable efficacy is meant to establish something *a limine* independent of my will, deliberation is the sounding-out and ordering of my preferences which *a limine* brings into play acts of choice not settled beforehand but formed *ad hoc* and thus the exercise of my free-will beyond its mere preliminary information. Aristotle was not unaware of this, for in book VII he argues that prudent judgement, i.e. correct thinking about singular *agibilia* (preparatory to concrete decision and action, that is), presupposes right willing, i.e. 'virtue'. Deliberation is in fact an exercise of freedom in some sense aiming at the *restriction* of freedom, namely at producing not simply action but action as it reasonably ought to be, should be or must be, analogously as it were to the correct solution of a theoretical problem. But Aristotle stretches the analogy: to paraphrase Hume's words, his own reason is still a slave to the Socratic-Platonic passion for installing reason as the master rather than the mere counsellor and interpreter of the will; that is why he transposes deliberation, i.e. the genesis of 'considered' or 'reasoned' willing, into the domain of means by reference to an unquestioned end, where reason is indeed sovereign and where free choice between alternative goods or mutually incompatible satisfactions is beside the point.

3

The position 'Deliberation is of means purely and simply and *not* of ends', as exemplified above, might however be dismissed as an extravaganza to which Aristotle is not committed by his general doctrine of practice. It reveals the dominant rationalistic trend of his thought rather than his outlook as a whole. He is, at any rate, on stronger ground if we take him to mean that deliberation is of means *and* ends; ends, that is to say, considered in their means-like aspect, or in other words, in their instrumental capacity or causal connection. Suppose I set up tentatively A as a particular end for its own sake; but either A itself or some means M which I could not help using to secure it is incompatible with another end of mine, B, which I cherish equally or even more; now on further reflection I find that A not only attracts me in itself but would also act as an effective means towards securing a further end, C, which ranks pretty high among my preoccupations. This sounds like a possible description of what happens when we deliberate, and it certainly refers to means; to be sure, means as they affect different established or provisional ends, not means to one end seen in isolation and taken for granted without reserve. On the contrary, when a man just makes a straightforward choice according to his preference he is not deliberating. Shall we then simply meet Aristotle half-way and conclude that deliberation is of means and ends jointly? This I am reluctant to do, mainly, on the face of it, for two reasons. First, Aristotle (book I, 1097a, b), while admitting that 'ends are plainly many',[1] is apt to object that any rational choice between two antithetic ends can only take place by reference to some higher end and that, thus, all particular ends directly or indirectly depend upon and are appraised as means to, a 'supreme good' the attainment of which constitutes the one 'ultimate end' (imposed by nature rather than freely chosen): consequently, that deliberation, even if apparently of ends, is essentially of means. Secondly, I on my part deny that the interrelationship of ends analyses without a remainder into simple, ultimate emotive preferences (stronger and weaker likes and dislikes) on the one hand and instrumental utilities in the service of some higher ends or a highest end on the other hand, and therefore deny that the weighing of ends against one another (when it's not a matter of straightforward non-deliberative choices) is reducible to a comparative assessment of means. I accordingly maintain that, quite apart from the unreflected choice of that which unequivocally attracts more or repels less, what stands in the thematic focus of deliberative choice are convergent and divergent ends, i.e. autonomous goods, values or satisfactions with their mutual *pro* and *con* accents and implications, whereas the apprehension of means and calculation of their effects play the part of a technical auxiliary. In the following section, I shall argue in support of this concept of non-instrumental connections, and that will issue directly in a criticism of Aristotle's mediatization of particular ends.

4

The frequent and indeed predominant multivalence of means is alone sufficient to confer upon them a character of relative or partial ends, while on the other hand any end may also be regarded as a means to various other ends;[2] but if the end-means pattern thus appears to slip into a mode of ambiguity and to exhibit one aspect of our practical approach to 'goods' (in the widest sense) rather than a permanent division of them into two classes (*bona delectabilia* and *honesta* and *bona utilia*), then it may more conveniently be said that in deliberating we confront mutually conspiring and mutually competitive ends with one another than that in deliberating we seek out the available and efficacious means to one determinate end. For the latter activity is a subsidiary requirement of the former, whereas the converse is not true.

But the relation between ends is by no means only causal, expressible, that is, in terms of conducive or harmful effects; it is also intrinsic. Some ends appear to be in keeping or consonance with each other; some are mutually jarring, unsuited, discordant, exhibiting a relation of contrariety up to the point of logical inconsistency. In actually setting up his ends (as distinct from unsanctioned desires, leanings or tentative visions), the agent is compelled to choose, on pain of behaving ineffectually and self-defeatingly; and of course in his choices such ends are more strongly weighted as display, in addition to their worth considered in itself, a particular 'fittingness' in respect of important other ends already established and as it were axiomatic. Thus, a man with dominant spiritual interests may control his penchant for gluttony not merely because in a consequential sense it is apt to interfere with his studies but because he is pained by a sense of essential incompatibility between these two passions; again, a traditional textbook example I think, an eminently sociable person will all the more tend to deliberately cultivate his taste for wine as a temperate enjoyment of good drinks not only promotes the forming of social ties but to some extent enriches and ennobles companionship. In view of the active, sanctioned pursuit and sustained cherishing of certain goods we may not unnaturally, if somewhat loosely, speak of 'ends' here, but the language of 'ends *and means*' is plainly inadequate.

Another line of argument leads in a similar direction. It has more than once been pointed out, by none so aptly and forcefully as by Sir David Ross,[3] that to set up an aim (be it even provisionally) and then to look about for the proper means to attain it is far from constituting the one universal model of practice. Often enough and quite normally, the machinery of tentative purposing and of deliberation is set in motion by occasions, finds, discoveries, offers, stimuli, temptations, suggestions, proposals and so forth. We come in possession, actual or virtual, of a good which may or may not awaken our desire to enjoy it, or a possible 'means' which starts us wondering whether we shall or shall not avail ourself of it, or to what use we might best put it. We ask ourself whether any of our 'ends' is served by this thing (would not, rather, our using it disserve one general end of ours, that of saving effort and time and per-haps money?); we look round for 'ends' to be achieved by the 'means' at our disposal. We deliberate whether we should adopt a suggested pur-pose—e.g. that of visiting a city, having received an invitation—or in the variant case, deliberate about possible ends for a given mean. Of course we do not form purposes out of nothing, without any conditioning elements whatever in our preexisting emotive structure and horizon of knowledge. However, for all the constants in our mental and affective outlook which make us receptive to some kinds of stimuli and unresponsible to others, our actual purpose-formation is largely contingent on occasions and sug-gestive influences which happen to cross our path. Our ends are not all ready-made, awaiting their fulfilment when the proper means should have been found; they may come to life and harden into shape in fairly unexpected contexts; and their fixation involves to some extent, at times it may be a considerable extent, a revision, modification and reorienta-tion of our preestablished structure of permanent or comparatively last-ing ends—I would rather say, our *concerns*—itself.[4] It is the choices, confrontations, inner dialogues, hesitations and new engagements implied in this process that *primo loco* constitute the field of deliberation.

Because the end-means relation is the simplest and the most evident of the different types of relations between the manifold single elements, phases, aspects and objects which make up the articulation of '*an action*' (or a course of action, or a project unfolding while carried into execution), there arises an intellectual temptation to extend the end-means model far beyond its true range. In proportion as a thing is means-like we know what it is for, i.e. what is its *raison d'être*:[5] a pencil-sharpener is incomparably more intelligible than, say, literature. Thus, objects of enjoyment and, worse, of reverent appreciation have been misinterpreted as means to the states of mind they or their presence or possession may evoke. It is a distorted way of speaking to call the *object* of an enjoyment a *means* to pleasure. The instrumentality implied in the *procuring* of the object (buying it in the market, etc.) is fallaciously transferred here to the object itself. Again, the components of a whole have been misnamed means to the end it is supposed to embody.[6] The earlier phases of a coherent unit of action and experience have sometimes been uncritically regarded as means to its terminal or culminating point, as if the courses of a festive dinner were means to the crowning delight of coffee, liqueur and Havana. And diverse kinds of subordination have boldly been equated to an end-means relation between the higher and the lower ranks of the hierarchy, as if (the conception is Aristotelian) slaves stood to masters as means to ends and the beef-steak was the entelechy of the cow. Similarly, there is a tendency to mistake for a mere matter of means-finding the *specification* or closer determination of an end, project or intention once conceived. To be sure, if I have to reach a given destination as soon as possible I shall take the shortest path or look for the most rapid *means* of communication; yet if I decide to go for a walk my choice of a direction—if at all a reflected choice—will not be, properly speaking, the choice of the most efficacious means but, although bearing on a very puny matter, a true deliberative choice which renders my purpose realizable by completing it and setting it in clearer outline.

5

If, to put it crudely, in deliberating we compare ends with the view of choosing between them, what are the criteria of the comparison and on what grounds do we choose or mean to choose in one sense as opposed to another? Here is a puzzle quite alien to the mere search for appropriate means, including even the cases when our knowledge of the efficacy of different means to an end is not certain but only probable. If you have decided to spend a few weeks at some southern place where you want to enjoy the warm climate but avoid the torrid summer heat, by all means go there in May or in September, though there just might be a heatwave in either of these months and a spell of cool weather in June or in August. But whether it is more worth while, say, to make this trip or to refurnish some of your rooms instead (supposing you cannot afford to do both) I am unable to tell you, and you may find it very awkward to '*decide*' which of the two you want more badly and what accessory advantages and drawbacks are implied on either side. ('Deciding' has its characteristic ambiguous sense here: it unites a quasi-theoretical act of examining and ascertaining what one most wants to a quasi-practical act, an inchoate act of willing.) Except in cases where we have a clear preference for one good over an alternative good and there is no reason why we should not follow it straightforwardly without any deliberation, we compare ends with ends *in the light of further ends* they are likely to promote or to hamper respectively, either in a causal sense or at any rate in the sense of concordance and disordance: do we then, after all, consider the ends between which we have to choose as if they were means to something else? No, for we feel inclined to pursue them for their own sake, without any logically necessary or previously given reference to further ends; again, these further ends or some of them may not be at all 'higher' or more important; again, some of the preferences that may ultimately play a part in our choice will perhaps only come to light, develop, mature and get more or less firmly established in the process of our deliberation. However enlightened by reason and based on or rather supported by reasons, choice is shot through with arbitrariness: that is why it centrally reveals the affirmation and exercise of our free-will, which is only marginally present in our theoretical thinking and conclusions.

The view here propounded is not wholly at variance with Aristotle's. His doctrine of the specificity of 'practical reason', open to serious objections to be sure, indicates his awareness of the gulf between theoretical elucidation and deliberative choice, including prudent or wise choice. His postulate (book I) of a single and paramount 'final' end which is pursued for its own sake *alone* is exposed in a wary and rambling fashion revealing a commonsensical moderation of his utilitarian and metaphysical emphasis. Aristotle admits here (1) that there are at least certain general categories of particular ends—concerns, I would say; Stevenson's 'focal aims' appear to express the same concept—such as knowledge, pleasure and honour, or some qualified forms thereof, which are desired, as it befits true ends, for their own sake, though also as 'means to happiness', i.e. subject to the arbitrament of an 'absolutely final end'.[a] He admits (2) that 'to call happiness the chief good' sounds like 'a mere truism', some 'clearer account of its real nature' being required. He explains (3) that happiness means a state of the soul and an ordering of conduct 'in accordance with Reason', a 'good life' and a 'complete life', which conveys the idea of a *comprehensive* condition of excellence rather than an isolated single 'end' from which all other ends were derivable as 'means'. And he concedes (4) that happiness thus understood, while it 'has no need of pleasure as an additional advantage but involves pleasure in itself', yet also 'requires the addition of external goods'.

Withal, the *problem* still remains whether it is not logically necessary to appeal to the arbitrament of an ulterior and unchallengeably valid end in order to choose *meaningfully* between competitive ends; in other words, whether the fact of deliberation does not *eo ipso* imply recourse to some practical ultimate or at any event, perhaps, to one of several—not intrinsically incompatible—axioms of this kind. One such ultimate standard of orientation would, I suppose, be provided by hedonic and biological utility, in direct continuity with the claims of nature; another, by deontic morality; yet another, by the aspiration for a unified meaning and dedication of life which points to the religious concept of salvation or holiness; and to these might be added the sense of a personal meaning and plan of life, centred in a specifically chosen set of values. Be that as it may, the Aristotelian notion of a 'chief good' or 'final end' is undoubtedly warped to some extent by an uncritical extension of the end-means model to a field of relationships of a more complex and reciprocal type.

At a second remove, Aristotle, obviously unsatisfied with the vague synthetic ideal of the 'complete life', distorts the blanket concept of 'happiness' into the more singularized and determinate supreme value of 'intellectual contemplation' as expanded in book X, the last. This arbitrary reinterpretation appears to introduce an 'ideal state of mind' out of contact with action and its problems, and suggesting a negation of practice rather than any directive for the ordering of it. Again, the 'complete life' is not so much subserved by particular goods in an instrumental capacity as constituted by them in the sense in which an ensemble is made up by its component parts. Any one of our particular ends may indeed be subordinate to the *conspectus* of our concerns, but unless the particular ends existed in their own right the conspectus would mean nothing at all. Even assuming that there is such a thing as a superior experience of all-round happiness, somehow separable from any explicit reference to particular dimensions of good, it *presupposes* particular ends and their fulfilment; the management of special concerns may at some points decisively depend on the endeavour to attain or maintain it, but the dependence is mutual. It is not enough to say, with Aristotle, that some particular ends of high standing are 'also' desired for their own sake and not 'merely' as a means to happiness. So far as happiness is conceived of as an all-embracing ideal, necessarily relevant to any definite and concrete provinces of fulfilment, it actually *consists* in these, and possibly in the feeling of their concordance; whereas so far as it is seen as seated in a supreme mode of fulfilment set apart from others, e.g. spirituality (taking the hint of the second Aristotelian version), it is no longer all-embracing and its nexus with other autonomous ends becomes contingent and open to vastly different interpretations. In either case, the *derivation* of single ends, including humble and highly particularized ones, from a superordinate and final end is doomed to failure as a merely imaginary construction, and significant choice is shown to take place not between different means to one end but between different ends. This, it is true, still implies various kinds of hierarchic and reciprocal relations between ends so as to account for the possibility of argument and the necessity of deliberation.

6

I can but touch in passing on the *ethical* side of the matter. With his doctrine of a marked-out final end and of choice bearing upon the proper means to an end, Aristotle lays himself open to the charge of debasing practical wisdom or 'prudence', and with it 'moral decision'—since he, like many other philosophers, fails to distinguish between the moral Ought and the practical 'I had better ...'—to the level of expediency: morality would then consist in the agent's finding the immanently right, i.e. effective, means to attain what he is ultimately striving for. But, though somehow in accord with his outlook, this is not the position he really, let alone consistently, holds. In book I, without realizing to be sure the altogether open field of the possible autonomous ends and special predilections of men, he notes that the blank of the abstract concept of 'the chief good' has been filled by different schools of thought with different kinds of more determinate things; i.e. he allows for different interpretations or specifications of the end as distinct from different views about the proper means to attain it. And in book VI (1144a), he expressly sets apart practical wisdom from 'cleverness', i.e. the skilful choice of means to any kinds of end whatsoever: only the virtuous person, who has opted for *the right end*, can reason properly about problems of practice, for he alone possesses the right premise for practical syllogisms. Aristotle appears to be trying to deal here with a basic ethical objection to his general doctrine of practice and morality; perhaps in so doing he lapses into self-contradiction, but anyhow he shows his aversion to sacrificing ethical intuition altogether to the exigencies of his metaphysical system, and is hinting at what is, if not a contradiction, at any rate a tension within our very experience of practice. The agent's own primary concerns are the only possible principles of his practice, for he cannot succeed or fail except in what *is* his endeavour, nor adopt objective principles except by reference to things he actually wants already. Nevertheless, can his practice in no way be wise or unwise, correct or false, *eupractic* or *dyspractic* apart from mere technical correction or miscalculation?

The following sentence by St Augustine (*De libero arbitrio*, book I) brings out more clearly and forcefully the fundamental insight that morality turns on cherishing one sovereign right end, not on applying the right means to another end; that, however closely related to happiness at least in the eternal or salvational sense, it can neither be derived from the concept of happiness nor take the place of happiness, and itself supply the sole comprehensive final end of man:

The wicked [i.e. the lost souls] are not unhappy because they did not desire happiness, for they desired that no less than the virtuous did; but the latter also desired to lead a life of justice, which the former did not.

Particular ends, including even permanent and life-shaping personal concerns, cannot be unequivocally deduced from any preestablished conceptual scheme or ideal, be it ever so fervently adopted; deliberation cannot be replaced by a mere technical 'application' of overall principles. If the concern of morality and the imperative of honesty cannot be conjured, except fictitiously, out of any conceptual apparatus of 'pleasure-and-pain economy', on the other hand even a man endowed with the keenest sense of honesty does not as a rule make business transactions from the motive of practising the virtue of honesty, and the rules of honesty tell him no more in what business transactions he should engage than the rules of chess tell the player what moves he should make in order to win the game.

Moreover, ideals are not only in need of being implemented by personal acts of choice but are themselves chosen, not imposed by nature or rational self-evidence;[b] and however defensible, commendable and extensive in scope they may be, they inevitably fall short of representing the totality of the worthy purposes of man. Whoever identifies the ideal of his choice with the 'ultimate end' of the universe or history or God in a sense exclusive of other points of view or experiences of value, is a prey to fictitious judgement and cramped pretension. This truth finds a masterly expression in Tennyson's verses:

And God fulfils Himself in many ways,
Lest one good custom should corrupt the world.

If not of Tennyson's, Plato and Aristotle and their system-happy followers might have taken heed of Heraclitus' warning:

Better is invisible than visible harmony.

7

I fear I must wind up by a dismaying anticlimax: the concept of deliberation I have tried to outline seems ineluctably to involve what I would venture to call somewhat pompously the fundamental paradoxy of Practice. If deliberation was not of ends but of means, i.e. if it were reducible to rational computation—which in my view merely belongs to its forecourt, as a technical auxiliary—no such paradoxy would arise; there is nothing paradoxical about the possibility of inaccurate knowledge or miscalculation. But again, if choice was a purely gratuitous affair, a display of the freedom of indifference, a wilful act of 'engagement' no matter for which cause or in what course; if significant choice bore on questions like 'Which boot shall I put on first when dressing?' then too we should be baffled by no paradox. Straightforward preferences are self-justifying and random hits stand in no need and do not admit of justification. But neither would deliberation then exist at all. In fact, it is not so. Placed before significant choices, man cannot but deliberate, weighing ends as if they were means, comparing them as if they were fixed data accessive to theoretical measurement, whereas their weight depends on the seesaw of his own tentative willing and on his emergent *parti-pris* as well as the other way round. In some sense, it is an inherently deceptive, not to say deceitful operation, with loaded dice as it were; the agent cannot help weighting what he is weighing, though neither can he do the weighting without a vague but imperative reliance on the results of his weighing, some would say the illusion of his manipulating objectively fixed weights. This circular and puzzling character of deliberation arises, not from plain irrationality as present in our spontaneous preferences and emotive whims, but from the interplay between an ineliminable irrationality (the fact that free-will alone, not reason, can choose and sanction) and an equally ineliminable rationality in the genesis of choice: a rationality whose primary habitat and starting-point is indeed, so far Aristotle's dictum remains valid, the consideration of means in view of ends. In other words, the paradoxy is rooted in the twofold fact that man cannot but choose freely, that, to give Sartre his due, he cannot abdicate his somehow gratuitous and groundless freedom, and that on the other hand he can only will goods and not the exercise of his freedom as such, and therefore *in choosing cannot but try to choose wisely*, i.e. to make a choice that *is* supported by grounds.

Wise or *eupractic* or correct (as opposed to false) choice is not a concept invented and foisted upon man by prigs or preachers; it is what man of necessity desires and hopes against hope to contrive. Nor is the concept as I here mean it and as men mean it confined to that of a well-informed and pondered choice, made in awareness of the factual circumstances and on the basis of a correct reasoning about foreseeable effects, as opposed to ignorance, error and precipitancy. Nor again, of course, is wise choice identified with one that actually happens to lead to success and beneficial results—the lucky hit as it were. Theoretical judgement also is largely conjectural; it may be as sound as possible and yet objectively wrong by accident, and inversely. But action may be sagaciously planned and carried out with complete success in the immanent or technical sense, and yet end up in a consciousness of practical failure. The fulfilment, secured at a high cost perhaps, of his purpose may leave the agent with a bitter tang of disappointment or worse in his mouth, and the definite feeling that he ought to have known this in advance and that he was a blundering fool or misguided by a perverse mood when taking his decision—not just ill informed or guilty of rashness or levity or miscalculation of probable effects, nor even just a different kind of man than he now is. (It is worth noting here that hesitancy and over-deliberation as well as thoughtless haste and audacity may adversely affect practice.)

If elaborate and pedantic rules of felicific practice, *Maximen der Lebensweisheit* as the Germans put it, are sometimes utterly fictitious or irrelevant and nearly always fallible, if it is derisory and often dangerous —a sure sign of unwisdom—to follow them slavishly, not to mention the contradictions between their respective emphases, it may nevertheless be useful to know and occasionally to consult some of them; and above all, they testify to man's *craving* for practical wisdom. An incurable but not really a morbid craving, for it is an absurd misuse of language to call our very being and constitution a disease (*une passion inutile*), whatever the incongruities and paradoxies inherent in it; yet it pertains to our constitution to deliberate with a view to arriving, not just 'to a decision' but to 'a wise' or to 'the right' decision, I do not mean to 'a wise decision or none'[7] but to a decision which shall be a wise decision. More briefly, it is part of our constitution *to deliberate*, since 'to deliberate' *is* to confront, compare, forecast and argue in view of a happy choice. By the same paradoxy, our free-will has to be exercised and can only be exercised in a self-restrictive fashion, for the ends we set up and stamp with the *fiat* of the 'sanctioning' imperative power of decision subject us to so many commitments and objectivizations, which are henceforth to circumscribe and govern our will though engendered by its ruling. We cannot want this to happen at random; we cannot help wanting that it should happen in a way attuned to what we most urgently, most perdurably, most evidently and most appreciatively want, and even that the emphasis of our wanting should be so ordered as to make this possible. Hence we cannot prescind from wishing to choose, not indeed 'from' reason or at the dictate of reason, but with reason, as if the ends we choose were underwritten by a pellucid will, unmarred by incertitude and tottering, which we do not actually possess; as if they bore the guarantee of rational evidence and the seal of objective truth.

Self-restrictive willing, the only mode of effective willing we can conceive of, is not for that reason self-destructive (though so many of our actions inevitably are); and the paradoxy of choice is not exactly a contradiction. Deliberation cannot be cleansed from an ingredient of sham rationality, but it does not follow that the problem of wise and unwise choice is itself a sham problem. It would be more difficult to construct paradigms of wise and unwise than of moral and immoral or, what is even easier, of technically prudent and imprudent action, mainly because the sorting-out of 'irrelevant circumstances' which conditions the force and applicability of hypothetical models and general criteria is more open to logical objections in the field of *eupractic* than in the fields of moral and of expediential judgement; and yet most of us, I suggest, could point at least to some sparse instances of arguably, if not demonstrably, wise and unwise choice in our own life-experience. The very fact of disbelieving altogether in the possibility of a wise choice would impair a man's deliberation and make him choose all the more unwisely; and so would an uncritical belief in rationality and disregard for the fact that all choice connotes and requires arbitrariness and entails risks. A choice that would on the face of it be deemed 'wise' on conventional grounds is likely to be wiser than an act of romantic irresponsibility; again, an apparently eccentric choice which expresses the 'authentic' bent of a fearless and passionate but reflective soul might be wiser than the obviously 'reasonable' choice in its place would be on that agent's part. It would always be ill-advised to act automatically on the principle expressed in William the Silent's motto '*Nul n'est besoin d'espérer pour entreprendre ni de réussir pour persévérer*', but it may be wise to act so in selected cases.

Aristotle's general concept of practical wisdom reveals the defects of an all too self-confident and short-circuited rationalism, ill compensated for by his rejection of all general criteria of wise choosing in the concrete case and his mystical idol of a postulated 'virtue of prudence' untestably operating on singulars. That is no reason, however, for turning a blind eye on the problem which this great pioneer of the theory of practice has bequeathed us. It may be elusive and bemusing but is not, I think, barren or nonsensical.

The thesis argued against in this paper, 'Deliberation is of Means not of Ends', is linked up with the following six Aristotelian positions, all of which except the last are touched upon in the text but which cannot be *in extenso* discussed here.

1. That, as Practice necessarily bears upon singulars (book I, 1097a), so also singulars constitute the object of practical knowledge only, Science proper being about universals. Thus all thinking about the particular circumstances of a concrete case, especially about means, is practical not theoretical thinking, and amounts to deliberation.
2. That, since Practice (as Plato decrees) has to be governed by Reason, yet (against Plato) demands a specific attention to singulars and cannot be determined by the 'scientific' or 'sapiential' knowledge of universals, there must be such an entity as Practical Reason or Prudence (book VI, 1141b). This confusing hybrid concept is, then, introduced so as both to safeguard Platonic rationalism and to tone it down as a concession to common sense. A valid insight into the *non-rigorous use of reason* is implied therein, though in fact non-rigorous rationality plays an immense part also in theoretical thought.
3. That *eupractic* and morally good conduct and *dyspractic* and morally bad conduct are respectively identical: an apparently self-evident

presupposition for Aristotle and countless others ever since. The roots of this confusion are partly sham-scientific, partly naturalistic and utilitarian, and partly moral-pedagogical; but it also arises, I suggest, from a misconception of the really arguable *consonance* between virtuous and *eupractic*, evil and *dyspractic* conduct. In the so-called Franciscan tradition (as contrasted with Thomism) in Christian-Scholastic thought, the distinction between (prudential) Practice and Morality is vigorously upheld, and a particular '*moral* practical reason' as well as a 'supernatural *moral* end of man' in discontinuity with the natural striving for 'happiness' (the latter necessarily present in all men, the former not) are asserted. See Jean Rohmer, *La finalité morale chez les théologiens de saint Augustin à Duns Scot*, especially the chapters on St Anselm of Canterbury and Duns Scotus. Evidently if moral valuations and norms were not autonomous but were just prudential rules, that would add to the plausibility of deliberation being 'of means'.

4. That Practical *Reason*, not the Will, takes the initiative for, and finally 'commands', action (book VI, 1143a). Cf. about this odd and much-disputed doctrine, G. E. M. Anscombe, *Intention*, §35 and pp. 74, 75 nn. If it were so, that again would displace the central emphasis of deliberation from ends to means. See P. Ricoeur's excellent criticism (*Philosophie de la volonté*, i, p. 161) of 'the intellectualist theory of choice', all the more significant as Ricoeur also justly rejects (p. 166) the voluntarist theory of choice as advanced by the existentialists, as apt to blur the experience of values and engulf valuation in decision.

5. That the higher a being ranks in the Universe or in the State the more it must be ordained to one determinate 'end', e.g. 'Man *qua* Man' more so than Man in his capacity as a craftsman (book I, 1097b). This fantastic notion is obviously rooted in Aristotle's cosmology and originates from the Eleatic (monistic and geometrical) concept of 'perfection'. For a devastating criticism of the 'cosmological theory of the will', the idea of 'particular goods as means to an end', and the alleged 'universal desire for a *bonum generale* from which anything might be derived by way of syllogisms', see Ricoeur, op. cit., pp. 180–186.

6. That, finally, the objects pursued by an unjust or vicious will are not real goods (wrongly coveted or unsuitable in the circumstances or even chosen in preference to *greater* goods) but '*apparent* goods' (book III, 1113a, b). Thus, immoral conduct and *a fortiori, dyspractic* conduct in general, though undoubtedly bound up with affective misdirection, would rest on a mistaken judgement and a consecutive choice of immanently

improper 'means' to the unequivocal 'final end' we all invariably pursue by metaphysical necessity.

Notes

1. ·'Honour, pleasure, intellect, in fact every excellence we choose for their own sake.' What Aristotle has in mind here are standard and (all but) permanent categories of 'ends', i.e. concerns or interests, rather than purposes proper such as 'to win this prize' or 'to get in at the next election'; in C. L. Stevenson's terminology, 'focal aims' rather than 'ends in view'. However, concrete here-and-now 'ends in view' are logically on a par with 'healing this patient', which Aristotle does state to be the physician's end (Bk I, 1097a).

2. Cf. Stevenson, 'Reflections on John Dewey's Ethics', *Proceedings of the Aristotelian Society* (December 1961): The 'large ends recommended in traditional ethics', such as 'the greatest happiness of the greatest number', are desired *partly but not alone for their own sake*. For 'focal aims' and their compatibility, nay consonance, with the *pluralism* of particular ends, see the most remarkable footnote on p. 203 in Stevenson, *Ethics and Language*, paperbound ed. 1960.

3. Ross, *Foundations of Ethics*, pp. 195–199. It looks as if Ross were less willing than I am 'to give up Aristotle's doctrine, that choice is not of ends but only of means'. According to him, we do not decide whether to *desire* but only whether to *seek* an end, and the latter means 'to take means to an end'. With this I must disagree. What we decide is whether to approve or to disapprove a desire of ours (absolutely and permanently, or relatively and temporarily); our 'taking (or not taking) means to an end' *presupposes* our decision to pursue (or not to pursue) that *end* as such. In an indirect and limited sense, we even choose our desires. It becomes, anyhow, apparent especially on p. 199 how 'widely' Ross himself, in his own words, 'departs from the Aristotelian model'. [The author appears to have had doubts about the views expressed in this footnote. This is indicated by a query written into the margin.—Francis Dunlop and Brian Klug]

4. Clearly our concerns (or 'enduring interests', or 'focal aims') do not constitute a denumerable set of distinct entities, making up all together our definitive 'self'. They can be described and classified in widely different ways; they mutually overlap and are also mutually at tension. Yet they form the matrix out of which our particular choices of ends emerge, and these in their turn react upon them and may in part modify or, to borrow another term from Stevenson, 'redirect' them. As Ricoeur puts it (*Philosophie de la volonté ii, Finitude et culpabilité*, 1960, p. 171): 'Le surgissement du choix est finalement, sous sa forme la plus authentique, une discontinuité au sein même de la motivation, parfois même un renversement de valeurs, une révolution dans l'évaluation.'

5. According to K. R. Popper ('Three Views concerning Human Knowledge', in *Contemporary British Philosophy*, iii, p. 369 n.), it is man-made things such as clocks, etc. that have an unequivocal and knowable *purpose*, and thus a definable 'essence'.

6. This traditional fallacy is exploded with peculiar vigour by Moore (*Principia Ethica*, §§20–21).

7. Practical decisions are not on the same logical footing with theoretical problems. Phrases conceived in the mode of doubt or a divided mind, such as 'We have no means of knowing . . .', 'More likely, it is so . . .', 'Partly this, partly that . . .', etc., are possible final answers to theoretical questions but not to practical alternatives. I cannot, e.g., for ever probably accept or probably turn down a concrete unique offer, nor in general partly accept and partly reject it.

Editors' Notes

a. [The author has written into the margin, next to the latter part of this sentence, the words 'then, not derivable'. This seems to be a comment about whether it is coherent to talk about desiring 'true ends' both for their own sake and as 'means to happiness'.—Francis Dunlop and Brian Klug]

b. [The text from here to the end of the paragraph has been marked by the author in a number of ways. It is difficult to ascertain his intentions and we have amended the text in only one place where the indication is relatively clear.—Francis Dunlop and Brian Klug]

Chapter 13

Deliberation and Practical Reason

David Wiggins

The matter of the practical is indefinite, unlimited.
Aristotle

1 THREE THESES OF ARISTOTELIAN INTERPRETATION

Consider the following three contentions:[1]

1. In book 3 of the *Nicomachean Ethics* (*NE*) Aristotle treats a restricted and technical notion of deliberation, which makes it unnecessary for him to consider anything but technical or so-called productive examples of practical reason. It is not surprising in the context of book 3 that deliberation is never of ends but always of means.

2. When he came to write books 6 and 7 of the *Nicomachean Ethics* and *De Anima* 3.7, Aristotle analysed a much less restricted notion of deliberation and of choice. This made it necessary for him to give up the view that deliberation and choice were necessarily of *ta pros to telos*, where it is supposed that this phrase means or implies that deliberation is only of means. Thereafter he recognized two irreducibly distinct modes of practical reasoning, *means-end* deliberations and *rule-case* deliberations.[2]

3. The supposed modification of view between the writing of book 3 and that of books 6–7, and the newly introduced (supposed) 'rule-case' syllogism, bring with them a radical change in Aristotle's view of the subject—even something resembling a satisfactory solution to the problems of choice and deliberation. Thus 6–7 do better in this way than vaguely suggest what complexities a lifelike account of practical deliberation would have to come to terms with.

Taken singly these doctrines are familiar enough in Aristotelian exegesis.[3] But my submission is that, both as a whole and in detail, the view constituted by (1), (2), (3) is damagingly mistaken. It obstructs improvement in our understanding of the real philosophical problem of practical reason. The examination of (1), (2), (3) will lead (in §§4–6 of this essay) into some general consideration of that problem and Aristotle's contribution to it.

I shall begin by trying to show that for all its simplicities and over-schematizations, Aristotle's book 3 account is in fact straightforwardly continuous with the book 6 account of deliberation, choice, and practical reasoning. Both accounts attempt to analyse and describe wide and completely general notions of choice and deliberation. Each is dominated, I think, by Aristotle's obsession with a certain simple solution of the kind described in book 3, 1112b—the geometer who searches for means to construct a given figure with ruler and compass. Aristotle is acutely and increasingly aware of the limitations of this analogy, but (in spite of its redeployment at 1143b1–5) he never describes exactly what to put in its place. Twentieth-century philosophy is not yet in a position to condescend to him with regard to these questions. For all its omissions and blemishes, Aristotle's account is informed by a consciousness of the lived actuality of practical reasoning and its background. This is an actuality that present-day studies of rationality, morality, and public rationality ignore at their cost, and ignore.

2   REJECTION OF THE FIRST THESIS: BOOK 3 OF THE NICOMACHEAN ETHICS

The supposition that book 3 set out to analyse a restricted notion of deliberation[4] or a restricted notion of choice gives rise to some internal difficulties within the book.

One apparent difficulty is this. *Bouleusis* (deliberation) is inextricably linked in book 3 to *prohairesis* (choice). 'Is the object of prohairesis then simply what has been decided on by previous deliberation?' Aristotle asks at 1112a15, en route to his defining it at 1113a10 as *deliberative desire of what is in our power*. About choice Aristotle remarks at 1111b5 'Choice is thought to be most closely bound up with (*oikeiotaton*) virtue and to discriminate characters better than actions do'. Now this is at least a peculiar remark if deliberation is construed as narrowly as some have been encouraged by the geometrical example at 1112b20 to construe it, and if we construe Aristotle's assertion that choice and deliberation are of what is toward the end (*tōn pros to telos*) to mean that choice and deliberation are concerned only with means. The most straightforward way to see it as a cardinal or conceptually prominent fact about choice that it accurately or generally distinguishes good from bad character, and has a certain constitutive relation to vice and virtue, is to suppose choice to be a fairly inclusive notion that relates to different specifications of man's end. The choices of the bad or self-indulgent man, the *mochthēros* or *akolastos*, would seem to be supposed by Aristotle to reveal this man for what he is because they make straightforwardly apparent his *misconceptions of the end*. The thought ought not to be that the choices such men make reveal any incapacity for technical or strictly means-end reasoning to get what they want or the ends they set themselves. For these they may well achieve—and, in Aristotle's view, miss happiness thereby. Their mistakes are not means-ends or technical mistakes. (*Cf.* 1142b18–20, and 6.12 on *deinotes*.)

It may be objected that the thought is neither of these things but that by seeing a man's choice one can come to guess what his ends are; and to arrive at a view of what his ends are is to arrive at a view of his character. But this interpretation, which scarcely does justice to *oikeiotaton*, must seem a little unlikely as soon as we imagine such an indirect argument to a man's ends. Typically, *actions* would have to mediate the argument. But actions are already mentioned by Aristotle in an unfavourable contrast. 'Choice . . . discriminates characters better than actions do.'

The interpretation of this passage is not perfectly essential to my argument, however. Let us go on, simply remarking that the onus of proof must be on the interpretation that hypothesizes that *prohairesis* or *bouleusis* means something different in book 3 and books 6 and 7. The first effort should be to give it the same sense in all these books. I hope to show that this is possible as well as desirable and that if anything at all gets widened in book 6, it is the *analysis* of choice and deliberation, not the sense of the words. Each must be one *analysand* throughout. As so often, there has been confusion in the discussion of this issue because a *wider analysis of notion N* has sometimes been confused with an *analysis of a wider notion N*. 'Wider conception' is well calculated to mask the difference between these fatally similar-looking things. But let us distinguish them.

There are certainly reasons of a sort why some scholars have seen the book 3 notions of deliberation and choice as technical notions that were superseded by wider notions and then by wider philosophical analyses of either or both notions. These reasons derive from Aristotle's frequent assertions that, unlike *boulesis* (wish), choice and deliberation are not *of the end* but of *what is toward the end* (*pros to telos*). See 1111b26, 1112b11–12, 1112b33–35, 1113a14–15, 1113b3–4. If *what is toward the end* in book 3 is taken (as it is for instance by Ross in his translation) to be a *means to an end*, then that must certainly suggest that as regards prohairesis and bouleusis we have a wider *analysand* as well as a wider analysis in books 6–7. But I argue that they need not be taken so.

It is a commonplace of Aristotelian exegesis that Aristotle never really paused to analyse the distinction between two quite distinct relations: (A) the relation x bears to *telos* y when x will bring about y, and (B) the relation x bears to y when the existence of x will itself help to constitute y. For self-sufficient reasons we are committed in any case to making this distinction very often on behalf of Aristotle when he writes the words *heneka* or *charin* (for the sake of). See, for example, book 1, 1097b1–5. The expression *toward the end* is vague and perfectly suited to express both conceptions.

The first notion, that of a means or instrument or procedure that is causally efficacious in the production of a specific and settled end, has as its clear cases such things as a cloak as a way of covering the body when one is cold, or some drug as a means to alleviate pain. The second notion that can take shelter under the wide umbrella of *what is toward the end* is that of something whose existence counts in itself as the partial or total realization of the end. This is a constituent of the end: *cf. Metaphysics* 1032b27 (N.B. *meros* there), *Politics* 1325b16 and 1338b2–4. Its simple presence need not be logically necessary or logically sufficient for the end. To a very limited extent the achievement of one end may do duty for that of another. Perhaps there might even be some sort of *eudaimonia* (happiness) without good health, or without much pleasure, or without recognized honour, or without the stable possession of a satisfying occupation. But the presence of a constituent of the end is always logically relevant to happiness. It is a member of a nucleus (or one conjunct, to mention a very simple possibility, in a disjunction of conjunctions) whose coming to be counts as the attainment of that end. Happiness is not identifiable in independence of such constituents (*e.g.* as a feeling that these elements cause or as some surplus that can be measured in a person's economic behaviour).

If it commits us to no new interpretative principle to import this distinction into our reading of book 3 and to suppose that both these relations are loosely included within the extension of the phrase *what is toward the end*, then, on this understanding of the phrase, Aristotle is trying in *NE* 3 (however abstractly and schematically) to treat deliberation about means and deliberation about constituents in the same way. Optimistically he is hoping that he can use the intelligibilities of the clear means-end situation and its extensions (how to effect the construction of this particular figure) to illuminate the obscurities of the *constituents-to-end* case. In the latter a man deliberates about what kind of life he wants to lead, or deliberates in a determinate context about which of several possible courses of action would conform most closely to some ideal he holds before himself, or deliberates about what would constitute eudaimonia here and now, or (less solemnly) deliberates about what would count as the achievement of the not yet completely specific goal which he has already set himself in the given situation. For purposes of any of these deliberations the means-end paradigm that inspires almost all the book 3 examples is an inadequate paradigm, as we shall see. But it is not easy to get away from. It can continue to obsess the theorist of action, even while he tries to distance himself from it and searches for something else.

There are two apparent obstacles in book 3 to interpreting the passages on choice and deliberation in this way and to making the crudities of the book continuous with the sophistications of books 6–7.

(*a*)

Three times Aristotle says 'We do not deliberate about *ends* but about *things that are towards ends*', and the plural may have seemed, to anyone who contemplated giving my sort of interpretation, to rule out the possibility that any part of the extension of *things that are towards ends*, that is, things that are deliberated, should comprise deliberable constituents of *happiness* (singular)—that is ends in themselves. If we do not deliberate about ends (plural), then it seems we do not deliberate about the constituents of happiness, which are ends, or about things that are good in themselves and help to make up happiness (*telē*). So it will be said, 'that which is toward the end' cannot ever comprehend any constituents of happiness—these being according to Aristotle undeliberable. But on my interpretation it may include such constituents. Therefore, it may be said, Ross's translation of *pros* in terms of *means* is to be preferred.

(*β*)

To deliberate about that which is toward happiness in the case where the end directly in question in some practical thinking is happiness might, if *that which is toward happiness* included constituents, involve deliberating happiness. But this Aristotle explicitly excludes.

Reply to (*a*)

The first passage of the three in question, 1112b11 following reads:

> We deliberate (*bouleuometha*) not about ends but about what is towards ends. For a doctor does not deliberate whether he shall heal, nor an orator whether he shall persuade, nor a statesman whether he shall produce law and order, nor does anyone else *deliberate about his end*. They assume the end and consider how and by what means it is to be attained, and if it seems to be produced by several means they consider by which it is best and most easily produced, while if it is achieved by one only they consider how it will be achieved by this, and by what means that will be achieved till they come to the first cause, which in the order of discovery is last. For the person who deliberates seems to investigate and analyse in the way described as though he were analysing a geometrical construction (not all seeking is deliberation *e.g.* mathematical seekings, but all deliberation is seeking), and what is last in the order of analysis seems to be the first in the order of being brought about.

I submit that the four words I have italicized show that the *bouleuometha* (we deliberate) and the use of the plural *telon* (ends) are to be taken distributively. Each of these three characters, the orator, doctor, or statesman, has *one* telos (for present purposes). He is already a doctor, orator, or statesman and already at work. That is already fixed (which is not to say that it is absolutely fixed), and to that extent the form of the eudaimonia he can achieve is already conditioned by something no longer needing (at least at this moment) to be deliberated. If I am right about this passage, then there seems to be no obstacle to construing the other two occurrences of the plural, 1112b34–35 and 1113a13–14 (both nearby), as echoes of the thought at 1112b15, and taking *toward the end* (singular) as the canonical form of the phrase (*cf.* 1113b3–4, 1145a4–5 for instance). Provided that difficulty (*β*) can be met, this end may (where required) be a man's total end, namely, happiness.

This reply prompts another and supplementary retort to the difficulty. Suppose I were wrong so far and that *that which is toward the end* (singular) had no special claim to be the canonical form of the phrase. Consider then the case where Aristotle is considering deliberations whose direct ends are not identical with happiness. (Presumably the indirect end will always be happiness: *cf.* 1094a.) Such ends need not be intrinsically undeliberable ends but simple ends held constant *for the situation: cf.* 1112b15, 'assuming the end' (*themenoi to telos*).

Reply to (β)

It is absurd to suppose that a man could not deliberate about whether to be a doctor or not; and very nearly as absurd to suppose that Aristotle, even momentarily while writing book 3, supposed that nobody could deliberate this question. It is so absurd that it is worth asking whether the phrase *deliberating about the end* or *deliberating about happiness* is ambiguous. It is plainly impossible to deliberate about the end if this is to deliberate by asking 'Shall I pursue the end?' If this end is eudaimonia, then *qua* animate humans we have to have some generalized desire for it (a generalized desire whose particular manifestations are desires for things falling under particular specifications of that telos). Simply to call eudaimonia the *end* leaves nothing to be deliberated about whether it should be realized or not. That is a sort of truism (*cf.* 1097b25 ff. *homologoumenon ti*), as is the point that if the desirability of eudaimonia were really up for debate, then nothing suitable by way of practical or ethical concern or by way of desire would be left over (outside the ambit of eudaimonia itself) to settle the matter. But this platitude scarcely demonstrates the impossibility of deliberating the question 'what, practically speaking, *is* that end?' or 'what shall *count* for me as an adequate description of the end of life?' And so far as I can see, nothing Aristotle says in book 3 precludes that kind of deliberation. The only examples we are given of things that we might conclude are intrinsically undeliberable are health and happiness (1111b27). The first is arguably (at least in the philosophy of the Greeks) an undetachable part of the end for human beings. The second is identical with the end as a whole (and no more practically definite an objective than 'the end'). So we are not given examples of logically detachable constituents of the end or of debatable specifications of the end to illustrate Aristotle's thesis in *NE* 3. But on the traditional interpretation of the undeliberability thesis, these were what was needed. So what I think he is saying that one cannot deliberate is *whether* to pursue happiness or health. It is not in any case excluded that (as described in *NE* 6) a man may seek by deliberation to make more specific and more practically determinate that generalized telos of eudaimonia which is instinct in his human constitution.

If this is right so far, then I think another step is taken beyond what was achieved in Allan's discussion to dissociate Aristotle's whole theory of deliberation from that pseudo-rationalistic irrationalism, insidiously propagated nowadays by technocratic persons, which holds that reason has nothing to do with the ends of human life, its only sphere being the efficient realization of specific goals in whose determination or modification argument plays no substantive part.[5]

3   REJECTION OF THE SECOND THESIS: THE TRANSITION TO BOOK 6

On the reading of book 3 so far defended, the transition from *NE* 3 to *NE* 6 is fairly smooth.

Regarding *practical wisdom* we shall get at the truth by considering who are the persons we credit with it. Now it is thought to be the mark of a man of practical wisdom to be able to deliberate well about what is good and expedient for himself, not in some particular respect, e.g. about what sorts of thing conduce to health or to strength, but about what sorts of things conduce to the good life in general (*poia pros to eu zen holos*). [1140a24–28, Ross's translation—note the *pros.*]

And again:

Practical wisdom on the other hand is concerned with things human and things about which it is possible to deliberate; for we say this is above all the work of a man of practical wisdom, to deliberate well.... The man who is without qualification good at deliberating is the man who is capable of aiming in accordance with calculation at the best for man of things attainable by action. Nor is practical wisdom concerned only with what is general—it must also recognize the particularized/ specific. That is why some who do not know, and especially those who have experience, are more practical than others who know. [1114b8–18, Ross]

Aristotle is saying here, among other things, that practical wisdom in its deliberative manifestations is concerned both with the attainment of particular formed objectives and also with questions of general policy—what specific objectives *to* form. He contrasts the two components, and in doing so he commits his investigation to the study of both (*cf.* 1142b30). On my view of *NE* 3, we ought not to be surprised by this. But there is a philosophical difficulty about this kind of deliberation which becomes plainer and plainer as *NE* 6 proceeds.

Aristotle had hoped in *NE* 3 to illuminate examples of nontechnical deliberation by comparing them with a paradigm drawn from technical deliberation. The trouble with both paradigm and comparison is this. It is absolutely plain what counts as my having adequate covering or as my having succeeded in drawing a plane figure of the prescribed kind using only ruler and compass. The practical question here is only what means or measures will work or work best or most easily to those ends. But the standard problem in a nontechnical deliberation is quite different. In the nontechnical case I shall characteristically have an extremely vague description of something I want—a good life, a satisfying profession, an interesting holiday, an amusing evening—and the problem is not to see what will be causally efficacious in bringing this about but to see what really *qualifies* as an adequate and practically realizable specification of what would satisfy this want. Deliberation is still *zetēsis*, a search, but it is not primarily a search for means. It is a search for the *best specification*. Till the specification is available there is no room for means. When this specification is reached, means-end deliberation can start, but difficulties that turn up in this means-end deliberation may send me back a finite number of times to the problem of a better or more practicable specification of the end, and the whole interest and difficulty of the matter is in the search for adequate specifications, not in the technical means-end sequel or sequels. It is here that the analogy with the geometer's search, or the inadequately clothed man's search, goes lame.

It is common ground between my interpretation and the interpretation of those who would accept the three tenets given at the outset, contentions (1), (2), (3), that Aristotle sensed *some* such difficulty in his dealings with practical reason. But according to the other interpretation [see (2) and (3)], Aristotle was led at this point to make a distinction between the situation where the agent has to see his situation as falling under a rule and the situation where the agent has simply to find means to encompass a definite objective.

Professor Allan gives the most argued form of this interpretation. Speaking of the practical syllogism he says 'in some contexts actions are subsumed by intuition under general rules, and performed or avoided accordingly.... In other contexts it is said to be a distinctive feature of practical syllogisms that they start from the announcement of an end [he then instances *NE* 1144a31, 1151a15–19, and *EE* 1227b28–32].... A particular action is then performed because it is a means or the first link in a chain of means leading to the end' (2). In support of this he claims to find Aristotle making such a distinction in the syllogisms mentioned at *De motu animalium* 701a9ff. In Forster's Loeb translation that passage reads as follows:

The conclusion drawn from the two premises becomes the action. For example, when you conceive that every man ought to walk and you yourself are a man, you immediately walk; or if you conceive that on a particular occasion no man ought to walk, and you yourself are a man, you immediately remain at rest. In both instances action follows unless there is some hindrance or compulsion.

Again, I ought to create a good, and a house is a good, I immediately create a house. Again, I need a covering, and a cloak is a covering. I need a cloak. What I need I ought to make: I need a cloak, I ought to make a cloak. And the conclusion 'I ought to make a cloak' is an action. The action results from the beginning of the train of thought. If there is to be a cloak, such and such a thing is necessary, if this thing then something else; and one immediately acts accordingly. That the action is the conclusion is quite clear; but the premises which lead to the doing of something are of two kinds, through the good and through the possible.

Now I think Allan understands this passage in a strange way. For he writes 'Aristotle *begins* with an example of the former [*sc.* rule-case] type [the walk syllogism] ..., but includes among other examples one of the latter type [the cloak syllogism] ... and he adds that the premises may be of two forms, since they specify either that something is good, or how it is possible (*hai de protaseis hai poietikai dia duo eidon ginontai, dia te tou agathou kai dia tou dunatou* [the premises that lead to the doing of something are of two kinds, concerning the good and the possible]).'[6] This is a strange reading. The walk syllogism, like the next syllogism, will need in any case to be treated as a dummy syllogism, a mere variable. For even if Allan's distinction between two kinds of syllogism could stand, the syllogism would be an idiotic example of either. No conclusion could safely rest on its 'rule-like' appearance. It would also be difficult to settle which sort the house-syllogism belonged to if any such distinction were intended.

In truth, the sentence about two kinds of premises seems to be no more than an allusion to the general form often manifestly displayed and always present (I believe) in Aristotelian action-syllogisms. The first or major premise mentions something that can be the subject of desire, *orexis*, transmissible to some practical conclusion (*i.e.*, a desire convertible via some available minor premise into action). The second premise details a circumstance pertaining to the feasibility, in the particular situation to which the syllogism is applied, of what must be done if the claim of the major premise is to be heeded. In the light of these *De motu* examples nothing could be more natural than to describe the first premise of a practical syllogism as *pertaining to the good* (the fact that it pertains to some good—either a general good or something which the agent has just resolved is good in this situation—is what beckons to desire) and to describe the second or minor premise as *pertaining to the possible* (where 'possible' connotes the feasibility, *given* the circumstances registered by the minor premise, of the object of concern mentioned in the first premise).

I can find no textual support for Allan's attempt to make the distinction into a distinction between different kinds of major premises. Indeed, no syllogism could be truly practical or be appropriately backed by orexis if its major premise were simply of the possible.

So much for the alleged presence of the distinction between rule-case and means-end syllogisms in the *De motu* passage. But even if I were wrong (and even if a distinctive rule-case type of syllogism were found at *NE* 7), contention (3) would still founder on other rocks. Allan's distinction of syllogisms is not the right distinction to solve Aristotle's problem, or *the* problem, of practical deliberation. The deliberative situations that challenge philosophical reflection to replace the means-ends description do not involve a kind of problem that anybody would think he could solve by subsuming a case under rules, whereas the comparatively trivial technical problems that are treated by Allan as means-end cases might often be resolved by recourse to rules. Nor can this difficulty be avoided by suggesting that if a policy question becomes too general or all-embracing, then there is no longer any rational deliberation about it. For Aristotle there is. He is convinced that the discovery and specification of the end is an intellectual problem, among other things, and belongs to practical wisdom. See 1142b31–33, for instance:

> If excellence in deliberation, *euboulia*, is one of the traits of men of practical wisdom, we may regard this excellence as correct perception of that which conduces to the end, whereof practical wisdom is a true judgment.

It is one of the considerable achievements of Allan's interpretation to have resolved the dispute about this sentence and to leave the relative clause meaning what the ancient tradition took it to mean and what it so obviously does mean. The good is the sort of thing which we wish for *because we think it good*, not something we think good because it is what we wish for. Thought and reason—not without desire, I must add—are the starting point.[7]

If all this were not enough to refute contentions (2) and (3) of §1, then Aristotle's own remarks elsewhere about the character of general rules and principles would be enough to discredit the rule-case approach. There *are* no general principles or rules anyway—except in so far as these are condensations of the judgment of aisthēsis (on which see the paraphrase of 1143a26 to be offered at §4):

> Matters concerned with conduct and questions of what is good for us have no fixity, any more than matters of health. The general account [of practical

knowledge] being of this nature, the account of particular cases is yet more lacking in exactness; for they do not fall under any art or precept, but the agents themselves in each case consider what is appropriate to the occasion, as happens also in the art of medicine and navigation (1104a3–10 *cf.* 1107a28).

From the nature of the case the subject matter of the practical is indefinite and unforeseeable, and any supposed principle would have an indefinite number of exceptions. To understand what such exceptions would be and what makes them exceptions would be to understand something not reducible to rules or principles. The only metric we can impose on the subject matter of practice is the metric of the Lesbian rule:

In fact this is the reason why not everything is determined by law and special and specific decrees are often needed. For when the thing is indefinite, the measure of it must be indefinite too, like the leaden rules used in making the Lesbian moulding. The rule adapts itself to the shape of the stone and is not rigid, and so too a special decree is adapted to the facts [1137b27–32, *cf. Politics* 1282b1–6].

I conclude that what Aristotle had in mind in book 6 was nothing remotely resembling what has been ascribed to him by neo-Kantian interpreters. Certainly contention (3) must seem absurdly overstated if the only new material which we can muster on Aristotle's behalf for the hard cases of deliberative specification is the 'rule-case' syllogism.

4   THE BOOKS 6–7 TREATMENT OF DELIBERATIVE SPECIFICATION—A GENERAL FRAMEWORK FOR ITS INTERPRETATION AND EVALUATION

NE 6 can be seen in a more interesting light than this. On the interpretation to be presented, the new materials largely consist, I admit, of sophistications, amendments, and extensions of the means-end paradigm. Nor is the alleged problem of the 'validity' of the practical syllogism solved. But Aristotle has a number of ideas to offer that seem to me to be of more fundamental importance than anything to be found now in utility theory, decision theory, or other rationality studies, however sketchily and obscurely he expressed them. That Aristotle's ideas are inchoate, however, is only one part of what is troublesome in establishing this claim. There is also the difficulty of finding a perspective or vantage point, over a philosophical terrain still badly understood, from which to view Aristotle's theory, and the difficulty (in practice rarely overcome) of sustaining philosophical momentum over a prolonged examination of a large number of obscure but relevant passages of the *Ethics* and *De Anima*.

To these difficulties my practical response is to adjourn all discussion of *akrasia* and, proceeding as if Aristotle had avoided what I regard as the errors of *NE* 7, to give the bare outline (a)–(g) of a neo-Aristotelian theory of practical reason. After that I shall amplify one point in this theory by giving an expanded paraphrase of two of the most obscure and most important passages about practical reason in *NE* 6. The reader's best defence against so prejudicial a method of exposition will be to compare the paraphrase with the Ross translation.

a. There are theories of practical reason according to which the ordinary situation of an agent who deliberates resembles nothing so much as that of a snooker player who has to choose from a large number of possible shots the shot that rates highest when two products are added. The first product is the utility of the shot's success (a utility that depends in snooker upon the colour of the ball to be potted and the expected utility for purposes of the next shot of the resulting position) multiplied by the probability P of this player's potting the ball. The second product is the utility (negative) of his failure multiplied by $(1 - P)$. It is neither here nor there that it is not easy to determine the values of some of these elements for purposes of comparing prospects. There is no problem about the end itself nor about the means. The end is to maximize points. Of course, there do exist deliberative situations, apart from snooker, which are a bit like this. But with ordinary deliberation it is quite different. There is nothing a person is under antecedent sentence to maximize; and probabilities, though difficult and relevant, need not be the one great crux of the matter. One usually asks oneself 'What shall I do?' not with a view to maximizing anything but only in response to a particular context. This will make particular and contingent demands on his moral or practical perception, but the relevant features of the situation may not all jump to the eye. To see what they are, to prompt the imagination to play upon the question and let it activate in reflection and thought-experiment whatever concerns and passions it should activate, may require a high order of situational appreciation, or, as Aristotle would say, perception (*aisthesis*). In this, as we shall see, and in the unfortunate fact that few situations come already inscribed with the names of all the concerns that they touch or impinge upon, resides the crucial importance of the minor premise of the practical syllogism.

b. When the relevant concerns are provisionally identified, they may still be too unspecific for means-end reasoning to begin. See the account of 'deliberative specification' in §3. Most of what is interesting and difficult in practical reason happens here, and under (a).

c. No theory, if it is to recapitulate or reconstruct practical reasoning even as well as mathematical logic recapitulates or reconstructs the actual experience of conducting or exploring deductive argument, can treat the concerns an agent brings to any situation as forming a closed, complete, consistent system. For it is of the essence of these concerns to make competing, inconsistent claims. (This is a mark not of our irrationality but of *rationality* in the face of the plurality of ends and the plurality of human goods.[8]) The weight of the claims represented by these concerns is not necessarily fixed in advance. Nor need the concerns be hierarchically ordered. Indeed, a person's reflection on a new situation that confronts him may disrupt such order and fixity as had previously existed and bring a change in his evolving conception of the point (*to hou heneka*), or the several or many points, of living or acting.

d. Someone may think it clear to him in a certain situation what is the relevant concern, yet find himself discontent with every practical syllogism promoting that concern (with major premise representing the concern). He may resile from the concern when he sees what it leads to, or what it costs, and start all over again. It is not necessarily true that he who wills the end must will the means. The same would have to apply to public rationality, if we had that. In a bureaucracy, where action is not constantly referred back to what originally motivated it, the acute theoretical and practical problem is to make room for some such stepping back, and for the constant remaking and reevaluation of concerns: also for the distinction that individual citizens make effortlessly for themselves between (i) ends that deliberation can realize by making projects and (ii) the constraints or concerns that delimit the space within which deliberation can operate freely. In this difficulty of referring back, and in the chronic inability of public agencies to render the relation *is found better overall than* transitive between situations envisaged and/or actually brought about by planning, lies one of the conceptual foundations for a reasoned hatred of bureaucracy, and for the demand for 'public participation' in planning. If one dislikes the last, or has no stomach for the expenditure of time and effort that it entails, then one should go back to the beginning, defy certain demands often represented as imperatives, and reexamine the ends for which a bureaucracy of such a size was taken to be needed, or at least the means chosen to realize the said ends. (These points come to life in a new way in Jean-Jacques Rousseau as Bertrand de Jouvenal interprets him. See Jouvenal's commentary on *The Social Contract*. They underline also certain distinctive merits of the Swiss democracies.)

e. The unfinished or indeterminate character of our ideals and value structure is constitutive both of human freedom and, for finite creatures who face an indefinite or infinite range of contingencies with only finite powers of prediction and imagination (*NE* 1137b), of practical rationality itself.

f. The person of real practical wisdom is the one who brings to bear upon a situation the greatest number of genuinely pertinent concerns and genuinely relevant considerations commensurate with the importance of the deliberative context. The best practical syllogism is that whose minor premise arises out of such a one's perceptions, concerns, and appreciations. It records what strikes the person as the *in the situation most salient feature of the context in which he has to act*. This activates a corresponding major premise that spells out the general import of the concern that makes this feature the salient feature in the situation. An analogy explored by Donald Davidson[9] between a *judgment of probability*, taken in its relation to judgments of probability relative to evidence, and a *decision*, taken in its relation to judgments of the desirability of an action relative to such and such contextual facts, will suggest this idea; the larger the set of considerations that issue in the singling out of the said feature, the more compelling the syllogism. But there are no formal criteria by which to compare the claims of competing syllogisms. Inasmuch as the syllogism arises in a determinate context, the major premise is evaluated not for its unconditional acceptability, nor for embracing more considerations than its rivals, but for its adequacy to the situation. It will be adequate for the situation if and only if circumstances that could restrict or qualify it and defeat its applicability at a given juncture do not in the practical context of this syllogism obtain. Its evaluation is of its essence dialectical, and all of a piece with the perceptions and reasonings that gave rise to the syllogism in the first place.

g. Since the goals and concerns that an agent brings to a situation may be diverse and incommensurable, and may not in themselves dictate any decision, they need not constitute the materials for some psychological theory (or any empirical theory above the conceptual level of a theory of matter) to make a prediction of the action.[10] Nor need anything else constitute these materials. There is simply no reason to expect that it will be possible to construct an (however idealized) empirical theory of the rational agent to parallel the predictive power, explanatory nonvacuity, and satisfactoriness for its purposes of an economic hypothesis—*e.g.* that under a wide variety of specifiable circumstances individual firms will push every line of action open to them to the point where marginal cost and marginal revenue are equal. If prediction were essential, then a phenomenologist or someone with a strong interest in the value consciousness of his subject might do best. But what is needed here is not prediction, but the subject's own decision processes, constantly redeployed on new situations or on new understandings of old ones.

5   TWO PARAPHRASES OF ARISTOTLE

My first paraphrase is of 1142a23 ff.:

That practical wisdom is not deductive theoretical knowledge is plain. For practical wisdom is, as I have said, of the ultimate and particular—as is the subject matter of action. In this, practical wisdom is the counterpart or dual of theoretical intuition. *Theoretical* intellect or intuition is of the ultimate, but in this sense—it is of ultimate universal concepts and axioms that are too primitive or fundamental to admit of further analysis or of justification from without. [At the opposite extreme] practical wisdom [as a counterpart of theoretical reason] also treats of matters that defy justification from without. Practical wisdom is of what is ultimate and particular in the distinct sense of needing to be quite simply perceived. By perception here I do not mean sense perception but the kind of perception or insight one needs to see that a triangle, say, is one of the basic or ultimate components [of a figure which one has to construct with ruler and compass]. [For there is no *routine* procedure for analysing a problem figure into the components by which one may construct it with rule and compasses.] The analysis calls for insight, and there is a limit to what one can say about it. But even this sort of insight is more akin to sense perception than practical wisdom is really akin to sense perception.

Comment

On this reading the geometer example turns up again. The method which the geometer discovers to construct the prescribed figure has a property unusual in a technical deliberation and ideal for making the transition to another kind of case, that of being in some sense constitutive of the end in view. It counts as the answer to a question he was asked (and would be proved to count so). *Caution.* Paraphrase and interpretation is not here confined to square-bracketed portions.

The other paraphrase I offer is of *NE* 1143a26 ff.:

... when we speak of judgment and understanding and practical wisdom and intuitive reason, we credit the same people with possessing judgment and having reached years of reason and with having practical wisdom and understanding. For all these faculties deal with ultimates or particularized specifics; and being a man of understanding and of good or sympathetic judgment consists in being able to judge about the things with which practical wisdom is concerned; for the equities are common to all good men in relation to other men. Now all action relates to the particular or ultimate; for not only must the man of practical wisdom know particular facts, but understanding and judgment are also concerned with things to be done, and these are ultimates. And intuitive reason is concerned with ultimates in both directions [i.e., with ultimates in two senses and respects, in respect of extreme generality and in respect of extreme specificity]. For intuitive reason [the general faculty] is of both the most primitive and the ultimate terms. Its proper province is where derivation or independent justification is impossible. In the case of that species of intuitive reason which is the theoretical intuition pertaining to demonstrative proof, its object is the most fundamental concepts and axioms. In its practical variety, on the other hand, intuitive reason concerns the most particular and contingent and specific. This is the typical subject matter of the minor premise of a practical syllogism [the one which is 'of the possible']. For here, in the capacity to find the right feature and form a practical syllogism, resides the understanding of the reason for performing an action, or its end. For the major premise and the generalizable concern that comes with it arise from this perception of something particular. So one must have an appreciation or perception of the particular, and my name for this is intuitive reason. [It is the source both of particular syllogisms and of all the concerns however particular or general that give a man reason to act.] ... we think our powers correspond to our time of life, and that a particular age brings with it intuitive reason and judgment; this implies that nature is the cause.... Therefore we ought to attend to the undemonstrated sayings and opinions of experienced and older people or of people of practical wisdom not less than to demonstrations; for, because experience has given them an eye, they see aright.

Comment

It is the mark of the man of practical wisdom on this account to be able to select from the infinite number of features of a situation those features that bear upon the notion or ideal of existence which it is his standing aim to make real. This conception of human life results in various evaluations of all kinds of things, in various sorts of cares and concerns, and in various projects. It does not reside in a set of maxims or precepts, useful though Aristotle would allow these to be at a certain stage in the education of the emotions. In no case will there be a rule to which a man can simply appeal to tell him what to do (except in the special case—see

1129b19 ff—where an absolute prohibition operates). The deliberator may have no other recourse but to invent the answer to the problem. As often as not, the inventing, like the frequent accommodation he has to effect between the claims of competing values, may count as a modification or innovation or further determination in the evolution of his view of what a good life is. *Caution.* As before, paraphrase has not been confined to square-bracketed sentences.

6 CONCLUSION

Against this account, as I have explained it, it may be complained that in the end very little is said, because everything that is hard has been permitted to take refuge in the notion of aisthesis, or *situational appreciation* as I have paraphrased this. And in aisthesis, as Aristotle says, explanations give out. I reply that, if there is no real prospect of an ordinary scientific or simply empirical theory of all of action and deliberation as such, then the thing we should look for may be precisely what Aristotle provides—namely, a conceptual framework which we can apply to particular cases, which articulates the reciprocal relations of an agent's concerns and his perception of how things objectively are in the world; and a schema of description *which relates the complex ideal the agent tries in the process of living his life to make real to the form that the world impresses, both by way of opportunity and by way of limitation, upon that ideal.* Here too, within the same schema, are knitted together, as von Wright says, 'the concepts of wanting an end, understanding a necessity, and setting oneself to act. It is a contribution to the moulding or shaping of these concepts.'[11] I entertain the unfriendly suspicion that those who feel they *must* seek more than all this provides want a scientific theory of rationality not so much from a passion for science, even where there can be no real science, but because they hope and desire, by some conceptual alchemy, to turn such a theory into a regulative or normative discipline, or into a system of rules by which to spare themselves some of the torment of thinking, feeling and understanding that can actually be involved in reasoned deliberation.

Acknowledgments

From *Proceedings of the Aristotelian Society*, vol. 76, 1975/76, with revisions. Because the first three sections of this essay circulated in typescript for more than a decade, I had the inestimable benefit (from which they must have felt I had the time and ought to have had the ability to profit better) of comments from J. L. Ackrill, M. J. Woods, M. F. Burnyeat, R. Sorabji (without the support of whose article 'Aristotle on the Role of Intellect in Virtue,' *Proceedings of the Aristotelian Society*, vol. 74, 1973/74, pp. 107–129, I might have felt I had to postpone publication yet further), J. C. Dybikowski, T. H. Irwin, Martha Craven Nussbaum, and G. E. L. Owen. To the last-named I also owed the invitation to continue the first three sections into §§4–6, and into a treatment of *akrasia* (see 'Weakness of Will, Commensurability and the Objects of Deliberation and Desire', in David Wiggins, *Needs, Values, Truth*, 3rd ed. [Oxford: Clarendon Press, 1998]), as James Loeb Visiting Fellow in Classical Philosophy at Harvard in Spring 1972. On the philosophical issue itself (as distinguished from the issue of Aristotelian interpretation) I would refer to Aurel Kolnai's 'Deliberation Is of Ends' (this volume, chap. 12).

Notes

1. It is possible that no scholar holds to all three. See also note 3.

2. I think that those who employ these or similar terms usually intend the distinction of two kinds of reasoning, and the two distinct kinds of non-theoretical syllogism allegedly recognized by Aristotle, to correspond in some way to Aristotle's distinction of production (poiēsis) and practice (praxis).

3. The conjunction of (1), (2), (3) is not intended to catch the flavour of a more subjectivist interpretation that has had some currency. This enlarges the role of moral virtue at the expense of intellect and, so far as possible, assimilates *NE* 6 to *NE* 3—where *NE* 3 is read in an exclusively means-end fashion. (1), (2), (3) is closer to the reason-oriented naturalist interpretation I shall commend and, like my interpretation, it owes much to Professor D. J. Allan. See his 'Aristotle's Account of the Origin of Moral Principles', *Proceedings of the XIth International Congress of Philosophy, Brussels, August 20–26, 1953* (Amsterdam, 1953), 12: 120–127 [hereinafter referred to as Allan (1)] and 'The Practical Syllogism,' in *Autour d'Aristote: Recueil offert à Mgr Mansion* (Louvain, 1955), pp. 325–340 [hereinafter referred to as Allan (2)]. These publications represent so considerable an advance in clearing away the mass of captious misinterpretation to which Aristotle's praxeology had been previously subjected that I have preferred to consider the composite view given above rather than dwell on Allan's special version of it. But I shall allude frequently to his treatment of single passages.

What principally distinguishes Allan's view from the composite view (1), (2), (3) is that Allan is inclined to say that the changes he postulates between the view of book 3 and the view of books 6–7 leave Aristotle's analysis of *deliberation* itself more or less unaffected. Against this I say that either the alleged rule-case reasoning, which is admitted by Allan to be *prohairetic*, can be properly termed deliberative or it cannot. If it can, then, if choice needed radical alteration, then so *on Allan's interpretation of it* did the book 3 account of deliberation. It could not remain unaffected. For precisely the same considerations then operate on both. If we say that choice cannot be termed deliberative, however, we contradict 1140a27–28. *Cf.* also 1139a23, 1141b8–15.

4. *Cf.* Allan (1), p. 124: '... the good propounded may be (a) distant or (b) general. Thus there is fresh work for practical reason to perform. In the former case, we have first to calculate the means which will, in due course, achieve the end. In the latter, we have to *subsume the particular case under a general rule*. Both these processes are analysed by Aristotle in a masterly fashion, *in different parts of his work, the former in the third book* of the Ethics, the latter in books VI and VII and in his psychological writings' (my italics). And *cf.* (2) 'His *first* position in the *Ethics* is that all virtuous action involves choice, that all choice follows up a deliberation and *that all deliberation is concerned with the selection of means*' (my italics).

5. *Cf.* at random, Jeremy Bray, *Decision in Government* (London, 1970), p. 72 '... the individual consumer's own decision processes which are the more complex for not being wholly rational in any economic sense'. Is there really, or should there be, a special sense of 'rational' in economics? Bray goes on to suggest that anyone who thinks there is room for reason in this sphere, or sets much store by the concept of *need*, must wish to deny freedom: 'However the concept of minimum need may be used in social security arrangements, it is a poor guide to consumer behaviour whether at the minimum income or other levels, and whether in an advanced or primitive society. The particular purchases made by a family reflect not only their immediate tastes such as a liking for warmth, bright colours, and tinned fruit, but also their spiritual life and fantasy world—the stone fireplace as a safe stronghold in a morally insecure world, the Jaguar car to release frustration or bolster a waning virility, the tingling toothpaste as a ritual purification. Far from being a matter for ridicule, consumer choice is something to nurture, cultivate and protect.' In the name of liberty, yes, but not because these ends are really outside the reach of reason or rational appraisal. Lest Bray's seem to be a purely Fabian doctrine, I quote a Chicago School economist, Milton Friedman: 'Differences about economic policy among disinterested citizens derive predominantly from different predictions ... rather than from fundamental differences in basic values, differences *about which men can only fight*' (my italics) (*Essays in Positive Economics* (Chicago, 1953), p. 5). For a protest see Alan Altshuler, *The City Planning Process* (Ithaca, N.Y., 1965), *ad init.*

6. Allan (2), pp. 336–337.

7. See *Politics* 1332b6–8 and *Metaphysics* 1072a2–9: 'We desire it because it seems good to us, it doesn't seem good to us because we desire it'. It is the beginning of wisdom on this matter, both as an issue of interpretation and as a philosophical issue, to see that we do not really have to choose between Aristotle's proposition and its apparent opposite (as at *e.g.*, Spinoza, *Ethics*, pt. III, proposition 9, note). We can desire it because it seems good *and* it seem good because we desire it. Compare 'A Sensible Subjectivism?', in David Wiggins, *Needs, Values, Truth*, 3rd ed. (Oxford: Clarendon Press, 1998), *passim.*

8. Jonathan Glover speaks of 'the aesthetic preference most of us have for economy of principles, the preference for ethical systems in the style of the Bauhaus rather than Baroque' (*The Aristotelian Society*, suppl. vol. 49, 1975, p. 183). Against this I say that only a confusion between the practical and the theoretical

could even purport to provide reasoned grounds for such a preference. (For the beginnings of the distinction, see Bernard Williams, 'Consistency and Realism', *The Aristotelian Society*, suppl. vol. 40, 1966, pp. 1–22.) Why is an axiom system any better foundation for practice than, *e.g.*, a long and incomplete or open-ended list of (always at the limit conflicting) *desiderata*? The claims of all true *beliefs* (about how the world is) are reconcilable. Everything true must be consistent with everything else that is true. But not all the claims of all rational concerns or even all moral concerns (that the world *be* thus or so) need be reconcilable. There is no reason to expect that they would be; and Aristotle gives at 1137b the reason why we cannot expect to lay down a decision procedure for adjudication in advance between claims, or for prior mediation. By the dragooning of the plurality of goods into the order of an axiom system I think practice will be almost as rapidly and readily degraded (and almost as unexpectedly perhaps) as modern building, by exploitation of the well-intentioned efforts of the Bauhaus, has been degraded into the single-minded pursuit of profit. (The last phase of Walter Gropius's architectural career, and the shady and incongruous company into which his ambitions for modern architecture drew him so irresistibly, will repay study by those drawn to Glover's analogy.)

9. *Cf.* 'How is Weakness of Will Possible?' in *Moral Concepts*, ed. Feinberg (Oxford University Press, 1969).

10. See Donald Davidson, 'Mental Events' in *Experience and Theory*, ed. Foster and Swanson (London, 1971). Also 'Towards a Reasonable Libertarianism', in David Wiggins, *Needs, Values, Truth*, 3rd ed. (Oxford: Clarendon Press, 1998). See also the concluding postscript (in the 3rd ed. only).

11. G. H. von Wright, *The Varieties of Goodness* (London, 1963), p. 171. Both for the quotation and in the previous sentence I am indebted to Martha Nussbaum. In her *Aristotle's 'De Motu Animalium'* (Princeton, 1978) she writes: 'the appeal of this form of explanation for Aristotle may lie in its ability to link an agent's desires and his perceptions of how things are in the world around him, his subjective motivation and the objective limitations of his situation ... animals are seen as acting in accordance with desire, but within the limits imposed by nature'.

Chapter 14

Consistency in Action

Onora O'Neill

UNIVERSALITY TESTS IN AUTONOMOUS AND IN HETERONOMOUS ETHICS

Many recent discussions of universality tests, particularly those in English, are concerned either with what everybody wants done or with what somebody (usually the agent; sometimes an anonymous moral spectator) wants done either by or to everybody. This is true of the universality tests proposed in Singer's Generalization Argument, in Hare's Universal Prescriptivism and generally of various formulations of Golden Rules as well as of Rule Utilitarianism. Since universality tests of these sorts all make moral acceptability in some way contingent upon what is *wanted* (or, more circumspectly expressed, upon what is preferred or found acceptable or promises the maximal utility), they all form part of moral theories that are *heteronomous*, in Kant's sense of that term. Such theories construe moral acceptability as contingent upon the natural phenomena of desire and inclination, rather than upon any intrinsic or formal features of agents or their intentions. If we rely on any of these proposed criteria of moral acceptability, there will be no types of act that would not be rendered morally acceptable by some change or changes in human desires.

By contrast Kant's proposed universality test, the Categorical Imperative, contains no reference either to what everybody wants done or to what somebody wants done either by or to everybody. Kant's first formulation of the Categorical Imperative, the so-called Formula of Universal Law, runs:

Act only on that maxim through which you can at the same time will that it should become a universal law. (*G*, IV, 421) [Abbreviations are given at the end of the chapter.—Ed.]

We are invited here to consider that we *can* will or intend, what it is *possible* or *consistent* for us to "will as a universal law" (not what we *would* will or *would* find acceptable or *would want* as a universal law). Since the principle contains no reference to what everybody or anybody wants, nor to anything that lies beyond the agent's own capacity to will, it is part of a moral theory for agents who, in Kant's sense of the term, act *autonomously.* The principle asserts that such agents need only to impose a certain sort of consistency on their actions if they are to avoid doing what is morally unacceptable. It proposes an uncompromisingly rationalist foundation for ethics.

Nevertheless, Kant interpretation, particularly in English, is rich in heteronomous readings of the Formula of Universal Law and in allegations that (despite claims to the contrary) it is impossible to derive non-trivial, action-guiding applications of the Categorical Imperative without introducing heteronomous considerations.[1] Textual objections apart (and they would be overwhelming objections), such heteronomous readings of Kant's ethics discard what is most distinctive and challenging in his ethical theory. These are the features of his theory on which I intend to concentrate. I want to challenge the view that Kantian ethics, and non-heteronomous ethical theories in general, must be seen as either trivially empty or relying covertly on heteronomous considerations in order to derive substantive conclusions. To do so I shall try to articulate what seem to me to be the more important features of a universality test for agents who, in a certain sense of the term, can act autonomously, that is, without being determined by their natural desires and inclinations.

I shall take Kant's Formula of Universal Law as the canonical case of such a universality test, and shall argue that it neither is trivially formalistic nor requires supplementing with heteronomous considerations if it is to be action-guiding. However, my main concern here is not to explicate Kant's discussion of his universality test, nor to assess the difficulty or adequacy of his various moves. I shall say nothing about his vindication of the Categorical Imperative, nor about his powerful critique of heteronomy in ethics, nor about his conception of human freedom. By setting aside these and other more strictly textual preoccupations I hope to open the way for a discussion of some features of universality tests for autonomous agents that have an interest that goes far beyond a concern with reading Kant accurately. I hope to show that Kant's formula, taken in conjunction with a plausible set of requirements for rational action, yields strong and interesting ethical conclusions that do not depend on what either everybody or anybody wants, and hence that reason can indeed be practical.

Over the last twenty years theorists have shed considerable light on the underlying structure of heteronomous ethical theories (as well as on other, particularly economic and political, decisions) by drawing on studies of the formal aspects of decision making under various conditions that have been articulated in various models of rational choice. In such discussions it is generally taken for granted that rational choosing is in some way or other contingent upon a set of desires or preferences.[2] I shall suggest that a similar concentration on certain requirements of rationality that are not contingent upon desires or preferences can help to provide a clearer picture of the underlying structure and strength of an ethical theory for autonomous beings.

The sequence of argument is straightforward. The following section provides an explication of Kant's Formula of Universal Law and of some of the ways in which it affects the character of an ethic for autonomous beings. The section entitled "Inconsistency without universalizing" discusses some ways in which action can fall into inconsistency even when the question of universalizing is not raised. The three sections that follow show how requirements for rational intending can be conjoined with Kant's universality test to yield determinate ethical conclusions.

MAXIMS AND MORAL CATEGORIES

The test that Kant's Formula of Universal Law proposes for the moral acceptability of acts has two aspects. In the first place it enjoins us to *act on a maxim*; secondly it restricts us to action on those maxims *through which we can will at the same time that they should be universal laws*. It is only the latter clause that introduces a universality test. However, for an understanding of the nature of this test it is essential in the first place to understand what Kant means by "acting on a maxim". For, contrary to appearances, this is not a trivial part of his criterion of morally acceptable action. Because a universality test for autonomous beings does not look at what is wanted, nor at the results of action, but merely demands that certain standards of consistency be observed in action, it has to work with a conception of action that has the sort of formal structure that can meet (or fail to meet) standards of consistency. Only those acts that embody or express syntactically structured principles or descriptions can be thought of as candidates either for consistency or for inconsistency.

Mere reflexes or reactions, for example, cannot be thought of as consistent or inconsistent; nor can acts be considered merely instrumentally as means for producing certain outcomes. In requiring action on a maxim Kant is already insisting that whatever is morally assessable should have a certain formal structure.

A maxim, Kant tells us, is "a subjective principle of action"; it is "a principle on which the subject *acts*" (*G*, IV, 421n; cf. 401n). A maxim is therefore the principle of action of a particular agent at a particular time; but it need not be "subjective" in the sense that it seeks to fulfill that particular agent's desires. In speaking of maxims as subjective principles Kant is not adopting any sort of heteronomous standard, but means to propose a standard against which the principles agents propose to act on, of whatever sort, may be tested. The Categorical Imperative provides a way of testing the moral acceptability of what we propose to do. It does not aim to generate plans of action for those who have none.

Although maxims are the principles of action of particular agents at particular times, one and the same principle might be adopted as a maxim by many agents at various times or by a given agent on numerous occasions. It is a corollary of Kant's conception of human freedom that we can adopt or discard maxims, including those maxims that refer to our desires.

On the other hand, acting on a maxim does not require explicit or conscious or complete formulation of that maxim. Even routine or thoughtless or indecisive action is action on *some* maxim. However, not all of the principles of action that a particular agent might exemplify at a given time would count as the agent's maxim. For principles of action need only incorporate *some* true description of an agent and *some* true description of the act and situation, whether these descriptions are vacuous and vague or brimming with detail. But an agent's maxim in a given act must incorporate just those descriptions of the agent, the act and the situation upon which the doing of the act depends.

An agent's maxim in a given act cannot, then, be equated simply with intentions. For an agent's intentions in performing a given act may refer to incidental aspects of the particular act and situation. For example, in making a new visitor feel welcome I may offer and make him or her some coffee. As I do so there will be innumerable aspects of my action that are intentional—the choice of mug, the addition of milk, the stirring—and there will also be numerous aspects of action that are "below the level of intention"—the gesture with which I hand the cup, the precise number of stirs and so on. But the various specific intentions with which I orchestrate the offer and preparation of coffee are all ancillary to an underlying principle. *Maxims are those underlying principles or intentions[3] by which we guide and control our more specific intentions.* In this particular example, had I lacked coffee I could have made my visitor welcome in other ways: The specific intention of offering and making coffee was subordinate to the maxim of making a visitor welcome. Had I had a quite different maxim—perhaps to make my visitor unwelcome—I would not in that context have acted on just those specific intentions. In another context, for example, in a society where an offer of coffee would be understood as we would understand an offer of hemlock, the same or similar specific intentions might have implemented a maxim of making unwelcome.

The fact that maxims are underlying or fundamental principles has important implications.[4] It means in the first place that it may not be easy to tell on which maxim a given act was performed. For example, a person who helps somebody else in a public place may have the underlying intention of being helpful—or alternatively the underlying intention of fostering a certain sort of good reputation. Since the helpful act might equally well be performed in furtherance of either underlying intention, there may be some doubt as to the agent's maxim. Merely asking an agent what his or her maxim is in such a situation may not settle the issue. The agent might be unsure. Both agents and others can work out that if the action would have been performed even if nobody had come to know of it, then the underlying principle would not have been to seek a certain sort of reputation. But an agent may after all be genuinely uncertain what his or her act would have been had he or she been faced with the possibility of helping, isolated from any effects on reputation. Isolation tests can settle such issues (*G*, IV, 398 f.; 407)—if we know their outcome; but since most such tests refer to counterfactual situations we often don't know that outcome with any great certainty. Further, isolation tests provide only a *negative* test of what an agent's maxim is not. Even those who have not adopted a maxim of seeking a good reputation may still be unsure whether they have adopted the maxim of helpfulness. They may perhaps wonder whether the underlying intention was not to preserve a certain sort of self-image or to bolster their sense of worth. Kant remarks on the opacity of the human heart and the difficulty of self-knowledge; he laments that for all we know there may never have been a truly loyal friend (*G*, IV, 407 f.; *DV*, VI, 440; 445 f.). And he does not view these as dispellable difficulties. Rather, these limits to human self-knowledge constitute the fundamental context of human action. Kant holds that we can know what it would be to try to act on a maxim of a certain sort, but can never be sure that what we do does not reflect further maxims that we disavow. However, the underlying intentions that guide our more specific intentions are not in principle undiscoverable. Even when not consciously formulated they can often be inferred with some assurance, if not certainty, as the principles and policies that our more specific intentions express and implement.

On a certain view of the purpose of a universality test, the fact that the maxim of a given action is neither observable nor always reliably inferable would be a most serious objection. For it would appear to render the outcome of any application of a universality test of dubious moral importance—since we might mistakenly have applied the test to a principle other than the agent's maxim. Further, even if the maxim had been correctly formulated, whether by the agent or by others, the maxim itself might reflect mistaken beliefs or self-deception in the agent, or the agent's act might fail to live up to its maxim. How then could any test applied to the agent's maxim be expected to classify acts into moral categories such as the right and the forbidden? For these categories apply to the outward and observable aspects of action. It is after all common enough for us to think of acts that are at least outwardly right (perhaps even obligatory) as nevertheless reflecting dubious intentions (I aim to kill an innocent, but mistakenly incapacitate the tiger who is about to maul him), and of acts whose intentions are impeccable as issuing tragically in wrong action (I aim for the tiger but dispatch the innocent).

The answer Kant gives to this problem is plain. It is that rightness and wrongness and the other "categories of right" standardly used in appraisal of outward features of action are *not* the fundamental forms of moral acceptability and unacceptability that he takes the Categorical Imperative to be able to discriminate.[5] Since the locus of application of Kant's universality test (and perhaps of any nonheteronomous universality test) is agents' fundamental principles or intentions, the moral distinction that it can draw is in the first place an intentional moral distinction, namely that between acts that have and those that lack moral worth. In an application of the Categorical Imperative to an agent's maxim we ask whether the underlying intention with which the agent acts or proposes to act—the intention that guides and controls other more specific intentions—is consistently universalizable; if it is, according to Kant, we at least know that the action will not be morally unworthy, and will not be a violation of duty.

The fact that Kant is primarily concerned with judgments of moral worth is easily forgotten, perhaps because he speaks of the Categorical Imperative as a test of *duty*, while we often tend to think of duty as confined to the *outward* aspects of action. It is quite usual for us to think of principled action as combining both duty and moral worthiness, which we regard as separate matters (e.g., showing scrupulous respect for others), or alternatively as revealing a moral worthiness that goes beyond all duty (e.g., gratuitous kindness that we think of as supererogatory). Correspondingly, it is quite usual for us to think of unprincipled action as in any case morally unworthy but still, in some cases, within the bounds of duty (e.g., the case of a could-be poisoner who mistakenly administers a life-saving drug). This is quite foreign to Kant's way of thinking, which sees the *central* case of duty as that of action that has moral worth, and regards as *derivative* that which accords merely in external respects with morally worthy action. On Kant's view the would-be poisoner who inadvertently saves life has violated a duty by acting in a morally unworthy way.

By taking an agent's fundamental or underlying principle or intention as the point of application of his universality test Kant avoids one of the difficulties most frequently raised about universality tests, namely that it seems easy enough to formulate *some* principle of action for any act, indeed possibly one that incorporates one of the agent's intentions, which can meet the criterion of any universality test, whatever the act. Notoriously some Nazi war criminals claimed that they were only "doing their job" or only "obeying orders"—which are after all not apparently morally unworthy activities. The disingenuousness of the claim that such acts were not morally unworthy lies in the fact that these Nazis were not only obeying orders, and indeed that in many cases their specific intentions were ancillary to more fundamental intentions *or principles* that might indeed have revealed moral unworthiness in the agent. (Such fundamental intentions or principles might range from "I'll do whatever I'm told to so long as it doesn't endanger me" to a fundamental maxim of genocide.) The fact that we can formulate *some* universalizable surface intention for any action by selecting among the agent's various surface intentions is no embarrassment to a universality test that is intended to apply to agents' maxims, and offers a solution to the problem of relevant descriptions.

It is equally irrelevant to a universality test that applies to maxims that we may be able to find some nonuniversalizable intentions among the more specific intentions with which an agent implements and fills out any maxim. If in welcoming my visitor with a cup of coffee I intentionally select a particular cup, my specific intention clearly cannot be universally acted on. The very particularity of the world means that there will always be aspects of action, including intentional aspects, that could not be universally adopted or intended. Kant's universality test, however, as we shall see, construes moral worth as contingent not on the universalizability or otherwise of an agent's specific intentions but on the universalizability of an agent's fundamental or underlying intention or principle.[6]

For Kant, then, the Categorical Imperative provides a criterion in the first place for duties to act on underlying intentions or principles that are morally worthy. It is only as a second and derivative part of his ethical theory that he proposes that the Categorical Imperative also provides a test of the outward wrongness and rightness of acts of specific sorts. He proposes in the *Groundwork* that acts that accord in outward respects with acts done on morally worthy maxims of action should be seen as being "in conformity with" or "in accord with" duty. The claim that we can provide a *general* account of which specific actions conform to the outward expressions of morally worthy maxims is highly controversial. We have already noted that there are many ways in which ancillary intentions may be devised in undertaking action on a given maxim, and there may be no single specific intention that is indispensable in all circumstances for action on a given maxim. Hence it is not generally clear what outward conformity conforms to. Kant appears to accept that the notion of outward conformity to duty is empty in many cases of duties of virtue, which are not sufficiently determinate for any particular more specific intentions to be singled out as required. He speaks of such duties as being "of wide requirement". But he also speaks of duties of narrow or strict requirement, and includes among these duties of justice and certain duties of respect to ourselves and to others.[7] Hence he takes it that there could in principle be a merely outward conformity to these strict or "perfect" duties. Whether this claim is justified depends on the success of his demonstration that the underlying maxims of justice and respect have determinate specific implications for all possible human conditions. If they do not, then there will be no wholly general account of the requirements of justice and respect for all possible situations. It is then at any rate not obvious that we can derive a standard for the outward rightness of acts from a standard for the moral worth of underlying intentions or principles. This is a major problem that I intend to set to one side in order to explore the implications of a universality test that applies to underlying intentions or principles and therefore aims, at least primarily, at a test of the moral worth rather than the outward rightness of actions.

The fact that Kant's universality test focuses on maxims, and so on the moral worth of action, implies that it is a test that agents must seek to apply to their own proposals for action. This is not, however, because agents are in a wholly privileged epistemological position with respect to their own underlying intentions. No doubt others may often have some difficulty even in discerning all of an agent's surface intentions, and may be quite unsure about the underlying intention. But Kant does not regard the agents' vantage points as affording infallible insight into their own intentions—self-consciousness is not transparent—and would not deny that on occasion others might arrive at a more accurate appreciation of an agent's underlying intention or principle than the agent could reach.

The reason why a universality test in a nonheteronomous ethical theory is primarily one for the use of agents rather than of moral spectators is that it is only an agent who can adopt, modify or discard maxims. Although a test of the outward moral status of acts might be of most use and importance to third parties (legislators, judges, educators—those of us who pass judgment on others), because it may be possible (or indeed necessary) to prevent or deter or praise or punish in order to elicit or foster outward action of a certain sort, it is difficult if not impossible for outward regulation or pressure to change an agent's maxim. Surface conformity can be exacted; intentional conformity is more elusive (*DV*, VI, 380 f.). Precisely because we are considering what a universality test for autonomous beings must be like, we must recognize that the test is one that we can propose to but not impose upon moral agents.

INCONSISTENCY WITHOUT UNIVERSALIZING

This account of acting on a maxim shows at least how action can be construed in a way that makes consistency and inconsistency possible, and provides some grounds for thinking that a focus on maxims may avoid some of the difficulties that have arisen in attempts to apply universality tests unrestrictedly to principles of action of all sorts. This opens the way for showing how action on a nonuniversalizable maxim is inconsistent and for considering whether such inconsistency constitutes a criterion of moral unworthiness. Before dealing with these topics it will be useful to run over some of the many ways in which action on a maxim may reveal inconsistency even when universalizing is not brought into the picture.

It is of course true that any act that is performed is possible, taken in itself. But it does not follow that the intentions that are enacted are mutually consistent. There are two sorts of possibilities here: In the first place there may be an internal inconsistency within an agent's maxim; in the second place there may be contradictions between the various specific intentions an agent adopts in pursuit of that maxim, or between some of these specific intentions and the agent's maxim. These two sorts of contradiction correspond closely to the two types of contradiction that Kant thinks may arise when attempts to universalize maxims fail, and that he characterizes as involving, respectively, "contradictions in conception" and "contradictions in the will" (*G*, IV, 424). Since I am also interested in charting the inconsistencies that can arise independently of attempts to universalize, as well as in those that arise when universalizing fails, I shall use the rather similar labels *conceptual inconsistency* and *volitional inconsistency* to distinguish these two types of incoherence in action. A consideration of the different types of incoherence that maxims may display even when the question of universalizability is not raised provides a useful guide to the types of incoherence that nonuniversalizable maxims display.

A maxim of action may in the first place be incoherent simply because it expresses an impossible aspiration. An agent's maxim might be said to involve a conceptual inconsistency if the underlying intention was, for example, both to be successful and to be unworldly, or alternatively, to be both popular and reclusive, or both to care for others and always to put his or her own advantage first, or both to be open and frank with everybody and to be a loyal friend or associate, or both to keep a distance from others and to have intimate personal relationships. Agents whose underlying maxims incorporate such conceptual inconsistencies do not, of course, succeed in performing impossible acts; rather, the pattern of their actions appears to pull in opposite directions and to be in various ways self-defeating. At its extreme we may regard such underlying incoherence in a person's maxim, and consequent fragmentation of the person's action, as tragic or pathological (and perhaps both), since there is no way in which he or she can successfully enact the underlying intention. In other cases we may think of the pattern of action that results from underlying conceptual incoherence as showing no more than ambivalence or presenting conflicting signals to others, who are consequently at a loss about what they should expect or do, finding themselves in a "double bind".

However, not all cases of disjointed action constitute evidence of an internally inconsistent maxim. For it may well be that somebody adopts some accommodation of the potentially inconsistent aspects of an underlying intention. For example, somebody may adopt the maxim of being competitive and successful in public and professional life but of disregarding such considerations in private life; or of being obedient and deferential to superiors but overbearing and exacting with all others. Provided such persons can keep the two spheres of action separated, their underlying intentions can be internally consistent. Hence one cannot infer an inconsistency in someone's underlying intentions merely from the fact that he or she exhibits tendencies in opposing directions. For these tendencies may reflect a coherent underlying intention to respond or act differently in different types of context or with different groups of people. A nonuniversalizable maxim embodies a conceptual contradiction only if it *aims* at achieving mutually incompatible objectives and so cannot under any circumstances be acted on with success.

A focus on maxims that embody contradictions in conception pays no attention to the fact that maxims are not merely principles that we can conceive (or entertain, or even wish) but principles that we *will* or intend, that is to say, principles that we adopt as *principles of action*. Conceptual contradictions can be identified even in principles of action that are never adopted or acted upon. But a second and rather different type of incoherence is exhibited in some attempts to will maxims whose realization can be quite coherently envisaged. Willing, after all, is not just a matter of wishing that something were the case, but involves committing oneself to doing something to bring that situation about when opportunity is there and recognized. Kant expressed this point by insisting that rationality requires that whoever wills some end wills the necessary means insofar as these are available.

Who wills the end, wills (so far as reason has decisive influence on his actions) also the means which are indispensably necessary and in his power. So far as willing is concerned, this proposition is analytic: for in my willing of an object as an effect there is already conceived the causality of myself as an acting cause— that is, the use of means; and from the concept of willing an end the imperative merely extracts the concept of actions necessary to this end. (*G*, IV, 417)

This amounts to saying that to will some end without willing whatever means are indispensable for that end, insofar as they are available, is, even when the end itself involves no conceptual inconsistency, to involve oneself in a volitional inconsistency. It is to embrace at least one specific intention that, far from being guided by the underlying intention or principle, is inconsistent with that intention or principle.

Kant, however, explicitly formulates only *one* of the principles that must be observed by an agent who is not to fall into volitional inconsistency. The Principle of Hypothetical Imperatives, as expressed in the passage just quoted, requires that agents intend any indispensable means for whatever they fundamentally intend. Conformity with this requirement of coherent intending would be quite compatible with intending no means to whatever is fundamentally intended whenever there is no specific act that is indispensable for action on the underlying intention. Further reflection on the idea of intending the means suggests that there is a *family* of Principles of Rational Intending, of which the Principle of Hypothetical Imperatives is just one, though perhaps the most important one. The following list of further Principles of Rational Intending that coherent intending (as opposed to mere wishing or contemplating) apparently requires agents to observe may not be complete, but is sufficient to generate a variety of interesting conclusions.

First, it is a requirement of rationality not merely to intend all *indispensable* or *necessary* means to that which is fundamentally intended but also to intend some *sufficient* means to what is fundamentally intended. If it were not, I could coherently intend to eat an adequate diet, yet not intend to eat food of any specific sort on the grounds that no specific sort of food is indispensable in an adequate diet.

Second, it is a requirement of rationality not merely to intend all necessary and some sufficient means to what is fundamentally intended but also to seek to make such means available when they are not. If it were not, I could coherently claim to intend to help bring about a social revolution but do absolutely nothing, on the grounds that there is no revolutionary situation at present, settling instead for rhetoric and gesture rather than politics. But if I do this, I at most wish for, and do not intend to help to bring about, a social revolution.

Third, it is a requirement of rationality not merely to intend all necessary and some sufficient means to whatever is fundamentally intended but also to intend all necessary and some sufficient *components* of whatever is fundamentally intended. If it were not, I could coherently claim to intend to be kind to someone to whom, despite opportunity, I show no kindness in word, gesture or deed, merely because acting kindly is not the sort of thing that requires us to take means to an end, but the sort of thing that requires that we act in some of the ways that are *constitutive* of kindness.[8]

Fourth, it is a requirement of rationality that the various specific intentions we actually adopt in acting on a given maxim in a certain context be mutually consistent. If it were not, I could coherently claim to be generous to all my friends by giving to each the exclusive use of all my possessions.

Fifth, it is a requirement of rationality that the foreseeable results of the specific intentions adopted in acting on a given underlying intention be consistent with the underlying intention. If it were not, I could coherently claim to be concerned for the well-being of a child for whom I refuse an evidently life-saving operation, on the grounds that my specific intention—perhaps to shield the child from the hurt and trauma of the operation—is itself aimed at the child's well-being. But where such shielding foreseeably has the further consequence of endangering the child's life, it is clearly an intention that undercuts the very maxim that supposedly guides it.

There may well be yet further principles that fully coherent sets of intentions must observe, and possibly some of the principles listed above need elaboration or qualification. The point, however, is to reveal that once we see action as issuing from a complex web of intentions, many of which are guided by and ancillary to certain more fundamental intentions or principles under particular conditions, the business of intending coherently and avoiding volitional inconsistency becomes a demanding and complex affair.

Reflection on the various Principles of Rational Intending reveals a great deal about the connections between surface and underlying intentions to which a rational being must aspire. Underlying intentions to a considerable extent express the larger and longer-term goals, policies and aspirations of a life. But if these goals, policies and aspirations are willed (and not merely wished for), they must be connected with some set of surface intentions that express commitment to acts that, in the actual context in which agents find themselves, provide either the means to or some components of any underlying intentions, or at least take them in the direction of being able to form such intentions, without at any point committing them to acts whose performance would undercut their underlying intentions. Wherever such coherence is absent we find an example of intending that, despite the conceptual coherence of the agent's maxim, is volitionally incoherent. In some cases we may think the deficiency cognitive—agents fail despite available information to appreciate what they need to do if they are indeed to act on their maxims (they may be stupid or thoughtless or calculate poorly). In other cases we might think of the deficiency as primarily volitional: agents fail to intend what is needed if they are to will their maxims and not merely to wish for them to be realized. Each of these types of failure in rationality subdivides into many different sorts of cases. It follows that there are very many different ways in which agents whose intentions are not to be volitionally inconsistent may have to consider their intentions.

Perhaps the most difficult of the various requirements of coherent willing is the last, the demand that agents not adopt specific intentions that in a given context may undercut their own maxims. There are many cases in which agents can reach relatively clear specific intentions about how they will implement or instance their maxims, yet the acts they select, though indeed selected as a means to or component of their underlying intentions, backfire. It is fairly common for agents to adopt surface intentions that, when enacted, foreseeably will produce results that defeat their own deeper intentions. Defensive measures generate counterattack; attempts to do something particularly well result in botched performances; decisive success in battle is revealed as Pyrrhic victory. It is perhaps unclear how long a view of the likely results of their action agents must take for us not to think action that leads to results incompatible with its underlying intention is irrational. But at the least the standard and foreseeable results of an action should not undercut the underlying intention of we are to think of an agent as acting rationally. Somebody who claims to intend no harm to others, and specifically merely intends to share a friendly evening's drinking and to drive others home afterward, but who then decides on serious drinking and so cannot safely drive, cannot plausibly claim to intend merely the exuberant drinking and bonhomie and not the foreseeable drunkenness and inability to drive safely. Given standard information, such a set of intentions is volitionally incoherent. For it is a normal and foreseeable result of exuberant drinking that the drinker is incapable of driving safely. One who intends the drinking also (given normal intelligence and experience) intends the drunkenness; and hence cannot coherently also intend to drive others home if the underlying intention is to harm nobody.[9]

This brief consideration of various ways in which agents' intentions may fail to be consistent shows that achieving consistency in action is a difficult matter even if we do not introduce any universality test. Intentions may be either conceptually or volitionally incoherent. The demand that the acts we perform reflect conceptually and volitionally coherent sets of intentions therefore constitutes a powerful constraint on all practical reasoning. This conclusion provides some reason for thinking that when these demands for consistency are extended in the way in which the second aspect of Kant's Formula of Universal Law requires, we should expect to see patterns of reasoning that, far from being ineffective or trivial, generate powerful and interesting results.

INCONSISTENCY IN UNIVERSALIZING

The intuitive idea behind the thought that a universality test can provide a criterion of moral acceptability may be expressed quite simply as the thought that if we are to act as morally worthy beings, we should not single ourselves out for special consideration or treatment. Hence whatever we propose for ourselves should be possible (note: not "desired" or "wanted"—but at least *possible*) for all others. Kant expresses this commonplace thought (it is, of course, not his argument for the Categorical Imperative) by suggesting that what goes wrong when we adopt a non-universalizable maxim is that we treat ourselves as special:

> whenever we transgress a duty, we find that we in fact do not will that our maxim should become a universal law—since this is impossible for us—but rather that its opposite should remain a law universally: we only take the liberty of making an *exception* to it for ourselves (or even just for this once) ... (*G*, IV, 424)

It is evident from this understanding of the Formula of Universal Law that the notion of a plurality of interacting agents is already implicit in the Formula of Universal Law. It is not the case that Kant introduces these notions into his ethics only with the Formula of the Kingdom of Ends, which would imply that the various formulations of the Categorical Imperative could not be in any way equivalent. To universalize is from the start to consider whether what one proposes for onself *could* be done by others. This seems to many too meager a foundation for ethics but not in itself an implausible constraint on any adequate ethical theory.

Clearly enough, whatever cannot be consistently intended even for oneself also cannot be consistently intended for all others. The types of cases shown to be conceptually or volitionally inconsistent by the methods discussed in the previous section are a fortiori nonuniversalizable. This raises the interesting question whether one should think of certain types of cognitive and volitional failure as themselves morally unworthy. However, I shall leave this question aside in order to focus on the types of failure in consistent intending that are *peculiar* to the adoption of nonuniversalizable intentions.

I shall therefore assume from now on that we are considering cases of maxims that are in themselves not conceptually incoherent, and of sets of underlying and surface intentions that are not themselves volitionally inconsistent. The task is to pinpoint the ways in which inconsistency emerges in some attempts to universalize such internally consistent intentions. The second part of Kant's Formula of Universal Law enjoins action only on maxims that the agent can at the same time will as universal laws. He suggests that we can imagine this hypothetical willing by working out what it would be like "if the maxim of your action were to become through your will a universal law of nature".[10] To universalize maxims agents must satisfy themselves that they can both adopt the maxim and simultaneously will that others do so. In determining whether they can do so they may find that they are defeated by either of the two types of contradiction that, as we have already seen, can afflict action even when universalizing is not under consideration. Kant's own account of these two types of incoherence, either of which defeats universalizability, is as follows:

We must *be able to will* that a maxim of our action should become a universal law—this is the general canon for all moral judgement of action. Some actions are so constituted that their maxim cannot even be *conceived* as a universal law of nature without contradiction, let alone be *willed* as what *ought* to become one. In the case of others we do not find this inner impossibility, but it is still impossible to *will* that their maxim should be raised to the universality of a law of nature, because such a will would contradict itself. (*G*, IV, 424)

Kant also asserts that those maxims that when universalized lead to conceptual contradiction are the ones that strict or perfect duty requires us to avoid, whereas those that when universalized are conceptually coherent but not coherently willable are opposed only to wider or imperfect duties.[11] Since we probably lack both rigorous criteria and firm intuitions of the boundaries between perfect and imperfect duties, it is hard to evaluate this claim. However, it is remarkably easy to display contradictions that arise in attempts to universalize maxims that we might think of as clear cases of violations of duties of justice and self-respect, which Kant groups together as perfect duties; and it is also easy to show how contradictions emerge in attempts to universalize maxims that appear to exemplify clear violations of duties of beneficence and self-development, which Kant groups together as imperfect duties. By running through a largish number of such examples I hope to show how groundless is the belief that universality tests need supplementing with heteronomous considerations if they are to be action-guiding.

CONTRADICTIONS IN CONCEPTION

A maxim that may lead to contradictions in conception when we attempt to universalize it often does not contain any conceptual contradiction if we merely adopt the maxim. For example, there is no contradiction involved in adopting the maxim of becoming a slave. But this maxim has as its universalized counterpart—the maxim we must attempt to "will as a universal law"—the maxim of everybody becoming a slave.[12] But if everybody became a slave, there would be nobody with property rights, hence no slaveholders, and hence nobody could become a slave.[13] Consider alternatively a maxim of becoming a slaveholder. Its universalized counterpart would be the maxim of everybody becoming a slaveholder. But if everybody became a slaveholder, then everybody would have some property rights; hence nobody could be a slave; hence there could be no slaveholders. Action on either of the nonuniversalizable maxims of becoming a slave or becoming a slaveholder would reveal moral unworthiness: It could be undertaken only by one who makes of himself or herself a special case.

Contradictions in conception can also be shown to arise in attempts to universalize maxims of deception and coercion. The maxim of coercing another has as its universalized counterpart the maxim that all coerce others; but if all coerce others, including those who are coercing them, then each party both complies with others' wills (being coerced) and simultaneously does not comply with others but rather (as coercer) exacts their compliance. A maxim of coercion cannot coherently be universalized and reveals moral unworthiness. By contrast, a maxim of coordination can be consistently universalized. A maxim of deceiving others as convenient has as its universalized counterpart the maxim that everyone will deceive others as convenient. But if everyone were to deceive others as convenient, then there would be no trust or reliance on others' acts of communication; hence nobody could be deceived; hence nobody could deceive others as convenient.

An argument of the same type can be applied to the maxim that is perhaps the most fundamental for a universality test, namely the maxim of abrogating judgment. One whose maxim it is to defer to the judgment and decisions of others—to choose heteronomy[14]—adopts a maxim whose universalized counterpart is that everyone defer to the judgments and decisions of others. But if everyone defers to the judgments and decisions of others, then there are no decisions to provide the starting point for deferring in judgment; hence it cannot be the case that everybody defers in judgment. Decisions can never be reached when everyone merely affirms, "I agree." A maxim of "elective heteronomy" cannot consistently be universalized.

Interpreters of Kant have traditionally made heavier weather of the contradiction in conception test than these short arguments suggest is necessary. There have perhaps been two reasons why. One is clearly that Kant's own examples of applications of the Categorical Imperative are more complex and convoluted than these short arguments suggest.[15] But even if detailed analysis of these examples is necessary for an evaluation of Kant's theory, it is clarifying to see whether a contradiction in conception test works when liberated from the need to accommodate Kant's particular discussion of examples.

But a second reason why the contradiction in conception test has seemed problematic to many of Kant's commentators is perhaps of greater importance for present concerns. It is that whereas many would grant that we can detect contradictions in attempts to universalize maxims simply of slaveholding or coercing or deceiving or deference, they would point out that no contradiction emerges if we seek to universalize more circumspect maxims, such as "I will hold slaves if I am in a position of sufficient power" or "I will deceive when it suits me and I can probably get away with it" or "I will defer in judgment to those I either admire or fear." Still less do contradictions emerge when we aim to universalize highly specific intentions of deception or deference, such as "I will steal from Woolworths when I can get away with it" or "I will do whatever my parish priest tells me to do."

However, the force of this objection to the claim that the contradiction in conception test can have significant moral implications is undercut when we remember that this is a test that applies to agents' maxims, that is, to their underlying or fundamental intentions or principles, and that as a corollary it is a test of moral worth. For what will be decisive is what an agent's fundamental intention or principle in doing a given act really is. What counts is whether the expression of falsehood expresses a fundamental attempt to deceive, or whether agreement with another (in itself innocent enough) expresses a fundamental refusal to judge or think for oneself. For an agent cannot truthfully claim that an underlying intent, plan or principle was of a very specific sort unless the organization of other, less fundamental, intentions reveals that it really was subject to those restrictions. Precisely because the Categorical Imperative formulates a universality test that applies to *maxims*, and not just to any intention, it is not rebutted by the fact that relatively specific intentions often can be universalized without conceptual contradiction. Conversely, further evidence for the interpretation of the notion of a maxim presented in the section entitled "Maxims and moral categories" is that it leads to an account of the Categorical Imperative that is neither powerless nor counterintuitive. However, for the same reason (that it applies to maxims and not to intentions of all sorts) the Categorical Imperative can most plausibly be construed as a test of moral worth rather than of outward rightness, and must always be applied with awareness that we lack certainty about what an agent's maxim is in a given case. This is a relatively slight difficulty when we are assessing our own proposed maxims of action, since we at least can do no better than to probe and test the maxim on which we propose to act (but even here we have no guarantee against self-deception). But it means that we will always remain to some extent unsure about our assessment of others' acts. Kant after all insists that we do not even know whether there *ever* has been a truly morally worthy act. But that is something we do not need to know in order to try to perform such acts. Self-deception may cloud our knowledge of our own maxims; but we are not powerless in self-guidance.

CONTRADICTIONS IN THE WILL

Just as there are maxims that display no conceptual incoherence until attempts are made to universalize them, so there are maxims that exhibit no conceptual incoherence even when universalized, but that are shown to be volitionally inconsistent when attempts are made to universalize them. Such maxims cannot be "willed as universal laws"; attempts to do so fail in one way or another to meet the standards of rationality specified by the group of principles that I have termed Principles of Rational Intending. For to will a maxim is, after all, not just to conceive the realization of an underlying intention; that requires no more than speculation or wishing. Willing requires also the adoption of more specific intentions that are guided by, and chosen (in the light of the agent's beliefs) to realize, the underlying intention, or, if that is impossible, as appropriate moves toward a situation in which such specific intentions might be adopted. Whoever wills a maxim also adopts more specific intentions as means to or constituents of realizing that underlying intention, and is also committed to the foreseeable results of acting on these more specific intentions. Since intending a maxim commits the agent to such a variety of other intentions, there are various different patterns of argument that reveal that certain maxims cannot be willed as universal laws without contradiction.

Clearly the most comprehensive way in which a maxim may fail to be willable as a universal law is if its universal counterpart is inconsistent with the specific intentions that would be necessary for its own realization. Universalizing such a maxim would violate the Principle of Hypothetical Imperatives. The point is well illustrated by a Kantian example.[16] If I seek to will a maxim of nonbeneficence as a universal law, my underlying intention is not to help others when they need it, and its universalized counterpart is that nobody help others when they need it. But if everybody denies help to others when they need it, then those who need help will not be helped, and in particular I will not myself be helped when I need it. But if I am committed to the standards of rational willing that constitute the various Principles of Rational Intending, then I am committed to willing some means to any end to which I am committed, and these must include willing that if I am in need of help and therefore not able to achieve my ends without help, I be given some appropriate help. In trying to universalize a maxim of nonbeneficence I find myself committed simultaneously to willing that I not be helped when I need it and that I be helped when I need it. This contradiction, however, differs from the conceptual contradictions that emerge in attempts to universalize maxims such as those considered in the last section. A world of non-benevolent persons is conceivable without contradiction. Arguments that reveal contradictions in the will depend crucially upon the role of the various Principles of Rational Intending—in this case on the Principle of Hypothetical Imperatives—in constraining the choice of specific intentions to a set that will implement all underlying intentions. It is only because *intending* a maxim of nonbeneficence as a universal law requires commitment to that very absence of help when needed, to which all rational intending requires assent, that nonbeneficence cannot coherently be universalized.

A second Kantian example,[17] which provides an argument to volitional incoherence, is a maxim of neglecting to develop any talents. A world of beings who develop no talents contains no conceptual incoherence. The maxim of an individual who decides to develop no talents, though imprudent, reveals no volitional inconsistency. For it is always *possible* that others fend for the imprudent, who will then find means available for at least some action. (It is not a fundamental requirement of practical reason that there should be means available to whatever projects agents adopt, but only that they should not have ruled out all action.) However, an attempt to universalize a maxim of neglecting talents commits one to a world in which no talents have been developed, and so to a situation in which necessary means are lacking not just for some but for any sort of complex action. An agent who fails to will the development, in self or others, of whatever minimal range of talents is required and sufficient for a range of action, is committed to internally inconsistent sets of intentions. Such agents intend both that action be possible and that it be undercut by neglect to develop even a minimal range of talents that would leave some possibility of action. This argument shows nothing about the development of talents that may be required or sufficient for any *specific* projects, but only points to the inconsistency of failing to foster such talents as are needed and sufficient for action of some sort or other. It is an argument that invokes not only the Principle of Hypothetical Imperatives but also the requirement that rational beings intend some set of means sufficient for the realization of their underlying intentions or principles.

These two examples of arguments that reveal volitional inconsistencies show only that it is morally unworthy to adopt maxims either of systematic nonbeneficence or of systematic neglect of talents. The duties that they ground are relatively indeterminate duties of virtue. The first of these arguments does not specify whom it is morally worthy to help, to what extent, in what ways or at what cost, but only that it would be morally unworthy to adopt an underlying intention of nonbeneficence. Similarly, the second argument does not establish which talents it would be morally worthy to develop, in whom, to what extent or at what cost, but only that it would be morally unworthy to adopt an underlying intention of making no effort to develop any talents. The person who adopts a maxim either of nonbeneficence or of nondevelopment of talents cannot coherently universalize the maxim, but must either make an exception of himself or herself, and intend, unworthily, to be a free rider on others' beneficence and talents, or be committed to some specific intentions that are inconsistent with those required for action on the maxim.

Another example of a maxim that cannot consistently be willed as a universal law is the maxim of refusing to accept help when it is needed. The universalized counterpart of this underlying intention would be the intention that everyone refuse to accept help when it is needed. But rational beings cannot consistently commit themselves to intending that all forgo a means that, if ever they are in need of help, will be indispensable for them to act at all.

A further example of a nonuniversalizable maxim is provided by a maxim of ingratitude, whose universalized counterpart is that nobody show or express gratitude for favors received. In a world of non-self-sufficient beings a universal maxim of ingratitude would require the systematic neglect of an important means for ensuring that help is forthcoming for those who need help if they are to realize their intentions. Hence in such a world nobody could coherently claim to will that those in need of help be helped. Yet we have already seen that to will that all in need of help be refused help is volitionally inconsistent. Hence, willing a maxim of ingratitude also involves a commitment to a set of intentions not all of which can be consistently universalized. The volitional inconsistency that overtakes would-be universalizers of this maxim arises in two stages: The trouble with ingratitude is that, practiced universally, it undercuts beneficence; the trouble with nonbeneficence is that it cannot be universally practiced by beings who have at least some maxims, yet (lacking self-sufficiency) cannot guarantee that their own resources will provide means sufficient for at least some of their projects.

The hinge of all these arguments is that human beings (since they are adopters of maxims) have at least some maxims or projects, which (since they are not self-sufficient) they cannot always realize unaided, and so must (since they are rational) intend to draw on the assistance of others, and so must (if they universalize) intend to develop and foster a world that will lend to all some support of others' beneficence and talents. Such arguments can reveal the volitional inconsistencies involved in trying to universalize maxims of entirely neglecting the social virtues—beneficence, solidarity, gratitude, sociability and the like—for beings who are rational yet not always able to achieve what they intend unaided. It follows from this point that the social virtues are very differently construed in Kantian and in heteronomous ethics. An ethical theory for nonheteronomous agents sees the social virtues as morally required, not because they are desired or liked but because they are necessary requirements for action in a being who is not self-sufficient. The content of the social virtues in this framework cannot be spelled out in terms of the provision of determinate goods or services or the meeting of certain set needs or the satisfaction of a determinate set of desires. Rather, the content of these virtues will always depend on the various underlying maxims and projects, both individual

and collaborative, to which agents commit themselves. What will constitute beneficence or kindness or care for others will depend in great part
on how others intend to act.

CONTRADICTIONS IN THE WILL AND FURTHER RESULTS

The patterns of argument that can be used to show underlying antisocial
intentions morally unworthy make use of various Principles of Rational
Intending in addition to the Principle of Hypothetical Imperatives. In
particular they draw on the requirements that rational agents intend not
merely necessary but also sufficient means to or components of their
underlying intentions or maxims, and that they also intend whatever
means are indirectly required and sufficient to make possible the adoption
of such specific intentions. However, the particular features of the fifth
Principle of Rational Intending—the Principle of Intending the Further
Results—have not yet been displayed. Attempts to evade this Principle of
Rational Intending lead to a peculiar sort of volitional inconsistency.

Good examples of arguments that rely on this principle can be developed by considering cases of maxims that, when universalized, produce
what are frequently referred to as "unintended consequences". For example, I can adopt the underlying intention of improving my economic well-
being, and the specific intention of doing so by competing effectively with
others. The maxim of my action can be consistently universalized: There
is no conceptual contradiction in intending everyone's economic position
to improve. The specific intention of adopting competitive strategies is
not inconsistent with the maxim to which it is ancillary; nor is universal
action on competitive strategies inconsistent with universal economic
advance (that indeed is what the invisible hand is often presumed to
achieve). But if an agent intends his or her own economic advance to be
achieved solely by competitive strategies, this nexus of intentions cannot
consistently be willed as universal law, because the further results of universal competitive activity, by itself, are inconsistent with universal economic advance. If everyone seeks to advance by these (and no other)
methods, the result will not put everybody ahead economically. A maxim
of economic progress combined with the specific intention of achieving
progress merely by competitive strategies cannot be universalized, any
more than the intention of looking over the heads of a crowd can be
universally achieved by everyone in the crowd standing on tiptoes.[18]
On the other hand, a maxim of seeking economic advance by means of

increased production can be consistently universalized. It is merely the particular specific intention of advancing economically by competitive strategies alone that leads to volitional inconsistency when universalized. Competitive means are inherently effective only for some: Competitions must have losers as well as winners. Hence, though it can be consistent to seek individual economic advance solely by competitive methods, this strategy cannot consistently be universalized. Once we consider what it would be to intend the consequences of universal competition—the usually *unintended* consequences—we can see that there is an inconsistency not between universal competitive activity and universal economic progress, but between the *further results of intending only universal competitive activity and universal economic progress*. Economic progress and competitive activity might each of them consistently be universal; indeed, it is possible for them to coexist within a certain society. (Capitalist economies do experience periods of general economic growth.) Nevertheless, there is a volitional inconsistency in seeking to achieve universal economic growth *solely by way* of universal adoption of competitive strategies.

This argument does not show that either the intention to advance economically or the intention to act competitively cannot be universalized, but only that the composite intention of pursuing economic advance solely by competitive tactics cannot be universalized. It does not suggest that either competition or economic progress is morally unworthy, but only that an attempt to achieve economic progress solely by competitive methods and without aiming at any productive contribution is not universalizable and so is morally unworthy.

Similarly, there is no inconsistency in an intention to engage in competitive activities of other sorts (e.g., games and sports). But if such competition is ancillary to an underlying intention to win, then the overall intention is not universalizable. Competitive games must have losers. If winning is not the overriding aim in such activities, if they are played for their own sake, the activity is consistently universalizable. But to play competitively with the fundamental intention of winning is to adopt an intention that makes of one's own case a necessary exception.

CONCLUSIONS

The interest of a Kantian universality test is that it aims to ground an ethical theory on notions of consistency and rationality rather than upon considerations of desire and preference. Kant's universality test meets many of the conditions that any such universality test must meet. In particular it focuses on features of action that are appropriate candidates for assessments of coherence and incoherence, namely the maxims or fundamental intentions that agents may adopt and the web of more specific ancillary intentions that they must adopt in a given context if their commitment to a maxim is genuine. Although Kant alludes specifically to conceptual inconsistencies and to those volitional inconsistencies that are attributable to nonobservance of the Principle of Hypothetical Imperatives in attempts to universalize intentions, there is in addition a larger variety of types of volitional inconsistency that agents who seek to subject their maxims to a universality test (and so not to make an exception of their own case) must avoid. A universality test applied to maxims and their ancillary, more specific, intentions can be action-guiding in many ways without invoking any heteronomous considerations.

However, precisely because it applies to intentions or principles, a universality test of this sort cannot generally provide a test of the rightness or wrongness of the specific outward aspects of action. It is, at least primarily, and perhaps solely, a test of the inner moral worth of acts. It tells us what we ought to avoid if we are not to act in ways that we can know are in principle not possible for all others. Such a test is primarily of use to agents in guiding their own moral deliberations, and can only be used most tentatively in assessing the moral worth of others' action, where we are often sure only about specific outward aspects of action and not about the maxim. This point will not be of great importance if we do not think it important whether an ethical theory enables us to pass judgment on the moral worth of others' acts. But specific outward aspects of others' action are unavoidably of public concern. The considerations discussed here do not reveal whether or not these can be judged right or wrong by Kant's theory. Kant no doubt thought that it was possible to derive specific principles of justice from the Formula of Universal Law; but the success of this derivation and of his grounding of *Rechtslehre* is beyond the scope of this chapter.

The universality test discussed here is, above all, a test of the mutual consistency of (sets of) intentions and univeralized intentions or principles. It operates by showing some sets of proposed intentions to be mutually inconsistent. It does not thereby generally single out action on any one set of specific intentions as morally required. On the contrary, the ways in which maxims can be enacted or realized by means of acts performed on specific intentions must vary with situation, tradition and culture. The specific acts by which we can show or fail to show loyalty to a friend or respect to another or justice in our dealings with the world will always reflect specific ways of living and thinking and particular situations and relationships. What reason can provide is a way of discovering whether we are choosing to act in ways (however culturally specific) that we do not in principle preclude for others. The "formal" character of the Categorical Imperative does not entail either that it has no substantive ethical implications or that it can select a unique code of conduct as morally worthy for all times and places. Rather than presenting a dismal choice between triviality and implausible rigorism, a universality test can provide a rational foundation for ethics and maintain a serious respect for the diversity of content of distinct ethical practices and traditions.

Abbreviations

References to and citations of Kant's writings are given parenthetically in the text, using the following abbreviations: *DV—The Doctrine of Virtue* (Pt. II, *Metaphysics of Morals*); *G—Groundwork of the Metaphysic of Morals*; *MM—The Metaphysics of Morals* (for citations of the introduction only). Citations give the volume and page number for the Prussian Academy edition (e.g., [*G*, IV, 424]). For full bibliographical details see the References.

Notes

1. Heteronomous readings of Kant's ethics include Schopenhauer's in *On the Basis of Morality*, but are most common in introductory works in ethics. Recent examples include William K. Frankena, *Ethics*, p. 25; Gilbert Harman, *The Nature of Morality*, p. 73; and D. D. Raphael, *Moral Philosophy*, p. 76. Allegations that Kant, despite his intentions, must invoke heteronomous considerations if he is to reach substantive conclusions can notoriously be found in J. S. Mill's *Utilitarianism*, p. 4, but are also now more common in more general discussions of Kant's ethics. Examples include C. D. Broad, *Five Types of Ethical Theory*, p. 130; and Marcus Singer, *Generalization in Ethics*, p. 262.

2. Even such a wide-ranging and reflective discussion of rational choice theory as Jon Elster's in *Ulysses and the Sirens* discusses no nonheteronomous conceptions or aspects of rational choice.

3. I would not now use the term *intention* here, or as I used it throughout this essay. Replacing it with (*underlying*) *practical principle* allows the same points to be made in more general form, and makes it easier to stress the extent to which maxims, unlike certain intentions, can be hidden from those whose maxims they are. Chapters 6–8 of Onora O'Neill, *Constructions of Reason*, lean less heavily on the term.

4. However, the claim that maxims are underlying or fundamental intentions or principles should not be collapsed into the claim, which Kant makes in *Religion within the Limits of Reason Alone*, that for any agent (rather than "for any act")

at a given time there is one fundamental maxim, to which all other principles that we might think maxims are ancillary.

5. See *G*, IV, 397 f.: "the concept of *duty*, which includes that of a good will ..." The persistence of the view that Kant is primarily concerned with right action perhaps reflects the modern conception that duty *must* be a matter of externals more than it reflects the Kantian texts. Cf. Onora Nell (O'Neill), *Acting on Principle*, and Onora O'Neill, *Constructions of Reason*, chapters 6–8.

6. The points mentioned in this and the preceding paragraphs suggest why a focus on maxims may make it possible to bypass a variety of problems said to plague universality tests when applied to principles that are "too general" or "too specific"; these problems include invertibility, reiterability, moral indeterminacy, empty formalism and the generation of trivial and counterintuitive results. See Singer, *Generalization in Ethics*; and Nell (O'Neill), *Acting on Principle*.

7. Kant does not then see all acts that are specifically required by strict or perfect duties as matters of justice. Some duties of virtue also have (limited) strict requirements, such as refraining from mockery or detraction or otherwise damaging others' self-respect. These are indispensable elements of any way of enacting maxims of respect. Cf. *DV*, VI, 421ff. and 463ff.; Nell (O'Neill), *Acting on Principle*, pp. 52–58; and Barbara Herman, "Mutual Aid and Respect for Persons".

8. Kant's discussions of duties of virtue in any case suggest that he would count the necessary constituents or components of an end, and not merely the instrumentally necessary acts, as means to that end.

9. The fifth requirement of rational intending clearly deals with the very nexus of intentions on which discussions of the Doctrine of Double Effect focus. That doctrine claims that agents are not responsible for harm that foreseeably results from action undertaken with dutiful intentions, provided that the harm is not disproportionate, is regretted, and would have been avoided had there been a less harmful set of specific intentions that would have implemented the same maxim in that situation. (The surgeon foresees, and regrets, the pain unavoidably inflicted by a lifesaving procedure.) Although the Doctrine of Double Effect holds that agents are not to be held responsible for such action, it allows that they do, if "obliquely" rather than "directly", intend it. It is compatible with the Doctrine of Double Effect to insist that an agent whose oblique intention foreseeably undercuts the action for the sake of which what is directly intended is done, acts irrationally. Where the fundamental intention is so undercut by a supposedly ancillary aspect of action, proportionality is violated, and the attribution of the fundamental intentions may be called in question.

10. This is the so-called Formula of the Law of Nature. Cf. *G*, IV, 421, and also 436: "maxims must be chosen as if they had to hold as universal laws of nature"; see also *MM*, VI, 225: "Act according to a maxim which can, at the same time, be valid as a universal law." In this discussion I leave aside all consideration of the relationships between different formulations of the Categorical Imperative, and in particular the differences between those versions that are stated "for finite rational beings" (typics) and those that are formulated in ways that make them relevant strictly to the human condition. These topics have been much discussed

in the literature: H. J. Paton, *The Categorical Imperative*; John Kemp, *The Philosophy of Kant*; Robert Paul Wolff, *The Autonomy of Reason*; Bruce Aune, *Kant's Theory of Morals*.

11. *G*, IV, 424; *MM*, IV, Introduction; *DV*, VI, esp. 389; see also chapters 11 and 12 of Onora O'Neill, *Constructions of Reason*.

12. For further discussion of the notion of the universalized counterpart of a maxim see Nell (O'Neill), *Acting on Principle*, pp. 61–63.

13. For an application of the Formula of Universal Law to the example of slavery see Leslie A. Mulholland, "Kant: On Willing Maxims to Become Laws of Nature."

14. To see why Kant thinks the abrogation of autonomy would be the most fundamental of failings see his *What Is Enlightenment?* and Barry Clarke's discussion of "elective heteronomy" in "Beyond the Banality of Evil."

15. See the various works of commentary listed in footnote 10 above; Jonathan Harrison, "Kant's Examples of the First Formulation of the Categorical Imperative"; and John Kemp, "Kant's Examples of the Categorical Imperative".

16. Cf. *DV*, VI, 447–464, for Kant's discussions of love and social virtues.

17. Cf. *DV*, VI, 443–447, for discussion of the duty not to neglect to develop talents (the "duty to seek one's own perfection"). "Talents" here are to be understood not as any particularly unusual accomplishments, but as any human powers that (unlike natural gifts) we can choose either to cultivate or to neglect. Kant tends to think the most important talents are second-order ones (e.g., self-mastery, self-knowledge) and that we can do little to develop these in others. Both restrictions seem to me unnecessary. See Onora O'Neill, *Faces of Hunger: An Essay on Poverty, Development and Justice*, chap. 8, for development of these thoughts.

18. See F. Hirsch, *The Social Limits to Growth*.

References

Aune, Bruce. *Kant's Theory of Morals*. Princeton University Press, Princeton, 1979.

Broad, C. D. *Five Types of Ethical Theory*. Littlefield Adams and Co., Totowa, N.J., 1965.

Clarke, Barry. "Beyond the Banality of Evil." *British Journal of Political Science* 10 (1980): 17–39.

Elster, John. *Ulysses and the Sirens*. Cambridge University Press, Cambridge, 1979.

Frankena, William K. *Ethics*. Prentice-Hall, Englewood Cliffs, N.J., 1963.

Harman, Gilbert. *The Nature of Morality*. Oxford University Press, New York, 1977.

Harrison, Jonathan. "Kant's Examples of the First Formulation of the Categorical Imperative." In *Foundations of the Metaphysics of Morals: Text and Critical Essays*, ed. R. P. Wolff, pp. 208–29. Bobbs-Merrill, Indianapolis, 1969.

Herman, Barbara. "Mutual Aid and Respect for Persons." *Ethics* 94 (1984): 577–602.

Hirsch, F. *The Social Limits to Growth*. Harvard University Press, Cambridge, Mass., 1976.

Kant, Immanuel. *Beantwortung der Frage: Was ist Aufklärung?* First published in 1784. In *Kants gesammelte Schriften*, edited by the Deutschen Akademie der Wissenschaften (formerly Königlichen Preussischen Akademie der Wissenschaften), vol. 8. Walter de Gruyter, Berlin, 1902–   .

Kant, Immanuel. *Grundlegung zur Metaphysik der Sitten*. First published in 1785. In *Kants gesammelte Schriften*, edited by the Deutschen Akademie der Wissenschaften (formerly Königlichen Preussischen Akademie der Wissenschaften), vol. 4. Walter de Gruyter, Berlin, 1902–   .

Kant, Immanuel. *Die Metaphysik der Sitten*. First published in 1797. In *Kants gesammelte Schriften*, edited by the Deutschen Akademie der Wissenschaften (formerly Königlichen Preussischen Akademie der Wissenschaften), vol. 6. Walter de Gruyter, Berlin, 1902–   .

Kant, Immanuel. *Die Religion innerhalb der blossen Vernunft*. First published in 1793. In *Kants gesammelte Schriften*, edited by the Deutschen Akademie der Wissenschaften (formerly Königlichen Preussischen Akademie der Wissenschaften), vol. 6. Walter de Gruyter, Berlin, 1902–   .

Kemp, John. *The Philosophy of Kant*. Oxford University Press, Oxford, 1968.

Kemp, John. "Kant's Examples of the Categorical Imperative." In *Foundations of the Metaphysics of Morals: Text and Critical Essays*, ed. R. P. Wolff, pp. 230–44. Bobbs-Merrill, Indianapolis, 1969.

Mill, J. S. *Utilitarianism*. In his *Utilitarianism, Liberty and Representative Government*, ed. Mary Warnock. J. M. Dent and Sons, London, 1968.

Mulholland, Leslie A. "Kant: On Willing Maxims to Become Laws of Nature." *Dialogue* 18 (1978): 92–105.

Nell (O'Neill), Onora. *Acting on Principle*. Columbia University Press, New York, 1975.

O'Neill, Onora. *Faces of Hunger: An Essay on Poverty, Development, and Justice*. George Allen and Unwin, London, 1986.

O'Neill, Onora. *Constructions of Reason*. Cambridge University Press, Cambridge, 1989.

Paton, H. J. *The Categorical Imperative*. Hutchinson, London, 1947.

Raphael, D. D. *Moral Philosophy*. Oxford University Press, Oxford, 1981.

Schopenhauer, F. *On the Basis of Morality*. Trans. E. F. J. Payne. Bobbs-Merrill, Indianapolis, 1965.

Singer, Marcus. *Generalization in Ethics*. Alfred Knopf, New York, 1961.

Wolff, Robert Paul. *The Autonomy of Reason*. Harper and Row, New York, 1973.

Chapter 15

Pleasure in Practical Reasoning

Elijah Millgram

Practical reasoning often strikes philosophers as ungrounded. It seems to them that desires are to be justified by reasoning that proceeds from, *inter alia*, further desires, and these further desires are to be justified by reference to still further desires. Avoiding circularity and infinite regress requires justification to terminate in desires that are themselves unjustified, and thus, from the point of view of reasons, simply arbitrary. If techniques of justification merely *transmit* reason-giving force from premises to conclusions, then if the premises are arbitrary, not different in this respect from whims, the conclusions will be arbitrary as well.

I'm going to argue that practical reasoning is no worse off than theoretical reasoning, as far as the arbitrariness of its premises goes. Philosophers, unless they are skeptics, are generally not worried about theoretical reasoning being ungrounded. One important reason why they are not is the role of observation in acquiring beliefs—even though it's notoriously difficult to say precisely what that role is. I will argue that practical reasoning can avail itself of an analog of belief formation underwritten by observational circumstances, so that practical reasoning has no *more* cause for embarrassment than theoretical reasoning.

In arguing this, I'm going to identify an element of practical reasoning that accompanies the analog of observational belief formation, and I'm going to *call* this element "pleasure." Then I will argue that this element *is* pleasure. I will provide a new argument against hedonism, and finally, I'll briefly discuss the consequences of these arguments for instrumentalist views of practical reasoning.

I TWO EXAMPLES

Here is an illustration of the relation between observation and pleasure in practical reasoning, borrowed from the experience of an acquaintance:[1]

Michelle works for a company that provides and maintains indoor plants for offices. Faced with a tree that was almost completely defoliated, she decided to try to bring it back to life, rather than go to the expense of replacing it. She pruned it back, cleaned off the dead material, watered the tree carefully, and applied rooting hormone. The tree, which had looked dead, revived, and "is today a beautiful tree."

Michelle describes bringing the tree back to life as having been "a big thrill." She says that meeting the challenge gave her real satisfaction: "It's really fun to see trees come back, go from bare branches to being covered with beautiful green leaves again." She has learned that she likes challenges that involve improving and reviving living things through her own perseverance, intelligence and skill, and that her next job will involve treating, nurturing, and learning about living things.

There is a good deal in this example that deserves careful attention. First, Michelle began her work on the dying tree for reasons that had nothing to do with the intrinsic rewards of caring for trees: she felt that an important part of her job was keeping expensive plant replacements to a minimum. Through her experience, Michelle came to have, first, a desire to care for trees, and second, a more general desire for the challenges and rewards of bringing living things back to a state of health. That is, in the course of the experience, Michelle acquired new ends; ends, moreover, for which she was able to adduce reasons.

Second, central to the process was Michelle's finding the challenge of reviving the dying tree to be *fun*. She found herself enthusiastic about what she was doing, engaged by it, wanting to do it. We are all familiar with the feeling of our work (or other things) going well, eliciting our attention and energy in a way that makes hard work seem almost easy. When one finds a task pleasant, one engages in it willingly, even eagerly; there is no need to force oneself to it, even when it is difficult. It is this feeling that I will call *pleasure* (begging whatever questions it is, for now, necessary to beg); and I will take this kind of case as the central or paradigmatic instance of pleasure.

I mean to distinguish feelings from sensations, so in calling pleasure a feeling, I am not suggesting that it is a sensation; in fact, I am implying that it is *not* a sensation. On this way of speaking, it is a central feature of sensations that having them involves being aware of them. Feelings, however, may be had unawares; a familiar example is the depressed person who does not realize that he is depressed. Unlike sensations, the feeling of pleasure may sometimes be recognized only in retrospect, or when one's attention is called to it by others. Feelings can *involve* sensations, sometimes in a way that makes it tempting to say that the sensations are part of the feelings; we often identify feelings by the sensations they involve (that sinking feeling). But feelings do not always involve the same sensations: a feeling of elation may be accompanied by a sensation of light-headedness in one case, by a sensation of butterflies in the stomach in another, and by no special sensation in a third; and I may be too intent on what I am doing to notice that I am elated. While pleasure often involves some sensation or other, there is no particular sensation, or class of sensations, that it necessarily involves.[2]

A third point to notice about the Michelle example is that something very like induction (or whatever pattern of reasoning it is that philosophers are trying to characterize when they talk about induction) is taking place here. Michelle learned from experience, first, that bringing a tree back to life is pleasurable, and second, that it is pleasurable *because* of the challenge it involves. This suggests that just as theoretical reasoning includes not only deductive reasoning (which does not itself respond to experience) but inductive reasoning (which does), practical reasoning includes an analog of induction, through which one can acquire new ends by learning from experience.

It might be objected that while there is something very much like induction going on here, that is because what is going on just *is* induction —that is, theoretical rather than practical reasoning. Michelle is out to attain pleasure, and learns inductively that certain things give her pleasure. Her decision to pursue these things is merely a matter of instrumental reasoning; now that she knows that tending trees is a way to get pleasure, she decides to tend trees. Michelle hasn't acquired any genuinely new ends; she has learned ways to address an end she already had.

We will see later just why this construal of the case is mistaken. For now, notice how alien this reading of the case is to the first-hand description. What Michelle (claims that she) wants to do is tend trees (which she has found to be pleasurable)—not to obtain pleasure *by* tending trees. This is a subtle but real difference, one which it is not obvious that an instrumentalist account can reconstruct.

Before going on to the account of pleasure, here is an example illustrating the use of its contrary, displeasure or unpleasantness, in practical reasoning:

Pat[3] had been supporting herself as a waitress in New York while pursuing a dancing career. As she went from job to job, the time she remained in each grew shorter and shorter. Although she began each job with a good deal of enthusiasm, she would soon find things to hate about the job, would fight with the boss, and get fired.

Over the course of this period, she found herself ever more unable to cope with the day-to-day details of living. She was unable to pay her rent or run her errands; she wasn't getting dates; and at one point she realized: "I'm crying all the time, so I must not be doing the right thing." She describes the time as dominated by "a feeling of complete despair. I just couldn't do it. There were these basic things that very stupid people could do, that I couldn't do."

Although she felt miserable, it took a long time until she understood what was making her feel that way. Eventually she realized that while some things were going very badly, "the things that were good for me were going well and easily." Finally, on the first day of a new job waiting tables, she quit. "I couldn't bring myself to do it. I didn't even get as far as taking the first order." At that point she was resolved not to waitress anymore. She now works for an architect and dances in the evenings.[4]

If the central case of pleasure is the feeling that things are going well, that one is performing smoothly and successfully, and that difficulties are manageable and can be overcome, the central case of displeasure is the converse: one must force oneself to engage in the unpleasant activity, and going ahead with it is like pulling teeth. In extreme cases, one cannot cope, simple tasks become impossible, doing what one is doing becomes unbearable.

Again, one might suppose that Pat's decision was taken on the basis of instrumental reasoning, the goal of which was to avoid displeasure. But this would misconstrue the example. Pat herself describes her feeling of despair and dysfunctionality as telling her that she was doing something wrong. She distinguishes her choosing to avoid waitressing (which was unpleasant and even painful) from a possible choice which she denies having made, that of choosing to avoid displeasure and pain by not waitressing. This is a distinction that most of us can discover in our own experience. It is quite often the case that decisions that attend to pleasure (and its contrary, displeasure) use pleasure (and displeasure) as signs or symptoms, evidence as to how well things are going. One then often chooses the more pleasurable (or less painful) option, but this is not because pleasure is one's *goal*: rather, pleasure is an indication of something else. Saying what that is will require discussing an analogy between beliefs and desires.

II   PLEASURE AS OBSERVATION

Just as someone's believing that p commits him to p's being true, so someone's desiring X commits him to X's being desirable. Imagine someone saying "I desire X, but X is in no way desirable"—gloomily insisting that obtaining X would bring only disappointment and regret, etc. If he continues to insist that he anticipates no benefit whatsoever from satisfying the desire, portraying its object in unrelievedly dark tones, we will find ourselves hard-put to keep saying that he *desires* it.[5] (Note that I'm *not* suggesting that the benefit has to be the agent's *own*; one may expect not to regret an action that benefits only others. The claim is not meant to preclude altruism.)

Now what does being committed to something's being desirable come to in practice? There is a point that used to be made by coherence theorists, that one is never in a position to compare one's beliefs with the world as it really is: all one is ever in a position to do is to check whether one's beliefs stand in inferential relations of conflict, compatibility, support, and so on, with *other* beliefs that one has. Being committed to something's being true cannot *in practice* be manifested in anything beyond one's inferential commitments. And a very important part of these inferential commitments amounts to anticipating *other* beliefs. (I do not mean to suggest that believing that p does not commit one to p *itself* being the case, nor to claim that p's being the case must amount to facts about my present, future or possible beliefs; I am not endorsing a form of verificationism. The words 'in practice' are meant to carry this qualification.)

Let's see an illustration of this. Suppose I inform you that I believe that there is milk in the refrigerator. I am committed to the milk's in fact being in the refrigerator: if it is not there, I am wrong. I expect that if I go and look, it will be there. Now what does going and looking amount to? I put myself in appropriate circumstances (by walking up to the refrigerator and opening the door): in these circumstances, I come to have a belief that there is a carton of milk on the top shelf. This belief is a *rock-bottom* belief, that is, it is not inferred from further beliefs. I may or may not be able to give further reasons for relying on this belief. But the belief is not *inferred* from these further reasons. It is clear that, on pain of an infinite regress, there must be such beliefs.

We can type this belief more tightly. There are rock-bottom (i.e., non-inferred) beliefs very different from this one: hunches or gut feelings, or the axioms of Euclidean geometry, understood the old-fashioned way, as self-evident truths. In contrast, the rock-bottom belief I acquire by looking in the refrigerator is *experiential*: I come to believe that there's milk in the refrigerator *by* looking in the refrigerator.

A belief's being rock-bottom carries no implication of indefeasibility: no matter how "observational" my belief, I may later retract it. Also, a belief's being rock-bottom carries no denial that there are necessary conditions of its acquisition that must be described in terms of further beliefs. A good deal of background is typically required for coming to have a rock-bottom belief. For example, if I were unacquainted with milk cartons and their contents, my opening the refrigerator would not have led to my believing that there was milk in the refrigerator. Beliefs whose acquisition requires such background may be, nonetheless, non-inferentially acquired, and be accordingly rock-bottom beliefs.[6]

The commitment to *p*'s truth involves, *in practice*, the expectation that various beliefs, some experiential and rock-bottom, and some not, will be compatible with my belief that *p*. To be sure, I cannot specify just which beliefs these are, but since I am not making a reductionist claim, this is not a difficulty. Now rock-bottom beliefs highlight a feature that beliefs have more generally. If my rock-bottom belief is impugned, I cannot fall back on the premises from which I inferred it, for what makes it a rock-bottom belief is that I acquired it non-inferentially.[7] In these circumstances, I may find myself becoming aware of a *feeling* (*not* a sensation) of belief, which I will call *a feeling of conviction*. "I just *looked* in the refrigerator. What do you mean, 'How do I know?' Of *course* I know." If I stop myself in the middle of such a tirade, the feeling I find there is typically a feeling of conviction.[8]

The feeling of conviction (or, as I will just say, *conviction*) plays an important role in one's epistemic economy—particularly when it is of the rock-bottom, experiential variety. If, on considering a proposition, I find it unconvincing—if I lack the *feeling* of conviction—I may decide that I am on the wrong track (or that someone else is). If I do not feel conviction in situations in which I'm face to face with the object of my would-be belief (that is, when experiential rock-bottom belief is at issue), then it's going to be very difficult to convince me. And if in such situations I *do* feel conviction, my views on the subject will be difficult to dislodge. Seeing is, often enough, believing; experiential rock-bottom conviction is the familiar feeling that goes along with believing because you're seeing.

I now want to argue that pleasure is practical reasoning's analog of experiential rock-bottom conviction. I claimed that when one desires *X*, one is committed to *X*'s being desirable. But what does that commitment amount to in practice? Often, to the expectation that when one puts oneself in the appropriate situations, e.g., that when one actually *gets X*, one will not be horribly disappointed and wish that one had never heard of *X*. Rather, one expects that when one gets *X*, *X* will *turn out* to be desirable. Now a primary indicator of whether X is desirable or not is *pleasure*. Pleasure is the rock-bottom judgment of desirability of (an object of) present experience—one's experiential rock-bottom judgment that, yes, this is desirable. Conversely, displeasure is the rock-bottom judgment of undesirability, directed towards present experience. That is, each is a response to an object of present experience that amounts to a (defeasible) estimate of the object's desirability.

Pleasure is not, of course, the sole indicator. Other indicators of whether or not X is desirable may be inferences regarding X's desirability, or rock-bottom judgments of desirability that, like hunches, are not experiential. It is therefore not the case that taking something to be desirable *entails* expecting it to be pleasurable, any more than believing something entails expecting face-to-face confrontation with it to produce conviction. (I believe that the earth revolves around the sun, but I don't expect it to *look* that way. I may think the policies I support to be for the best, even though I expect that I will only *see* the unfortunate side-effects I know they will have.) Even when one comes face to face with X, one may mistakenly think it is desirable, or one may be mistakenly disappointed. Like experiential rock-bottom conviction, pleasure is not infallible. The drug addict is a trite case of pleasure not properly corresponding to desirability. Perhaps another is the altruistic act. The fallibility of both pleasure and the evidence of one's own eyes is relied upon by magicians, pickpockets, and con artists. That fact does not, however, make either dispensable.

It may sound peculiar to identify a feeling with a judgment. Possibly this is because one feels that there must be more to a judgment than a feeling; possibly because one can make judgments that do not *feel* like much at all. But recall that I am not using 'feeling' as a synonym for sensation: because it is not a sensation, a feeling is not precluded from having cognitive content in the way one might think sensations were; and, as I remarked earlier, one can have feelings of which one is hardly, or not at all, aware. I am avoiding distinguishing feelings from judgments because the distinction seems too forced here to be useful. But one can just as well think of these feelings as *aspects* or *accompaniments* of judgments.

Finally, there is a terminological asymmetry between conviction and pleasure. Conviction is to be found across the spectrum of belief; we do not have a word that picks out conviction specifically arrived at in the course of experience. Pleasure, on the other hand, is restricted to experiential judgments of desirability. But I do not believe that the asymmetry is more than terminological. Just as there are non-experiential judgments, rock-bottom and otherwise, that play important roles in theoretical reasoning (for example, the judgment that a particular step in a mathematical proof is correct), so there may be non-experiential judgments of desirability (rock-bottom and otherwise) that play equally important roles in practical reasoning.

III   WHAT'S WRONG WITH HEDONISM?

Practical reasoning tends to take one from a position of lesser pleasure to a position of greater pleasure. When I decide on Korean scallion pancakes instead of another round of marinated tofu, the likely upshot is that my subsequent life will be more pleasant than otherwise. Some philosophers have noticed this tendency, and concluded that pleasure is one's sole and necessary goal. In this they could not be more mistaken. Hedonists err in roughly the way that someone who thinks that the goal of enquiry is to maximize conviction might err. Normally, one's enquiries tend to take one from a position of lesser conviction to a position of greater conviction: after the inquiry, one has more beliefs, and believes things more strongly. However—and this is very important—in general one's goal is *not* conviction: one's goal is truth. Conviction is epistemically important as a guide to truth, but conviction *per se* is not the object of my efforts.

To conclude that because one tends to move to positions of greater conviction one's goal is *the conviction*, rather than *true and relevant belief* would be seriously to misconstrue the normal case of epistemic endeavor. One's feelings of conviction guide one's changes of belief, but this does not make them one's goal. Hedonists assume that because desires and goals change in response to experienced pleasure and displeasure, these must be the actual goals. But this view is naïve: pleasure and displeasure are indications and signs of desirability we use in determining what our goals should be. Michelle did not become devoted to trees as a way of pursuing pleasure (if she were only interested in pleasure, she would not have genuinely cared about the trees); rather, her pleasurable experiences helped her decide that one of her (non-instrumental) ends ought to be tending trees.

Similarly, time spent with my friend is, by and large, pleasurable; and were this not the case, eventually we should cease being friends. Nonetheless, it would be a mistake to construe the friendship instrumentally—

to conclude that I befriend him solely in order to obtain pleasure. The correct account of the counterfactual is, rather, this: if time spent together becomes, by and large, unpleasant, I shall start to wonder whether something is wrong with the friendship.

Notice that the argument not only cuts against egoistic hedonism, but against universal hedonism, or pleasure-utilitarianism, as well. If pleasure is a kind of estimate of desirability, the utilitarian's Good consists in maximizing the number and force of these estimates. This is a quite unlikely conception of the Good.

Earlier I claimed that it would be a mistake to construe the Michelle case as amounting to induction (i.e., theoretical reasoning about what produces pleasure) plus instrumental reasoning directed toward the goal of pleasure. We're now better positioned to say just what is wrong with that construal.

Such inductive reasoning can of course take place: one can learn that tending trees produces pleasure in much the way one can learn that one can't help finding well-groomed and sincere-sounding young men with attaché cases convincing. But this conclusion is theoretical rather than practical; it does not underwrite subsequent action in the way that a very similar-*looking* inference (say, from 'A_1 is desirable', 'A_2 is desirable', 'A_3 is desirable' ... to 'All As are desirable') would.

Normally, the conclusion about what tends to produce pleasure is related, more or less directly, to the desirability of objects of pleasure. But suppose that one is instead interested simply in the pleasure produced, and not in any further desirability the pleasure may indicate, and that one proposes to use the knowledge of what gives one pleasure to put oneself in situations that one will find pleasurable, without regard to the reliability of one's judgments of desirability in those circumstances. That would be a little like putting oneself in the way of lots of well-groomed and sincere-sounding young men with attaché cases, without too much regard to what they are likely to persuade one of, just in order to acquire convictions. It is evidence of the strategy's motivational incoherence that knowingly putting oneself in the way of acquiring convictions in this manner will impede one's ability actually to acquire them. Similarly, if one puts oneself in situations where one takes it that one's pleasure fails to be responsive to actual desirability, one's ability to make the judgments of desirability that pleasure consists in will be corroded.[9] (The realization makes pleasures seem hollow; and hollow pleasures are very soon no longer pleasures at all.) This suggests, first, that acting on the hedonist proposal would end up giving you not more pleasure, but less.[10] Second, the inability of a pattern of reasoning to survive awareness in this way strongly suggests that there is something seriously wrong with it. And finally, it is in any case clear that this is not what is going on in the Michelle example; her reasoning is quite able to survive her own scrutiny, and that is because it is directed toward the desirability of tending trees, rather than her own pleasure.

In developing an account of pleasure that construes it as a guide to the choice of ends, rather than an end itself, we have addressed the problem of the ungroundedness of practical reasoning. If a form of reasoning is just the manipulation of arbitrary desires, the question remains: why should the outcome of such manipulation guide action? Attention to the role of pleasure in determining those desires allows us to understand them as reflecting (more or less) informed estimates of desirability, and so as being not merely arbitrary.

Theoretical reasoning that did not attend to the world—say, solely deductive reasoning—would be useless; thinking that matters has to be informed by the way things are. If practical reasoning is to be useful, if it is to matter, it too will have to be informed by the way things are. Instrumentalist views of practical reasoning take it that the world has its say only by determining what is a means to what; but this is not enough. Attention to the role of pleasure shows how the world is enabled to have a further say in practical reasoning. Practical reasoning is informed by something that can be considered the practical analog of observation.

IV   SOME COMMONPLACES ABOUT PLEASURE

The objection likely to be pressed most strongly against the foregoing is this: what does what I am calling 'pleasure' have to do with *pleasure*? Now the claim that practical reasoning is no more the manipulation of arbitrary desires than theoretical reasoning is the manipulation of arbitrary beliefs does not depend on my successfully identifying experiential rock-bottom judgments of desirability with pleasure. But my argument against hedonism does depend on this identification. So I will try to show how the observationalist account I have presented accommodates the insights that motivate competing theories of pleasure, as well as the objections that have been traditionally urged against them. Showing how those insights are accommodated by my account will show it to be an account of that very thing into which they are insights—*viz*., pleasure.

I have been developing the observationalist account of pleasure in opposition to the instrumentalist construal, on which pleasure serves the function of an ultimate goal or end. The insight that makes the instrumentalist view seem plausible is nicely rendered by Anscombe.[11] She remarks that

'It's pleasant' is an adequate answer to 'What's the good of it?' or 'What do you want that for?' I.e., the chain of 'Why's' comes to an end with this answer.

This point seems to support the instrumentalist or hedonist view in the following way. It is taken that the chain of 'Why's' is a series of requests for further goals. "Why are you going shopping?" "To get some more moong dal." "Why do you want more moong dal?" "To make cucumber soup." "Why are you going to make the soup?" (And so on.) It is presumed that the final answer ("It's pleasant") states the final goal, that the reason it terminates explanation is that there is no further goal.

On my view, 'It's pleasant' does indeed terminate explanation, but it does so in much the way that 'I just believe it' terminates explanations in the theoretical realm, or rather, recalling the experiential aspect, the way 'That's just how it looks to me' does. 'It's pleasant' more or less amounts to: 'In experiencing it, I find it desirable'. One is not adducing a further goal, but affirming that the goal one has just mentioned is desirable.

Anscombe continues the passage we just quoted:

a claim *that* 'it's pleasant' can be challenged, or an explanation asked for ('But what *is* the pleasure of it?') ...

The instrumentalist must explain just *how* the final answer ('It's pleasant') can be challenged. And he seems to have only two choices: the challenge could consist in a denial that pleasure is one's goal (not an option for the hedonist), or in a claim that the penultimate goal is not in fact a satisfactory or efficient means of attaining pleasure. This latter is an unlikely gloss on "But what is the pleasure of it?"; however, I will not press this point now. Perhaps the instrumentalist can find a way to handle challenges like this one. The observationalist account, however, is able to explain the possibility of a challenge without undue forcing. Just as "I just believe it" can (in appropriate circumstances) be challenged by "Well, you shouldn't," so "it's pleasant" can be challenged by, "No, it isn't," or "Well, it shouldn't be": roughly, by claiming that it's *not*, after all, desirable.

The observationalist account, then, accommodates one of the two insights most partial to the instrumentalist view. (The other is the already discussed fact that "You wouldn't have chosen it if it weren't pleasant" is so often true.) But pleasure also seems plausible as a primary goal because it is closely connected with the good—closely enough to be identified with it, or confused with it. Anscombe, for example, criticizes the hedonist account herself, on the grounds that pleasure seems to involve a prior judgment about good.[12] John Stuart Mill famously equates happiness with pleasure, pleasantness with desirability, 'happiness' again with 'desirable', and these with utility. Bentham calls utility "that property in any object, whereby it tends to produce benefit, advantage, pleasure, good, or happiness, (all this in the present case comes to the same thing) ...".[13] Three famous philosophers can't all be wrong: there must be some kind of very close tie between the notions of pleasure, of an object of choice, and of what is good.

Being able to explain this tie is thus a demand legitimately made of an account of pleasure. Conveniently enough, this connection lies at the heart of the observationalist account. From the first-person point of view, they are tied together in just the way that p and 'I believe that p' are. First, a rock-bottom judgment of desirability immediately directed towards the experienced object—that is, on the present account, *pleasure*—just *is* taking it to be desirable. Second, one desires only what one thinks desirable, that is, what one anticipates will turn out to be desirable. But expecting something to turn out to be desirable is, usually, expecting it to be pleasurable.

The roles of pleasure as a terminator of explanation, and as something supposedly invoked by all desire, have been taken as objections to construing pleasure as a sensation: as Anscombe remarks in one of her more authentically Wittgensteinian moods, "Pleasure cannot be an impression; for no impression could have the consequences of pleasure."[14] Nonetheless, philosophers have often been tempted to understand pleasure on the model of sensations. One motivation may have been the instrumentalist's need for a detachable (yet always available) goal. Another may have been linguistic reflex: we talk about something's *feeling* pleasant, for example, and feelings are often confused with sensations. And I think there is a further point. Pleasure seems subject to something like first-person privilege: who to know better whether and how the experience is pleasant than the experiencing individual himself? The experiencing individual *just knows*—he does not have to investigate, or find out, the way one must with other matters of fact. Traditionally, sensations were thought to be the home of this kind of privilege and of privacy, so it is not surprising that pleasure was assimilated to sensation.

On closer examination, neither first-person privilege nor privacy have turned out to be nearly as philosophically robust as it used to be acceptable to assume. Nonetheless, what remains is accommodated by my account. Pleasure plays a role in many ways analogous to that of certain facets of belief. Now belief naturally carries with it a certain first-person privilege; the modest one of being able, usually, to know what one believes without asking or otherwise investigating, and to know how strongly one feels one's beliefs. (There is, of course, no claim of infallibility being made here.) The analogy should make it unsurprising that pleasure exhibits similar features.

It is often objected to sensation accounts of desire that pleasure is too heterogenous to be plausibly taken to be a sensation. What, it is asked, do all the different pleasurable sensations—those experienced while skiing, while reading poetry, while dozing in the sun, and so on—have in common save the trivial property of being pleasant? As Aristotle noticed, there are diverse pleasures proper to particular activities and senses (*EN* 1175a22ff). This fact is a problem for a view that would identify a *single* sensation or quality as the objective of rational deliberation and action; for in what sense is pleasure a *single* objective?[15] Again, rather than consider whether advocates of sensation accounts can parry this objection, I will just note that the fact it adduces is accommodated comfortably by the observationalist account. What do all convictions have in common (what could they be expected to have in common) save the property of being convictions? Beliefs are very different from one another because what each belief is, is mostly a matter of what it is about; and beliefs may be about very dissimilar things. If pleasure is the practical analog of conviction, we should expect pleasures to be very different from one another, and to share only apparent desirability. This is why pleasures are so diverse.

Philosophers uncomfortable with sensation models of pleasure have often adopted adverbial accounts. These philosophers recognize that pleasure is normally experienced in the course of doing something, and they take pleasure to be something about the manner in which the activity is done. This view has its problems: It is hard to say just what it is that all pleasurable activity has in common. (Words like "exuberance" turn up in what are correctly taken to be the central cases; but these are ill-suited to describe naps on a warm summer day.) And it is hard to explain the role of pleasure in justification and choice under this construal.[16] Once more leaving aside the question of whether adverbial views can be defended against these objections, note that on the view I am defending it is clear why pleasure taken in activity seems relatively central. Not only do we make our rock-bottom judgments in the course of whatever it is we are doing, but our deliberative attention to pleasure will be most importantly focused on our activities: we want to know whether what we are doing is going well, if we ought to be doing it, and so we pay special attention to the pleasure or displeasure we take in it. But there will be no adverb (save the uninformative ones, 'pleasurably' and, possibly, 'enjoyably') sure to characterize all pleasurable activities, for activities of the most various kinds may be found desirable.

It should now be far more plausible that when I say "pleasure," I mean *pleasure*. The apparently incompatible motivations of competing theoretical views of pleasure are jointly accommodated by the account developed here. What better indication that this is a theory whose subject matter is that of the other theories of pleasure—that is, pleasure? Perhaps, however, I should acknowledge that there is one motivation for theories of pleasure that I have chosen not to try to make room for. That is the thought that there must be some commensurable quantity to be maximized if rational choice is to be always possible. (There may be a further thought, that our moral life would be much simpler if there were such a commensurable quantity.[17]) I believe the conception of practical reasoning expressed by this thought to be seriously mistaken, and I do not feel that I need to be concessive toward it.

V   OBJECTIONS

I will now examine three further objections. First, consider someone who desires a piece of chocolate cake because it will be pleasurable. On my account, the anticipated pleasure just is the experience of finding the cake desirable; so I must say he desires the cake because he wants to find it desirable. But this is unenlightening, peculiar-sounding, and simply misses the point of the appeal to *pleasure*.[18]

The way out of this problem requires not accepting too quickly the claim that he desires the cake because he wants the pleasure he gets when he eats it. Rather, what the person desires are the *sensations* he will get when eating the cake, and these will be pleasurable—that is, the kind of sensations he will find to be rock-bottom desirable. Normally one does not have to distinguish feelings from the sensations they involve, but here we have no choice. Pleasure is not a sensation, and what the man wants from the chocolate cake is sensations, sensations that will be desirable when he gets them.[19]

I have been arguing that pleasure permits the analog, in practical reasoning, of observation: that is, that reasoning that involves pleasure is a practical form of *empirical* reasoning. But it might be objected that the theoretical and practical versions of empirical reasoning differ fundamentally, and that this is displayed in the fact that theoretical empirical reasoning exhibits convergence, whereas practical empirical reasoning does not. The difference, it will be suggested, is this. Genuine observation is intersubjective, but pleasures are idiosyncratic. This raises the question whether our initial worry regarding the ungroundedness of practical reasoning has in fact been addressed.

The objection needs to be qualified before it can be answered. First, there is not quite as much convergence in theoretical empirical reasoning as the objection seems to suppose; observation is not always as intersubjective as all that. Science converges, but not all empirical reasoning is science. In Almodovar's *Women on the Verge of a Nervous Breakdown* there is a character who looks like a Picasso: as though her face were one of those figures both of whose eyes are on the same side. I see the resemblance, and so do some other people I have spoken to; but not everyone, even among those familiar with Picasso, does. And I am not quite willing to insist that anyone who does not see the resemblance is wrong. Not all observation is properly understood on the model of identifying the colors of medium-sized dry-goods under good light.[20] Second, there is somewhat more convergence in judgments of desirability than the objection supposes. After all, many pleasures are sufficiently standardized to support large industries.

But even with the contrast between theoretical and practical empirical reasoning muted by these qualifications, there still seems to be a remainder of tolerated nonconvergence unaccounted for. We are more tolerant of disagreement as to what is pleasurable than of disagreement in observation: "There's no accounting for taste." "*Chacun son goût.*"

There is, however, a simple way to accommodate this toleration. It is an unmysterious fact that different things are desirable for different people. To the extent that pleasure covaries with these differences, variation in pleasure may be accounted for in terms of the reliability of (the practical analog of) observation. True, there will be cases in which we do not want to say that differences in desirability account for differences in pleasure, and in which we are unwilling to correct the pleasures of either party. But these are likely to be cases in which the disagreement does not matter very much. Here the toleration may be on a par with the toleration of diverging beliefs that we do not think matter very much.

A further difficulty lies in the transience of pleasure. As identical rock-bottom beliefs accumulate, conviction strengthens, but as identical "observations" of desirability accumulate, pleasure—it will be objected —gives way to boredom. Pleasure cannot be, consequently, a proper analog of conviction.

This objection, however, rests on a simple confusion. If I look twenty times for the milk in the refrigerator, each time I find it confirms a constant fact: that the milk has been in the refrigerator throughout. In contrast, the twentieth cup of milk is not as desirable as the first; that I find it less pleasurable is a sign of the reliability of my judgment. In this, it is no different from belief: were I to make repeated observations of some changing state of affairs (say, a state of affairs that was changing *because* I was making repeated observations of it) I should find that my convictions changed with it. For example, I can request a record of my checking account's activity, for a three dollar charge. If I do this repeatedly, I shall find less and less in my account.[21]

I have argued that pleasure plays an important role in practical reasoning, but not the role the hedonist supposes it has: pleasure is not (usually) the goal of instrumental reasoning; rather, it makes possible a practical analog of induction to be used in deliberation of ends. In so arguing, I have proposed an account of pleasure: pleasure is a rock-bottom judgment of desirability immediately directed towards (objects of) present experience. As the objections just treated show, my account involves some forcing. (For example, we must say that what I desire of the chocolate cake is not pleasure, but sensations, which are pleasurable.) But I think the forcing is not excessive, and I think the account does better than competing accounts. Each of these is developed around one insight regarding pleasure, and has its strength in its ability to represent that insight; but each is vulnerable to attack by an account developed around a competing insight. The account I have proposed tries to accommodate the central insights of the other competing accounts of pleasure jointly. To the extent that it succeeds in this, it is a plausible theory of pleasure in its own right.

VI INSTRUMENTALISM AND SPECIFICATIONISM

If my account of pleasure is correct, it provides reasons for thinking that instrumentalist views of practical reasoning, that is, views on which all practical reasoning consists in choosing means to given ends, are mistaken. First, the inductive or empirical practical reasoning in which pleasure figures is not a technique for determining means to given ends, but a way of determining the ends themselves. Our discussion of pleasure thus provides us with a counterexample to the instrumentalist thesis by exhibiting an alternative form of practical reasoning.

Second, instrumentalist views tend to transform themselves, when pressed, into positions that attribute to agents single and necessary goals. Consider a train of reasoning which begins with my desire for a blender, and which ends with my deciding that I want a food processor instead— even though getting a food processor is not a way of getting a blender. Instrumentalist construals of such cases typically posit background desires to which both my initial and terminal desires stand in relations of instrumental justification: my real desire, the instrumentalist will claim, is for (say) a glitzy counter appliance, and acquiring a food processor is a better way of satisfying that desire than acquiring a blender.

The instrumentalist wishes to posit background desires in a way that does not seem simply *ad hoc*. But the attribution of a particular desire (such as a desire for a new counter appliance) can be called into question in various ways. For example, I can continue the train of reasoning: upon further deliberation, I discard the desire for a food processor in favor of a new assortment of expensive spices. Now the posited background desire cannot be for a counter appliance; it will have to be for something more general, e.g., excitement in the kitchen.

As the instrumentalist is pressed toward more general desires, he is likely to look for a desire whose ascription cannot be dislodged in this way; and he is likely to look for desires to ascribe that will resist the charge of *ad hoc*-ness. Very general desires, with objects like pleasure, happiness, or desire-satisfaction, tend to get invoked at this point: they are a natural resting place. (Appeal to these desires can also address the problem of the apparent arbitrariness of one's ultimate ends: even if they are not instrumentally justifiable, they may be supposed to be psychologically necessary, and at least in that sense not arbitrary.)

Attempting to save instrumentalism by construing happiness as an ultimate goal has the following problem: While it is plausibly said that everyone does desire happiness, happiness is a dummy goal, one that itself has no content. Happiness cannot be used as a starting point for instrumental reasoning without determining in what happiness would consist; the components of happiness must be identified, and arranged into a coherently organized goal that can be pursued.[22] Attempting to use happiness to save the thesis that all practical reasoning is instrumental has the effect of implausibly declaring the reasoning by which one arrives at one's conception of happiness to be theoretical rather than practical reasoning.[23]

If happiness is shown to be an unpromising option for the instrumentalist, he is likely to turn to pleasure, which has the advantage of appearing to be a more substantive notion than happiness.[24] But to take pleasure as one's ultimate and necessary end is just to adopt some form of hedonism. In short, if I am right about the ways in which instrumentalist views of practical reasoning can be pushed towards hedonism, then the account of pleasure developed here, by showing that hedonism is mistaken, provides a further reason for thinking that instrumentalist accounts of practical reason are mistaken.

In dismissing the instrumentalist's appeal to happiness, I invoked an occasionally discussed alternative to means-ends reasoning, the specification of ends; I will conclude by considering briefly the role of pleasure in exercising this alternative.[25] Deliberation consists, on the specificationist account, not, or not only, in determining what would be a means to one's already given ends, but in coming to understand what would constitute realizing a vaguely specified end, such as *eudaemonia*, having an entertaining evening, a good constitution for the body politic, or a cure for an illness.[26]

Now while it is clear enough that we do engage in mental activity of this kind, it may be less clear that this activity is subject to the normative constraints that would allow us to regard it as reasoning or as deliberation, properly so-called. In fact, two of the four just-cited expositors of the specificationist view deny that specification of ends is a form of reasoning. Kolnai describes it as "shot through with arbitrariness," and "an inherently deceptive, not to say deceitful operation ...";[27] and Broadie, in a passage that perhaps clarifies Kolnai's qualms about the specification of ends, presents an argument to the effect that such specification cannot be "inferential": because the specification of an end

is a move from the less to the more determinate, which latter, precisely because it is more determinate, cannot be entailed by what is less so. It might seem that with suitable extra premises there could be a logically acceptable inference from the indeterminate to the determinate end. After all, there is no acceptable inference from the determinate end to the means except via additional [empirical] premises.... But ... what additional premises would do the trick? (a) Factual premises, whether particular or general, would not help; nor (b) would any purely logical propositions. The addition (c) of some formal propositions about *eupraxia* [the particular end whose specification Broadie is discussing], such as that it is 'self-sufficient' or 'lacking in nothing', would not logically enable one to interpret the pursuit of *eupraxia* as the pursuit of *S* (where *S* is something more specific); whereas (d) inserting a premise that specifies *eupraxia* substantially might of course sustain the inference to a no less substantial conclusion, but only by thrusting back to an earlier stage the problem of how such propositions are obtained in the first place.[28]

Suppose I am faced with the problem mentioned by Williams, that of deciding what would make for an entertaining evening. Mummenschanz is at the McCarter Theater, and I have not seen them, nor, I gather, anything like them, before. I have factual premises, in the form of a friend's description ("they mime inanimate objects"), and these premises do not help. Logical and formal propositions do not help either. What I need is a premise of Broadie's type (d), one that specifies my end of being entertained substantially and in the relevant respects: I need to know whether Mummenschanz will *count as* entertainment, that is, whether it will *be* entertaining.

As Broadie insists, the demand for such premises raises "the problem of how such propositions are obtained in the first place." She evidently intends mention of the problem to have the force of a rhetorical question, since she concludes that no such premises are available. But consideration of a concrete situation in which the demand arises makes it obvious how such premises *are* obtained: I can *go* to McCarter, and discover, by *observation*, whether Mummenschanz is entertaining or not. That is, specification of ends can be understood to be a form of rational deliberation, but one that, like the practical analog of induction, relies essentially on practical experience. (Testimony may of course take the place of experience, as when I am told not only that the performance is mime of such-and-such a kind, but that it is vastly entertaining. But here I rely on experience indirectly.)

The example reminds us that actual judgments of desirability, experiential or otherwise, are normally a good deal richer than those to which I have, for expository convenience, largely confined myself. To attend the performance and thereby discover that Mummenschanz is vastly entertaining is of course to discover that attending the performance is in certain respects desirable, and it is to have taken a good deal of pleasure in the performance, but my response, and what I have found out, is not exhausted by these descriptions. A more adequate account of practical observation would take up the task of characterizing these richer experiences.

Acknowledgments

I'm grateful to Alyssa Bernstein, Hilary Bok, Arthur Collins, Christoph Fehige, Tamar Laddy, Robert Nozick, Hilary Putnam, Henry Richardson, Tim Scanlon, Mark Shelton, Candace Vogler, and Leif Wenar for commenting on earlier drafts and for helpful discussion; and to the participants in Harvard's *n*th-year seminar for their objections and suggestions.

Notes

1. I'm grateful to Michelle Desaulniers for the example.

2. On this point, see Gosling, 1969, pp. 46f, and below, sec. 5.

3. Real name withheld on request.

4. Although traditionally 'pain' has been used to mean the converse of pleasure I will use words like 'displeasure' and 'unpleasant' instead, since, first, while pain is generally unpleasant, many things are unpleasant but not painful, and second, we need a name for the sensations we normally call 'pain', and since pleasure is a feeling rather than a sensation, its contrary should be a feeling as well. The example makes the traditional usage understandable; it is all too natural to describe Pat's experience as painful. Because physical sensations of pain typically make it difficult or impossible to continue doing what one is doing, physical pain occupies much the same role as the more central cases of unpleasantness that we are now considering. This explains why it is natural to extend the word 'pain' to instances such as this one.

5. For related considerations, see Anscombe, 1985, pp. 70ff. Notice that I am not claiming that one cannot desire something under one aspect while failing to judge it desirable in another respect, or even while judging it undesirable, all things considered.

   I have found that it is still difficult for some philosophers to believe the claim put forward in the text. For their benefit, it is worth noting that its role here is heuristic: it is used to introduce my account of pleasure, but the account itself does not depend on it.

6. It may be argued that inference *must* have taken place, perhaps unconsciously. But if unconscious inference is taking place in cases like these, then we can either restrict the term 'rock-bottom belief' to cases in which not even unconscious inferences occur, or we can allow it to apply where unconscious inferences are found. I will be using the notion of rock-bottom belief to help the reader pick out a certain kind of experience or feeling. Since distinguishing between cases in which unconscious inferences are being made, and those in which they aren't, wouldn't be useful for this purpose, adopting the restriction wouldn't be helpful.

7. Or, at any rate, I am not aware of the unconscious inferences by which I acquired it. I may be able to provide arguments from other (background) beliefs from which I *could* have inferred it; and sometimes I will actually fall back on these. The situation I am now interested in is one in which I do not fall back on further beliefs.

8. This technical use of the word 'conviction' is not as far a cry from its ordinary use as might be thought. When asked to list one's convictions—the things about which one has this feeling—one normally produces, say, points of religious or political or moral doctrine, rather than beliefs about what's in the refrigerator. And this might suggest that conviction is rather rare. But I am claiming that conviction is a feeling, rather than a sensation, which is to say that one is not always aware of it. One may be made aware of the feeling by a challenge; if someone exerts pressure on my claim to know where I live, I shall become aware of a feeling of conviction as deeply-rooted as those attached to any of my political views. One may be inclined to say of cases in which one may have conviction on a particular point without being aware of it that one has the conviction without the feeling. Similarly (to anticipate) one may take pleasure in an activity without being aware of it; in such circumstances one may be inclined to say that one is having pleasure, but not a *feeling* of pleasure. (Cf. Gosling, 1969, pp. 47–53.) But since I am distinguishing feelings from sensations in part by the claim that one can be unaware of one's feelings, I will use 'conviction' and 'feeling of conviction' indifferently (and 'pleasure' and 'feeling of pleasure' as well).

9. See Millgram, 1997, chap. 2, for related discussion.

10. I am tempted to think that a partial explanation for the paradox of hedonism (that is, the fact that many of the activities we engage in could not yield pleasure if their goal were understood to be pleasure) may be found here. Cf. Sidgwick, 1907/1981, pp. 48ff.

11. Anscombe, 1985, p. 78.

12. If I am correct, this is not quite right: the judgment is not *prior*; rather, the pleasure just is the judgment.

13. Mill, 1861/1969, pp. 209f., 234, 237; Bentham, 1789/1996, p. 12.

14. Anscombe, 1985, p. 77.

15. On this point, see Gosling, 1969, pp. 28–53.

16. For a fuller discussion, see Gosling, 1969, pp. 54–85.

17. Cf. Nussbaum, this volume, chap. 8.

18. This objection is due to Alyssa Bernstein.

19. More generally, it may be experiencing the desirable features of the cake that one is looking forward to; one need not think of oneself as a consumer of sensations.

This distinction, incidentally, makes masochism conceptually unproblematic. Masochists are people who take pleasure in pain, and the existence of such people presents a problem for philosophers who hold pain to be the converse of pleasure. (Athletes might be a less exotic case of people who can find painful sensations pleasurable.) But if the pain masochists allegedly take pleasure in is a *sensation*, then it is not the converse of pleasure, since pleasure is not, on my account, a sensation. What sensations are found pleasurable is not a matter of the logic of the notion of pleasure: while there may be good reasons for pain being not *normally* pleasurable, there is no reason in principle why sensations of pain could not engender rock-bottom judgments of desirability, that is, be pleasurable.

20. There is no general, nontrivial account of what makes observation, observation: the explanation of what makes seeing that a chair is brown an observation will have precious little in common with the explanation of what makes seeing that a face looks like a Picasso an observation. So we should not expect a general, nontrivial account of what makes a practical observation, a practical observation.

21. The objection is also in error in its claim that repeated pleasures always become less pleasurable: repeated wine tasting, or sexual experiences with a particular partner, or encounters with an exotic cuisine, may make those things much more pleasurable than they were found to be at first acquaintance.

Notice that although Nature has equipped us with rock-bottom dispositions to judge this or that desirable—say, to find food desirable after a moderately lengthy fast—pleasure depends in large part on one's tastes. Now tastes, when educated, amount to taste (if not necessarily to good taste), and taste plays much the same role in our rock-bottom judgments of desirability that certain kinds of background beliefs play in our acquiring rock-bottom convictions. For example, while I do not *infer* that I enjoy the painting from my knowledge of its merits, the pleasure I take in it does depend on my having that knowledge. This is why taste can be both spontaneous and informed by belief, discrimination, and so on. Explaining how this can be the case is one of the problems a theory of taste must address. (Cf. Schaper, 1987.) That the present account of pleasure provides means of addressing this difficulty suggests that it may be on the right track.

22. Desire-satisfaction theories must address this problem as well. Given that one's desires typically are too much at cross-purposes to be thought of as a single, coherent goal, before embarking on instrumental reasoning proceeding toward the goal of desire-satisfaction, a way must be found to rank, arrange and organize the desires that one proposes to try to satisfy.

23. This is not to say that the notion of happiness plays *no* role in practical reasoning: of course it does. I am inclined to think that its function is very like that of what Kant called regulative ideals. One must act on the assumption that it is possible to arrange one's central (and, maybe, not-so-central) goals into a coherent and (in principle) satisfiable goal or life-plan: taken together, the things one (really) wants make up a picture of a life well-lived. This may not in fact be the case; having to act as though one's ends allow this does not entail that they actually do. (Kant distinguished regulative ideals from the necessary preconditions of the possibility of experience.)

24. This advantage may be only apparent. We remarked on the diversity of pleasures above. If pleasures are so different from one another that they are not immediately commensurable, organizing one's pleasures into a single coherent goal is also a precondition of using pleasure as a starting point for instrumental reasoning.

25. Prominent advocates include Kolnai (this volume, chap. 12), Richardson (1986; 1990), Wiggins (this volume, chap. 13) and Broadie (1987).

26. For these examples, see *EN* 1095a16–21, Williams, this volume, p. 80, Kolnai, this volume, pp. 259–260.

27. Kolnai, this volume, pp. 268, 272.

28. Broadie, 1987, pp. 238f. Her argument involves a problematic premise: that the more determinate cannot be inferentially extracted from the less. After all, if the determinateness of one's starting point is not *stipulatively* linked to the determinateness of one's conclusion, we may expect to find any number of counter-examples in which determinateness increases as the inference is traversed. (Turning over several indistinct and obscure recollections of the previous day, I suddenly realize *exactly* what Sandra is up to.) I believe that the problematic premise may be defended; however, I will not further consider the issue here.

References

Anscombe, G. E. M. 1985. *Intention*. Second ed. Cornell University Press, Ithaca, N.Y.

Bentham, Jeremy. 1789/1996. *An Introduction to the Principles of Morals and Legislation*. Edited by J. Burns and H. L. A Hart. Clarendon Press, Oxford.

Broadie, S. W. 1987. "The Problem of Practical Intellect in Aristotle's *Ethics*." In J. Cleary, editor, *Proceedings of the Boston Area Colloquium in Ancient Philosophy*, vol. 3, pages 229–252. University Press of America, Lanham, Md. With a response by Henry Richardson.

Gosling, J. C. B. 1969. *Pleasure and Desire: The Case for Hedonism Reviewed*. Clarendon Press, Oxford.

Kolnai, A. 1978. "Deliberation Is of Ends." This volume, chap. 12.

Mill, J. S. 1861/1969. *Utilitarianism*. In his *Collected Works*, vol. 10, edited by J. Robson. University of Toronto Press, Toronto.

Millgram, E. 1997. *Practical Induction*. Harvard University Press, Cambridge.

Nussbaum, M. 1986. "The *Protagoras:* A Science of Practical Reasoning." This volume, chap. 8.

Richardson, H. S. 1986. "Rational Deliberation of Ends." Ph.D. thesis, Harvard University.

Richardson, H. S. 1990. "Specifying Norms as a Way to Resolve Concrete Ethical Problems." *Philosophy and Public Affairs* 19 (4): 279–310.

Schaper, E. 1987. "The Pleasures of Taste." In E. Schaper, editor, *Pleasure, Preference, and Value*, pages 39–56. Cambridge University Press, Cambridge.

Sidgwick, H. 1907/1981. *The Methods of Ethics*. Hackett, Indianapolis.

Wiggins, D. 1980. "Deliberation and Practical Reason." This volume, chap. 13.

Williams, B. 1981. "Internal and External Reasons." This volume, chap. 4.

Chapter 16

How to Make Decisions: Coherence, Emotion, and Practical Inference

Paul Thagard

Students face many important decisions: What college or university should I attend? What should I study? What kind of job should I try to get? Which people should I hang out with? Should I continue or break off a relationship? Should I get married? Should I have a baby? What kind of medical treatment should I use? A theory of practical reasoning should have something to say about how students and other people can improve their decision making.

I regularly teach a first-year course on critical thinking intended to help students improve their reasoning about what to believe and what to do. After spending about two thirds of the course on ways of improving judgments about the truth and falsity of controversial claims in areas such as medicine and pseudoscience, I devote the last third to practical reasoning, with the focus on how people can make better decisions. I discuss the kinds of erroneous reasoning that decision makers commonly fall into, and some systematic models proposed by psychologists, economists, and philosophers to specify how people *should* make decisions.

Many students in the course dislike these models and resist the claim that using them is preferable to making decisions simply by intuition. They trust their "gut feelings" more than they trust the analytical methods that require a systematic and mathematical comparative assessment of competing actions that satisfy multiple criteria. The textbooks I use (most recently Gilovich 1991, Russo and Schoemaker 1989, Schick and Vaughn 1999) encourage people to avoid the use of intuition and instead to base their judgments and decisions on reasoning strategies that are less likely to lead to common errors in reasoning. From this perspective, decision making should be a matter of calculation, not intuition.

While I agree that intuition-based decision making can lead to many problems, I also think that calculation-based decision making of the sort recommended by psychologists and economists has some serious pitfalls. In this chapter I will try to offer a synthesis and partial reconciliation of intuition and calculation models of decision making, using a recently developed theory of emotional coherence (Thagard 2000). This theory builds on a previous coherence-based theory of decision making developed in collaboration with Elijah Millgram. Understanding decision making in terms of emotional coherence enables us to appreciate the merits of both intuition and calculation as contributors to effective practical reasoning.

DECISION AS INTUITION

Suppose that you are a student trying to decide whether to study a liberal-arts subject, like philosophy or art history, in which you have a strong interest or a subject, such as economics or computer science, that may lead to a more lucrative career. To make this decision intuitively is just to go with the option supported by your emotional reactions to the two alternatives. You may have a strongly positive gut feeling toward the more interesting subject along with a strongly negative feeling about the more career-oriented one, or your feelings may be just the opposite. More likely is that you feel positive feelings toward both alternatives, along with accompanying anxiety caused by your inability to see a clearly preferable option. In the end, intuitive decision makers choose an option based on what their emotional reactions tell them is preferable.

There is much to be said for intuitive decision making. One obvious advantage is speed: an emotional reaction can be immediate and lead directly to a decision. If your choice is between chocolate and vanilla ice cream, it would be pointless to spend a lot of time and effort deliberating about the relative advantages and disadvantages of the two flavors. Instead, an emotional reaction such as "Chocolate—yum!" can make for a quick and appropriate decision. Another advantage is that basing your decisions on emotions helps to ensure that the decisions take into account what you really care about. If you are pleased and excited about a possible action, that is a good sign that the action promises to accomplish the goals that are genuinely important to you. Finally, decisions based on emotional intuitions lead directly to action: the positive feeling toward an option will motivate you to carry it out.

But emotion-based intuitive decision making can also have some serious disadvantages. An option may seem emotionally appealing because of failure to consider other available options. Intuition may suggest buying chocolate ice cream only because you have failed to consider a lower-fat alternative that would be a healthier choice. Intuition is also subject to the intense craving that drug addicts call "jonesing." If you are jonesing for cocaine, a pizza, or a Mercedes-Benz convertible, your intuition will tell you to choose what you crave, but only because the craving has emotionally swamped other desires that you will be more aware of when the craving is less intense.

Another problem with intuition is that it may be based on inaccurate or irrelevant information. Suppose that you need to decide whom to hire for a job. If you are prejudiced against people of a particular sex, race, or ethnicity, then your intuition will tell you not to hire them, even if they have better qualifications for doing the job well. It is difficult to determine introspectively whether your intuitions derive from reliable and relevant information.

Finally, intuitive reasoning is problematic in group situations where decisions need to be made collectively. If other people disagree with your choices, you cannot simply contend that your intuitions are stronger or better than the intuitions of others. Defending your emotional reactions and attempting to reach a consensus with other people requires a more analytical approach than simply expressing your gut feelings.

DECISION AS CALCULATION

Experts on decision making recommend a more systematic and calculating approach. For example, Bazerman (1994, 4) says that rational decision making should include the following six steps:

1. Define the problem, characterizing the general purpose of your decision.
2. Identify the criteria, specifying the goals or objectives that you want to accomplish.
3. Weight the criteria, deciding the relative importance of the goals.
4. Generate alternatives, identifying possible courses of action that might accomplish your various goals.
5. Rate each alternative on each criterion, assessing the extent to which each action would accomplish each goal.
6. Compute the optimal decision, evaluating each alternative by multiplying the expected effectiveness of each alternative with respect to a criterion times the weight of the criterion, then adding up the expected value of the alternative with respect to all criteria.

We can then pick the alternative with the highest expected value and make a decision based on calculation, not on subjective emotional reactions. Using slightly different terminology, Russo and Schoemaker (1989, chap. 6) recommend essentially the same kind of decision-making process based on multiple weighted factors.

Some students dismiss this kind of process as robotlike and find it offensive that important decisions in their lives might be made mathematically. A cartoon in the *New Yorker* (Jan. 10, 2000, p. 74) shows a man sitting at a computer and saying to a woman, "I've done the numbers, and I will marry you." Some decisions, at least, seem inappropriately based on doing the numbers. But is the emotional dismissal of Bazerman's 6-step calculation method justified? We can certainly see some notable advantages of the calculation method over the intuition method. First, it is set up to avoid neglecting relevant alternatives and goals. Second, it makes explicit the consideration of how the various alternatives contribute to the various goals. Third, it puts the decision-making process out in the open, enabling it to be carefully reviewed by a particular decision maker and also by others involved in a group decision process.

However, the calculation method of decision making may be more difficult and less effective than decision experts claim. Suppose that you are trying to decide between two courses of study, say philosophy versus computer science, and you systematically list all the relevant criteria such as how interesting you find the subjects and how well they fit with your career plans. You then weight the criteria and estimate the extent to which each option satisfies them and proceed to a calculation of the expected value of the competing choices. Having done this, you find that the expected value of one option, say philosophy, exceeds that of the other. But what if you then have the reaction "I don't want to do that!" Your emotional reaction need not be crazy, because it may be that the numerical weights that you put on your criteria do not reflect what you really care about. Moreover, your estimates about the extent to which different actions accomplish your goals may be very subjective and fluid, so your unconscious estimation is at least as good as your conscious one. I once knew someone who told me that she made decisions by first flipping a coin, with heads for one option and tails for another. When the coin came up heads, she would note her emotional reaction, which gave her a better idea of whether she really wanted the option associated with heads. She then used this emotional information to help her make a choice between the two options.

There is empirical evidence that calculation may sometimes be inferior to intuition in making good judgments. Damasio (1994) describes people with injuries that have disconnected the parts of their brains that perform verbal reasoning and numerical calculation from emotional centers such as the amygdala. With their abstract-reasoning abilities intact, you might think that the patients become paragons of rationality, like Spock or Data in *Star Trek*. On the contrary, these patients tend to make poor interpersonal decisions. Damasio conjectures that the deficiencies arise because the brain damage prevents the patients from making emotional evaluations with the aid of *somatic markers*, bodily states that indicate the positive or negative emotional value of different possibilities. The problem is that the patients just do not know what they care about. Wilson and Schooler (1991) report research that shows that there are domains where people's intuitive judgments may be more effective than their more systematic, deliberative ones. They studied college students' preferences for brands of strawberry jam and for college courses, and they found that students who were asked to analyze the reasons for their preferences ended up with choices that corresponded less with expert opinion than did the choices of less analytical students. Wilson and Schooler conjecture that this happens because analyzing reasons can focus people's attention on relatively unimportant criteria. Lieberman (2000) argues that intuitions are often based on unconscious learning processes that can be interfered with by attempts at explicit learning.

It seems, therefore, that we need a model of decision making that is more psychologically natural and more normatively effective than the calculation model. I will now argue that we can get better accounts of how decisions are made and of how they should be made by understanding practical inference in terms of emotional coherence.

DECISION AS COHERENCE

Decision making is a kind of inference, but what is inference? Many philosophers have taken deductive logic as the model for inference. Here is a sort of deductive practical inference:

Whenever you want ice cream, you should order chocolate.
You want ice cream.
Therefore, you should order chocolate.

Unfortunately, we rarely have general rules that tell us exactly what to do, so deduction is not a good model for practical inference. A second familiar model of inference is calculation, useful for example in solving arithmetical problems and working with probability theory. But there is a third general model of inference that advocates the following rule: accept a representation if and only if it coheres maximally with the rest of your representations. Many philosophers have advocated coherence theories of inference but have left rather vague how to maximize coherence (see, e.g., Harman 1986, Brink 1989, and Hurley 1989). A precise and general model of coherence-based inference can be constructed in terms of constraint satisfaction (Thagard and Verbeurgt 1998, Thagard 2000).

When we make sense of a text, picture, person, or event, we need to construct an interpretation that fits with the available information better than alternative interpretations. The best interpretation is one that provides the most coherent account of what we want to understand, considering both pieces of information that fit with each other and pieces of information that do not fit with each other. For example, when we meet unusual people, we may consider different combinations of concepts and hypotheses that fit together to make sense of their behavior.

Coherence can be understood in terms of maximal satisfaction of multiple constraints, in a manner informally summarized as follows:

1. Elements are representations such as concepts, propositions, parts of images, goals, actions, and so on.
2. Elements can cohere (fit together) or incohere (resist fitting together). Coherence relations include explanation, deduction, facilitation, association, and so on. Incoherence relations include inconsistency, incompatibility, and negative association.
3. If two elements cohere, there is a positive constraint between them. If two elements incohere, there is a negative constraint between them.
4. Elements are to be divided into ones that are accepted and ones that are rejected.
5. A positive constraint between two elements can be satisfied either by accepting both of the elements or by rejecting both of the elements.
6. A negative constraint between two elements can be satisfied only by accepting one element and rejecting the other.
7. The coherence problem consists of dividing a set of elements into accepted and rejected sets in a way that satisfies the most constraints.

Computing coherence is a matter of maximizing constraint satisfaction and can be approximately accomplished by several different algorithms. The most psychologically appealing models of coherence optimization are provided by connectionist algorithms. These use neuronlike units to represent elements and excitatory and inhibitory links to represent positive and negative constraints. Settling a connectionist network by spreading activation results in the activation (acceptance) of some units and the deactivation (rejection) of others. Coherence can be measured in terms of the degree of constraint satisfaction accomplished by the various algorithms. In general, the computational problem of exactly maximizing coherence is very difficult, but there are effective algorithms for approximately maximizing coherence in terms of constraint satisfaction (Thagard and Verbeurgt 1998).

I will now make this account of coherence more concrete by showing how it applies to inference about what to do. Elijah Millgram and I have argued that practical inference involves coherence judgments about how to fit together various possible actions and goals (Millgram and Thagard 1996, Thagard and Millgram 1995). On our account, the elements are actions and goals, the positive constraints are based on facilitation relations (the action of going to Paris facilitates my goal of having fun), and the negative constraints are based on incompatibility relations (you cannot go to Paris and London at the same time). Deciding what to do is based on inference to the most coherent plan, where coherence involves evaluating goals as well as deciding what to do.

More exactly, deliberative coherence can be specified by the following principles:

Principle 1: Symmetry   Coherence and incoherence are symmetrical relations: if factor (action or goal) F_1 coheres with factor F_2, then F_2 coheres with F_1.

Principle 2: Facilitation   Consider actions $A_1, \ldots, A_n$ that together facilitate the accomplishment of goal G. Then (a) each A_i coheres with G, (b) each A_i coheres with each other A_j, and (c) the greater the number of actions required, the less the coherence among the actions and goals.

Principle 3: Incompatibility   (a) If two factors cannot both be performed or achieved, then they are strongly incoherent. (b) If two factors are difficult to perform or achieve together, then they are weakly incoherent.

Principle 4: Goal priority   Some goals are desirable for intrinsic or other noncoherence reasons.

Principle 5: Judgment   Facilitation and competition relations can depend on coherence with judgments about the acceptability of factual beliefs.

Principle 6: Decision   Decisions are made on the basis of an assessment of the overall coherence of a set of actions and goals.

In order to assess overall coherence, we can use the computer program DECO (short for "Deliberative Coherence"). DECO represents each element (goal or action) by a neuronlike unit in an artificial neural network and then spreads activation through the network in a way that activates some units and deactivates others. At the end of the spread of activation, the active units represent elements that are accepted, while the deactivated ones represent elements that are rejected. DECO provides an efficient and usable way to compute the most coherent set of actions and goals.

At first glance, deliberative coherence might seem like a variant of the calculation model of decision making. Figuring out which action best coheres with your goals sounds like Bazerman's calculation of the expected value of alternatives based on the extent to which they satisfy weighted criteria. But there are some crucial differences. Unlike Bazerman's proposal, the deliberative-coherence model of decision does not take the weights of the goals as fixed. In DECO, units representing some of the goals get initial activation in accord with principle 4, goal priority, but their impact depends on their relation to other goals: even a basic goal can be deactivated, at least partially, by other goals. The impact of goals on decision making depends on their activation, which depends on their relation to other goals and to various actions. For example, students trying to decide what to do on the weekend might start off thinking that what they most want to do is to have fun, but then they realize that having fun is not so important, because it conflicts with other goals, such as studying for an important exam or saving money to pay next term's tuition.

Psychologically, decision as coherence is very different from decision as calculation. Calculations are conscious and explicit, displayable to everyone on pencil and paper. In contrast, if coherence maximization in human brains is similar to what happens in the artificial neural networks used in DECO, then assessment of coherence is a process not accessible to consciousness. What comes to consciousness is only the result of the process of coherence maximization: the realization that a particular action is the one I want to perform. Thus, as an account of how decisions are made by people, deliberative coherence is closer to the intuition model of decision than to the calculation model. Coherence is maximized not by an explicit, consciously accessible calculation but by an unconscious process whose output is the intuition that one action is preferable to others. There is, however, a major difference between the deliberative-coherence account of decision making and the intuition account: intuitions about what to do are usually emotional, involving feelings that one action is a good thing to do and that alternatives are bad things to do. Fortunately, coherence theory can naturally be extended to encompass emotional judgments.

EMOTIONAL COHERENCE

In the theory of coherence stated above, elements have the epistemic status of being accepted or rejected. We can also speak of the degree of acceptability, which in artificial neural-network models of coherence is interpreted as the degree of activation of the unit that represents the element. I propose that elements in coherence systems have, in addition to acceptability, an emotional *valence*, which can be positive or negative. Depending on the nature of what the element represents, the valence of an element can indicate likability, desirability, or other positive or negative attitude. For example, the valence of Mother Theresa for most people is highly positive, while the valence of Adolf Hitler is highly negative. Many other researchers have previously proposed introducing emotion into cognitive models by adding valences or affective tags (Bower 1981, 1991; Fiske and Pavelchak 1986; Lodge and Stroh 1993; Ortony, Clore, and Collins 1988; Sears, Huddy, and Schaffer 1986). Kahneman (1999) reviews experimental evidence that evaluation on the good/bad dimension is a ubiquitous component of human thinking.

Just as elements are related to each other by the positive and negative deliberative constraints described in the last section, so they also can be related by positive and negative valence constraints. Some elements have intrinsic positive and negative valences, for example, *pleasure* and *pain*. Other elements can acquire valences by virtue of their connections with elements that have intrinsic valences. These connections can be special valence constraints, or they can be any of the constraints posited by the theory of deliberative coherence. For example, if someone has a positive association between the concepts of *dentist* and *pain*, where *pain* has an intrinsic negative valence, then *dentist* can acquire a negative valence. However, just as the acceptability of an element depends on the acceptability of all the elements that constrain it, so the valence of an element depends on the valences of all the elements that constrain it.

The basic theory of emotional coherence can be summarized in three principles analogous to the qualitative principles of coherence above:

1. Elements have positive or negative valences.
2. Elements can have positive or negative emotional connections to other elements.
3. The valence of an element is determined by the valences and acceptability of all the elements to which it is connected.

As already mentioned, coherence can be computed by a variety of algorithms, but the psychologically most appealing model, and the model that first inspired the theory of coherence as constraint satisfaction, employs artificial neural networks. In this connectionist model, elements are represented by units, which are roughly analogous to neurons or neuronal groups. Positive constraints between elements are represented by symmetric excitatory links between units, and negative constraints between elements are represented by symmetric inhibitory links between units. The degree of acceptability of an element is represented by the activation of a unit, which is determined by the activation of all the units linked to it, with the strength of the various excitatory and inhibitory links taken into account.

It is straightforward to expand this kind of model into one that incorporates emotional coherence. In the expanded model, called "HOTCO" for "hot coherence," units have valences as well as activations, and units can have input valences to represent their intrinsic valences. Moreover, valences can spread through the system in a way very similar to the spread of activation, except that valence spread depends in part on activation spread. An emotional decision emerges from the spread of activation and valences through the system because nodes representing some actions receive positive valence and nodes representing other actions receive negative valence. The gut feeling that comes to consciousness is the end result of a complex process of cognitive and emotional constraint satisfaction. Emotional reactions such as happiness, anger, and fear are much more complex than positive and negative valences, so HOTCO is by no means a general model of emotional cognition. But it does capture in a general way how emotional inference produces positive and negative attitudes toward objects, situations, and choices.

It might seem that we can now abandon the cognitive theory of deliberative coherence for the psychologically richer theory of emotional coherence, but that would be a mistake for two reasons. First, emotional coherence must interconnect with other kinds of coherence that involve inferences about what is acceptable as well as about what is emotionally desirable. The valence of an element depends not just on the valences of the elements that constrain it but also on their acceptability. Attaching a negative valence to the concept *dentist*, if it does not already have a negative valence from previous experience, depends both on the negative valence for *causes pain* and the acceptability (confidence) of *causes pain* in the current context. The inferential situation here is analogous to expected utility theory, in which the expected utility of an action is calculated by summing, for various outcomes, the result of multiplying the probability of the outcome times the utility of the outcome. The calculated valence of an element is like the expected utility of an action, with degrees of acceptability analogous to probabilities and valences analogous to utilities. There is no reason, however, to expect degrees of acceptability and valences to have the mathematical properties that define probabilities and utilities. Because the valence calculation depends on the acceptability of all the relevant elements, it can be affected by other kinds of coherence. For example, the inference concerning whether to trust someone depends largely on the valence attached to them based on all the information you have about them, where this information derives in part from inferences based on explanatory, analogical, and conceptual coherence (Thagard 2000).

The second reason for not completely replacing the cold (nonemotional) theory of deliberative coherence with the hot theory of emotional coherence is that people can sometimes come up with incompatible hot and cold judgments about what to do. Unconsciously using deliberative coherence may produce the judgment that you should not do something, while emotional coherence leads you in a different direction. For example, students seeing the first nice spring day at the end of a long Canadian winter might decide emotionally to go outside and enjoy it, while at the same time reasoning that the alternative of finishing up overdue end-of-term projects is more coherent with their central goals, such as graduating from university. I am not the only person capable of thinking, "The best thing for me to do is x, but I'm going to do y." Jonesing in reaction to vivid stimuli can make emotional coherence swamp deliberative coherence.

The theory of emotional coherence provides a psychologically realistic way of understanding the role of intuition in decisions. My gut feeling that I should go to Paris is the result of an unconscious mental process in which various actions and goals are balanced against each other. The coherence process involves both inferences about what I think is true (e.g., I'll have fun in Paris) and inferences about the extent to which my goals will be accomplished. But the coherence computation determines not only what elements will be accepted and rejected but also an emotional reaction to the element. It is not just "Go to Paris—yes" or "Go to Paris—no," but "Go to Paris—yeah!" or "Go to Paris—yuck!"

As we just saw, however, emotional coherence may be better as a descriptive theory of how people make decisions than as a normative theory of how people should make decisions. Judgments based on emotional coherence may be subject to the same criticisms that I made against intuitive decisions: susceptibility to jonesing and to failure to consider the appropriate range of actions and goals. I doubt, however, that people are capable of making decisions without recourse to emotional coherence—that is just how our brains are constituted. For normative purposes, therefore, the best course is to adopt procedures that interact with emotional coherence to produce intuitions that are informed and effective.

USING INTUITION AND EMOTION TO MAKE GOOD DECISIONS

The theory of emotional coherence shows how people's gut feelings about what to do may sometimes emerge from integrative unconscious judgments about the actions that might best accomplish their goals. But it also applies to cases where people's intuitions are too quick and uninformed. How can students and other people be helped to ensure that their decisions are based on *informed* intuition?

For important decisions, I recommend that, rather than leaping to an immediate intuitive choice, people should follow a procedure something like the following:

Informed intuition
1. Set up the decision problem carefully. This requires identifying the goals to be accomplished by your decision and specifying the broad range of possible actions that might accomplish those goals.
2. Reflect on the importance of the different goals. Such reflection will be more emotional and intuitive than just putting a numerical weight on them, but it should help you to be more aware of what you care about in the current decision situation. Identify goals whose importance may be exaggerated because of jonesing or other emotional distortions.

3. Examine beliefs about the extent to which various actions would facilitate the different goals. Are these beliefs based on good evidence? If not, revise them.

4. Make your intuitive judgment about the best action to perform, monitoring your emotional reaction to different options. Run your decision past other people to see if it seems reasonable to them.

This procedure combines the strengths and avoids the weaknesses of the intuition and calculation models of decision making. Like the intuition model, it recognizes that decision making is an unconscious process that involves emotions. Like the calculation model, it aims to avoid decision errors caused by unsystematic and unexamined intuitions. One drawback of the informed-intuition procedure is that it is not so intersubjective as the calculation model, in which the numerical weights and calculations can be laid out on the table for all to see. It would certainly be a useful exercise in many cases for people to go through the steps of producing a calculation in order to provide some information about how different people are seeing the situation. Ultimately, however, the individual decision makers will have to make decisions based on their own intuitive judgments about what is the right thing to do. The members of the group may be poor at specifying the emotional weights they put on different goals, and they may be unaware of their assumptions about the extent to which different actions facilitate different goals. Achieving consensus among a group of decision makers may require extensive discussion that reveals the goals and beliefs of decision makers to themselves as well as to others. It is much easier to identify jonesing and other emotional distortions in others than in yourself. The discussion, including the exercise of working through a calculation together, may help the members of the group converge on evaluations of goal importance and belief plausibility that produce a shared reaction of emotional coherence. Scientific consensus concerning competing scientific theories can emerge from a process of individual coherence and interpersonal communication (Thagard 1999, chap. 7), but conflict resolution concerning what to do requires a more complex process of comparing and communicating the diverse goals driving the various decision makers. A crucial part of this process is becoming aware of the emotional states of others, which may benefit as much from face-to-face interactions involving perception of people's physical communication as from their purely verbal communication.

Informed intuition is a much more complicated process of decision making than the practical syllogism commonly discussed by philosophers. Millgram (1997, 41) gives the following example:

1. Delicious things should be eaten. [Major premise]
2. This cake is delicious. [Minor premise]
3. Eat the cake. [Conclusion]

The practical syllogism gives an inadequate picture of decision making, both descriptively and normatively. Descriptively, it fails to notice that the decision to eat the cake is crucially influenced by the emotional value of the action of eating the cake. Normatively, it fails to see that deciding is a matter of deliberative coherence that has to balance competing goals (e.g., eat something delicious, be slim, be healthy) and to evaluate competing actions (e.g., eat the cake, eat an apple, drink Perrier). On the coherence model of inference, reasoning and inference are very different. Reasoning is verbal and linear, like the practical syllogism and proofs in formal logic. But inference is an unconscious mental process in which many factors are balanced against each other until a judgment is reached that accepts some beliefs and rejects others in a way that approximately maximizes coherence.

This does not mean that practical and theoretical reasoning should be sneered at. Reasoning is a verbal, conscious process that is easily communicated to other people. People are rarely convinced by an argument directly, but the fact that reasoning does not immediately translate into inference does not make it pointless. Making reasoning explicit in decisions helps to communicate to all the people involved what the relevant goals, actions, and facilitation relations might be. If communication is effective, then the desired result will be that each decision maker will make a better-informed intuitive decision about what to do.

Improving inference is both a matter of recognizing good inference procedures, such as informed intuition, and watching out for errors that people commonly make. Such errors are usually called fallacies by philosophers and biases by psychologists. Psychologists, economists, and philosophers have identified a variety of error tendencies in decision making, such as overrating sunk costs, using bad analogies, and being overconfident in judgments. Noticing the role of emotional coherence in decision making enables us to expand this list to include emotional determinants of bad decision making, such as jonesing and failing to perceive the emotional attitudes of other people. In this paper I have emphasized the positive strategy of making decisions with a recommended procedure, informed intuition, but a fuller account would also develop the negative strategy of avoiding various tendencies that are natural to human thinking and that often lead to poor decisions.

The coherence model of decision making allows goals to be adjusted in importance while evaluating a decision, but it does not address the question of how we adopt new goals. Millgram's (1997) account of practical induction is useful for describing how people in novel situations can develop new interests that provide them with new goals. A full theory of decision making would have to include an account of where human goals come from and how they can be evaluated. People who base their decisions only on the goals of sex, drugs, and rock and roll may achieve local coherence, but they have much to learn about the full range of pursuits that enrich human lives.

CONCLUSION

I have tried in this paper to provide students and other people with a model of decision making that is both natural and effective. Practical inference is not simply produced by practical syllogisms or cost-benefit calculations but also requires assessment of the coherence of positively and negatively interconnected goals and actions. This assessment is an unconscious process that is based in part on emotional valences attached to the various goals to be taken into consideration and yields a conscious judgment that is not just a belief about what is the best action to perform but also a positive emotional attitude toward that action. Reason and emotion need not be in conflict with each other if the emotional judgment that arises from a coherence assessment takes into account the relevant actions and goals and the relations between them. The procedure I recommend, informed intuition, shows how decisions can be both intuitive and reasonable.

Acknowledgments

This research is supported by the Natural Sciences and Engineering Research Council of Canada. The sections on decision as coherence and emotional coherence contain excerpts from Thagard (2000). I am grateful to Elijah Millgram for comments on an earlier draft. Various papers on coherence can be found on my web site: http://cogsci.uwaterloo.ca.

References

Bazerman, M. H. 1994. *Judgment in Managerial Decision Making*. New York: John Wiley.

Bower, G. H. 1981. "Mood and Memory." *American Psychologist* 36: 129–148.

Bower, G. H. 1991. "Mood Congruity of Social Judgments." In J. P. Forgas, ed., *Emotion and Social Judgments*, pp. 31–53. Oxford: Pergamon Press.

Brink, D. 1989. *Moral Realism and the Foundations of Ethics*. Cambridge: Cambridge University Press.

Damasio, A. R. 1994. *Descartes' Error*. New York: G. P. Putnam's Sons.

Fiske, S., and Pavelchak, M. 1986. "Category-Based vs. Piecemeal-Based Affective Responses: Developments in Schema-Triggered Affect." In R. Sorrentino and E. Higgins, eds., *Handbook of Motivation and Cognition*, vol. 1, pp. 167–203. New York: Guilford.

Gilovich, T. 1991. *How We Know What Isn't So*. New York: Free Press.

Harman, G. 1986. *Change in View*. Cambridge: MIT Press.

Hurley, S. 1989. *Natural Reasons*. Oxford: Oxford University Press.

Kahneman, D. 1999. "Objective Happiness." In D. Kahneman, E. Diener, and N. Schwarz, eds., *Well-Being: Foundations of Hedonic Psychology*. New York: Russell Sage Foundation.

Lieberman, M. D. 2000. "Intuition: A Social Cognitive Neuroscience Approach." *Psychological Bulletin* 126: 109–137.

Lodge, M., and Stroh, P. 1993. "Inside the Mental Voting Booth: An Impression-Driven Process Model of Candidate Evaluation." In S. Iyengar and W. J. McGuire, eds., *Explorations in Political Psychology*, pp. 225–295. Durham: Duke University Press.

Millgram, E. 1997. *Practical Induction*. Cambridge: Harvard University Press.

Millgram, E., and Thagard, P. 1996. "Deliberative Coherence." *Synthese* 108: 63–88.

Ortony, A., Clore, G. L., and Collins, A. 1988. *The Cognitive Structure of Emotions*. Cambridge: Cambridge University Press.

Russo, J. E., and Schoemaker, P. J. H. 1989. *Decision Traps*. New York: Simon and Schuster.

Schick, T., Jr., and Vaughn, L. 1999. *How to Think about Weird Things*. Second ed. Mountain View, Calif.: Mayfield.

Sears, D., Huddy, L., and Schaffer, L. 1986. "A Schematic Variant of Symbolic Politics Theory, as Applied to Racial and Gender Equality." In R. Lau and D. Sears, eds., *Political Cognition*, pp. 159–202. Hillsdale, N.J.: Erlbaum.

Thagard, P. 1999. *How Scientists Explain Disease*. Princeton: Princeton University Press.

Thagard, P. 2000. *Coherence in Thought and Action*. Cambridge: MIT Press.

Thagard, P., and Millgram, E. 1995. "Inference to the Best Plan: A Coherence Theory of Decision." In A. Ram and D. B. Leake, eds., *Goal-Driven Learning*, pp. 439–454. Cambridge: MIT Press.

Thagard, P., and Verbeurgt, K. 1998. "Coherence as Constraint Satisfaction." *Cognitive Science* 22: 1–24.

Wilson, T. D., and Schooler, J. W. 1991. "Thinking Too Much: Introspection Can Reduce the Quality of Preferences and Decisions." *Journal of Personality and Social Psychology* 60: 181–192.

Chapter 17

A Difficult Choice in Preference Theory: Rationality Implies Completeness or Transitivity but Not Both

Michael Mandler

1 INTRODUCTION: RATIONALITY IN PREFERENCE THEORY

The economic theory of rational choice enjoys ever-widening popularity. Various social sciences now routinely endow agents with preference orderings or utility functions and explain social outcomes as the product of maximizing behavior. Curiously, the boom in rational-choice theory outside economics has coincided with growing doubts about the theory on the home turf. After long ignoring the substantial evidence that individuals do not choose as theories of rationality wish them to, economists have increasingly turned to positive models of choice, often derived from psychology, that make no mention of ideal or rational conduct (see Rabin 1998 for a recent survey).

At first glance, it seems odd that economics ever aspired to a normative theory of rationality. A science in the business of prediction can seemingly ignore the question of how agents ought to choose, and thus sidestep the controversies that inevitably surround definitions of what is rational. The risks of embracing a dubious theory of rationality are not mere abstract possibilities. For decades, economics has been taken to task for claiming that agents are self-interested pleasure seekers. Partly as a reaction, the economic theory of rationality has evolved considerably over the last hundred years. Originally, to be rational was indeed to choose options that deliver the greatest pleasure. But at least since the 1930s, rationality in economics has been identified instead with the more modest standard that preference be internally consistent; agents in economics no longer pursue the fictional substance called utility. This shift, which remains underappreciated outside of economic theory, is one key to why rationality has remained central to preference analysis. When narrowed to internal consistency, rationality seems to place only weak plausible restrictions on behavior.

The claims of preference theory are also less ambitious than is sometimes supposed. Economic analysis does not assert the absurdity that agents always choose the preference-maximizing action. The theory claims only that when agents systematically violate the dictates of economic rationality—which posit that agents can rank any pair of options and that rankings are transitively ordered—they suffer harm. Consequently, given practice and opportunity to learn, their behavior will in time conform more closely to the axioms of rationality. For many, this long-run link to behavior explains the role of rationality in preference theory: rationality can ultimately guide action.

But despite the common belief that the axioms of economic rationality are incontestable features of reasonable conduct, preference theory does not adequately explain why behavior should obey those axioms. Instead, the axioms of rationality have taken on a life of their own. In the absence of clear justifications for the rationality axioms, the behavioral evidence that contradicts these axioms is difficult to assess. Does the problem lie with the behavior or the axioms? That is, are agents indeed acting self-destructively, or do the axioms of rationality mischaracterize which patterns of choice are reasonable?

My primary aim in this essay is to show that it is the axioms that are to blame. To accomplish this, I reconstruct those partial arguments in favor of the rationality axioms that do exist. As we will see, there are strong cases for the rationality of the completeness axiom—the assumption that agents can rank any pair of options—and for the rationality of transitivity, but the arguments in favor of each axiom employ different definitions of preference. Completeness applies to preference as choice, while transitivity applies to preference as a set of judgments of well-being. Convincing arguments for the axioms taken together cannot be assembled on either definition.[1]

I distinguish between preference theories that put forward *ordering principles*, which explain how agents come to their preference rankings, and those that do not. The hedonism advocated by the inventors of economic utility theory was decidedly in the first camp. Such theories give grounds for why agents should have well-defined judgments about what promotes their welfare; that is, they explain why preferences in the welfare sense should be complete. In view of hedonism's manifest implausibility as a theory of motivation, its expulsion from economics has seemed an unqualified gain. But the need for ordering principles remains, although nowadays it is rarely acknowledged. As we will see, the difficulties of current-day preference theory stem from its attempt to impose completeness and transitivity as universal axioms, when in fact their plausibility hinges on whether or not an ordering principle is present.

To illustrate the role of ordering principles in preference analysis, I begin the essay with a brief look at hedonistic preference theory. Conveniently, this will allow a detour to the theory of cardinal utility, which is the natural model of utility for pleasure-seeking agents. I then turn to the movement that overturned hedonism and cardinal utility, ordinal preference theory, which remains the cornerstone of preference analysis to this day. After exploring my central topic—the limits of ordinalism's ability to defend its account of rationality—I return to cardinality. As we will see, cardinal utility provides an ordering principle for the theory of choice under uncertainty. Analogously to the difficulties facing standard choice theory in the absence of the ordering principle once supplied by hedonism, the theory of choice under uncertainty cannot easily justify completeness in the absence of cardinality.

Sections 3 and 7 below, on cardinality, are the more technical parts of this essay. They are self-contained and the remainder, with the exception of a stray remark on cardinality in section 4, can be read without them.

2 PREFERENCE BASED ON UTILITY

The theory of utility maximization originally relied on a narrow view of motivation. Particularly in the work of Jevons (1871), one of the founders of neoclassical economics, the only pertinent feature of a good or commodity is the quantity of utility or pleasure it delivers to its consumer. An agent's total satisfaction is the sum of these pleasures across all goods, and agents strive to maximize this sum.

Jevons took utility or pleasure as his primitive concept: utility objectively determines which choices best promote an agent's well-being. Faced with various arrays of goods, it is objectively in the agent's interest to choose the array that delivers the greatest quantity of pleasure. Individuals may on occasion err and fail to choose the array of goods that delivers the greatest pleasure, but with time and leeway for experimentation, individuals will gravitate to the correct, utility-maximizing decision. Utility thus originally served as an ordering principle; it prescribed which choices are rational.

Jevons and other early utility theorists were careful to limit the domain of their analysis to standard consumption goods. They reasoned that material satisfactions, whatever their source, are always commensurable. Shelter from the cold, for instance, delivers the same sort of pleasure-stuff, though a different quantity, as a fine meal. When choices cannot be reduced to homogeneous pleasure—for example, when deciding between altruistic sacrifice and self-interested gain—decision-making cannot proceed via the pleasure calculus, and therefore is not the subject of utility analysis. Jevons and his follower Alfred Marshall took particular care to exempt ethical decisions from the domain of utility theory; hedonism does not supply an adequate ordering principle for such questions. Jevons understood that when decisions do have an ethical dimension, one can still *define* chosen options to embody more pleasure than rejected options. But since it is merely a label, such a concept of pleasure does not prescribe action or determine an ordering; it only certifies after the fact that chosen alternatives have more "pleasure" than rejected alternatives. Jevons consequently rejected this approach.

3   SEPARABILITY AND CARDINALITY

The previous section implicitly treats the pleasure of a good as unaffected by the quantities of other goods consumed. This feature, which I call the *separability postulate*, was an explicit part of the work of Jevons and other early utility theorists. If we let the consumption of good i be denoted x_i and the pleasure or utility of good i as u_i, the separability postulate can be expressed as the assumption that u_i is a function of x_i alone. If there are a total of l goods, the agent's total pleasure or total utility is then $u_1(x_1) + \cdots + u_i(x_i) + \cdots + u_l(x_l)$, which I also represent as $u(x_1, \ldots, x_l)$. Functions u of this mathematical form are called *additively separable*. I will use x as shorthand for a "consumption bundle" of the l goods $(x_1, \ldots, x_l)$.

In current-day preference theory, any *increasing transformation* of $u(x)$, say $F(u(x))$, is considered to be an accurate summary of the agent's preferences. A transformation F is increasing if it satisfies the property: if $u > u'$ then $F(u) > F(u')$. Consequently, if $\hat{x}$ delivers greater utility than x' according to the utility function $u(x)$ and if F is increasing, then $F(u(\hat{x}))$ will be greater than $F(u(x'))$. Evidently, the utility function $F(u(x))$ records the agent's relative ranking of consumption bundles just as accurately as the original utility $u(x)$.

The separability postulate, however, imposes further restrictions on which utility functions constitute fully accurate psychological measuring sticks. Among the functions that can be generated via some increasing transformation F from an additively separable $u(x)$, Jevonian theory effectively deemed only those $F(u(x))$ that preserve the property of additive separability to be acceptable. The other $F(u(x))$, even though they summarize the agent's relative ranking of consumption bundles correctly, fail to record the agent's judgment that the pleasures of distinct goods do not interact with each other.

Consider a couple of examples. Suppose that there are two goods and that $u(x) = x_1 + \log x_2$ is a fully accurate utility function for some agent. That is, $u(x)$ records both the agent's relative rankings of consumption bundles and his or her sensation that goods deliver utility without interaction effects. Since multiplying by 2 is an increasing transformation and preserves additive separability, the utility $2x_1 + 2 \log x_2$ is also fully accurate. But consider instead $(x_1 + \log x_2)^3$. Although cubing is also an increasing transformation, $(x_1 + \log x_2)^3$ does not satisfy additive separability, as the reader can confirm by multiplying this expression out.

These examples hint at a remarkable feature of additively separable utility functions. If we insist that only additively separable utility functions are fully accurate descriptions of some agent's preferences, then we are effectively specifying a cardinal utility function for that agent. To say that utility is cardinal means that if a function u is a psychologically accurate utility function for an agent, then the function v is also psychologically accurate if and only if v is an increasing linear transformation of u. An increasing linear transformation of a function u is a function of the form $au + b$, where $a > 0$. It is easy to see that if u is additively separable, then so is $au(x) + b$, as the case of multiplying by 2 (i.e., $a = 2$, $b = 0$) illustrates. Also, though it is a little trickier to prove this formally, if F is *not* linear, then $F(u(x))$ will be not be additively separable, as the case of cubing illustrates.[2] (Equivalently, if $F(u(x))$ is additively separable, then F is linear.) Thus, if u is additively separable and if we insist that only additively separable functions can serve as accurate utility functions, the entire set of admissible utility functions is precisely the set of increasing linear transformations of u; in other words, utility is cardinal.

Cardinality of utility means that an agent's satisfaction is measurable in the same sense that some physical magnitudes, for example, temperature, are measurable. Specifically, the ratios of utility differences take on a fixed value: given any four consumption bundles x, y, z, w such that z and w do not deliver the same utility level, the ratio

$$\frac{u(x) - u(y)}{u(z) - u(w)}$$

will equal the same number, whichever function u in a set of cardinal utility functions is plugged in. (This fact is easy to confirm: for each appearance of the function u above, simply substitute any given increasing linear transformation $au(x) + b$ and cancel terms.) Cardinality therefore implies that agents can not only judge which changes are more preferred —for example, that a switch from y to x delivers a bigger pleasure boost than a switch from w to z—but can also assign an exact number to the ratio of these changes—the first switch delivers, say, 2.3 times the pleasure of the second. The separability postulate, which at first glance seems to be an innocuous and plausible restriction, ends up implying that pleasure behaves like a tangible, corporeal quantity. Of course, in the nineteenth century this physicality seemed fitting; if homogeneous pleasure is indeed the motivating force behind preference, it is only natural for utility to be cardinally scalable.

4   ORDINAL PREFERENCES AND DERIVED UTILITY

Even restricted to standard consumption goods, hedonism offers a narrow and implausible psychology. While some consumption goods are nothing more than vehicles for pleasure, many are not; they deliver incommensurate benefits and communicate diverse messages. Ways of life require certain commodities; decisions about such commodities cannot be made on the basis of pleasure any more than can the underlying decisions about life. A summer devoted to self-improvement—studying a new language, say—calls for one set of commodities; a summer of fun at the beach calls for another. Yet a decision between scholarship and sunbathing is not made by comparing quantities of homogenous pleasure; it involves judgment of the value of learning, assessment of how to balance recreation and education, awareness of the risks of skin cancer, etc. A fortiori, when we leave the realm of standard goods and consider the intangibles over which preferences are nowadays defined—it is standard, for example, for agents to be endowed with well-defined preferences over the well-being of others—the inapplicability of hedonistic psychology becomes indisputable.

It is therefore unsurprising that economic theory has deserted hedonism wholesale. Faced with criticism of utilitarian psychology, economists began as early as the late nineteenth century to disavow hedonism (Lewin

1996). By the early twentieth century, it had become routine for economists to assert that utility theory was not wedded to any specific psychological model. Utility, economists have claimed ever since, is just a concise way to summarize an agent's relative or ordinal ranking of commodity bundles; it is not supposed to explain how those rankings are psychically crafted.

Ordinal preference theory formalized this new understanding of utility in the 1930s and rapidly achieved theoretical dominance. Current-day economic theories of preference and choice continue to follow ordinalist methodology. The primitive concept of ordinalism is an agent's *preference relation*, usually denoted by the symbol $\succeq$. The expression $x \succeq y$ means that the agent prefers x to y in the weak sense that the agent either strictly prefers x to y or is indifferent between the two. Strict preference and indifference are defined formally in terms of $\succeq$: x is strictly preferred to y, denoted $x \succ y$, if $x \succeq y$ and it is not the case that $y \succeq x$, and x and y are indifferent if both $x \succeq y$ and $y \succeq x$.

Ordinal rankings have two primary interpretations. In the first, to say that an agent strictly prefers bundle x to bundle y, or $x \succ y$, means no more than that the agent systematically chooses x over y. In the second, strict preference for x over y implies in addition that the agent judges him or herself to be better off with x than with y. The first interpretation explicitly avoids psychological content, but even in the second understanding, the meaning of "better off" is intentionally left vague. Economists frequently think of being better off as an experience of greater "well-being" or "welfare," and, for brevity's sake, I will use these expressions too. But the agents of ordinalist theory need not judge what makes them better off by comparing quantities of "welfare." Instead, agents can deliberate about what values take precedence; they may, for instance, reason that religious law rather than sensory pleasure should dictate what foods they eat. That preferred choices deliver greater "welfare" thus means simply that an agent's deliberation has reached resolution. Contemporary preference theory, therefore, is not subject to the criticism that it reduces the multiplicity of values to a common denominator, while utility theory in the hedonist era certainly did. Still, much confusion and pointless criticism would be avoided if locutions such as "welfare" or even "better off" were dropped. The second account of preference would be better phrased as saying that an agent prefers x to y if, in addition to the agent systematically selecting x over y, the agent also believes that there is greater justification for choosing x rather than y. For many purposes, the criterion of justification may be left as a black box.[3]

Rationality in ordinal preference theory is identified with two properties of $\succeq$: completeness and transitivity. A preference relation $\succeq$ is defined to be *complete* if, for all pairs of consumption bundles (x, y), either $x \succeq y$ or $y \succeq x$ (or both). An agent with complete preferences thus can at least weakly rank every pair of bundles. (The bundle x may be identical to the bundle y, and therefore complete preferences are always reflexive; that is, $x \succeq x$ for all x.) A preference relation $\succeq$ is defined to be *transitive* if, for all triples of consumption bundles (x, y, z), $x \succeq y$ and $y \succeq z$ imply $x \succeq z$. For the moment, think of transitivity as an internal consistency requirement. I will discuss rationales for completeness and transitivity in detail in the next section.

Like hedonism, ordinal preference theory employs utility functions, but it holds that their sole purpose is to summarize the information in preferences. A utility function is said to *represent* a preference relation if, for every pair of choices (x, y), the function reports that x has at least as much utility as y if and only if x is weakly preferred to y. In symbols, u represents $\succeq$ if, for every pair (x, y), $u(x) \geq u(y)$ if and only if $x \succeq y$. According to ordinal theory, a function that represents $\succeq$ is considered to be as good a summary of $\succeq$ as any other function that represents $\succeq$.

Ordinal utility functions, therefore, do nothing more than rank consumption bundles from best to worst. For you to grasp how limited this conception of utility is, let me simplify matters a little and assume that agents choose from only a finite number of different consumption bundles. (Real agents, of course, never have the chance to choose from sets that are any larger.) In this case, if $\succeq$ is complete and transitive, a utility function that represents $\succeq$ will always exist. Hence, the claim that agents maximize utility amounts to nothing more than an assertion that their preferences are complete and transitive. Specific functions that represent $\succeq$ can be assembled in a number of ways; perhaps the simplest is to let $u(x)$ equal the total number of options that x is strictly preferred to. So, for instance, a bundle x that is strictly preferred to none of the options is assigned utility 0, as are all options classified as indifferent to x.[4]

Ordinal utility functions are not cardinal (as defined in the preceding section). Beginning with a $u(x)$ that represents some preference relation $\succeq$, we could add a constant k, perhaps a very large number, to the utility of every bundle weakly preferred to some arbitrary bundle z. The new function, say $v(x)$, would thus assign the utility number $u(x) + k$ to all $x \succeq z$ and continue to assign $u(x)$ to the remaining x. The function $v(x)$ still represents $\succeq$ according to the ordinal definition of representation. But clearly, as long as z is not the least preferred bundle and there are at least three bundles, $v(x)$ will not be an increasing linear transformation of $u(x)$; equivalently, some of the ratios of utility differences must change. In fact, the utility functions that represent $\succeq$ are precisely the set of increasing transformations of $u(x)$ (or, equivalently, the increasing transformations of $v(x)$) discussed in the previous section. Thus, unlike Jevonian theory and its additively separable utility functions, ordinalism does not suppose that cardinal yardsticks lie behind preference rankings.

Current official theory, therefore, substantially contracts the meaning of utility maximization. Ordinalists do not claim that agents form preferences by gauging how much utility their options deliver, or indeed that preference tracks any single psychological objective, much less a quasi-physical substance. Utility maximization means at most that agents' judgments about how to achieve well-being are complete—every pair of options is ranked—and that those judgments are transitively ordered, from which it follows (in the finite case) that the options can be put in a list from best to worst. Current economic theory thus makes more modest psychological claims than is often supposed. If there are difficulties in the economist's view of rationality, and I will argue that there are, they cannot be found in an allegiance to Benthamite or Jevonian psychology. Indeed, the concept of utility that economics now embraces is precisely the definition of utility, discussed at the end of section 2, that Jevons rejected as vacuous.

A Mathematical Note

If agents have complete and transitive preferences over a countably infinite set, utility functions representing those preferences will again always exist. If preferences are defined over an uncountable set of items, however, then complete and transitive preferences need not always be representable; there may be no function that assigns utility numbers to all potential items of choice that is consistent with the preference relation. But with an added technical condition—that there is a countable subset of items such that for each pair of items (x, y) with $x \succ y$, there exists a z in the subset that satisfies $x \succeq z \succeq y$—utility functions that represent $\succeq$ are again guaranteed to exist. (For details, see, e.g., Fishburn 1970 or Kreps 1988.)

5   COMPLETENESS *OR* TRANSITIVITY

At first glance, the ordinal preference model seems to be an unqualified improvement over its hedonist predecessor. By holding psychological content to a minimum, preference theory rebuts the charge that it needs a reductionist account of human nature and avoids committing itself to a specific—and thus inevitably imperfect—psychology.

Ordinalism has also been able to lift the domain restrictions imposed by the first generation of utility theorists. Freed from the assumption that agents make decisions by weighing quantities of pleasure, ordinalists have happily extended preference theory to broader classes of decisions. Depending on the application at hand, agents are presumed to have rational preferences over abstract goods such as the absence of environmental degradation, over allocations that trade off material gain against ethical concerns, over the welfare of others, or even occasionally over political goals.[5] Moreover, since ordinalists take completeness and transitivity to characterize rationality per se, they deploy in these new domains the same axioms originally designed to model choice over material consumption goods. The removal of domain restrictions has opened even classically philosophical terrain to preference analysis; witness Harsanyi's (1953) claim that distributional equity should be determined by the decisions of rational agents who are ignorant of who in society they will ultimately be. Thus, the very topics that Jevons and others were reluctant to include in utility theory are now embraced by it.

But does ordinalism provide a convincing theory of rationality? More precisely, can it explain why a rational agent must obey the completeness and transitivity axioms? Hedonism, despite its implausibilities, did provide such an explanation. If each possible consumption experience can be placed on a single numerical scale of pleasure, any pair of consumption experiences can be compared and ranked—completeness is therefore satisfied. And since numbers are transitively ordered, the consumption experiences that generate these pleasure numbers are transitively ranked as well.

Of course, ordinalism is more general than hedonism in that hedonism provides just one way to justify completeness and transitivity. It may be possible to form preference judgments without carrying out a pleasure calculus, and as we will see presently, there are alternative rationales for transitivity as well. But because of hedonism's weaknesses, the formal generality of ordinalism does not by itself vindicate the ordinalist theory of rationality. Pleasure served an indispensable prescriptive function in early utility theory; agents who at first do not know how to choose between a pair of consumption bundles can resolve their impasse by investigating how much pleasure their potential choices deliver. In the absence of a credible ordering principle, agents may not know how to rank their options. In formal terms, preferences can be incomplete: for some pairs of options x and y, agents may be unable to assert either $x \succeq y$ or $y \succeq x$. Ordinalism's open-mindedness about the motivations behind preferences, which is its main attraction, thus at the same time undermines its ability to justify one of its two key axioms.[6]

The difficulties caused by the lack of an ordering principle are less apparent in the case of traditional consumption goods; they stand out in the expanded domains that preference theory now tries to cover. Consider an agent trying to decide rationally how much of society's resources should be devoted to keeping the environment unspoiled. The agent acknowledges the force of several arguments: that both material wealth and keeping nature pristine are genuine goods, that nature should be treated with respect and even reverence, and that respect for nature does not entail that every glen should be preserved intact. Despite an awareness of these points—indeed, because of that awareness—the agent does not know where to draw the line in the conflict of ends. Recognizing the economic dimension to the problem, the agent approaches a specialist in the economic theory of rationality for help. The expert informs the agent, "You have a complete and transitive preference relation defined over ordered pairs of environmental cleanliness and material wealth. Choose a feasible ordered pair that is at least weakly preferred to all other feasible ordered pairs." The agent is at a loss; it was precisely in order to construct such preferences that the agent approached the specialist.

This story underscores a distinctive feature of rationality theory in economics: it does not take a stand on normative questions even though the agents it studies may well desire to have preferences that are normatively legitimate. This disengagement marks a clear departure from philosophical explanations of rationality that offer specific, substantive accounts of what is good, just, and legitimate. From this vantage point, the economic theory of rationality appears conspicuously incomplete.

Rational choice theorists will no doubt respond that the normative content of preference theory is limited to internal consistency; they are therefore excused from normative debates over substantive questions. But because of its agnosticism about motivation, ordinalism must concede that agents may want preferences that can be rationally defended. Such agents must deliberate about which normative criteria are appropriate and how they should be applied. To defenders of preference theory, this possibility presents no particular difficulty: they would claim that the sources of preferences are not part of what the theory tries to explain. Hence, preference theory need not concern itself with, let alone resolve, deliberative predicaments. By this line of argument, it does not matter how normative questions ought to be resolved; it matters only that agents decide such questions one way or another. But the positive facts of preference are linked to normative theory since, as I mentioned, agents may desire preferences that are rationally defensible. Consequently, if agents are unsure about what is legitimate or substantively rational, their preferences may be ill-defined. Difficulties in normative theory thereby seep into the positive theory of preference.[7]

A standard challenge is put to any ostensible occurrences of incompleteness: force agents to choose. To find a preference between some pair x and y, inform agents that unless they choose one of the options, they will be assigned a third item that they are known to rank below both x and y. These forced choices are then identified as preferences. Since sufficiently dire threats can easily be devised, these elicitations will indeed generate an ordering of x and y. (If an agent responds that either x or y is acceptable, then both $x \succeq y$ and $y \succeq x$ are inferred, which, by definition, means that the agent is indifferent between x and y.)

Recall from section 4 that ordinal preferences have two main interpretations: they can refer either to agents' judgments of how best to promote their welfare or to choices. Evidently, our earlier argument for the incompleteness of ordinal preferences employed the welfare definition. The forcing procedure, in contrast, invokes the choice definition. Since this latter definition is, if anything, the dominant understanding of preference in economics, the forcing procedure presents a formidable case in favor of completeness.

But what of transitivity? Before scrutinizing forced choices on this score, let us return to the welfare interpretation of preference, and consider whether preference in this sense should satisfy transitivity. The welfare definition of preference is more demanding than the choice definition in that agents who think they will experience greater welfare with x than with y have a compelling reason to choose x over y. If they do not, they will end up with a worse outcome.[8] (In contrast, an agent who merely chooses x when y is available may be picking x only because of the need to make some choice.) The strongest arguments for transitivity cleverly exploit the fact that choices should track welfare judgments. Consider an agent who has well-defined welfare judgments over a set of three alternatives. That is, assume that completeness is satisfied for each pair of items. If these preferences do not satisfy transitivity, we can label the options so that $x \succeq y$, $y \succeq z$, and $z \succ x$ hold. Suppose that option z is originally the status quo and we give the agent the opportunity to shift to y. Since the agent at least weakly prefers y to z, he or she will be amenable to the switch. Similarly, once y is the status quo, the agent should then agree to shift to x, which is strictly dispreferred to the original option z. Intransitivity can thus sequentially lead agents to inferior outcomes.[9]

A variant of this argument is the famous money-pump, originally due to Davidson, McKinsey, and Suppes (1955). Here agents exhibit a more blatant violation of transitivity: for some triple of options (x, y, z), preferences satisfy $x \succ y$, $y \succ z$, and $z \succ x$. Because each of these preferences is strict, such an agent, when originally endowed with z, will agree to part with a small amount of money to switch to y, then pay more money to switch from y to x, and then pay more money still to return to z, thereby ending up with the original status quo but with less money. If the judgments $x \succ y$, $y \succ z$, and $z \succ x$ are not altered by the loss of wealth, the agent can be subjected to more rounds of pumping.

The money pump has wielded remarkable influence. In its wake, even many critics of economic rationality have conceded that failures of transitivity will expose agents to a dire hazard. And the money pump does indeed provide grounds for why rational welfare judgments should satisfy transitivity. But, as I argued earlier, preference in the welfare sense is liable to be incomplete. Thus, any defense of the full ordinalist conception of rationality hinges on preference-as-choice and on whether preference in this sense, which is guaranteed to be complete, should be transitive as well.

Specifically, do the above sequential consistency arguments apply to choice? They may appear to apply. When preference is defined as choice, we may interpret the expression $a \succeq b$ to mean "Out of the set $\{a, b\}$, a is chosen" and $a \succ b$ to mean "Out of the set $\{a, b\}$, a is chosen and b is not." If we assume that at least one element is chosen out of every set— in accordance with the forcing procedure—then this preference-as-choice relation must be complete. Consequently, a violation of transitivity implies there is a triple (x, y, z) that satisfies $x \succeq y$, $y \succeq z$, and $z \succ x$. We now deploy the same sequence of exchanges used earlier: if z is the original status quo, the agent will agree to switch to y and then to x. Moreover, since $a \succeq b$ in effect means "The agent will accept a when b is available," we do not need to worry at this point in the argument about any distinction between welfare and choice or about agents who agree to exchanges only when they have a strict welfare judgment.

To conclude that this sequence of choices is irrational, we must enrich the interpretation of $\succeq$ somewhat. As things stand, we have shown only that an intransitive chooser can end up with an option that is never directly chosen over the original status quo. If absolutely no welfare significance is imputed to $\succeq$, no irrationality can be inferred. But even a sliver of psychological content will bridge the gap. If we suppose that $a \succ b$ implies that the agent judges himself or herself to be better off with a than with b, then we may conclude that intransitive choosers are irrational: they end up with x even though they judge z to be superior. This interpretation of $\succeq$ is much less demanding than the ordinary welfare interpretation of $\succeq$, in which $a \succeq b$ implies that agents hold themselves to be at least as well off with a as with b. Here we impose interpretation only on agents' strict choices; that is, if agents *never* agree to accept b when a is available, we assume the agents are better off with a.

The above reasoning offers the strongest argument yet produced for equating rationality with the completeness and transitivity of preferences: interpret preference as choice and show that intransitive choices will expose agents to manipulation. Unfortunately, the manipulation conclusion hangs on a restrictive view of how agents must choose. In our interpretation of $\succeq$ as choice, we have assumed that $a \succeq b$ means that an agent will *always* choose a from the set $\{a, b\}$. But in the crucial case of agents who are unable to make welfare judgments over potential alternatives, that assumption is arbitrary and counterintuitive. Agents who cannot rank a pair of options a and b will sometimes choose a and sometimes choose b. Specifically, they may display *status quo bias*, in which they stick to the status quo until offered an alternative that they judge to make them better off. In our manipulation example, assume that y is unranked in welfare terms relative to both x and z, and in accord with the interpretation of strict choice given above, that z is ranked as superior to x. For concreteness, think of the alternatives as embodying different quantities of two rival goods and suppose that the agent is unable to rank trade-offs between the goods. The goods, for example, could be personal wealth for the agent and environmental quality, with x and z each containing more wealth but less environmental quality than y, and with z containing slightly more wealth and slightly more environmental quality than x. Thus y would indeed be unranked relative to both x and z but z would be superior to x. How will an agent with these rankings choose? If z is the original status quo and the agent exhibits status quo bias, the agent, unable to judge how much wealth the environment is worth, will refuse to switch to y from z. Potentially manipulating sequences of exchanges thus never commence.[10]

It is crucial that status quo maintenance and other manipulation-avoidance strategies do not succeed by requiring that choice be transitive; otherwise, the traditional account of rational choice would be vindicated. To see the intransitivity of status quo maintenance, I need to introduce a new, less-restrictive definition of preference-as-choice. Observe that the forcing procedure, which I used to establish that preference-as-choice must satisfy completeness, by no means shows that agents must always choose the same element from any given set. The necessity of choice implies only that *some* option must be picked, and agents may want to vary their selections, perhaps to avoid manipulation or maybe out of whim. So let us instead interpret $a \succeq b$ to mean "There exist circumstances under which a is chosen from the set $\{a, b\}$," which is precisely what the forcing procedure demonstrates. Under this interpretation, the ability of agents to vary how they choose—say as a function of which option is the status quo—allows $\succeq$ to exhibit intransitivity while ensuring that agents are not manipulated. To confirm that intransitivity can occur in our example, note that although y is not chosen from the set $\{y, z\}$ when z is the status quo, it may well be chosen when y itself is the status quo. And similarly, x may well be chosen from the set $\{x, y\}$ when x is the status quo. We therefore have $y \succeq z$ and $x \succeq y$. Since the agent must always choose z from the set $\{x, z\}$ (z ranks strictly higher than x on welfare grounds), we have $z \succ x$ (that is, there are no circumstances under which x is chosen from $\{x, z\}$). Transitivity is therefore violated, and the case for the rational necessity of completeness and transitivity fails.

Status quo bias and other discordant evidence have been widely interpreted, by both economists and others, as a strong repudiation of the standard economic model of rationality. And status quo bias indeed contradicts the standard model. But, as I have indicated, the phenomenon is not a sign of irrationality in the sense that status quo bias puts agents in harm's way. Hence, it is not any thesis about the prevalence of genuinely rational behavior that must be overturned; it is the economic account of rationality that must give way.[11]

If we take a bird's eye view of the various arguments in favor of the ordinalist theory of rationality, a curious symmetry in their flaws appears. If preference is defined as a set of welfare judgments, then rational agents will satisfy transitivity but need not obey completeness; if preference is defined as choice, then although agents will definitionally satisfy completeness, rationality does not imply that they must obey transitivity.

The duality between preference-as-choice and preference-as-welfare-judgment illuminates some of the quarrels that perpetually beset preference theory. As I remarked, the domains nominally covered by preference analysis have steadily expanded. These expansions, moreover, have often been motivated by complaints that preexisting models of preference are psychologically too confining, that they do not allow agents' decisions to vary in a sufficiently rich way. This pattern of complaint and domain expansion is firmly established and will no doubt continue. For example, although there are exceptions, current economic models usually posit preferences that are defined over allocations of goods and not over the procedural rules that determine allocations. For instance, agents are typically assumed to care only about the decisions their government makes, not whether those decisions are determined by fiat or democratic vote. But if this tradition were subjected to sustained criticism, models would no doubt proliferate in which agents have preferences over allocations conjoined with procedural rules. Many critics protest that such conceptual moves leave preference theory vacuous and unfalsifiable. Defenders of orthodox preference theory, rarely persuaded by these charges, in turn reply that models with expanded domains do make falsifiable predictions. Transitivity, for example, is testable independently of the domain over which preferences are defined.[12] The present analysis points instead to a different drawback of mechanical domain expansions. Expansions occur when hitherto neglected aspects of decisions are incorporated into the definitions of the objects of choice. The new domains therefore usually describe a more complex class of decision problems. In the example above, for instance, agents would have to judge the equity and politics of various procedural rules and weigh those judgments against their attitudes towards allocations of goods. Incompleteness of preference is therefore far more likely, or if preference is defined as choice, intransitivity is more likely. The problem with domain expansions is not that they make preference theory unfalsifiable; rather, they render the ordinalist rationality axioms inapplicable.

6 PREFERENCE AS A SUBSTITUTE FOR ORDERING PRINCIPLES

I have illustrated the difficulty of constructing complete welfare orderings with the example of decisions that have a normative dimension; when agents want to do what is right, it is plain that they need a principle that shows them how to rank their options. But the incompleteness problem is not intrinsically tied to normativity. When agents have to choose between everyday consumption goods that deliver incommensurate but nonnormative benefits, they may not know which of their options best promote their well-being. Every inhabitant of the modern world is now and then defeated by the multiplicity of market choices. It is not just that we have too much information to process; the world of commodities simply cannot be reduced to a single ordering. Many decision quandaries are trivial— what flavor ice cream?—and have no abiding significance. But just as with momentous choices that pit the value of undisturbed nature against material wealth, the trivial dilemmas leave agents without a well-formed set of welfare judgments. And so people end up choosing in some other way. As I indicated in the previous section, these choices may end up displaying intransitivity, which in itself is evidence that agents' welfare judgments are incomplete (Raz 1986), but agents are not thereby exposed to the money pump or other hazards.

When available, ordering principles resolve the dilemmas of how to rank alternatives, often by showing that multidimensional decisions can be reduced to simpler choices over alternatives that agents already know how to order. Hedonism functioned in just this way in economics. It declared that seemingly complex consumption options, each of which combines apparently disparate and incomparable attributes, in reality all convey some quantity of a single sensation. The appeal of such a global ordering principle is manifest. In addition to the convenience of modeling agents with utility functions, pleasure ensures a determinacy to consumption decisions analogous to what profitability accomplishes in the business realm. The scale of profits, calculated in terms of money, provides firms with an external criterion that orders their production decisions objectively and unambiguously. In fact, many have considered the ready calculability of profits to be an essential cause of the dominance of means-ends calculations in modern societies. Hedonism extended the reach of instrumental rationality to cover all species of human decision making; each object of decision is made comparable in terms of its efficiency in delivering pleasure.

Hedonism in economics quickly came under rightful attack and had to be discarded. By substituting complete preferences for the ordering function previously performed by pleasure, ordinalism seemingly retained the advantages of utility maximization without its embarrassing psychological baggage. This strategy of replacing judgments about pleasure with preferences or choices followed the course set by the history of utilitarianism in moral philosophy. In Benthamite psychology, as it was commonly understood, all forms of desire—whether material wants, sympathy for others, or even a love of justice—are reduced to homogeneous pleasure. This reduction cannot be carried through, however, even for the desires of a single individual, and consequently Benthamism cannot guide preference and action. The young John Stuart Mill, for instance, complained that Bentham's philosophy was of little use to individuals deciding how to mold their "character" (Mill 1838). Of course, one can vacuously repair this incompleteness, though not its lack of prescriptive content, by declaring that the options that agents in the end choose are the ones that deliver the greatest pleasure. Mill himself took this tack in his later return to the utilitarian fold. Mill famously decomposed homogeneous Benthamite pleasure into qualitatively distinct types of pleasure (Mill 1861). How should one decide among the kinds of pleasure? Mill did not lay down any ordering principle; instead, one kind of pleasure is more valuable than another if those who are familiar with both prefer it. Moreover, in the cases he discussed, Mill claimed that the knowledgeable do in fact tend to choose as one. If this claim were correct, some prescriptive substance might be salvaged from Mill's position, but it is not.

Most, though by no means all, utilitarians in the twentieth century have followed Mill in rejecting the homogeneity of pleasure, in assigning primacy instead to agents' preferences, and in identifying whatever agents prefer as the more valuable pleasure or goal. The principal difficulty with this triad of moves is not the presumption that agents always opt for the more valuable goal. Since utilitarians typically place few restrictions on the ordering principles that agents may use to construct their preferences, this assumption need not impose a reductionist decision-making rule on agents. Indeed, when agents have a good grip on the comparative value of competing goals, and value is defined expansively, their preferences (and choices) will be guided by that understanding. This concordance between value and preference has no doubt bolstered the plausibility of preference-based utilitarianism. But the implication is only one-way: if agents cannot reach a firm conclusion about value, their choices obviously cannot reveal what they deem to be valuable. Like ordinal decision theory, therefore, post-Benthamite utilitarianism lacks prescriptive content: it cannot guide preference or choice.

7 EXPECTED UTILITY THEORY: CARDINALITY REVISITED?

The theory of expected utility has long stood as the primary economic model of preference in the face of uncertainty. In the early days of neo-classical economics, Jevons and other pioneers offered little in the way of justification; they just asserted that agents maximize the mathematical expectation of their pleasure. For example, if $u(x)$ is the pleasure of option x and $u(y)$ is the pleasure of option y, the anticipated pleasure of receiving x with probability p and y with probability $(1 - p)$ is given by the expected utility formula $pu(x) + (1 - p)u(y)$. More generally, I assume in this section that there are a finite number of options, labeled $x^1, \ldots, x^n$. A typical prospect, often called a *lottery*, is denoted $(p^1, \ldots, p^n)$, where each p^i is the probability of receiving option x^i and where $\sum_{i=1}^{n} p^i = 1$. An agent who assigns the utility numbers $u(x^1), \ldots, u(x^n)$ to the n options therefore ascribes the pleasure level $\sum_{i=1}^{n} p^i u(x^i)$ to the lottery $(p^1, \ldots, p^n)$. (The superscripts in x^i and p^i serve as indices of the options and do not indicate that a quantity is raised to some power.) From our discussion of additive separability in section 3, it should be clear that expected utility functions are cardinal. That is, the functions u and v represent the same preferences over uncertain prospects (when each is inserted into the expected utility formula) if and only if v is an increasing linear transformation of u.

For Jevons and other early utility theorists, taking utility as a primitive fit nicely with their psychological views. But following the ordinalist revolution of the 1930s, utility could serve only as a tool to represent preferences and not as a theoretical starting point. With the raw material of the Jevonian approach missing, expected utility numbers could no longer be calculated. Conveniently, the mathematician John von Neumann and his coauthor Oscar Morgenstern soon accomplished the seemingly impossible, an axiomatization of the expected utility formula that takes ordinal preferences as primitive, even though expected utility functions are themselves cardinal. Like the ordinalist theory of section 4, the von Neumann–Morgenstern model begins with a preference relation $\succeq$ over a set of potential choices, but now that set consists of lotteries. Rationality is again identified with preference relations that satisfy the completeness and transitivity axioms. However, completeness and transitivity do not by themselves generate utility functions that satisfy the expected-utility formula; two additional axioms are necessary. To explain these, I need to introduce compound lotteries, which are lotteries whose outcomes are themselves lotteries. For instance, a compound lottery might deliver lottery p with probability π and lottery q with probability $(1 - \pi)$. Denote this lottery $(\pi p + (1 - \pi)q)$. The von Neumann–Morgenstern theory supposes that agents regard a simple lottery as interchangeable with those compound lotteries that deliver the same final probabilities of outcomes; so $(\pi p + (1 - \pi)q)$ is interchangeable with the simple lottery that delivers x^1 with probability $\pi p^1 + (1 - \pi)q^1$, x^2 with probability $\pi p^2 + (1 - \pi)q^2$, etc.

The first of the additional axioms, known as the *continuity* or *Archimedean* axiom, states that for every lottery r such that some lottery p is ranked strictly above r and some other lottery q is ranked strictly below r, there exists a lottery $(\pi p + (1 - \pi)q)$ with $\pi > 0$ ranked strictly above r and another lottery $(\rho p + (1 - \rho)q)$ with $\rho > 0$ ranked strictly below r. Continuity is so called because it presumes that if π is set near 1, then $(\pi p + (1 - \pi)q)$ will be almost as desirable as p, while if ρ is set near 0, then $(\rho p + (1 - \rho)q)$ will be almost as undesirable as q. The plausibility of the axiom hinges on whether or not the value of an outcome varies discontinuously as its probability changes. Although certainly not a feature of rationality per se, there obviously are many contexts in which agents will agree that their preferences should satisfy such a property.

The second and far more controversial additional axiom, *independence*, states that an agent weakly prefers lottery p to lottery q if and only if, for each lottery r and probability π, the agent also weakly prefers $(\pi p + (1 - \pi)r)$ to $(\pi q + (1 - \pi)r)$. In other words, if the agent prefers p to q, then he or she should still prefer p to q even after hearing the news that he or she might receive r rather than p or q. One argument in favor of the axiom goes as follows. Suppose that independence is violated, i.e., that for some p, q, and r, both $p \succeq q$ and $(\pi q + (1 - \pi)r) \succ (\pi p + (1 - \pi)r)$ hold. Now imagine that the agent has to choose between the compound lotteries $(\pi p + (1 - \pi)r)$ and $(\pi q + (1 - \pi)r)$. The choice proceeds in two stages. First, a coin that turns up heads with probability π and tails with probability $(1 - \pi)$ is flipped. If tails, the agent receives r (and if r is a lottery, the remaining uncertainty about what option the agent receives is then resolved). If heads, the agent moves to stage 2, where he or she chooses between p and q. If the agent were to commit in advance to a choice at stage 2, the agent's options would represent the same alternatives as a one-stage lottery with options $(\pi p + (1 - \pi)r)$ and $(\pi q + (1 - \pi)r)$. It seems reasonable, therefore, for the agent simply to plan to choose at stage 2 according to the dictates of $\succeq$. Given the preferences posited, the agent will plan to choose q. The coin is tossed. If tails, the agent receives r. But if heads, the agent, who by assumption has the preference $p \succeq q$, will want to choose p at stage 2, not q. The agent apparently cannot hold to preestablished plans, even in the absence of new information. (Remember: at the commitment stage, the agent knew that the choice between p and q would apply only if the coin were to come up heads.)

This inconsistency can readily be converted into a manipulation reminiscent of the money pump discussed in section 5. Suppose that an agent with the same preferences as above begins in possession of the compound lottery $(\pi p + (1 - \pi)r)$. Since $(\pi q + (1 - \pi)r)$ is strictly preferred to $(\pi p + (1 - \pi)r)$, it is plausible that the agent will agree to switch from $(\pi p + (1 - \pi)r)$ to $(\pi q^- + (1 - \pi)r)$, where q^- has the same probabilities as q but each of the n options is now made slightly less attractive by subtracting a small amount of money from the agent's wealth. Suppose as before that the lottery $(\pi q^- + (1 - \pi)r)$ proceeds sequentially. In stage 1, a coin is flipped that turns up heads with probability π and tails with probability $(1 - \pi)$. If heads, the agent receives q^-, and if tails, the agent receives r. Stage 2 then resolves any remaining uncertainty in the lotteries q^- and r. The coin is now tossed. If tails, the agent receives r as planned. If heads, the agent is offered the chance to switch from q^- to p^-, a lottery with the same probabilities as p but with each of its n options diminished by a small amount of money. Since the agent regards p to be at least as good as q, he or she should strictly prefer p to q^- (by transitivity); hence if p^- is a small enough diminishment of p, the agent will prefer p^- to q^- and accept the offer. The agent has thus moved from an original position in which he or she receives r with probability $(1 - \pi)$ and p otherwise to a position where he or she again receives r with probability $(1 - \pi)$ but now receives p^- rather than p otherwise. The agent has traded away some expected wealth with no offsetting gain.[13]

This argument, known sometimes as "making book (or Dutch book) against oneself," has convinced many economists and decision theorists that independence is an inherent feature of rational conduct. But the Dutch-book argument relies on the implicit premise that $p \succeq q$ implies the agent ought also to prefer p to q (or p^- to q^-) *after* the coin toss. As Machina (1989) has argued convincingly, this premise is unwarranted. By supposition, the agent has the preference $(\pi q + (1 - \pi)r) \succ (\pi p + (1 - \pi)r)$. That is, when exposed to the possibility of receiving r with probability π, the agent strictly prefers q to p. After hearing the news that he or she will not receive r, shouldn't the agent hold to this preference rather than to revert to the valuation that would have held had there never been a possibility of r? The fact that the agent did not receive r does not erase the earlier exposure to risk, and that exposure is as legitimate an influence on preference as past material consumption, which, according to all schools of preference theory, can properly affect current decision making. If the agent does treat past risk as equivalent to prospective risk, he or she will refuse the final switch to p^- and escape manipulation. This rebuttal does not completely settle matters—the relation $\succeq$ does not formally entail what preferences the agent will have after exposure to some uncertainty— but it weakens the case that violating independence necessarily invites manipulation.

But even if past exposure to risk can influence current preferences, there are certainly cases where individuals will concede that past risk ought not to bear on the present. One way to shift the persuasive ground in favor of independence is to change slightly the choice situation facing the agent with preferences $p \succeq q$ and $(\pi q + (1 - \pi)r) \succ (\pi p + (1 - \pi)r)$. Suppose that we present the agent with prospects p and q. The agent chooses p. We then announce that unbeknownst to the agent, there had earlier been a $(1 - \pi)$ chance that the agent would have received r and not have been offered the choice between p and q. As it turned out, this eventuality did not materialize. Even though no barrier of logic or self-interest prohibits the agent from then reversing his or her choice between p and q, many would regard the news of the earlier possibility of r as irrelevant. To be free from Dutch-book manipulations, however, violators of independence must regard past and prospective risks as equivalent. Self-interest therefore requires that the preference between p and q be reversed. In circumstances where agents do not concur with the need for such reversals, the case for the rationality of independence gains ground.

Whether independence is intrinsic to rationality or not, a separate methodological consideration argues for applying normative preference theory only to decision-making problems in which independence can be expected to hold. To test the internal consistency of an agent's choices, we must observe several of the agent's decisions, and to ensure that these decisions are not spurious, there must be a chance that each choice determines which option the agent ultimately receives. The decisions therefore fall under the theory of choice under uncertainty. But if the agent can freely violate the independence axiom, almost any pattern of choice will be consistent with virtually any rationality axiom. Suppose, for example, that we want to know whether an agent's preferences over the prospects p, q, and r are transitive. We present the agent in sequence with the choice sets $\{p,q\}$, $\{q,r\}$, and $\{p,r\}$, where each decision has the probability 1/3 of being the determining choice. If the agent were to choose p from the first set and q from the second, the agent—if he or she does not satisfy independence—may choose r from the third without violating transitivity. The first two choices, in fact, do not even reveal a preference for p over q or for q over r. The agent's objects of choice are triples of the form (p,q,r) that denote the decision made at each of the three choice sets; the agent therefore never makes a direct choice between p and q, between q and r, or between p and r. Indeed, without independence, we may infer only that one set of triples is preferred and that another set of triples is rejected. (I use "set" here because the agent may be willing to accept both items at one or more of the choice sets.) So, for example, if the agent were to choose (p,q,r), we would be able to infer only that the agent prefers (p,q,r) over (p,q,p), (p,r,r), (p,r,p), (q,q,r), (q,q,p), (q,r,r), and (q,r,p). Since the antecedent of transitivity—that some triple a is preferred to some triple b and that b is preferred to some triple c—does not obtain, testing transitivity is impossible. With independence, on the other hand, the preferences operative at one choice set must hold at the other two choice sets and overall. Axioms on preferences are then testable.

To sum up this lengthy digression, continuity and independence, even if they lack an ironclad claim to rationality, are certainly plausible in some circumstances. And independence is needed for empirical confirmation of any axiom on preferences.

When a preference relation $\succeq$ satisfies all four of the axioms we have discussed—completeness, transitivity, continuity, and independence—the von Neumann–Morgenstern expected utility theorem states that there exists a function u such that $p \succeq q$ if and only if $\sum_{i=1}^{n} p^i u(x^i) \geq \sum_{i=1}^{n} q^i u(x^i)$ (see, e.g., Fishburn 1970). How is it that the von Neumann–Morgenstern axioms on ordinal preferences generate a cardinal utility function? Various schools of preference theory have their answers to this question. Early on, some die-hard hedonists claimed that the von Neumann–Morgenstern theory resurrected the claim that utility is a measurable quantity. And some ordinalists have conceded that measurability of utility does obtain when the von Neumann–Morgenstern axioms are satisfied. But the majority position has held that the apparent cardinality of von Neumann–Morgenstern preferences is a mathematical illusion (see, e.g., Arrow 1963, 10). While it is true that *within the expected utility formula*, u is unique up to an increasing linear transformation—that is, if $\sum_{i=1}^{n} p^i u(x^i)$ represents $\succeq$ and F is nonlinear, then $\sum_{i=1}^{n} p^i F(u(x^i))$ will not represent $\succeq$—we may apply a nonlinear transformation to the formula as a whole without changing the ranking of prospects. So if G is an increasing transformation, whether linear or not, then $G(\sum_{i=1}^{n} p^i u(x^i))$ must represent the same preference relation as $\sum_{i=1}^{n} p^i u(x^i)$. For example, with two options x^1 and x^2, $p^1 \log u(x^1) + p^2 \log u(x^2)$ does not represent the same preferences as $p^1 u(x^1) + p^2 u(x^2)$, since logarithms are nonlinear, but $\log(p^1 u(x^1) + p^2 u(x^2))$ does. It follows that agents who satisfy the von Neumann–Morgenstern axioms (or indeed any set of axioms on $\succeq$) need not experience well-defined ratios of differences in expected utility. And even when agents *can* report specific ratios of utility differences, agents with the same $\succeq$ can report ratios that differ.[14] Von Neumann–Morgenstern theory therefore does not present a genuine case of measurable utility.

The ordinalist consensus has used these arguments to try to remove any taint of measurability from the theory of choice under uncertainty. And it is certainly true that just as with choice over certain outcomes, agents do not need to assess uncertain options using a measurable concept of satisfaction or pleasure. Moreover, if we could be sure that preferences over uncertain options were complete, it would not matter for the theory how those preferences were formed. But how might agents go about assembling preferences over uncertain prospects? We saw in section 5 that simply compelling agents to choose will not generate preferences that satisfy transitivity. Agents must come to a reasoned judgment about how well the prospects available to them serve their interests. Yet it is not easy to gauge the value of lotteries. Agents must not only make judgments about the certain outcomes—say that x^1 is superior to x^2 and that x^2 is superior to x^3. To generate a complete ordering, they must also name a probability weighting of x^3 and x^1 that is indifferent to x^2. The obvious way to form such a judgment is to ask, "How does the gain from switching from x^2 to x^1 compare to the gain from switching from x^3 to x^2?" If we use the function u to gauge these "gains," the agent is in effect asking, "What is the following ratio?"

$$\frac{u(x^1) - u(x^2)}{u(x^2) - u(x^3)}$$

Not surprisingly, with this number in hand the needed probability is easy to calculate. (If we label the above ratio k, the agent will regard x^2 to be indifferent to the combination of x^1 with probability $1/(1+k)$ and x^3 with probability $k/(1+k)$.) If agents form preferences in this way, they are making explicit welfare judgments that single out the expected utility formula (or any of its increasing linear transformations) as psychologically accurate. Indeed, this method of building preferences amounts to a substantial return to Jevonian utility theory; agents have to *begin* with a utility or welfare judgment and derive their preferences from this primitive. A scalable sense of satisfaction would once again assume a pivotal prescriptive role in the theory of preference.

Assessing the cardinality of the von Neumann–Morgenstern construction is therefore delicate. By itself, the theory does not imply that agents form cardinality judgments or assess choices using a measurable gauge of satisfaction. But relative to choice under certainty, preferences over uncertain prospects constitute precisely the type of domain expansion that places the completeness axiom in doubt (see section 5). To qualify as an adequate account of uncertain choice, therefore, the von Neumann–Morgenstern approach must explain how agents come to rank the prospects they choose among. Conceivably, agents might assemble preferences without comparing measurable amounts of satisfaction. But until this missing psychological link is closed, cardinality remains the obvious device for forming preference judgments. Preference theory thus continues to rely on the Jevonian heritage it has worked so hard to jettison.

8   CONCLUSION: THE DOMAIN OF PREFERENCE ANALYSIS

Preference incompleteness diminishes the role that economic analysis can play in social decision making. Economics has long aimed to cut through the difficult debates that surround normative and political claims. Society does not need to resolve disputes over justice and right and the content of the good, it is said, since economic analysis can prescribe social reforms using only individual preferences as its raw material. While various economic theories of social choice do not agree on how individual preferences should be aggregated into social decisions, most camps agree that some principles are uncontroversial. For instance, virtually every normative theory in economics holds that Pareto-inefficient decisions should not be selected; that is, society should not adopt a policy if there is some other policy that leaves every agent at least as well off and that improves the welfare of some agents. Such nostrums of policy advice presuppose that "at least as well off" and "improves the welfare of" are well-defined. These judgments about individual well-being are identified with individual preference orderings, which are, of course, assumed to be complete and transitive. This combination of taking preference as given and applying a mechanical aggregation procedure (such as Pareto efficiency) has given economic advice a technocratic air: a mechanical rule can generate correct, or at least better, social decisions. But if the presupposition of completeness is removed and the need for substantive ordering principles acknowledged, preferences no longer provide an adequate basis for policy analysis. Agents may not possess firm judgments about their own welfare, let alone about the well-being of the social whole, and their nascent judgments will be influenced by the very normative debates that economists have wanted to bypass.

These warnings do not mean that there are no domains to which preference analysis can be applied. In areas where agents do make welfare judgments—that is, where preference in the welfare sense satisfies the completeness axiom—rationality *does* require that choice satisfy the other classical rationality axiom, transitivity. The argument in section 5 that agents can choose intransitively without exposing themselves to manipulation applies only to options that are unranked on welfare grounds. Rational agents must always choose options that they think will deliver greater well-being; otherwise, they can end up with a worse outcome. The disjunction between choice and welfare judgment therefore occurs only when welfare judgments cannot be formed. Hence, when an ordering principle allows agents to come to definitive judgments about what promotes their well-being, the constraints of rationality are binding; if their choices do not satisfy transitivity, agents can be led to welfare-diminishing trades. And in those environments of uncertainty, discussed in section 7, where independence and continuity are plausible, the full machinery of expected utility maximization can be invoked.

The prerequisite of preference analysis, therefore, is to discover whether agents do have credible welfare rankings in the domain under study. Unfortunately, the standard vocabulary of economic theory, which simply equates choice and well-being, is poorly equipped to answer this question. Certainly, there are many cases of economic decision making in which agents find welfare rankings easy to construct. Decisions where income is the only interest at stake are clear cases; such decisions resemble the profitability orderings mentioned in section 6, which form the prototypical models of instrumental rationality. But just as certainly, there are numerous cases, particularly outside of economic life, where the completeness axiom is suspect at best. Harsanyi's model of social justice in terms of how individuals would choose if ignorant of what personality they will ultimately have provides a telling example. I began this essay by mentioning the expansion of economic preference analysis into other social sciences. No blanket assessment of this development is possible. The value of such analyses depends on where they fit on the spectrum between choice over monetizable goals and choice behind a veil of ignorance.

Acknowledgments

I am grateful for the detailed comments of Alyssa Bernstein, Elijah Millgram, and Jorge Restrepo.

Notes

1. Sen (1973, 1982, 1997) has long emphasized the differences between the choice and welfare definitions of preference. Levi (1986) also presses the distinction; his treatment of preference over uncertain prospects is particularly relevant to economic applications and to section 7 of this paper.

2. This result, whose history begins with Fisher (1892), requires that there are at least two goods k and j such that u_k and u_j are not constant functions. A technical restriction is also necessary, e.g., that the range of each u_i is an interval (as when the u_i are continuous). See Mandler (1999) for a relatively short proof and Krantz, Luce, Suppes, and Tversky (1971) for an extended treatment.

3. The persistent use of the word "welfare" in preference theory no doubt betrays a lingering belief that individuals *do* form their preference rankings by comparing welfare magnitudes. But many do not hold this view, and ordinalism in any event is not tied to this error.

4. It is easy to confirm that u represents $\succeq$. To show that if $x \succeq y$ then $u(x) \geq u(y)$, note that transitivity implies, for all z, that if z satisfies $y \succ z$, then $x \succ z$. The set of choices that x is strictly preferred to therefore contains the set of choices that y is strictly preferred to, and hence $u(x) \geq u(y)$. To show that if $u(x) \geq u(y)$ then $x \succeq y$, suppose to the contrary that $u(x) \geq u(y)$ and $y \succ x$. Reasoning as before, if z satisfies $x \succ z$, then $y \succ z$, and so the set of choices that y is strictly preferred to contains the set of choices that x is strictly preferred to. But the set of choices that y is strictly preferred to must have strictly more elements than the set of choices that x is strictly preferred to since, given $y \succ x$, x is in the former set but not the latter. Hence $u(y) > u(x)$, a contradiction.

5. The move to absorb ethical decision-making into preference analysis occurred early on, well prior to formal versions of ordinalism (see, e.g., Wicksteed 1910, book 2).

6. Many philosophical accounts of practical rationality offer alternative ordering principles, which could conceivably fill the prescriptive role once played by plea-

sure in utility theory. But until one of these accounts definitively explains how to justify preference, incompleteness is likely to persist: if agents are unaware of or unpersuaded by a proposed logic of decision-making, they will remain unable to order their alternatives.

7. The link between preference-as-it-is and preference-as-it-rationally-should-be is by itself compatible with orthodox preference analysis. As discussed in the introduction, that momentary behavior frequently violates rationality is widely conceded; rationality exerts its pull only gradually. The extra ingredient here is that there may be no identifiable set of welfare judgments that anchors preferences and that induces a well-defined ordering even in the long run.

8. "Welfare" is here defined as expansively as necessary, incorporating all due consideration for equity and the well-being of others. Still, even granting an expansive definition, there are cases that cloud the principle that rational agents should always choose the option that furthers their welfare. The act of choice may take on an independent meaning, as in Sen's (1973) famous example of the polite guest who desires the biggest slice of cake but chooses the second-biggest. Choice and the welfare definition of preference then need not coincide if the definition of welfare does not incorporate the symbolic import of choice. This problem disappears, however, if preference is defined as justified choice, following my suggestion in section 4.

9. If preferences obey continuity and nonsatiation conditions, the same conclusion will hold if agents agree to switch only to strictly preferred options (see Mandler 1998, where these conditions are defined precisely).

10. Agents can face more complex manipulations against which status quo bias does not provide adequate protection. For instance, consider an agent with the same welfare judgments over x, y, and z as in the example and who in addition strictly ranks a fourth option w strictly below x, y, or z. The agent faces a sequence of four choice sets, the first three of which are $\{y, w\}$, $\{y, z\}$, and $\{x, w\}$. The fourth set contains x and whichever option the agent chooses from the second set. To ensure that choice is not spurious, suppose that at each set the agent does not know whether there will be another round of choice. Status quo bias and optimization imply that y, y, and x, respectively, are chosen from the first three sets. The fourth set is therefore $\{x, y\}$. Since the agent selects x from the third set, status quo bias implies that x is also chosen from the fourth set. But, had the agent chosen z from the second set, he or she could then select z from the fourth set and be strictly better off (assuming the fourth set is the final round). Status quo bias therefore harms the agent relative to choosing according to a complete and transitive choice relation that agrees with the welfare judgments that the agent is capable of making. As I have shown elsewhere (Mandler 1998), however, more sophisticated choice procedures can immunize the agent from such manipulations and still exhibit intransitivity of choice.

11. Usually, evidence of status quo bias is taken as a sign that agents do not have preferences that are fixed through time (see, e.g., Tversky and Kahneman 1991). But although choice does indeed change through time depending on which option

is the status quo, there is no need to infer that welfare judgments also change. The choices that shift are likely to be between options that agents do not know how to order. Agents latch on to the status quo partly for this reason; when no ordering principle is apparent, the non-decision of holding to the status quo provides a convenient default decision.

12. Assuming, that is, that the domain is fixed during the time frame in which choice is observed. For example, to subject transitivity to empirical test, one cannot claim, after sequentially observing $x \succeq y$, $y \succeq z$, and $z \succ x$, that the x rejected in the third round is actually distinct from the x that is accepted in the first round. An independence assumption is also required; see section 7.

13. See Green 1987 for a more formal treatment and Machina 1989 for critical discussion. The antimanipulation rationale for independence was anticipated by early probabilists who argued that if agents' subjective probabilities do not conform to the rules of probability theory they will agree to bets under which they lose money with certainty (see de Finetti 1937 and Kyburg and Smokler 1964).

14. If G is nonlinear, and p, q, r, and s are four lotteries, the following ratios need not be equal:

$$\frac{\sum_{i=1}^{n} p^i u(x^i) - \sum_{i=1}^{n} q^i u(x^i)}{\sum_{i=1}^{n} r^i u(x^i) - \sum_{i=1}^{n} s^i u(x^i)}$$

$$\frac{G(\sum_{i=1}^{n} p^i u(x^i)) - G(\sum_{i=1}^{n} q^i u(x^i))}{G(\sum_{i=1}^{n} r^i u(x^i)) - G(\sum_{i=1}^{n} s^i u(x^i))}$$

The same $\succeq$ is therefore consistent with different ratios of utility differences.

References

Arrow, K. 1963. *Social Choice and Individual Values*. 2nd ed. New Haven: Yale University Press.

Davidson, D., J. McKinsey, and P. Suppes. 1955. "Outlines of a Formal Theory of Value, I." *Philosophy of Science* 22: 140–160.

De Finetti, B. 1937. "Foresight: Its Logical Laws, Its Subjective Sources." In *Annales de l'Institut Henri Poincaré* 7. Reprinted in *Studies in Subjective Probability*, edited by H. Kyburg and H. Smokler, pp. 93–158. New York: Wiley, 1964.

Fisher, I. 1892. *Mathematical Investigations in the Theory of Value and Price*. New Haven: Yale University Press, 1925.

Fishburn, P. 1970. *Utility Theory for Decision Making*. New York: Wiley.

Green, J. 1987. "'Making Book against Oneself,' the Independence Axiom, and Nonlinear Utility Theory." *Quarterly Journal of Economics* 102: 785–796.

Harsanyi, J. 1953. "Cardinal Utility in Welfare Economics and in the Theory of Risk-Taking." *Journal of Political Economy* 63: 434–435.

Jevons, W. S. 1871. *Theory of Political Economy*. London: Macmillan.

Krantz, D., R. D. Luce, P. Suppes, and A. Tversky, 1971. *Foundations of Measurement*. Vol. 1. New York: Academic Press.

Kreps, D. 1988. *Notes on the Theory of Choice*. Boulder: Westview.

Kyburg, H., and H. Smokler. 1964. Introduction. In *Studies in Subjective Probability*, edited by H. Kyburg and H. Smokler, pp. 1–15. New York: Wiley.

Levi, I. 1986. *Hard Choices: Decision Making under Unresolved Conflict*. Cambridge: Cambridge University Press.

Lewin, S. 1996. "Economics and Psychology: Lessons for Our Own Day, from the Early Twentieth Century." *Journal of Economic Literature* 34: 1293–1323.

Machina, M. 1989. "Dynamic Consistency and Non-expected Utility Models of Choice under Uncertainty." *Journal of Economic Literature* 27: 1622–1668.

Mandler, M. 1998. "Incomplete Preferences and Rational Intransitivity of Choice." Harvard University.

Mandler, M. 1999. "Compromises between Cardinality and Ordinality, with an Application to the Convexity of Preferences." Mimeo, Royal Holloway College, University of London.

Marshall, A. 1920. *Principles of Economics*. 8th ed. London: Macmillan.

Mill, J. S. 1838. "Bentham." Reprinted in *Collected Works of John Stuart Mill*, edited by J. Robson, vol. 10, pp. 75–115. Toronto: Toronto University Press, 1969.

Mill, J. S. 1861. "Utilitarianism." Reprinted in *Collected Works of John Stuart Mill*, edited by J. Robson, vol. 10, pp. 203–259. Toronto: Toronto University Press, 1969.

Rabin, M. 1998. "Psychology and Economics." *Journal of Economic Literature* 36: 11–46.

Raz, J. 1986. *The Morality of Freedom*. Oxford: Clarendon Press.

Sen, A. 1973. "Behaviour and the Concept of Preference." *Economica* 40: 241–259.

Sen, A. 1982. Introduction. In his *Choice, Welfare, and Measurement*, pp. 1–38. Oxford: Blackwell.

Sen, A. 1997. "Maximization and the Act of Choice." *Econometrica* 65: 745–780.

Tversky, A., and D. Kahneman. 1991. "Loss Aversion in Riskless Choice: A Reference-Dependent Model." *Quarterly Journal of Economics* 106: 1039–1061.

Wicksteed, P. 1910. *The Common Sense of Political Economy*. London: Macmillan.

Chapter 18

The Idea of Perfection

Iris Murdoch

It is sometimes said, either irritably or with a certain satisfaction, that philosophy makes no progress. It is certainly true, and I think this is an abiding and not a regrettable characteristic of the discipline, that philosophy has in a sense to keep trying to return to the beginning: a thing which it is not at all easy to do. There is a two-way movement in philosophy, a movement towards the building of elaborate theories, and a move back again towards the consideration of simple and obvious facts. McTaggart says that time is unreal, Moore replies that he has just had his breakfast. Both these aspects of philosophy are necessary to it.

I wish in this discussion to attempt a movement of return, a retracing of our steps to see how a certain position was reached. The position in question, in current moral philosophy, is one which seems to me unsatisfactory in two related ways, in that it ignores certain facts and at the same time imposes a single theory which admits of no communication with or escape into rival theories. If it is true that philosophy has almost always done this, it is also true that philosophers have never put up with it for very long. Instances of the facts, as I shall boldly call them, which interest me and which seem to have been forgotten or 'theorized away' are the fact that an unexamined life can be virtuous and the fact that love is a central concept in morals. Contemporary philosophers frequently connect consciousness with virtue, and although they constantly talk of freedom they rarely talk of love. But there must be some relation between these latter concepts, and it must be possible to do justice to both Socrates and the virtuous peasant. In such 'musts' as these lie the deepest springs and motives of philosophy. Yet if in an attempt to enlarge our field of vision we turn for a moment to philosophical theories outside our own tradition we find it very difficult to establish any illuminating connection.

Professor Hampshire says, in the penultimate chapter of *Thought and Action*, that 'it is the constructive task of a philosophy of mind to provide a set of terms in which ultimate judgements of value can be very clearly stated.' In this understanding of it, philosophy of mind is the background to moral philosophy; and in so far as modern ethics tends to constitute a sort of Newspeak which makes certain values non-expressible, the reasons for this are to be sought in current philosophy of mind and in the fascinating power of a certain picture of the soul. One suspects that philosophy of mind has not in fact been performing the task, which Professor Hampshire recommends, of sorting and classifying fundamental moral issues; it has rather been imposing upon us a particular value judgment in the guise of a theory of human nature. Whether philosophy can ever do anything *else* is a question we shall have to consider. But in so far as modern philosophers profess to be analytic and neutral any failure to be so deserves comment. And an attempt to produce, if not a comprehensive analysis, at least a rival soul-picture which covers a greater or a different territory should make new places for philosophical reflection. We would like to know what, as moral agents, we have got to do because of logic, what we have got to do because of human nature, and what we can choose to do. Such a programme is easy to state and perhaps impossible to carry out. But even to discover what, under these headings, we *can* achieve certainly demands a much more complex and subtle conceptual system than any which we can find readily available.

Before going on to consider the problems in philosophy of mind which underlie the inarticulate moments of modern ethics I should like to say a word about G. E. Moore. Moore is as it were the frame of the picture. A great deal has happened since he wrote, and when we read him again it is startling to see how many of his beliefs are philosophically unstatable now. Moore believed that good was a supersensible reality, that it was a mysterious quality, unrepresentable and indefinable, that it was an object of knowledge and (implicitly) that to be able to see it was in some sense to have it. He thought of the good upon the analogy of the beautiful; and he was, in spite of himself, a 'naturalist' in that he took goodness to be a real constituent of the world. We know how severely and in what respects Moore was corrected by his successors. Moore was quite right (it was said) to separate the question 'What does "good" mean?' from the question 'What things are good?' though he was wrong to answer the second question as well as the first. He was right to say that good was indefinable, but wrong to say that it was the name of a quality. Good is indefinable because judgments of value depend upon the will and choice of the individual. Moore was wrong (his critics continue) to use the quasi-aesthetic imagery of vision in conceiving the good. Such a view, conceiving the good on the analogy of the beautiful, would seem to make possible a contemplative attitude on the part of the moral agent, whereas the point about this person is that he is essentially and inescapably an *agent*. The image whereby to understand morality, it is argued, is not the image of vision but the image of movement. Goodness and beauty are not analogous but sharply contrasting ideas. Good must be thought of, not as part of the world, but as a movable label affixed to the world; for only so can the agent be pictured as responsible and free. And indeed this truth Moore himself half apprehended when he separated the denotation from the connotation of 'good'. The concept 'good' is not the name of an esoteric object, it is the tool of every rational man. Goodness is not an object of insight or knowledge, it is a function of the will. Thus runs the correction of Moore; and let me say in anticipation that on almost every point I agree with Moore and not with his critics.

The idea that 'good' is a function of the will stunned philosophy with its attractiveness, since it solved so many problems at one blow: metaphysical entities were removed, and moral judgments were seen to be, not weird statements, but something much more comprehensible, such as persuasions or commands or rules. The idea has its own obviousness: but it does not depend for its plausibility solely upon its usefulness or upon an appeal to our ordinary knowledge of the moral life. It coheres with a whole moral psychology, much of which has been elaborated more recently. I want now to examine certain aspects of this psychology and to trace it to what I think is its origin and basis in a certain argument of Wittgenstein. First I shall sketch 'the man' which this psychology presents us with, then I shall comment on this man's most important features, and then I shall proceed to consider the radical arguments for such an image.

I shall use for my picture of 'the man' of modern moral philosophy two works of Professor Hampshire, his book *Thought and Action* and his lecture *Disposition and Memory*. Hampshire's view is, I think, without commanding universal agreement, fairly central and typical, and it has the great merit that it states and elaborates what in many modern moral philosophers is simply taken for granted. Hampshire suggests that we should abandon the image (dear to the British empiricists) of man as a detached observer, and should rather picture him as an object moving among other objects in a continual flow of intention into action. Touch and movement, not vision, should supply our metaphors: 'Touching, handling and the manipulation of things are misrepresented if we follow the analogy of vision.' Actions are, roughly, instances of moving things about in the public world. Nothing counts as an act unless it is a 'bringing about of a recognizable change in the world'. What sorts of things can be such recognizable changes? Here we must distinguish between 'the things and persons that constitute the external world and the sensations and impressions that I or anyone else may from moment to moment enjoy'. What is 'real' is potentially open to different observers. The inner or mental world is inevitably parasitic upon the outer world, it has 'a parasitic and shadowy nature'. The definiteness of any thought process depends upon 'the possibility of [its] being recognized, scrutinized and identified by observers from different points of view; this possibility is essential to any definite reality'. 'The play of the mind, free of any expression in audible speech or visible action is a reality, as the play of shadows is a reality. But any description of it is derived from the description of its natural expression in speech and action.' 'The assent that takes place within the mind and in no process of communication when no question has been actually asked and answered is a shadowy assent and a shadowy act.' 'Thought cannot be thought, as opposed to day-dreaming or musing, unless it is directed towards a conclusion, whether in action or in judgement.' Further: thought and belief are separate from will and action. 'We do try, in ordinary speech and thought, to keep the distinction between thought and action as definite as possible.' Thought as such is not action but an introduction to action. 'That which I do is that for which I am responsible and which is peculiarly an expression of myself. It is essential to thought that it takes its own forms and follows its own paths without my intervention, that is, without the intervention of my will. I identify myself with my will. Thought, when it is most pure, is self-directing. . . . Thought begins on its own path, governed by its universal rules, when the preliminary work of the will is done. No process of thought could be punctuated by acts of will, voluntary switchings of attention, and retain its status as a continuous process of thought.' These are very important assumptions. It will follow from this that a 'belief' is not something subject to the will. 'It seems that I cannot present my own belief in something as an achievement, because, by so presenting it, I would disqualify it as *belief*.' These quotations are from *Thought and Action*, the later part of Chapter Two.

In the Ernest Jones lecture, *Disposition and Memory*, Hampshire does two things: he puts the arguments of *Thought and Action* more polemically in a nutshell, and he introduces, under the protection of Freud, an idea of 'personal verification' which I shall discuss at length below. From *Disposition and Memory*: 'Intention is the one concept that ought to be preserved free from any taint of the less than conscious.' And 'it is characteristic of mental, as opposed to physical, concepts that the conditions of their application can only be understood if they are analysed genetically'. These are succinct statements of what has already been argued in *Thought and Action*. Hampshire now gives us in addition a picture of 'the ideally rational man'. This person would be 'aware of all his memories as memories.... His wishes would be attached to definite possibilities in a definite future.... He would ... distinguish his present situation from unconscious memories of the past ... and would find his motives for action in satisfying his instinctual needs within the objectively observed features of the situation.' This ideal man does not exist because the palimpsest of 'dispositions' is too hard to penetrate: and this is just as well because ideal rationality would leave us 'without art, without dream or imagination, without likes or dislikes unconnected with instinctual needs'. In theory, though not in practice, 'an interminable analysis' could lay bare the dispositional machinery and make possible a perfect prediction of conduct; but Hampshire emphasizes (and this is the main point of the lecture) that such ideal knowledge would not take the form of a scientific law but would have its basis and its verification in the history of the individual. I shall argue later that the very persuasive image with which Hampshire has presented us contains incompatible elements. Roughly, there is a conflict between the 'logical' view of the mind and the 'historical' view of the mind, a conflict which exists partly because logic is still tied to an old-fashioned conception of science. But this is to anticipate.

I shall find it useful later to define my own view in fairly exact section-by-section contrast with Hampshire's; and as his view is rich in detail, extensive quotation has been necessary. As I have suggested, Hampshire's man is to be found more or less explicitly lurking behind much that is written nowadays on the subject of moral philosophy and indeed also of politics. Hampshire has thoroughly explored a background which many writers have taken for granted: and for this one is grateful. This 'man', one may add, is familiar to us for another reason: he is the hero of almost every contemporary novel. Let us look at his characteristics, noting them as yet without discussion. Hampshire emphasizes clarity of intention. He says 'all problems meet in intention', and he utters in relation to intention the only explicit 'ought' in his psychology. We ought to know what we are doing. We should aim at total knowledge of our situation and a clear conceptualization of all our possibilities. Thought and intention must be directed towards definite overt issues or else they are merely day-dream. 'Reality' is potentially open to different observers. What is 'inward', what lies in between overt actions, is either impersonal thought, or 'shadows' of acts, or else substanceless dream. Mental life is, and logically must be, a shadow of life in public. Our personal being is the movement of our overtly choosing will. Immense care is taken to picture the will as isolated. It is isolated from belief, from reason, from feeling, and is yet the essential centre of the self. 'I identify myself with my will.' It is separated from belief so that the authority of reason, which manufactures belief, may be entire and so that responsibility for action may be entire as well. My responsibility is a function of my knowledge (which tries to be wholly impersonal) and my will (which is wholly personal). Morality is a matter of thinking clearly and then proceeding to outward dealings with other men.

On this view one might say that morality is assimilated to a visit to a shop. I enter the shop in a condition of totally responsible freedom, I objectively estimate the features of the goods, and I choose. The greater my objectivity and discrimination the larger the number of products from which I can select. (A Marxist critique of this conception of bourgeois capitalist morals would be apt enough. Should we want many goods in the shop or just 'the right goods'?) Both as act and reason, shopping is public. Will does not bear upon reason, so the 'inner life' is not to be thought of as a moral sphere. Reason deals in neutral descriptions and aims at being the frequently mentioned ideal observer. Value terminology will be the prerogative of the will; but since will is pure choice, pure movement, and not thought or vision, will really requires only action words such as 'good' or 'right'. It is not characteristic of the man we are describing, as he appears either in textbooks or in fiction, to possess an elaborate normative vocabulary. Modern ethics analyses 'good', the empty action word which is the correlate of the isolated will, and tends to ignore other value terms. Our hero aims at being a 'realist' and regards sincerity as the fundamental and perhaps the only virtue.

The very powerful image with which we are here presented is behaviourist, existentialist, and utilitarian in a sense which unites these three conceptions. It is behaviourist in its connection of the meaning and being of action with the publicly observable, it is existentialist in its elimination of the substantial self and its emphasis on the solitary omnipotent will, and it is utilitarian in its assumption that morality is and can only be concerned with public acts. It is also incidentally what may be called a democratic view, in that it suggests that morality is not an esoteric achievement but a natural function of any normal man. This position represents, to put it in another way, a happy and fruitful marriage of Kantian liberalism with Wittgensteinian logic solemnized by Freud. But this also is to anticipate; what confronts us here is in fact complex and difficult to analyse. Let me now try to sort out and classify the different questions which need to be answered.

I find the image of man which I have sketched above both alien and implausible. That is, more precisely: I have simple empirical objections (I do not think people are necessarily or essentially 'like that'), I have philosophical objections (I do not find the arguments convincing), and I have moral objections (I do not think people *ought* to picture themselves in this way). It is a delicate and tricky matter to keep these kinds of objections separate in one's mind. Later on I shall try to present my own rival picture. But now first of all I want to examine in more detail the theory of the 'inner life' with which we have been presented. One's initial reaction to this theory is likely to be a strong instinctive one: either one will be content with the emphasis on the reality of the outer, the absence of the inner, or one will feel (as I do) it cannot be so, something vital is missing. And if one thinks that somehow or other 'the inner' is important one will be the more zealous in criticizing the arguments concerning its status. Such criticisms may have far-reaching results, since upon the question of 'what goes on inwardly' in between moments of overt 'movement' depends our view of the status of choice, the meaning of freedom, and the whole problem of the relation of will to reason and intellect to desire. I shall now consider what I think is the most radical argument, the keystone, of this existentialist-behaviourist type of moral psychology: the argument to the effect that mental concepts must be analysed genetically and so the inner must be thought of as parasitic upon the outer.

This argument is best understood as a special case of a yet more general and by now very familiar argument about the status of what is 'private'. Our tradition of philosophy, since Descartes until very recently, has been obsessed by an entity which has had various names: the *cogitatio*, the sense-impression, the sense-datum. This entity, private to each person, was thought of as an *appearance* about which the owner had infallible and certain *knowledge*. It was taken by Descartes as the starting point of a famous argument, and was pictured by the British empiricists as an instrument of thought. The conception of the *cogitatio* or sense-datum, oddly attractive and readily grasped, suggests among other things that what is inward may be private in one of two senses, one a contingent sense and one a logical sense. I can tell you, or refrain from telling you, a secret; but I cannot (logically) show you my sense-data.

After a long and varied history this conception has now been largely abandoned by philosophers. The general argument for abandoning it has two prongs. Briefly, the argument against the *cogitatio* is that (a) such an entity cannot form part of the structure of a public concept, (b) such an entity cannot be introspectively discovered. That is, (a) it's no use, (b) it isn't there. The latter point may be further subdivided into an empirical and a logical contention. The empirical contention is that there are very few and pretty hazy introspectabilia, and the logical contention is that there are in any case difficulties about their identification. Of the two moments in the general argument (a) has received more attention than (b), since as (a) has been regarded as knock-down (b) has been treated as subsidiary. If something is no use it does not matter much whether it's there or not. I shall argue shortly that because something is no use it has been too hastily assumed that something else is not there. But let us first look at the argument in more detail.

I said that the argument about mental concepts was a special case of the general argument. The general argument is at its most felicitous when applied to some simple nonmental concept such as 'red'. 'Red' cannot be the name of something private. The structure of the concept is its public structure, which is established by coinciding procedures in public situations. How much success we can have in establishing any given public structure will be an empirical question. The alleged inner thing can neither be known (Descartes) nor used (the British empiricists). Hume was wrong to worry about the missing shade of blue, not because a man could or couldn't picture it, or that we could or couldn't be persuaded that he had, but because the inner picture is necessarily irrelevant and the possession of the concept is a public skill. What matters is whether I stop at the traffic lights, and not my colour imagery or absence of it. I identify what my senses show me by means of the public schemata which I have learned, and in no other way can this be *known* by me, since knowledge involves the rigidity supplied by a public test. Wittgenstein in the *Untersuchungen* sums the situation up as follows: 'If we construe the grammar of the expression of sensation on the model of "object and name", the object drops out of consideration as irrelevant.'

This argument, which bears down relentlessly upon the case of 'red', might seem to be even more relentless in the case of the very much more shadowy inner entities which might be supposed to be the 'objects' of which mental concepts are 'names'. After all, one might say to oneself in a quasi-nonsensical way, my sensation of red does, when I am doing philosophy, look like something which I have privately 'got'; and if I am not allowed to 'keep' even this clear little thing as my own private datum, why should I expect to 'keep' the hopelessly hazy inner phenomena connected with concepts such as 'decision' and 'desire'? Surely I should in the latter cases be even happier to rely upon the 'outer' face of the concept, since the inner one is so vague. Let me clarify this so as to make plain the force of the genetic argument in the case of mental concepts.

Wittgenstein of course discusses in this context mental as well as physical concepts. But his discussion is marked by a peculiar reticence. He does not make any moral or psychological generalizations. He limits himself to observing that a mental concept verb used in the first person is not a report about something private, since in the absence of any checking procedure it makes no sense to speak of oneself being either right or mistaken. Wittgenstein is not claiming that inner data are 'incommunicable', nor that anything special about human personality follows from their 'absence', he is merely saying that no sense can be attached to the idea of an 'inner object'. There are no 'private ostensive definitions'. Whether Wittgenstein is right to say that we can attach no sense to the idea of being mistaken about how things *seem*, and whether any legitimate conclusions about human nature can be drawn from his position I shall consider later. I want now to go on to look at the conclusions which *have* (not by him) been drawn, and at the developed form of the argument as we find it, with variations, in Hampshire, Hare, Ayer, Ryle and others.

As I have said, the argument seems to bear even more strongly in proportion as the alleged inner datum becomes more obviously shadowy and even tends to be irresponsibly absent. In such cases purely empirical considerations (the empirical subdivision of (b) above) are especially strong. I say, 'Well, I must decide. All right. I'll go.' Perhaps nothing introspectible occurs at all? And even if it does *that* is not the decision. Here we see what is meant by speaking of a genetical analysis. How do I *learn* the concept of decision? By watching someone who says 'I have decided' and who then acts. How else could I learn it? And with that I learn the essence of the matter. I do not 'move on' from a behaviouristic concept to a mental one. (Since ordinary language, which 'misleadingly' connects the mental with the inner, straightforwardly connects the physical with the outer, a genetic analysis of physical concepts would not be especially revealing.) A decision does not turn out to be, when more carefully considered, an introspectible movement. The concept has no further inner structure; it *is* its outer structure. Take an even clearer example. How do I distinguish anger from jealousy? Certainly not by discriminating between two kinds of private mental data. Consider how I *learned* 'anger' and 'jealousy'. What identifies the emotion is the presence not of a particular private object, but of some typical outward behaviour pattern. This will also imply, be it noted, that we can be mistaken in the names which we give to our own mental states.

This is the point at which people may begin to protest and cry out and say that something has been taken from them. Surely there is such a thing as deciding and not acting? Surely there are *private* decisions? Surely there are lots and lots of objects, more or less easily identified, in orbit as it were in inner space? It is not, as the argument would seem to imply, silent and dark within. Philosophers will reply coolly to these protests. Of course a sense can be attached to: he decided to but did not. That is, he said he would go, and we had reasons to believe that he would, but a brick fell on his head. Or, the notion of his going cohered with many other things he was doing and saying, and yet he did not go. But all this is just as overt, just as little private, as the actual carrying out of the decision. And it must be admitted to be, when one reflects, difficult to attach sense by any other method to the idea of an unfulfilled decision, in our own case just as much as in the case of someone else. Are there 'private' decisions? I said some words to myself. But did I really decide? To answer that question I examine the *context* of my announcement rather than its private core.

However, it will be said, surely there *are* introspectible objects which we can identify? We *do* have images, talk to ourselves, etc. Does the genetic argument imply that these are nothing? Well, it might be answered, let us look at them. One might roughly divide these data in order of shadowiness into visual images, verbal thoughts, other images, other thoughts and feelings which while not exactly verbal or visual seem nevertheless to be 'entities'. It will be true of all these that I cannot show them to other people. Of course I can to a limited extent describe them,

I can describe my imagery or mention words which I 'say' in my head. I can also give metaphorical descriptions of my states of mind. (Ryle discusses these 'chronicles' and 'histories' of thought in *Aristotelian Society*, supplementary volume 1952.) But what does this amount to? These data, vaguer and more infrequent than one might unreflectively suppose, cannot claim to be 'the thing itself' of which my uttered thoughts are the report. Note that I offer my descriptions in ordinary public words whose meaning is subject to ordinary public rules. Inner words 'mean' in the same way as outer words; and I can only 'know' my imagery because I know the public things which it is 'of'. Public concepts are in this obvious sense sovereign over private objects; I can only 'identify' the inner, even for my own benefit, via my knowledge of the outer. But in any case there is no check upon the accuracy of such descriptions, and as Wittgenstein says, 'What is this ceremony for?' Who, except possibly empirical psychologists, is interested in alleged reports of what is *purely* inward? And psychologists themselves now have grave doubts about the value of such 'evidence' from introspection. Whether I am *really* thinking about so-and-so or deciding such-and-such or feeling angry or jealous or pleased will be properly determined, and can only be determined, by the overt context, however sketchy and embryonic. That I decided to do *X* will be true if I said sincerely that I was going to and did it, even if nothing introspectible occurred at all. And equally something introspectible might occur, but if the outward context is entirely lacking the something cannot be called a decision. As Wittgenstein puts it, 'a wheel that can be turned though nothing else moves with it is not part of the mechanism'.

These radical arguments are, it seems to me, perfectly sound over a certain range. They really do clearly and definitively solve certain problems which have beset British empiricism. By destroying the misleading image of the infallible inner eye they make possible a much improved solution of, for instance, problems about perception and about universals. A great deal that was, in Hume and Berkeley, repugnant to common sense can now be cleared away. But, as I have said, while Wittgenstein remains sphinx-like in the background, others have hastened to draw further and more dubious moral and psychological conclusions. Wittgenstein has created a void into which neo-Kantianism, existentialism, utilitarianism have made haste to enter. And notice how plausibly the arguments, their prestige enhanced from undoubted success in other fields, seem to support, indeed to impose, the image of personality which I have sketched above. As the 'inner life' is hazy, largely absent, and any way 'not part of the mechanism', it turns out to be *logically* impossible to take up an idle contemplative attitude to the good. Morality must be action since mental concepts can only be analysed genetically. Metaphors of movement and not vision seem obviously appropriate. Morality, with the full support of logic, abhors the private. Salvation by works is a conceptual necessity. *What* I am doing or being is not something private and personal, but is imposed upon me in the sense of being identifiable only via public concepts and objective observers. Self-knowledge is something which shows overtly. Reasons are public reasons, rules are public rules. Reason and rule represent a sort of impersonal tyranny in relation to which however the personal will represents perfect freedom. The machinery is relentless, but until the moment of choice the agent is outside the machinery. Morality resides at the point of action. What I am 'objectively' is not under my control; logic and observers decide that. What I am 'subjectively' is a foot-loose, solitary, substanceless will. Personality dwindles to a point of pure will.

Now it is not at all easy to mount an attack upon this heavily fortified position; and, as I say, temperament will play its part in determining whether or not we *want* to attack or whether we are content. I am not content. Let me start cautiously to suggest an alternative view, taking however for a rubric the warning words of Wittgenstein: 'Being unable—when we surrender ourselves to philosophical thought—to help saying such-and-such; being irresistibly inclined to say it—does not mean being forced into an *assumption*, or having an immediate perception or knowledge of a state of affairs.'

For purposes of the rest of this discussion it will be useful to have an example before us: some object which we can all more or less see, and to which we can from time to time refer. All sorts of different things would do for this example, and I was at first tempted to take a case of *ritual*, for instance a religious ritual wherein the inner consent appears to be the real act. Ritual: an outer framework which both occasions and identifies an inner event. It can be argued that I make a promise by uttering the words 'I promise': a performative utterance. But do I, in a religious context, repent by sincerely uttering the words 'I repent', am I 'heartily sorry' simply by saying in an appropriate situation that I am heartily sorry? Is this so even if I then amend my life? This is not so clear and is indeed a difficult and interesting question. I decided however not to take a religious example, which might be felt to raise special difficulties, but to take something more ordinary and everyday. So here is the example.

A mother, whom I shall call *M*, feels hostility to her daughter-in-law, whom I shall call *D*. *M* finds *D* quite a good-hearted girl, but while not exactly common yet certainly unpolished and lacking in dignity and refinement. *D* is inclined to be pert and familiar, insufficiently cere-monious, brusque, sometimes positively rude, always tiresomely juvenile. *M* does not like *D*'s accent or the way *D* dresses. *M* feels that her son has married beneath him. Let us assume for purposes of the example that the mother, who is a very 'correct' person, behaves beautifully to the girl throughout, not allowing her real opinion to appear in any way. We might underline this aspect of the example by supposing that the young couple have emigrated or that *D* is now dead: the point being to ensure that whatever is in question as *happening* happens entirely in *M*'s mind.

Thus much for *M*'s first thoughts about *D*. Time passes, and it could be that *M* settles down with a hardened sense of grievance and a fixed picture of *D*, imprisoned (if I may use a question-begging word) by the cliché: my poor son has married a silly vulgar girl. However, the *M* of the example is an intelligent and well-intentioned person, capable of self-criticism, capable of giving careful and just *attention* to an object which confronts her. *M* tells herself: 'I am old-fashioned and conventional. I may be prejudiced and narrow-minded. I may be snobbish. I am certainly jealous. Let me look again.' Here I assume that *M* observes *D* or at least reflects deliberately about *D*, until gradually her vision of *D* alters. If we take *D* to be now absent or dead this can make it clear that the change is not in *D*'s behaviour but in *M*'s mind. *D* is discovered to be not vulgar but refreshingly simple, not undignified but spontaneous, not noisy but gay, not tiresomely juvenile but delightfully youthful, and so on. And as I say, *ex hypothesi*, *M*'s outward behaviour, beautiful from the start, in no way alters.

I used above words such as 'just' and 'intelligent' which implied a favourable value judgment on *M*'s activity: and I want in fact to imagine a case where one would feel approval of *M*'s change of view. But of course in real life, and this is of interest, it might be very hard to decide whether what *M* was doing was proper or not, and opinions might differ. *M* might be moved by various motives: a sense of justice, attempted love for *D*, love for her son, or simply reluctance to think of him as unfortu-nate or mistaken. Some people might say 'she deludes herself' while others would say she was moved by love or justice. I am picturing a case where I would find the latter description appropriate.

What *happens* in this example could of course be described in other ways. I have chosen to describe it simply in terms of the substitution of one set of normative epithets for another. It could also be described, for instance, in terms of *M*'s visual imagery, or in simple or complex metaphors. But let us consider now what exactly 'it' is which is being described. It may be argued that there is nothing here which presents any special difficulty. For purposes of moral judgment we may define 'actions' in various ways. One way in this case would be to say that *M* decided to behave well to *D* and did so; and *M*'s private thoughts will be unimportant and morally irrelevant. If however it is desired to include in the list of *M*'s moral acts more than her overt behaviour shows, one will have to ask of the extra material: in what sense 'moral' and in what sense 'acts'? Of course if *M*'s reflections were the prologue to *different* outer acts, then the reflections might be allowed to 'belong' to the acts as their 'shadows' and gain from them their identity and their importance: though the difficulty of discerning the inward part and connecting it with the outer as a condition of the latter could still be considerable. But what are we to say in the present case?

Hampshire tells us: 'Thought cannot be thought as opposed to day-dreaming or musing, unless it is directed towards a conclusion, whether in action or in judgement.... The idea of thought as an interior mono-logue ... will become altogether empty if the thought does not even pur-port to be directed towards its issue in the external world.... Under these conditions thought and belief would not differ from the charmed and habitual rehearsal of phrases or the drifting of ideas through the mind.' Let us exclude from this discussion something which might at this point try to enter it, which is the eye of God. If *M*'s mental events are not to depend for being and importance upon this metaphysical witness, do we want to, and if so how can we, rescue them from the fate of being mere nothings, at best describable as day-dreams?

It would be possible of course to give a *hypothetical* status to *M*'s inner life, as follows. '*M*'s vision of *D* has altered *means* that *if M* were to speak her mind about *D* now she would say different things from the things she would have said three years ago.' This analysis avoids some difficulties but, like phenomenalism, encounters others. The truth of the hypothetical proposition could be consistent with nothing in the interim having occurred in *M*'s mind at all. And of course a change of mind often does take the form of the simple announcement of a new view without any introspectible material having intervened. But here *ex hypothesi* there is at least something introspectible which has occurred, however hazy this may be, and it is the status of this which is in question. At any rate the idea which we are trying to make sense of is that *M* has in the interim been *active*, she has been *doing* something, something which we approve of, something which is somehow worth doing in itself. *M* has been morally active in the interim: this is what we want to say and to be philosophically permitted to say.

At this point the defender of what I have called the existentialist-behaviourist view may argue as follows. All right. Either *M* has no introspectible material, in which case since *M*'s conduct is constant it is hard to see what could be meant by saying that she had changed her mind, other than saying that a hypothetical proposition is true which no one could know to be true; or else *M* has introspectible material and let us see what this might be like. *M* may imagine saying things to *D*, may verbally describe *D* in her mind, may brood on visual images of *D*. But what do these goings-on mean? What is to count here as serious judgment as opposed to 'the charmed and habitual rehearsal of phrases?' *M*'s introspectabilia are likely on examination to prove hazy and hard to describe; and even if (at best) we imagine *M* as making clear verbal statements to herself, the identity and meaning of these statements is a function of the public world. She can only be thought of as 'speaking' seriously, and not parrot-like, if the outer context logically permits.

The point can also be made, it may be said in parenthesis, that the identity of inward thoughts is established via the public meaning of the symbolism used in thinking. (See, e.g., Ayer, *Thinking and Meaning*.) This should refute claims to 'ineffable experience', etc. Philosophers have more recently chosen to emphasize the 'shadow' view, that is to consider the particular sense of the thought via context rather than the general sense of the thought via symbols. But I think the points are worth separating. They represent two complementary pictures of the 'self' or 'will' as outside the network of logical rules, free to decide where to risk its tyranny, but thereafter caught in an impersonal complex. I can decide what to say but not what the words mean which I have said. I can decide what to do but I am not master of the significance of my act.

Someone who says privately or overtly 'I have decided' but who never acts, however favourable the circumstances (the existentialist-behaviourist argument continues), has not decided. Private decisions which precede public actions may be thought of as the 'shadow' of the act, gaining their title from being part of a complex properly called 'decision': though even here the term 'decision' if applied to the inner part only would be a courtesy title since there is no check upon the nature or existence of the inner part and its connection with the outer. Still, that is the situation in which we innocuously and popularly speak of 'private decisions' or 'inner acts', i.e., where some kind of outer structure is present and we may if we like picture, perhaps we naturally picture, an inner piece too. In M's case, however, since there is no outward alteration of structure to correspond to an alleged inner change, no sequence of outer events of which the inner can claim to be shadows, it is dubious whether any sense can be given here to the idea of 'activity'. The attempted categorical sense of M's inner progress has to fall back on the hypothetical sense mentioned above. And the hypothetical proposition cannot be known to be true, even by M, and could be true without anything happening in M's mind at all. So the idea of M as *inwardly* active turns out to be an empty one. There is only outward activity, ergo only outward moral activity, and what we call inward activity is merely the shadow of this cast back into the mind. And, it may be bracingly added, why worry? As Kant said, what we are commanded to do is to love our neighbour in a practical and not a pathological sense.

This is one of those exasperating moments in philosophy when one seems to be being relentlessly prevented from saying something which one is irresistibly impelled to say. And of course, as Wittgenstein pointed out, the fact that one is irresistibly impelled to say it need not mean that anything *else* is the case. Let us tread carefully here. In reacting against the above analysis there is certainly one thing which I do *not* wish to maintain, and that is that we have infallible or superior knowledge of our mental states. We can be mistaken about what we think and feel: that is not in dispute, and indeed it is a strength of the behaviourist analysis that it so neatly accommodates this fact. What is at stake is something different, something about *activity* in a sense which does not mean privileged activity.

Let me try in a rough ordinary way and as yet without justification to say what I take to be, in spite of the analysis, the case about M: a view which is not congruent with the analysis and which if true shows that the analysis cannot be correct. The analysis pictures M as defined 'from the outside in': M's individuality lies in her will, understood as her 'movements'. The analysis makes no sense of M as continually active, as making progress, or of her inner acts as belonging to her or forming part of a continuous fabric of being: it is precisely critical of metaphors such as 'fabric of being.' Yet can we do without such metaphors here? Further, is not the metaphor of vision almost irresistibly suggested to anyone who, without philosophical prejudice, wishes to describe the situation? Is it not the natural metaphor? *M looks* at *D*, she attends to *D*, she focuses her attention. *M* is engaged in an internal struggle. She may for instance be tempted to enjoy caricatures of *D* in her imagination. (There is curiously little place in the other picture for the idea of *struggle*.) And *M*'s activity here, so far from being something very odd and hazy, is something which, in a way, we find exceedingly familiar. Innumerable novels contain accounts of what such struggles are like. Anybody could describe one without being at a loss for words. This activity, as I said, could be described in a variety of ways, but one very natural way is by the use of specialized normative words, what one might call the secondary moral words in contrast to the primary and general ones such as 'good'. *M* stops seeing *D* as 'bumptious' and sees her as 'gay', etc. I shall comment later upon the importance of these secondary words. Further again, one feels impelled to say something like: *M*'s activity is peculiarly *her own*. Its details are the details of *this* personality; and partly for this reason it may well be an activity which can only be performed privately. *M* could not *do this* thing in conversation with another person. Hampshire says that 'anything which is to count as a definite reality must be open to several observers'. But can this quasi-scientific notion of individuation through unspecified observers really be applied to a case like this? Here there is an activity but no observers; and if one were to introduce the idea of potential observers the question of their *competence* would still arise. *M*'s activity is hard to characterize not because it is hazy but *precisely because it is moral*. And with this, as I shall shortly try to explain, we are coming near to the centre of the difficulty.

What *M* is *ex hypothesi* attempting to do is not just to see *D* accurately but to see her justly or lovingly. Notice the rather different image of freedom which this at once suggests. Freedom is not the sudden jumping of the isolated will in and out of an impersonal logical complex, it is a function of the progressive attempt to see a particular object clearly. *M*'s activity is essentially something progressive, something infinitely perfectible. So far from claiming for it a sort of infallibility, this new picture has built in the notion of a necessary fallibility. *M* is engaged in an endless task. As soon as we begin to use words such as 'love' and 'justice' in characterizing *M*, we introduce into our whole conceptual picture of her situation the idea of progress, that is the idea of perfection: and it is just the presence of this idea which demands an analysis of mental concepts which is different from the genetic one.

I am now inclined to think that it is pointless, when faced with the existentialist-behaviourist picture of the mind, to go on endlessly fretting about the identification of particular inner events, and attempting to defend an account of M as 'active' by producing, as it were, a series of indubitably objective little things. 'Not a report' need not entail 'not an activity'. But to elaborate this what is needed is some sort of change of key, some moving of the attack to a different front. Let us consider for a moment the apparently so plausible idea of identity as dependent upon observers and rules, an idea which leads on directly to the genetic analysis of mental concepts. This is really red if several people agree about the description, indeed this is what being really red means. He really decided, roughly, if people agree that he kept the rules of the concept 'decide'. To decide means to keep these rules and the agent is not the only judge. Actions are 'moving things about in the public world', and what these movements *are* objective observers are actually and potentially at hand to decide.

Wittgenstein, as I have said, does not apply this idea to moral concepts, nor discuss its relation to mental concepts in so far as these form part of the sphere of morality. (That mental concepts enter the sphere of morality is, for my argument, precisely the central point.) But no limit is placed upon the idea either; and I should like to place a limit. What has enabled this idea of identification to go too far is partly, I think, an uncriticized conception of science which has taken on where Hume left off.

Hume pictured a manifold of atoms, hard little indubitable sense-data or appearances, whose 'subsequent' arrangement provided the so-called material world. The Copernican Revolution of modern philosophy ('You can't have "knowledge" of "appearances"') removes the notion of certainty from the inside to the outside: public rules now determine what is certain. It may still be disputed whether one cannot sometimes give a sense to 'being mistaken about an appearance'. There is certainly an area for discussion here, but this discussion has never become a very radical one. It has remained within the general terms of the revolution; and although it would be impossible to dispute the importance of that revolution it has nevertheless been so far in effect a continuation of Hume by other means. (The work of J. L. Austin for instance is a detailed and brilliant exorcism of the notion of the sense-impression. Yet by substituting an impersonal language-world for the old impersonal atom-world of Hume and Russell he in a way 'saves' the latter.) What the philosopher is trying to characterize, indeed to justify, is still the idea of an impersonal world of facts: the hard objective world out of which the will leaps into a position of isolation. What defines and constitutes fact has been removed from one place to another, but the radical idea of 'fact' remains much the same. Logic (impersonal rules) here obliges science with a philosophical model.

What makes difficulties for this model is the conception of persons or individuals, a conception inseparable from morality. The whole vocabulary, so profoundly familiar to us, of 'appearance' and 'reality', whether as used by the old British empiricists or by modern empiricism, is blunt and crude when applied to the human individual. Consider for instance the case of a man trying privately to determine whether something which he 'feels' is repentance or not. Of course this investigation is subject to some public rules, otherwise it would not be *this* investigation: and there could be doubts or disputes about whether it is this investigation. But these apart, the activity in question must remain a highly personal one upon which the *prise* of 'the impersonal world of language' is to say the least problematic: or rather it is an activity which puts in question the existence of such an impersonal world. Here an individual is making a specialized personal *use* of a concept. Of course he derives the concept initially from his surroundings; but he takes it away into his privacy. Concepts of this sort lend themselves to such uses; and what use is made of them is partly a function of the user's *history*. Hume and Kant, the two patron saints of modern philosophy, abhor history, each in his own way, and abhor the particular notion of privacy which history implies. A certain conception of logic and a certain conception of science also abhor history.

But once the historical individual is 'let in' a number of things have to be said with a difference. The idea of 'objective reality', for instance, undergoes important modifications when it is to be understood, not in relation to 'the world described by science', but in relation to the progressing life of a person. The active 'reassessing' and 'redefining' which is a main characteristic of live personality often suggests and demands a checking procedure which is a function of an individual history. Repentance may mean something different to an individual at different times in his life, and what it fully means is a part of this life and cannot be understood except in context.

There is of course a 'science' which concerns itself especially with the history of the individual: psychoanalysis. And with a determination at all costs not to part company with a scientific conception of 'the objective' it is to psychoanalysis that Professor Hampshire finally appeals: he very properly lets in the historical individual, but hopes to keep him by this means upon a lead. Hampshire reads in an impersonal background to the individual's checking procedure with the help of the notion of an ideal analysis. The analyst is pictured as somehow 'there', as the ultimate competent observer playing the part of the eye of God. Hampshire allows that it is possible in theory though not in practice to 'approach complete explanations of inclination and behaviour in any individual case through an interminable analysis'. But why should some unspecified psychoanalyst be the measure of all things? Psychoanalysis is a muddled embryonic science, and even if it were not there is no argument that I know of that can show us that we have got to treat its concepts as fundamental. The notion of an 'ideal analysis' is a misleading one. There is no existing series the extension of which could lead to such an ideal. This is a *moral* question; and what is at stake here is the liberation of morality, and of philosophy as a study of human nature, from the domination of science: or rather from the domination of inexact ideas of science which haunt philosophers and other thinkers. Because of the lack until fairly recently of any clear distinction between science and philosophy this issue has never presented itself so vividly before. Philosophy in the past has played the game of science partly because it thought it was science.

Existentialism, in both its Continental and its Anglo-Saxon versions, is an attempt to solve the problem without really facing it: to solve it by attributing to the individual an empty lonely freedom, a freedom, if he wishes, to 'fly in the face of the facts'. What it pictures is indeed the fearful solitude of the individual marooned upon a tiny island in the middle of a sea of scientific facts, and morality escaping from science only by a wild leap of the will. But our situation is not like this. To put it simply and in terms of the example which we have considered of *M* and her daughter-in-law: even if *M* were given a full psychoanalytical explanation of her conduct to *D* she need not be confined by such an explanation. This is not just because *M* has a senseless petulant freedom which enables her to be blind, nor is it just because (the more subtle view favoured by Hampshire) she is then enabled to redeploy her psychic forces on a ground of greater knowledge. It is because *M* is not forced to adopt these concepts at all, in preference say to any particular set of moral or religious concepts. Science can instruct morality at certain points and can change its direction, but it cannot contain morality, nor ergo moral philosophy. The importance of this issue can more easily be ignored by a philosophy which divorces freedom and knowledge, and leaves knowledge (via an uncriticized idea of 'impersonal reasons') in the domain of science. But M's independence of science and of the 'world of facts' which empiricist philosophy has created in the scientific image rests not simply in her moving will but in her seeing knowing mind. Moral concepts do not move about *within* a hard world set up by science and logic. They set up, for different purposes, a different world.

Let me try now to explain more positively what it is about moral concepts which puts them entirely out of relation with the behaviourist view with its genetic explanation of mental phenomena. I want here to connect two ideas: the idea of the individual and the idea of perfection. Love is knowledge of the individual. M confronted with D has an endless task. Moral tasks are characteristically endless not only because 'within', as it were, a given concept our efforts are imperfect, but also because as we move and as we look our concepts themselves are changing. To speak here of an inevitable imperfection, or of an ideal limit of love or knowledge which always recedes, may be taken as a reference to our 'fallen' human condition, but this need be given no special dogmatic sense. Since we are neither angels nor animals but human individuals, our dealings with each other have this aspect; and this may be regarded as an empirical fact or, by those who favour such terminology, as a synthetic *a priori* truth.

The entry into a mental concept of the notion of an ideal limit destroys the genetic analysis of its meaning. (Hampshire allowed the idea of perfection to touch one concept only, that of intention: but he tried to save this concept from morality by making the ideal limit a scientific one.) Let us see how this is. Is 'love' a mental concept, and if so can it be analysed genetically? No doubt Mary's little lamb loved Mary, that is it followed her to school; and in some sense of 'learn' we might well learn the concept, the word, in that context. But with such a concept that is not the end of the matter. (Nor indeed the beginning either.) Words may mislead us here since words are often stable while concepts alter; we have a different image of courage at forty from that which we had at twenty. A deepening process, at any rate an altering and complicating process, takes place. There are two senses of 'knowing what a word means', one connected with ordinary language and the other very much less so. Knowledge of a value concept is something to be understood, as it were, in depth, and not in terms of switching on to some given impersonal network. Moreover, if morality is essentially connected with change and progress, we cannot be as democratic about it as some philosophers would like to think. We do not simply, through being rational and knowing ordinary language, 'know' the meaning of all necessary moral words. We may have to learn the meaning; and since we are human historical individuals the movement of understanding is onward into increasing privacy, in the direction of the ideal limit, and not back towards a genesis in the rulings of an impersonal public language.

None of what I am saying here is particularly new: similar things have been said by philosophers from Plato onward; and appear as commonplaces of the Christian ethic, whose centre is an individual. To come nearer home in the Platonic tradition, the present dispute is reminiscent of the old arguments about abstract and concrete universals. My view might be put by saying: moral terms must be treated as concrete universals. And if someone at this point were to say, well, why stop at moral concepts, why not claim that all universals are concrete, I would reply, why not indeed? Why not consider red as an ideal end-point, as a concept infinitely to be learned, as an individual object of love? A painter might say, 'You don't know what "red" means.' This would be, by a counterattack, to bring the idea of value, which has been driven by science and logic into a corner, back to cover the whole field of knowledge. But this would be part of a different argument and is not my concern here. Perhaps all concepts could be considered in this way: all I am now arguing is that some concepts must be.

In suggesting that the central concept of morality is 'the individual' thought of as knowable by love, thought of in the light of the command, 'Be ye therefore perfect', I am not, in spite of the philosophical backing which I might here resort to, suggesting anything in the least esoteric. In fact this would, to the ordinary person, be a very much more familiar image than the existentialist one. We ordinarily conceive of and apprehend goodness in terms of virtues which belong to a continuous fabric of being. And it is just the historical, individual, nature of the virtues as actually exemplified which makes it difficult to learn goodness from another person. It is all very well to say that 'to copy a right action is to act rightly' (Hampshire, *Logic and Appreciation*), but what is the form which I am supposed to copy? It is a truism of recent philosophy that this operation of discerning the form is fairly easy, that rationality in this simple sense is a going concern. And of course for certain conventional purposes it is. But it is characteristic of morals that one cannot rest entirely at the conventional level, and that in some ways one ought not to.

We might consider in this context the ambiguity of Kant's position in the *Grundlegung*, where he tells us that when confronted with the person of Christ we must turn back to the pattern of rationality in our own bosoms and decide whether or not we approve of the man we see. Kant is often claimed as a backer of the existentialist view: and these words may readily be taken to advocate that return to self, that concern with the purity of the solitary will, which is favoured by all brands of existentialism. Here I stand alone, in total responsibility and freedom, and can only properly and responsibly do what is intelligible to me, what I can do with a clear intention. But it must be remembered that Kant was a 'metaphysical naturalist' and not an existentialist. Reason itself is for him an ideal limit: indeed his term 'Idea of Reason' expresses precisely that endless aspiration to perfection which is characteristic of moral activity. His is not the 'achieved' or 'given' reason which belongs with 'ordinary language' and convention, nor is his man on the other hand totally unguided and alone. There exists a moral reality, a real though infinitely distant standard: the difficulties of understanding and imitating remain. And in a way it is perhaps a matter of tactics and temperament whether we should look at Christ or at Reason. Kant was especially impressed by the dangers of blind obedience to a person or an institution. But there are (as the history of existentialism shows) just as many dangers attaching to the ambiguous idea of finding the ideal in one's own bosom. The argument for looking outward at Christ and not inward at Reason is that self is such a dazzling object that if one looks *there* one may see nothing else. But as I say, so long as the gaze is directed upon the ideal the exact formulation will be a matter of history and tactics in a sense which is not rigidly determined by religious dogma, and understanding of the ideal will be partial in any case. Where virtue is concerned we often apprehend more than we clearly understand and *grow by looking*.

Let me suggest in more detail how I think this process actually happens. This will I hope enable me to clarify the status of the view I hold and to relate it to linguistic philosophy in particular. I have spoken of a process of deepening or complicating, a process of learning, a progress, which may take place in moral concepts in the dimension which they possess in virtue of their relation to an ideal limit. In describing the example of *M* and her daughter-in-law I drew attention to the important part played by the normative-descriptive words, the specialized or secondary value words. (Such as 'vulgar', 'spontaneous', etc.) By means of these words there takes place what we might call 'the siege of the individual by concepts'. Uses of such words are both instruments and symptoms of learning. Learning takes place when such words are used, either aloud or privately, in the context of particular acts of attention. (*M* attending to *D*.) This is a point to be emphasized. That words are not timeless, that word-utterances are historical occasions, has been noted by some philosophers for some purposes. (Strawson notes it when attacking the Theory of Descriptions.) But the full implications of this fact, with its consequences for the would-be timeless image of reason, have not, in our modern philosophy, been fully drawn. As Plato observes at the end of the *Phaedrus*, words themselves do not contain wisdom. Words said to particular individuals at particular times may occasion wisdom. Words, moreover, have both spatio-temporal and conceptual contexts. We learn through attending to contexts, vocabulary develops through close attention to objects, and we can only understand others if we can to some extent share their contexts. (Often we cannot.) Uses of words by persons grouped round a common object is a central and vital human activity. The art critic can help us if we are in the presence of the same object and if we know something about his scheme of concepts. Both contexts are relevant to our ability to move towards 'seeing more', towards 'seeing what he sees'. Here, as so often, an aesthetic analogy is helpful for morals. *M* could be helped by someone who both knew *D* and whose conceptual scheme *M* could understand or in that context begin to understand. Progress in understanding of a scheme of concepts often takes place as we listen to normative-descriptive talk in the presence of a common object. I have been speaking, in relation to our example, of progress or change for the better, but of course such change (and this is more commonly to be observed) may also be for the worse. Everyday conversation is not necessarily a morally neutral activity and certain ways of describing people can be corrupting and wrong. A smart set of concepts may be a most efficient instrument of corruption. It is especially characteristic of normative words, both desirable and undesirable, to belong to sets or patterns without an appreciation of which they cannot be understood. If a critic tells us that a picture has 'functional colour' or 'significant form' we need to know not only the picture but also something about his general theory in order to understand the remark. Similarly, if *M* says *D* is 'common', although the term does not belong to a technical vocabulary, this use of it can only be fully understood if we know not only *D* but *M*.

This dependence of language upon contexts of attention has consequences. Language is far more idiosyncratic than has been admitted. Reasons are not necessarily and *qua* reasons public. They may be reasons for a very few, and none the worse for that. 'I can't explain. You'd have to know her.' If the common object is lacking, communication may break down and the same words may occasion different results in different hearers. This may seem on reflection very obvious; but philosophy is often a matter of finding a suitable context in which to say the obvious. Human beings are obscure to each other, in certain respects which are particularly relevant to morality, unless they are mutual objects of attention or have common objects of attention, since this affects the degree of elaboration of a common vocabulary. We develop language in the context of looking: the metaphor of vision again. The notion of privileged access to inner events has been held morally suspect because, among other things, it would separate people from 'the ordinary world of rational argument'. But the unavoidable contextual privacy of language already does this, and except at a very simple and conventional level of communication there is no such ordinary world. This conclusion is feared and avoided by many moralists because it seems inimical to the operation of reason and because reason is construed on a scientific model. Scientific language tries to be impersonal and exact and yet accessible for purposes of teamwork; and the degree of accessibility can be decided in relation to definite practical goals. Moral language which relates to a reality infinitely more complex and various than that of science is often unavoidably idiosyncratic and inaccessible.

Words are the most subtle symbols which we possess and our human fabric depends on them. The living and radical nature of language is something which we forget at our peril. It is totally misleading to speak, for instance, of 'two cultures', one literary-humane and the other scientific, as if these were of equal status. There is only one culture, of which science, so interesting and so dangerous, is now an important part. But the most essential and fundamental aspect of culture is the study of literature, since this is an education in how to picture and understand human situations. We are men and we are moral agents before we are scientists, and the place of science in human life must be discussed in *words*. This is why it is and always will be more important to know about Shakespeare than to know about any scientist: and if there is a 'Shakespeare of science' his name is Aristotle.

I have used the word 'attention', which I borrow from Simone Weil, to express the idea of a just and loving gaze directed upon an individual reality. I believe this to be the characteristic and proper mark of the active moral agent. 'Characteristic' and 'proper' suggest in turn a logical and a normative claim; and I shall discuss below how far what I say is to be taken as recommendation and how far as description. In any case a theory, whether normative or logical, is the more attractive the more it explains, the more its structure may be seen as underlying things which are familiar to us in ordinary life. I want now to go on to argue that the view I am suggesting offers a more satisfactory account of human freedom than does the existentialist view. I have classified together as existentialist both philosophers such as Sartre who claim the title, and philosophers such as Hampshire, Hare, Ayer, who do not. Characteristic of both is the identification of the true person with the empty choosing will, and the corresponding emphasis upon the idea of movement rather than vision. This emphasis will go with the anti-naturalistic bias of existentialism. There is no point in talking of 'moral seeing' since there is nothing *morally* to see. There is no moral vision. There is only the ordinary world which is seen with ordinary vision, and there is the will that moves within it. What may be called the Kantian wing and the Surrealist wing of existentialism may be distinguished by the degree of their interest in *reasons* for action, which diminishes to nothing at the Surrealist end.

Our British philosophers are of course very interested in reasons, emphasizing, as I have said, the accessibility, the non-esoteric nature of moral reasoning. But the production of such reasons, it is argued (and this is indeed the point of emphasizing their impersonal character), does not in any way connect or tie the agent to the world or to special personal contexts within the world. He freely chooses his reasons in terms of, and after surveying, the ordinary facts which lie open to everyone: and he acts. This operation, it is argued, *is* the exercise of freedom. This image of man as a highly conscious self-contained being is offered by some philosophers as a *donné* and by others, e.g. Hampshire, as a norm; although Hampshire is careful to give the norm a scientific background.

Let us now ask quite simply if this is realistic, if this is what, in our experience, moral choice is like. It might seem at first that the existentialists have an advantage in that they do account for a peculiar feature of moral choice, which is the strange emptiness which often occurs at the moment of choosing. Of course choices happen at various levels of consciousness, importance, and difficulty. In a simple, easy, unimportant choice there is no need to regard 'what goes on' as anything beyond the obvious sequence of reason, decision, action, or just reason, action; and such choices may properly be regarded as 'impersonal'. 'Shall I go? Oh yes, I promised to.' I receive my bill and I pay it. But difficult and painful choices often present this experience of void of which so much has been made: this sense of not being determined by the reasons. This sensation is hailed with delight by both wings of existentialism. The Kantian wing claims it as showing that we are free in relation to the reasons and the Surrealist wing claims it as showing that there are no reasons. Indeed this experience of emptiness seems perfectly to verify the notion that freedom is simply the movement of the lonely will. Choice is outward movement since there is nothing else there for it to be.

But is this the case, and ought we really to be so pleased about this experience? A more sombre note concerning it is struck at one point by Sartre, who on this problem veers wildly between Kantianism and Surrealism. *Quand je délibère les jeux sont faits.* If we are so strangely separate from the world at moments of choice are we really choosing at all, are we right indeed to identify *ourselves* with this giddy empty will? (Hampshire: 'I identify myself with my will.') In a reaction of thought which is never far from the minds of more extreme existentialists (Dostoevsky for instance), one may turn here towards determinism, towards fatalism, towards regarding freedom as a complete illusion. When I deliberate the die is already cast. Forces within me which are dark to me have already made the decision.

This view is if anything less attractive and less realistic than the other one. Do we really have to choose between an image of total freedom and an image of total determinism? Can we not give a more balanced and illuminating account of the matter? I suggest we can if we simply introduce into the picture the idea of *attention*, or looking, of which I was speaking above. I can only choose within the world I can *see*, in the moral sense of 'see' which implies that clear vision is a result of moral imagination and moral effort. There is also of course 'distorted vision', and the word 'reality' here inevitably appears as a normative word. When *M* is just and loving she sees *D* as she really is. One is often compelled almost automatically by what one *can* see. If we ignore the prior work of attention and notice only the emptiness of the moment of choice we are likely to identify freedom with the outward movement since there is nothing else to identify it with. But if we consider what the work of attention is like, how continuously it goes on, and how imperceptibly it builds up structures of value round about us, we shall not be surprised that at crucial moments of choice most of the business of choosing is already over.

This does not imply that we are not free, certainly not. But it implies that the exercise of our freedom is a small piecemeal business which goes on all the time and not a grandiose leaping about unimpeded at important moments. The moral life, on this view, is something that goes on continually, not something that is switched off in between the occurrence of explicit moral choices. What happens in between such choices is indeed what is crucial. I would like on the whole to use the word 'attention' as a good word and use some more general term like 'looking' as the neutral word. Of course psychic energy flows, and more readily flows, into building up convincingly coherent but false pictures of the world, complete with systematic vocabulary. (*M* seeing *D* as pert-common-juvenile, etc.) Attention is the effort to counteract such states of illusion.

On this view we are certainly in a sense less free than we are pictured as being on the other view, in that the latter presents a condition of perfect freedom as being either our unavoidable fate (the Surrealists) or our conceivably attainable goal (the Kantians). Freedom for Hampshire is a matter of having crystal-clear intentions. But on the view which I suggest, which connects morality with attention to individuals, human individuals or individual realities of other kinds, the struggle and the progress is something more obscure, more historically conditioned, and usually less clearly conscious. Freedom, itself a moral concept and not just a prerequisite of morality, cannot here be separated from the idea of knowledge. That *of* which it is knowledge, that 'reality' which we are so naturally led to think of as revealed by 'just attention', can of course, given the variety of human personality and situation, only be thought of as 'one', as a single object for all men, in some very remote and ideal sense. It is a deep paradox of moral philosophy that almost all philosophers have been led in one way or another to picture goodness as knowledge: and yet to show this in any sort of detail, to show 'reality' as 'one', seems to involve an improper prejudging of some moral issue. An acute consciousness of this latter difficulty has indeed made it seem axiomatic to recent philosophers that 'naturalism is a fallacy'. But I would suggest that at the level of serious common sense and of an ordinary non-philosophical reflection about the nature of morals it is perfectly obvious that goodness *is* connected with knowledge: not with impersonal quasi-scientific knowledge of the ordinary world, whatever that may be, but with a refined and honest perception of what is really the case, a patient and just discernment and exploration of what confronts one, which is the result not simply of opening one's eyes but of a certainly perfectly familiar kind of moral discipline.

What then of the 'void', the experience of *Angst* of which the existentialists have told us so much? If it cannot be understood in their sense as an experience of pure freedom, what is it, and does it really occur at all? Perhaps there are several different conditions involved here. But the central one, the heart of the concept, I think I would describe rather as a kind of fright which the conscious will feels when it apprehends the strength and direction of the personality which is not under its immediate control. Innumerable 'lookings' have discovered and explored a world which is now (for better or worse) *compulsively* present to the will in a particular situation, and the will is dismayed by the feeling that it ought now to be everything and in fact is not. *Angst* may occur where there is any felt discrepancy between personality and ideals. Perhaps very simple people escape it and some civilizations have not experienced it at all. Extreme *Angst*, in the popular modern form, is a disease or addiction of those who are passionately convinced that personality resides solely in the conscious omnipotent will: and in so far as this conviction is wrong the condition partakes of illusion. It is obviously, in practice, a delicate moral problem to decide how far the will can coerce the formed personality (*move* in a world it cannot *see*) without merely occasioning disaster. The concept of *Angst* should of course be carefully distinguished from its ancestor, Kant's *Achtung*, in which dismay at the frailty of the will is combined with an inspiring awareness of the reality which the will is drawn by (despair at the sensuous will, joy in the rational will). The loss of that awareness, or that faith, produces *Angst*, which is properly a condition of sober alarm. Those who are, or attempt to be, exhilarated by *Angst*, that is by the mere impotence of the will and its lack of connection with the personality, are, as I have suggested above, in danger of falling into fatalism or sheer irresponsibility.

The place of choice is certainly a different one if we think in terms of a world which is *compulsively* present to the will, and the discernment and exploration of which is a slow business. Moral change and moral achievement are slow; we are not free in the sense of being able suddenly to alter ourselves since we cannot suddenly alter what we can see and ergo what we desire and are compelled by. In a way, explicit choice seems now less important: less decisive (since much of the 'decision' lies elsewhere) and less obviously something to be 'cultivate'. If I attend properly I will have no choices and this is the ultimate condition to be aimed at. This is in a way the reverse of Hampshire's picture, where our efforts are supposed to be directed to increasing our freedom by conceptualizing as many different possibilities of action as possible: having as many goods as possible in the shop. The ideal situation, on the contrary, is rather to be represented as a kind of 'necessity'. This is something of which saints speak and which any artist will readily understand. The idea of a patient, loving regard, directed upon a person, a thing, a situation, presents the will not as unimpeded movement but as something very much more like 'obedience'.

Will and reason then are not entirely separate faculties in the moral agent. Will continually influences belief, for better or worse, and is ideally able to influence it through a sustained attention to reality. This is what Simone Weil means when she says that 'will is obedience not resolution'. As moral agents we have to try to see justly, to overcome prejudice, to avoid temptation, to control and curb imagination, to direct reflection. Man is not a combination of an impersonal rational thinker and a personal will. He is a unified being who sees, and who desires in accordance with what he sees, and who has some continual slight control over the direction and focus of his vision. There is nothing, I think, in the foreground of this picture which is unfamiliar to the ordinary person. Philosophical difficulties may arise if we try to give any single organized background sense to the normative word 'reality'. But this word may be used as a philosophical term provided its limitations are understood. What is real may be 'non-empirical' without being in the grand sense systematic. In particular situations 'reality' as that which is revealed to the patient eye of love is an idea entirely comprehensible to the ordinary person. *M* knows what she is doing when she tries to be just to *D*, and we know what she is doing too.

I said that any artist would appreciate the notion of will as obedience to reality, an obedience which ideally reaches a position where there is no choice. One of the great merits of the moral psychology which I am proposing is that it does not contrast art and morals, but shows them to be two aspects of a single struggle. The existentialist-behaviourist view could give no satisfactory account of art: it was seen as a quasi-play activity, gratuitous, 'for its own sake' (the familiar Kantian-Bloomsbury slogan), a sort of by-product of our failure to be entirely rational. Such a view of art is of course intolerable. In one of those important movements of return from philosophical theory to simple things which we are certain of, we must come back to what we know about great art and about the moral insight which it contains and the moral achievement which it represents. Goodness and beauty are not to be contrasted, but are largely part of the same structure. Plato, who tells us that beauty is the only spiritual thing which we love immediately by nature, treats the beautiful as an introductory section of the good. So that aesthetic situations are not so much analogies of morals as cases of morals. Virtue is *au fond* the same in the artist as in the good man in that it is a selfless attention to nature: something which is easy to name but very hard to achieve. Artists who have reflected have frequently given expression to this idea. (For instance, Rilke praising Cézanne speaks of a 'consuming of love in anonymous work'. Letter to Clara Rilke, 13 October 1907.)

Since the existentialist-behaviourist view wished to conceive of will as pure movement separated from reason and to deprive reason of the use of normative words (since it was to be 'objective'), the moral agent so envisaged could get along, was indeed almost forced to get along, with only the most empty and general moral terms such as 'good' and 'right'. The empty moral words correspond here to the emptiness of the will. If the will is to be totally free the world it moves in must be devoid of normative characteristics, so that morality can reside entirely in the pointer of pure choice. On my view it might be said that, *per contra*, the primary general words could be dispensed with entirely and all moral work could be done by the secondary specialized words. If we picture the agent as compelled by obedience to the reality he can see, he will not be saying 'This is right', i.e., 'I choose to do this', he will be saying 'This is *A B C D*' (normative-descriptive words), and action will follow naturally. As the empty choice will not occur the empty word will not be needed. It would however be far from my intention to demote or dispense with the term 'good': but rather to restore to it the dignity and authority which it possessed before Moore appeared on the scene. I have spoken of efforts of attention directed upon individuals and of obedience to reality as an exercise of love, and have suggested that 'reality' and 'individual' present themselves to us in moral contexts as ideal end-points or Ideas of Reason. This surely is the place where the concept of good lives. 'Good' : 'Real' : 'Love'. These words are closely connected. And here we retrieve the deep sense of the indefinability of good, which has been given a trivial sense in recent philosophy. Good is indefinable not for the reasons offered by Moore's successors, but because of the infinite difficulty of the task of apprehending a magnetic but inexhaustible reality. Moore was in a way nearer the truth than he realized when he tried to say both that Good was *there* and that one could say nothing of what it essentially was. If apprehension of good is apprehension of the individual and the real, then good partakes of the infinite elusive character of reality.

I have several times indicated that the image which I am offering should be thought of as a general metaphysical background to morals and not as a formula which can be illuminatingly introduced into any and every moral act. There exists, so far as I know, no formula of the latter kind. We are not always the individual in pursuit of the individual, we are not always responding to the magnetic pull of the idea of perfection. Often, for instance when we pay our bills or perform other small everyday acts, we are just 'anybody' doing what is proper or making simple choices for ordinary public reasons; and this is the situation which some philosophers have chosen exclusively to analyse. Furthermore, I am well aware of the *moral* dangers of the idea of morality as something which engages the whole person and which may lead to specialized and esoteric vision and language. Give and take between the private and the public levels of morality is often of advantage to both and indeed is normally unavoidable. In fact the 'conventional' level is often not so simple as it seems, and the quaintly phrased hymn which I sang in my childhood, 'Who sweeps a room as for Thy laws makes that and the action fine', was not talking foolishly. The task of attention goes on all the time and at apparently empty and everyday moments we are 'looking', making those little peering efforts of imagination which have such important cumulative results.

I would not be understood, either, as suggesting that insight or pureness of heart are more important than action: the thing which philosophers feared Moore for implying. Overt actions are perfectly obviously important in themselves, and important too because they are the indispensable pivot and spur of the inner scene. The inner, in *this* sense, cannot do without the outer. I do not mean only that outer rituals make places for inner experiences; but also that an overt action can release psychic energies which can be released in no other way. We often receive an unforeseen reward for a fumbling half-hearted act: a place for the idea of grace. I have suggested that we have to accept a darker, less fully conscious, less steadily rational image of the dynamics of the human personality. With this dark entity behind us we may sometimes decide to act abstractly by rule, to ignore vision and the compulsive energy derived from it; and we may find that as a result both energy and vision are unexpectedly given. To decide when to attempt such leaps is one of the most difficult of moral problems. But if we do leap ahead of what we know we still have to try to catch up. Will cannot run very far ahead of knowledge, and attention is our daily bread.

Of course what I have been offering here is not and does not pretend to be a 'neutral logical analysis' of what moral agents or moral terms are like. The picture offered by, e.g., Hampshire is of course not neutral either, as he admits in parenthesis. (*Thought and Action*, Chapter Two.) 'A decision has to be made between two conceptions of personality.... It may be that in a society in which a man's theoretical opinions and religious beliefs were held to be supremely important, a man's beliefs would be considered as much part of his responsibility as his behaviour to other men.' And he contrasts this with 'a utilitarian culture'. Hampshire speaks here of a 'decision'; and there is always an existentialist 'short way' with any rival theory: to say, 'You use that picture, but you *choose* to use it.' This is to make the existentialist picture the ultimate one. I would wish to exclude any such undercutting of my theory. To say that it is a normative theory is not to say that it is an object of free choice: modern philosophy has equated these ideas but this is just the equation I am objecting to. I offer frankly a sketch of a metaphysical theory, a kind of inconclusive non-dogmatic naturalism, which has the circularity of definition characteristic of such theories. The rival theory is similarly circular; and as I have explained I do not find that its radical arguments convincingly establish its sweeping moral and psychological conclusions.

Philosophers have always been trying to picture the human soul, and since morality needs such pictures and as science is, as I have argued, in no position to coerce morality, there seems no reason why philosophers should not go on attempting to fill in a systematic explanatory background to our ordinary moral life. Hampshire said, and I quoted this at the start, that 'it is the constructive task of the philosophy of mind to provide a set of terms in which ultimate judgments of value can be very clearly stated'. I would put what I think is much the same task in terms of the provision of rich and fertile conceptual schemes which help us to reflect upon and understand the nature of moral progress and moral failure and the reasons for the divergence of one moral temperament from another. And I would wish to make my theory undercut its existentialist rivals by suggesting that it is possible in terms of the former to explain why people are obsessed with the latter, but not vice versa. In any case, the sketch which I have offered, a footnote in a great and familiar philosophical tradition, must be judged by its power to connect, to illuminate, to explain, and to make new and fruitful places for reflection.

Chapter 19

Anscombe on Practical Inference

Candace Vogler

1 INTRODUCTION

> Let us consider a man going round a town with a shopping list in his hand. Now it is clear that the relation of this list to the things he actually buys is one and the same whether his wife gave him the list or it is his own list; and that there is a different relation when a list is made by a detective following him about. If he made the list himself, it was an expression of intention; if his wife gave it to him, it has the role of an order. What then is the identical relation to what happens, in the order and the intention, which is not shared by the record? It is precisely this: if the list and the things that the man actually buys do not agree, and if this and this alone constitutes a *mistake*, then the mistake is not in the list but in the man's performance (if his wife were to say: 'Look, it says butter and you have bought margarine', he would hardly reply: 'What a mistake! we must put that right' and alter the word on the list to 'margarine'); whereas if the detective's record and what the man actually buys do not agree, then the mistake is in the record.[1]

Elizabeth Anscombe's shopper story inspired the idea that there are two kinds of propositional attitudes, belief and desire, which have different "directions of fit."[2] Like the detective, belief has a world-to-mind direction of fit (that is, belief aims to track the truth of its matter). Like the shopper, desire has a mind-to-world direction of fit (that is, desire aims to make its matter true). But Anscombe's story isn't an allegory where lists represent propositions and men represent attitudes. It's a plain example introducing her discussion of practical and theoretical knowledge.

Notice, e.g., that if both men do their tasks well, their lists will match. Under such circumstances, we won't know, just from the *contents* of a list, whether it was produced as a record of what happened, given as an order, or made up by someone to guide his purchases.[3] For all that, record keeping is not the same as intending (on one's own account or in obedience to an authority), and the distinction between practical and theoretical knowledge concerns the lists' *uses*. The *lists* have different directions of fit because each is made for a different purpose. Making a record involves theoretical knowledge. Making purchases involves practical knowledge.

Anscombe's work on practical inference likewise aims to investigate the difference between practical and theoretical reason, while giving due place to what they share. As you might expect from the widespread allegorical rendering of the shopper story, *how* Anscombe treats practical inference is at angles with much contemporary work. That is not to say that Anscombe has nothing to say to us, or that she isn't addressing topics that are germane to current work. Rather, she has to devote a lot of attention to clearing ground for her positive points about practical reasoning. My task in this essay is to cover her ground-clearing operations and trace some of her positive points.

The ground she has to clear is held by diverse opponents. I'll call them *inferentialists*.[4] Inferentialism is the target of this complaint:

[Practical reasoning] is commonly supposed to be ordinary reasoning leading to such a conclusion as: 'I ought to do such-and-such.' By 'ordinary reasoning' I mean the only reasoning ordinarily considered in philosophy: reasoning towards the truth [or probable truth] of a proposition, which is supposedly shewn to be true [or probable] by the premises. (1963, sec. 33)[5]

Put that way, it may seem like almost all contemporary philosophers who think that there is such a thing as practical reasoning will be, to some extent, inferentialists. That is not far wrong. And, in Anscombe's view, it is not so much that inferentialists have nothing to contribute to the study of practical reasoning as that they have no way of getting at the sense in which practical reasoning is practical. To get at *that*, one needs to explain such things as the fact that the detective's list and the shopper's list have distinct uses. Inferentialists try to capture what's distinctive about practical inference by content restrictions on practical argument (e.g., the conclusion of a practical argument is an action, a decision to act, or a judgment that such-and-such action is desirable/required/called for— each of which suggests that the conclusion concerns some matter that the agent can affect by her act), together, sometimes, with insistence that one of the premises of a practical inference mention (at least one of) the reasoner's ends or desires. Anscombe argues that such attempts fail.

Her best arguments for this claim come in her extended treatment of practical inference, in the middle of her attack on three common inferentialist assumptions, namely,

1. that we can treat action as a given in our work on practical reason,
2. that inferential relations among the contents of propositional attitudes determine the course of practical reasoning, and
3. that in practical reasoning, action or intention is compelled by inference; in theoretical reasoning, belief is compelled by inference.[6]

The latter two are obviously inferentialist. Here is how the first assumption is inferentialist: in treating an action as given, we take up some true description of a human behavior, stipulate that the description is a description of an action, and then busy ourselves finding content-sensitive links between this description and, say, propositional attitudes, with an eye toward illuminating practical reason by exploring the inferential links between the relevant contents. What we miss in doing so is the *structure* in descriptions of intentional actions as such, and it is this structure, Anscombe thinks, that helps to illuminate practical knowledge, practical inference, and practical reasoning.

Much of my essay will be devoted to giving Anscombe's arguments against the three assumptions. I will begin with some remarks about Donald Davidson and where Anscombe thinks he goes wrong. Anscombe doesn't give extensive treatment of Davidson's work. But Davidson's work is more familiar than hers, so it's fruitful to use their quarrel as a starting point for discussing her views.

2   PRACTICAL REASONING AS A CAUSE OF ACTION

Davidson holds that my beliefs, judgments, con- and pro-attitudes show the point of what I do, they "rationalize" my action.[7] Moreover, rationalization is a species of causal explanation. But sometimes attitude-based causal explanations miss the mark. Here is one of Davidson's examples:

A climber might want to rid himself of the weight and danger of holding another man on a rope, and he might know that by loosening his hold on the rope he could rid himself of the weight and danger. The belief and want might so unnerve him as to cause him to loosen his hold, and yet it might be the case that he never *chose* to loosen his hold, nor did he do it intentionally.... Since there may be wayward causal chains, we cannot say that if attitudes that would rationalize x cause an agent to do x, then he does x intentionally. (1980, 79)[8]

Davidson thinks that introducing practical reasoning into the discussion might improve the account of intentional action: "For a desire and a belief to explain an action in the right way, they must cause it in the right way, perhaps through a chain or process of reasoning that meets standards of rationality" (1980, 232).

And here we might ask, Why bother? Why not just claim that it is nevertheless *necessary* that an agent's *A*-ing be caused by attitudes that constitute reasons for *A*-ing if the agent's *A*-ing is to count as intentional action? Intentional action is a pretty broad topic. It is hard to see why we would expect to get a singular, abstract causal framework that will characterize the antecedents of intentional action generally. Practical reasoning seems a likely addition in cases where I work out some practical problem in advance of taking action. It looks much less plausible in cases where my act is grounded in a skill that I acquired before reaching the age of reason, as when I make such-and-such movements in order to rise from my chair and walk. Executing an elaborate political stratagem in order to win a campaign and standing up in order to move about are, alike, intentional actions. The latter is not only rarely the product of explicit practical deliberation, but my ability to do it without thinking about it developed well before I was a fully-fledged rational animal.[9]

In fact Davidson argues that we should *not* expect to get a single account of the "right" sort of causal link between action and attitudes.[10] But now look how odd his response to the climber case is—the action wasn't caused in the right way; it may be impossible to give a general account of the right causal link; had the climber's act been caused by practical reasoning, *that* would be a right causal link. In short, had the climber case not been a climber case, it would not have involved climber-style wayward causation. When a philosopher responds in this sort of way to a potential counterexample one suspects that the case has struck too close for comfort.

The project of investigating reasons-based explanation as a species of causal explanation began for Davidson in seeking to understand the *because* in "the agent performed the action *because* he had [such-and-such] reason" (1980, 9). Davidson's thought was that this *because* indicates that reasons-based intentional action explanation is causal. Since reasons-based action explanation casts action in the favorable light that it has for agents, Davidson supposed that reasons for acting were given by propositional attitudes toward actions of the kind at issue.

Now, the problem lurking in the climber example may not be merely that the agent met the necessary conditions for intentionally loosening his grip but failed to meet the sufficient conditions. Potentially, at least, the problem is much more serious. Davidson identifies reasons with suitably connected propositional attitudes. In the climber example, we have suitably connected action-directed propositional attitudes and we have the action *because* of *those very* psychological states. But the very idea that he could just drop his companion *unnerves* the climber. From the climber's point of view, notice, these psychological states may not provide *any* reason for action *at all*. The threat is that the "rationalizing" relation *can't* be cashed out as a relation between the contents of psychological states, on the one side, descriptions of behavior, on the other. As Anscombe puts it, Davidson "realizes that even identity of description of *act done* with *act specified in the belief,* together with causality by belief and desire, isn't enough to guarantee the act's being done *in pursuit of the end* and *on grounds of the belief*" (1989, 378 [2]). That is, tight links between the contents of propositional attitudes and true descriptions of behavior caused by those attitudes may shed *no* light on the character of intentional action and reasons for acting.

Anscombe makes her remark in charging Davidson with assuming that we can treat action as given. I will discuss this first inferentialist assumption in the next section. Before doing that, I will discuss how Davidson's thought about practical reasoning involves the other two assumptions.

Davidson thinks that it might be possible to avoid the problem posed by the climber example if, instead of just looking for a causally efficacious, content-sensitive link between what a man has on his mind and what he does, we ask whether the man's action was a product of practical reasoning, or backed by considered judgment. Practical reasoning is reasoning toward action. Such reasoning surely should rationalize any action that it explains. I will focus on two interpretations of Davidson's suggestion.

First, my *judgment* about what I should do might be treated as the conclusion of my practical reasoning, my action then caused by my judgment. This won't solve the problem of freak causal chains, however. Here is Davidson's example:

A man might have good reasons for killing his father, and he might do it, and yet the reasons not be his reasons in doing it.... Suppose, contrary to the legend, that Oedipus ... was hurrying along the road intent on killing his father, and, finding a surly old man blocking his way, killed him so he could (as he thought) get on with the main job. Then not only did Oedipus want to kill his father, and actually kill him, but his desire caused him to kill his father. (1980, 232)

In the example, Oedipus judges that he has good reason to kill his father, means to kill his father, and kills his father because he has set out to kill his father. But, again, the causal chain is "wrong."

On the second interpretation, A-ing itself might be treated as the *con-clusion* of practical reasoning in two senses: it *follows* logically from the practical inference and it is the *outcome* of the deliberative episode. The suggestion has the advantage of perfecting the fit between the inferential and causal orders in action: one As in response to a compelling practical argument, as one might come to believe that p in response to a compel-ling theoretical argument. On this interpretation, notice, we have versions of all three inferentialist assumptions: *given* action, we treat it as the conclusion of practical reasoning governed by "standards of rationality," i.e., reasoning which leads to action in the way that theoretical inference leads to belief.

There are several ways that the second interpretation might go. Here's one likely to be favored by inferentialists: the action itself could be understood as intentionally making-the-proposition-that-one-As-true. In the Oedipus example, Oedipus *unintentionally* brings it about that he As. By requiring that he deliberately make it the case that he do what reason recommends, and treating the "good reason" clause as suggesting that his action arises from solid practical deliberation, we unite the causal and inferential orders in action in the right sort of way.

Anscombe's response to this kind of move is subtle. Rather than enter into the fray in attempting to explain what practical reasoning contrib-utes to the causes of action, she dismantles the inferentialist assumptions that give rise to Davidson's difficulty and to various other problems.

3   FIRST ASSUMPTION: WE MAY TREAT ACTION AS GIVEN

The most important assumption Anscombe rejects is that we may treat action as given in work on practical reason. *Action* functions as a primi-tive in many contemporary accounts. By *primitive* I mean that we don't bother analyzing the structure of intentional action as such. Anscombe's explicit discussion of this assumption goes by very quickly. She gives an open question argument against Davidson in order to leave behind worries about the causal antecedents of intentional action, and, hence, worries about wayward causation:

[Davidson] can do no more than postulate a 'right' causal connexion in the happy security that none such can be found. If a causal connexion were found we could always still ask: 'But was the act done for the sake of the end and in view of the thing believed?' (1989, 378 [2])

In both the climber example and the Oedipus example, the answer to the open question is no.

How does Davidson manage to miss that the *persistent* possibility of asking, no matter what caused the action, whether it was done in pursuit of the end and on grounds of the belief suggests that seeking out the causal antecedents of action won't help us to understand practical reason? Anscombe writes,

I conjecture that the cause of this failure of percipience is the standard approach by which we first distinguish between 'action' and what merely happens, and then specify that we are talking about 'actions'. So what we are considering is already given as—in a special sense—an action, and not just any old thing which we do, such as making an involuntary gesture. Such a gesture might be caused, for example, by realising something (the 'onset of a belief') when we are in a certain state of desire. Something I do is not made into an intentional action by being caused by a belief and desire, even if the descriptions fit. (1989, 378 [2–3])

Her most obvious target here is the climber example. In the climber example we don't have intentional action at all. Davidson knows this, but seems to think that there is an action, nonetheless. Anscombe's point is that if you aren't going to restrict *action* to *intentional action*, and you are willing to treat the climber's response as action, you have opened the door to the whole gamut of involuntary gestures.[11] What we have in the climber case *isn't* action missing the extra "intention" ingredient. What we have is a startle response. Any number of things might have startled the climber as he was making his way up the face, resenting the extra weight. Since there is no action in such cases, there is no wayward cause of action in such cases. We were confused by combining his passing thought with a description of his ensuing movement. This is exactly the kind of thing Anscombe means by charging us with assuming that we can take action as given: supposing that since we have a true description of the event, since the event involved movement, and since the agent might have made such movements intentionally, we have a true description of an action. The motor here is inferentialist: we assume that a *content-sensitive* link between psychological cause and behavioral effect is enough to give us action.[12]

What of the oedipal drama? There we have intentional killing of the killer's father, we have a killer who means to kill his father, but we don't have intentional patricide. Now, elsewhere Anscombe argues that an action is an event to which the reasons-for-acting-seeking-question-"Why are you *A*-ing/did you *A*?" is given application.[13] If, gesturing toward the old man's corpse, we asked Oedipus why he killed his father, Oedipus would refuse to give the relevant question "Why?" application by responding that he didn't know that he had done.[14] The action isn't intentional "under" this description.

Davidson tries to capture this by insisting that "the expression that introduces intention ... must be intensional," i.e., we are not licensed to substitute co-referring expressions into a statement of intention (1980, 122). The stipulation captures *one* part of Anscombe's observation that actions are intentional under some descriptions but not others (the inferentialist, logic-related point, to be exact). What it misses *entirely* is her detailed account of *how* those descriptions under which action is intentional *hang together* ordinarily.

Here is what I mean. Without even *posing* the question "Why have you killed your father?" we can see that we don't have intentional patricide in Davidson's example because Oedipus will (we assume) *continue* searching for his father, intent on killing him, after the deed is done. Anscombe argues that intentional actions are, ordinarily, representable under a series of *linked* descriptions involving means and ends or parts of an action and the whole of it.[15] I *A* in order to *B*. *A*-ing is a means to, or part of *B*-ing. Indeed, in the normal case we will expect to find me *A*-ing in order to *B*, *B*-ing in order to *C*, and so on. So, for example, I make ink marks on a printed slip of paper *in order to* make out and sign a check, I make out and sign a check *in order to* instruct my bank to effect a transfer of funds from my account to my creditor, I instruct the bank to do so *in order to* pay the whole or some part of my debt to the indicated creditor, and I pay the bill, say, *in order to* keep my credit in good standing. Anscombe's "Why?"-question is a device that seeks to elicit the calculative form *in* the action.

It would take me considerably far afield to trace her arguments that intentional action will, paradigmatically, have a means-end or part-whole calculative form. Suffice it to say that much of *Intention* is devoted to giving the argument and I will suppose good grounds for her claim. Where she sees Davidson getting himself in a muddle is in thinking that we need to look to what is in place *before* Oedipus kills the old man in order to handle the case. Obviously, if we explain an action, *A*, by reference to a cause, *C*, then we are committed to holding that *C* happened or obtained, that *C* happened or obtained before *A* happened, and that *C* brought it about that *A* happened.[16] But, given that Davidson's Oedipus intends to commit patricide, we can as fruitfully direct our attention to what happens *after* he kills the old man.

It belongs to the rational structure in intentional action that once the intended end is *attained*, there is no reason to continue to pursue its attainment. An "end" is, in this sense, a *stopping-place* for intentional action. Davidson's Oedipus kills Laius, and will then keep seeking to kill Laius. His failure to *stop* his pursuit once the natural, intended stopping-place is reached signals that something has gone wrong. Either he does not grasp his own success or else he is exhibiting a serious failure of practical rationality, in roughly the way that I would if, having succeeded in discharging my debt to my creditor, and knowing this, I kept seeking to repay that very same debt to that very same creditor. By failing to notice that reason informs what people do as they go along, rather than just being in people before they do things, and causing them to act, Davidson is unable to take advantage of the rational structure in action to handle his own examples.[17] But once we notice that there is reason in intentional action, we should, Anscombe thinks, drop the assumption that the scene of reason is confined to some states or events which are in place *before* action happens, and this is enough to call off the hunt for the rational cause. It is also enough to show that we can't treat actions as given.

What we see in intentional action is pursuit of an end on grounds of the thing believed. It should be true of the agent that he seeks to attain his end just as long as he is in pursuit of it, and that what he does in pursuit of his end is done for the sake of attaining his end and on account of his insight that doing these things will contribute to attaining that end. Anscombe uses the asking and answering of "Why are you *A*-ing/ did you *A*?"-questions as a device to reveal this fit between what one has in mind and what one does, step-by-step, as one goes along. Imagining the exchange of questions and answers *closes* off the open question by allowing us to display the calculative, rational articulation of the event as it is taking place.

Getting an accurate description of the event in question, *of* the intentional action *as* an intentional action, *is* (at least) getting a description of its calculative articulation, of the intended end and the means or parts done in order to attain, or make it possible to attain, the end. Moreover, *getting* an accurate description of an event *qua* intentional action takes us a long way toward *showing* the grounds of the act. This is why she thinks that we get ourselves in a mess if we treat the action as given. We can't so much as accurately *describe* our explanandum, *qua* intentional action, without attending to its intended means-end or part-whole articulation. The inferentialist exploits connections among contents for the sake of understanding practical reason. In the lion's share of cases, getting the right description of intentional action, the right *content*, turns on understanding the calculative articulation of the action. This, in turn, opens a window on practical reason. The reason in the act shows us part of the agent's grounds for acting, part of what she has in view in doing what she does.

Once we have appreciated the calculative structure in intentional action, Anscombe takes it, we can approach discussion of practical reasoning from a different angle. It is not that we have, on the one side, someone with a lot of things in mind, on the other an event describable in indefinitely many ways, and now confront the onerous task of connecting mental representation to event. It is that some of the salient descriptions of what one has in mind will (if all goes well) line up with the salient descriptions of what one does (as the shopper's *list* lines up with what he *buys*, if all goes well). Representation of practical inferences, for Anscombe, is centrally a device for understanding intentional action, *not* by giving its cause, but by revealing its grounds, by showing "what good, what use, the action is" (1989, 380 [5]). It may or may not happen that the agent thinks out what to do explicitly along the lines suggested by the argument. Whether or not she does, the argument gives the grounds, the point, of the action by showing what the agent has in view *in* doing what she does. The practical argument displays an order in action which could likewise be retrieved by asking the agent why she is *A*-ing or *B*-ing, and tracing the order in her responses to the questions that are given application. The questions are given application when our descriptions, *A*-ing, *B*-ing, *C*-ing, are accepted by the agent as descriptions of what she is doing and shown to be relevant to her understanding of her own end and to the grounds she has for thinking that what she is doing contributes to its attainment. Both Oedipus and the climber will refuse to give the relevant question application, notice.

For Anscombe, then, there is no mystery about explaining the connection between the agent's rational powers and the agent's intentional action. Rather, understanding practical reason is understanding how the reason in the agent is likewise in the acts. Because there is no mystery about the connection between intention in agents and the calculative order in their intentional actions (these come to us bound up together), there is no temptation to try to solve the mystery by giving a special kind of causal account of the act. Davidson assumed that he needed some such account, Anscombe thinks, because he wasn't paying attention to the rational structure *in* action, and thereby wasn't noticing that, if the event-to-be-explained involved intentional action, then it had an intended means-end or part-whole articulation relevant to its representation and to understanding its grounds.[18]

4   SECOND ASSUMPTION: INFERENTIAL RELATIONS AMONG THE PROPOSITIONAL CONTENTS OF PSYCHOLOGICAL STATES DETERMINE THE COURSE OF PRACTICAL REASONING

The second assumption Anscombe attacks is that investigating practical reasoning will consist in investigating the inferential relations among propositions toward which the agent takes attitudes and which she seeks to make true by her action. The thought here is that all we need to do to theorize practical reasoning is to set out the relevant inferences and stipulate that in practical reasoning such inferences are conducted in the service of determining what to do. Anscombe's argument against this assumption turns on the claim that it takes time both to set forth the grounds of an act and to act.[19] This allows her to produce a paradox. I will trace the argument by showing how the paradox arises.

4.1   Practical Reasoning and Practical Inference

When I engage in practical deliberation I entertain one thought, then another, and then another in the service of figuring out what to do. If this train is to count as *reasoning*, there must be some inferential connections between the contents of the thoughts, and my moving from thought to thought must be explained by the inferential connection. So, noticing that it's raining outside, then remembering how pleasant it was to swim the other day, then thinking *Moby Dick* a fine novel, then wondering how George is doing, then considering wearing a hooded coat when I go out to purchase the newspaper, then deciding to make stew for dinner will probably *not* count as an episode of practical reasoning. Whereas noticing the rain, considering the coat, and thinking it too warm a day for coats *may* count as practical reasoning. The conclusion of this reasoning might be going out in my shirtsleeves, carrying an umbrella (or deciding to do so). The conclusion might instead be waiting for the rain to let up before getting the paper, or sending someone else to fetch the paper, or driving to the newsstand, etc.—umbrella-carrying is not *necessitated* by my inference. But suppose I decide on the umbrella. My practical argument can be given this way:

If I walk, uncovered, to the newsstand, I will get drenched.
If I wear a hooded coat on my walk, the coat will keep me dry.
If I carry an umbrella on my walk, the umbrella will keep me dry.
It's too warm for coats.

Followed by heading off with my umbrella, or deciding to take an umbrella when I go. In practical reasoning, I use such arguments in deciding what to do.

Now, since it takes time to construct, produce, or conduct a practical inference (i.e., to make use of the argument), indefinitely many things might derail the deliberative process. I stand poised beside the coat rack and umbrella stand, considering how to protect myself from the rain in pursuit of my paper, and then something happens—the phone rings, armed assassins burst through the windows, or the roof caves in. I might never again take up my coat-versus-umbrella quandary. Continuing to debate the umbrella question might be *crazy* under the circumstances.

Of course, the *rational order* obtaining between taking an umbrella and my inference is completely *undisturbed* by whatever stopped me from going on about my business. It is in place. But because it takes time to figure out what to do, the process can be interrupted. And when the process is interrupted, it looks as though it isn't the *inferential relations* among practical considerations, but rather *contingent* facts about the sort of day I am having, that determines the course of my deliberations. And so, it can be objected, what determines the course of practical reasoning *isn't* the inferential relations among propositions, but rather whether or not (for instance) the roof caves in. Will it do to reply that the inferential relations nevertheless determine how things *ought to* go? Apparently not. For notice how *insane* it would be to require that I decide the umbrella question, on pain of irrationality, *before* attending to the cave-in or take it up again *afterwards*. And yet, the very fact that almost *anything* could happen to someone who is trying to figure out what to do virtually guarantees that we can neither predict *nor* prescribe the course of practical deliberation on the basis of the inferential links among the contents of thoughts.

4.2   An Inferentialist Response and the Paradox It Generates

One way for an inferentialist to respond to this objection would be to require the *instantaneous* setting forth of grounds which might then be acted upon *instantaneously*.[20] This would remove the time gap. If we require that the grounds be set forth instantaneously, however, we have preserved the inferential order at the expense of our claim that in practical reasoning I make use of arguments in order to figure out what to do. Anscombe writes,

> Now one can hardly be said to make use of an argument that one does not produce, inwardly or outwardly. But the production takes time. If I [set forth the grounds] 'on the instant', there isn't time. (1989, 378–79 [3])

She concludes that the demand for instantaneous justification (in the name of getting perfect overlap between the inferential content of my practical argument and what I do or decide) has the curious result of making the practical argument inferentially sound *by* making it *useless* as a bit of practical reasoning. It is guaranteed the practical analog of (something like) validity just in case there is *no time* to make the argument. Which is to say, just in case there is no time to move from thought to thought in the way which is supposed to explain and justify the action.

On my reading, Anscombe produces the paradox in the service of drawing our attention to two points about practical reasoning. I will return to the paradox below. For now, I will discuss the points about practical reasoning.

4.3   The First Point about Practical Reasoning

Anselm Müller has discussed the first insight we can draw from the paradox at some length.[21] Practical reasoning takes time and is done for the sake of figuring out what to do. Müller writes,

> When I reflect in order to find out how to attain a given end—and, finally, in order to attain it—that is not like sweating in order to lose heat as a result of evaporation. Nor is the difference just one of consciousness: I may be conscious not only that I am sweating but also what it is good for; still, I cannot be said to be led to perspire by the latter consideration. Practical thinking is, in this, rather like its typical result: acting with an intention. The action is done *with a view to* an end and *on account of* my insight that it helps to bring this end about. This also seems to be the way I engage in practical reasoning for the sake of an end of mine. (More often than not, actions are done for reasons without any prior 'engaging in practical reasoning'. But this does not prevent us from attributing to the agent thoughts that articulate those reasons. Their expression can be elicited, for example after the action, and function as a criterion of its purpose and character. So there is nothing fictitious about these 'dispositional' thoughts, and what I have to say about the goal-directed character of practical considerations is to apply to them, too). (1979, 96–97)

What the inferentialist misses in his attempt to treat practical inference as plain inference is the goal-directed character of episodes of practical reasoning and of the agent's state of mind when deliberating. Any ordinary goal-directed process is temporally extended. Because it is temporally extended, it can be prevented from attaining its goal. In attempting to get rid of this feature of practical reasoning, the inferentialist attempts to get rid of the deliberative process. Which is to say, he attempts to remove the inference from the context in which it is put to use. In practical reasoning, I employ or construct arguments in order to determine what to do. Getting rid of this is getting rid of the "practical" aspect of practical reasoning.

What gave rise to the paradox, recall, was getting rid of deliberation in the name of preserving inferential integrity. But once we appreciate that practical reasoning is goal-directed, hence, very like intentional action, we can find a different solution. I may set out to make a cake and then change course dramatically when the roof caves in. We do not explain my cave-in responsive acts as belonging to the same calculative order involving beating eggs, measuring flour, etc. I *stop* cake-baking and *start* digging out of the rubble when the roof caves in. In assessing the soundness of my cake-baking, we look to see whether I was, in fact, taking appropriate steps toward producing a cake. Similarly, in assessing my umbrella-deliberation, we see whether or not I was doing a good job calculating—was I on the track of a do-able thing that might allow me to stay dry and cool in pursuit of the paper? Again, when the roof caves in, I stop all that and turn my energies elsewhere. Noticing the goal-directedness of practical reasoning allows us to see that the inferential relations among contents don't give the whole story about how practical reasoning will or should go, any more than a good recipe is sufficient basis to predict or prescribe what should take place when someone sets out to follow the recipe, should the heavens fall.

4.4   The Second Point about Practical Reasoning

What drives the inferentialist to seek out instantaneous justification for action is his urge to treat practical inference as plain inference. But practical inference, partly owing to the action-directed action-like character of practical reasoning, is variously distinct from theoretical inference. This is the second point about practical reasoning that Anscombe draws our attention to with her paradox. Basically, inferentialism fixates upon the content of practical inferences, ignoring the character of practical reasoning. Anscombe argues that content-fixation is useless for understanding what's distinctive about practical reasoning.

Her insistence on this point shouldn't surprise us if, thinking back to the shopper and the detective, we are struck by the fact that a purchase list could exhibit *either* practical *or* theoretical knowledge. Anscombe will argue that inspection of the *content* of an inference concerning things one can affect by one's action can't establish that we have before us a practical inference drawn in the course of practical reasoning. Now, if Anscombe succeeds in establishing this, then she will have undermined inferentialism. Either (i) there will be no such thing as practical inference, or else (ii) there *will* be, but inferentialism, bound as it is to thought about inferential relations among *contents*, won't be equipped to explain what's distinctive about it.

The first horn of the dilemma is a bad place to land. Again, recall the shopper and the detective. Think about the asymmetry in the errors they might make. The shopper's list said *butter* and he'd bought margarine. He *couldn't* correct the mistake by erasing *butter* and writing *margarine*. Buying margarine was an error in *action*, an error in performance in accordance with practical reason. The failure was *in* what he did, given his end (to buy butter; to make it true that he bought butter). But if the *detective's* list didn't match the contents of the basket, he could correct the error by changing the *list*. This difference was supposed to alert us to a difference in theoretical and practical reason: these have different directions of fit. The record has a world-to-list direction of fit. The shopper's list has a list-to-world direction of fit. For all that, both are reason governed. If the shopper buys margarine, he's made a mistake. If the detective then writes *margarine*, he's done his job well.

The inferentialist method of handling the distinction usually involves one or both of the following. He may restrict the content of practical inference to matters which can be affected by the reasoner's own future action.[22] This makes practical reasoning rather like theoretical reasoning about the doer's own future deeds. Or, the inferentialist may insist that one of the premises make mention of one of the reasoner's own wants or ends. Anscombe argues that neither will do the trick.

4.5   Content Restriction

Anscombe begins her attack on the content-restriction thought by considering how a bit of Euclidean geometry might be used in practical reasoning

Table 1
A Euclidean practical inference and its justification

Justification	Practical consideration
The center of a circle is the midpoint of a diameter.	If I construct the perpendicular bisector of a diameter, that will give me the center of a circle.
The perpendicular bisector of a chord, produced to the circumference, is a diameter.	If I produce a chord to the circumference and construct a perpendicular bisector of the chord, that will give me a diameter.
Whereupon I construct a chord to the circumference.	

(1989, 382–383 [8–9]). The objective is to construct the center of a circle. Here in table 1 is the practical inference and its justification.

In figuring out how to construct the center of the circle, I could entertain the practical considerations on the right (the conditionals), or I could remind myself of the points listed in the justification at the left. Because the content of my practical argument could be the points listed on the left, it isn't *necessary* that the premises make explicit mention of my own future actions in order to count as premises of practical inference. Neither is it *sufficient*—notice that you can't tell the *use* to which the premises are being put by examining the *content* of the list on the right *either*. Although the conditionals mention actions I might perform, I could be entertaining them in the course of remembering a geometry lesson, or theorizing about Euclidean constructions. Anscombe writes,

> The considerations and their logical relations are just the same whether the inference is practical or theoretical. What I mean by 'considerations' are all those hypotheticals ... and also any propositions which show them to be true. The difference between practical and theoretical is mainly a difference in the service to which these conditionals are put. Thus, if we should want to give conditionals which are logical truths, which we might think of as giving us the logically necessary connexions which 'stand behind' the inferences, *they will be exactly the same conditionals* for the practical and for the corresponding 'theoretical' inferences. (1989, 392 [21])

In short, inspecting the content of an inference won't establish whether it's practical or theoretical. The use to which an inference is put is not established by its content, even if its content has been restricted to matters that the agent can affect by her action.

And here the inferentialists might take comfort: practical inference is very like theoretical inference after all! The problem in using our under-

standing of theoretical inference to shed light on practical inference
appears to be this: practical inference stands in a special relation to the
agent's own future actions, a special relation that is more than having as
its topic something that the agent could affect by action. But suppose we
were to stipulate that representations of practical inference must both
concern what the agent can affect by action *and* include a premise mentioning the reasoner's wants or ends. Then, not only would we have
restricted the topic to her potential future actions, we would have added
information to our description of the facts of the case that would show
that what we had set forth was practical inference. At which point, we
could rely upon our understanding of theoretical inference to illuminate
the practical analog.

4.6   Mention of Desires/Ends in the Premises Is neither Necessary nor Sufficient for Practical Inference

Anscombe borrows an example from Müller as a softening-up point
against this attempt:

I desire that I murder my father and marry my mother.
If I *A*, I will murder my father.
If I *B*, I will avoid being apprehended for the murder, and be in a posi-
tion to disguise my identity from my mother.
If I *A* and *B*, I can *C* (court her).

Whereupon I seek help from a psychiatrist, judging that the need to free
myself of this desire has become acute.

That a desire is mentioned in the premises is not sufficient to show that
what we have before us is practical reasoning directed at satisfying the
want. Neither is it necessary. In arguing for this, Anscombe asks that we
consider cases involving subordinates whose lot is to execute the orders of
their superiors. The subordinate is given the following instruction:

Objective: to make it the case that *p*
p iff *q*

Accordingly, the subordinate works it out that if *r*, then *q*, whereupon
he sets out to make it the case that *r*. Notice that it is possible to do all
of this without taking *any* personal interest in seeing to it that *p*, and
without believing that *p* iff *q*. Anscombe writes that such an agent "con-
ducts the inference" and acts in conclusion, "perhaps ... as it were ironically," adding, "Surely slaves and other subordinates must often act so"

(1989, 396 [25]). Since you can engage in practical reasoning on the basis of premises you don't believe in the service of an end that is nothing to you, and then act on the grounds set forth in the inference, it is clear that mention of one of your own ends (in any but the thinnest possible sense of "own") is not necessary for successful employment of practical inference. Hence, it isn't necessary that any of your ends be given as the objective, or that grounds you take to be good function as premises. She uses this point partly in the service of arguing against the third inferentialist assumption.

5   THIRD ASSUMPTION: IN PRACTICAL REASONING, ACTION IS COMPELLED BY INFERENCE; IN THEORETICAL REASONING, BELIEF IS COMPELLED BY INFERENCE

In Anscombe's view, the idea that in theoretical reasoning, sound inference compels belief while in practical reasoning, sound inference compels action shapes various aspects of work on practical reason. She thinks that this assumption confuses the dual aspects of belief:

Beliefs, believings, are psychological states, something in the history of minds. But also a belief, a believing, is internally characterized by the proposition saying what is believed. This is (mostly) not about anything psychological; its meaning and truth are not matters of which we should give a psychological account. Propositions, we say, are what we operate the calculi of inference with, for example, the calculus of truth functions. . . . Certainly what [such a calculus] is *for* is, e.g., to pass from beliefs to beliefs. But we should throw everything into confusion if we introduced belief into our description of the validity of inferences. In setting forth the forms of inference we put as elements the propositions or we use propositional variables to represent them. (1989, 397 [26–27])

She makes a corresponding point about practical inference: we display the inferential structure of practical reasoning by showing its content. There would be no point in discussing the content of practical inference without supposing that the content might get "plugged into" agents' minds or wills, just as there would be no point in mapping out theoretical inference with an eye toward understanding theoretical reasoning if we did not think that such inference might inform belief. But we handle the content by means of the truth-connections between *propositions*, not by means of the historical relations among believings or intendings. As Anscombe puts it, "We would never think that the validity of 'p, if p then q, q' was to be expounded as the entailment of 'X believes q' by 'X believes that p and that if p then q.' It is, we feel, the other way around" (1989, 397 [26]).[23]

She urges that we develop corresponding scruples for practical inference. Not only is mentioning the agent's psychological states neither necessary nor sufficient to mark an inference as practical, mention of psychological states has *no* place in the premises (*unless*, as in the psychiatric example, these states are among the things that the agent seeks to *alter* by action). As we do for theoretical inference, we should focus upon the truth-connections among the propositions in discussing practical inference. Of course, if our objective is to understand *episodes of reasoning* (practical or theoretical) in the life histories of agents, we will restrict our attention to what we take it that the agents know, and how what they know shapes what they come to do or think. But representing inferential connections isn't chronicling events.

Nor need it involve genuine belief or willing. Recall our ironical slave who was told that *p* iff *q* and instructed to make it the case that *p*. He set about seeing to it that *r* since if *r* then *q*. He *didn't* believe that *p* iff *q* and had *no* personal stake in making *p* true. You don't have to *believe* the premises in order to draw such conclusions. We might note here how often philosophical argument is based in displaying the unsavory consequences of opposing positions. Standard philosophical practice *relies* upon our ability to appreciate the inferential connections between contents we take to be dead false, implausible, wicked, or otherwise deficient. The dual aspects of contentful psychological states are, for all their interconnectedness, separable.

Belief has a logical aspect. Intentional action has a rational structure. Any train of thought that leads one from belief to belief by means of the truth-connections among the contents, or from practical considerations to action by means of the truth-connections among the contents, will count as reasoning. But that doesn't mean that there is some relation between believings aptly called "logical compulsion," or a relation between psychological states and intending aptly called "practical compulsion." What there *are* are truth-connections between contents, not a special "logical" or "practical" compulsion to be in one psychological state after one has been in another, or to intend to *A* after having got into some psychological state.

5.1   Diagnosis of the Third Assumption

Anscombe thinks that we are led to suppose logico-psychological "compulsion" by failing to keep the two aspects of inference distinct. On the one side, there is the logical aspect concerning the truth relations among the contents (e.g., *p* and that *p* makes it probable that *q*). This aspect is the logician's topic. On the other, there is the use to which consideration of truth-connections is put in actual episodes of (non-ironical) reasoning. If we run these two together, she thinks, we assume that we have a grip on something like a logical step, "an act of mind which is making a step from premise to conclusion [and makes this] step *in logic*, making a *movement* in a different, *pure*, medium of logic itself" (1989, 393 [21]).

It is very easy to make the assumption about belief since beliefs are individuated in terms of their contents, the contents stand in logical relations to other actual or possible belief-*contents via* the truth-connections among contents (so much so that one tends to suppose that there could be no such thing as the utterly inferentially isolated belief), logic supplies ample resources for representing the truth-connections, etc.—all of which can, in turn, lead one to conceive advances in thinking as "movements" in a field of possibilities sketched out by logicians. Then it is as if we picture logic as a medium through which belief is transmitted (1989, 390–398 [19–28]). (Put *that* way, I think, most of us would deny that we had any such view; but Anscombe is here trying to sketch a picture on the basis of a fairly common inferentialist assumption.) Having conceived of well-grounded belief as the result of logical steps, which compel changes in psychological states, it then appears that the question is whether there is a logic step in the practical case:

The dispute seemed one between people who all agreed that there was such a thing as 'stepping' for assertions or suppositions; but some thought they could see such a 'step' also in the case of practical inference, while others just couldn't descry it at all. But there is no such thing in either case! (1989, 393 [21])[24]

And here we are finally in a position to appreciate how the paradox about practical inference arose on the assumption that inferential relations among the contents of psychological states determine the course of practical reasoning. The problem was that almost anything could interrupt practical reasoning, or intervene before one took action on its basis. These occurrences did *not* interrupt or intervene in the inferential relations among contents, however. So it looked like the only way to get inferential relations to *determine courses of events* was to demand instantaneous grounds followed by instantaneous action. But in thereby preserving the practical argument's inferential integrity, we rendered the argument useless, i.e., nonpractical. There was no longer time to *make* the argument, hence no longer time to *use* the argument in deciding what to do. However, if we are clear that we have, on the one side, a discussion of truth-connections among contents, on the other, a description of states and processes informed by those connections, we can avoid the paradox. When practical reasoning, as reasoning, goes well, it goes well because the agent does a good job of figuring out what to do. This will involve having some grip on some inferential relations obtaining among the contents of the practical considerations. But to take this to mean that inferential relations obtain among psychological states, or psychological states and subsequent actions, is to blur the dual aspect distinction. The "step" assumption tacitly or explicitly treats inferential relations *as* relations among states, processes, or states and processes, rather than taking it that discussion of inferential relations is sometimes useful in understanding courses of events (e.g., when the events involve episodes of reasoning).

6 THE STORY SO FAR

Anscombe has argued against the assumptions

1. that we can treat action as a given in our work on practical reason,
2. that inferential relations among the contents of propositional attitudes determine the course of practical reasoning, and
3. that in practical reasoning, action is compelled by inference; in theoretical reasoning, belief is compelled by inference.

She has made these points about practical inference while doing so:

· The conclusion of a practical inference is something one can affect by one's action.
· The content of a practical inference reveals something of the rational articulation of the action it underwrites, e.g., the premises and conclusion often include descriptions "under which" the action is intentional.
· The agent need not have conducted an inference that underwrites her act before taking action; the relevant contents might be represented as answers to reasons-for-acting-seeking-questions of the form "Why are you *A*-ing?" as she goes along; such questions are given application just in case the agent's act is intentional qua *A*-ing.

These points show that giving practical arguments is not only useful in deciding what to do, but also useful in understanding intentional action as such.

She has also made these points:

· One cannot tell the use to which an inference is being put from the content of the inference (recall the Euclidean inference).
· Both practical and theoretical inference rely upon the truth-connections of the propositions involved, and these can be shared across practical and theoretical inferences (again, recall the Euclidean inference).
· We cannot distinguish the two by insisting that at least one of the premises of a practical inference make mention of one of the agent's ends or wants, first because this is neither necessary nor sufficient to establish that inference is practical (recall the psychiatric patient and the ironical slave), more importantly because mention of psychological states has *no* proper place in setting out the content of any inference (this was the point of her discussion of the dual character of propositional attitudes).

Now, we can finally have a look at practical inference in particular.

7   SPECIFYING THE OBJECTIVE OF PRACTICAL REASONING

Anscombe has argued that mention of ends has no place among the premises of a practical inference. Further, placing the end among the premises, on Anscombe's view, flies in the face of a very long tradition of work on this subject. Traditionally—again, on Anscombe's reading—the starting point for practical reasoning is an objective. The objective is not *listed* among the premises. Rather, practical premises are about how to attain the objective. For all that, Anscombe thinks it worthwhile to give the objective off to the side of the practical inference. There are two reasons to do so.

First, giving the objective shows how things are supposed to come out. Suppose that we are given the following:

Strong alkaloids are deadly poison to humans.
Nicotine is a strong alkaloid.
What's in this bottle is nicotine.

From these facts, practical reasoning might lead to careful avoidance of a lethal dose, or to drinking down the whole bottle. Anscombe remarks,

That being so, there is a good deal of point in having the end somehow specified if we want to study the form. This at least is true: if you know the end, you know what the conclusion should be, given these premises. Whereas if you do not know the end, (a) the conclusion may be either positive *or* negative . . . , but also (b) how do we know where the reasoning should stop and a decision be made? (1989, 382 [7])

Table 2
Parallels between practical inference and theoretical inference

Practical inference	Theoretical inference
Objective: that s	r (or: Suppose r)
p	If q and r, then s
If p, then q	If p, then q
If q and r, then s	p
Decision: r!	Therefore, s

Second, listing the objective sometimes sets up a nice parallel between practical and theoretical inference. As Anthony Kenny has pointed out, the objective in practical inference can be represented as the conclusion of a corresponding theoretical inference.[25] For example, let $s =$ "I commit suicide"; let $r =$ "I drink the contents of the bottle"; let $q =$ "What's in the bottle is a lethal quantity of nicotine"; let $p =$ "Nicotine is a strong alkaloid, strong alkaloids taken in sufficient quantity are deadly poison, and the bottle contains such and such quantity of nicotine." In both cases p is the warrant for q. Now notice the inferences in table 2.

Anscombe points out that once we have noticed such parallels, it doesn't much matter whether or not we treat practical inference as having a distinctive form. The objective in the practical case is analogous to the conclusion of a corresponding theoretical inference. The conclusion in the practical case is analogous to the supposition or starting point for the corresponding theoretical inference. The same truth-connections are relevant to both. Etc. This is another way of showing what the inferentialists get right, in Anscombe's view.

8   A MAJOR DIVIDE BETWEEN PRACTICAL AND THEORETICAL REASONING

That practical reasoning is a goal-directed process that leads to goal-directed processes, i.e., intentional actions, nevertheless sets special limits on the "inferential consequences" of practical deliberation.

Inferentialists ignore this. Consider Robert Brandom's discussion of the shared structure of practical and theoretical commitments:

If a doxastic commitment to p has as a scorekeeping consequence doxastic commitment to q, then a practical commitment to make-true p has as a scorekeeping consequence a practical commitment to make-true q. (1994, 243)

A commitment to make-true is an intention. A scorekeeping consequence is, in effect, an inferential consequence. Brandom sees no obvious distinction between "transmission" of belief in light of inferential consequences and "transmission" of intention in light of inferential consequences. Anscombe will insist upon a distinction.

An intentional action is intentional (at least) under a series of linked descriptions that have a means-end or part-whole calculative form. There will be a wide range of descriptions of any of my actions that I can predict will be made true by my act, but are not intended effects of my action. At the most basic level, my intended effects are the ones that stand in means-end or part-whole relations to each other. For example, putting one foot in front of the other is a part of walking, and, in intentionally walking, I intend putting one foot in front of the other. Walking may be a means to getting to school, in which case, I intend putting one foot in front of the other to that end (namely, getting to school). But walking likewise wears down the soles of my shoes.

Now, given a moment's thought, I will *of course* predict that in walking to school, I will be wearing down my shoes. I will also be creating a breeze, casting shadows on the pavement, etc. Consequently, if I know these things, they belong among the "doxastic commitments" that I undertake upon being prepared to assert that I will walk to school today. They are *not* among the intended consequences of walking. I do not intend walking as one means among many I might take to wearing down my shoes. Wearing down my shoes isn't a stage in some other proceeding I have undertaken. You can see this in part because it isn't as though I will be "committed" to finding some *alternate* means of wearing down my shoes if the walk doesn't do the trick.

A strict inferentialist will have a lot of trouble making sense of the intended-foreseen distinction in practical philosophy. But if we notice that the first line of transmission of intention in practical reasoning, practical inference, *and* intentional action is along the means-end, part-whole calculative lines, we will see that merely foreseen consequences, however epistemically warranted, fall outside the calculative order in intentional action. This, in turn, reveals a very significant difference between theoretical and practical knowledge.

I suggested early on that the most important of the three assumptions Anscombe argues against is that we can treat action as given. Part of the reason that noticing the calculative order in action is vital to understanding practical reason is just this: as Anscombe thinks that Aristotle taught us, the first line of transmission of intention in practical reasoning and in action is calculative. One acts *in pursuit of an end* on grounds of what is believed. The end-directedness of *the whole business*—practical reasoning, the ends or means it generates, the pursuit of these on the grounds set forth in the practical argument—is fitted together in practice by the calculative form of the reasoning and of the course of action that is its conclusion. This calculative form gives the underlying shape of the operation of practical reason, in Anscombe's view, even if one engages in practical deliberation because one is clueless what to pursue, and must first find some suitable thing to go for. *Finding* the suitable end becomes, in such cases, the *objective* of practical reasoning, which will, accordingly, succeed just in case one settles upon a suitable pursuit and acts accordingly. Having a grip on such matters as the intended/foreseen distinction is a first step in understanding how knowledge in intention is different from theoretical knowledge.

9   CONCLUDING REMARKS

Anscombe makes various other points about practical reasoning in her essay. She suggests an interpretation of Aristotle's practical syllogisms as revealing the calculative order in action. She urges that we may not be able to imagine leading a practically rational human life without pursuing some "generic" ends (e.g., wanting *a* suitable place to live, *a* friend, *a* meal) by way of urging that we will need to do at least some practical reasoning as we go along (if only reasoning toward finding specific and get-able things the obtaining of which will constitute attaining our generic ends). She doesn't address questions about noncalculative practical reasoning. The burdens in making sense of noncalculative practical reasoning will include explaining how it is supposed to come out and where it is supposed to stop—recall her remarks about why specifying the objective is useful if we want to study forms of practical inference; in noncalculative practical deliberation, we presumably lack the specific objective that answers these questions and enables study of forms. In short, she does not give a tidy, systematic theory of practical reasoning or practical inference. What she does do, however, is raise a great many points that merit the attention of anyone interested in the topic and, I think, gives us good reason to doubt the three assumptions against which she argues.

Notes

1. Anscombe 1963, sec. 32.

2. The attribution is standard. See, e.g., Mark Platts 1979, 256–257.

3. The equivalent psychological claim might be that you couldn't tell *attitude* from propositional content. It isn't obvious how Anscombe's point about *use* can be reduced to attitude difference.

4. Philip Clark uses "inferentialism" to describe his position. Clark's views are in line with Anscombe's; he is not, I think, in my target group.

5. I have inserted the allusion to probabilistic inference.

6. Anscombe 1989; see also Anscombe 1963, secs. 33–37. Anscombe 1989 is reprinted in *Virtues and Reasons*, edited by Rosalind Hursthouse, Gavin Lawrence and Warren Quinn (Clarendon Press: Oxford, 1998), pp. 1–34. Hereafter, reprint page references are given in brackets.

7. Davidson 1980, essays 1, 2, 4, 5, 12.

8. Ernest LePore and Brian McLaughlin (1988, 5) take it that in such cases a primary reason ([belief, pro-attitude] pair) causes action without rationalizing it.

9. Two *caveats* about the stand-and-walk example. First, I have in mind a case where the Davidsonian should be content with an explanation in terms of beliefs and pro-attitudes—I just want to stretch my legs, know that I need to get out of my chair to do so, etc.—Davidson leaves ample room for such examples.

Second, on some views, skill will be grounded in practical reasoning insofar as grounded in learning. See, e.g., Millgram 1997. Now, if a man has learned how to lead climbs, he has learned why keeping hold of the rope matters. By parity of reasoning, he has learned how to let a companion fall. Davidson suggests that finding practical reasoning among the causal antecedents could make the difference between treating the case as intentional action and treating it as a climbing accident. The suggestion makes no sense if the climber's know-how automatically makes his behavior a product of practical reasoning.

10. Davidson 1980, essay 4.

11. Anscombe 1963, sec. 19: treating intention as an added ingredient to "action" obliterates the voluntary/involuntary distinction, making it well nigh impossible to give a principled account of action.

12. Anscombe 1963, secs. 9–11, analyzes such cases.

13. Anscombe 1963, secs. 5–9.

14. Anscombe 1963, sec. 6.

15. Anscombe 1963, secs. 23, 26.

16. Consider Davidson 1980, essay 7.

17. In the climber case, thinking we have action would generally involve thinking that the climber intends to injure his companion or else to break their agreement. Suppose that the companion manages to catch hold of a rocky outcrop and hang there. If the lead climber intended injury, we'd expect to see him backtrack and,

say, stomp on her fingers. If he just meant to break the agreement, he might just move on. The point is that if he *acted*, it was in pursuit of an end and the calculative structure should inform his course.

18. Anscombe is sometimes charged with "behaviorism" because she makes the study of intentional action the starting point for work on practical reason. The charge seems rooted in the first assumption: if you take action as given, you will likely suppose that directing our attention to action is directing our attention to behaviors that require no analysis. Anscombe then seems determined to account for the psychology of rational action (for intention, e.g.) by staring at these "givens." But Anscombe's point *isn't* that we can confine our attention to behavioral regularities in order to get a grip on intention. Her point is that isolating a *criterion* for intentional action (not mere behavior, but rationally informed action, intentional "under" a calculative series of descriptions) illuminates intention and reasons for acting. The criterion works not by "reducing" psychology to behavior, but by teaching us to see reason *in* action.

19. She also points out that action is rarely necessitated by practical grounds: "Practical grounds may 'require' an action, when they shew that *only* by its means can the end be obtained, but they are just as much grounds when they merely shew that the end *will* be obtained by a certain means. Thus, in the only sense in which practical grounds *can* necessitate a conclusion (an action), they need not, and are none the less grounds for that" (1989, 384 [11]). I will simply make the point in passing. Very few of us (save some Kantians—Kant may have thought that reasons necessitate action) take a strictly deductivist view of practical reasoning.

20. Georg Henrik von Wright (1972) makes the suggestion. Von Wright is acutely sensitive to the difficulty in tracing the connection between practical reasoning and action.

21. Müller 1979.

22. Anthony Kenny treats practical inference as involving contents of the form "Fiat *p*!" partly because fiats only attach to propositions that can be made true by the addressee's future actions. Anscombe discusses imperatival inference at length (1989, 384–390 [11–19]).

23. I hope that her point is clear. In case it isn't, notice the following. Inferential validity guarantees that *anyone* who ever believed that *q* on the grounds that *p* and that if *p* then *q* would have the *same* warrant for her belief as *X* does. On the interpretation that Anscombe takes to be recognizably daft, we would treat the study of valid inference as empirical investigation of routine connections between believings within and across individuals. Logicians don't work that way. Moreover, on any such approach it would be hard to get at what was wrong with *Y* if *Y* believed that not-*q*, that *p*, and that if *p* then *q*. The criticism would appear to boil down to the charge that *Y*'s position was *unpopular*, or harmful to *Y*'s practical interests. But if *p* and *q* concern matters which have no practical impact, and if *Y* tends often enough to go along with the crowd, *modus ponens*-wise, then the charges are toothless. There are other troubles. For example,

propositional attitude contexts are generally taken to exhibit failures of logical closure. It is hard to understand this if we think that the topic of logic is propositional attitudes.

24. For recent attempts to find the practical "step," see, e.g., Christine Korsgaard's discussion of the need to supplement Kant's argument about the hypothetical imperative: "[there remains] a problem about how the analytic proposition is supposed to make it possible for the agent to combine willing the end with knowing the means to *arrive at* a rational requirement of willing the means" (1997, 238). The use of "arrive at" (italicized, notice) suggests that we need an account of how the agent *makes the step* in willing from end to means in accordance with Kant's postulated *formal* requirement. For a related but very different example, see Robert Brandom 1994. For Brandom it isn't that there is a special pure medium of logic in which one takes steps, exactly. Rather how we understand inferential relations is by imagining moving from proposition to proposition, all the while being scorekeepers of our own and each other's "moves." Logical schemata become like various sorts of scorecards we might employ in keeping track of logic steps.

25. Kenny 1966.

References

Anscombe, G. E. M. 1989. "Von Wright on Practical Inference." In *The Philosophy of Georg Henrik von Wright*, ed. P. A. Schlipp and L. E. Hahn, pp. 377–404. La Salle, Ill.: Open Court. Reprinted in *Virtues and Reasons*, ed. R. Hursthouse, G. Lawrence, and W. Quinn, pp. 1–34. Oxford: Clarendon Press, 1998.

Anscombe, G. E. M. 1963. *Intention*. Ithaca, N.Y.: Cornell University Press.

Brandom, R. 1994. *Making It Explicit: Reasoning, Representing, and Discursive Commitment*. Cambridge: Harvard University Press.

Davidson, D. 1980. *Essays on Actions and Events*. Oxford: Clarendon Press.

Kenny, A. 1966. "Practical Inference." *Analysis* 26 (January): 65–73.

Korsgaard, C. 1997. "The Normativity of Instrumental Reason." In *Ethics and Practical Reason*, ed. G. Cullity and B. Gaut, pp. 215–254. Oxford: Clarendon Press.

LePore, E., and McLaughlin, B. 1988. "Actions, Reasons, Causes, and Intentions." In *Actions and Events: Perspectives on the Philosophy of Donald Davidson*, ed. E. LePore and B. McLaughlin, pp. 1–24. Oxford: Basil Blackwell.

Millgram, E. 1997. *Practical Induction*. Cambridge: Harvard University Press.

Müller, A. 1979. "How Theoretical Is Practical Reasoning?" In *Intention and Intentionality: Essays in Honour of G. E. M. Anscombe*, ed. C. Diamond and J. Teichman, pp. 91–108. Ithaca, N.Y.: Cornell University Press.

Platts, M. 1979. *Ways of Meaning*. London: Routledge and Kegan Paul.

Von Wright, G. H. 1972. "On So-Called Practical Inference." *Acta Sociologica* 15: 39–53.

Chapter 20

Action, Norms, and Practical Reasoning

Robert Brandom

I BACKGROUND

In this paper I aim to do three things, corresponding to the three pieces of my title:

• To explain the expressive role that distinguishes specifically *normative* vocabulary. That is, to say what it is the job of such vocabulary to make explicit. Doing this is saying what 'ought' means.
• To introduce a non-Humean way of thinking about *practical reasoning*.
• To offer a broadly Kantian account of the *will* as a rational faculty of practical reasoning.

The idea is to do that by exploiting the structural analogies between discursive exit transitions in action and discursive entry transitions in perception to show how the rational will can be understood as no more philosophically mysterious than our capacity to notice red things.

Practical reasoning often leads to action, so it is clear that there is an intimate connection between these two elements of my title. But one might wonder: why action and *norms*?

Let me start with some background. The beginning of wisdom in thinking about these matters (as for so many others) is to look to Kant: the great, grey mother of us all. For we are in the privileged position of being downstream from the fundamental conceptual sea-change effected by the replacement of concern with Cartesian certainty by concern with Kantian necessity—that is, of concern with our grip on concepts (is it clear? is it distinct?) by concern with their grip on us (is this rule binding on us? is it applicable to this case?). Kant's big idea is that what distinguishes judgment and action from the responses of merely natural creatures is neither their relation to some special stuff nor their peculiar transparency, but rather that they are what we are in a distinctive way *responsible* for. They express *commitments* of ours: commitments that we are answerable for in the sense that our *entitlement* to them is always potentially at issue, commitments that are *rational* in the sense that vindicating the corresponding entitlements is a matter of offering *reasons* for them.

Another big idea of Kant's—seeing the *judgment* as the smallest unit of experience—is a consequence of the first one. The logic he inherited started with a doctrine of *terms*, divided into the singular and the general, proceeded to a doctrine of *judgment* (understood in terms of the predication of a general term of a singular one), and thence to a doctrine of *consequences* or inferences. Kant starts with judgment because that is the smallest unit for which we can be *responsible*. (This thought is taken over by Frege, who begins with the units to which pragmatic force can attach, and Wittgenstein, who looks at the smallest expressions whose utterance makes a move in the language game.) It is under this rubric that judgment is assimilated to action. A third Kantian idea is then to understand both judgment and action as the application of *concepts*. He does that by understanding concepts as the *rules* that determine what knowers and agents are responsible *for*—what they have committed themselves to.

I am going to discuss the topics of my title—action, norms, and practical reasoning—in the idiom I develop in my book, *Making It Explicit*.[1] To begin with, I will work within the context of what I call there a *normative pragmatics*. Specifically, I think of discursive practice as deontic scorekeeping: the significance of a speech act is how it changes what commitments and entitlements one attributes and acknowledges. I work also within the context of an *inferential semantics*. That is, discursive commitments (to begin with, doxastic ones) are distinguished by their specifically inferential articulation: what counts as evidence for them, what else they commit us to, what other commitments they are incompatible with in the sense of precluding entitlement to. This is a reading of what it is for the norms in question to be specifically *conceptual* norms. The overall idea is that the rationality that qualifies us as *sapients* (and not merely sentients) can be identified with being a player in the social, implicitly normative game of offering and assessing, producing and consuming, reasons.

I further endorse an *expressive* view of *logic*. That is, I see the characteristic role that distinguishes specifically logical vocabulary as being making explicit, in the form of a claim, features of the game of giving and asking for reasons in virtue of which bits of *non*logical vocabulary play the roles that they do. The paradigm is the *conditional*. Before introducing this locution, one can *do* something, namely endorse an inference. After introducing the conditional, one can now *say* that the inference is a good one. The expressive role of the conditional is to make *explicit*, in the form of a claim, what before was *implicit* in our practice of distinguishing some inferences as good.

Giving and asking for reasons for *actions* is possible only in the context of practices of giving and asking for reasons generally—that is, of practices of making and defending *claims* or *judgments*. For giving a reason is always expressing a judgment: making a claim. That is, practical reasoning requires the availability of beliefs (doxastic commitments) as premises. On the side of the *consequences* of acquisition of practical deontic statuses, it appears in the essential role that propositional, that is, assertible, contents play in specifying conditions of *success*: that is, what would count as fulfilling a commitment to act. Forming an intention (undertaking a commitment) to put a ball through a hoop requires knowing what it is to put a ball through a hoop—what must be *true* for that intention to *succeed*. (This is a point about explanatory *autonomy*: I claim that one can explain the role of beliefs in theoretical reasoning (leading from claims to claims) first, without needing to appeal to practical reasoning, while I do not believe one can do things in the opposite order.)

II MOTIVATION

The treatment of action I am sketching is motivated by three truisms, and two more interesting ideas. First, beliefs make a difference both to what we *say*, and to what we *do*. We license others to infer our beliefs (or, as I will say, our doxastic commitments) both from our explicit claims and from our overt intentional actions. Next is a (by now familiar) lesson we have been taught by Anscombe and Davidson.[2] Actions are performances that are intentional under some specification.[3] Such performances can genuinely be things *done* even though they have many specifications under which they are *not* intentional. A third, companion idea is that at least one way a specification of a performance can be privileged as one under which it is intentional is by figuring as the conclusion of a piece of practical reasoning that exhibits the agent's reasons for producing that performance.

Davidson's original idea was to eliminate *intentions* in favor of primary *reasons*, understood in terms of *beliefs* and *pro-attitudes* (paradigmatically, *desires*). My first idea is to start instead with normative statuses and attitudes corresponding to *beliefs* and *intentions*. I'll try to explain *desires*, and more generally, the pro-attitudes expressed by *normative* vocabulary, in terms of those beliefs and intentions. The thought is that there are two species of discursive commitment: the cognitive (or doxastic), and the practical. The latter are commitments to *act*. Acknowledgments of the first sort of commitment correspond to *beliefs*; acknowledgments of the second sort of commitment correspond to *intentions*. The first are takings-true, the second makings-true. Practical commitments are like doxastic commitments in being essentially inferentially articulated. They stand in inferential relations both among themselves (both means-end and incompatibility) and to doxastic commitments.

The second basic idea motivating the present account is that the non-inferential relations between acknowledgments of practical commitments and states of affairs brought about by intentional *action* can be understood by analogy to the noninferential relations between acknowledgments of doxastic commitments and the states of affairs they are brought about by through conceptually contentful *perception*.

a. Observation (a discursive *entry* transition) depends on reliable dispositions to respond differentially to states of affairs of various kinds by acknowledging certain sorts of commitments, that is, by adopting deontic attitudes and so changing the score.
b. Action (a discursive *exit* transition) depends on reliable dispositions to respond differentially to the acknowledging of certain sorts of commitments, the adoption of deontic attitudes and consequent change of score, by bringing about various kinds of states of affairs.

Elaborating the first idea (modeling intention on belief as corresponding to inferentially articulated commitments) involves examining the sense in which practical reasons are *reasons*; elaborating the second idea (modeling action on perception, discursive exits on discursive entries) involves examining the sense in which practical reasons are *causes*. It is this latter idea that makes sense of the distinction, so crucial to Davidson, between acting *for* a reason, and merely acting *with* a reason.

Put in terms of the deontic scorekeeping model of discursive practice, the idea is that *intentions* are to *reasons* as *commitments* are to *entitlements*. It follows that on this model, Davidson would be wrong to say that "someone who acts with a certain intention acts for a reason." For just as one can undertake doxastic or theoretical commitments to which one is not entitled by reasons, so one can undertake practical commitments to which one is not entitled by reasons. What makes a performance an *action* is that it is, or is produced by the exercise of a reliable differential disposition to respond to, the acknowledgment of a practical commitment. That acknowledgment need not itself have been produced as a response to the acknowledgment of other commitments inferentially related to it as entitlement-conferring reasons. (Though that it *could* be so elicited *is* essential to its being the acknowledgment of a practical commitment.)

III PRACTICAL REASONING AND MATERIAL INFERENCE

The strategy of trying to understand desires, and the pro-attitudes expressed by normative vocabulary more generally, in terms of their relation to beliefs and intentions—instead of the more orthodox Humean and Davidsonian strategy of starting with beliefs and desires—requires thinking about practical reasoning somewhat differently. Consider the following three bits of practical reasoning:

α. Only opening my umbrella will keep me dry, so
   I shall open my umbrella.
β. I am a bank employee going to work, so
   I shall wear a necktie.
γ. Repeating the gossip would harm someone, to no purpose, so
   I shall not repeat the gossip.

'Shall' is used here to express the significance of the conclusion as the acknowledging of a practical commitment. ('Will' would be used correspondingly to express a doxastic commitment to a prediction.)

The Davidsonian approach treats these as enthymemes, whose missing premises might be filled in by something like:

a. I want (desire, prefer) to stay dry.
b. Bank employees are obliged (required) to wear neckties.
c. It is wrong (one ought not) to harm anyone to no purpose.

(Orthodox contemporary humeans would insist that something is missing in the second two cases, even when (b) and (c) are supplied. More on that thought later.) This enthymematic thesis is parallel on the side of practical reasoning to the insistence that theoretical reasoning be ⁵completed⁵ by the addition of conditionals, which assert the propriety of the material inferences involved, and transform the move into something that is *formally* valid. Sellars teaches us that that move is optional. We need not treat all correct inferences as correct in virtue of their form, supplying implicit or suppressed premises involving logical vocabulary as needed. Instead, we can treat inferences such as that from "Pittsburgh is to the West of Philadelphia," to "Philadelphia is to the East of Pittsburgh," or from "It is raining," to "The streets will be wet," as *materially* good inferences—that is inferences that are good because of the content of their *non*logical vocabulary.[4] I propose to adopt this nonformalist strategy in thinking about practical inferences.

One reason to do so is that the notion of *formally valid* inferences is definable in a natural way from the notion of *materially correct* inferences, while there is no converse route. For given a subset of vocabulary that is privileged or distinguished somehow, an inference can be treated as good in virtue of its form, with respect to that vocabulary, just in case it is a materially good inference and it cannot be turned into a materially bad one by substituting *non*-privileged for *non*-privileged vocabulary, in its premises and conclusions. This substitutional notion of formally good inferences need have nothing special to do with *logic*. If it is specifically *logical* form that is of interest, then one must antecedently be able to distinguish some vocabulary as peculiarly logical. Once that is done, it can be treated as the vocabulary that is privileged in the sense that motivates us to look for proprieties of inference that are invariant under substitutions for all but that logical vocabulary. But if one were instead to pick out *theo*logical (or aesthetic) vocabulary as privileged, then looking at which substitutions of non-theological (or non-aesthetic) vocabulary for non-theological (non-aesthetic) vocabulary preserve material goodness of inference will pick out inferences good in virtue of their theological (or aesthetic) form. According to this way of thinking, the formal goodness of inferences derives from and is explained in terms of the material goodness of inferences, and so ought not to be appealed to in explaining it.

This account contrasts with the standard order of explanation, which treats all inferences as good or bad solely in virtue of their form, with the contents of the claims they involve mattering only for the truth of the (implicit) premises. According to this way of setting things out, there is no such thing as material inference. This view, which understands "good inference" to mean "formally valid inference", postulating implicit premises as needed, might be called a *formalist* approach to inference. It trades primitive goodnesses of inference for the truth of conditionals. I am not claiming that one *cannot* decide to talk this way. The point is just that one *need* not.

If one rejects the formalist order of explanation, what should one say about the role of conditional claims, such as "*If* Pittsburgh is to the West of Philadelphia, *then* Philadelphia is to the East of Pittsburgh"? The claim is that although such conditionals need not be added as explicit premises in order to license the inference from their antecedents to their consequents, they nonetheless serve to make explicit—in the form of a claim—the otherwise merely implicit endorsement of a material propriety of inference. Before we have conditionals on board, we can *do* something, namely treat certain material inferences as correct. Once we have the expressive power of those logical locutions, we come to be able to *say that* they are good. The expressivist line about logic sees conditionals as making implicit material inferential commitments explicit, in the form of claims—but as *not* required to make the inferences they explicitate *good* inferences. Indeed, on this view, playing such an explicitating expressive role is precisely what distinguishes some vocabulary as distinctively *logical.*

IV   ENTHYMEMES AND MONOTONICITY

I want to treat

(A)   It is raining
──────────────────
     ∴ I shall open my umbrella

like

(B)   It is raining
──────────────────
     ∴ The streets will be wet

and say that *neither* one is an enthymeme.

The Davidsonian will respond that we can see that the reason offered in the first case is incomplete, because the inference would not go through if I did not want to stay dry. But I think that what we really know is rather that the inference would not go through if I had a *contrary* desire: say, the Gene Kelly desire to sing and dance in the rain, and so to get wet. But the fact that conjoining a premise incompatible with the desire to stay dry would infirm the inference (turn it into a bad one) does not show that the desire was all along already functioning as an implicit premise. There would be a case for that conclusion only if the reasoning involved were *monotonic*—that is, if the fact that the inference from p to q is a good one meant that the inference from $p\&r$ to q must be a good one. (So that the fact that the latter is *not* a good argument settled it that the former isn't either.)

But material inference is not in general monotonic—even on the theoretical side. It can be in special cases, say in mathematics and fundamental physics. But it never is in ordinary reasoning, and almost never in the special sciences. (Reasoning in clinical medicine, for instance, is resolutely nonmonotonic.) Consider the arguments that are codified in the following conditionals:

i. If I strike this dry, well-made match, then it will light. $[p \rightarrow q]$
ii. If p and the match is in a very strong electromagnetic field, then it will *not* light. $[p \; \& \; r \rightarrow \sim q]$
iii. If p and r and the match is in a Faraday cage, then it will light. $[p \; \& \; r \; \& \; s \rightarrow q]$
iv. If p and r and s and the room is evacuated of oxygen, then it will *not* light. $[p \; \& \; r \; \& \; s \; \& \; t \rightarrow \sim q]$
⋮

The reasoning we actually engage in always permits the construction of inferential hierarchies with oscillating conclusions like this. A certain kind of formalist about logic will want to insist, for reasons of high theory, that material inference *must* be like formal inference in being monotonic. And at this point in the dialectic, such a *monotonous formalist* will invoke *ceteris paribus* clauses. I do not want to claim that invoking such clauses ("all other things being equal") is incoherent or silly. But we must be careful how we understand the expressive role they play. For they cannot (I want to say, in principle) be cashed out; their content cannot be made explicit in the form of a series of additional premises. They are not shorthand for something we *could* say if we took the time or the trouble. The problem is not just that we would need an *infinite* list of the conditions being ruled out—though that is true. It is that the membership of such a list would be *indefinite*: we don't know how to specify in advance what belongs on the list. If we try to solve this problem by a *general* characterization, we get something equivalent to: "*ceteris paribus*, q follows from p" means that "q follows from p unless there is some *infirming* or *interfering* condition." But this is just to say that *q* follows from *p* except in the cases where for some reason it doesn't.

I would contend that *ceteris paribus* clauses should be understood as explicitly marking the nonmonotonicity of an inference, rather than as a *deus ex machina* that magically *removes* its nonmonotonicity. The material inference (i) above is just fine as it stands. But if one wants explicitly to acknowledge that, even so, it can form the base of an oscillating hierarchy of inferences of the form of (ii), (iii), (iv), and so on, then one can do so by reformulating it as:

i'. If I strike this dry, well-made match, then *ceteris paribus*, it will light.

Like their theoretical brethren, material proprieties of *practical* reasoning are nonmonotonic. So the fact that if I add "I want to get wet," as a second premise to inference (A) above the resulting inference no longer goes through does *not* show that the *denial* of that premise was already implicit. That would be the case only if material practical inferences were monotonic. In any case, as we will see, there is another way to go. We could think of the expressive role of avowals of desire as being analogous, on the practical side, to that of the conditional, on the theoretical side: as functioning not as a *premise*, but as making explicit the *inferential* commitment that permits the transition.

V   INFERENTIAL SIGNIFICANCE OF NORMATIVE VOCABULARY

With this background, I can state my fundamental thesis: *normative vocabulary* (including expressions of preference) *makes explicit the endorsement (attributed or acknowledged) of* MATERIAL *proprieties of* PRACTICAL *reasoning*. Normative vocabulary plays the same expressive role on the *practical* side that *conditionals* do on the *theoretical* side.

The idea is that the broadly normative or evaluative vocabulary used in (a), (b), and (c) ('prefer', 'obliged', and 'ought')—which Davidson understands as expressing the pro-attitudes needed to turn the incomplete reasons offered as premises in (α), (β), and (γ) into complete reasons—is used to make explicit in assertible, propositional form the endorsement of a *pattern* of material practical inferences. Different patterns of inference should be understood as corresponding to different sorts of norms or pro-attitudes.

For instance, an attributor who takes (α) to be entitlement preserving will also take

α'. Only standing under the awning will keep me dry, so
   I shall stand under the awning.
α''. Only remaining in the car will keep me dry, so
   I shall remain in the car.

and a host of similar inferences to have that status. Doing so is implicitly attributing a preference for staying dry. (Notice that because desires can compete, they provide only *prima facie* reasons for acting. Acknowledging the nonmonotonicity of practical reasoning, however, already provides for the features of reasoning that are normally dealt with by introducing such a notion.)

The norm, rule, or requirement that bank employees wear neckties is what makes going to work into a reason for wearing a necktie, for bank employees. Taking it that there is such a norm or requirement also just is endorsing a pattern of practical reasoning: taking (β) to be a good inference for anyone who is a bank employee. This inferential pattern is different from that exhibited by (α) in two ways. First, there need not be for each interlocutor for whom (β) is taken to be a good inference a set of other inferences corresponding to (α), (α'), (α''). Instead, there will be related inferences such as:

β'. I am a bank employee going to work, so
   I shall not wear a clown costume.
β''. I am a bank employee going to work, so
   I shall comb my hair.

But these are not licensed by the norm made explicit in (b), but only by others associated with the same social institutional status (being a bank employee).

Second, the scorekeeper will take (β) to be a good inference for any interlocutor A such that the scorekeeper *undertakes* doxastic commitment to the claim that A is a bank employee—as opposed to *attributing* a desire or acknowledgment of a commitment. Here the norm implicitly underwriting the inference is associated with having a certain status, as employee of a bank, rather than with exhibiting a certain desire or preference. Whether one has a good reason to wear a necktie just depends on whether or not one has occupies the status in question. This pattern, where what matters is the scorekeeper's undertaking of a commitment to A's occupying the status, rather than A's acknowledgment of that commitment, corresponds to an *objective* sense of 'good reason for action' (according to the scorekeeper). In this sense, that A is preparing to go to work can be a good reason for A to wear a necktie, even though A is not in a position to appreciate it as such. (Compare the sense in which one's reliability as a reporter can entitle one to a claim [in the eyes of a score-keeper], even if one is not aware that one is reliable, and so not aware of one's entitlement.)

Endorsement of practical reasoning of the sort of which (γ) is representative, codified in the form of a normative principle by (c), corresponds to an inferential commitment exhibiting a pattern different from those involved in either (α) or (β). For a scorekeeper who takes (γ) to be entitlement-preserving for A takes it to be entitlement-preserving for *anyone*, regardless of desires or preferences, and regardless of social status.

These *prudential* (or instrumental), *institutional*, and *unconditional* norms (made explicit by corresponding 'ought's) are meant only as three representative varieties, not as an exhaustive list. But they show how different sorts of norms correspond to different patterns of practical reasoning. The idea is that normative vocabulary is a kind of *logical* vocabulary, in my expressive sense: its expressive function is to make explicit commitments to inferences.

To endorse a practical inference as entitlement preserving is to take the doxastic premises as providing reasons for the practical conclusion. To exhibit a piece of good practical reasoning whose conclusion is a certain intention is to exhibit that intention, and the action (if any) that it elicits, as *rational*, as reasonable in the light of the commitments exhibited in the premises. Thus *all* of the 'ought's that make explicit species of practical reasoning taken as examples here, the prudential 'ought', the institutional 'ought', and the unconditional 'ought', are different kinds of *rational* 'ought'. There is no *a priori* reason to assimilate all such 'ought's to any one form—for instance the prudential (Humean totalitarianism), as rationality-as-maximizing theorists (such as Gauthier) do. Recall also that the entitlement provided by prudential or institutional reasons need *not* be endorsed by the attributor; as Davidson points out, we need not take the agent's reasons to be *good* reasons.

From the point of view of this botanization of patterns of practical reasoning (which I do not pretend is complete) the humean and the kantian each have too restricted a notion of reasons for action. Each pursues a Procrustean order of explanation:

· The humean assimilates all reasons for action to the *first* pattern. (Thus the humean will see the inferences like (β) and (γ) as incomplete, even with the addition of premises (b) and (c).)
· The kantian assimilates all reasons for action to the *third* pattern.

The humean denies that a mere obligation or commitment could provide a reason for action, unless accompanied by some desire to fulfill it. And the kantian denies that a mere desire (sinnliche Neigung) could provide a reason for action, unless accompanied by the acknowledgment of some corresponding obligation or commitment.

VI SOME CONSEQUENCES

A picture of the rational will emerge if we combine these three ideas:

· The belief model of intending—the idea of modeling practical commitments on doxastic ones
· The picture of practical reasoning as relating beliefs as premises to intentions as conclusions
· The modeling of actions as discursive exit transitions on perceptions as discursive entry transitions

It is important to remember to begin with that acknowledging a practical commitment is *not* understood on the model of *promising*, but of *claiming*.[5] In particular, the commitment is not *to* anyone in particular, and one can change one's mind anytime, essentially without penalty. In both these respects, the practical commitments that correspond to intentions are like doxastic commitments, rather than like promises. But while a commitment *is* in force, it has consequences: for other practical commitments (and hence entitlements to practical commitments), via means-end reasoning and consideration of practical incompatibilities, and for doxastic commitments (and hence entitlement to doxastic commitments). Scorekeepers are licensed to infer our beliefs from our intentional actions (in context, of course), as well as from our speech acts.

Acting with reasons is being *entitled* to one's practical commitments. Having this status is being intelligible to oneself and to others. This status can be vindicated by offering a suitable sample piece of practical reasoning (which need not actually have preceded the acknowledgment or performance in question). That piece of practical reasoning explains *why* one did as one did: what *reasons* one had. This means that in particular cases, one can act intentionally but without reasons. But the capacity to acknowledge propositionally contentful practical commitments will be attributed only to those whose performances are largely intelligible.

The modeling of action on perception registers the crucial fact that acknowledgments of commitments can cause and be caused. Kant defines the rational will as the capacity to derive performances from conceptions of laws.[6] I am suggesting that we can replace "conception of a law," in this formulation by "acknowledgment of a commitment." 'Law' is Kant's term for a binding rule—a norm. One's conception of a law is what one takes oneself to be obliged to do. Having a rational will, then, can be understood as having the capacity to respond reliably to one's acknowledgment of a commitment (of a norm as binding on one) by differentially producing performances corresponding to the content of the commitment acknowledged. But perception is strictly analogous, on the input side. It is a capacity to respond differentially to the presence of, say, red things, by acknowledging a commitment with a corresponding content. The one capacity should in principle appear as no more mysterious than the other. According to this picture, we are rational creatures exactly insofar as our acknowledgment of discursive commitments (both doxastic and practical) makes a difference to what we go on to *do*.

Prior intentions are acknowledgments of practical commitments that are distinct from and antecedent to the responsive performances they are reliably differentially disposed to elicit. In other cases (intentions-in-action) the production of the performance may *be* the acknowledgment of the practical commitment. Prior intentions involve practical commitments to produce performances meeting *general* descriptions. Intentions-in-action are acknowledgments of practical commitments consisting of performances that are intentional under *demonstrative* specifications (e.g. "I shall jump *now*."). (These are Sellars' 'volitions'—"prior intentions whose time has come,"[7] a category rescued from the mistake of conceiving 'tryings' as minimal *actions* that are safe in that they preclude the possibility of *failure*, just as, and for the same reasons, 'seemings' are conceived as minimal *knowings* that are safe in that they preclude the possibility of *error*.[8]) One is a reliable agent (compare: reliable perceiver) with respect to a range of circumstances and a range of contents of practical commitments when one is so disposed that under those circumstances one's prior intentions with those contents conditionally *mature* into corresponding intentions-in-action.

One nice feature of this story is that what is expressed by the normative 'should' is related to what is expressed by the intentional 'shall' as third-person usage to first-person usage—that is, as attributing practical commitments (to others) is related to acknowledging practical commitments (oneself). The use of normative vocabulary such as 'should' expresses the attribution to an agent of commitment to a pattern of practical reasoning, while the use of 'shall' expresses acknowledgment by the agent of the sort of practical commitment that can appear as the conclusion of such practical reasoning. It is those acknowledgments that in competent agents are keyed to the production of the corresponding performances under favorable conditions. This relationship provides a way to make sense of weakness of the will (*akrasia*). For that phenomenon arises when self-*attributions* of practical commitments (which would be made explicit by statements of the form "I *should* ...") do not have the causal significance of *acknowledgments* of practical commitments (which would be made explicit by statements of the form "I *shall* ..."). In this form, the possibility of incompatible intentions is no more mysterious than that of incompatible claims (or for that matter, promises).

Notice that Davidson started off only with intentions-in-action—the case, on the present account, where the performance *is* the acknowledgment of a practical commitment. He later introduces intendings, but he construes them as judgments that some performance is "desirable, good, or what ought to be done". Since he does not tell us what these normative terms mean, this is objectionably circular. By starting elsewhere, we have seen how to make independent sense of the expressive role of normative vocabulary.

Finally, notice that this account distinguishes

a. acting intentionally, which is acknowledging a practical commitment, either in, or by producing, a corresponding performance,
b. acting with reasons, which is being entitled to such a commitment,
c. acting for reasons, which is the case where reasons are causes, when acknowledgment of practical commitment is elicited by proper reasoning.

VII   CONCLUSION

I said at the outset that in this paper I aimed to do three things:

• To explain the expressive role that distinguishes specifically *normative* vocabulary. That is, to say what it is the job of such vocabulary to make explicit.
• To introduce a non-Humean way of thinking about *practical reasoning*.

• To offer a broadly Kantian account of the *will* as a rational faculty of practical reasoning, by exploiting the structural analogies between discursive exit transitions in action and discursive entry transition in perception to show how the rational will can be understood as no more philosophically mysterious than our capacity to notice red things.

Although the account I have offered has of necessity been telegraphic, its goal has been to fulfill that discursive practical commitment.

Notes

1. Harvard University Press, 1994. The ideas presented here are discussed there in more detail in the second half of chapter 4.

2. G. E. M. Anscombe, *Intention* (Blackwell, 1959), and Donald Davidson, originally in "Actions, Reasons, and Causes," reprinted in *Actions and Events* (Oxford University Press, 1984).

3. Not necessarily a *description*, at least if that category is conceived narrowly. For, as will emerge below (in section V), it is important that the specifications in question can include *demonstrative* and indexical elements.

4. Wilfrid Sellars, "Inference and Meaning," reprinted in J. Sicha (ed.), *Pure Pragmatics and Possible Worlds: The Early Essays of Wilfrid Sellars* (Ridgeview Publishing, Reseda, Calif., 1980).

5. In particular, the notion of the sort of commitment undertaking by making a claim that is elaborated in chapter 3 of *Making It Explicit*.

6. *Critique of Practical Reason*, section 7.

7. "Thought and Action," p. 110 in Keith Lehrer (ed.), *Freedom and Determinism* (Random House, 1966).

8. I discuss Sellars on 'seems' in my Study Guide, included in Wilfrid Sellars' *Empiricism and the Philosophy of Mind* (Harvard University Press, 1997), in the commentary to section 16, pp. 139–144. I discuss the parallel with 'try' in *Making It Explicit*, pp. 294–295.

Contributors

Robert Brandom is Distinguished Service Professor at the University of Pittsburgh and author of *Making It Explicit* (1994).

Michael Bratman is Durfee Professor in the School of Humanities and Sciences and Professor of Philosophy at Stanford University. He is the author of *Intention, Plans, and Practical Reason* (1987), *Faces of Intention: Selected Essays on Intention and Agency* (1999), and various articles in philosophy of action and related fields.

James Dreier is Associate Professor of Philosophy at Brown University. He received his Ph.D. from Princeton University in 1989.

Christoph Fehige is a Research Scholar at the University of Constance. He has written on the value of life, the foundations of ethics, and practical reason.

Brad Hooker is Senior Lecturer in Philosophy at the University of Reading, and author of *Ideal Code, Real World: A Rule-Consequentialist Theory of Morality* (2000). He has written on reasons for action in *Philosophical Papers* (1991) and the *Australasian Journal of Philosophy* (1992).

Aurel Kolnai was Visiting Lecturer at Bedford College, University of London, at his death in 1973. He was the author of *The War against the West* (1938), *Ethics, Value, and Reality* (1978), *The Utopian Mind* (1995), *Privilege and Liberty* (1999), and *Political Memoirs* (1999).

Christine M. Korsgaard is Arthur Kingsley Porter Professor of Philosophy at Harvard University. She is the author of *The Sources of Normativity* (1996), in which she examines modern views about the normative force of obligation and defends a Kantian view of her own, and *Creating the Kingdom of Ends* (1996), a collection of essays on Kantian ethics.

Michael Mandler is Professor of Economics at Royal Holloway College, University of London. He studies microeconomic theory, mathematical economics, and social choice theory. He previously taught at Harvard University and the University of Pennsylvania. His recent book, *Dilemmas in Economic Theory* (1999), examines foundational problems in preference analysis and the theory of economic equilibrium.

Elijah Millgram is Associate Professor of Philosophy at the University of Utah. The author of *Practical Induction* (1997), he is interested in practical reasoning, truth, and John Stuart Mill.

Dame Iris Murdoch taught philosophy at St. Anne's College in Oxford and was well-known as a novelist. Her philosophical essays have been recently collected in *Existentialists and Mystics*, edited by Peter Conradi (1997).

Martha Nussbaum is Ernst Freund Distinguished Service Professor of Law and Ethics at the University of Chicago, with appointments in the Philosophy Department, Law School, and Divinity School; she is an Associate of the Classics Department, a member of the Board of the Center for Gender Studies, and an Affiliate of the Committee on Southern Asian Studies.

Onora O'Neill is Principal of Newnham College, Cambridge, and works in ethics and political philosophy. She has worked extensively on Kant's practical philosophy, and in particular on his accounts of practical reason and autonomy. Her books include *Towards Justice and Virtue* (1996) and *Bounds of Justice* (2000).

John Robertson is Assistant Professor of Philosophy at Syracuse University. He is the author of "Internalism about Moral Reasons" (1986) and "Hume on Practical Reason" (1990), and is the coauthor (with Michael Stocker) of "Externalism and Internalism," in the *Encyclopedia of Ethics* (1992).

David Schmidtz is Joint Professor of Philosophy and Professor of Economics at the University of Arizona. He recently edited *Robert Nozick* for Cambridge University Press and coedited (with Elizabeth Willott) *Environmental Ethics: What Really Matters, What Really Works* for Oxford University Press.

Michael Slote is Professor of Philosophy at the University of Maryland, College Park. He has written extensively in moral psychology and ethics, and his book *Morals from Motives* has just been published by Oxford University Press.

Paul Thagard is Professor of Philosophy, Adjunct Professor of Psychology and Computer Science, and Director of the Cognitive Science Program at the University of Waterloo. His most recent books are *Coherence in Thought and Action* (2000) and *How Scientists Explain Disease* (1999).

Candace Vogler is Associate Professor of Philosophy at the University of Chicago. Her research interests include practical reason, ethics, social and political philosophy, gender and sexuality studies, and critical race theory. She is the author of *John Stuart Mill's Deliberative Landscape* (2001) and of *Reason in Action* (forthcoming).

David Wiggins is Wykeham Professor of Logic in Oxford University, and he is author of *Identity and Spatio-temporal Continuity* (1967), of *Sameness and Substance* (1980), and of *Needs, Values, Truth* (3rd ed., 1998).

Bernard Williams is Deutsch Professor of Philosophy at the University of California, Berkeley, and a Fellow of All Souls College, Oxford. He has held chairs in London, Cambridge, and Oxford, and from 1979 to 1987 he was Provost of King's College, Cambridge. His publications include *Morality* (1972), *Problems of the Self* (1973), *Descartes: The Project of Pure Enquiry* (1978), *Moral Luck* (1982), *Ethics and the Limits of Philosophy* (1985), *Shame and Necessity* (1993), and *Making Sense of Humanity* (1995).

Index

Index of Examples